Basic Marketing

Richard T. Hise
Texas A & M University

Peter L. Gillett
Northern Illinois University

John K. Ryans, Jr.
Kent State University

Basic Marketing

CONCEPTS AND DECISIONS

Winthrop Publishers, Inc.   Cambridge, Massachusetts

Library of Congress Cataloging in Publication Data
Hise, Richard T
    Basic marketing.
    Includes index.
    1. Marketing.   I. Gillett, Peter L., joint
author.   II. Ryans, John K., joint author.
III. Title.
HF5415.H543   658.8   78-17563
ISBN 0-87626-056-3

Cover and interior design by David Ford
Line illustrations by Phil Carver & Friends
Photo research by Carole Frohlich

Photo Credits

pg. 3: *top left*, © Howard Harrison 1976; *top right*, courtesy Bulova; *bottom left*, John Urban/Stock, Boston; *bottom right*, Cary Wolinsky/Stock, Boston
pg. 141: *top left*, © Howard Harrison 1978; *top right*, Daniel S. Brody/Stock, Boston; *bottom left*, Frank Siteman; *bottom right*, © Howard Harrison 1978
pg. 199: *top left*, © Howard Harrison 1976; *top right*, courtesy General Telephone and Electronics Corporation; *bottom left*, Ellis Herwig/Stock, Boston; *bottom right*, courtesy Coopers & Lybrand
pg. 473: *top left*, Frank Siteman; *top right*, Jim Ritscher/Stock, Boston; *bottom left*, Peter Menzel/Stock, Boston; *bottom right*, © Howard Harrison 1976
pg. 523: *top left*, photograph reproduced with the permission of PepsiCo, Inc., owner of the trademarks *Pepsi* and *Pepsi-Cola* in English and Cyrillic in the U.S.S.R. and elsewhere for soft drinks; *top right*, courtesy *Photography for Industry*; *bottom left*, George Belierose/Stock, Boston; *bottom right*, T. D. Lovering/Stock, Boston

© *1979 by Winthrop Publishers, Inc.*
17 Dunster Street, Cambridge, Massachusetts 02138

10 9 8 7 6 5 4 3 2 1

This book is dedicated to
Carol, Richie, Amy, and Emily
Karen
Cinda

Contents

Part I   Background for Marketing Decisions

Part II   Preparing to Make Marketing Mix Decisions

Part III   Marketing Mix Decisions

Contents

Contents

Part IV   Implementing and Evaluating Marketing Mix Decisions

---

Part V   International Marketing Management

Contents

List of Cases

Preface

Success in the marketing field requires a clear understanding of certain fundamental marketing concepts. Our text focuses on these key concepts, helping prospective marketers build the knowledge base necessary for effective decision making. We've made an effort to provide complete, careful explanations of these key concepts, reinforced with illustrations of real, often familiar products and companies.

Organization

In the first chapter we introduce a decision-making model which outlines the seven basic steps involved in most marketing decisions: 1) analysis of the market, 2) analysis of the environment, 3) establishment of objectives, 4) development of product/market combinations, 5) development of a marketing mix, 6) development of the marketing organization, and 7) development of a control system. This model reflects the sequence of the subsequent chapters and serves as a reference point for students.

The importance of basing decisions on sound marketing concepts is underscored by our chapter organization. Chapters on decision making in three critical areas—product, channels of distribution, and pricing—are preceded by chapters that fully discuss the concepts involved in such decisions.

Coverage

In addition to our coverage of those fundamental areas discussed in most introductory marketing texts, we've included full chapters on important topics that have, we feel, been slighted by other books: marketing strategy, physical distribution, marketing organization, marketing control, and international marketing. We outline career opportunities in marketing, and investigate such special aspects of marketing as product elimination, product positioning, management by objectives for marketing, the marketing audit, and channels of distribution conflict.

Readability and Learning Aids

We believe we've succeeded in producing a text that is truly readable and interesting. Certainly every effort has gone into making it so. The manuscript was carefully evaluated by reading specialists to ensure the appropriate reading level, and a number of learning aids were built in to make it a little easier for students to absorb the wide range of material we've covered. These learning aids include:

- *Key terms,* listed at the beginning of every chapter, set off in bold type where they appear in context, and defined in a glossary at the end of each chapter;
- *Learning objectives,* in question form, preceding every chapter;
- *Two case studies* with questions, following each chapter;
- Numerous *tables, charts, diagrams,* and *cartoons;*
- *Chapter summaries,* keyed to the objectives; and
- End-of-chapter *discussion questions.*

Supplementary Materials

To further assist students in mastering the textual material, we have also prepared a Student Guide, which includes chapter summaries, sample true/false and multiple-choice questions (with answers), studying tips, and reviews of important concepts. An Instructor's Manual with transparency masters and a test bank is available to adopters of *Basic Marketing.*

Acknowledgments

As with any text, *Basic Marketing* has been a collaborative effort involving the contributions of many. We would like to thank the following individuals who read the manuscript at various stages and offered numerous incisive comments: H. Robert Dodge, Northern Illinois University; James S. Gould, Bryant College; K. Lee McGown, Concordia University; Alan G. Sawyer, University of Massachusetts, Amherst; George A. Smith, Northeastern University; John H. Sullivan, North Shore Community College; Sumner White, Massachusetts Bay Community College; and Frederick Wiseman, Northeastern University.

We owe them all a deep debt of gratitude. Our thanks also to the many people who participated in the research, typing, and preparation of the manuscript. They include: Leslie Gruver, Carol Nelson, David Fette, Terry Dupuis, Cindy Fullerton, Debbie Roedder, Debbie Laufman, Rosemary Pacheco, Anton Bricker, and Nancy Burns.

We would also like to give thanks to our former students who helped shape our thoughts about the basic course in marketing and, thus, significantly influenced the direction and scope of this text. These individuals include: Raj Aggarwal, Toledo University; Robert Barath, California State University at Fullerton; Victoria Berger, Market Facts, Inc.; Ronald Zallocco, Cleveland State University; James H. Donnelly, University of Kentucky; David Fry, Northwood Institute; Jim Grimm, Illinois State University; Raymond Horton, Lehigh University; John M. Ivancevich, University of Houston; Steve Keiser, University of Delaware; Steven Kelly, DePaul University; Charles Lamb, Texas A&M University; Cyril Logar, West Virginia University; Herbert Lyon, University of Houston; Kenneth Mast, University of Akron; George Prough, University of Akron; Peter Sanchez, Temple University; William Shanklin, Kent State University; Terence Shimp, University of South Carolina; Willem Van't Spijker, University of Rennes; Ivan Vernon, Baylor University; Ronald Webb, Stonehill College; Wayne Weeks, Eastern Michigan University; and James Wills, University of Hawaii.

A special thanks to Michael E. Meehan, editor, Winthrop Publishers, Inc., who worked so well and so closely with us on this project for three years. Our appreciation also to Pat Torelli, production editor at Winthrop, who did such a splendid job with the manuscript during the production stage.

While we leaned heavily upon all of these individuals during the last three years, the responsibility for any omissions, errors, or deficiencies must remain with us.

Basic Marketing

PART 1

Background for Marketing Decisions

Introduction to Marketing Decisions

After you finish this chapter, you should be able to answer the following questions:

1. What are the major aspects of marketing as contained in its definition?
2. How important is marketing in our society?
3. What is the marketing concept?
4. What are the seven basic marketing functions?
5. What is the marketing mix?
6. What are the seven basic steps that must be followed in making marketing decisions?
7. How do strategic and tactical objectives differ?
8. Why are decisions in marketing difficult to make?
9. How attractive are career opportunities in marketing?

KEY TERMS *Advertising   Channels of Distribution Management   Control System Demarketing   Environment   Marketing   Marketing Concept Marketing Mix   Marketing Research   Personal Selling   Physical Distribution   Pricing   Product Management   Strategic Objectives Tactical Objectives*

INTRODUCTION   Marketing is certainly one of the most pervasive and dynamic forces in the United States today. Marketing's importance has increased over the last 30 years and there is little to suggest that there will be any significant decrease in its importance in the future. If anything, the importance of marketing in our society should be even greater.

Marketing has been a major factor in making our economy the most envied economy in the world. It produces and supports millions of jobs. Marketing is used by virtually every type of business and nonbusiness organization in this country. A large percentage of the final cost of goods and services is composed of marketing costs. Vast quantities of resources are devoted each year to the marketing of goods and services. In short, marketing is worthy of our attention.

DEFINITION OF MARKETING

Although there are a number of definitions for marketing, we believe that **marketing** is best defined as the *determination of the needs and desires of the market so that goods and services can be provided that satisfy these needs and desires.* Let's examine the various aspects of this definition.

Determining Needs and Wants Before Goods and Services Are Developed

The reader will notice that the above definition implies that the market's needs and desires are determined *before* goods and services are developed. We do not develop products and services without knowing if they are desired by the market. Consumers and business firms do not buy products they do not want. They do purchase products and services that satisfy their needs and desires.

Kenner, a General Mills subsidiary, did not adequately research the needs of the market and thus its "Steve Scout" doll failed to compete with Hasbro Industries' "G.I. Joe" doll. The market's needs were not satisfied by the Steve Scout doll; boys wanted dolls to portray a "tough guy" image, which "Steve Scout" failed to do.[1]

Needs and Desires Are Incorporated Into Goods and Services

After the needs and desires of the market have been determined, products and services are developed that recognize these needs and desires. The specific features of the products and services must be related directly to the market's needs and desires. A good example of this is the Volkswagen Rabbit. Through an analysis of the market, Volkswagen found that car purchasers' most important needs and desires were (1) low purchase price,

---

[1] Keith T. Stephens and Edward M. Mazze, "Planning—The Marketing Skill You Must Master," *Product Management* (September, 1976), p. 56.

(2) fuel economy, and (3) inside roominess. The Rabbit sells for under $3,500, gets 40 miles to the gallon, and has interior dimensions equivalent to those found in medium-sized cars.

Needs and Desires Must Be Satisfied

Determining customer needs and desires before developing products and services will to a large extent ensure that their needs and desires will be satisfied, but we must be positive that this is happening. The needs and desires of customers can, and often do, change. Another problem is that the needs and desires may have been incorrectly determined in the first place. Thus, a company should be constantly questioning whether or not its products and services are satisfying customer needs and desires.

Making sure that customer needs and wants are being satisfied is considered by many companies to be so important that company *presidents* often mingle with customers in order to get customer reactions to company products and services. Figure 1.1 provides some examples of this.[2] Also, consumer affairs departments in many large firms, which were established in the 1960's and 1970's to represent the customer viewpoint in their firms, have become involved with measuring customer satisfaction. Two of the

[2] *The Wall Street Journal*, July 1, 1976, pp. 1, 20.

Figure 1.1   Company Presidents Who Determine the Extent to Which Customer Needs and Wants Are Satisfied

1. Winston V. Morrow, Jr., president of Avis, frequently waits in line at airports for a rental car to "get the feel of things." Occasionally, he helps out behind the counter.

2. Bill Veeck and Ted Turner, owners of the Chicago White Sox and Atlanta Braves baseball teams, sit in the bleachers to get fan reactions to their teams.

3. Richard Ferris, president of United Airlines, travels coach on United flights because "If you don't ride back there, you can't know what the hell is going on."

4. Gerald S. Office, Jr., chairman and president of Ponderosa System, a chain of cafeteria steak houses, samples the food four or five times a week.

5. Harry Jersig, president of Lone Star Brewing, samples the company's draft beer in bars to see if it is being properly served. He also tests from 3 to 5 bottles of Lone Star beer a day. With the company for 36 years, he has not missed a single working day.

Introduction to Marketing Decisions

authors of this text found in studying 153 consumer affairs departments that 72% investigated the level of customer satisfaction. Other mechanisms also exist to deal with customer satisfaction. Whirlpool has initiated cool-line, which is a nationwide toll-free number available to customers with problems and complaints.

An Exchange Takes Place

The above definition suggests an important concept: that in a transaction between buyer and seller an exchange process exists. Each side in the transaction gives up something in order to obtain something. The purchaser gives up money in order to obtain a product or service, while the seller gives up the product or service to obtain money. Both sides expect that what they receive will have more value than what they have given up. For example, the purchaser of a $79 bicycle would expect to obtain more than $79 worth of benefit; he would not pay $79 to obtain only $60 worth of benefits. The seller of the bicycle, on the other hand, would expect the $79 price he receives to exceed the total cost of manufacturing and marketing the product.

IMPORTANCE OF MARKETING IN OUR SOCIETY

All Organizations in Our Society Use Marketing

There is probably no organization in the United States that does not practice marketing to some extent. Our previous discussion primarily dealt with business firms that provide products and services, but other organizations in our society have come to increasingly rely on marketing to achieve their objectives.

Political parties now determine the needs and desires of voters. Surveys are often used to determine what these needs and desires are. Candidates and party platforms reflect them. Candidates use such marketing tools as advertising in an effort to be elected.

Hospitals in 1976 were encouraging their "customers" (patients) to schedule non-urgent surgery in order to avoid overuse or underuse of hospital facilities. Blue-Cross/Blue-Shield is using advertising to convince individuals to have minor surgery performed in doctors' offices rather than occupy a hospital bed.

In the 1970's a number of universities began adding marketing experts to their staffs in order to attract more students and better students and to find out if the needs of their various publics (students, faculty, community, alumni, etc.) were being satisfied.

In 1974 the United States Post Office hired a number of highly skilled product managers to aggressively market a number of new services.

Many churches have begun to rely upon various marketing techniques such as analysis of the market and advertising in an effort to attract more members and contributions.

Charitable organizations, for example, the American Red Cross, March of Dimes, and United Givers Fund, have come to use marketing concepts in order to achieve their contribution requirements.

The cities of Charlotte, North Carolina, Macon, Georgia, and Tampa, Florida used marketing strategies in an effort to reduce litter. Through the Clean Community System, developed by Keep America Beautiful, Inc., litter was decreased by 75% in these cities.

In 1974 federal drug enforcement agencies hired marketing consultants whose responsibility it was to develop models of the distribution networks for heroin. From these models it was hoped that more could be learned about the operations of heroin dealers and that the flow of heroin into the United States could be reduced.

Marketing Has Helped Produce the World's Highest Standard of Living

There is little doubt that marketing has helped produce the highest standard of living in the world for the inhabitants of the United States. Americans have better housing and more durables, such as washing machines, than does any other country. They are more likely to own an automobile than people in other countries. Americans have a great deal of leisure time that can be enjoyed through travel and recreation. They eat better than people in other countries, and a smaller percentage of farm workers and owners are required than for any other country.

It is interesting to compare our standard of living to that of Russia, which has an economy and social system very unlike ours. The average worker in the United States must work 762 hours to own a medium-sized car; in Russia the average worker must work 7,907 hours. A Russian works 1,111 hours to purchase a color television; an American works only 147 hours. An American works only 53 hours to acquire an automatic washing machine, but a Russian must toil 204 hours.[3]

Marketing Provides Employment

Marketing provides a great many jobs in the United States. Although exact numbers are not possible, marketing jobs probably account for one-fourth to one-third of all jobs in the civilian labor force.

What are included in marketing jobs? All workers employed by the 2,329,000 retail stores and 548,000 wholesaling firms, employees of advertising agencies and marketing consulting firms, many of those who work for transportation companies, employees of manufacturing firms who perform marketing functions (such as advertising and marketing research), em-

---

[3] *The New York Times*, February 2, 1971, Section E, p. 5.

Introduction to Marketing Decisions

ployees in other nonmarketing firms (banks, insurance companies, etc.) who are involved in marketing activities are all considered marketing employees.

Marketing Costs

It is generally recognized that about 50% of the final cost of most consumer products is made up of marketing costs. This means that for every dollar a consumer spends in a retail store, $.50 goes for the performance of marketing activities. Probably no other figure more strongly indicates the importance of marketing in our economy.

This high percentage is often used to criticize marketing, but such a criticism is largely unfounded. Much of this cost occurs because the marketing system is responding to genuine consumer needs. A good example of this is packaging. Consumers have demanded packages that can be easily stored, freeze more varied foods longer, provide easier opening, and are lighter in weight. As a result, total expenditures on packaging materials increased from $9.6 billion in 1958 to $16.6 billion only 10 years later. Outlays for aerosol and plastic containers, two packaging materials particularly desired by consumers, experienced phenomenal growth in this decade. Expenditures for aerosol containers rose from $90 million in 1958 to $365 million in 1968. In 1968, $521 million were spent on plastic containers, compared to only $20 million in 1958.[4] Obviously, these increases in costs have contributed to the high percentage of product cost attributable to marketing.

International Marketing

The effort of American companies to market products and services abroad is called *international marketing*. The extent to which these efforts are successful have important effects on our domestic economy. Companies that sell overseas provide employment for American workers that otherwise might not exist. Sales of these companies to foreign purchasers help to offset our country's purchases of foreign goods and services, especially those from Japan, West Germany, and Italy. With a trade deficit of almost $27 billion in 1977 for the United States, the importance of international marketing is accentuated.

Demarketing

In the 1970's it became necessary for American companies to consider the possibility of **demarketing.** Demarketing means persuading purchasers to consume *fewer* goods and services, instead of more, in order to save scarce resources.

[4] *Modern Packaging Encyclopedia*, 1968, p. 24, as reported in Robert F. Hartley, *Marketing: Management and Social Change* (Scranton, Pa.: Intext Educational Publishers, 1972), p. 6.

Background for Marketing Decisions

Demarketing was stimulated by the Arab Oil boycott of 1973, which demonstrated to America the need to reduce its consumption of oil and, hence, its reliance on foreign sources. Examples of demarketing efforts included urging Americans to drive 55 miles per hour, to get regular automobile tuneups, and to keep the thermostats in their homes at 65° in winter.

Other raw materials and products were also in short supply in the 1970's and, thus, were logical candidates for demarketing efforts. These included sugar, paper, tin, coffee, and chromium.

Efficient Use of Resources

Resources are important to an economy. Since there is a fixed amount of many of these resources, they must be used as efficiently as possible. Oil, natural gas, and various other minerals are examples. Other resources can be replenished, but at a cost, and considerable time is involved. Examples of these include timber and fish. Other resources, like manpower and money, must also be used efficiently. If they are not, they will cost more and will probably result in higher product costs.

Marketing can be a powerful weapon in the battle for efficient resource usage in that the cornerstone of marketing should be the determination of customer needs and wants *before* goods and services are produced. If these needs and wants are reflected in goods and services, there should be less waste of valuable resources because the goods and services that are available in the marketplace are more likely to be purchased. Thus, there will not be a lot of unsold products in the marketplace and valuable resources will not be misused. Also, if goods and services that actually satisfy customer needs and wants are produced, not as much money has to be spent for advertising and these funds (resources) can be used elsewhere.

THE MARKETING CONCEPT

The marketing concept refers to the basic philosophy of marketing that a company should have. In order for a company to be a success, its marketing philosophy must emphasize (1) customer needs and desires, (2) goal achievement, (3) societal requirements, and (4) a systems approach.

Customer Needs and Desires

The importance of customer needs and desires was discussed earlier when we defined marketing. When a company adopts the marketing concept, it must follow three specific steps in order to ensure the proper commitment to customer needs and desires. First, the company must determine customer needs and desires before it develops goods and services for these customers. Second, these needs and desires must be incorporated into the products and services developed for these customers. Third, the company must make sure that these products and services are indeed satisfying customer needs and wants.

Goal Achievement

Any organization's marketing effort will be directed toward achieving goals. A church, for example, may want its marketing program to increase its membership. The major goal of most business firms is profit. Without adequate profit, the firm's very existence will eventually be in jeopardy.

Marketing departments historically emphasized sales volume and, unfortunately, relegated profit to a secondary position. A company that has adopted the marketing concept does not do this. Sales volume is still important, but it must be obtained at satisfactory profit levels.

The astute firm constantly measures the profitability of various aspects of its marketing operations. For example, it measures the profitability of its various products, customers, salesmen, and territories. In Chapter 6, we will discuss other major goals for business firms besides profit, including market share, sales volume, product protection, and growth.

Permission: From the *Wall Street Journal*.

"Do you realize that this railroad is in worse financial condition than we are?"

Societal Requirements

The marketing concept also includes a concern for society's needs. Customer needs and desires and goals are focal points of the company's operations, but the broader needs of society must also be recognized. Some major concerns include the quality of air and water, providing safe and properly functioning products, as well as the quality of life itself.

Permission: From the *Wall Street Journal*.

"I agree with you about air pollution, but I don't think you should protest by not breathing."

A Systems Approach

A systems approach is another important aspect of the marketing concept. The systems approach has two important dimensions. First, it means that marketing decisions are made within a *systems* context, that is, no decision of a marketing nature can be made without first noting its effect on other marketing decisions and, in turn, their effect on it. For example, we might not want to make a change in a product's price without also considering a change in the product's advertising. Second, the *entire firm* must function as a smoothly operating system with one major objective: to provide customers with products and services that satisfy their wants and needs. This is often very difficult to achieve in practice. Production often believes that its primary objective is to produce a given product, with given specifications, at the lowest possible cost per unit. And finance may believe that its major function is to obtain needed funds at the very best terms available. These goals are, of course, important to the success of the firm, but the most important goal is to provide goods and services that recognize customer needs and desires. Unless all areas of the firm have this as their paramount goal, there will be no need to produce products at the lowest possible cost or secure funds at the most favorable rate because the firm will no longer be in existence.

HAVE COMPANIES ADOPTED THE MARKETING CONCEPT?

To what extent has the marketing concept been adopted by American firms? A study of 273 large manufacturing firms provides some answers.

If the marketing concept has been adopted, some area of the firm must be given the responsibility of determining what consumer needs and desires are. This is usually the task of the marketing research department. Of the 273 firms studied, 77% had established marketing research departments consisting of one or more full-time employees. To what extent had these companies attempted to find out customer needs and desires in advance of marketing their last new product? Obviously, this is a key question concerning the extent to which these firms had adopted the marketing concept. Approximately 92% of the firms indicated that customer needs and desires had been determined before marketing their last new product.

The study also covered the extent to which the profitability dimension of the marketing concept was recognized by these 273 firms. Nearly 97% indicated that they examine the profitability of their products. About 67% measured the profitability of territories, about 57% measured the profitability of salespeople, and about 54% measured the profitability of customers.[5]

THE SEVEN BASIC MARKETING FUNCTIONS

The reader will recall that in the preface we said that this text has a decision-making orientation. We also said that its major objective is to offer suggestions that would help marketing employees make more effective decisions.

We believe that there are seven basic marketing functions that must be performed by most companies. (See Figure 1.2) In this chapter each of these functions will be briefly discussed so that the reader can obtain a basic understanding of them. A number of basic decisions that have to be made for each of these marketing management functions will be discussed.

[5] Richard T. Hise, "Have Manufacturing Firms Adopted the Marketing Concept?" *Journal of Marketing* (July, 1965), pp. 9–12.

Figure 1.2   The Basic Marketing Functions

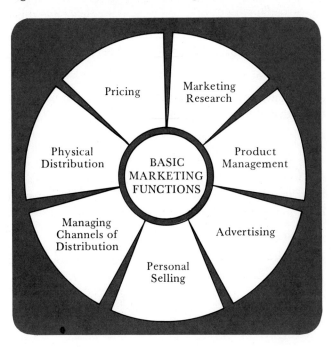

Separate chapters later in this book will cover these fundamental functions in greater detail.

Marketing Research

The major task of **marketing research** is to provide marketing decision makers with *timely and accurate information* so that *better* decisions can be made.

Information About the Market.   Perhaps the most important information required of the marketing research function is that pertaining to the market. As indicated earlier, the market's needs and desires must be determined. Once these are established, products and services can be developed to satisfy needs and desires of various target markets. After these products and services are marketed, the marketing research effort must measure the extent to which the market's needs and desires are actually being satisfied.

Other dimensions of the market must also be determined. Some of these are included in Figure 1.3. Although not all of these can be discussed, the

Introduction to Marketing Decisions

Figure 1.3   Examples of Information About the Market That the Marketing Research Function Must Obtain

1. Population in geographical areas and population trends.

2. Income obtained by the market and income trends.

3. Estimates of market potentials (total number of units of a product that could be purchased by a given market).

4. Sales volume forecasts (how many units of a product an individual firm expects to sell).

5. Which kinds of purchasers account for the largest percentage of total units sold.

6. Who are the purchasers who consistently purchase a specific brand.

7. Who makes the actual decision to buy.

8. Which segments of the market are profitable and which segments are unprofitable.

9. How the product is actually used by the market.

experiences of the Canada Dry Company can be cited to show the importance of knowing how the market is actually using a product (item 9). In analyzing its market for its ginger ale, the company was surprised to find that 90% of the time ginger ale was being used as a soft drink; prior to this analysis, the company assumed that its ginger ale was being primarily used as a mixer. This was valuable information because as Ed Cott, Canada Dry's director of marketing put it, "This information opened up a whole new world for us. Our growth opportunity was selling ginger ale as a soft drink, not as a mixer."[6]

Information About the Environment.   Information about those areas outside the firm that affect its marketing decisions is very important. Thus, the marketing research effort, for example, should be monitoring the economy, government, culture, and technology. Significant trends and developments should be identified and reported to decision makers so that appropriate responses can be made.

Competition is an especially important part of the environment. A firm must know what new products the competition is bringing out, what

---

[6] Curt Schleier, "Premiums and Incentives—Tools for Repositioning," *Product Management* (September, 1976), p. 37.

changes are occurring in the competition's marketing strategies, what the competition's market share is, and so on.

Some examples of developments in the environment include the following:

1. The Federal Trade Commission suggested in 1976 that food products should not carry the words "natural" or "organic" because they have no commonly understood definition.
2. In the 1960's Americans turned to milder bourbons and ryes and to premixed cocktails.
3. The migration of Americans to the West and South will result in these areas replacing the East as America's trend setters.
4. More working women will find less time for shopping, thus increasing dollars spent on mail-order business and out-of-home consumption of food and beverages.[7]

Information About Other Marketing Functions.   Other marketing areas look to marketing research to provide them with data on their own operations. For example, the advertising department would like to know how many readers of a particular magazine noticed the company's recent advertisement. The product management group would like an indication of which products are profitable and which products are unprofitable. In the personal selling function, the sales manager would appreciate knowing how much time each salesman spends on nonselling activities, such as on paper work and traveling.

Product Management

The major task of the **product management** function is to develop new products and services that satisfy customer needs and wants. New product management is a responsibility that the marketing area generally shares with the research and development and production departments. After these new products and services have been developed, a plan must be developed for marketing them over their lifetimes. Finally, each product or service will eventually have to be considered for elimination.

There are several specific decisions that must be made for each product marketed, for example,

1. The precise physical characteristics (or features) to be included. These involve decisions about size, color, raw materials, and so on.
2. The quality level. Here, we are concerned with durability, productivity, efficiency, etc.
3. The package. Two kinds of packages are important: (1) the package to protect the product when it is being shipped and (2) the package at the retail store that is designed to stimulate sales.

[7] *Product Management* (September, 1976), p. 28.

4. The brand name. This involves deciding on a specific name for each product carried.
5. Warranties. Warranties refer to guarantees about the product given to purchasers. For example, most of us are familiar with the 12-month or 12,000-mile warranties on new cars.
6. After-the-sale service. Some products have to be installed, repaired, or maintained.
7. How many varieties of each product to produce and market. From the basic product it is possible to develop a great many varieties based on sizes, styles, colors, and so on.

Advertising

Advertising is a major means whereby the market is informed of the existence and availability of products and services that can satisfy needs and desires. Advertising uses various *nonpersonal* sources, such as television and magazines, to communicate to the market and to secure its purchase of products and services.

A number of important responsibilities are carried out by individuals in advertising. These include:

1. Determining the size of the advertising budget (appropriation).
2. Choosing the media to use (newspapers, magazines, television, or radio, for example).
3. Developing copy (what the advertising message should say).
4. Choosing and working with advertising agencies.
5. Testing the effectiveness of advertisements.

Personal Selling

Personal selling uses *personal* sources to communicate the existence and availability of products that can satisfy the needs and desires of the market. Salespeople call on customers and attempt to influence them to purchase their products and services.

Figure 1.4 lists some of the major responsibilities of the personal selling function.

Advertising and personal selling are major components of an organization's promotional mix. The promotional mix is the organization's total effort to inform the market about products and services and to persuade the market to purchase them. Besides advertising and personal selling, **sales promotion** and **publicity** are part of the promotional mix. Examples of sales promotion efforts include samples, coupons, and exhibits. Publicity refers to news stories about a company, its products, or employees that appear in such media as television, newspapers, and magazines.

Background for Marketing Decisions

Figure 1.4   Major Personal Selling Responsibilities

1. Determining which customers to call on.

2. Determining when to call on these customers.

3. Recruiting sales force.

4. Selecting sales force.

5. Training sales force.

6. Compensating sales force.

7. Motivating sales force.

8. Supervising sales force.

9. Evaluating sales force's performance.

Managing Channels of Distribution

Channels of distribution are the middlemen a company uses to market its products. The majority of middlemen include wholesalers and retailers.

Some of the major responsibilities in the channels of distribution area include:

1. Deciding whether or not to use channels of distribution.
2. Determining which general types of middlemen to use.
3. Choosing specific middlemen to market products.
4. Obtaining the cooperation of channel members.
5. Analyzing the effectiveness of a company's channels of distribution.

Physical Distribution

Physical distribution refers to the physical movement of finished products from production areas to customers. This function involves two major areas, transportation and storage of finished products. Figure 1.5 lists some of the specific responsibilities in the physical distribution area.

Pricing

Pricing is another major functional area of marketing. Some of the important decisions to be made by those who are responsible for pricing include the following:

1. Deciding on basic objectives for prices.
2. Deciding on a basic approach to price setting. For example, are prices

Figure 1.5   Major Responsibilities in the Physical Distribution Function

1. Determining the level of customer service, such as how many shipments per month to make to customers.

2. Determining where to locate warehouses.

3. Deciding on the number of warehouses.

4. Deciding on the type of warehouse, such as single-story versus multiple-story.

5. Choosing the mode of transportation, that is, whether to use pipeline, water, rail, truck, or air transportation.

6. Determining the size of shipments.

7. Deciding the best level of inventory to maintain.

for products to be generally established because of the costs they incur or are they to be related to the demand in the market?
3. Placing a specific price on each product.
4. Deciding if and when these specific prices are to be changed.
5. Putting prices on new products.
6. Establishing markup, markdown, and discount policies.
7. Ensuring that pricing policies adhere to legal requirements.

THE MARKETING MIX

A very important idea is the **marketing mix.** The marketing mix refers to the *combination of marketing decisions that is used to market specific products to specific markets over a specific time period.* As such, it involves decisions in all of the marketing functions discussed above, with the exception of marketing research. It is generally assumed that the marketing mix is made up of decisions from the product, advertising, personal selling, channels of distribution, physical distribution, and pricing areas that are instituted *after* the marketing research effort has examined the market and such elements of the environment as the economy, competition, culture, and technology. The information gathered by marketing research about the market and the environment greatly determines the marketing mix to be used.

Figure 1.6 provides examples of marketing mixes for two products: a consumer product (soap powder) and an industrial product (machine tools). The reader should in particular notice the differences in the marketing

Figure 1.6   Possible Marketing Mixes for Soap Powders and Machine Tools

Marketing Mix Element	Soap Powder	Machine Tools
1. Product	Blue-colored powder having a high level of cleaning action boxed in red and yellow package with brand name of Kleenzo.	Heavy-gauge steel stamping machine able to punch out 200 forms per hour. Called Model X-20, it carries a 5-year unconditional guarantee.
2. Advertising	$200,000 advertising budget allocated to television and newspapers. Advertisements are run weekly.	$80,000 advertising budget allocated between trade magazines and brochures sent directly to potential buyers. Four ads per year are placed in trade magazines. Brochures are sent when decisions to purchase machine tools are most likely to be made.
3. Personal selling	Forty salesmen call on retailers. Their function is to take orders and keep shelves stocked.	Ten salesmen solve problems for their current customers and potential customers and show them how Model X-20 can increase their output.
4. Channels of distribution	Company uses 10,000 retail stores through which the product is distributed. Supermarkets and drugstores are chiefly used.	Two experienced manufacturers' agents work with a few special customers. Most customers are contacted directly by the company's sales force.
5. Physical distribution	Company owns fleet of trucks that makes deliveries once every two weeks to large customers and once every month to smaller customers. Ten large warehouses are used throughout the country.	Company hires trucking firm when machine tools have to be shipped. Air shipments are made when customers need machine tools in a hurry or when spare parts are required. One warehouse next to production facility is used.
6. Pricing	A 48-ounce size of Kleenzo is sold for $1.20 to retailers who sell it for $1.39.	The price for a basic Model X-20 is $6,000. Since customers frequently want modifications of the basic model, the price often varies from $6,000.

mixes that may exist for these products. These differences result chiefly from differences in the products themselves and the differences in their markets.

It is important for the reader to analyze the above definition of the marketing mix carefully. Each product that a company carries usually has a marketing mix different from the market mixes of the other products it carries. Even the same product may carry a different marketing mix for different markets. For example, vinyl upholstery in automobiles might be chosen more by women, but leather might be chosen more by men. The marketing mix should be in effect for a specific time period. At the end of this time period, its effectiveness should be determined. If its effectiveness is not good, the marketing mix may have to be changed. For example, the price on hair dryers may have to be reduced from $24.95 to $19.99.

The marketing mix is very important in achieving tactical (short-term) objectives. These are objectives specified for one year or less.

Decisions in the marketing mix should be made in a systems context. For example, decisions about price cannot be made without considering product quality and the size of the advertising budget for a product.

Marketing mix decisions use a company's scarce resources. Advertising budgets, for example, take up money. Decisions on the size of the sales force require manpower allocations. Product decisions involve the use of raw materials. Because the marketing mix is important in achieving tactical objectives and uses scarce resources, marketing mix decisions must be made carefully.

A MODEL FOR MARKETING DECISIONS

We are now ready to look at a model for making marketing decisions. The model consists of the seven basic steps required for most marketing decisions. The seven fundamental steps, and their sequence, are shown in Figure 1.7. We will now briefly discuss each of these steps.

Step One: Analysis of the Market

Obviously, the first step in making marketing decisions is to analyze the market. In this step we especially want to know what the market's needs and desires are. After these have been identified, the firm can decide on those specific markets that it wants to serve, and it can begin to match its products to these specific markets' needs and desires. Then, it can begin to plan how best to market to these markets.

Step Two: Analysis of the Environment

The second step involves analyzing the **environment.** In this text we consider the environment to include those areas, in addition to the market, over

Figure 1.7   A Model for Making Marketing Decisions

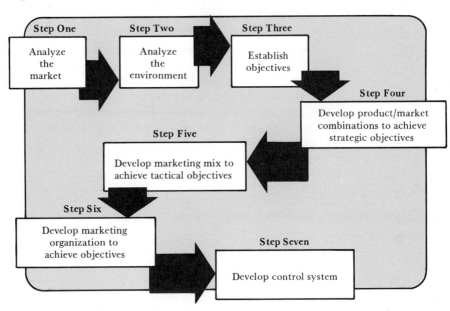

which the marketing department cannot exert direct control. We include the following in our definition of the environment:

1. The company in which the marketing department is located.
2. Competition.
3. Technology.
4. Legal/political area.
5. The economy.
6. Culture.
7. Foreign countries.

The environment should be analyzed for two major reasons. First, the environment often indicates *opportunities* for products and services to satisfy the market's needs and desires. Some examples include:

1. Changing cultural values that make certain products more acceptable, such as pants and bikini bathing suits for women and hair spray for men.
2. The competition's dropping a product that can be profitably marketed by another firm.

3. The research and development department's developing a new material that can be used in products to satisfy market needs and desires.
4. The space program's developing a number of new materials that could be used in consumer products. Teflon is a good example.

Second, the environment often presents *obstacles* to the marketing of products and services. Competition, for example, may bring out a clearly superior offering that makes current products and services obsolete. Or the federal government may rule that certain product components can no longer be used. When cyclamates and hexachlorophene were banned in the 1970's, the production of some artificially flavored soft drinks and soaps had to be curtailed until substitutes could be developed. A certain kind of product would perhaps be successful if technology existed to reduce its price so that people could afford it. Home video taping units for recording television programs appear to be a potentially successful product, but their current price of $1,200 or more precludes their large-scale acceptance.

Step Three: Establish Objectives

Once we have analyzed the market and the environment, we are in a position to establish feasible objectives for our products and services. In this regard, a company is concerned with strategic and tactical objectives.

Strategic objectives are the long-run, basic objectives of a company. By long run, we mean objectives that take longer than one year to achieve. Some strategic objectives include profit, market share, sales volume, product protection, and growth.

Tactical objectives involve a time frame of one year or less. Tactical objectives can be assigned specifically to the marketing department and other departments to achieve. Strategic objectives, on the other hand, are generally those that the entire firm is trying to attain. Tactical objectives are established in order to enable the strategic objectives to be obtained. For example, having salesmen increase the number of calls they make on customers by 10% may be a major means of increasing profit by 8%. Other examples of tactical objectives are decreasing delivery times to customers by 8 hours and adding 200 new customers in 1980.

Step Four: Develop Product/Market Combinations to Achieve Strategic Objectives

In step four, management and the marketing department must decide how they are going to achieve the basic strategic objectives. This is done primarily through various combinations of products and markets. In general, there are four combinations that can be used:

1. Selling the same product to the same market.
2. Selling the same product to a different market.
3. Selling a different product to the same market.
4. Selling a different product to a different market.

Step Five: Develop the Marketing Mix to Achieve Tactical Objectives

Tactical objectives are essentially achieved through the marketing mix. Some additional examples include:

1. Better routing of salesmen to reduce travel time by 15%.
2. Changing advertising media from newspapers to television to increase the number of potential customers seeing our ads by 10%.
3. Acquiring new materials handling equipment to increase the speed of moving finished products by 20%.
4. Reducing prices by 10% to encourage 1,000 additional retail stores to stock our products.

Step Six: Develop the Marketing Organization to Achieve Objectives

After it has been decided how the strategic objectives (step four) and the tactical objectives (step five) are going to be achieved, the marketing organization most appropriate for achieving these objectives should be established. The major decisions involved here include:

1. Deciding on a basic organizational approach. The alternatives include organizing on a product, customer, geographical, or functional basis.
2. Deciding on the degree of *specialization* required in the marketing organization. That is, how specialized do we want the marketing positions to be.
3. Deciding on the degree of *centralization/decentralization* required. That is, where in the marketing organization do we want decisions to be made: by higher-level executives (centralization) or by lower-level employees (decentralization)?
4. Determining the number and types of subdepartments to be included in the marketing department. (This refers to the *departmentalization* decision). For example, are we going to have a separate advertising department?
5. Determining how large the *span of control* should be. That is, how many subordinates can one superior effectively manage?
6. Deciding how to *motivate* marketing personnel most effectively. That is, how to stimulate marketing employees to work hard to achieve company objectives.

Step Seven: Develop a Control System

A **control system** is designed to measure the effectiveness of the marketing department's performance, and it involves six major steps. First, we must decide on the *aspect of the marketing operation* to be evaluated. Let's assume that it is the salesperson's performance. Second, we have to establish a *criterion* on which the salesperson's performance will be measured. Let's assume this to be the percentage of time spent on calling on new customers. Third, we must decide on a *standard of performance* for the measurement criterion. This might be that 20% of the individual's time should be spent on calling on new customers. Fourth, we must decide how to *monitor* the marketing operation to see if the standard of performance is achieved. In this example, we might use the salesperson's call report in which he or she indicates the time spent on established and new customers. Fifth, we must compare these results to the standard of performance. We might find, for example, that salesman Smith spent only 5% of his total time calling on new customers compared to the desired standard of 20%. Sixth, we must engage in *performance improvement analysis* if the performance deviates significantly from the standard of performance established. In this case, we might recommend that salesman Smith do a better job of identifying prospective new customers.

Figure 1.8 has been developed so that the reader may get a feel for how these seven basic steps might appear in practice. It shows how a company that is developing a new product (lawn chairs) might handle these seven steps.

DECISION MAKING IN MARKETING: PROBLEMS AND DIFFICULTIES

The following model for making decisions in marketing provides a useful sequence of steps that should result in a more effective performance by the marketing department. At this point, however, it is necessary to discuss some of the problems and difficulties that the marketing decision maker must face in spite of the existence of such a helpful model.

Marketing Decisions Must Contend with Uncontrollable Variables

Marketing decisions are affected by variables over which the marketing department has little or no control. In general, the environment includes many examples of uncontrollable variables. For example, the marketing department can neither control nor influence competition to any great extent. Little can be done about the governments of foreign countries and their policies. Changes in culture are largely beyond the control of the marketing decision maker. Federal, state, and local governments pass laws that are detrimental to marketing and little can be done to prevent this.

Probably the most important uncontrollable variable is the market itself. Its needs and desires are constantly changing and marketing can do little to influence these changes. At best, it can monitor the market and adjust its products and services to conform to the market's needs and desires.

Marketing Decisions Are Involved with People

Marketing decisions involve people. People make marketing decisions and are affected by them. Marketing decisions must recognize the needs and desires of people (the market). People cannot be scrutinized and understood

Figure 1.8 Using the Seven-Step Model for Making Marketing Decisions to Develop and Market a New Product

Step One: Analyze the Market

A manufacturer of aluminum products for industrial uses analyzes the consumer market and decides that there is an excellent opportunity for manufacturing outdoor, folding lawn chairs by using aluminum tubing for the frame. The primary market is designated as homeowners living in warm weather states such as Arizona, Florida, and California.

Step Two: Analyze the Environment

The company believes that it has the required technology for manufacturing these chairs. The trend in the United States toward more leisure time should have a positive effect on sales, as should the increased populations in warm weather states. An investigation of competitive firms selling aluminum to the industrial market indicates that none is considering adding outdoor folding lawn chairs to their product lines.

Step Three: Establish Objectives

At the end of five years, the company wants the profit from these chairs to be bringing in a 20% return on investment (strategic objective). In order to help achieve this objective, it is estimated that the chairs must be available in 5,000 retail stores during the first year (tactical objective).

Step Four: Develop Product/Market Combinations to Achieve Strategic Objectives

Because the company is selling a new product to a new market and because it lacks production capacity, it acquires a small Tampa, Florida, company that has manufactured lawn chairs in the past.

Step Five: Develop Marketing Mix to Achieve Tactical Objectives

Two kinds of chairs will be sold: a chaise lounge and a regular type chair. Each kind of chair will be available in red and white, green and white, or blue and white. These are the colors desired by the market. The regular chair will be priced at $5.95; the chaise lounge will go for $12.95. These prices will provide middlemen with adequate profit. The sales force will call on the buyers of chain variety stores and department stores. The company's fleet of trucks will be used to transport the finished products in order to minimize late deliveries for retailers. Color advertisements will appear in *Better Homes and Gardens, Woman's Day,* and *Family Circle.* These advertisements will build demand among consumers and thus will induce retailers to carry the chairs.

Figure 1.8—*continued*

Step Six: Develop Marketing Organization to Achieve Objectives

The newly acquired company in Tampa, Florida, will become the lawn chair division of the parent company. This division will be headed up by a division manager who will report directly to the president of the parent company. A director of marketing for the lawn chair division will report to the division manager and will be responsible for carrying out the marketing program for the lawn chairs.

Step Seven: Develop Control System

Return on investment data for the lawn chair division will be analyzed each year to see if the five-year strategic objective is likely to be achieved. If this objective appears to be in jeopardy, revision of the marketing program will be considered. The number of retailers carrying the product at the end of the first year will be determined in order to see if the tactical objective has been obtained.

---

like a scientist can do in physics or chemistry with matter and elements. People do not permit the development of laws for marketing as can be done in the physical sciences. People change their minds, often they do not know what they want, they have fears, they make mistakes, and so on. Thus, there will always be a great deal of risk involved in making marketing decisions. That is, the decision maker is never 100% certain what the outcome of his decisions will be.

Marketing Decisions Usually Involve a Great Number of Marketing Mix Combinations

Another characteristic of marketing decisions that causes difficulties is the large number of marketing mix combinations that generally confront the decision maker. To illustrate: a decision involving five different prices for a product, four different colors, six different advertising appropriations, and three different channels of distribution forces the marketing executive to consider 360 possible combinations ($5 \times 4 \times 6 \times 3 = 360$). This is a simple example. Many decisions involve many more combinations. Although a computer can be used to analyze these situations, the decision maker is often left to contend with an overwhelming array of marketing mix combinations.

Marketing Operations Involve Much Time

Marketing operations frequently are extended over long periods of time and thus add to the decision maker's problems. The longer the time involved, the more likely market conditions will change, competition can adjust its marketing mix, unfavorable legislation can be passed, and so on.

Some marketing decisions are notorious for taking up time. For example, most new products take two or more years to market. It can often take from three to five years, or longer, to put together effective sales forces or channels of distribution systems.

Marketing Decisions Involve Heavy Use of Valuable Resources

Because marketing decisions involve heavy use of valuable resources, such as money and manpower, the marketing executive is under pressure to make decisions that use these resources effectively.

In developing new products, it is not unusual to incur costs running in the millions of dollars. (Polaroid's SX-70 camera was estimated to have cost $600 million to develop.) Therefore, marketing executives want to minimize the possibility that costly new products will fail.

It frequently costs a company $30,000 or more annually to compensate and support one salesperson. A sales force of 100 people, for example, could incur a cost as high as $3 million. Given such an expenditure, marketing executives want to ensure that these individuals are carefully selected, trained, and motivated.

Marketing Decisions Are Interdisciplinary in Nature

Today, marketing decisions recognize the contributions of other disciplines. Chief among these are the areas of economics, mathematics, psychology, and sociology. While these contributions are helpful, they force the marketing decision maker to be more knowledgeable about areas other than marketing.

The above comments on making decisions in marketing imply that a marketing executive has a tough job. This is certainly true. The executive must heavily rely upon his judgment, training, and experience when he makes a decision.

If the marketing executive's job is demanding, it would be expected that employment opportunities in the marketing field should be numerous and rewarding for *successful* individuals.

CAREER OPPORTUNITIES IN MARKETING

Career opportunities in marketing are excellent. Demand appears to be high for individuals who have been trained in marketing. The compensation is good, fringe benefits are attractive, work assignments are exciting, and advancement opportunities are exceptional. Increasingly, women are finding attractive opportunities in marketing, especially in retailing and advertising. Other minorities, especially blacks, are being aggressively recruited.

We will discuss the available marketing positions on the following pages.

Introduction to Marketing Decisions

The chief marketing executive generally carries the title of vice-president of marketing, director of marketing, marketing manager, or vice-president of sales. Whatever the title, that person is responsible for the firm's overall marketing effort. Usually, the chief marketing executive reports directly to the company's president or chief executive officer.

In large firms that are organized on a division basis, one person may not be responsible for the marketing effort of the entire firm. Instead, each division has a top marketing executive who reports to the vice-president or president in charge of that division. An example of this is Pfizer Company, the well-known manufacturer of pharmaceuticals, toiletries, and cosmetics. In 1976 the chief marketing executives were found at the division level for the following divisions: chemicals; diagnostics; minerals, pigments, and metals; laboratories; and medical systems.

The demand for chief marketing executives is high. Many companies are expanding their operations, both nationally and internationally, and need qualified chief marketing executives. One executive search firm, for example, indicated in 1976 that the chief marketing executive was the

Figure 1.9   1974 Compensation and Value of Stock for 15 Chief Marketing Executives

Company	1974 Compensation	Value of Stock
1. Russ Togs	$240,051	$1,215,000
2. Sears, Roebuck	231,000	883,000
3. Revlon	209,111	790,000
4. Goodyear Tire and Rubber	178,686	128,000
5. Standard Oil of California	150,692	251,000
6. Upjohn	137,572	43,000
7. F. W. Woolworth	132,751	102,000
8. Jos. Schlitz Brewing	131,700	None
9. Georgia Pacific	130,000	537,000
10. Zenith Radio	125,250	None
11. Firestone Tire and Rubber	123,600	196,000
12. S. S. Kresge	110,000	489,000
13. Hewlett-Packard	102,083	3,843,000
14. American Airlines	83,425	None
15. Wm. Wrigley, Jr.	55,960	23,000

single most sought after employee. Demand ran 40% higher than in 1975. Salaries were up also 30%.[8]

Typical chief marketing executives are in their middle forties, have had about 20 years of marketing experience, have been with their present company for most of those 20 years, and have probably changed companies only once. They usually have a bachelor's degree.[9] Many have MBA's. Most have sales backgrounds.[10]

Chief marketing executives are in demand to fill presidents' positions. In 1975, 25% of the presidents of 688 large companies had marketing backgrounds, more than any other job category.[11]

Figure 1.9 shows the 1974 compensation figures for the chief marketing executives of 15 well-known companies as reported by *Sales Management*.[12] Also included is the value of stock they owned as of July 12, 1976. These data indicate that the chief marketing executive is generally a well-paid individual.[13]

In addition to their compensation and stock holdings, these executives were provided a generous fringe benefit package. Most received the following:

1. Pension plans.
2. Life insurance.
3. Hospitalization insurance.
4. Company cars.
5. Social club memberships.
6. Free legal advice.
7. Low-cost loans.
8. Use of company recreational facilities.
9. Financial, investment, and estate planning.
10. Profit sharing.
11. Stock options.

Personal Selling

There are attractive opportunities for those who wish to go into the selling profession. Compensation is good and sales experience is often helpful in getting into marketing management. Increasingly, salespeople are expected to have had some college education. This is particularly true for those who are selling for manufacturing firms. Many salespeople selling technical industrial products, for example, hold undergraduate degrees in engineering.

[8] *Sales and Marketing Management*, April 12, 1976, p. 7.
[9] *Business Management*, September, 1971, pp. 36–37.
[10] Victor P. Buell, "Developing Future Marketing Managers," *Sales Management* (March 4, 1966), p. 36.
[11] *Business Week*, August 12, 1972, p. 27.
[12] *Sales Management* (October 6, 1975), pp. 51–56.
[13] Ibid., p. 50.

Introduction to Marketing Decisions

In 1976 starting salespeople were earning from $11,000 to $12,000 per year. Salespeople are usually provided company automobiles and expense accounts when they travel. Experienced salespeople are generally well-paid. One study indicated that 25% of the salespeople analyzed in 1974 received $21,000 or more a year. This was higher than salaries paid accounting managers, purchasing agents, engineers, and general foremen. Sales managers, who are responsible for a company's entire sales force and usually report directly to the company's chief marketing executive, were paid more than plant managers, personnel managers, and electronic data processing managers. One-fourth of these sales managers were paid more than $27,000 per year.[14]

Sales experience appears to be a prerequisite for advancement in marketing. Particularly is this the case for chief marketing executives. Chief marketing executives in one study cited sales experience as the second most important reason for their success (first was education). Over one-half of the individuals started in a selling capacity. The importance of a sales background for chief marketing executives is underscored by Robert W. Lear, vice-president of marketing, the Carborundum Company: "He must have some extensive line sales management in his record."[15]

Advertising

The field of advertising can be a rewarding career in terms of compensation and job satisfaction. As in the sales area, it is desirable that the individual has had some college training. Advertising is a field that has attracted many women in past years.

There are a number of positions available in advertising. Some of the more common ones include the following:

1. *Artists and layout specialists* create the visual parts of advertisements.
2. *Media directors* purchase time and space from advertising media such as radio, television, newspapers, and magazines.
3. *Production managers* convert copy and art work into print.
4. *Copywriters* take the basic advertising theme and translate it into headlines, slogans, and texts.
5. *Advertising managers* are responsible for directing a company's entire advertising program. They make broad policy decisions, such as the type of advertising, the size of the advertising budget, and which advertising agency to use.
6. *Account executives* work for advertising agencies. Their major job is to solicit new business by studying a company's advertising needs and developing an advertising plan to satisfy those needs. Successful account executives for large advertising agencies may earn over $100,000 a year.

[14] Ibid., p. 56.
[15] Buell, op. cit., p. 44.

Marketing Research

Marketing research specialists collect information about markets, products, competition, and company marketing operations. They analyze these data, draw conclusions, and make recommendations to decision makers.

A bachelor's degree is the usual entry requirement for marketing research personnel. However, graduate training is becoming more necessary. Courses in marketing, statistics, economics, psychology, and computers are desirable.

Most marketing research positions are found in manufacturing companies, advertising agencies, research firms, advertising media, government agencies, and university research centers.

In 1976 starting salaries for marketing research personnel was around $11,000. Those who had master's degrees were getting around $14,000. Experienced directors of marketing research frequently earn from $30,000 to $35,000 annually.

Retailing

Employment opportunities in retailing appear to be excellent. Many of the large retailing firms in the United States are opening a number of new stores each year, and qualified personnel are hard to find.

Most of the positions available are with large department stores, national or regional variety store chains, and supermarket and drugstore chains. Entry positions usually require a college degree or attendance at a two-year college.

A two-year training program is usually required of men and women in retailing. During this time they combine on-the-job experience with formal classroom instruction. Then after a probationary period they may become assistant buyers if they are working for department stores or if they are employed by a drug, supermarket chain, or variety chain, they may become assistant store managers or department heads.

Men or women managing stores or serving as head buyers are usually paid as much as $30,000 a year.

Physical Distribution

Career opportunities in physical distribution are exciting and challenging. Increasingly, college experience is being required. Helpful courses include physical distribution management, transportation, marketing, law, economics, statistics, and management.

Most large manufacturing firms have physical distribution departments. Other opportunities exist in transportation firms such as trucking, railroads, and airlines.

In 1976 the annual salary for trainees in physical distribution departments in manufacturing firms was about $11,000. Salaries of from $35,000 to $40,000 per year are not unusual for the top person.

A 1976 graduate of a large university illustrates the career potential in transportation firms. Bob worked his way through college by loading and unloading freight at a terminal of a medium-sized regional trucking firm. After graduation, he accepted an offer to participate in the company's management training program. His first year's salary was $15,000. Within five years, he expected to be a terminal manager. His projected annual income then was a base of around $30,000 plus a bonus that could add as much as 20%.

Product Managers

Product managers are responsible for the marketing program for a single brand or group of products. They frequently decide on the products' advertising media, channels of distribution, budgets, market, and price.

Most product managers have some college training. In some companies, a master's degree in business administration is required. The product manager position is generally filled by an individual who has several years experience with a company. Women are finding good career opportunities as product managers, especially with companies marketing products purchased by women.

In 1976, it was not uncommon for brand managers to be paid $26,000 to $30,000 per year. They are also prime candidates for promotion to higher level positions. For example, the product manager of a well-known toothpaste recently became the vice-president of marketing for one of the divisions of a large, diversified corporation.

In short, the above indicates that the career opportunities in marketing in the future are likely to be very good. What makes the outlook even more exciting is that many *nonprofit organizations* are beginning to hire marketing specialists. Below are some examples of these kinds of organizations:

1. Political parties.
2. Hospitals.
3. Universities.
4. Museums.
5. Symphony orchestras.
6. Churches.
7. Charitable organizations.
8. Welfare agencies.
9. City governments.

PLAN OF THIS TEXT

The remaining chapters in this text are arranged in a logical sequence. This sequence follows the decision model indicated in Figure 1.7 and discussed earlier. Chapters 2 and 3 deal with market analysis. Chapter 2 looks at various types of markets while Chapter 3 deals with consumer (market) behavior.

Chapter 4 discusses the marketing environment. Chapter 5 is concerned with the marketing research function. It is positioned here because it discusses how markets and the environment are analyzed (prior chapters) and because it is also important for establishing objectives and developing the marketing mix (subsequent chapters). Chapter 6 covers steps three, four, and five of the decision-making model: establishing objectives, achieving strategic objectives, and achieving tactical objectives.

Chapters 7 through 15 discuss the various elements of the marketing mix in detail. Product decisions are contained in Chapters 7 and 8. Chapter 9 deals with the advertising function. Personal selling is the subject of Chapter 10. Channels of distribution decisions are contained in Chapters 11 and 12. Chapter 13 discusses the physical distribution function. Pricing decisions are handled in Chapters 14 and 15.

Step six of the decision-making model, marketing organization, is the subject of Chapter 16. Chapter 17 discusses the development of control systems, which is the seventh and last step of the decision-making model.

International marketing is covered in Chapter 18. We feel that today this is such an important marketing topic that it deserves inclusion as a separate chapter.

SUMMARY

Marketing is a major function of business and nonbusiness firms that is very important in our economy and in our daily lives. Marketing is concerned with (1) determining the needs and desires of customers and (2) developing products and services that satisfy these needs and desires. Marketing's significance in our economy is illustrated by the amount of jobs it provides, the resources it uses, the level of marketing costs involved, the variety of organizations practicing marketing, and so on.

The marketing concept provides a focus for an organization's marketing operations. It stresses the need to achieve goals while satisfying customer needs and desires through a systems orientation while being aware of societal objectives.

There are seven basic marketing functions: (1) marketing research, (2) product management, (3) advertising, (4) personal selling, (5) channels of distribution management, (6) physical distribution, and (7) pricing. Except for marketing research, these management functions are included in the firm's marketing mix. The marketing mix refers to the combination of marketing decisions used to market specific products to specific markets over a specific period of time.

The seven basic steps that marketing executives must consider in making decisions are: (1) analyzing the market, (2) analyzing the environment, (3) establishing objectives, (4) achieving strategic objectives through product/market combinations, (5) achieving tactical objectives through marketing mix decisions, (6) developing the marketing organization, and (7) developing the control system.

Marketing executives are responsible for achieving objectives. Strategic objectives are long-run goals of the firm for which marketing executives

Introduction to Marketing Decisions

may have partial responsibility. Tactical, or short-run goals, are marketing objectives used to obtain strategic objectives. The marketing executive has direct responsibility for achieving the tactical objectives assigned to his department.

Marketing decisions are difficult to make because they involve people, deal with uncontrollable variables, take a great deal of time, use up valuable resources, involve a great number of marketing mix variables, and are interdisciplinary in nature.

Career opportunities in marketing are excellent. The pay is good, rapid advancement is possible, and the jobs are interesting and challenging. There appears to be a healthy demand for individuals who have marketing skills.

QUESTIONS

1. Do you believe that the marketing concept is as applicable to companies selling industrial products as it is to those marketing consumer products?
2. Do you believe that the chief marketing executive is worth the compensation and fringe benefits discussed in this chapter? Why or why not?
3. Why is the marketing mix an important concept?
4. From your own experience can you provide several specific examples of nonbusiness firms that have used marketing techniques to secure their objectives?
5. When might a company not want or be able to use the seven-step model for making marketing decisions.
6. Why must a company analyze the environment before it makes decisions about its marketing mix?

GLOSSARY

Advertising: the marketing function that uses nonpersonal means of informing customers of the existence of products and services that can satisfy their needs and desires and attempts to obtain their purchase

Channels of Distribution Management: the marketing function that involves establishing and maintaining a network of middlemen to market a company's products or services

Control System: the procedures used to measure the effectiveness of the marketing department's performance

Demarketing: efforts to persuade purchasers to consume fewer goods and services in order to save scarce resources

Environment: those areas, except the market, over which the marketing department cannot exert direct control

Marketing: the determination of needs and desires of the market so that goods and services can be provided that satisfy these needs and desires

Marketing Concept: the basic orientation of a firm's marketing effort involving an emphasis on goal achievement, satisfying customer needs and wants, recognizing societal requirements, and using a systems approach

Marketing Mix: the combination of marketing decisions used to market specific products to specific markets over a specific time period

Marketing Research: the marketing function that provides marketing decision makers with timely and accurate information

Personal Selling: the marketing function that uses personal means of informing customers of the existence of products and services that can satisfy their needs and desires and attempts to obtain their purchase by the market

Physical Distribution: the marketing function that concerns moving finished goods from a company's production area to the purchasers of these products

Pricing: the marketing function concerned with the establishment and maintenance of an overall pricing program

Product Management: the marketing function that involves developing new products and services that satisfy customer needs and wants, management of these products and services over their lifetimes, and consideration of marginal products and services for elimination

Strategic Objectives: Long-run, basic objectives of a company

Tactical Objectives: short-run objectives assigned to the marketing department that aid in achieving strategic objectives

CASES

Case 1: Ward Cookie and Cracker Co.

Harry L. Ward, founder and president of a firm that manufactures cookies and crackers, decided to install the marketing concept in his company. He had been exposed to the marketing concept while attending a marketing conference in Chicago. He believed that the marketing concept, if properly implemented in his company, would increase the firm's profits.

As a first step, he created a new position, the vice-president of marketing. The person in this position was to be responsible for the entire range of marketing functions, including management of the sales force, advertising, physical distribution, and marketing research. The vice-president of marketing was to report directly to Mr. Ward.

As a second step, Mr. Ward created another new position, the director of marketing research. The person in this position was to report directly to the vice-president of marketing. The major function of this position was to determine the basic needs and desires of consumers that could be satisfied by cookies and crackers. Then the director of marketing research was to survey the company's current customers in order to determine how effectively the firm's ten major products were satisfying these basic needs and desires.

1. Do you agree with the president's belief that adoption of the marketing concept should improve the company's profit?
2. Do you believe that what the president has done demonstrates an adequate knowledge and understanding of the marketing concept?
3. What else might the president do to successfully implement the marketing concept in his company?

Case 2: Baxter Printing Co.

The Baxter Printing Company, a medium-sized printing firm, was acquired by a large news media conglomerate that owns a number of television and radio stations and newspapers in the South.

Management of the Baxter Printing Company decided to expand its business. To accomplish this, Baxter acquired a new web-fed press. This was a large capital investment that increased the company's fixed costs by 250%. The web-fed press was designed to serve customers who had high-volume, high-quality printing needs.

Because of Baxter's other responsibilities, management did not have time to generate a list of potential customers for this new machine. Also, because management did not have a customer list, it had no way of developing an estimate of potential business for this press.

Baxter employed as a consultant a marketing professor from a local university to assist them with these tasks. The marketing professor was asked to (1) develop a list of companies that would be customers for the web-fed printing press and (2) from that list estimate potential sales volume for the new acquisition.

The consultant found that of all expenditures in the United States in 1975 for web-fed printing, 34% went for magazines and periodicals, 20% went for direct mail, 16% went for catalogs, 11% went for newspapers, 11% went for brochures, pamphlets, and folders, and 8% went for miscellaneous expenses.

Since most newspapers have their own printing presses, newspapers were eliminated as a prospect. The consultant believed that good prospects for the web-fed press consisted of (1) magazines and periodicals, (2) manufacturing firms doing extensive direct mail and catalog advertising, (3) large retailers or mail order firms, and (4) colleges and universities. A list (derived from published sources) of over 1,700 prospects found within the area covered by Baxter's salesmen was developed. The consultant was able to project a potential sales volume from this list.

1. Could the Baxter Printing Company have benefited from using the seven-step approach to making marketing decisions discussed in this chapter?
2. What do you think of Baxter's decision to acquire the web-fed press *before* it developed an estimate of sales potential?
3. Do you agree with the consultant's prospect categories? Are there any other organizations you believe could also have been listed as prospects?

Identifying and Selecting Markets

After you finish this chapter, you should be able to answer the following questions:

1. What is a market? What are consumer markets and industrial markets?

2. What basic questions should a marketer be able to answer in pinpointing markets?

3. What are several options a firm may choose in selecting markets to serve?

4. What are the benefits and limitations of market segmentation? How are market segments identified?

5. How are the physical characteristics of United States consumer markets changing? How do these market trends influence consumer spending patterns: population size and geographic location, age and family life cycle trends, and income trends?

6. What factors seem to suggest that future consumer markets will grow much more slowly, if at all? How can firms anticipate and adapt their marketing strategies to this slow growth era?

7. How do industrial buyers differ from final consumers? Why do they differ? What are some of the important buying characteristics of producers, resellers, and government customers?

Benefit Segmentation   *Consumer Market*   *Demographic Factors*
Discretionary Income   *Family Life Cycle*   *Industrial Market*   *Market*
Market Segments   *Psychographic Segmentation*   *Target Market*

INTRODUCTION Choosing target customers is both critical to the firm's success, and it is a complicated task. It is critical because the success of any marketing program hinges upon how well the marketer can identify customer needs and select those specific, most profitable groups to serve. It is complicated because markets exist in changing environments and because important market characteristics are complex and often not easily measured. Our task in this and the next chapter will be to describe some important characteristics of markets, look at how they may be changing, and explore how these characteristics influence buying decisions and thus marketing management. A descriptive look at customers is the subject of this chapter. Determining *why* customers buy is usually much more complex, and it often requires extensive research into consumer motivations, preferences, and shopping experiences. The following chapter explores some of the "whys" of consumer behavior.

What Is a Market?

Defining the term *market* is a problem because the term is used in so many different ways. Often we think of markets as people, alone or in organizations—teen-agers, factory purchasing agents, department store fashion buyers. There are *product* markets—for peanuts, ten-speed bikes, machine tools. Markets often are thought of as *places of exchange*—shopping centers or more temporary places, like weekend "flea markets," or trade shows, such as furniture markets for manufacturers and distributors. *Geography* can describe markets—the Asian market, the Boston market.

All of these terms are useful in *describing* and *identifying* markets, but they are not by themselves definitions of the term market. Marketing has been considered as a human exchange process to satisfy wants and needs. With this in mind, we can think of a **market** as people or organizations that have wants and needs and that have the ability and willingness to exchange something of value for them. Notice that people who have wants and needs alone do not make a market. The market for a $90,000 Rolls Royce Camargue is not just anyone wanting a prestige automobile. The exchange price obviously limits this market to those who have exceptional purchasing power.

As a starting point, we need some sort of language to help in classifying and describing markets. The most basic scheme classifies markets into two broad types: the **consumer market** and the **industrial market.** Consumers, alone or as part of a family or household, buy products and services for their own use. The industrial market buys products and services primarily to use in running the business, or to resell, or to produce further goods and services. Since industrial markets include a wide variety of institutions that have unusual characteristics, it is helpful to divide this market further into producers, resellers, and governmental institutions. The classifications of both consumer and industrial markets are shown in Figure 2.1. From a marketing management viewpoint, the broad classification shown in Figure 2.1 is clear and useful because each of these markets differs in important ways—in buying motivations, in purchasing methods, and often in the types of products and services they buy. Consumer and industrial markets both can be further subdivided in much finer detail. For instance, consumer markets frequently are subdivided by geographic area (Northeast, Pacific Coast states), by demographic characteristics (teen-agers, middle-income, female, etc.), by product usage (heavy user, non-user), and countless other ways.

Very detailed classifications of industrial markets are available and widely used. The federal government, for example, has developed a Standard Industrial Classification System (SIC) for all types of producers, so that firms as diverse as shipbuilders and children's shoe manufacturers can be easily identified and located. Since there are hundreds of thousands of industrial customers, it is important to know what classification systems are available and how to use them.

Figure 2.1   Classifications of Markets

| | Industrial Customers | | |
Consumers	Producers	Resellers	Governmental
Persons, households, or families buying for personal consumption	Manufacturers and processors, utilities, construction, transportation, service industries, nonprofit institutions acquiring goods and services used in producing further products and services for sale or nonprofit exchange	Wholesalers serving both consumer and industrial markets; retailers purchasing from producers or other resellers for resale or rental	Political subdivisions: federal, state, regional, and local buying or renting goods and services for performing governmental functions

Background for Marketing Decisions

SEGMENTED MARKETS

Marketers perform two basic tasks in meeting their exchange objectives: first, they identify potential markets and select certain target markets to serve; then they design and implement marketing strategies to meet these target market objectives. Marketing strategies, or action plans for accomplishing objectives, then, are thought of in terms of particular markets. Thus, identifying and selecting target markets are critical early tasks of marketing managers, and they are the subject of this and the next chapter.

In affluent economies there are few completely *homogeneous* markets, that is, markets of people who want identical products at identical prices and quantities. For instance, think about a product as basic as drinking water. Most people in the United States turn on the water faucet when they want a drink of water. But a few people pay extra for a refrigerator accessory that provides water and ice cubes without opening the door. And more and more people are buying their favorite brand of drinking water in bottles from the supermarket shelf. Among a group of young people, all sharing a common need for housing, many rent apartments in cities, others insist on houses in the suburbs, while one or two will scan the ads in *Mother Earth News* for a few timbered acres in Maine where they can build their own log cabins. The point is that most markets are segmented into different groups sharing preferences for a specific set of product characteristics.

Why Segment Markets?

Henry Ford made history with his decision to mass produce the Model T Ford at a very low price for the mass market. His famous quip, "The public can have any color it wants, as long as it's black!" clearly illustrated his marketing philosophy. A wise choice at the time, but not for long. Other manufacturers, notably General Motors, began producing cars in a variety of price levels, styles, brands, and colors, believing that the auto market was becoming bigger and more affluent—a **segmented market.** They were right. GM built a market lead over Ford that it has never relinquished.

Today, most firms pursue a market segmentation strategy. In fact, it is probably safe to say that market segmentation is one of the most visible features of an affluent society. As people increase their wealth and leisure time, they become able to enjoy a much greater variety of life-styles, and the many different products and services that go with them.

For instance, tennis, like golf before it, was once a game for the wealthy. Today, it is played by people from all walks of life. Many tennis racket manufacturers have responded with inexpensive rackets for children, beginners, and people who have little money; very expensive, stylish rackets for more affluent players; rackets designed for power, others for control; rackets designed for two-handed backhands. Today, trying to sell a single model to the entire tennis market would satisfy few customer groups.

In short, market segmentation is popular because it often pays off in higher sales and profits. By designing specific products for different customer groups, the firm can more closely match the needs of its different target customers. This offers the firm some protection from competitors who are not as closely matched to these segments' needs.

Market segmentation brings other related benefits, too. It keeps the firm tuned more closely to the market and alert to new opportunities. And it encourages higher management efficiency in using the firm's resources.

Limitations of Market Segmentation

Logically, the concept of a market segment can be extended to the needs of individual customers or firms. In fact, the term "custom-made" refers to just this idea—creating a product or service to the specifications of a particular customer. Custom-built homes, customized vans, and custom-tailored clothing for individuals or factory buildings or computerized inventory control systems for firms are just a few examples. Since customized products and services are more costly to produce than are standardized products, the total market that can afford to be individually served is very small. Even segmenting to larger groups can be extremely expensive. At some point, the production and marketing costs will outweigh the benefits of segmentation. The firm, then, faces a trade-off between the added costs and benefits of more precise segmentation.

Firms also must guard against creating too many different products or excessive or frivolous product features beyond those desired by enough customers. Not only will the firm wind up with a large percentage of unprofitable items, the excessive products may confuse and irritate some customers who would rather face fewer and less demanding choices.

Whether markets are uniform or segmented, they usually are too large for a single organization to serve effectively with its limited resources. Therefore, firms select certain **target markets** from the segments it has identified. Marketing mix strategies are then developed to match these target market needs and also the objectives and resources of the firm.

In segmented markets the firm could pursue several options in choosing potential target markets and marketing mixes:[1]

1. Aim at the entire market (all segments) with a single product offer. This is called *undifferentiated marketing*.
2. Focus on just one or a very few segments of the broader market, again with a single product. This is called *concentrated marketing*.
3. Pursue several different segments with different products for each segment. This is called *market segmentation*.

We can illustrate these options by using the example of the young-adult housing market. Following the undifferentiated marketing approach, a

[1] Philip Kotler, *Marketing Management*, 3rd. ed. (Englewood Cliffs, N.J.: Prentice-Hall, Inc., 1976), p. 142.

Background for Marketing Decisions

housing developer might build only three-bedroom houses for young people who have all types of housing needs. Following a concentrated marketing strategy, the developer might design apartment complexes for just single people. Seeking more customers, the developer might pursue a market segmentation strategy, offering single-family houses, apartments for singles, and log cabin kits to separate segments of this market.

Conditions Necessary for Successful Market Segmentation

The primary condition for segmentation is the existence of real differences in buying and consumption within the total market; otherwise, the marketer will be wasting resources in creating separate marketing mixes. Since market segmentation is often very expensive, it is also important that the segments are *large enough* to be served profitably. Market segments must also be *measurable*. This means that although real customer differences may exist, the marketer cannot segment the market if individual factors that distinguish the segments cannot be identified. For instance, perhaps the buyer's personal moods may have a lot to do with her purchases of such things as cosmetics or record albums. But since moods change quickly, the marketer cannot afford to measure individual buyers' changing emotions anyway. Therefore, segmenting by emotional states may be impractical. Segments should also be *accessible* by the firm. For example, perhaps the purchasers of a new men's after-shave lotion are likely to be more innovative males. But if innovators do not differ from other men in responsiveness to advertising themes or in their media preferences or shopping patterns, it may not be practical to try to reach them separately.

Finally, the firm must consider its competitors. A small segment ignored by competitors may be far more profitable than a large segment that everyone else is aggressively serving.

Identifying Market Segments

Logically, buyer needs and preferences should be the basis for identifying market segments. But especially for new products, the firm still must decide which potential buyers have these particular needs and preferences. The task of identifying market segments can be difficult. Often, marketers rely upon their past experience and intuition, or perhaps they hang back and follow the lead of other firms. These methods are less likely to work today because the consumer market is more complex and changes quickly and competition for new segments is too intense. In recent years, market researchers have developed and refined a number of methods for locating and classifying market segments. There is no one best method. It is a question of what works best in a given situation.

Most firms segment markets by *geographic* differences (nations, regions, city, etc.) and by **demographic factors** (age, family income, occupation, sex, etc.). Since both geographic and demographic market statistics are widely available and the market classifications are fairly well standardized, marketers find them easy to use. More important, for many products, geographic and demographic factors are strongly related to buying patterns. Skis and snowmobiles and snorkels and suntan lotion are examples of products where geography counts; large families buy big packages of food, children's clothing, and station wagons.

Used alone, demographic factors often are not precise enough measures of buying preferences. For example, certain style-conscious young people who have relatively low incomes are known to buy 10 or 15 pairs of shoes each year, spending considerably more than many business and professional adults who have much higher incomes. It is really the buyer's attitudes and interests toward clothing and shoe fashions that influence shoe buying preferences, not age, income level, or other demographic characteristics per se. Measuring buyers' attitudes, preferences, and activities is known as **psychographic** or *life-style segmentation* and is discussed more fully in the next chapter. Here, researchers try to uncover customer characteristics that group them into such categories as "leisure-oriented retiree," "traditional housewife," or "ecologically conscious consumer."

Benefit segmentation involves classifying markets on the basis of par-

"Now remember, kids, call them 'city folk' and say things like 'aye, Gramps' and 'by cracky'. They're impulse buyers looking for organically grown produce in a country setting with a home-grown, cornball atmosphere."

ticular benefits different customer groups receive from similar products. Then, the product design and other marketing factors, such as price or advertising, are developed to emphasize these different benefits. One study of the toothpaste market found that different kinds of people were seeking pleasant flavor, sparkling teeth, decay prevention, and low price as major benefits and that specific brands differed in their appeal to customers on these features. Those most interested in bright teeth, for example, preferred Plus White, MacLeans, and Ultra-Brite, while Crest was preferred by users concerned with decay prevention. Families with small children bought Crest, while the "sparkling teeth" benefit segment tended to be single people and tobacco users. Segmenting by product benefits seems an ideal approach, but marketers often find that, especially for new products, it is difficult to determine in advance just what benefits will be most important to which kinds of people.

Another way of getting at benefit segments is through *marketing factor* segmentation. Markets often differ in their responsiveness to marketing factors such as price and "deals," service, assortment, or quality. Marketers can emphasize various marketing mix factors for different segments. Avon cosmetics, sold door-to-door, seem to appeal especially to women who want or need a lot of personal service from the seller. These women also tend to be stay-at-homes, older, lower-income, and less innovative in buying. For products that are bought frequently or in multiple units, it is important to know that a small percentage of buyers account for most of the sales. These heavy users can be identified and segmented by *usage rate.* Heavy users can be extremely important segments. For instance, one-half of the cola beverage purchasers buy 90% of the cola sold. Similar percentages are found for such products as beer, bourbon, dog food, and many other items.

In summary, the marketer can segment customers in many different ways. The goal is to determine the most decisive method. The fact that there is no one best way of segmenting markets is a continuing challenge to marketing creativity.

THE CHANGING CONSUMER MARKET

Our description of American consumer markets will begin with a look at important attributes of the American population: its size, geographic location, and basic *demographic* information including age, income, and family status. Since population data are always changing, understanding basic *trends* in consumer markets is vital in predicting market characteristics in the future.

Population Size and Growth

Marketers are interested in population growth figures because these figures suggest the numbers of people who will be demanding goods and services. The United States population is projected to grow from a current 215 million to about 225 million by 1980 and to about 245 million by 1990 (see Figure 2.2). Any way you look at it, this is a huge and growing consumer market. But the *rate* of growth has been slowing recently, thanks to a sharply lower birthrate. In 1973 the birthrate in the United States dropped to about 1.9 children per family. This is now below the *zero population growth* (ZPG) average of 2.1 children per family needed to replace both parents. Since 1973 the birthrate has remained below the ZPG rate. If this low birthrate continues, in about 70 years the total population in the United States will stop growing and actually decline.

Accurate population forecasting is very difficult. Just ten years ago, for instance, the most sophisticated forecasters estimated that there would be 340 million people in the United States by the year 2000. Today, these same forecasters have revised their estimates sharply downward, to 262 million.[2] Where did all these 78 million hypothetical people go? They disappeared in the declining birthrate. In 1966 population experts were figuring on 3.1 children per family instead of the current 2.1 estimate used today.

What does the revised population forecast mean for marketers? For one thing, it means that firms no longer can count on total population growth to bring higher sales and profits. Therefore, firms will be trying to discover fast-growing market segments within the total population. It also means

[2] "The Future Revisited," *The Wall Street Journal*, March 15, 1976, p. 1.

Figure 2.2   United States Population Trends

U.S. Population (millions)		Population Projections to 2025*			
			Series		
			I	II	III
1900	76				
1920	106	1980	226	223	220
1940	132	1990	258	245	235
1960	181	2000	287	262	245
1974	212	2010	322	279	250
		2020	362	294	252
		2025	382	300	250

* These projections reflect three different assumptions about the average number of lifetime births per woman. Series II, for example, was set at 2.1 births per woman, representing replacement level.

Source: U.S. Department of Commerce, Bureau of the Census, *Population Estimates and Projections* (Series P-25, No. 541), February, 1975, p. 1.

Background for Marketing Decisions

Figure 2.2—*continued*

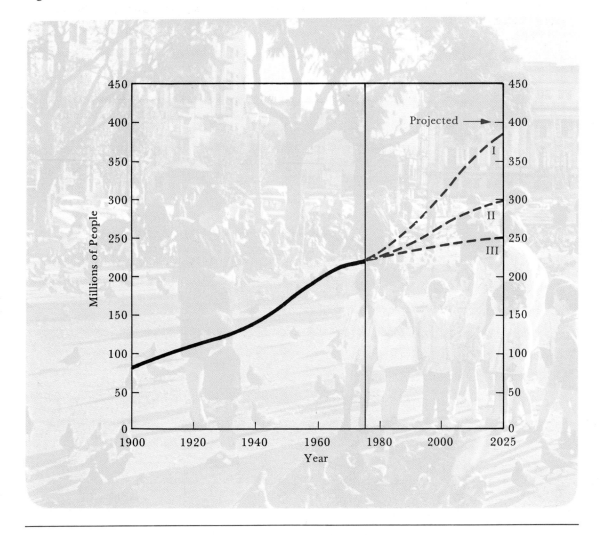

Identifying and Selecting Markets

that marketers will have to match their products more carefully with the needs of their market segments.

Some firms have already started adjusting to the new population trend facts of life. Gerber's dropped its famous slogan, "Babies are our business— our *only* business," and entered other markets, such as life insurance for young adults and retirees, two fast-growing age segments. Johnson & Johnson successfully broadened its "no tears" baby shampoo appeal to include teen-agers and adults.[3]

[3] "The Baby Bust," *The Wall Street Journal*, January 4, 1972, p. 1.

Age Distribution Is Changing

Although the total United States population is gradually increasing, a closer look at population growth by age groups reveals some surprises (see Figures 2.3 and 2.4). Over the next 10 years, nearly all of this growth will be in just two age groups, younger adults aged 25 to 39 and people 60 years and over. The number of teen-agers will actually shrink about 14% by 1985. Alert markets are switching emphasis to these growth segments. Honda, alarmed at the decline in its teen-age market, is adding automatic transmissions to its motorcycle line to appeal to older buyers.[4] PepsiCo. sees a slowing growth in soft drink sales but increases in diet and citrus-flavored drinks used as mixers. And Federated Department Stores is switching its fashion emphasis from teens and young twenties to people in their thirties.[5]

[4] "Motorcycles: The Dip Continues," *Business Week*, May 3, 1976, pp. 80, 85.
[5] "How the Changing Age Mix Changes Markets," *Business Week*, January 12, 1976, pp. 74–78.

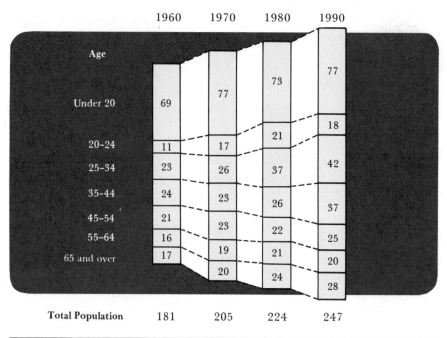

Figure 2.3   Population Shifts by Age Group, 1960–1990 (millions of persons)

Background for Marketing Decisions

Figure 2.4   Population Shifts by Age Group, 1960–1990 (percentage changes)

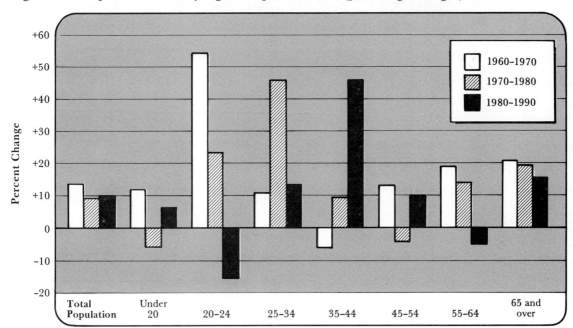

Source: Based on data from Bureau of the Census, Current Population Reports, Series P-25 using Series E for projections.

Family Life Cycle Affects Spending

Consumer age and family status directly influence spending. Together, age and family status show *life cycle stages* of families. The **family life cycle stages** of adults (six major categories) looks like this:

1. Young single adults
2. Young couples without children
3. Young couples with children
4. Older couples with dependent children
5. Older couples with no children at home
6. Older single adults

The typical financial status and buying patterns of adults at different life cycle states are described in Figure 2.5. By knowing a family's current life cycle stage and when the family will enter a new stage, marketers have a good idea of what a family may purchase and why. Young working adults without children, for example, are good prospects for apartment furniture, restaurant meals, and skiing vacations. But when children appear, young couples will begin spending much more heavily on food and children's clothing, will seek more spacious housing, buy more life insurance, and perhaps cut back on new cars, vacations, and savings to meet their new spending needs. Middle-aged couples whose children have grown and left home tend to have higher savings and discretionary buying power compared with other middle-aged consumers whose children are still at home or in college. These examples suggest that the family life cycle stage is often much more meaningful than consumers' ages alone as an indicator of their financial status and buying patterns.

Figure 2.5   Consumption Patterns at Different Life Cycle Stages

Stages in Life Cycle

1. Bachelor stage: young, single people not living at home	Few financial burdens. Fashion opinion leaders. Recreaction-oriented. Buy basic kitchen equipment, basic furniture, cars, equipment for the mating game, vacations.
2. Newly married couples: young, no children	Better off financially than they will be in near future. Highest purchase rate and highest average purchase of durables. Buy cars, refrigerators, stoves, sensible and durable furniture, vacations.
3. Full nest 1: youngest child under six	Home purchasing at peak. Liquid assets low. Dissatisfied with financial position and amount of money saved. Interested in new products. Buy washers, dryers, TV, baby food, chest rubs and cough medicines, vitamins, dolls, wagons, sleds, skates.
4. Full nest 2: youngest child six or over six	Financial position better. Some wives work. Less influenced by advertising. Buy larger-sized packages, multiple-unit deals. Buy many foods, cleaning materials, bicycles, music lessons, pianos.
5. Full nest 3: older couples with dependent children	Financial position still better. More wives work. Some children get jobs. Hard to influence with advertising. High average purchase of durables. Buy new, more tasteful furniture, auto travel, non-necessary appliances, boats, dental services, magazines.

Figure 2.5—*continued*

Stages in Life Cycle

---

6. Empty nest 1: Older couples, no children living with them, head in labor force

Home ownership at peak. Most satisfied with financial position and money saved. Interested in travel, recreation, self-education. Make gifts and contributions. Not interested in new products. Buy vacations, luxuries, home improvements.

7. Empty nest 2: older married couples, no children living at home, head retired

Drastic cut in income. Keep home. Buy medical appliances, medical-care products that aid health, sleep, and digestion.

8. Solitary survivor in labor force

Income still good, but likely to sell home.

9. Solitary survivor, retired

Same medical and product needs as other retired group. Drastic cut in income. Special need for attention, affection, and security.

Source: Reprinted from William D. Wells and G. Gubar, "Life Cycle Concept in Marketing Research," *Journal of Marketing Research*, November 1966, p. 362, published by the American Marketing Association.

Young Adults Set the Buying Pace Today

The fastest-growing age groups and life cycle stages are younger adults and the elderly. Both groups are worth further discussion, for not only are they growing fast, their life styles are also changing.

Babies grow up and reach what is called the "prime marriage age" in a very short time (about 20 to 25 years). Because so many babies were born between 1945 and 1965 (the "baby boom" years), the United States today has more young people in this prime marriage age than ever before. In 1975, there were about 2.2 million marriages. This is expected to climb to over 2,500,000 by 1980 and reach 2,700,000 per year in 1990. Coupled with a projected increase in the *fertility rate* (births per 1,000 women aged 15–44) from 69 in 1975 to 73 by 1990,[6] this increase in marriages is getting marketers excited. As the family life cycle illustration shows (Figure 2.5), these young adults will be heavy consumers of durable goods and services.

This young adult market is also much different in life style from earlier generations of newly forming families. Understanding these differences is critically important for today's marketer. Some of these life-style differences are:

1. More young singles
2. Postponement of marriage

[6] *U.S. News & World Report*, October 27, 1975, p. 32.

Identifying and Selecting Markets

3. Delay of first child, and fewer children
4. More working women, especially young mothers
5. More education and higher-level occupations and incomes

Young singles and couples will have higher incomes than earlier generations. And with fewer little mouths to feed, they will spend this income on
themselves. Although it is true that some younger people favor a simpler,
less materialistic life-style, many others buy expensive stereos and sports
and outdoor equipment, travel widely, and consume many other products
and services often considered luxuries by their parents. Thus, Drexel
Heritage Furnishings predicts that the market will move to higher-priced
furniture.[7] Much of the furniture industry is reacting to changing life-styles
by designing smaller, more portable furniture for today's mobile, apart-
ment-oriented young singles and childless couples.

Convenience is very important to young singles and couples, too, especially when both partners are working. Some shopping centers are busier at
night, especially on weekend nights, than during the day. Who are they
attracting? Working women who can't shop during the day.[8]

Young Women Buy for Themselves

Today's younger woman is more likely to work, remain single longer, and
plan her family around her career. More independent today, she also makes
more of her own purchasing decisions. Auto manufacturers are well aware
that women buy one-fourth of all new cars. Mercury's Capri, Mustang,
Toyota, and Datsun are just a few makes designed largely for women
owners. But many marketers still have a long way to go in meeting women's
needs. When was the last time you saw a woman selling cars? Or life
insurance?

The Booming Elderly Market

The fast-growing "over-60" market is more complex than it might first
appear. For one thing, we tend to stereotype older people as retired, physically deteriorating, and having little desire or ability to buy much. Certainly
some older people fit this description. But consider the following facts about
the older population: People retire earlier today, often well before 65;
therefore, the "retiree" market contains many more people who think and
act and buy like younger adults. And 25% of the population 65 years of
age or older are working. Thus, income varies widely among older consumers. Retired elderly persons on low fixed incomes must struggle harder
than ever today to make ends meet, for inflation robs their purchasing
power. Yet, millions of elderly people are better off than ever before.

Many firms are just beginning to cater to the needs and buying power of

[7] *Business Week*, January 12, 1976, p. 76.
[8] *The Richmond News-Leader*, April 4, 1976.

this affluent segment. Older consumers are responding eagerly to planned retirement communities, organized travel services, shopping facilities, and even restaurant menus designed for their particular needs. Yet, today's older people often do not like being singled out and marketed to as "different" consumers. Even the term "senior citizen" turns off many older people who want to act and look young and buy young. These shoppers purposely avoid clothing styles and colors designed and promoted to appeal to "mature" customers.

Geographic Distribution of Consumer Markets

The United States market is so large and diverse that most firms do not aim at the entire national population. Instead, they serve certain segments within the total population. One basic way of subdividing the population is by geographic region.

Marketers are well aware that the United States population is not at all evenly distributed. (See Figure 2.6 for population per square mile by state.)

Figure 2.6   Population per Square Mile by States, 1970

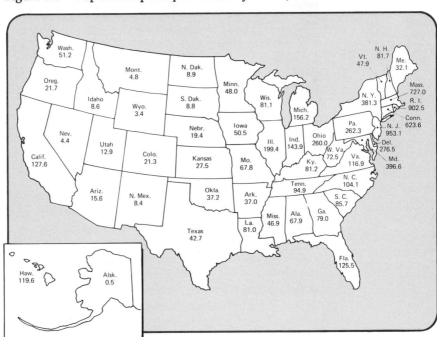

Source: *Statistical Abstract of the United States*, 1976, p. 13.

Identifying and Selecting Markets

The majority of people live in the largest urban areas. Most of these big cities are on the two coasts and in the Great Lakes states. Contrasts in population density sometimes are startling. For example, more people live in the 81 square miles of Brooklyn, New York (about 2.6 million) than live in the 6 least populated western states that have a combined land area of *one million* square miles. Less than 5% of the population now live on farms, while about 70% reside in just the 264 urban areas defined as Standard Metropolitan Statistical Areas (SMSAs).* Metropolitan areas have been growing so fast and sprawling over such wide areas that in 1975 the Federal Office of Management and Budget created a new category, bigger than the present SMSA, to better measure the growth of these cities. The Bureau now lumps together such cities as Miami and Ft. Lauderdale, Florida, and Cleveland and Akron, Ohio. Some demographers see this urban growth eventually joining cities into a new kind of urban–suburban *supercity* called *interurbia* or *megalopolis*. The largest megalopolis, called *Boswash*, will be the 600-mile-long string of cities and suburbs stretching from Boston through New York, Philadelphia, and Baltimore to Washington, D.C.

Where the United States Population Is Moving

Anticipating where the population is shifting is extremely important to businesses, especially to those that have national markets. But it is not easy to predict accurately where the United States population will be moving. Therefore, good forecasting here can give a firm a competitive advantage.

Some broad, long-term population movements are well-known, for example:

1. The migration from rural to urban and suburban areas
2. A population shift from the interior states to coastal and "sunbelt" states, especially to Florida and the Southwest
3. A more recent shift from North to South, reversing the earlier movement from the rural South to northern industrial centers

For the next ten years or so, it appears that smaller cities, especially those in sunbelt states, will grow the fastest. One forecast (Figure 2.7) shows the ten fastest-growing areas to 1980. These areas offer well-above-average marketing opportunities over at least the next few years, for several reasons. First, more people means larger markets. Second, fast-growing areas contain very high percentages of "new arrivals," people who spend heavily in moving into their new homes. Since new residents must learn new shopping patterns, they are especially responsive to alert marketers willing to help them locate new sources of goods and services.

* SMSAs are defined by the U.S. Census Bureau as counties or groups of contiguous counties with a combined population of at least 100,000 and a central city of at least 50,000 people.

Figure 2.7   Ten of 100 Top United States Markets That Will Grow the Fastest by 1980

Baltimore, Maryland
Colorado Springs–Pueblo, Colorado
Denver, Colorado
Memphis, Tennessee
Miami–Fort Lauderdale, Florida
Nashville, Tennessee
Norfolk–Portsmouth–Newport News–Hampton, Virginia
Orlando–Daytona Beach, Florida
Tampa–St. Petersburg, Florida
Tucson, Arizona

Source: "Growth Seen Shifting Away from Biggest Markets," *Advertising Age*, December 15, 1975, p. 93.

Finally, market competition may be less severe in smaller cities since the largest, most aggressive national firms tend to concentrate their efforts in the largest urban markets.

Income Trends

In 1960 most marketers used family incomes of "over $10,000 a year" as the top income category in classifying consumer markets. And for good reason; in 1960 only 32% of United States families earned more than $10,000. But look at what has happened to family incomes since then (see Figure 2.8).

Today, higher-income classifications have been added to account for income growth. But much more important, even when adjusted for inflation gains, family income has jumped remarkably over the last several decades. By 1985, the second largest proportion of family income will be in the $25,000-and-over category. In the middle 1970's, however, these gains in real income largely disappeared. This will be discussed more fully in Chapter 4.

Marketing Significance of Income Gains

To appreciate the marketing importance of these income gains, it is necessary to classify *purchases* into two types: (1) expenditures for *necessities*, such as basic foods, clothing, rent or mortgage payments, utilities, local transportation, and basic health care and (2) *discretionary* purchases that

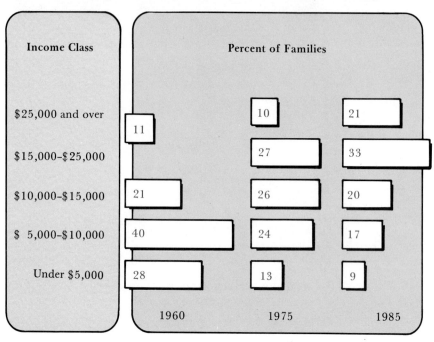

Figure 2.8   Changes in Family Income (in 1971 dollars)

Income Class	Percent of Families		
	1960	1975	1985
$25,000 and over	11	10	21
$15,000–$25,000		27	33
$10,000–$15,000	21	26	20
$ 5,000–$10,000	40	24	17
Under $5,000	28	13	9

Source: Fabian Linden, "Age and Income—1985," *Conference Board Record*, 13 (June 1976). With permission of The Conference Board, Inc.

households can make after buying necessities. We might expect that expenditures for necessities would not rise as fast as gain in total real income, leaving more **discretionary income** to save or to spend on non-essentials.

Government surveys have revealed how United States families at different income levels spend their money. Notice in Figure 2.9 that families in higher-income groups spend more dollars in every category (not included here is any breakdown of how much of the family income goes for taxes or savings). The dollar differences in spending by family income level are very substantial in clothing, recreation, gifts and contributions, and other more *discretionary* purchases. But notice also that for categories that are largely *necessities*, the dollar expenditures increase more slowly as family incomes climb. In fact, calculations would show that the *percentages* of family income spent on food and health care, for example, will decrease as incomes rise, leaving more for discretionary buying. Spending patterns have changed somewhat since these figures were published, of course. Families are spending an even higher proportion of their incomes today for

Figure 2.9   Annual Family Spending by Income Groups, 1973

Spending For:	All Families	By Family Income Before Taxes					
		$8000–9999	$10,000–11,999	$12,000–14,999	$15,000–19,999	$20,000–24,999	$25,000 and up**
Food	$1568	$1392	$1563	$1750	$2010	$2293	$2651
Housing (total)*	2468	2128	2342	2591	3027	3495	4682
Clothing	671	517	617	692	867	1082	1564
Transportation	1639	1466	1714	1956	2257	2712	3234
Health care	491	466	487	513	584	706	896
Personal care	103	98	111	115	139	166	233
Education	105	194	221	232	347	551	833
Reading materials	49	43	53	59	69	86	112
Recreation	669	485	597	690	896	1297	1842
Alcoholic beverages	79	95	124	110	134	144	202
Tobacco products	130	226	232	243	264	272	256
Personal insurance	258	237	298	326	415	510	857
Retirement and pensions	584	537	715	773	988	1245	1721
Gifts and contributions	430	354	356	424	518	689	1637

* Includes fuel and utilities, maintenance, home furnishings and equipment

** Average income about $38,500

Source: Derived by Citibank from Consumer Expenditure Survey Series: Interview Survey, 1972 and 1973 (Report 455-3), 1976, U.S. Department of Labor.

housing, home fuels, and gasoline, for example, and so have cut back their spending elsewhere.

This information provides marketers with a good idea about the total sales of broad types of products and services at different family income levels. Although not shown here, substantial differences in family expenditures also are found by comparing families of different sizes, by family life-cycle stage, and by geographic region.

Serving Disadvantaged Consumers: A Continuing Challenge

In an era of growing concern for putting "people first, things second," [9] one of the greatest challenges to marketing is how to meet the special needs of disadvantaged consumers—the poor, the handicapped, and many older

[9] Leonard L. Berry, "Marketing Challenges in the Age of the People," *MSU Business Topics* (Winter, 1972), p. 7.

people. Certainly their buying needs are just as real as other people's. But because they have less money to spend, and often are costly to serve, disadvantaged consumers are often seen as an unattractive market from a sales and profit standpoint. Therefore, they may be ignored, abandoned, or even discriminated against as consumers. Consider these problems:

1. An estimated 700 million people throughout the world suffer chronic hunger and often the grim prospect of starvation. At the same time, the livestock population in the United States annually consumes enough food to feed 1.3 billion people.
2. Nearly one-fourth of this nation's elderly, and one-half of all elderly black and other minority persons, live in poverty. In times of rapid price inflation, older Americans living on low retirement incomes have a hard time affording even the basic necessities of life. The elderly consumer is said to be a "forgotten group" in our society.
3. For years, retailers have been abandoning decaying inner cities for the fast-growing, more affluent and profitable suburbs. The smaller retailers who remain are often less efficient, face higher costs, and sometimes must charge higher prices to the very consumers who can least afford to pay—the poor.
4. Most stores in this nation are designed to serve automobile traffic. This is a problem for many elderly and handicapped people and for those who cannot afford to drive a car. Very few retail stores or shopping centers have designed adequate facilities for the physically handicapped.
5. Low-income shoppers most in need of efficient buying are the least qualified to make good buying decisions. They are often poorly trained in shopping skills and have less access to buying information. They are the easiest prey for the dishonest merchant.

Can marketers profitably serve the special needs of disadvantaged consumers? In some cases, yes. Modern supermarkets have helped bring lower food prices to less-developed nations throughout the world, often with good profits. Recent downtown redevelopment efforts seem to be succeeding in some cities. In United States cities some stores and even entire shopping centers offer price discounts to elderly shoppers on normally slow business days. As a result, they report large sales increases on these days. Some black-owned and -managed shopping centers, such as Progress Plaza in Philadelphia, report success in their inner-city locations. But many black retail firms, like other business, have found it difficult to make a profit there.

Marketers, and society at large, must define more clearly just what are the responsibilities of the marketplace to all of its consumers. One viewpoint is that government, and the people themselves, should meet the task of helping disadvantaged consumers. Increasingly, society is demanding that marketers must bear more of the responsibility to serve all consumer's needs as efficiently and fairly as possible. Yet, in many instances, marketers have not yet found profitable ways of serving disadvantaged consumers. This market remains one of marketing management's vital challenges in the years ahead.

Future Markets—A Turning Point?

Marketing's task is to discover and exploit demand—to create customers.[10] As Peter Drucker states so well, it is through marketing's efforts in discovering customer-creation opportunities that economic resources are converted into wealth. Business firms, through customer creation, gain a differential advantage over competition, enjoy growth and profits, and thus increase the rate of economic growth. This economic growth has brought a higher material standard of living, more jobs, greater productivity with more time for leisure, and more money for social welfare, wars, space programs, and many other things.

Today, most marketers are optimistic that their efforts will continue bringing greater sales and profit rewards. Their optimism is based on a number of important *assumptions* about the climate for economic growth, for example:

1. The long period of prosperity following World War II will continue, with only minor and temporary periods of recession.
2. Rates of inflation and unemployment will be mild and manageable.
3. Natural resources will remain inexpensive and plentiful.
4. Advances in technology will continue to improve production efficiency, solve energy shortages and pollution problems, and raise living standards.
5. People will continue to want more and better products and services and will want to work hard to get them.

You may already be questioning some of these assumptions. Today many experts (economists, demographers, biological scientists, and others) claim that these assumptions are unrealistic for the future. Who is right? Only time will tell. But marketers must seriously consider the possibility that future markets will grow more slowly.

Limits to Growth: Some Evidence

Today, expert opinion differs on how close modern society is to its growth limits. "Technological optimists" like R. Buckminster Fuller argue that science and technology have the potential to cure the problems of mankind and the world.[11] But other experts estimate that the world cannot possibly keep its present material standard of living or its quality of life. Using com-

---

[10] Peter Drucker, *The Practice of Management* (New York: Harper & Row, 1954), pp. 37–41.
[11] Michael Pilburn, *The Environment: A Human Crisis* (Rochelle Park, N.J.: Hayden, 1974), p. 118.

Identifying and Selecting Markets

puter models to simulate the future, one team of researchers forecasted that population increases and people's appetites for the earth's resources will outstrip the world's capacity to produce. Thus, in the next three or four decades the Western world will see a sharp decline in its standard of living and the developing nations will not be able to increase their living standards.[12]

These more pessimistic forecasts are based on a growing awareness that our environment is fragile and its resources are limited. Barry Commoner argues that mankind is putting demands on the earth's air, water, and biological resources beyond its natural ability to cope. Eventually we will have to pay the price of this damage.[13] Paul Ehrlich and many others believe that overpopulation is the basic threat to the earth's environment and to mankind's future.[14] Unless world population growth is curbed, future generations can exist only by sharply restricting personal freedoms and lowering the material standards of living.[15]

In the early 1970's the United States had a glimpse of what a different future might be like. This event was the 1973–1974 oil shortage crisis. It helped send the economy into a tailspin of inflation, recession, and high unemployment. These forces seriously hurt United States consumers. The middle classes, the backbone of the economy, became more cautious in their spending habits and less willing to believe that in consumption "more is better." Some marketers believe that many people permanently lost some of their appetites for consumption, even after the recession ended and people had more money to spend.[16]

Another factor slowing the consumption rate may be the changing values of young people, tomorrow's heavy consumers. They seem to be less interested in "quantity of consumption" and more concerned with "quality of life." For many, the self-denial and hard work necessary to "get ahead" is not worth it. The result: perhaps less emphasis on buying and consuming products and services, perhaps much more concern with consuming more efficiently and wasting fewer resources. Perhaps more emphasis will be on developing "markets of the mind," on consuming more experiences, on self-improvement and greater self-awareness.

In summary, let us briefly review what the critics of the "continued growth and prosperity" forecast are saying. Essentially, despite a population increase, the economic growth rate will slow down dramatically. And with this slowing growth, United States consumers will change their basic attitudes toward consumption. "Quality of life" concerns will replace "quantity of consumption" values. In short, for marketers in the decades ahead, consumer markets may be a whole new ball game.

[12] Donella Meadows, et al., *The Limits to Growth* (New York: Universe Books, 1972).
[13] Barry Commoner, "A Businessman's Primer on Ecology," eds. L. L. Berry and J. S. Hensel, *Marketing and the Social Environment* (New York: Petrocelli Books, 1973), pp. 86–101.
[14] Paul Ehrlich, *The Population Bomb* (New York: Ballantine Books, 1968).
[15] D. Meadows, *The Limits to Growth.*
[16] "The Squeeze on the Middle Class," *Business Week*, March 10, 1975, pp. 52–60.

How can marketers succeed if the future does not continue to bring steady growth? First, if it really is a new ball game, then past experience will be less useful in guiding the firm's future. Marketers thus will have to *monitor their total environment* more carefully. Not only must customers and competitors be measured but also the broad political and social trends, technology, and economic forces. All of these forces will be changing, and all will influence the shape of future markets. Today, firms such as General Electric employ *corporate futurists* to help in the difficult task of exploring the impact of all of these environmental forces on future markets.[17]

Firms willing to carefully study the broader societal changes often find that exciting marketing opportunities lie hidden in the problems of slowing economic growth and the consumer's *new functionalism*. One example is Rival Manufacturing, which scores well with its Crock Pot slow-cooker (convenient, inexpensive to operate, and cooks inexpensive foods well). And Miles Homes, which supplies the "build-it-yourself" housing market, enjoys booming sales among inflation-squeezed buyers.[18]

Contingency planning will become more important as markets experience greater and more rapid change. Firms will have to plan alternative strategies for a variety of possible market conditions. With their broad views of environmental trends, corporate futurists may be especially helpful in planning alternative strategies for uncertain futures.

In times of shortages, supplying firms may be unable to meet their customer demands. Therefore, sellers may have to switch from market growth strategies to *market retention strategies*. Here, sellers aim at keeping their best customers from switching to other suppliers or to substitute products. This could happen when resources become scarce, as during the 1973–1974 oil embargo.

At times, increased demand for products and services greatly exceeds the marketer's ability to supply it. The excessive demand may be temporary (Ft. Lauderdale, Florida, during Spring vacation) or permanent (continual overcrowding of too popular wilderness camping areas near major cities).

Through careful demarketing, marketers can actively discourage customers from buying or consuming too much.[19] For example, many public utilities now teach their customers how to reduce their energy consumption. To firms following market growth strategies, the idea of demarketing may seem novel, but it is likely that demarketing will become more important as future markets face shortages.

---

[17] "More Companies Use 'Futurists' to Discern What Is Lying Ahead," *The Wall Street Journal*, March 31, 1975, pp. 1, 16.

[18] *Business Week*, May 24, 1976, pp. 85–88.

[19] Philip Kotler and Sidney Levy, "Demarketing, Yes, Demarketing," *Harvard Business Review* (November–December, 1971), pp. 74–80.

As consumers ourselves, we know something about how many consumers there are, where they live and shop, and what they buy. But most of us know much less about industrial markets. With the exception of retailers, the buying and selling activities of other industrial customers (manufacturers, wholesalers, schools, governments, etc.) are generally hidden from view and are not well-publicized. Yet, this is a vast and complex market. The bulk of purchasing is done by the industrial market, and it is very likely that marketing students will spend a good part of their careers in serving this market.

The importance and variety of industrial markets are seen in Figure 2.10. Compared with the over 200 million final consumers, the 13 million-plus industrial buyers are much fewer. But they are so diverse in size and in types of jobs performed that it is useful to separate this market into several types with similar buyer characteristics. Figure 2.10 groups the ten different types of industrial customers into the three basic classifications mentioned earlier in the chapter: producers, resellers, and governmental units. While this is only one possible way of grouping the industrial market, each of these three groups has some common dimensions as buyers. In our discussion we will look first at producers, concentrating upon the

Figure 2.10   Types and Numbers of Industrial Customers, 1973

Types of Customers	Number of Establishments
Producers:	
Agriculture, forestry, and fisheries	3,586,000
Mining	86,000
Service industries	3,367,000
Finance, insurance, and real estate	1,576,000
Contract construction	1,099,000
Manufacturing	449,000
Transportation, communications, other utilities	434,000
Resellers:	
Wholesalers	548,000
Retailers	2,329,000
Government:	
Governmental units (1971)	78,000

Source: U.S. Department of Commerce.

Background for Marketing Decisions

buying characteristics of the best-known type of producer—manufacturers. Then we will discuss some of the characteristics of wholesalers and retailers (resellers) and government markets.

Producer Markets: Manufacturers

Compared with that of consumer markets, buying power among manufacturers is highly concentrated among very few firms, as shown in Figure 2.11. Notice that less than 5% of all United States manufacturers have more than 250 workers. Yet, these firms employed (in 1972) about 60% of the nation's production employees and produced about 65% of its manufactured output. In addition, manufacturing is highly concentrated by industry and by geographic area. Boeing Corporation, located in Seattle, Washington, and Douglas Aircraft in Long Beach, California, produce the bulk of the nation's commercial jet aircraft. Steel, autos, cereals, and many other industries show similar geographic concentrations. The Great Lakes and the Middle Atlantic states and California, plus major cities elsewhere, do most of the nation's manufacturing. Home offices, where the important buying decisions are made, are even more geographically concentrated. A few square miles of Manhattan in New York City contain the headquarters for many of the nation's largest manufacturing firms.

Figure 2.11   Size Distribution of Manufacturing Establishments in the United States, by Number of Employees

Number of Employees	Number of Establishments	Percentage of Firms	Percentage of Value Added	Percentage of Employees
1–4	112,289	35.9	1.1	1.1
5–9	46,696	14.9	1.4	1.7
10–19	43,736	14.0	2.8	3.4
20–49	49,892	16.0	7.2	8.7
50–99	25,628	8.2	8.2	9.9
100–249	20,807	6.7	15.9	17.9
250–499	8,031	2.6	14.5	15.4
500–999	3,483	1.1	11.4	13.1
1,000–2,499	1,527	.5	17.0	12.5
2,500 or more	582	.2	20.6	16.2
Total	312,671	100.0	100.0	100.0

Source: 1972 Census of Manufactures.

Identifying and Selecting Markets

The market characteristics of manufacturers greatly influence the strategies of firms serving this market. First, since manufacturers vary greatly by size, market segmentation by customer size is very important. The largest manufacturers buy in huge quantities, and their buying procedures tend to be more complex and formalized than those of much smaller firms. When manufacturers are few and geographically concentrated, sellers often can use a sales force to contact customers personally on a regular basis. With more emphasis on personal selling to reach and influence manufacturers, advertising becomes less important. The concentration of manufacturing firms also means that suppliers may serve them directly instead of using the more involved marketing channels often required for reaching consumer markets.

Like final consumers, manufacturers should be thought of as problem solvers who buy goods and services to satisfy consumption needs. But while consumers buy for personal or family consumption, manufacturers buy goods and services to use in further production. Their purchases are made for eventual sales and profits. Thus, manufacturers, like all industrial buyers, are considered more "economic" and less "emotional" in their buying motivations.

Purchasing Agents Are Buying Specialists

Manufacturers large enough to have specialized management teams often use purchasing agents as full-time buying specialists (other business and public institutions do, too). These professional buyers are skilled in evaluating purchases in terms of their costs and contributions to the firm's goals. Purchasing agents must consider many factors in making buying decisions. Reliability and reputation for good service can be critical factors in selecting suppliers. Even for small, inexpensive items, the manufacturer cannot afford supply delays or inconsistency in product quality. Production lines might have to be shut down until the supplier comes through. Often several firms are capable of meeting the buyer's product requirements, so that price and service competition among suppliers becomes intense. In this case, the supplier firm that understands the manufacturer's needs better and has a stronger personal relationship through effective personal selling may have a decided advantage.

Purchasing Agents Have Personal Goals

Personal relationships between suppliers and intermediate customers can serve important human needs of buyers, too. Purchasing agents are more than just efficient buying machines; they also are employees who seek to protect and improve their own positions in the firm. And they want to lead rewarding personal lives. Purchasing agents thus avoid taking too many risks and seek personal support for their decisions within and outside their firm. To prevent mistakes, they may be reluctant to choose new, untried products or suppliers. Successful marketers selling to intermediate customers recognize that both economic and personal needs must be satisfied here, just as in consumer markets.

Buying Processes of Manufacturers

Selling to manufacturers is complex, and competition among suppliers is often intense. Therefore, suppliers today study the *total buying process* for clues for marketing strategy. For manufacturers and other producers, it seems useful to classify purchasing decisions into three categories based on the newness of the situation for the buyer and thus the buyer's need for information. The three purchasing decision classifications are (1) new tasks, (2) modified rebuy, and (3) straight rebuy.[20]

New tasks are brand-new buying situations that call for much information gathering and evaluation. In a *modified rebuy* situation the buying firm is considering different suppliers for an item previously bought on a straight rebuy basis. The *straight rebuy* situation is more routine and well-known and thus little decision effort or time is needed.

For highly complex or expensive purchases, the manufacturer's top executives probably will make the final buying decisions. Straight rebuys of less expensive or frequently bought items are much simpler. They may even be ordered automatically by computer. Potential suppliers should examine buying situations carefully and then adjust their marketing strategies to fit the buyer's particular decision process.

Reseller Markets

Resellers include wholesalers and retailers who acquire goods for resale at a profit. Like producers, resellers are found in all sizes and degrees of specialization. Industrial wholesalers (often called industrial distributors) may stock several hundred thousand items for producers of all types. Other wholesalers may be highly specialized, such as importers of diamonds or tobaccos for retail store distribution. Retailers range in size from sidewalk hotdog vendors to giant chains like Sears that has annual sales in the billions of dollars and a staff of thousands of professional buyers. With so many different sizes and kinds of operations, segmenting the reseller market presents a real challenge.

Good Buying Is Critical for Resellers

Resellers typically do not see themselves as selling agents for their suppliers. Rather, they act as purchasing agents for their customers: they buy what their customers need and want. So it is safe to say that buying is absolutely critical to their sales success. The old maxim, "Goods well bought

[20] F. E. Webster, Jr., and Y. Wind, *Organizational Buying Behavior* (Englewood Cliffs, N.J.: Prentice-Hall, Inc., 1972), pp. 23–24.

are half sold," probably states the typical wholesaler or retailer's philosophy very well.

In smaller reseller firms the buyer and seller may be the same person—the owner. In large retailing firms, such as department stores, buying is highly professional and specialized. Buyers have much authority and are important, well-paid members of the retailer's management team.

Inventory Management Is Important, Too

Inventory management is highly important for wholesalers and retailers. Resellers try to have the right products at the right place and time to satisfy their customers, while holding their own inventory storage and shipping costs to a minimum. Therefore, in addition to good buying, much of the reseller's effort goes into regulating the quantity and timing of his purchases for optimum inventory turnover.

Resellers often carry so many different products that it is difficult to give individual attention to each item. A Sears general merchandise catalog, for instance, lists well over 100,000 items, and Sears distributes more than a dozen specialty catalogs that list additional thousands of products. Each item requires Sears to make a buying decision months in advance of the first retail sale.

Resellers often have many more *new* products to consider buying than they can possibly handle. For example, each year the grocery industry introduces perhaps 10,000 new products. This is enough to replace every existing item on the typical supermarket shelf, and then some! Since many products currently stocked are proven winners and extra shelf space is limited, most of these new items cannot be added. In fact, just listening to all of the new product sales pitches would take up all of a store manager's time. As a result, many wholesale and retail food chains use buying committees for new product decisions. These committees are usually made up of executives and managers from several functional areas in the firm. Professional grocery buyers listen to new product sales presentations and then screen the new products being offered, dropping most items and keeping the rest for the buying committee to consider. Often the new product salesperson is not even allowed to talk with the buying committee. Thus, competition for the grocery buyer's attention is fierce in this market. Perhaps 90% of the new food items presented to grocery firms are rejected.

The Government Market

The government market (all governmental units at the federal, state, and local level) is the nation's largest consumer. In 1975 government purchases were about $340 billion, almost 25% of the gross national product.[21] Since governments are involved in just about every kind of activity—schools,

[21] Source: U.S. Department of Commerce, Office of Economic Analysis, cited in *1976 Information Please Almanac*, p. 59.

food service, offices, as well as federal military operations—they buy just about every kind of product or service. And government expenditures, especially at state and local levels, are constantly expanding. Thus, the government market is potentially an attractive customer for most suppliers.

Successful selling to governments, like selling to other intermediate customers, demands professional and specialized marketing effort. Many governmental agencies require that competitive bidding procedures be followed. The government buyer's job is to describe what is to be purchased and the terms of sale. Then the buyer may be required to accept the lowest-priced bid. This procedure is especially likely when purchase specifications are exact. In other cases, contracts are negotiated between buyer and seller. For example, consider the task of buying products for the Apollo space program. The complex space vehicles and their supporting systems are assembled over a period of years after contracts are signed. Often the necessary technology and exact costs for developing these new and highly complex products are not completely known when the buying contracts are signed. Therefore, the seller's reputation and demonstrated abilities to perform influence the contract award decision. Contracts are often re-negotiated several times over the life of the contract project, as production costs and program needs change.

Firms that sell to governments must also know how to find out about selling opportunities and how to locate the appropriate target customers within vast government agencies. Trade associations and trade magazines often provide useful information on selling to hospitals, schools, laboratories, and many other kinds of government markets. Many governments also are very helpful. The federal government, for example, advertises its upcoming contracts and offers directories for prospective sellers.

The federal government has centralized much of its buying to improve buying efficiency. Centralized buying also simplifies the seller's task of locating and dealing with various governmental units. One central buying agency is the Federal Supply Service (FSS), which buys most of the non-military products for the government. The FSS buys over $4 billion worth of products each year from birdseed for the Washington Zoo to computers, its single biggest item. Almost all of its purchases are made on a low-bid basis. This does not mean that only giant firms can afford to sell to the very price-conscious FSS. Much of its business winds up in small companies through subcontracts. The Federal Supply Service also gives small companies that have fewer than 600 employees a 6% price edge in direct bidding.

SUMMARY

In this chapter we saw that markets are so large and diverse that few firms can hope to serve all markets that might possibly want their products and services. Therefore, marketers must carefully identify potential customers and select specific *target markets* from them. Indeed, identifying and selecting specific target markets are the necessary starting points in marketing strategy planning.

The growing complexity of consumer characteristics and needs creates unique market segments that will respond profitably to different marketing mixes. Market segmentation strategy offers some distinct advantages over an undifferentiated marketing approach to target customers. But because market segmentation is costly, it must be carefully planned and managed in order to yield success. There are many different ways to segment markets. Demographic and geographic segmentation are most popular, but benefit, market factor, psychographic, and other segmentation methods often prove to be superior. The marketer must be innovative, flexible, and practical in choosing and applying segmentation methods.

Markets can be grouped at a very general level into consumers and industrial customers. Industrial customers, in turn, were classified into three categories: producers, resellers, and governments, each with basic differences in buying needs and characteristics. We also showed that industrial customers differ tremendously by type of business, size, buying volume, and other factors. Because of these wide differences, firms selling to industrial customers must thoroughly study and segment their customers before designing their marketing approaches. We learned that industrial customers are highly influenced by economic factors and that final consumers more often buy according to their personal tastes and preferences. But industrial customers are people, too, and their personal needs must be considered. Later chapters on personal selling and advertising will emphasize their complex buying characteristics.

In studying United States consumers we looked first at population data and noted that geographic markets are ever-changing. We are a very mobile people. Population shifts must be continually monitored because today's growth markets may decline and new opportunities may quickly appear. Although the total population is growing more slowly today, hidden in these figures are some fast-growing and very promising age segments—younger adults and the elderly.

Population trends are not enough by themselves to suggest just where market potential lies. Income trends and changing consumer life-styles are critical too. In fact, life-style trends are of primary importance because they determine how people will spend their incomes. In today's relatively affluent economy, few purchases are absolute necessities. Along with higher incomes, smaller families, working women, and the growing demand for leisure are shaping our future markets.

A threatening cloud on the market horizon is the possibility of resource shortages and slowing market growth. For marketers, the lengthy postwar period of market expansion may be facing a crucial turning point. Firms will have to monitor their total environment and do contingency planning in order to anticipate and help prepare for this much different future. Market retention strategies will help preserve falling demand, while demarketing efforts can be used when resource shortages prevent the firm from supplying its customer demand.

For the marketer, the consumer data discussed in this chapter can be very useful in estimating the market's general buying requirements and potential. But these data have not been so helpful in predicting just which products and brands will be bought or which stores, advertisements, or selling approaches will be most effective. To answer these specific questions, marketers must have a more sophisticated analysis of *why* consumers behave as they do. In the next chapter we will explore some insights from marketing and behavioral science research that are helping marketers understand people and households as consumers.

QUESTIONS

1. What are some major differences between consumer and industrial markets?
2. What are the advantages of a market segmentation approach over an undifferentiated approach to selecting target markets?
3. Suggest some potential market segments within the market for citizen band radios. Now suggest how the seller's marketing mix could be altered to serve each segment.
4. Mail order marketers rely heavily on usage rate segmentation in selecting target customers. Why do you think that this approach is especially valuable for them?
5. Basing your opinion on geographic population mobility patterns, where do you think that a national retail chain should locate its new stores over the next five to ten years?
6. Which industries may benefit most from the declining birthrate?
7. Which stages of the family life cycle will grow fastest over the next ten years? How might these trends influence the decisions of a clothing retailer? A furniture manufacturer?
8. Why is the family life cycle likely to be better in market analysis than consumer age?
9. Some analysts believe that future consumer markets will grow much more slowly. Why do they think so? What can firms do to adjust to a possible "slow growth" era?
10. "Resellers see themselves as purchasing agents for their customers." Why is this statement important to marketers who are trying to sell products to resellers?

Identifying and Selecting Markets

Benefit Segmentation: classifying market segments on the basis of particular benefits or values received from products and services by different consumer groups

Consumer Market: individuals (or households) buying or using goods and services for personal or household consumption

Demographic Factors: physical characteristics describing a population, such as age, income level, sex, occupation, national origin, and many others

Discretionary Income: spendable personal or household income beyond that which is needed to purchase basic necessities of food, clothing, housing, and transportation

Family Life Cycle: important stages of life that a typical family passes through from marriage and family formation, maturation of children, children leaving home, and sole survivor

Industrial Market: producer, reseller, and governmental organizations buying goods and services for use in producing other goods or services or for use in other operations

Market: people or organizations that have wants and needs and that have the ability to exchange something of value for them

Market Segments: within the broader market, groups of similar consumers with similar product needs and wants

Psychographic Segmentation: classifications of personal activities, interests, and opinions that attempt to measure consumer life-style patterns

Target Market: that market segment (group of current or potential customers) for whom a specific market offer is created

CASES

Case 1: Hi-Value Foods, Inc.

Hi-Value Foods, Inc., a regional chain of 40 supermarkets, is considering ways of expanding its sales and profits. One of Hi-Value's executives believes that more specialty food departments, such as bakeries, delicatessens, and wine shops, would not only attract new customers but would also increase sales among current customers. He has been noticing the growth of health food sales and believes that health food departments within the supermarkets would be successful. "The variety of health food specialty products is growing fast, and health foods can be sold at higher-than-average markups and prices. Health foods will attract older shoppers who tend to have special dietary needs. And look at the statistics—the number of people 65 years of age and older is growing tremendously, from 20 million in 1970 to about 26 million by 1985. That's a 30% gain! We should introduce health food departments aimed toward older shoppers."

Another executive disagrees. She argues that health food buyers are more likely to be young people who are concerned with ecology and who seek a simpler way of life. She says, "These young people don't like super-markets and therefore won't buy enough other foods to be worthwhile for us. And elderly customers cannot pay health food prices, and they buy groceries in small amounts. So they aren't a profitable market segment, either."

Hi-Value's president wants to resolve the issue. "We need to find out who the health food buyers and users are and whether or not they represent new markets that will help us grow. We must know this before we consider designing, stocking, and promoting health food departments to older customers or anyone else."

1. Would the elderly market be an attractive one for the proposed health food department?
2. Do you feel that the elderly market is important enough to do market segmentation research?
3. Which segmentation approaches would you suggest?

Case 2: Schoolhouse, Inc.

Schoolhouse, Inc. manufactures and markets notebook covers, pen and pencil sets, crayon sets, tape dispensers, and similar school-supply items to school-age children and their parents. Schoolhouse licensed the rights to display a popular cartoon character on its products and in its promotion. This cartoon character is the central theme in all advertising, which appears in children's magazines, comics, and as inserts in several gift catalogs. To date, all selling was through mail order direct to final customers.

Schoolhouse executives believed that the present market was losing some of its promise. Competition was intense from similar products promoted with other cartoon characters, and licensing rights were becoming more costly. In the past year, the firm had been exploring other market opportunities for its product line.

One promising opportunity seemed to be the institutional market. Executives thought they could sell essentially the same products, minus the cartoon feature, to school systems, hospitals, governmental agencies, and

Identifying and Selecting Markets

reach other industrial customers through office supply houses. Some additions to the product line would be necessary, and obviously not all items (such as crayons) would sell well here. But management felt that, on the whole, the production adjustments would be minor.

The marketing director was concerned that marketing requirements would be quite different. Advertising and personal selling would play quite different roles in the two markets. The present emphasis on colorful packaging and heavy advertising support would have to change, the marketing manager believed. Also, pricing requirements would be different. In fact, the industrial market and the present consumer market might require adjustments almost everywhere in the present marketing program.

1. Do you agree with the marketing manager's appraisal?
2. How do the two types of markets differ in their buying requirements? Why?
3. In what specific ways do you think Schoolhouse will need to adjust its marketing effort to serve this new market?

Understanding Consumer Behavior

After you finish this chapter, you should be able to answer the following questions:

1. Why do marketers need to go beyond demographic analysis of markets?
2. What are the contributions and limitations of the "economic man" model of consumer behavior?
3. What is meant by *selective processes in perception,* and how do they influence marketing strategy?
4. What are *self-image* and *social role*? How are they related to buying and consumption?
5. How does the family act as a *reference group* for the individual consumer? Why is it important to study family decision making?
6. How and why does *social class* influence consumer behavior?
7. What are some basic cultural values in American society that shape consumer behavior? How are *cultural values* changing, and what do these changes mean for consumer behavior and marketing management?
8. What is a *consumer decision process?* Why do marketers study consumer decision processes?

Consumer Decision Process   Culture   Economic Man   Hierarchy of Needs   Life-Style   Motive   Product Image   Reference Groups   Role   Selective Processes of Perception   Self-Concept   Social Class

INTRODUCTION

Consumer demographic factors are vital in identifying market opportunities and predicting basic market trends. Knowing population size, consumers' age distribution, and income levels, the clothing industry can estimate with reasonable accuracy the number of pairs of men's pants that will sell in a year. But estimating the sales of various styles and brands by using demographics is another matter. Demographic information is not much help in predicting the phenomenal success of Levi's denim jeans. And demographics cannot explain why 16-year-old girls in Los Angeles can't wait to own a pair of bib overalls, while farm boys in Missouri cannot wait to put on something else.

To better understand consumer behavior, marketers rely on insights from economics and the behavioral sciences of psychology, sociology, and anthropology. Each of these sciences concentrates on different aspects of human behavior. Together, they provide the marketing manager with a richer, more complete view of consumers.

Figure 3.1 shows the major influences on the consumer decision maker. The reader will recognize each factor as an important subject of a different academic discipline. For example, learning and perception are studied in psychology, and social class is a topic in sociology. Of course, the "real world" as viewed by the individual decision maker is not as compartmentalized as Figure 3.1 might suggest. All of these factors interact in complex fashion in the consumer's mind to influence his buying response.

We will study each factor individually in this chapter. Toward the end of the chapter we will suggest how today's consumer researchers are incorporating these factors into more complex models to better explain consumer decision making.

ECONOMIC VIEWS OF CONSUMER BEHAVIOR

Economics provides many valuable insights about consumers. The economist sees people essentially as economic problem solvers. Here, consumers try to make the most rational and efficient spending decisions that their budgets will allow. Consumers understand their needs, and they know the various products, their need-satisfying qualities, and their prices. With this information, buyers simply decide how much of each product to buy in order to maximize their satisfaction within their budgets.

Knowing how their customers buy, marketers will want to measure their current ability to buy (income levels). Marketers also will examine past sales records to find out how different demographic types of buyers have

Figure 3.1 Determinants of Consumer Behavior

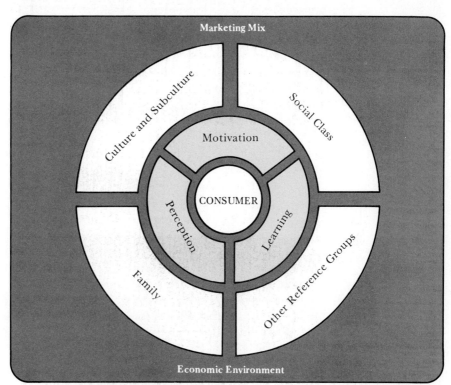

responded to different price levels of desirable products. Using all of these data, marketers supposedly can forecast purchases of their product line by different consumer groups.

The economic problem solving view probably is most useful for explaining purchases of homogeneous products, such as agricultural commodities (wheat, eggs, etc.) or basic industrial raw materials or supplies (copper wire, paper supplies). Consumers usually know these products well and understand why they need them. Since competing brands are practically identical, price differences may well decide which supplier will sell the most.

Economic theory also explains much of the buying behavior of industrial customers. Manufacturers, retailers, and other institutions buying to improve their own sales and profits are strongly motivated by economic factors. But as we pointed out in Chapter 2, many other personal and social factors may also be involved in industrial buying.

For heterogeneous products and brands, consumer differences in product

Understanding Consumer Behavior

knowledge, personal tastes, and social factors may be more important than economic factors. Auto manufacturers, for example, often have difficulty forecasting sales using economic and demographic data. In recent years, Detroit has consistently failed to anticipate the dramatic swings in buyer preferences, first for small cars and then for big cars.[1] George Katona's pioneering studies show that people's attitudes and expectations about the future strongly influence their decisions to buy or to postpone buying automobiles and other durable goods. According to Katona, if better forecasting is to be achieved, traditional economic analysis should be blended with modern psychological research on people's attitudes and feelings of confidence and pessimism about the future.[2] Consumer behavior is too complex to be captured in the traditional **economic man** model.

In going beyond economic theory, we will have to expand our view of the consumer in two directions: (1) the individual psychological makeup of the buyer that affects individual decision making and (2) the social and cultural environment of the individual buyer.

INDIVIDUAL FACTORS INFLUENCING CONSUMER BEHAVIOR

Buying decisions may be simple, *routine* responses requiring little or no information gathering, evaluating, and deciding. Or decisions may require *limited* or *extensive* problem solving. The purchase of industrial drills involves several different levels of buying complexity. Here, past experience, or *learning*, allows the buyer to simplify the buying task.

Consumer Learning

Most human behavior, including consumer problem solving, is *learned* behavior. Therefore, understanding learning is basic to understanding consumers. Psychologists classify many *types* of learning; we will look at three broad types of learning that are particularly useful in studying consumer behavior. These are as follows:

1. Acquiring *information.*
2. Learning *preferences* (learning to like).
3. Developing *habits* of thought, perception, and action.[3]

Much learning is acquiring information. Learning may require but a single "lesson"—glancing at a menu and noting that the price of your favorite super whopper hamburger has just been raised a dime. But learning enough about a programmable pocket calculator to buy one might take

[1] "Thinking Bigger: Detroit Discovers Buyers Don't Want Small Cars," *The Wall Street Journal*, February 11, 1975, pp. 1, 14.
[2] George Katona, *Psychological Economics* (New York: Elsevier, 1975).
[3] Chester R. Wasson, *Consumer Behavior: A Managerial Viewpoint* (Austin, Texas: Austin Press, 1975), p. 90.

Background for Marketing Decisions

several demonstrations by skilled salespeople. The complexity of the learning task involved in acquiring information is important in developing promotional strategy.

Most of our tastes and preferences are acquired (learned). We tend to like people, products, and places that are familiar to us, even though we cannot recall receiving any particular rewards for learning to like them. Thus, frequently repeated advertisements are important not only in building brand awareness, but also in building liking for that brand.

Does that mean that the slogan, "Try it, you'll like it!" is true if people do try it often enough? Not necessarily. Researchers have found that if an audience is initially either favorable or neutral toward the product, repeated experiences will bring liking of the product. But if the audience's original attitude is unfavorable, further contact with the product will produce even stronger dislike. That is, if the idea of raw oysters turns you off, chances are that you will like them even less after eating one. The point is that marketers must understand the attitude starting point of their target market before trying to persuade the market to prefer a product or brand.

For the marketer, building or changing the consumer's buying and consumption habits can be even more challenging, especially if the consumer must break well-established habits to learn new ones. Sellers of "no wax" vinyl floor coverings, for example, continually instruct their customers *not* to wax their new floors; they instruct the customers that the floors only need to be washed to keep them glossy. But out of habit, some customers will wax them anyway and then complain to the seller when the unnecessary wax builds up on the floor surfaces and dulls them.

Perception

Perception strongly influences how we deal with our environment. We receive information or cues from our environment as various sensations— sight, smell, sound, for example. We then translate or attribute meanings to this sensory information. That is, we perceive the information. What we perceive and how we perceive it are the complex results of two interacting factors:

1. *Stimulus factors,* such as the size and color of a billboard advertisement, or the weight, color, scent, and firmness of an orange.
2. *Individual or personal factors.* These include our sensory abilities and our learned experiences, attitudes, motivations, and expectations by which we interpret the stimulus factors. We judge an orange's ripeness and juiciness from whatever sensory information we received, interpreting that information from our learned experiences.

It is useful for the marketer to distinguish between sensation and perception, because both human processes influence the consumer's reaction to the market environment. The different roles that sensation and perception play in consumer choice is well-illustrated by laboratory experiments. For instance, many people cannot identify different brands of beer in taste tests when the brand labels are disguised. Their sensory abilities are not that well-developed. But when brand labels are identified, taste ratings for their favorite brands will rise sharply, suggesting that their perceptual biases now are operating. Past expectations and motivations are coloring what the subjects think they are actually tasting as flavor differences.

The laboratory taste test results often serve as important ammunition for brand advertising battles. In 1976 Coca-Cola and Pepsi-Cola disagreed in their advertisements over whose taste was preferred by customers. Pepsi claimed victory in its tests because Coke drinkers voted 2 to 1 that Pepsi tasted better than Coke. But Coke cried "foul" in its ad, claiming that consumers naturally preferred the letter M (the disguised Pepsi brand) to the letter Q (the Coke brand) in the Pepsi-sponsored test. It was the letters, not the taste, that influenced the brand choices, claimed Coke.[4]

Our Perception Is Selective

Whatever the reason for the brand choices, the point is that people deal with information selectively. Psychologists recognize three **selective processes of perception:** (1) selective exposure or attention, (2) selective perception, and (3) selective retention or recall.

People seek out and pay attention to certain stimuli (brands, stores, etc.) and ignore other information (selective exposure). Most advertising messages, for example, never pass through our perceptual "filters," and thus they register no impact on our behavior.

Advertisers know this. They continually work to stimulate our awareness and recognition of their messages by using color (an effective contrast in a mostly black-and-white newspaper), motion (flashing lights), novelty, sexual themes, and many other techniques to capture and hold attention.

The advertiser also tries to assure that his message is interpreted in the intended manner. Selective perception results from the unique experiences, preferences, social influences, and emotional moods of audiences. Thus, Art Carney asked us in a television advertisement, "What is a drink?" He was reminding us that too many adults almost automatically think of "a drink" as an alcoholic beverage. This perception influences our expectations of what we think other people will want to drink and what we feel we should offer them. Art Carney heightened our awareness that we selectively perceive social drinking in an unfortunately narrow way.

Finally, we also practice *selective recall*. Last year's camping trip probably gave us some bad moments, but we will recall the good times more easily.

Understanding human selective processes is vitally important to marketers. The selective processes help explain why many people remain brand loyal and why it is so difficult for competitors to win them away through

[4] "PepsiCo Ad Insists: No Question—Coke Drinkers Prefer Pepsi," *Advertising Age*, July 19, 1976, pp. 2, 66.

Background for Marketing Decisions

advertising. Satisfied customers tend to "tune out" information on competing brands and evaluate their own brand choices more favorably. Even when new information is received, it may be easily forgotten if it does not confirm the consumers' beliefs about their present brand choice.

Consumer Motivation

Exploring why consumers behave as they do eventually brings us to the concept of motivation. Simply put, our behavior is motivated by our needs. All of us have many different needs. Under certain circumstances, some of these latent needs will become aroused or motivated and will direct us toward certain goals that will satisfy these needs.

We can avoid scientific controversies as to which human needs, if any, are innate and which are acquired through experience because for marketing management purposes virtually all consumer needs involving products and services are learned.

As humans mature, the basic, uncomplicated needs of infancy become much more numerous and specific. Desires for enough nutrients and liquids to maintain bodily balances quickly move to wanting soda pop, toast and jelly, hamburgers, and eventually steaks. With sufficient reinforcement, children can learn to want virtually anything.

For marketers, the concept of motivation is important because it is believed that by understanding consumer motivations, the marketer has the basis for explaining and predicting consumer behavior. Thus, marketers have searched diligently for **motives** to help them anticipate consumer's actions.

As usual, though, things are hardly that simple. Consumer behavior is not so easily predicted from motives, for several reasons:

1. Motives are internal psychological states. They are hidden from direct observation and measurement and must be *inferred* from people's behavior or from self-reports. Thus, it is difficult to link specific consumer actions with needs and motives.
2. Often specific consumer behavior is *multiply* motivated. New cars, for example, are bought for many reasons—"economic" needs for transportation, for status reasons, for a sense of satisfaction of being able to afford one. Which motives predominate, and when do they predominate?
3. A general motive (desire for transportation) may lead to numerous specific behaviors—leasing versus owning a car, different types and makes of cars, or to buying a motorcycle or bicycle.
4. Many other factors in addition to motives influence our behavior. Spending power, availability of brands, differences in knowledge and experience are just a few. Knowing motives is helpful, but it is only a starting point for the marketer.

Figure 3.2 Maslow's Hierarchy of Needs

Self–Need	Self–Actualization (Need to know, understand, achieve for personal awareness and satisfaction)	Self–Need
Social Needs	Esteem and Status (Striving to achieve a high position relative to others, including reputation, prestige)	Social Needs
	Belongingness and Love (Seeking acceptance by family, friends, others with whom the person feels close)	
Physical Needs	Safety Needs (Ordinary prudence, desire to protect oneself from harm; may be overlooked in trying to satisfy basic physiological needs)	Physical Needs
	Physiological Needs (Needs basic to survival, including food, drink, and shelter)	

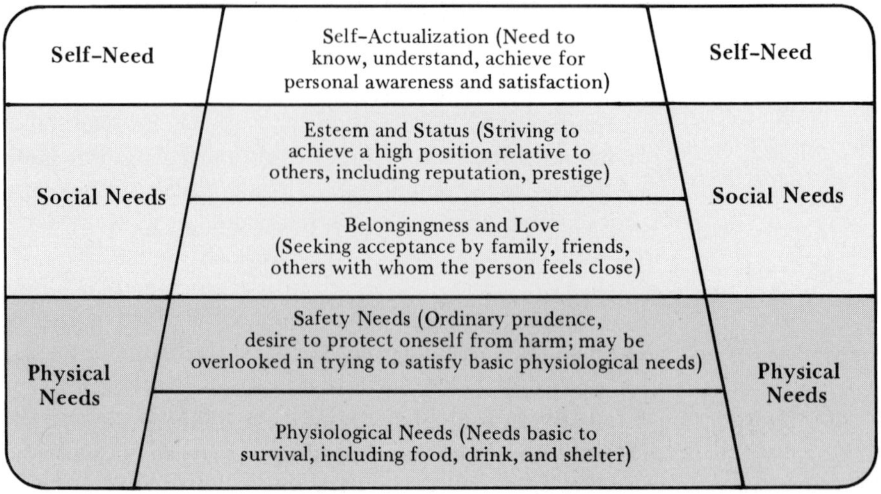

Thus, relying on lists of motives to account for consumer behavior is of limited value. Instead, marketers need organized theories of motivation to explain which motives produce buying actions under particular circumstances.

One popular theory is Maslow's **hierarchy of needs.**[5] Maslow believed that human needs are arranged in a priority, or hierarchy, as shown in Figure 3.2.

Essentially, the basic needs must be adequately met before higher-level needs will be sought. Thus, once man's basic physiological needs for food, sex, shelter, etc., are satisfied, safety needs (job safety, insurance for the family) become important, and so on. Using this theory, the marketer would identify the need state that is activated (or *prepotent*) within his target markets. These needs should be satisfied before attempting to meet higher-order ones.

It is often argued that in affluent societies most people are able to reach status, self-esteem, and even self-fulfillment motive levels. This may account for the current interest in luxury goods and in all forms of participative activities, including development of self-awareness and education for its own sake.

While the hierarchy of needs is important, in reality this theory is too

[5] Abraham H. Maslow, *Motivation and Personality* (New York: Harper and Bros., 1954).

Background for Marketing Decisions

general to be considered a good predictive theory for marketing management. It fails to account for multiple motivations behind certain buying actions (insurance policies may be bought for safety reasons, but they are also successfully promoted as a status item). And it cannot specify at what point a certain motive or need will become satisfied. But Maslow's efforts suggest the directions that research on consumer motivations should take.

Consumer Self-Image

Look at Figure 3.3 for a moment and describe yourself in terms of the four components of the **self-concept.** Probably there are similarities among your *self-image* (the way you see yourself), your *ideal self* (as you would like to be), and your *looking-glass self* (how you think others see you), but these components will not be exactly alike. Your *real self* is the person you really are, but it is especially difficult to pin down.

According to many psychologists, our self-concept is one of our most valued possessions. We strive to maintain a positive image of ourselves. And we try to improve our self-image. Since we want others to think well

Figure 3.3   Components of Self-Concept

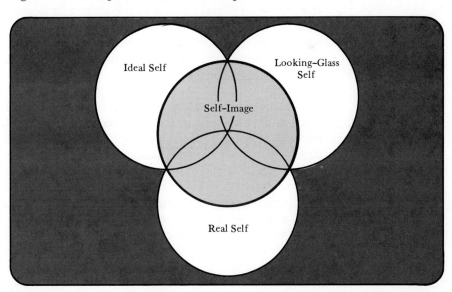

Source: Adapted from John Douglas, George A. Field, and Lawrence X. Tarpey, *Human Behavior in Marketing* (Columbus, Ohio: Charles E. Merrill Books, Inc., 1967), p. 65. Reproduced by permission.

Understanding Consumer Behavior

of us, we express or symbolize this image to others through our conversations, our emotions, and our actions. Self-image is valuable in understanding consumer behavior, for one of the important ways of enhancing positive feelings about ourselves and symbolizing our self-images to others is through consumption. The possessions we own and the activities we enjoy all reflect something we want to say about ourselves.

Examples of this *symbolic communication of self* are everywhere.[6] The hostess concerned with serving the *right* wine at a dinner party and the professor who rehearses colorful stories and jokes for class are presenting their self-images. We also buy and consume to symbolize a positive image to ourselves. Think how good you feel about yourself when you have updated your wardrobe with some new fashions.

Advertisers constantly dramatize the idea of buying products to enhance the consumer's self-image. Consider the TV ads that portrayed the young wife who is unhappy because she can't make a good cup of coffee—and her husband's comments don't help, either. Mrs. Olsen, of course, always comes to the rescue with her Folger's coffee!

This example illustrates the intriguing idea of matching desired self-image with the **product image** (brand image). Here, a brand of coffee is advertised as a good-tasting, "fool-proof" coffee that works well for anyone. If serving good coffee is important to you (that is, if good coffee symbolizes a capable and caring homemaker and promises love and respect in return), then the brand image is seen as an appropriate match for your desired self-image, and you will probably choose this brand.

Today the word *image* is part of everyone's vocabulary. We all understand what is generally meant by the image of a product, a brand, and even a political candidate. Some brands have strong and distinct images. These well-defined images appeal differently to different people, and they apparently have much influence on consumer choices. Most males, for instance, would feel uncomfortable smoking Virginia Slims cigarettes in public, or even in private.

Thus, marketers must research the different images their products and brands have among different target markets. They should create and reinforce (through package, price, label, advertising, and other methods of communicating to markets) a close matching of their products with desired self-images of their target customers. Some marketing experts, though, caution against creating and promoting product images that are *too* clear and specific. They believe that somewhat ambiguous images allow different customers to interpret the product image in terms of their own valued self-images.[7] Thus, Winston cigarettes, for example, undoubtedly appeal to a broader range of masculine, feminine, and other self-images than do Virginia Slims.

[6] Erving Goffman, *The Presentation of Self in Everyday Life* (New York: Doubleday & Co., Inc., 1959).

[7] For example, Franklin B. Evans, "The Brand Image Myth," *Business Horizons*, Fall, 1961, p. 26.

Background for Marketing Decisions

Finally, we should recognize that not all buying is *expressive* in purpose. Canned peaches, for instance, are probably bought on the basis of flavor, menu needs, and price, not to tell your neighbor something about yourself. Products must be *socially visible* and somewhat *unusual* if they are to serve as expressive symbols of the self. Thus, the notion of product image–self-image matching does not explain all buying behavior.

INFLUENCE OF OTHERS ON INDIVIDUAL BUYING BEHAVIOR

Up to now we have concentrated on some of psychology's insights into personal buying behavior. Yet, the individual buyer's relationships with others also determine his consumption choices. We can turn to social psychology and sociology for insights into how the consumer interacts with his family, other reference groups, and social class.

Social Roles and Consumer Behavior

A good starting point in bringing together the individual consumer with the many social influences on his behavior is through the concept of social role.

The term **role** means the same to the social psychologist as it does to the actor on the stage. A social role is a set of rights and duties belonging to a social position. Thus, the role of "father" is given to people in certain positions (males with children) by the larger society. Society determines how the role is to be played (what is expected of fathers) and evaluates role performance.

Marketers have long known that you can predict quite a lot about a person's behavior, including his buying behavior, by identifying the many roles he plays because one of the important ways a person demonstrates his social position and acts out his social roles is through consumption.

People who are new to important social roles quickly learn appropriate social behavior for these roles. They may be especially open to guidance from others, including marketers, on how these new roles should be played

For example, choosing a diamond engagement ring is a highly symbolic, emotional experience for many young couples. It is also expensive, and few young people feel competent to judge value in a diamond ring. Instead of deciding by themselves, the couple may turn to an experienced jeweler for advice. The jeweler will carefully point out hidden quality features, advise them on a diamond's lasting value, and discuss their budget requirements. He skillfully guides the couple toward a satisfactory purchase and compliments them on their wise choice.

Buyers Play Multiple Roles

Most consumers in modern, affluent societies play a great variety of roles, moving from one to another as the occasion demands. Usually the roles are *complementary*, making the role transition easy, but roles may also *conflict*, such as the wife and mother role versus the career role conflict many women experience today.

The diversity of social positions people hold and the roles they play makes their buying behavior very complex and thus not easy to predict. The marketer must determine which roles are being played and when they are being played. On the same shopping day, a student may buy a t-shirt for dorm lounging, a floor-length gown for a Saturday night party, and hiking boots for weekend camping.

Reference Groups Influence Consumer Role Behavior

A **reference group** consists of people individuals look to in forming their opinions, attitudes, and beliefs. Family, friends, and other face-to-face groups, as well as other groups the individual just wishes to emulate, may be important reference groups. Each reference group has its own values and perspectives that its members adopt.

Because different reference groups may view the same social role very

Permission: From the *Wall Street Journal*.

"If you must know, I dress like this because I want to be accepted by my peer group."

differently, social role behavior is seldom rigidly prescribed. Depending on which reference groups are most important, individual consumers may choose to express a role very differently.

For example, consider the role of housewife. Women whose reference groups stress traditional values probably adopt a traditional housewife role for themselves. These women may view daily housecleaning as very important in their lives. The liberated wife may consider housecleaning an unimportant symbol of the housewife role; to her, housecleaning is boring. The marketer of furniture polish may recognize two distinct housewife segments here. The traditional wife polishes furniture often and insists on a polish that gives a perfect finish. The liberated wife usually polishes just before company arrives and demands a quick and easy spray polish. Different advertising appeals and product designs might be created for the two groups.

THE FAMILY'S ROLE IN CONSUMER BEHAVIOR

To the marketer, the family is important in at least three ways:

1. As a reference group, the family strongly influences the attitudes, beliefs, and actions of the individual consumer.
2. Family members, especially parents, act as purchasing agents for other family members.
3. The family itself frequently acts as a *buying unit*. Expenditures on housing, automobiles, vacations, and food often are joint family decisions.

The Family as a Reference Group

The family is the most important reference group for the individual. It is largely through the family that we learn standards of what is appropriate behavior, which attitudes are correct and which are not, how to dress, which foods taste good and which ones taste bad.

Training in consumption begins early. Young children learn from their parents the value of money, how to shop, and what is important to buy.[8] As children mature, they grow in buying ability and gain more independence from family influence. By the time a young girl reaches her mid-teens, for example, she may spend little time shopping for clothing with her mother. Instead, she relies on her friends for buying advice and support.

In our affluent society, youth have become an important market segment

---

[8] James U. McNeal, "An Exploratory Study of the Consumer Behavior of Children," in *Dimensions of Consumer Behavior*, James U. McNeal, ed. (New York: Appleton-Century-Crofts, 1969), pp. 256–57; William D. Wells, "Children as Consumers," in *On Knowing the Consumer*, Joseph W. Newman, ed. (New York: Wiley, 1966), pp. 138–39.

for many goods. One author notes that over 60% of all tape recorders and over 30% of all radios are owned by children under 12 years old. Teen-agers buy over 80% of all records sold and over one-half of all movie tickets.[9]

Young people are important consumers in other ways, too, for example:

1. They are highly *innovative,* often the first to try new products.
2. They are highly *communicative,* influencing other consumers well beyond their own age groups. Miniskirts, jeans, hamburgers, and pizza are just a few examples of huge markets created largely by youth.
3. They are *tomorrow's family consumers.* Future-oriented marketers are seeking to understand young people's consumption needs and build strong ties with them before they reach their adult buying years.

Purchasing Decisions Within the Family

One person in the family may act as the family's purchasing agent. But the purchasing agent is not necessarily the family's decision maker. Decisions on what to buy often result from complex social interactions among several family members.

The wife is usually thought of as the family's buying specialist. She shops for the children and the home. Often she buys most of her husband's clothing. But as more women take jobs outside the home, and as family leisure time increases, husbands and children may be doing more deciding and shopping.

For more expensive items, both husband and wife become involved in the buying decision. As Figure 3.4 shows, their roles may vary considerably, depending on the type of purchase. Wives tend to dominate in the expressive features of a purchase, such as the model and color of the automobile and the fabric, style, and color of furniture. Husbands apparently have more influence in functional aspects of the purchase, such as when and where to buy, how much to spend, and which mechanical features are necessary.

Other factors also complicate the family decision process. Which partner contributes the most income, which one has the strongest interest in the purchase, and who personally dominates the household all determine the pattern of decision making in a particular family.

Although each family behaves differently, marketers can learn how families typically decide and shop for different products so that they can tailor their marketing to fit the general pattern. In furniture retailing, for instance, some salespeople follow an old rule of thumb that a couple shopping together is a better sales prospect than an individual customer. Figure 3.4 suggests why: furniture purchases usually require a decision from both partners, after each has contributed to certain aspects of the buying deci-

[9] R. J. Markin, Jr., *Consumer Behavior* (New York: Macmillan, 1974), p. 437.

Figure 3.4   Husbands and Wives Report on Their Decision-making Influence

| | Who in Your Family Decides? | | | | | | | |
| Who decides | When it's time to buy a car | | About savings | | Money and bills (from a non-panel study) | | When it's time to buy household goods, appliances, furniture, etc. | |
	Husbands	Wives	Husbands	Wives	Husbands	Wives	Husbands	Wives
Wife only	3%	3%	27%	26%	39%	43%	24%	25%
Wife predominantly	1	1	2	6	b	2	12	10
Both equally	31	23	47	49	31	26	53	51
Husband predominantly	5	9	3	4	2	2	4	5
Husband only	51	54	18	13	27	27	4	6
Don't buy (don't save)	7	9	3	2	b	b	2	2
Not ascertained	2	1	a	a	1	—	1	1
Number of cases	354	297	343	301	454	505	354	307

a. "Not ascertained's" were excluded here

b. Less than .5%

Source: Reprinted from Elizabeth H. Wolgast, "Do Husbands or Wives Make the Purchasing Decisions?" *Journal of Marketing*, Vol. 23, No. 2 (October 1958), p. 153, published by the American Marketing Association.

sion. The individual customer is probably just looking and is not yet ready to make a buying decision.

The Family as a Consuming Unit

In Western societies most individuals belong to at least two families during their lifetimes: the family of their parents and then the one formed when they marry. New families bring new demands for housing, appliances, furniture, and hundreds of other products and services that families use. Most of these purchases duplicate the product assortments of the families left behind. Therefore, marketers carefully watch trends in new family formations, because the growing number of family units, not the number of individual consumers, determines their sales potential.

The changing composition of the family is also important. As families move through their life cycles, family needs and purchasing abilities change.

Today and tomorrow the fastest growth will be in one- and two-person households: (1) young singles and marrieds and (2) elderly consumers without children. These households will adopt very different life-styles from conventional family units. They will prefer smaller apartments or condominiums to the single-family home and they will have and want fewer possessions.

Since the United States has never experienced such an abundance of relatively well-off "nonfamily" households, it will be interesting to see just how buying patterns will change. Exciting marketing opportunities will be created by these emerging market needs.

We will now shift our attention from smaller, face-to-face social groups to the larger groups to which individual consumers belong—their culture, subculture, and social class. The influence of larger groups on our behavior is not as direct and thus not so easy to measure, but it can strongly shape our beliefs and action.

SOCIAL CLASS

One important social group is **social class.** Every society stratifies its members into social classes according to their value to their society. In more traditional cultures the social class distinctions are sharp and the boundaries between classes are rigid. In modern Western societies, such as the United States, occupation and earning power are especially important determinants of social class. As a result, social classes are more open and people can move among the classes more freely, although a definite social hierarchy still exists.

Members of a social class share common values, goals, and ways of thinking, speaking, and behaving. Their influence on the individual is often so broad and subtle that he is hardly aware of it. And social class is only one of many social forces shaping his thoughts and actions. Yet social class has much to do with his behavior as a consumer. The products he buys and uses, the way he displays them to show where he "fits into" society, and the way he feels about them all reflect the influence of his social class membership.

The task of marketing management is to understand social class characteristics and how they influence consumer behavior. Armed with this knowledge, the marketer can create marketing mixes designed to appeal to social class differences.

The American Social Class Structure

Descriptions of American social classes vary, depending on which methods sociologists use to measure social class. Probably the most widely accepted view of the social class structure is provided by Lloyd Warner. His six-class structure is shown in Figure 3.5.

Figure 3.5   Warner's Social Class Structure

Social Class	Membership	Population Percentage
Upper-upper	Old rich	0.5
Lower-upper	New rich	1.5
Upper-middle	Managers, professionals	10.0
Lower-middle	White-collar employees	33.0
Upper-lower	Blue-collar workers	40.0
Lower-lower	Unskilled laborers	15.0

Source: W. Lloyd Warner, et al. *Social Class in America* (Chicago: Science Research Associates, Inc., 1949).

Sociologists and consumer researchers have produced a wealth of insights into social class characteristics and buying patterns. Here we will briefly highlight several important characteristics of each social class and suggest some of the consumer attitudes and buying characteristics of each class.

1. *Upper Classes*

    These are the social elite, made up of families of inherited wealth (upper-upper class) and the newly rich (lower-upper class) who rank somewhat lower on the social scale. The upper-upper class often emulates British aristocracy in their preferences for traditional homes, private schools, and activities such as riding and sailing. Lower-uppers are very achievement-oriented. They have been socially mobile, often having risen from middle-class backgrounds. Thus, they tend to be conspicuous in their consumption of expensive homes and cars, stylish clothing, and other symbols of their newly acquired wealth and status.

    A small fraction of the total market, upper classes are of little interest to many marketers. But they are especially important market segments for certain luxury goods and services.

2. *Upper-Middle Class*

    These are career-oriented professionals and business executives earning well-above-average incomes. They are the most highly educated class, often holding graduate or professional degrees. Their lifestyle and consumption behavior are centered upon the household head's career. Thus, having a fashionable home in a good neighborhood, dressing well, and living and entertaining graciously are very important. Typically, the wife, children, and home are symbols of the husband's career success, although career women are also becoming important in this class.

Understanding Consumer Behavior

3. *Lower-Middle Class*

Many people think of this second-largest social class as "typical Americans." They are smaller shopkeepers, office workers, teachers, technicians, salespeople—the bottom of the "white-collar" occupations. Their values are the traditional ones of American society—practicality, respectability, hard work, church-going, and family-centered. Often they have worked into this class from a lower class, and they work hard to maintain their status.

This class is conforming and is not as innovative as others in new fashions, tastes, and behaviors. Like the higher classes, lower-middle-class women are very home-conscious. Their expectations are lower, though. They want a good, but not fashionable, home in a respectable neighborhood, and they work hard to keep it neat and pretty.

4. *Upper-Lower or "Working" Class*

This is the largest social class. It consists of factory production workers, craftsmen and tradesmen, service occupations like TV repair work and waitress, and other blue-collar manual labor occupations. Their values and behavioral patterns are similar to the lower-middle class. But upper-lower class people are generally less educated and less involved in the world outside their families.

Since their jobs may be less stable or less open to advancement, they tend not to be social climbers, and they pursue shorter-range goals. Thus, they are less interested in stylish homes or acquiring and displaying other symbols of social advancement. Together with the lower-middle class, this group forms the American *mass market* and includes over two-thirds of the total population.

5. *Lower-Lower Class*

This class includes unskilled laborers, people chronically on welfare, and others in occupations considered nonrespectable in the society. Incomes and education levels are likely to be very low and unemployment rates high.

With little occupational security or status and few prospects for advancement, the lower-lower class views life more on a day-to-day basis. They buy and consume more for the moment or when cash is available. Although a sizable proportion of the population is in this class, marketers tend to ignore them because of their very low buying power.

Social class researchers point out that American social class structure continually changes, so that social stratification concepts must be updated to remain useful. Thus one authority suggests that the Warner six-class structure might today be more appropriately divided into three main groupings—Upper Americans, Middle Americans, and Lower Americans, with important life-style divisions within each level. For example, Middle Americans, comprising about two-thirds of all urban households, would consist of both "white-collar" and "blue-collar" occupations of Warner's lower-middle and upper-lower classes. The standard of living appears more important today than does "collar color," or how that living is earned. Within the broad Middle-American grouping, two major life-styles are pursued—*respectability* (in neighborhood, formal associations, and public appearance) and *modernity* and *life enjoyment*.[10]

Social class profiles suggest that social classes differ in much more than the amount of money they have to spend. They also think about and perceive their worlds differently. Figure 3.6 lists the psychological differences between the middle and the lower social classes.

Because their perceptions, values, and goals differ, different social class families earning identical incomes may spend them very differently. For example, an upper-lower class household headed by a Teamster truck driver and an upper-middle class lawyer's family each earn $25,000 per year. The

[10] Richard P. Coleman, a retrospective comment on his "The Significance of Social Stratification in Selling," in *Classics in Consumer Behavior*, Louis E. Boone, ed. (Tulsa: The Petroleum Publishing Company, 1977), pp. 300–302.

Figure 3.6 Psychological Differences Between the Middle and Lower Social Classes

Middle Class	Lower Class
1. Pointed to the future.	1. Pointed to the present and past.
2. Viewpoint embraces a long expanse in time.	2. Lives and thinks in a short expanse of time.
3. More urban in identification.	3. More rural in identification.
4. Stresses rationality.	4. Nonrational essentially.
5. Has well-structured sense of the universe.	5. Has vague, unclear, and unstructured sense of the world.
6. Horizons vastly extended or not limited.	6. Horizons sharply defined and limited.
7. Greater sense of choice making.	7. Limited sense of choice making.
8. Self-confident, willing to take risks.	8. Very much concerned with security.
9. Immaterial and abstract in his thinking.	9. Concrete and perceptive in his thinking.
10. Sees himself tied to national happenings.	10. World revolves around family and self.

Source: Reprinted from Pierre D. Martineau, "Social Classes and Spending Behavior," *Journal of Marketing* (October, 1958), p. 129, published by the American Marketing Association.

truck driver's family lives in a good home in a less expensive working-class neighborhood. Their home is well-stocked with appliances, and the family probably has a new car, perhaps a camper, boat, or other recreational vehicles, and a substantial savings account. The young lawyer pours his income into a more expensive home in a prestige neighborhood, joins the best country club he can afford, and buys more expensive furniture and clothing—all symbols of upward mobility, not security.

In this case, the truck driver's family earns substantially more than the average income *of its social class*, while the lawyer may be struggling to maintain a life-style appropriate to professionals earning much more than $25,000. Within their respective social classes the truck driver is considered "overprivileged" and the lawyer "underprivileged." The truck driver's family actually enjoys substantially more *discretionary* purchasing power and is an especially good market for expensive luxury items.[11]

Social classes also shop differently. Lower-class women prefer local, face-to-face shopping situations where they can find friendly clerks and easy credit. They tend to lack shopping information and are more impulsive and less organized in their shopping. Upper-middle class women organize their shopping more efficiently. They know what they want and where to buy it. Their shopping is more selective and wide-ranging. Upper-middle class shoppers are more critical of advertising claims and are suspicious of emotional appeals.[12]

CULTURES AND SUBCULTURES

Each society develops a unique **culture,** or learned way of life, which it hands down to future generations. Culture consists of shared beliefs, values, customs, and rules or norms of appropriate behavior. How we act toward others, what is important to us, what we wear, eat, and otherwise buy and consume are greatly influenced by our culture.

Consider just these examples of cultural and subcultural influences in national and international markets:

1. The youth culture easily crosses international boundaries today. In the mid-1970's faded and worn Levi's sold for $30 or more in Europe. British rock musicians enjoyed international celebrity status.
2. Brown eggs bring higher prices than white eggs in New England. But just the opposite is true in New York City.[13]

[11] Richard P. Coleman, "The Significance of Social Stratification in Selling," in *Marketing: A Maturing Discipline*, Martin L. Bell, ed. (Chicago: American Marketing Association, 1960), pp. 171–85. Peter L. Gillett and Richard A. Scott, "The Over-privileged/Underprivileged Consumer: A Useful Concept in Market Analysis?" *Proceedings of the Southern Marketing Association*, November, 1975.

[12] Sidney J. Levy, "Social Class and Consumer Behavior," in *On Knowing the Consumer*, Joseph W. Newman, ed. (New York: John Wiley & Sons, Inc., 1966), pp. 146–60.

[13] Wasson, *op. cit.*, p. 206.

Background for Marketing Decisions

3. Physical distance is culturally important. Latin Americans stand very close and often touch each other when discussing business. This embarrasses a typical U.S. businessperson, who feels more comfortable standing 5 to 8 feet away.[14]
4. Cultures view *time* differently. Being late for an appointment is interpreted as an insult in the United States, while Middle Easterners resent deadlines.[15]

Like our social class, our broader culture is so much a part of us that we often are unaware of its influence. But our unconscious acceptance of culture may change to conscious awareness when we experience a foreign culture. Here we begin to appreciate the similarities and differences in the cultures mentioned above. Unawareness of subtle but important cultural differences can cause serious misunderstandings in international markets. Therefore, international corporations are hiring native personnel in sensitive corporate positions or are training their executives in cultural differences and how to respond to them.[16]

The American Core Culture

The American marketplace strongly reflects its traditional cultural values. For the majority of the population, these values are rooted in the Puritan ethic. Striving to better oneself and deferring pleasures until success is earned are basic cultural themes. Leisure time is idle time better spent working and accumulating material wealth. The family is important, and woman's place is in the home.

For the most part, marketing operates within these cultural values. Possessions, such as cars, homes, and clothing, are sold and promoted as improving one's material standards of living and they are displayed by consumers as symbols of economic success.

Advertising provides us with excuses for relaxing and enjoying luxuries that otherwise might conflict with traditions of being thrifty and working hard. Thus, Cadillacs or expensive liquors are to be enjoyed "because you have worked hard, succeeded, and *deserve* them." Modern appliances help mother save time so that she can spend more time with her husband and children.

Marketing Responds to Changing Culture

The American core culture is changing; it is creating new values, lifestyles, and patterns of consumption. The forces of culture change are complex and are not easily measured. But several pressures for change are evident:

[14] Edwin T. Hall, "The Silent Language of Overseas Business," *Harvard Business Review* (May–June, 1960), pp. 87–96.
[15] *Ibid.*
[16] Theodore O. Wallin, "The International Executive's Baggage: Cultural Values of the American Frontier," *MSU Business Topics*, Spring, 1976, pp. 49–58.

1. Rising affluence, which also reduces the amount of work and opens up a leisure-oriented society.
2. Rising education levels, which produce more critical and questioning attitudes and which challenge traditional values.
3. Increasing communications and mobility, which brings together different peoples, ideas, and consumption patterns.
4. Declining influence of the family and organized religion on the values of the young.

Alert marketers respond to culture changes by adjusting their marketing programs to the new values and life-styles. Other firms try to do even better by anticipating new value trends and new consumption patterns before they are fully developed. Their strategy is to focus on market segments at the cutting edge of change—groups such as young people, career-oriented women, and ecologically conscious consumers.[17]

The changes in modern American culture are many. Several trends especially important to marketing management are reviewed below.

Decline of the Puritan Ethic

In the affluent society, traditional religious values are being challenged by a "theology of pleasure."[18] "Do it now" replaces self-denial; today's young couple buys expensive stereophonic systems and a color TV before the first paycheck arrives—thanks to the credit card revolution.

The Importance of Leisure

The values of long, hard work are challenged by the demand for leisure and the pursuit of self-expression outside the work role. The "leisure boom" created a tremendous demand for recreational products and services. Campgrounds and beaches overflow; Disneyland is imitated in amusement parks everywhere. Sports and hobby equipment enjoy huge sales.

Does the leisure trend mean that careers are unimportant and that young people no longer seek meaning and achievement in their work? Apparently not. A Louis Harris poll shows that many young high-school and college-age students still claim that money is one ingredient in their search for

---

[17] For a sampling of excellent books and articles on the subject, see: Lee Adler, "Cashing in on the Cop-out," *Business Horizons*, February, 1970, pp. 19–30; William Lazer et al., "Consumer Environments and Life-Styles of the Seventies," *MSU Business Topics*, Spring, 1972, pp. 5–17; Alvin Toffler, *Future Shock* (New York: Random House, Inc., 1970); E. B. Weiss, "New Life Styles of 1975–80 Will Throw Switch on Admen," *Advertising Age*, May 15, 1972; Ian Wilson, "Sociopolitical Forecasting: A New Dimension to Strategic Planning," *Michigan Business Review*, July, 1974.

[18] James F. Engel, D. Kollat, and R. Blackwell, *Consumer Behavior*, 2nd ed. (New York: Holt, Rinehart & Winston, Inc., 1973), p. 103.

personal fulfillment. But many people look beyond their jobs. Asked how they would use their leisure time if their regular job took care of family needs, 88% said that they would "relax and enjoy life with family and friends," while only 26% said they would get a second job.[19]

Whether today's young people will reject the middle-class virtues of job-related success, one change is certain. Affluence brings the desire for leisure and the means to afford it. The five-day workweek and the more recent trends toward the four-day workweek and flexible working hours have brought tremendous changes in life-styles, shopping, and consumption patterns. Shorter workweeks allow many Americans to move to distant suburbs and to spend much more leisure time in travel, sports activities, or watching television.

Youthfulness Is Highly Valued

In a rapidly changing, high-technology society the new knowledge and creativity of the young become more valued than the experience and wisdom of their elders. Society emphasizes youth so much that everyone wants to feel and be seen as youthful.

Marketers stress youthful themes in products and advertising. Advertisements for cigarettes, cosmetics, clothing, and nearly everything else feature young-looking models in youth-oriented surroundings. Shopping centers feature boutique displays and fashions designed for young people.

As we noted in Chapter 2, young people are large and important market segments. But youthfulness also influences the buying behavior of older people. Today this youth trend shows little signs of changing, but as the nation's average age increases, marketers will be watching closely for signs that youthful values and life-styles may also be declining in importance.

Sex Roles Are Changing

The roles of women, and to a lesser extent of men, are changing rapidly in modern society. Today, women are demanding and accepting wider roles. They seek more independence from their families and new careers outside the home. Because of their greater economic independence, women are able to buy more and their influence is growing.

"Men's liberation," a more recent, less vocal movement, challenges the aggressive, dominating image of males. Younger middle- and upper-class males are adopting somewhat more feminine modes of dress and self-expression. They are taking a more active part in family shopping, child-rearing, and even housework.

[19] Charles E. Silberman, "Identity Crisis in the Consumer Markets," *Fortune*, March, 1971, pp. 92–95, 159–60.

Understanding Consumer Behavior

Less Emphasis on Material Consumption; More Environmental Concern

Once society acquires a reasonably high material standard of life, it seeks a higher quality of life.[20] As people seek greater flexibility in life-styles and greater mobility, ownership of possessions becomes less important than using them. Today, marketers lease and rent virtually any product or service that consumers want to use.[21]

Although large homes and big cars are desired less by today's young people, we should not overlook the fact that they spend heavily on expensive stereos, record collections, customized vans, and camping gear.

Some consumers are reducing their levels of consumption or are seeking less ecologically harmful product alternatives. More people are willing to recycle waste materials and to forego needlessly wasteful convenience packaging. They conserve energy in the home and avoid using dangerous pesticides.

Subcultures Are Market Segments

Marketers frequently segment the national population by *subculture*. A subculture is a smaller group within the larger society. The subculture shares much of the larger culture, but it also has its own beliefs, attitudes, and life-styles. New York City, for example, has significant black, Jewish, Puerto Rican, Italian, Irish, and other subcultures. We usually think of subcultures as racial, religious, and ethnic groups, but subcultures may organize around an age group (teen-agers), activity (motorcycle cult), or other unusual ways of life (communes).

Each subculture has a separate identity, its own shopping areas, and products that it consumes. For example, pizza may be a universal dish, but collards, bagels, and red beans and rice are not.

Great mobility and instantaneous national communications have spread many of the consumption patterns well beyond their original subcultures. Italian, Chinese, and Mexican foods are a few examples of products that now have become Americanized.

The Black Subculture

Subcultures, such as blacks and other ethnic groups, may be large enough to generate considerable attention as market segments. Blacks are by far the most important ethnic subculture in the United States. The 24.1 million blacks and 3.2 million other nonwhites spent $73 billion in 1976, making them the ninth largest consumer market in the world, says the Gibson

[20] William J. Stanton, *Fundamentals of Marketing*, 4th ed. (New York: McGraw-Hill, 1975), p. 99.
[21] Leonard L. Berry and Kenneth E. Maricle, "Consumption-Without-Ownership: Marketing Opportunity for Today and Tomorrow," *MSU Business Topics*, Spring, 1973, pp. 33–41.

Background for Marketing Decisions

Report, a marketing newsletter specializing in the black marketplace. The black subculture, however, is so diverse that it must be treated as a series of separate market segments.

Overall, the similarities between black and white markets are greater than the differences.[22] But there are differences, and they reflect more than just the lower incomes of black consumers. Blacks share common experiences of social and economic discrimination in jobs, housing, education, and other areas.

Blacks spend more for clothing and non-automobile transportation and less for food, housing, medical care, automobile transportation than whites who have comparable incomes. Blacks apparently are more brand loyal than are whites.

The growing urban black population has created opportunities for a fast-rising, black-oriented media.[23] Black-owned and managed retail stores and shopping centers are also growing, although not without the many problems associated with low-income urban locations.[24] Travel services, cosmetics, and other services and products designed for blacks are enjoying sales success.[25]

Recent years have brought a resurgence of black consciousness. Yet, several researchers have concluded that most blacks implicitly accept middle-class white consumption values, while remaining at a disadvantage in reaching their goals.

Profiling Consumers by Life-styles

In these two chapters we have looked at consumers from a number of viewpoints: their demographic characteristics, personal characteristics, social roles, and group memberships. For the consumer researcher, adding up each piece of information about the consumer and his buying behavior is something like putting together a puzzle. The researcher attempts to fit together enough pieces to get an idea of the consumer's overall pattern of behavior.

One of the patterns researchers try to construct is consumer *life-style*. What consumer life-style means and how life-style is related to consumer behavior are well expressed by Joseph T. Plummer:

Life-style deals with everyday, behaviorally oriented facets of people as well as their feelings, attitudes, and opinions . . . [it] attempts to answer questions like: What do women think about the job of housekeeping? Are they interested in contemporary fashions? Do they participate in community activities? Are they optimistic about the future? Do they see themselves as homebodies or swingers? When the answers to questions like these correlate significantly with product usage, magazine readership, television program preferences, or other mass com-

[22] Engel, Kollat, and Blackwell, *op. cit.*, p. 183.
[23] "Black Market," *Newsweek*, July 17, 1972, pp. 71–72.
[24] "Black Shopping Centers," *Black Enterprise*, September, 1972, pp. 43, 45–47, 49.
[25] " 'Black Is Beautiful' Market Brings New Dollars to Supers," *Progressive Grocer*, April, 1972, pp. 142–50.

Figure 3.7   Demographic Profile of the Heavy User of Shotgun
Ammunition

	Percent who spend $11+ per year on shotgun ammunition (141)	Percent who don't buy (395)
Age		
Under 25	9	5
25–34	33	15
35–44	27	22
45–54	18	22
55+	13	36
Occupation		
Professional	6	15
Managerial	23	23
Clerical-Sales	9	17
Craftsman	50	35
Income		
Under $6,000	26	19
$6,000–$10,000	39	36
$10,000–$15,000	24	27
$15,000+	11	18
Population Density		
Rural	34	12
2,500–50,000	11	11
50,000–500,000	16	15
500,000–2 million	21	27
2 million+	13	19
Geographic Division		
New England–Mid-Atlantic	21	33
Central (N, W)	22	30
South Atlantic	23	12
E. South Central	10	3
W. South Central	10	5
Mountain	6	3
Pacific	9	15

Source: Reprinted from William D. Wells, "Psychographics: A Critical Review," *Journal of Marketing Research* (May 1975), p. 197, published by the American Marketing Association.

Figure 3.8 Psychographic Profile of the Heavy User of Shotgun
Ammunition

Base	Percent who spend $11+ per year on shotgun ammunition (141)	Percent who don't buy (395)
I like hunting	88	7
I like fishing	68	26
I like to go camping	57	21
I love the out-of-doors	90	65
A cabin by a quiet lake is a great place to spend the summer	49	34
I like to work outdoors	67	40
I am good at fixing mechanical things	47	27
I often do a lot of repair work on my own car	36	12
I like war stories	50	32
I would do better than average in a fist fight	38	16
I would like to be a professional football player	28	18
I would like to be a policeman	22	8
There is too much violence on television	35	45
There should be a gun in every home	56	10
I like danger	19	8
I would like to own my own airplane	35	13
I like to play poker	50	26
I smoke too much	39	24
I love to eat	49	34
I spend money on myself that I should spend on the family	44	26
If given a chance, most men would cheat on their wives	33	14
I read the newspaper every day	51	72

Source: Reprinted from William D. Wells, "Psychographics: A Critical Review," *Journal of Marketing Research* (May 1975), p. 198, published by the American Marketing Association.

munication variables, a picture emerges that goes beyond flat demographic descriptions, program ratings, or product-specific measures.[26]

Life-style research usually involves getting information on demographic and social group membership, along with measures of consumer's activities, interests, and opinions (often called AIO inventories or *psychographics*). The researcher can then relate these characteristics to the consumer's use of media, products, and brands.

To get some idea of the insights provided by life-style analysis, take a look at Figures 3.7 and 3.8. Both are profiles of heavy buyers of shotgun ammunition.[27] Figure 3.7 shows that the heavy user of shotgun shells is younger, lower in income and education, more rural and Southern than nonusers. This is not too surprising, perhaps, but it doesn't suggest *why* people shoot and what else they like to do.

In the AIO profile (Figure 3.8) we learn that shooters enjoy other rugged outdoor activities, even working outdoors. These relationships suggest other products—camping and fishing equipment, hardware and tools—that might be promoted to hunters. And they suggest other outdoor activities and settings for advertising shotgun ammunition. Since ammunition buyers are also more attracted by violence, either action and adventure magazines or police and Western TV programs may be good *media* for advertising.

One of the most extensive psychographic analyses of consumers has been done by Needham, Harper & Steers, the Chicago advertising agency. From this study, 10 life-style types were developed—five female and five male (see Figure 3.9). Specific profiles were then developed for each type. For example, "Eleanor, the Elegant Socialite," is "racy, social, cosmopolitan, aware, self-assured, high-strung, weight conscious, somewhat conservative on social issues, and attractive."[28]

While psychographic analysis has not been fully accepted by some practitioners, it does appear to offer a useful alternative to the more traditional approaches of determining why consumers buy.

THE CONSUMER DECISION PROCESS ADDS INSIGHTS

Looking at consumer behavior as a *decision process* offers valuable insights for the marketer. Here, the focus is on individual buyers and how they reach a purchase decision. Figure 3.10 illustrates a simplified **consumer decision process.**

Looking at each decision stage, the marketer can examine a number of questions about the buyer behavior. For example, what kinds of information do buyers seek? Will they rely heavily on the advice of trusted friends?

[26] Joseph T. Plummer, "The Concept and Application of Life-Style Segmentation, *Journal of Marketing*, January, 1974, pp. 33–37.

[27] This example is discussed in William D. Wells, "Psychographics: A Critical Review," *Journal of Marketing Research*, May, 1975, pp. 196–251, at pp. 197 and 198.

[28] Peter W. Bernstein, "Psychographics Is Still an Issue on Madison Avenue," *Fortune*, January 16, 1978, p. 79.

Figure 3.9   An Example of a Psychographic Analysis of American Consumers

Source: Based on an original illustration by Robert Logrippo for *Fortune* magazine.

How many dealers and brands will they compare? How much influence does the dealer have on the buyers' decisions? After the purchase, will buyers want additional information to support their choices? Answers to these questions provide clues for appropriate marketing strategy at each purchase decision stage.

PUTTING IT ALL TOGETHER

In recent years consumer researchers have developed comprehensive theories of consumer decision making.[29] They are integrating the important behavioral concepts to yield a more complete picture of how consumers act

[29] For example, see Engel, Kollat, and Blackwell, *op. cit.*; John A. Howard and Jagdish Sheth, *The Theory of Buyer Behavior* (New York: John Wiley & Sons, Inc., 1969).

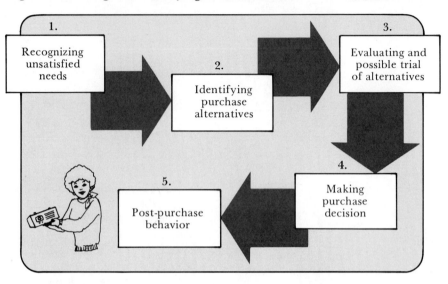

Figure 3.10   Stages in the Buying Decision Process

1. Recognizing unsatisfied needs

2. Identifying purchase alternatives

3. Evaluating and possible trial of alternatives

4. Making purchase decision

5. Post-purchase behavior

in complex market environments. At this point, researchers are only beginning to test their theories in the marketplace. But these theories promise
to give marketing managers a framework for organizing their data and
insights and for suggesting appropriate marketing responses.

Yet, understanding how consumers behave seldom gives the marketer
automatic answers. Ultimately, managers must exercise their own intuition
and judgment in selecting marketing strategy.

SUMMARY

This chapter has explored behavioral science contributions to understanding
and predicting consumer actions.

First, we considered the consumer as an economic problem solver. Economics offers valuable theories and tools for predicting how people will
purchase products under given market conditions. But the economic perspective ignores much of the complexity of human decision making. Many
personal and social factors must also be included.

Marketers look to psychology for insights into personal factors influencing buyer behavior. Consumer learning, perception, and motivation are
important foundations for building a psychology of consumers.

Acquiring information, learning preferences, and developing habit patterns are several types of learning important to marketing managers.

Developing effective advertising and promotion strategy requires careful assessment of consumer learning patterns.

Since human perception is selective, marketers often have little choice but to tailor their market offers to fit the different perceptions of their target markets. The consumer's way of experiencing his or her world often lies outside the marketers' ability to alter these perceptions.

We discussed that since most consumer needs are learned, marketers theoretically have unlimited opportunity to encourage consumer needs for their particular products and services. Thus, measuring consumer motivations is important, but motives are only one key to understanding and predicting the consumer's specific behavior. People strive to maintain and display positive images to themselves and others. As social beings, people must also learn to play various social roles. These roles are defined and rewarded by important reference groups.

Thus, much of our consumption is symbolic, designed to express personal self and social role. Looking at much of human consumption as expressive or symbolic behavior adds new and useful dimensions to the consumers.

The social class, subcultures, and the broader culture we belong to are important social forces that shape our values, attitudes, and actions, and thus our buying and consumption. Marketers find it helpful to identify and segment consumers as members of these social groups. As values and attitudes of society change, they produce definite shifts in market behavior.

Marketers need to pull together many of these behavioral factors in order to build more comprehensive models of the consumer. Consumer life-style analysis is one recent research approach. Life-style segments offer richer, more meaningful consumer portraits than do demographic or psychological factors alone.

Finally, the consumer decision process offers a useful framework for designing marketing strategy. In studying consumer decision making, marketers can ask important questions about how consumers acquire and process information and about the actions consumers take during and after the purchase. With answers to these questions, marketers can design more complete and effective marketing programs based on fuller insights into how and why consumers make their decisions.

QUESTIONS

1. *Households* are forming at a faster rate than *families* today. Why? How is the faster growth in households changing national consumption patterns?
2. Why must advertising copywriters be aware of and understand selective processes among audiences?

Understanding Consumer Behavior

3. Discuss gift-giving as "symbolic communication." Is it important for marketers to know whether their products are being bought as gifts or for personal use? Select a product example and suggest how the seller's marketing mix strategy might differ for each case.

4. The following cultural values seem to be changing, especially among younger people: emphasis on quality of life rather than material standard of living; changing sex roles; decline in the "postponement of gratification" ethic. How are consumption patterns changing in response to these cultural trends? How are marketers adjusting to these changes?

5. Marketers can profitably measure and respond to both demographic and life-style patterns of target customer groups. What insights are added by each consumer pattern?

6. As a manufacturer of clothing for pre- and early teen-age girls, you are interested in how and where to advertise your product line. A consumer analyst suggests that research on family interaction patterns might be especially helpful in your advertising decisions. Do you agree? What questions might this research help answer?

7. How is the concept of reference group related to social role? To self-image?

8. Using a recent purchase you made as your subject, outline the purchase decision process you followed. Use the five-step model presented in Figure 3.10. What were some of the major questions you had to answer? Did your decision sequence flow in this manner?

GLOSSARY

Consumer Decision Process: the procedure or steps an individual uses in reaching a buying decision. A five-stage process would include: (1) need or problem recognition, (2) identifying purchase alternatives, (3) evaluating alternatives, (4) deciding and buying, (5) post-purchase evaluation

Culture: the unique way of life, or shared beliefs, rules of behavior, customs, and artifacts of a society that is learned and handed down through generations

"Economic Man": a rather mechanistic view of consumers as economic problem solvers. Some basic assumptions are that consumers understand their needs and know all available means of satisfying them; thus buying decisions involve simply deciding how much of each product to buy within the financial budget

Hierarchy of Needs: a classification of motives that assigns priority to basic needs, which must be at least partially satisfied before the next order of needs becomes activated. The hierarchy proceeds from physiological needs, to safety, to belongingness and love, to esteem and status, to self-actualization needs

Life-Style: the overall pattern of attitudes, values, roles, and self-concept that an individual expresses through consumption, work, and play

Motive: inner striving conditions, variously described as wishes, need, drive, etc., that activate or move behavior toward goals

Product Image: the sum total of attitudes and knowledge that people hold of a product. The particular images different people hold usually develop from their personal and cultural patterns, experience, and the social influence of others, including marketers

Reference Groups: groups with whom an individual identifies in forming his attitudes, values, and perspectives. Reference groups influence role behavior and self-evaluation

Role: a set of rights and duties belonging to a social position

Selective Processes of Perception: generally recognized as three processes by which people notice and filter (exposure or attention), interpret (perceive), and remember (recall) information selectively in accordance with their individual experiences, beliefs, and motivations

Self-Concept: the idea that a person has of himself, thinks others view him, and wishes to see himself in a unique manner. The interaction of these views of self (self-concept) influences behavior

Social Class: groups of individuals sharing common goals, values, and ways of thinking and behaving. Societies stratify or rank social classes according to the relative social value of their occupations, specific knowledge, or wealth

CASES

Case 1: Bilge Brothers

Bilge Brothers, a small California brewer, was planning to capitalize on the trend toward diet or low-calorie beers by introducing their own brand. The brewer created Lo-Cal in 12-oz and 7-oz bottles and cans to compete with the two national brands of diet beers selling in their market area.

Lo-Cal was carefully brewed in taste and appearance to match the formulas of the two major low-calorie brands. Advertising, cartons and labeling, and point-of-purchase promotional materials were designed to appeal especially to women supermarket shoppers. The Lo-Cal beer was then test marketed for several months in two medium-sized cities in Bilge's marketing region. Management enthusiastically awaited the test results.

Test market sales were disappointing, well below the performance levels established for the test market period. Supermarket audits showed that neither men nor women were buying much Lo-Cal. Shopper surveys in supermarkets where all low-calorie brands were sold revealed that both sexes who had an opinion on the brand thought it was weaker tasting, more watery, and less satisfying than the other brands of low-calorie beers. Shoppers claiming to be regular drinkers of the national brands were especially critical of Lo-Cal.

Bilge Brothers' management decided to employ a marketing consulting firm before making a final decision on whether or not to market Lo-Cal. The consultant performed a two-phase tasting experiment with consumers. Randomly selected adult beer drinkers in Bilge's market area were asked to state their beer brand preferences. In the first tasting experiment, they sample tasted carefully disguised brands of all of the light beers. The great majority of drinkers were unable to distinguish among any of the low-calorie brands by taste and appearance alone. "Favorite" brands thus scored no better than Lo-Cal.

When the taste tests were repeated with the brand labels identified, ratings for Lo-Cal worsened, while ratings for other brands increased. The marketing consultant noted the test results and prepared a report explaining (1) what the results meant for Lo-Cal's product formula design and marketing strategy and (2) what Lo-Cal should do now, and why.

1. Assume that your task is to write this report. What will you say in the report?

Case 2: Miller Optical Co.

Miller Optical Co. sold glasses and contact lenses through five retail stores in a medium-sized city. Sam Miller, the owner, was concerned that his sales were not keeping pace with growth in his local market. Well-established in the community for over 30 years, Miller Optical was a traditional optician, Sam Miller thought. It offered a full line of services, including examinations, fitting and repairs, and an extensive line of high-quality lenses and frames for the entire family, sold at full-margin prices usually suggested by their optical suppliers. Sam Miller did not promote his stores aggressively, believing that the quality of service and the products would "sell themselves" through satisfied customers. Promotion was limited to telephone book yellow pages advertising and small but steady advertising in the city newspapers "to let people know we're still around."

Sam knew that the market was changing, and competition was intensifying. Eyeglasses were now fashion items; prescription sunglasses were selling especially well. A tremendous variety of metal and plastic frames were being offered, and styles were moving in and out of fashion more rapidly than ever. The retail response to this market growth was apparent in Miller's local area. In recent years, a large regional chain was gaining entry into the new shopping centers. The downtown discount optician seemed to be thriving. And just last year, Brite Eyes, a new discounter, moved into the local college area and was doing very well.

Sam knew that he didn't have the time or the ability to manage a more aggressive marketing program, so he hired Amy Cole, a young woman with three years' experience in bank marketing, to develop and manage a new marketing program for the stores.

Amy decided that her first task was to gather extensive background information on the prescription glasses market, customer buying patterns, and the national and local competitive environment. Over the next several weeks she informally interviewed Miller Optical personnel, talked with optical supply wholesalers, and visited local competitors to observe their marketing practices and talk with customers about buying and wearing glasses. She also read as much of the recent trade literature as she could. After several weeks of investigation, she began to summarize her information and develop a number of questions and suggestions that would lead to more specific research and then a firm marketing proposal. Some of her findings are summarized here.

Market Trends

—The market is growing rapidly. Glasses are losing much of their negative image, and in fact are a style asset, particularly in fashion sunglasses and in tinted contact lenses. Youth leads the way in making glasses a fashion accessory. Many more people are buying several different pairs for different uses or modes of dress. The optical industry has exploited the rising affluence and growing diversity of life-styles by offering a wide variety of products and through aggressive promotion of eyewear as fashionable.

—People whose prescriptions must be changed have always faced the expense of new glasses, but with inflation, shorter fashion cycles, and the desire to own several pairs of glasses, the costs of eyewear have been escalating for more customers. As a result, more opticians are offering less expensive imported frames and adopting mass merchandising discount selling techniques and pricing policies.

Customer Profiles

1. Young children wear glasses primarily to correct eyesight deficiencies. Parents concerned with thorough examinations. Families with several children especially budget conscious and seek economical glasses, but avoid compromising on quality. Parents prefer to buy through optometrists or local opticians; some buy from downtown discount optician, but not Brite Eyes discounter.

2. Teens and young adults of both sexes are style conscious, follow fashion trends, and are likely to own more than one pair of glasses. Sunglasses of all prices and types, both prescription and non-prescription, are bought and worn everywhere. Locally, they are the best customers of Brite Eyes, although they may buy from any of the types of retailers.

3. Middle-aged and older adults have high demand for examination services. Many have worn glasses for years, are reasonably experienced shoppers, and are concerned with performance features and services. Women seem more fashion conscious than do men, but are concerned with a pleasing appearance rather than up-to-date styling. Most are likely to patronize a local optometrist or conventional optician, but lower-income adults are good customers of downtown discounter. Few have heard of Brite Eyes; none had shopped there.

Local Competition

1. Optometrists (O.D.'s) are physicians certified to examine and prescribe lenses identical to those offered by opticians, at equivalent or slightly lower prices.
2. Large optical chains feature a wide variety of high quality products, full services, and full-margin prices. Aggressive in promotion and store location, they are apparently growing somewhat faster than the total market.
3. Local chains (like Miller Optical) are quite similar to large chains, except that they are usually less aggressive in promotion, relying more upon reputation, personal knowledge of customers, convenient service.
4. Conventional discounters are located in downtown or lower-rent areas, and emphasize low price ($29.95 Complete!) and feature a rather wide variety of less-expensive imported frames. Examinations are standardized and low-priced.
5. Brite Eyes is also a discounter featuring low-priced imported merchandise, but concentrated in fashion lines for adults. Located near the University, the store has a somewhat shabby, noisy boutique atmosphere. Examinations are standardized and low-priced. Salespeople are college students employed part time. Brite Eyes advertises heavily in campus newspapers, local rock music stations, and some newspaper advertising.

Selected Comments from Informal Interviews

elderly woman shopper: "I can't afford to buy my glasses from my optometrist, so that's why I'm here (downtown discount store). I guess they're as good as any. Nothing fancy."

college sophomore: "I can get new glasses at Brite Eyes for about 30 bucks—who can afford $80? Besides, I'll get a pair of sunglasses too, and still save money. Unless you've got real eye problems, there's no need to pay for an elaborate exam, either."

parent: "This is my child's first visit to the optometrist, and I want to be sure she gets her eyes checked carefully and fitted right. My neighbor recommended him."

Miller Optical salesperson: "We're not supposed to tell customers this, but those imported frames you can buy from Brite Eyes won't hold up more than a year. They look like ours, but the quality is just not there. You get what you pay for. If a customer asks me, I'll tell him."

another salesperson: "I doubt that most people ever shop around much before buying glasses. Store location and reputation mean a lot. But the young people are looking at styles a lot. They like places with a lot of selection."

1. How important is store image to success in retailing here? Can Miller Optical successfully appeal to present customers and still compete with discounters?
2. Does the life-style approach seem to make sense in promoting the sale of eyewear and services? How about demographic segmentation?
3. How would you go about segmenting this market based on benefits and/or life-styles that you think are involved?
4. What else about consumer behavior would you suggest that Amy investigate before completing her market analysis?

Background for Marketing Decisions

The Environment for Marketing Decisions

After you finish this chapter, you should be able to answer the following questions:

1. How does the environment impact on marketing decisions?
2. What are the major aspects of the environment?
3. What kinds of decisions do companies make that affect their marketing departments?
4. What are some indications that competition is getting stronger?
5. What is the major input that the marketing department must provide the company's research and development effort?
6. What major economic trends occurred in the United States in the 1970's?
7. In what ways can the legal/political area impact on marketing decisions?
8. What major cultural changes in the past two decades have affected a company's marketing operations?
9. Are there any problems in foreign countries that can affect a company's marketing operations?

INTRODUCTION

In the first chapter we talked about the need to understand the market for goods and services. We also discussed the importance of the environment, which was defined as those areas outside the marketing department, in addition to the market, over which the marketing department cannot exert direct control. Included in the environment is the company in which the marketing department is located, competition, technology, the economy, legal/political area, culture, and foreign countries.

The environment impacts strongly on marketing decision making in two ways. First, it provides opportunities that must be recognized and acted upon by the marketing department. Second, the environment frequently presents obstacles and constraints that must be recognized and adjusted to as marketing decisions are made.

In this chapter we will deal at length with the environment. Any company that chooses to ignore developments in the environment does so at its peril. Thus, in this chapter we will trace the major developments that have occurred in each of these areas of the environment with a view toward indicating opportunities and obstacles that have resulted. We will also indicate the implications of these developments for marketing strategies.

THE MARKETING DEPARTMENT'S COMPANY

A company's top management makes a number of crucial decisions that directly affect its marketing operations. Whether the marketing department likes it or not, it must adjust to and recognize these decisions as it plans its own operations.

What kinds of decisions do we mean? Some of the more important decisions are listed in Figure 4.1. In the following discussion we will discuss some of the more important trends that are occurring when these kinds of decisions are made by companies.

Most large companies appear to be giving additional emphasis to their marketing operations for a number of reasons, but probably mainly because these firms have adopted the marketing concept. Once the marketing concept has been operationalized, it is likely that marketing's status in the firm will be enhanced. Frequently the top marketing man is given vice-presidential status and the marketing effort is consolidated so that the marketing department has major responsibility for the various marketing functions.

Although adoption of the marketing concept suggests that marketing's share of the firm's scarce resources should increase, data are lacking in this regard. It is known that, on the average, consumer goods manufacturers

Figure 4.1 Company Decisions That Affect the Marketing Department

1. Determining the overall emphasis to be given to the company's marketing operations.
2. Allocating scarce resources to the marketing department.
3. Preparing various budgets for the marketing department.
4. Establishing overall company objectives that the marketing department must assist in achieving.
5. Establishing specific objectives that the company's marketing operations are supposed to achieve.
6. Determining who the company's chief marketing executive will be.
7. Deciding how much status in the organization the marketing department will get.
8. Deciding which marketing functions should be emphasized and which ones should be deemphasized.

increased expenditures for marketing research by 142% between 1962 and 1968 and that manufacturers of industrial goods increased expenditures by 75%. However, it should be pointed out that these consumer goods manufacturers devoted only .3% of their sales to marketing research, compared to but .12% of sales for industrial products manufacturers. Compared to expenditures for research and development, the total of $300 million to $400 million spent annually for marketing research represents only 4%.[1]

Companies seem to be stressing significantly more than ever the achievement of profit objectives. This means that the marketing department, as a result, will either have to obtain profit objectives or be more concerned with objectives designed to aid in achieving profit. Given the profit emphasis embodied in the marketing concept, it might be argued that this emphasis should not present a problem for the marketing department. However, if the marketing area has been used to emphasizing such nonprofit objectives as sales volume, the transition to a profit orientation may not be a smooth one.

COMPETITION

There is little doubt that companies are facing, and will continue to face, increasingly rugged competition. We believe this to be true for a number of reasons.

[1] Theodore N. Beckman, William R. Davidson, and W. Wayne Talarzyk, *Marketing* (New York: The Ronald Press Company, 1973), pp. 555–56.

The Environment for Marketing Decisions

Marginal, small operations are being forced out of business at accelerated rates. This means that the firms that remain are large and highly efficient and thus present severe competitive problems. Their highly efficient production methods result in lower costs that are often reflected in tough to match prices. Economies of scale in the storage and transportation areas also contribute to lower costs; these operations also provide rapid distribution to customers, which is an important competitive edge.

Many industries tend to be dominated by a small nucleus of huge firms. It is not at all unusual in such industries as rubber, flat glass, steel, aluminum, and petroleum for the four or five largest companies to account for 75% or more of the industry's total sales. This leaves the rest of the industry's companies slicing up a very small piece of pie. The dominance of these industries by a few giants makes it virtually impossible for new firms to be successful and thus few attempt to enter the market. For example, except for foreign imports—manufactured by huge operations—when have there been any new automobiles in the United States not manufactured by the "big four"?

The constant stream of new products turned out by competitive firms puts pressures on other companies. Frequently, they lack the expertise and financial backing to introduce successful new products. And in the near future, at least, it is highly doubtful that the stream of new products will run dry, for companies realize that they will not survive five years unless a large percentage of their sales volume is accounted for products not currently carried.

Many companies today find it more difficult to determine just who their competitors are; thus, they have a difficult time competing effectively. More companies are bringing out new, competitive products. Conglomerates are acquiring companies to manufacture and market products totally beyond their normal product lines. Also contributing to this difficulty is that many companies take a limited view as to who their competitors are, not realizing that companies beyond their own industry may be more of a threat than those within. This is especially true when consumer discretionary income is involved. For example, the vacation industry (hotels, restaurants, and air lines) may be tougher competitors for the consumer's dollars than other companies in the retail jewelry industry.

The increasing emphasis by competitors on nonprice competition creates problems. Product differentiation is a major weapon. Product packages, advertising, and channels of distribution are also weapons. These competitive actions are not as easy to match as meeting prices. Also, companies have more difficulty in assessing the impact of nonprice competitor tactics on sales and profits and, hence, are reluctant to follow suit.

The increased use of sophisticated decision techniques is giving many firms a distinct competitive edge. When applied to the production area, for example, these decision techniques result in better scheduling of facilities, less wastage, and lower production costs. In recent years these techniques have been vigorously applied to the marketing area as well. They have helped firms decide, for example, where to locate warehouses, what are the best routes for their salesmen, which accounts their salesmen should call on and how frequently, the best timing for advertisements, and so on.

One major weapon that companies have is their technological expertise. This expertise may result in successful new products, modifications of old products, and new and better ways of producing and marketing products and services.

TECHNOLOGY

The Past Scope of Technological Effort

In 1972 a total of $28 billion was spent on research and development in the United States. Of this total, 68.7% was accounted for by industry, 14.3% by the federal government, 13.5% by universities, and 3.6% by other organizations engaged in research (see Figure 4.3).

Figure 4.2 shows the commitment to research and development in the United States in 1964 and 1972. This figure presents the percentage of the nation's gross national product allocated to total research and development and to R&D expenditures accounted for by industry, the federal government, universities, and other organizations doing research. Examination of Figure 4.2 reveals a number of significant findings. In 1964, slightly more than 3% of the gross national product in the United States was devoted to all types of expenditures. By 1972, this figure had dropped to 2.52%. Expenditures as a percentage of gross national product declined for the various kinds of R&D expenditures. Large decreases occurred for federal government research (.45% to .36%) and industrial research (2.14% to 1.73%).

Figure 4.3 shows the percentage of total research and development outlays accounted for by the four major kinds of expenditures in 1957 and 1972. Research by industry accounted for 77.9% of total expenditures in 1957, but dropped to 68.7% in 1972. Federal government research as a percentage increased slightly between these years. Research by universities as a percentage of total R&D outlays showed a significant increase, going from 8.0% to 13.5%.

The data presented in Figures 4.2 and 4.3 suggest a decrease in technological effort within American industry. Specific figures support this hypothesis. Since 1968 total government and industry spending for research and development has dropped 6% when inflation has been accounted for. The National Science Foundation indicates that between 1965 and 1975 industry spending for basic research (research with no immediate payoff or application) dropped 12%. Also, during the same period federal expenditures for basic research within industry dropped 45%.[2]

2 *Business Week*, February 16, 1976, p. 56.

Figure 4.2   Percentage of Gross National Product Spent on Various Types of Research and Development, 1964 and 1972

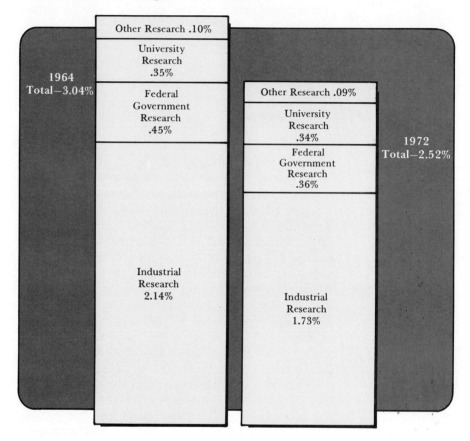

Source: This figure was developed from data provided in Harry A. Lipson and John R. Darling, *Marketing Fundamentals* (New York: John Wiley & Sons, 1974), p. 175.

Some of the factors that explain this decreased research and development effort are as follows:

1. Soaring research and development costs.
2. Increased governmental regulation.
3. Lack of adequate and inexpensive capital with which to finance R&D projects.
4. Continuing high rates of new product failure.

Background for Marketing Decisions

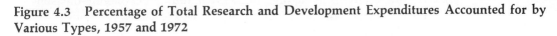

Figure 4.3 Percentage of Total Research and Development Expenditures Accounted for by Various Types, 1957 and 1972

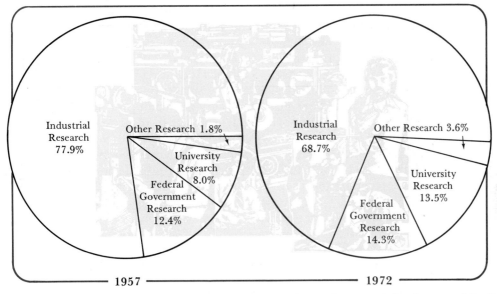

Industrial Research 77.9%

Other Research 1.8%

University Research 8.0%

Federal Government Research 12.4%

Industrial Research 68.7%

Other Research 3.6%

University Research 13.5%

Federal Government Research 14.3%

1957 ——————— 1972

Source: This figure was developed from data provided in Lipson and Darling, op. cit., pp. 161, 175.

5. An increasingly conservative management that is more interested in a sure thing and is afraid to take risks.[3]

As a result of this negative thinking, a number of reactions appears to be occurring in industry. New products are being assigned more stringent performance demands. New products now stay longer in the research and testing stages and are expected to pay back their investment in half the time thought reasonable several years ago. Top management appears to be getting more involved with new products. For example, Roger R. Robbins, executive vice-president of Purex, stated: "In the last year, on the basis of high capital risk, I turned down new products at a rate at least twice what I did a year ago."[4] Many companies now direct their innovative effort to modifying existing products instead of developing new products. For example, a new grain-spirits drink reformulated from an old recipe was introduced in 1976 by Glenmore Distillers. In the same year Quaker Oats repackaged a hot wheat cereal that it has been selling for 68 years.[5]

[3] Ibid., pp. 56–57.
[4] Ibid., p. 57.
[5] Ibid.

The Environment for Marketing Decisions

Risks from Technological Inertia

Despite the decreased technological effort noted above, companies run great risks by drastically reducing their R&D expenditures and playing the game too conservatively. Some companies have refused to pull in their horns. For example, Eastman Kodak produced and marketed over 120 new or improved products in 1972. Hewlett-Packard introduced between 85 and 100 new offerings in 1971 and 1972; it introduced 70 in 1967. A manufacturer of toys introduced 107 new items in the first 6 months of 1971; that was the same number they produced during the whole of 1970. Black and Decker brought out 15 new products in 1970, and it doubled this figure for 1971.[6]

Why are these and countless other companies taking such an aggressive technological stance? First, many companies are looking for that one outstanding new product success that will guarantee them an excellent return on investment for years to come. Second, they are afraid to reduce their technological effort because they do not see tough competitors doing so. Third, they may be caught without the necessary technological expertise that may revolutionize an entire industry. Timex, for example, for years did not have and could not acquire the technology necessary to produce electronic time pieces. Fourth, innovative companies often perform better than noninnovative firms. Between 1945 and 1974 five high-technology companies—IBM, 3M, Polaroid, Xerox, and Texas Instruments—had an annual compounded growth rate of 16.5% in sales and 10.8% in jobs. For six companies considered to be less innovative over this time period—General Foods, General Electric, Bethlehem Steel, DuPont, Procter and Gamble, and International Paper—the growth rates were only 7.8% in sales and 1.9% in jobs.[7]

The Role of Marketing in Technology

The marketing department has a most important role to play in a company's technological effort: Marketing must direct these efforts so that new products and modifications of existing products are designed to satisfy the needs and desires of the market. There is nothing as likely to fail as a technologically superior product that the market does not want. Consider the case of the Scan Data Company which developed the highly powerful and flexible OCR machine that can read not only typewritten copy, but also computer printouts and handwriting. Unfortunately, the machine was too technologically advanced for the market which did not need its power and flexibility and did not want to pay the accompanying high price. As a result, in 1971 the firm had a net loss of $.79 a share.

Technologically strong companies must have a marketing orientation in order to succeed. Tektronix, a producer of electronic instruments with great technical knowledge, realized in 1975 that it lacked a corresponding marketing knowledge. As a result, Tektronix established a separate marketing-

---

[6] *The Wall Street Journal*, April 13, 1972, p. 1.
[7] *Business Week*, February 16, 1976, pp. 57–58.

Background for Marketing Decisions

Figure 4.4 How Different Areas of the Firm View the Customer

1. What marketing said the customer wanted.

2. What the R&D department developed.

3. What the production department manufactured.

4. What the customer actually wanted.

oriented organization in an effort to develop new products that would be successful.[8]

The marketing department must be sure that it understands what the market wants. After this has been established, research and development must develop the product that will satisfy the market's needs and desires. The marketing department must then work with production to ensure that the product that is eventually manufactured is what the consumer wants. By working closely with R&D and manufacturing, the situation depicted in Figure 4.4 may be avoided.

Sources of Technological Expertise

A company has a number of sources that it can tap the order to develop technological expertise. These include its own R&D department, other companies, independent inventors, the federal government, and consulting firms.

[8] Ibid., p. 91.

A major source of technological expertise should be a company's own *research and development* department. This department should be taking recommendations from the marketing department and converting them into prototype models that can be used in test markets and also be produced by the production area if the market accepts the product. Also, R&D should be developing ideas that have potential as products. These ideas can then be taken by the marketing department and presented to the market for its approval or disapproval.

R&D should also be analyzing the company's already existing products in order to see how they can be improved to more adequately satisfy the market's requirements. It also should be analyzing the company's marketing operations to see if they can be made more efficient. Especially important are materials handling equipment, warehouse design, and transportation vehicles.

Other companies and independent inventors are often important sources of technological expertise. Other companies can be absorbed by a larger company, and independent inventors' patents can be acquired.

These two sources for technology are very important because in spite of the well-heeled internal R&D departments that exist in many companies, many significant inventions in the twentieth century have come from these two areas. They include:[9]

1. Xerography: Chester Carlson
2. Cyclotron: Ernest O. Lawrence
3. Jet engine: Frank Whittle and Hans von Ohain
4. Power steering: Francis Davis
5. Air conditioning: Willis Carrier
6. Polaroid camera: Edwin Land

An example of one company absorbing another company for its technological expertise is the recent acquisition of S.C.I. by Docutel. Docutel, a supplier of automatic teller machines to the banking industry, was searching for companies that have additional expertise in this area. S.C.I., located in Huntsville, Alabama, was formed at the height of the space program. Because of the decline in the space program, S.C.I. decided that financial institutions would be a viable market for its technological knowledge. Accordingly, S.C.I. developed several applications that interested Docutel and Docutel thus acquired S.C.I.

The *federal government* is a major source of technological expertise. In particular, the United States effort in the space program has made available countless industrial applications (see Figure 4.5).[10] Most important is the fact that the federal government has encouraged private industry to make use of these applications, but thus far the response has not been encouraging.

[9] Robert J. Holloway and Robert S. Hancock, *Marketing in a Changing Environment* (New York: John Wiley & Sons, Inc., 1973), p. 156.
[10] *Popular Science*, March, 1974, p. 87 and *Space World*, July, 1976, pp. 16–32.

Figure 4.5   Technological Spinoffs from the Space Program

1. Orbiting satellites that can monitor the earth and provide valuable data on crops, weather, and earthquakes.
2. Carbon fibers used in jet aircrafts, golf clubs, and tennis rackets. They are lighter than steel, but they are stronger and stiffer.
3. Advances in health and medical areas, such as better splints for broken limbs, and more effective cancer detection devices.
4. New alloys used in tools, kitchenware, and household appliances.
5. Trajectory and moon landing analyses have resulted in a fully computerized auto traffic control system for a nine-square mile area in Los Angeles. The system calculates the best traffic-light sequence during rush-hour traffic. Mobility has been increased by 15% during tests, resulting in gas consumption savings and less air pollution.
6. Wind deflectors for trucks have been developed to reduce wind resistance by 24%, resulting in a 10% fuel savings.
7. Life rafts equipped with radar reflective canopies greatly increase the distance that they can be seen from the air.
8. Orbiting satellites have been responsible for the virtual elimination of the screwworm in the United States. It destroys cattle, poultry, and wildlife.
9. Land surveying satellites can spot 99% of the fresh water sources currently not being used in the United States.
10. Aluminized plastic used to keep fluids cold in space programs are used in lightweight jackets, sleeping bags, and parkas.
11. Silicone plastic from airplane seats has been used in football helmet liners.
12. A computer image process used to enhance satellite photos can indicate missing chromosomes in fetuses, thus identifying possible inherited diseases before the infant is born.

Consulting firms that specialize in new product development (NPD firms) or firms that act as brokers between manufacturers and inventors are being used more and more by companies that are beset by rising technology costs and risks.

Tips for Managing the Firm's Technological Effort

We will conclude this section by offering some recommendations that will enhance the firm's technological effort, especially as it relates to the marketing area. Technological breakthroughs are only valuable if they satisfy the needs and desires of the market. These needs and desires must guide the

The Environment for Marketing Decisions

firm's technological efforts and the marketing department should have the responsibility of determining what these needs and desires are.

A company and its marketing area should take a broad view of what technology is all about. This means that, in addition to emphasizing the development of new products, technology should be concerned with modifying existing products. Making production and marketing operations more efficient is another significant objective for a firm's technological effort. Successes in these areas, for example, often result in lower prices which in turn make products competitive and available to mass markets. A good example of the need for technological endeavor concerns the field of fiber optics that has tremendous promise in locating hidden cancers, easing telephone tie-ups, examining internal organs without exploratory surgery, and reducing aircraft operating expenses. A major problem is that staggering high costs have prevented full-scale production. Developing technology, however, is expected to bring the price of the fiber down to a few cents a foot compared to about $.35 a foot.[11]

In establishing an R&D effort, companies must emphasize both **applied** and **basic research.** This is often difficult for marketing departments to accept, because they tend to be suspicious of any kind of research (basic) that does not have an immediate payoff. However, many breakthroughs with long-run potential for new products frequently result from such research.

Companies should consider several different sources for technological advances, not just their own R&D departments. Other companies, independent inventors, and the federal space program are examples.

THE ECONOMY

Some significant aspects of the United States economy in the 1970's and their implications for marketing decisions should be discussed. Perhaps the most important of these aspects are the following:

1. Inflation
2. Decline in rate of growth of real income
3. Slow growth in gross national product
4. High level of unemployment
5. Recession
6. Shortages
7. Energy problems

Inflation

The 1970's saw an increase in prices in the United States that far surpassed the normal rate that prevailed in the previous two decades. Particularly pronounced increases occurred in 1973, 1974, and 1975. In 1973 there was

[11] *The Wall Street Journal*, November 30, 1976, p. 1.

Permission: From the *Wall Street Journal*.

"Remember when a piece of eight really bought something?"

a 6.2% increase in prices, followed by an 11% rise in 1974. In 1975 the increase was 9.1%. Accounting for much of these increases were price rises for food, fuel, and utilities. For 1973, 1974, and 1975, respectively, food price increases were 14.5%, 14.4%, and 8.5%. For fuel and utilities, they were 5.7%, 18.4%, and 11.7%.

Inflation results in an erosion of purchasing power. That inflation in the 1970's has cut deeply into the purchasing power of individual Americans and United States business firms can be seen in the following figures. In 1976 the average consumer had to pay $1.70 to purchase items that cost only $1.00 in 1967. Business firms in 1976 purchasing from wholesale establishments had to pay $1.82 for products that cost only $1.00 in 1967.[12]

Decline in Rate of Growth of Real Income

Real income is the increase in income that is over and above the rate of inflation. For example, if an individual were to receive an increase of 10% in his income and if the rate of inflation were 6%, he would be enjoying a

[12] *Statistical Abstract* (Washington, D.C.: U.S. Bureau of the Census, 1976), p. 432.

The Environment for Marketing Decisions

rise in real income. On the other hand, if his income were to increase 10% and if the rate of inflation were 12%, he would not have an increase in real income.

In 1974 and 1975 in the United States there was a decrease in real income. Disposable per capita personal income based on 1972 prices was $4,068 in the United States in 1973. In 1974 it dropped to $3,981 and dipped to $3,928 in 1975.[13] Thus, in these two years the average worker in the United States was finding that the rate of inflation was above his salary increase.

Slow Growth in Gross National Product

Figure 4.6 provides some gross national product figures for the United States from 1970 through 1975.[14] Gross national product refers to the dollar value of all goods and services produced and is one of the most important measures of a country's economic health. This figure shows that the rate of growth in our gross national product has slowed in 1974 and 1975 in comparison with what occurred in 1972 and 1973. When gross national product is expressed in 1972 dollars, it can be seen that the United States experienced *declines* in GNP of 1.7% and 1.8% in 1974 and 1975.

[13] Ibid., p. 396.
[14] Ibid., p. 394.

Figure 4.6   Gross National Product in the United States, 1970–1975

Year	Gross National Product (Billions of Dollars)	Percentage Change	Gross National Product in 1972 Dollars (Billions of Dollars)	Percentage Change
1970	983	5.0	1,075	—.3
1971	1,063	8.2	1,108	3.0
1972	1,171	10.1	1,171	5.7
1973	1,307	11.6	1,235	5.5
1974	1,413	8.2	1,214	−1.7
1975	1,516	7.3	1,192	−1.8

Background for Marketing Decisions

High Levels of Unemployment

The level of unemployment in the United States increased sharply in 1974, 1975, and 1976. In 1974 the unemployment rate was 5.6%, up from 4.9% in 1973. In 1975 the rate jumped to 8.5%, followed by 8.3% percent in 1976.

Recessions

Lack of growth in the GNP and high levels of unemployment are two indications of a recession, that is, a general downturn in the economy. Because of the GNP and unemployment rate in the United States in 1974–1976, it is apparent that this country was experiencing a recession. Recessions are not new to the United States, but they do present problems for the marketing decision maker. These will be discussed later.

Shortages

During the middle 1970's there were a number of shortages in the United States. Business firms had problems obtaining raw materials needed to manufacture products and consumers experienced difficulty in securing a wide range of consumer products. Examples of items in short supply include sugar, coffee, paper, petroleum derivatives, plastics, and home canning supplies.

Reprinted by permission from *Sales & Marketing Management* magazine. Copyright 1975.

"I sell scarce items, and I never get a chance to complete my sales talk."

Energy Problems

During the 1970's a number of energy problems surfaced in the United States. Our country's dependence on foreign petroleum sources increased to where we imported 47% of our petroleum needs. The natural gas crisis of the winter of 1976–1977 closed schools and businesses and was responsible for adding from 1 million to 2 million individuals to the ranks of the unemployed.

What are the implications of these trends in our economy for marketing operations? Some of these trends appear to be long-run and, thus, deserve the attention of marketers. They include inflation and energy problems. The other trends appear to be short-run in nature. However, since these do represent severe disruptions and are likely to occur intermittently in the future, their effects cannot be ignored.

A reexamination of the products currently being marketed appears necessary. Given the rate of inflation and its negative impact on real income, companies may want to consider eliminating higher priced lines that may not be as popular. Products that are only marginally profitable may also be dropped because they use valuable resources that are in short supply. Management may want to consider producing and marketing substitute products for hard to get products, for example, sweaters because of home fuel oil scarcities. Other raw materials will have to be uncovered for those that are difficult to get so that profitable products can be continued to be marketed. An example of this is Lever Brothers' use of sunflower oil as an ingredient in its highly polyunsaturated margarine instead of safflower oil, which has been in short supply.

Other elements of the marketing mix will have to be adjusted as a result of economic developments. During the recession of 1974 and 1975 one study found that consumers dramatically increased their emphasis on the price of products as opposed to their quality. They read fewer advertisements and were not as willing to travel as far to shop. Thus, during recessions companies might consider stressing a greater pricing orientation and using other advertising media than newspapers.[15]

A major decision that all companies must make is whether or not to reduce the level of their marketing effort during a recession. For example, should the advertising and marketing research budgets be curtailed and should the company lay off salespeople? The general consensus is that firms that maintain the level of their marketing effort during recessions are more likely to perform better when an upswing occurs than those that have reduced the level of their marketing effort.

If shortages are to persist in the future, companies may want to undertake demarketing efforts. These involve programs that encourage companies and consumers to use less of scarce resources. Many such programs have con-

[15] Richard T. Hise and Myron Gable, "Shopping Behavior in a Stagflation Economy: An Empirical Analysis," in Henry W. Nash and Donald P. Robin, eds., *Proceedings: Southern Marketing Association* (1976), pp. 261–263.

centrated on getting Americans to use less home heating oil and natural gas and consuming less gasoline. Some industries have, of course, been able to benefit by such efforts, as witness the increased sale of home insulation.

LEGAL/POLITICAL AREA

The legal/political area of the environment can affect marketing in several ways. Laws have been passed to regulate marketing activities, and state and federal agencies have been developed to administer these laws. Federal, state, and local governments are major purchasers of goods and services in our economy. Monetary and fiscal policies of the federal government can be utilized to slow down an overheated economy or stimulate one that is in a recession. The various levels of government also provide financial support and data for companies. We will now consider some of these aspects of governmental impact on companies' marketing operations.

Laws Affecting Marketing

The major laws and their major provisions affecting marketing are described in Figure 4.7. Figure 4.7 reveals that these laws tend to be of two major types: those affecting competition and those dealing with specific aspects of marketing operations. The basic act dealing with competition is the Sherman Anti-Trust Act of 1890 which essentially made monopolies and efforts to create monopolies illegal. Additional legislation strengthened the Sherman Anti-Trust Act by outlawing specific ways that monopolies could be created.

Several laws have been passed that deal with specific aspects of marketing operations. Figure 4.7 provides a representative sample of these laws and reveals that the areas of branding and labeling, pricing, advertising, packaging, and credit have been the major activities dealt with.

A vast federal bureaucracy has been established to administer the various laws that regulate American business firms. Some of the more important regulating bodies that affect marketing operations are described in Figure 4.8.[16] The growth in the scope of federal governmental intervention in business is illustrated by the fact that the budgets for the major economic regulatory agencies increased from $166 million in 1970 for eight agencies to $428 million in 1975 for ten agencies. In 1976 it appeared that the Justice Department, the chief investigative agency, was concentrating on anti-trust and price-fixing violations.

Compliance with these various regulatory agencies is costly and time-consuming. Dow Chemical estimates that it spends almost $150 million per year on compliance. General Motors calculated that the documents it has

[16] *Business Week*, April 4, 1977, pp. 52–56.

Figure 4.7   Major Laws Affecting Marketing

Laws Dealing with Competition

1. *Sherman Anti-Trust Act (1890)*: Made monopolies and efforts to create monopolies illegal.
2. *Clayton Anti-Trust Act (1914)*: Specified unlawful monopolistic activities, such as discriminatory pricing, tying contracts, acquiring shares of competing companies, and interlocking directorates.
3. *Federal Trade Commission Act (1914)*: Listed unreasonable methods of competition and created the Federal Trade Commission to administer the Act.
4. *Celler Antimerger Act (1950)*: Made it illegal to acquire assets of competing firms when the effect was to create a monopoly.

Laws Dealing Specifically with Marketing Operations

1. *Pure Food and Drug Act (1906)*: Outlawed the adulteration and misbranding of foods and drugs sold in interstate commerce.
2. *Robinson–Patman Act (1936)*: Outlawed price discrimination when the purpose was to lessen competition or create a monopoly.
3. *Miller–Tydings Act (1937)*: Allowed manufacturers of products in interstate commerce to specify prices below which retailers could not sell these products.
4. *Wheeler–Lea Act (1938)*: Outlawed deceptive advertising of foods, drugs, and cosmetics.
5. *Food, Drug, and Cosmetic Act (1938)*: Extended the scope of the Pure Food and Drug Act to include cosmetics and therapeutic devices. Outlawed injurious cosmetics, false and misleading labels, and deceptive containers.
6. *Wool Products Labeling Act (1939)*: Required that the percentages of new wool, reprocessed wool, and other fibers be shown on the labels of products containing wool.
7. *Fur Products Labeling Act (1951)*: Required that fur labels indicate whether the fur is new or used and whether it is bleached or dyed.
8. *Hazardous Substances Labeling Act (1960)*: Power was given to the Food and Drug Administration to require household products containing dangerous substances to provide warnings on the labels.
9. *Truth-in-Packaging Act (1966)*: Required that the quantity and composition of the contents of packaged consumer products be indicated on their labels.
10. *Truth-in-Lending Act (1968)*: Required that written notice of all finance charges be furnished before the transaction occurred.
11. *Toy Safety and Child Protection Act (1969)*: Required that children's toys that are potentially dangerous carry such warnings on the labels.

Figure 4.8   Major Federal Regulatory Agencies Affecting Marketing

Agency	Budget	Number of Employees	Function
Anti-Trust Division of the Justice Department	$27 million	900	Regulates interstate commerce activities
Civil Aeronautics Board	$22 million	800	Regulates air fares and routes
Consumer Product Safety Commission	$39 million	890	Reduce injuries from products
Environmental Protection Agency	$865 million	10,000	Develops and enforces standards for clean air and water
Federal Reserve System	$700 million	26,000	Sets monetary and credit policies and regulates Federal Reserve System banks
Federal Trade Commission	$55 million	1,700	Prevents unfair trade practices and promotes competition
Food and Drug Administration	$240 million	7,000	Is responsible for drug product safety and effectiveness and regulates labeling for drug products
Interstate Commerce Commission	$57 million	2,100	Regulates rates and routes of railroads and trucking firms

to file in connection with certification of its cars for sale in a single year would result in a stack 15 stories high.[17]

Governments as Purchasers of Goods and Services

Federal, state, and local governments are important sources of purchases in our economy. As such, many firms are vitally dependent upon these governments for a large percentage of their total sales volume.

In 1975, 22.1% of all production in the United States was accounted for by government purchases. Little variation from the 20% to 22% range has

[17] Ibid., p. 47.

Permission: From the *Wall Street Journal*.

"Oh, That's just our financial report and prospectus."

occurred over the last 25 years. What has changed, however, are the percentages accounted for by the federal, state, and local governments. In 1952, 15.1% of all production in the United States was purchased by the federal government, compared to 6.7% for state and local governments. In 1975 the federal government's purchases amounted to 8.2% of production; the figure for state and local governments was 13.9%.[18]

Figure 4.9 gives an idea of the extent to which certain companies are dependent upon government expenditures and indicates that some companies would probably go out of business if drastic cuts in defense spending occurred. Other smaller, less well-known companies may potentially share the same fate.

Monetary and Fiscal Policies

Over the last 25 years the federal government has pursued various monetary and fiscal policies designed to have a stabilizing effect on our economy. When inflation is rampant, various strategies can be effected that will help

[18] John Lindauer, *Economics* (Philadelphia: W. B. Saunders Company, 1977), p. 263.

Figure 4.9   Dependency of U.S. Companies on Defense Contracts,
1968–1974

Company	Percentage of Total Sales from Defense Contracts	Total Sales Volume from Defense Contracts (millions of dollars)
Grumman Aircraft	86	5,521
Lockheed Aircraft	62	12,097
General Dynamics	55	10,004
Northrop	55	2,131
McDonnell Douglas	54	8,102
Martin-Marietta	44	1,822
Raytheon	41	3,758
Boeing Company	40	6,098
Avco	39	1,897
Textron	38	3,090
North American-Rockwell	36	4,753
General Tire	36	1,415
United Aircraft	33	6,873

Source: This figure was developed from John Lindauer, *Economics* (Philadelphia: W. B. Saunders, 1977), p. 263.

to reduce the rate of increases in prices. **Fiscal policies** such as increasing taxes and decreasing government spending are possibilities, as are such **monetary policies** as increasing the interest rate charged banks that want to borrow money from the Federal Reserve and increasing the level of deposits banks must have with the Federal Reserve. During recessions, when the objective is to stimulate the economy so that the percentage of unemployment will be lowered, the opposite strategies may prove effective. These include decreasing taxes, increasing government spending, decreasing the interest rate that the Federal Reserve charges borrowing banks, and decreasing the percentage of deposits member banks must keep with the Federal Reserve.

Financial Support and Data

Business firms may use governmental sources for financial aid. For example, the following federal governmental agencies extend loans, underwrite costs, or provide research funds: Department of Health, Education and Welfare;

Department of Housing and Urban Development; Department of Commerce; Department of the Interior; Small Business Administration; and Office of Economic Opportunity.

Governments are vital sources of free or inexpensive data and information. Figure 4.10 lists some of the data and information that are of value to marketers and that can be obtained from government sources. At the federal level, various departments and agencies can be contacted directly for information on the data they provide; the Government Printing Office is also a valuable source.

CULTURE

Culture refers to the norms and values (beliefs) of a society. These beliefs have an impact on what, why, when, how, and where consumers purchase. Many norms and values are consonant with a company's products and the strategies used to market these products and, thus, little modification of the firm's marketing programs is required. Over time some norms and values may change and be in conflict with the products being marketed and their marketing strategies; thus, modifications are required. Other long-run cultural changes, however, may open up new opportunities for firms that recognize these changes and are willing and able to adjust to them.

These ideas will become clearer as we discuss some of the more significant cultural changes in the United States that have, we believe, the greatest impact on a company's marketing sector.

Figure 4.10 Data and Information of Value to Marketers That Are Available from Government Sources

1. Population and population trends.
2. General indicators of the strength of the economy.
3. Commodity prices.
4. Labor force employment and earnings.
5. Level of various kinds of consumer credit.
6. Inventory levels in various industries.
7. Income and savings data on the United States population.
8. Value of exports and imports.
9. Number of new housing starts.
10. Sales and employment figures for retailing and wholesaling firms.
11. Educational levels in standard metropolitan statistical areas.
12. Federal expenditures by geographical region.
13. Marriage, divorce, birth, and death rates by states.

Declining Birthrate

In 1955 there were about 25 births for every 1,000 individuals in the United States and around 118 births for every 1,000 women aged 15–44. By 1974 the birthrate per 1,000 individuals dropped to about 15 and the birthrate for every 1,000 women aged 15–44 declined to about 68.[19]

What are the implications of the declining birthrate? First, companies that produce and market infant products are going to be faced with a shrinking market potential. Second, this decline may eventually result in a stagnant total population for the United States, causing lower demand for products whose sales are largely a function of population size. Third, various age groups may account for increasingly larger percentages of the total United States population, thus making them more attractive market segments. The over-65 group is a good example.

While there are some indications that the birthrate decline may have eased in the United States (see Chapter 2), the consequences of a possible continued declining birthrate should not be ignored.

Increasing Level of Education

Between 1964 and 1975 the number of individuals enrolled in college more than doubled, from 4.6 million to 9.7 million. During this same period the number of people in college per 1,000 persons 23 years old increased from 501 to 944.[20]

The increasing level of education suggests that in the future consumers may be more discriminating consumers. They also are likely to be heavier purchasers of books, travel, entertainment, and recreation. They are less likely to accept merchandise that is dangerous, shoddy, or fails to work.

Geographical Mobility

Within the last several decades Americans have exhibited a tendency to move frequently. It is not unusual for 20% of the population to move in one year's time. About 66% of that number move within the same county.

Mobile people are very likely to be in the market for new products. They also have a tendency to switch brands. Therefore smart marketers will direct a good deal of their marketing effort to the important mobile market segment.

Favorable Attitude Toward Credit

In 1975 total consumer credit outstanding was $197 billion, up from $22 billion in 1950. As a percentage of disposable personal income, total consumer credit was 10.5% in 1950 and 18.3% in 1975. Whereas consumer credit in the past was generally used to finance big ticket items like auto-

[19] *Statistical Abstract*, p. 53.
[20] Ibid., pp. 110–11.

The Environment for Marketing Decisions

mobiles, the financing of lower priced items and services (such as vacations) has increased greatly through the use of bank credit cards and charge accounts.[21] As a result, an increasingly larger number of companies will have to consider the extension of credit as an important competitive weapon. For well-financed firms, this may not be a problem, but companies that have minimal financial assets may be in trouble.

Increasing Leisure Time

The length of the average work week in the United States has been dropping. As a result, Americans are finding that they have more leisure time to enjoy nonwork related pursuits. More time and money are being devoted to recreation, sports (both as a spectator and participant), symphonies, operas, travel, books, and entertainment.

Women in the Work Force

More and more women are obtaining gainful employment in the work force. In 1975 around 40% of the United States work force was made up of women. Many of these women are heads of households (divorced or widowed), but most women work in order to increase the family income and the family's standard of living. This increased standard of living is often reflected in expenditures for better housing, travel, education, and entertainment.

Because a job takes the woman out of the house, marketers of new products should take this into consideration. Convenience food items are examples of those new products. Since women may have less time for shopping, it may mean that husbands well become more involved in shopping. Therefore advertising efforts may have to be redirected.

The Body Beautiful

Many Americans are concerned with how they look and feel. This has resulted in increased sales for such products and services as vitamins, bicycles, health salons, cosmetics, and diet foods. For other products, this concern has caused a decrease in sales. For example, because of the link between cholesterol and heart problems, the annual per capita consumption of eggs plummeted from 403 in 1945 to 278 in 1974. As a result, egg substitutes have come on the market.

FOREIGN COUNTRIES

The value of exports to foreign countries from the United States increased threefold between 1967 and 1975. In 1967 America's exports were valued at $31 billion; by 1975 they were valued at $107 billion. Perhaps even more

[21] Ibid., p. 492.

significant is the fact that exports as a percentage of gross national product increased from 3.9% in 1960 to 7.1% in 1975. Specific product lines that showed the greatest increase in sales from 1967 to 1975 were crude foods (455%), crude materials (331%), and finished manufactures (353%).[22]

Between 1960 and 1972 an additional 800,000 jobs in the United States were attributed to exports. In all, in 1972 there were 3.6 million jobs dependent on export trade.[23]

These data indicate that the United States is becoming more dependent on foreign trade in order to maintain a vigorous economy. And for many companies, their overseas operations are vital to their success. For example, from foreign sources they obtain valuable raw materials, including petroleum, tin, copper, rubber, cocoa beans, coffee, chromium, etc. Such countries as Japan, Italy, Canada, West Germany, and France are important purchasers of United States exports.

Although opportunities for investment in foreign markets has proved wise in the past, recent developments have caused more firms to become more cautious. Expropriation by local governments and unstable governments and economies are examples. In addition, some countries, such as Nigeria, require foreign companies to hire certain percentages of indigenous nationals.

Selling abroad is not easy. Differences in economic conditions, norms, and customs must be recognized. Because of these differences product modifications are frequently necessary and different advertising strategies must be developed.

COPING WITH THE ENVIRONMENT

Because the **environment** is so crucial to a company's success, some mechanism must be established whereby the firm can monitor and respond to the environment. Some means must be developed so that a company can find out what is occurring in the environment and this information must be quickly channeled to the appropriate decision maker.

Most firms do not have a formalized approach for monitoring the total environment. This is unfortunate because opportunities for new products and product modifications are missed and changes in other areas of the marketing mix cannot be made or are made too late. Adjustments to competitive actions are ineffective, the impact of unfavorable governmental legislation is more pronounced, changes in the economy result in serious disruptions, changing norms and values are not recognized until it is too late, and the company lags technologically.

We suggest that some area in the company should be responsible for monitoring the environment. Those aspects of the environment that should

[22] Ibid., p. 840.
[23] Ibid., p. 848.

The Environment for Marketing Decisions

be monitored are the competitive, cultural, technological, economic, and legal/governmental aspects. When the firm has extensive overseas operations, the foreign environment should also be monitored.

A step in the right direction appears to be the "think tank," a group of futurist individuals employed by a few enlightened companies. These individuals look at developing trends throughout the environment and attempt to make projections for 20 to 30 years in the future. From these projections it is possible for a company to develop appropriate marketing strategies.

SUMMARY

A firm's marketing department should monitor the environment so that it is aware of the opportunities and obstacles that exist. The most significant aspects of the environment include the company in which the marketing department is located, the competition, technology, the economy, legal/political area, culture, and foreign countries.

Companies make many decisions that affect marketing departments. Examples of these are budgets, resource allocations, and marketing objectives. Most companies are probably giving additional emphasis to their marketing operations, but it is not known if, on the whole, marketing departments are getting greater resources.

Competition is getting tougher all the time. Larger, more efficient firms tend to dominate many industries. They are bringing out a constant stream of new products and can emphasize nonprice competition. Their successful application of decision-making tools allows them to operate more efficiently.

While spending for technology appears to have declined in the United States within the last decade, a company jeopardizes its success and possibly its very existence if it reduces its effort to produce new products, to modify existing products, and to find better ways to manufacture and market their offerings. In implementing its technological effort, a firm must first recognize the needs and desires of the market and then develop new products and modify existing offerings that satisfy these needs and desires.

A number of significant trends occurred in the economy of the United States in the 1970's. Some of these involved inflation, high level of unemployment, shortages, and energy problems. All of these present significant opportunities and potential obstacles for marketers and, if these trends persist during the remainder of this decade, marketing plans and strategies may have to be modified significantly.

In the legal/political area, marketers should be familiar with the major laws that affect their operations. The current positions of regulatory agencies that interpret and apply these laws must also be known. Companies that are dependent on government contracts should anticipate changes that could adversely affect these sales so that other options can be pursued.

Cultural changes should be monitored because they affect what, why, when, how, and where consumers purchase. These cultural changes should be recognized while marketing plans are being developed. Some of the more important cultural changes that have occurred in the United States within the last 20 years are the declining birthrate, increasing level of education, geographical mobility, increasingly positive attitude toward credit, more leisure time, and a greater concern with how one looks and feels.

Good opportunities for favorable returns on investment have existed in foreign countries. However, the increasing instability in many of these nations suggests that companies in the United States should proceed with caution as they contemplate initial ventures or expansion of existing operations.

In order to recognize the opportunities and obstacles that exist in the environment, companies must have a definite, formalized procedure for monitoring the environment.

QUESTIONS

1. What is the major reason why many firms have been giving additional emphasis to their marketing operations?
2. Why is it difficult to compete with nonprice competition?
3. What explanation can you give for the decline in technological expenditures in the United States since 1965?
4. How should marketing and research and development work together in developing new products? What should their objectives be?
5. How can you explain the fact that many significant technological breakthroughs in the twentieth century have come from small companies and independent inventors?
6. Distinguish between basic and applied research. Which one tends to be favored by the marketing department?
7. What are the basic trends in the United States economy? What are their implications for marketing strategies?
8. Distinguish between the monetary and fiscal policies of the federal government. Which tend to have the most direct effect on a firm's marketing operations? Why?
9. How can you explain the declining birthrate in the United States from 1955 to 1975? What are its implications for marketing?
10. Why has the population of the United States been so mobile in the last several decades? What can companies do to reach this market segment?

The Environment for Marketing Decisions

Applied Research: research effort that has a practical, relatively immediate application

Basic Research: fundamental research that does not have an immediate objective or application

Environment: areas outside the marketing department, in addition to the market, over which the marketing department cannot exert direct control

Gross National Product: the total dollar value of goods and services produced in a year in the United States

Fiscal Policies: policies of the federal government that are designed to minimize the effects of recession and inflation; they include increasing taxes and decreasing government spending

Monetary Policies: policies of the federal reserve that are designed to affect the money supply so that the effects of recessions and inflations can be minimized; they include manipulating the interest rate charged banks that want to borrow from the Federal Reserve and the level of deposits banks must keep with the Federal Reserve

Real Income: an increase in income that exceeds the rate of inflation

CASES

Case 1: The Redfield Co.

In the last two years the Redfield Company has been badly hurt by competitors. The firm is a manufacturer of precision engineering tools and does $50 million in business every year. The competitive actions that caused problems for Redfield were as follows:

1. An across-the-board price cut of 10% by the leading manufacturer of precision engineering tools.
2. The development of a new cutting device by a competitor that increased efficiency by 40% and provided the developer with a decided competitive edge.
3. The discarding of selling agents by 20% of the companies in the industry in favor of going directly to industrial purchasers.

In each case, the strategies had been planned for at least six months in advance, yet Redfield was not aware of them. As a result, Redfield's reactions were slow and very ineffective.

1. Is it likely that the Redfield Company has a formal mechanism for monitoring competition?
2. What alternatives exist for the Redfield Company to monitor competition?
3. Which of these alternatives would have probably discovered the contemplated changes brought out by competition?

Case 2: The Roper Co.

Jason Swift is vice-president of marketing of the Roper Company, a large manufacturer of plastics. The company's sales were $100 million in 1977. The company sells to other manufacturing firms.

Mr. Swift is concerned with his company's research and development effort and performance. Since 1970 top management has allocated increasingly smaller budgets to research and development. In 1970 R&D's budget amounted to 2% of sales. In 1977 the budget was 1% of sales. During this time no new products and no new modifications of existing products were developed that had a significant impact on the market. Of the six new products developed, four were removed from the market within a year. The other two were profitable, but not nearly as profitable as management had hoped. Product modifications improved profits only slightly.

Research and development deadlines were seldom achieved. In most cases, there were time overruns of six months or more.

1. Does Mr. Swift have reason to be concerned?
2. What factors might explain the R&D situation?
3. Could the marketing department be part of the problem?
4. What would you do if you were Mr. Swift?

PART 2

Preparing to Make Marketing Mix Decisions

Marketing Research

After you finish this chapter, you should be able to answer the following questions:

1. The marketing research function needs to collect information about a number of areas. One area is probably more important than the others. Which area is this and why?

2. Why are time and cost factors so important to marketing research?

3. What is *cost-benefit* analysis? Why is it valuable to marketing research?

4. What is involved in a preliminary investigation and why is it an important step in the marketing research process?

5. What are the other steps in the marketing research process?

6. What is probably the single most important determinant of the effectiveness of the various functional areas that marketing research may be called upon to measure?

7. How can we measure the effectiveness of the marketing research department?

Consumer Panel   Internal Data   Marketing Information System
Personal Interviews   Primary Data   Reliability   Response Rate
Scientific Method   Sample   Secondary Data   Validity   Value of
Information

INTRODUCTION

Marketing decisions of all kinds cannot be made without accurate information. In addition, the information must be timely and it must be gotten to the decision maker who must make the decision. These are the major responsibilities of the marketing research function.

In this chapter we will be concerned with the following areas: First, we must understand the kinds of information the marketing research department ought to obtain. We will discuss these for the market, the environment, and the basic marketing mix decisions. Second, we will present a basic seven-step marketing research methodology. Third, we will indicate various methods whereby the effectiveness of the marketing research function can be determined. Fourth, we will describe common mistakes made in marketing research. Fifth, we will present a number of suggestions that will make marketing research more effective. Sixth, we will discuss a new responsibility in many marketing research departments, that of developing and implementing a marketing information system.

INFORMATION REQUIRED OF THE MARKETING RESEARCH FUNCTION

There is a great deal of information that marketing research is responsible for obtaining. Some of this will be needed on a continuing, periodic basis, but the rest will be obtained as needed.

In the following discussion we will indicate the information needed for the market, the environment, and the seven basic marketing functions. The items under each heading are by no means all that may be required of the marketing research effort. They do, however, provide a good idea of what might be needed. Figure 5.1 shows the 11 most important areas of marketing research as practiced by 1,700 companies.[1] The reader will notice that these involve the major areas of the market, the environment, and the seven basic marketing functions.

Information About the Market

Information about the market may very well be the most important concern of marketing research since the market is so vital to the success of the firm. The reader will realize that many of these were discussed in previous chapters, but a brief review is in order.

[1] Dik Warren Twedt, ed., *1968 Survey of Marketing Research* (Chicago: American Marketing Association, 1969), pp. 41–44.

Figure 5.1   Eleven Most Important Marketing Research Activities As Reported by 1,700 Companies

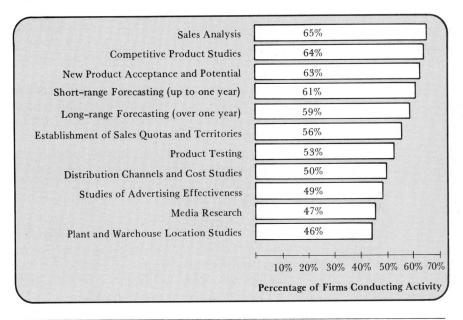

Sales Analysis	65%
Competitive Product Studies	64%
New Product Acceptance and Potential	63%
Short–range Forecasting (up to one year)	61%
Long–range Forecasting (over one year)	59%
Establishment of Sales Quotas and Territories	56%
Product Testing	53%
Distribution Channels and Cost Studies	50%
Studies of Advertising Effectiveness	49%
Media Research	47%
Plant and Warehouse Location Studies	46%

10% 20% 30% 40% 50% 60% 70%

Percentage of Firms Conducting Activity

Population.   People make up markets. Therefore, the marketing research department must carefully analyze population and population trends. For example, it needs to know how many people live in various states or sales territories and whether they are losing or attracting people. For many kinds of products, such as consumer convenience goods (cereal, toothpaste), population may be the major factor in predicting their sales.

Income.   People need money (*income*) to purchase products. The marketing research staff should be aware of trends in income of the purchasers of its products. Increasing income may result in more purchases of various products. Additional *discretionary* income (what is left after a basic standard of living has been achieved) means the greater likelihood of purchase of such items as vacations, luxury cars, college educations, and restaurant meals. As a greater percentage of the nation's income is concentrated in the hands of more people, a mass market exists for more products, thereby giving marketers a better opportunity to sell more of their products.

Market Potentials.   *Market potentials* are estimates of the amount of a product that could possibly be purchased from all firms in a given geographical area during a specific time period. Estimating these is a very important task for the marketing research department. Market potentials tell, for example, how much marketing effort (advertising, salesmen, etc.) should be put into a specific area. Generally, a company should put more effort into areas where the marketing potential is greatest.

Market potentials are usually predicted by using various data. For example, higher levels of populations and income in a given area may mean that a greater potential will exist than in an area where population and income are lower. It is the responsibility of the marketing research staff to isolate factors that predict market potential and use them in making such predictions.

Sales Volume Forecasts.   Estimates of market potentials are often the first step in predicting sales volumes for various products. If the market potential is known, the percentage of this obtained by the product in the past can be used to estimate sales volume. For example, if the market potential is 4,000 units and a specific product has historically obtained 20% of the market potential, the sales volume forecast would be 800 units (4,000 × .20 = 800).

Sales volume estimates are important because they serve as a bench mark for judging the effectiveness of the marketing program. If actual sales fall below predicted sales, the company knows that its marketing program is probably not as effective as it should be. They also help the marketing department determine how much resources, such as salesmen and advertising dollars, are needed for specific products. In general, more resources are needed in order to secure greater sales volumes.

Who Are the Heavy Purchasers?   It is commonly known that a relatively small percentage of customers accounts for a large percentage of purchases. For example, one study found that 9% of the households accounted for 85% of the purchases of liquid starch.[2]

Figure 5.2 shows who the heavy purchasers are of travel magazines. In this example, the heavy purchasers are women. Those under 50 years of age account for only 20% of the market, but they purchase 30% of the units bought. Even heavier users are those 50 years of age and over. They purchase 50% of the travel magazines but represent only 20% of the market. In the last column are shown average numbers of units purchased per customer. This is another way to determine who the heavy users are. These figures show that the heavy users are women, especially those over 50 years of age.

The heavy purchasers obviously are an important market segment. As such, they must be aggressively marketed to. Much less effort should be directed to the light purchasers. The marketing research department should identify these two market segments for the various products the firm markets.

Who are the Loyal Purchasers?   Loyal purchasers are those who tend to buy a specific brand to the virtual exclusion of competitive brands. *Brand*

---

[2] *Soap Products: TV Guide Market Report,* 1968, p. 2.

Preparing to Make Marketing Mix Decisions

Figure 5.2 Identifying the Heavy Purchasers of Travel Magazines

Type of Customer	Number of Purchasers	Percentage of Purchasers	Number of Units Purchased	Percentage of All Units Purchased	Average Number of Units Purchased per Customer
Teen-agers	1,000	10	500	5	1/2
Men under 50 years of age	2,000	20	500	5	1/4
Men 50 years of age and older	3,000	30	1,000	10	1/3
Women under 50 years of age	2,000	20	3,000	30	1 1/2
Women 50 years of age and older	2,000	20	5,000	50	2 1/2
	10,000	100	10,000	100	

loyalty is usually measured by the number of consecutive purchases of a given brand. The greater the number of consecutive purchases, the greater the level of loyalty to that brand. This is important because these people are more likely to purchase the same brand the next time than are disloyal customers.

Marketing research effort must be directed toward finding who the loyal and unloyal purchasers are. Loyal customers should not be taken for granted; much marketing effort should be directed to keeping these customers satisfied. If unloyal customers can be fairly easily switched to your product and if they will remain loyal, they should also receive some attention.

New Product Innovators and Non-Innovators.   An important responsibility of the marketing research effort is to determine which individuals tend to purchase new products first (*innovators*) and which individuals purchase them long after they have been on the market, if at all (*non-innovators*). Once the innovators and the non-innovators are identified, the firm knows who should be informed first of the existence of new products.

The Core Market.   The core market is that market segment whose needs and desires are best satisfied by the product's *features* (characteristics) and *benefits* (value to purchaser). If the core market is known, the firm can then consider modifications of features and benefits to satisfy the needs and desires of noncore marketing individuals.

Who Makes the Buying Decision?   Analysis of the market should determine who actually makes the decision to purchase. Once this is determined, marketing knows who needs to be emphasized in its marketing efforts. Obtaining this information is not, however, easy. For industrial goods, for example, a large number of individuals may be involved, making it difficult to isolate who, in fact, makes the actual purchase decision.

In one study of purchasing offset printing machines, it was found that, contrary to expectations, purchasing department personnel had little involvement with purchasing these machines. The individual supervising the printing function was the one much more likely to be involved.[3]

Who is Involved with Other Steps in the Purchasing Process? There are other steps in the purchasing process besides the actual buying decision. These include deciding whether or not a purchase is necessary, what the product's characteristics should be, how many different products will be evaluated, and who the suppliers will be. The marketing research effort should determine which individuals have responsibility for these steps. Obviously, a firm cannot expect to sell its product unless it is successful in the steps prior to the actual purchase decision. For example, a company will have no chance of making a sale if it is not asked to present its products for consideration.

Are Buyers Satisfied or Dissatisfied? A large portion of the marketing research effort must be directed toward finding out if buyers of the company's products are satisfied or dissatisfied. In either case, it must be determined why. If purchasers are satisfied, the reasons why they are satisfied can be stressed in the company's marketing effort. If purchasers are not satisfied, the company should obtain information on how the product can be improved to better suit customer needs and desires.

A $400,000 market analysis conducted by Hanes found that women were dissatisfied with the lack of uniform quality control for hosiery. "For a while, I always bought medium-tall in the same brand for $.79 a pair," says Pat Sasha, a New Jersey social worker. "One week they sagged and bagged, the next week I could hardly sit down, they were so tight."[4]

Although gathering data about the market is probably the most important marketing research responsibility, analyzing the environment is also important. In this regard, we will discuss competition, the economy, and the legal/political area.

Competition

New Products and Improvement of Existing Products. The marketing research department should constantly monitor the competition. Attention should be directed to finding out what new products their competitors are developing and what improvements they are planning for existing products.

[3] J. Patrick Kelly, "Functions Performed in Industrial Purchasing Decisions with Implications for Marketing Strategy," *Journal of Business Research* (October, 1974), p. 427.
[4] "Our L'eggs Fit Your Legs," *Business Week*, March 25, 1972, p. 36.

Changes such as these can have disastrous effects on a company's sales and profits. The sooner it knows these, the better its opportunity to make the necessary adjustments.

Shifts in Marketing Strategy. These shifts include new advertising campaigns, lower or higher prices, opening or closing of warehouses, and adding or dropping channels of distributions. A firm must know about these changes so that it can revise its own marketing efforts to combat the competition.

Market Shares. The percentage of total units sold of a specific product by any one particular firm is the market share. For example, if 10,000 total units of a product were sold and a firm sold 2,500, its market share would be 25% (2,500/10,000). The firm must know the market shares for its products and competitive products. The higher the market share, generally speaking, the better the profit. Thus, if the market share is high, it probably means that the marketing mix is effective. If it is low, the marketing mix is probably not too effective and should be changed.

Acquisitions and Mergers. A firm must know if competitive firms are acquiring or are merging with other companies. These organizational changes indicate important shifts in competitor strategies. They indicate new products, attempts to reduce risk and cost, a new geographical emphasis, attempts to assure supplies of raw materials, and so on. They also mean that these firms will probably be stronger competitors than in the past because of their resulting larger size.

The marketing research department can use various techniques to monitor competition. These include reading newspapers and trade magazines, visiting trade shows and exhibits, having salespeople make an effort to notice what the competition is doing, and reading the competition's annual reports.

A number of large, well-known companies have established formal methods of keeping tabs on customers. For example, Westinghouse has its consumer-product research department responsible for monitoring competition. Citicorp has an executive whose title is Manager of Competitive Intelligence. Sperry Rand has a staff group that reports directly to the president on the actions of competitors.[5]

The Economy

The marketing research department has to know how the economy is doing. This information will aid in planning the marketing effort. Increasing gross national product (the total value of the nation's goods and services) and disposable income (the amount of money people have to spend)are favorable signs about the economy. When these occur, marketing effort should be increased. When a downturn in the economy is predicted, marketing effort may have to be stabilized until an upswing occurs.

[5] Richard T. Hise, *Product/Service Strategy* (New York: Petrocelli/Charter, 1977), p. 17.

Whether consumers are expected to save or spend their incomes has to be determined. If the tendency to save increases, the available funds for spending decreases, thereby making it more difficult to sell products and services.

Predicting the availability of raw materials (like oil) is an important aspect of monitoring the economy. If shortages are anticipated, the amount of finished goods produced and marketed will obviously decrease. Inventory levels must be predicted. If these drop, business and industry may have to bring these levels back up. This could mean an opportunity for a company to increase its sales.

As far as gathering these data are concerned, the marketing research department probably can use already existing sources, such as those published by the federal, state, and local governments, trade associations, banks, newspapers, and trade magazines.

Legal and Governmental Environment

Since the various levels of government regulate business and industry, the marketing research department must be familiar with the legal and governmental aspect of the environment. Thus, it needs to know what monetary and fiscal policies are being planned and it must adjust accordingly. Such factors as tax rates, interest rates, and level of spending directly affect the economy, and thus a company's ability to sell its products.

The marketing research department must know not only the laws that affect marketing operations but also proposed laws that will affect them. These may be in such areas as pricing, channels of distribution, and personal selling. Finally, it must know how these laws are being interpreted. Thus, it must be aware of what is occurring in the various regulatory agencies, such as the Federal Trade Commission, Food and Drug Administration, and the Interstate Commerce Commission, and it must be aware of the court decisions that may affect marketing operations.

Much of what the marketing research department needs to know about the legal/governmental area may be found in published sources, such as newspapers, magazines, and government documents.

Now that we have an idea of what information the marketing research department must have about some of the aspects of the environment, let's turn our attention to the data it needs about the various marketing functional areas.

Marketing Research

The marketing research department must analyze its own operations so that it can do a better job. It needs to, for example, determine what the likely **response rates** will be for mail surveys. The response rate is found by dividing the number of returned questionnaires by the number *sent out*.

Productivity standards for interviewers must be estimated. That is, the likely number of each kind of interview that could be completed within a certain time period, say, 8 hours, must be established.

The **reliability** of internal and external data is an area that needs to be investigated. (**Internal data** are data found inside the company, such as company records; external data are data found outside the company, such as company records. Reliability refers to how accurate the data are.)

Data **validity** must also be determined. This refers to how suitable the data are for the research objective involved. For example, is market share really an acceptable measure of how well a product is doing?

The marketing research department must frequently determine how large a **sample** is needed when it is collecting information. In many cases, it is too costly and time-consuming to contact all members of a given population. Therefore, only a percentage of them (a sample) is studied. The sample size is a function of various factors, such as how accurate the estimate has to be, how much confidence must be put into the estimate, and what research funds are available. (See Figure 5.3 for an example of how sample size can be determined).

Another responsibility of the marketing research department is that of estimating the **value of information.** It should be given in dollars and it tells us how worthwhile the information is. The value of information should be compared to the cost of securing information to determine if the data should be collected. For example, if the value of the information is $20,000, but the cost of obtaining it is $30,000, it is not beneficial to obtain the information. In all cases, the value of the data must exceed the cost of obtaining the data.

Products

The marketing research departments must supply data about a firm's products.

Share of Market.   The share of market for each product must be determined regularly. In addition, the trend of these market shares must be noticed. Management would be especially concerned with those products that have had steadily decreasing market shares.

Profitability.   The revenue (sales) for each product must be compared to the costs (expenses) involved in securing these sales. Obviously, products for which costs exceed revenues are in trouble.

Another measure of profitability is *return on investment.* This refers to a product's net profit divided into its investment dollars. For example, if investment in a product is $100,000 and its profit is $10,000, then its return on investment is 10% ($10,000/$100,000). The investment figure for a product consists of such items as research and development, test markets, and the cost of special-purpose production machinery. The return on investment for a product must exceed the cost of securing the funds used to develop the product.

20/80 Principle.   The marketing research department should determine

Figure 5.3 Establishing the Sample Size

One of the authors worked with a large bank that was trying to determine the sample size needed to estimate the percentage of BankAmericard holders making less than $8,000 per year that would default on payments. The bank would issue BankAmericards to this sample size for a year to see the percentage that became delinquent. The bank was interested in increasing its revenues from its BankAmericard operations by extending credit to these individuals, but the bank knew that a high percentage of defaults from these low-income individuals would jeopardize this objective.

The bank's experience was that about seven-tenths of 1% of individuals making over $8,000 per year defaulted. Using this statistic, the company's director of marketing research estimated that it was highly unlikely that the delinquency rate for low-income BankAmericard holders would be more than 5% (or seven times as great). He also said that the sample size should be large enough so that the sample results would be off by no more than 2% from the delinquent rate to be actually found if all low-income applicants were issued BankAmericards. He also said that he wanted to be 95% certain that the sample percentage of delinquent BankAmericard holders would represent the true percentage of delinquent accounts that would be found for all low-income applicants.

The consultant took the above data and presented the bank with the following formula, which suggested that a sample size of 320 would be sufficient:

$$n = (P) \, (1 - P) \left[\frac{Z}{E} \right]^2$$

$$n = (.05) \, (.95) \left[\frac{1.64}{.02} \right]^2$$

$$n = 320$$

if the 20/80 principle exists in its product line; that is, does a large number of products account for a small percentage of total company sales? If so, it is very likely that many of these products may be unprofitable. The relatively few products that obtain a large percentage of total sales must be monitored carefully. Any problem with these products could seriously damage the firm's profit.

In addition to these very basic aspects of product analysis, the marketing research department may be called upon to provide other kinds of information about products, some examples of which are included in Figure 5.4.[6]

[6] *Advertising Age*, August 21, 1972, pp. 37–40; James C. Tanner, "Name Change Brings Excedrin Headaches and Costs Approximately $100 Million," *The Wall Street Journal*, January 9, 1972, p. 32; and David Shaw, "Grocery Shelf Psychology–It Aims to Please," *The Los Angeles Times*, August 18, 1970, p. 33.

Figure 5.4   Examples of Product Research

1. A study was conducted of the extent to which consumers recognize products when brand names are omitted from the packages. The product groups analyzed were rice, bathroom tissue, freeze-dried coffee, liquid cleaners, liquid dishwashers, and salad oils. The most frequently recognized brand was Charmin's bathroom tissue (recognized by 97% of the consumers). Others with high ratings were Taster's Choice freeze-dried coffee (92%), and Janitor in a Drum liquid cleaner (87%).
2. Exxon, Inc. spent $100 million to develop and market the name Exxon. In all, 10,000 four- and five-letter names were originally generated. Research and testing reduced this list to 6 names that were tested worldwide in 56 languages involving 5 million people.
3. A broker researched a new spray-can spot cleaner and concluded that it was an impulse item. He recommended that grocers display it next to coffee, which is a big-volume seller. The product captured 85% of the market.

They involve analyses of brand names and consumers' perceptions of products.

Advertising

A number of aspects of the firm's advertising program must be evaluated by the marketing research department.

Which Media to Use.   Which media to use (newspapers, magazines, television, radio, etc.) is an important decision with which the marketing research department can help. Many mathematical models can be used here. They look at such factors as size of the audience reached by the media, cost of using the media, and impressions or attitudes obtained. Such a model was used by Anheuser-Busch. It found that national TV was more effective than other media and that billboard advertising was very ineffective. As a result, Anheuser-Busch dropped outdoor advertising and put its money into TV.[7]

Size of Advertising Budget.   Determining how large the advertising budget should be is a decision with which the marketing research department can be involved. A major factor here is at what expenditure level does there appear to be little, if any, additional sales volume obtained.

Allocation of Advertising Budget.   Once the total advertising appropriation has been determined, it must be spent on specific products, media, and geographical locations. The marketing research department can provide assistance in making these decisions. The major factor to consider in making these decisions is which allocations will result in the most profit.

[7] "A Struggle to Stay First in Brewing," *Business Week*, March 24, 1973, pp. 42–49.

Which Appeals to Use.   The central theme of an advertisement is called its *appeal*. The appeal might be convenience, relaxation, sex, comfort, etc. The appeals must be tested in order to see which appeals are the most effective. They may vary according to the type of product, the audience to which the advertisement is directed, and the medium used.

Effectiveness of Advertising.   Many firms attempt to determine how effective their advertising is. They would like to know the extent to which advertising is achieving their objectives. For example, in 1975 AT&T began a study of the effectiveness of their trade show materials. Testing occurred at the National Computer Conference Trade show where AT&T had a $40,000 display of its Dataspeed 40 data communications terminal. Thirty visitors were interviewed at the show and 600 show registrants were telephoned after the show and asked to tell what they could recall about the AT&T display.[8]

Many companies on a regular basis measure the effectiveness of their printed advertisements, for example, those appearing in magazines or newspapers. The extent to which readers recall the advertisement or can remember anything about it are areas usually investigated.

Personal Selling

Sales and expenses for each salesperson must be determined. These data make it possible to determine the profitability of each salesperson so that management will know which are in trouble and can work with them to improve their performance.

The total number of calls that each salesperson makes is another important figure. This should be broken down into calls made on established accounts and those made on new accounts. The percentage of calls of each type resulting in a sale for each member of the sales force should be calculated. For example, if a salesperson made 100 calls on new accounts and got 10 orders, the success percentage would be 10% (10/100). Management should help individuals whose percentages fall significantly below the company averages. They might, for example, need help with their presentation.

The *average sales volume* for each salesperson for new and established accounts should be determined by the marketing research department. Persons who have low average sales volumes should be identified and the reasons for their poor performance should be determined. Perhaps the salespeople are concentrating on too many small accounts.

The percentage of each salesperson's time spent on traveling, calling on customers, servicing customers, and doing paper work must be determined. These percentages can be very informative. For example, they can show which individuals are spending too much time in getting to their accounts and which are spending too much time on paper work.

Cost-per-sales call and *cost-per-mile* for each person on the sales force

---

[8] *Sales and Marketing Management*, July 12, 1976, p. 21.

must also be determined, but they are easy to calculate. For example, if a salesperson's compensation and expenses were $20,000 for the year and he or she made 500 calls during that time, the cost-per-sales call would be $40 ($20,000/500). Cost-per-mile is obtained by dividing the total miles traveled by the total costs. If a salesperson traveled 40,000 miles during the year and his or her compensation and expenses were $20,000, the cost-per-mile would be $.50 ($20,000/40,000 = $.50). Salespeople who have high costs-per-sales call and high costs-per-mile must be identified so that management can determine why these costs are so high. For example, perhaps the individual is doing a poor job of routing, resulting in too few sales calls. This could increase the cost-per-sales call and cost-per-mile figures.

Channels of Distribution

The marketing research department should help decide if the firm needs channels of distribution or if the firm should go directly to its customers. In making this decision, it should assign revenues and costs to the alternative of using or not using middlemen and decide on a profitability basis which decisions to make.

If the decision is to use middlemen, the firm must decide what kind to employ. For example, should they be wholesalers and, if so, what kind? Selling agents, merchant wholesalers, rack jobbers? Or should the firm use retailers, such as supermarkets, department stores, or drug stores? A key variable here is what the firm's customers are used to.

Next, the *best location* for these middlemen must be determined. This decision largely depends on what the marketing research department has found out about the market. For example, retail stores should be located where there is a concentrated market.

It must also be determined *which individual channel members are profitable and which members are not.* Thus, the marketing research effort should determine the costs associated with each channel and subtract these costs from the sales volume each channel accounts for. Unprofitable channels may be dropped, or a way to increase their sales or decrease their costs, or both, should be determined.

Physical Distribution

In analyzing the firm's physical distribution system, the marketing research department must concern itself with a number of decision areas. In most cases, it will be called upon to present the potential profit for various alternatives. Analysis of the location of customers, their service requirements (such as frequency of delivery and size of shipment), and the costs of the various alternatives are important questions that should be answered in making any of the following decisions.

Determining Which Modes to Use.   Railroad, truck, and air transportation are alternative modes that management can consider for a wide range of products, especially consumer products and some industrial products. Some raw materials and agricultural products may be moved effectively by water barge. Fuels, such as oil, may be transported by pipeline.

Deciding Whether to Own or Lease Transportation Facilities. The marketing research department may be able to suggest whether transportation facilities, such as trucks and warehouses, should be owned or rented. Owning facilities may result in better performance because the facilities satisfy the company's needs better (special-purpose warehouses, such as refrigerated warehouses), but they reduce the firm's flexibility (a warehouse built for a company has a fixed location that cannot change if the market's location changes).

Determining the Size of a Profitable Order. Many small-sized orders from customers may not be profitable because the cost of processing them exceeds their cost. The marketing research department must determine what size order is profitable so that the firm can decide what to do about the "small-order" problem.

Determining the Optimum Size of a Shipment. Small shipments are good for customers because the shipments do not need a large storage area. Large shipments, however, benefit the shipper because they do not need large storage areas and the shipper can get discounts on larger-sized shipments. The marketing research department can help decide what the best shipment size is for the shipper.

Determining the Best Frequency of Delivery. More frequent delivery is helpful to the customer because he will need less storage space and there is less likelihood that he will experience shortages. More frequent delivery is not advantageous to the shipper because he loses quantity discounts. The best frequency of delivery should be determined by the marketing research department.

Deciding on Location of Warehouses. Determining where warehouses should be located is an important decision because various aspects of the market are crucial. Such factors as size, location, and makeup should be determined by the marketing research department.

Deciding on Optimum Size of Warehouses. The total size of a warehouse, especially square footage, must be determined. Such factors as customer demand patterns (quantity, shipment size, frequency, and the like) and location are important considerations. The marketing research department can indicate what these are.

A good example of how marketing research can help physical distribution decisions is the mail-order house that found that 30% of its merchandise was being returned. The director of marketing research suspected that merchandise was more likely to be returned the longer customers had to wait to receive shipment of orders. Research confirmed his suspicion. As a result, company delivery times were shortened and the percentage of returned merchandise was reduced.[9]

[9] Horace C. Levinson, "Experiences in Commercial Operations Research," *Operations Research*, August, 1953, pp. 220–39.

Pricing

The marketing research department can help in many pricing areas. Perhaps its most important task is to help determine the price for the product to be sold that will *maximize total profits* or *return on investment*. In order to arrive at this price, the marketing research department must have some idea of the *demand curve* for each product, that is, how many units would be bought at each price. It also must know the *average cost curve* for each product, that is, its cost-per-unit.

The marketing research department must also determine the *price elasticity* for a firm's products. This refers to changes in the quantity of a product sold resulting from changes in prices. A somewhat similar concept is the *cross-elasticity of demand*, which refers to the change in demand for one product as a result of changes in the price of another product. Cross-elasticities should be calculated for competitive products in relation to the firm's products. Also, the effect of price changes in *a firm's own* products on sales of *the firm's other* products should also be measured.

An important and difficult pricing decision is the determination of the best price to put on a *new product*. Here, the marketing research department has to consider demand, the product's costs, and the price of competitive products.

The importance of the marketing research effort in the pricing area can be seen in Figure 5.5 which indicates some pricing strategies for three beers in the San Antonio market.[10]

[10] Charles G. Burck, "While the Big Brewers Quaff, the Little Ones Thirst," *Fortune* (November, 1972), pp. 103–107, 176–78.

Figure 5.5   Marketing Research Analysis of Pricing Tactics for Beer

When Anheuser-Busch sells Budweiser at a discount in San Antonio, many drinkers of Pearl and Lone Star, two local popular-priced beers, switch to Bud. Some of these converts keep drinking Bud even after the price goes up again. But Pearl and Lone Star cannot lure the Budweiser drinker by cutting their own prices, because Budweiser's premium image attracts and holds customers who are relatively unconcerned about price. Pearl and Lone Star can only steal customers from each other. And if one of them raises its price, it risks losing market share to the other, without making any impression on the Budweiser drinkers.

PERFORMING MARKETING RESEARCH

Now that we have a good idea of the *kind* of information the marketing research department may have to gather, let's see *how* it might get this information. In the following material we will use a specific example so that the seven steps described will be more meaningful. These steps are shown in Figure 5.6.

Step One: Define the Problem

The problem troubling the company must be clearly understood by the marketing research staff. It helps to define the problem as precisely as possible. The problem also should be put in writing. Failure to define the problem accurately can be disastrous because all of the subsequent marketing research effort will be wasted.

In our example, we will assume the following problem: "The national market share of Kleenzo Floor Cleaner has dropped from 30% to 20% from 1975 to 1976."

Step Two: Conduct Preliminary Investigations

The purpose of the preliminary investigation is to get some idea of *what is causing the problem.* Once this has been determined, then recommendations on solving the problem can be made.

Figure 5.6   Basic Steps in the Market Research Process

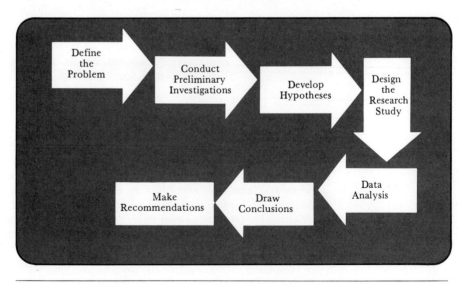

The preliminary investigation should include *outside reading, analysis of internal data, informal talks with involved executives,* and *discussion with the market.* These procedures very frequently will result in an indication of what is wrong without having to resort to the time-consuming and costly gathering of additional information.

Outside Reading.   The researcher must gain a basic understanding of the product, its market, and competition. In many cases, it is helpful and informative for the researcher to read newspapers, business magazines, and trade association reports. In our example, the marketing research department would like articles dealing with any of the three basic areas indicated above. Articles covering the following might be helpful: Which products are the best cleaners? What are the effects of the products on the environment? Do the products present safety hazards? Does the market prefer liquid or powder cleaners?

Analysis of Internal Data.   Company records, letters, memos, purchase orders, invoices, annual reports, and documents should be examined because they frequently indicate why the problem exists. For example, there may be a number of letters from customers complaining about Kleenzo's strong smell.

Informal Talks with Involved Executives.   These individuals may be willing to suggest why Kleenzo's market share has declined. The marketing manager may believe that its price is too high, the advertising manager may think that its package is too drab, and the vice-president of production may believe that the package is difficult to open.

Discussions with the Market.   This is a very critical part of the preliminary investigation because the market's attitudes toward a product will determine the level of its effectiveness. In the Kleenzo study, for example, the market should be asked what it likes and what it does not like about the product. Of special significance, given the declining market share, is to find out from consumers who stopped using the product why they stopped using it. These reasons may be very helpful in the next step.

Step Three: Develop Hypotheses

After performing the preliminary investigation, the marketing research department may conclude that it knows the reason for the drop in Kleenzo's market share. If so, it could skip this step, as well as steps four through seven, and begin recommending what should be done to restore Kleenzo's market share. Elimination of these steps would be desirable because time and money would be saved. For many problems, however, these additional steps must be performed because the preliminary investigation will be indecisive.

Step three involves the development of some possible reasons for the problem. These are called *hypotheses.* They must be tested through additional research.

Let's assume that the results of the preliminary investigation suggest that the odor of Kleenzo may be the cause of its market share loss. The resultant hypothesis might be as follows: "The major reason for the drop in market share for Kleenzo is its offensive odor."

Step Four: Design the Research Study

The research study is a comprehensive plan for testing the hypothesis developed in the previous step. It includes two major aspects: *planning the sample* and *collecting data*.

Planning the Sample. It would be too costly and too time-consuming to contact all the consumers in the United States who clean floors in order to find out why Kleenzo's popularity is decreasing. It would not be necessary, either; we could get just as accurate an idea with far fewer people. This is called a *sample*.

Determining the actual size of the sample (the *number* of consumers to be contacted) and how they will be reached can be complicated and will not be discussed at length. However, the firm will need a larger sample the more closely it wants the responses of the sample of consumers to actually represent the feelings of *all* consumers and the more confident the firm wants to be with these results. (See Figure 5.3 for an example of determining sample size.)

In the Kleenzo example, we will assume that the research staff interviews a sample of 1,000 consumers who have *stopped using* Kleenzo.

Collecting Data. Data can be collected in a number of ways. These include personal interviews, mail questionnaires, telephone surveys, laboratory experiments, direct observation, consumer panels, and analyzing secondary sources.

Personal interviews involve trained interviewers who ask questions of the selected sample. In the Kleenzo example, interviewers could call on customers and ask them why they stopped using the product. Personal interviewing tends to be costly and time-consuming, but it allows interviewers the opportunity to ask additional questions in order to obtain the information desired.

Another approach is to send the sample a *questionnaire* through the *mail*. Customers would be asked to answer questions about why they no longer use Kleenzo and to return the questionnaires to the company. Mail questionnaires may be less costly and time-consuming than personal interviews, but a large percentage of the sample may not bother to complete the questionnaires.

Telephone surveys could be used to contact customers about Kleenzo. Telephone surveys are fairly inexpensive and can be completed rather quickly. They allow the caller to deviate from the initial questions in order to secure additional information, and respondents may have questions that they do not understand clarified. It is not an appropriate alternative for sampling the general population because not every household has a telephone. Also, people may not be at home when the survey is being made.

Laboratory experiments involve putting subjects into a situation and then observing their reactions to it. In the Kleenzo example a number of people could be brought to the firm's headquarters and asked to use Kleenzo. Then their reactions to the product could be observed. Laboratory experiments have the advantage of keeping out factors that might affect the results, but they are conducted in artificial surroundings.

Direct observation is similar to laboratory experiments except that the sample is observed in a more natural setting. For example, some procedure could be established for observing people's reactions to Kleenzo after they have used it in their own homes. This data collection method eliminates the artificiality of the laboratory experiment approach, but it is often difficult to put into operation and could be very costly and time-consuming.

Consumer panels would involve having customers keep track of their purchases by having them record them in a diary. Consumer panels are advantageous because they allow for the examination of purchasing patterns over time. A consumer panel might indicate how long the average customer used Kleenzo before switching to another brand. *Secondary sources*, such as magazines and technical reports, could be examined to see if previous research has indicated any problems with floor cleaners.

In addition to planning the sample and collecting data, other steps in the research study may have to be performed. For example, if personal interviews are used, the interviewers must be trained. Training should include instructing interviewers which houses to approach, how to get cooperation of the respondents, how to interpret the respondents' answers, and how to end interviews.

If interviewers are used, it may be necessary to check their work because, unfortunately, there are interviewers who do not carry out assignments as instructed or who deliberately falsify results. There are a number of ways to check an interviewer's work. For example, some of the addresses the interviewer is asked to call on can be nonexistent (see Figure 5.7). If the results obtained by one interviewer differ significantly from those of the other interviewers—assuming there is no reason that they should—this may indicate a falsification. Another approach is to telephone some of the customers who the interviewers indicate they called on and ask them if they were contacted. If interviewers are told in advance that this will be done, they are less likely to do a dishonest or shoddy job.

In the Kleenzo example, it is assumed that the marketing research department has decided to determine the reason for its market share decline by sending interviewers to the homes of 1,000 customers who stopped using Kleenzo and asking them the following question: "Would you please tell me why you stopped using Kleenzo?"

Step Five: Data Analysis

As each questionnaire is returned, the responses given by the respondents should be read and analyzed (*edited*). In the case of the Kleenzo study, the response must be categorized into a small number of specific reasons. These reasons are shown in Figure 5.8.

Figure 5.7   Checking on Interviewers' Work

"I'm very interested in the response you got at 1135 Elm Avenue, Mr. Jones. 1135 Elm Avenue is located in the exact center of the city dump."

If the data are numerous and are to be analyzed by the computer, the *coding* function must be performed. This involves assigning numbers to pieces of information so that they are easier to work with. In Figure 5.8 code numbers one through seven have been assigned to the seven reasons given for no longer using Kleenzo. Code numbers could also be used to indicate other information, such as various categories of ages for customers and the family income.

Tabulating data refers to basic counting and is necessary to get the data ready for statistical analysis. If the data are sizable, the tabulating step should be done on the computer.

Figure 5.8 shows the number of respondents indicating various reasons for discontinuing the use of Kleenzo. It is assumed that a total of 800 of the 1,000 customers contacted participated in the study.

In many cases, the data analysis step may involve using *tests of significance*. The purpose of these, and less sophisticated analysis procedures, is to help determine whether the hypothesis we are testing can be accepted.

Figure 5.8 Results of the Study to Determine Why Kleenzo's Market Share Has Dropped

1. 40 (5%) Kleenzo did not do a good job of cleaning my floors.
2. 400 (50%) Kleenzo has a bad odor.
3. 20 (2.5%) Kleenzo's price was too high.
4. 100 (12.5%) Kleenzo's package was too difficult to open.
5. 40 (5%) Kleenzo's package was not attractive.
6. 100 (12.5%) I found another product that I like better.
7. 100 (12.5%) Kleenzo was frequently not available at the store where I shop.

Step Six: Drawing Conclusions

In this step it is decided whether the hypothesis being tested can be accepted. This follows from the data analysis step. In the Kleenzo study, it can be concluded with some certainty that the odor of Kleenzo is the major reason customers switch to other brands. This is because four times as many customers cited this reason than any other reason (see Figure 5.8), and 50% of the sample indicated the odor as the reason for dropping the product.

Step Seven: Making Recommendations

After a conclusion has been reached, the marketing research department must then make some specific recommendations. In this case, it appears appropriate for it to recommend that the company determine some way to make the odor of Kleenzo less offensive. For many marketing research studies, management would be presented with a written report of the project.

MEASURING THE EFFECTIVENESS OF MARKETING RESEARCH

Like all other areas of marketing, the effectiveness of the marketing research function must be determined, and there are a number of ways that this can be accomplished, for example, by asking the following:

1. How good is the "batting average" of the marketing research department? Do its recommendations more often than not prove to be incorrect?

2. Are its recommendations generally accepted by top management or are they consistently ignored?
3. Is the information obtained correct or is it frequently found to be misleading or even false?
4. Is the information obtained timely or does it always seem to be secured too late to make use of?
5. Once information is generated, is it gotten quickly to the right person, that is, the person who must act on it? Or does the information get sidetracked or channeled to the wrong person?
6. Are research projects completed on time or does the marketing research department consistently fail to meet deadlines?
7. Are research projects completed within budget limitations or are the allotted budgets frequently exceeded by wide margins?

COMMON MISTAKES IN MARKETING RESEARCH

If the marketing research department wants to increase its effectiveness, it must recognize the mistakes that many departments commonly make. If it recognizes these mistakes, it will be in a better position to function more effectively. These mistakes will be discussed below and will be followed by suggestions on how to improve marketing research effectiveness.

The Cost of Information Exceeds Its Value

Marketing research directors frequently engage in projects whose costs are not justified by the value of the information obtained. An example will illustrate the point. Suppose a firm believes that it could reduce its transportation costs by $50,000 if it were to ship larger lots to its customers. If the cost of finding out customer reaction to this plan were $70,000, the research would not be justified because its cost ($70,000) would exceed the benefit ($50,000). Clearly, the firm would be worse off by $20,000.

Too Much Data Are Accumulated

Many marketing research firms generate too much data. As a result, they do not know what to do with all of them. Much time and effort are wasted in reading reams of computer printouts and lengthy reports. (See Figure 5.9.)

Too Much Emphasis on Primary Data

Accumulating **primary data** through such means as questionnaires and experimental designs is often overemphasized by the marketing research staff. They are expensive and time-consuming, and frequently they are not necessary. Internal company data, talks with executives, and readily avail-

Figure 5.9   Too Much Data

"All I wanted was last month's sales figures in Omaha."

able **secondary data** should not be under utilized. In addition, primary data usually take longer to secure and are more costly than secondary data.

Inadequate Training of Research Personnel

An otherwise good research design could be ruined if it is not carried out as planned. This often results when interviewers and others involved in the study are not properly trained. Many marketing research staffs spend much time and effort developing feasible research plans but mistakenly assume that the plans will be successful even though the people who will be using the plans have not been trained how to use the plans efficiently.

Not Enough Support for Marketing Research

Another common mistake that firms make in marketing research is that the firms do not adequately support the marketing research departments. Many of the nation's largest firms frequently have skeleton marketing research departments. Smaller companies have a tendency to have one-person departments or, worse, an individual who has other responsibilities. In addition, there is a tendency to not provide the marketing research department with an adequate budget to allow it to collect all the information needed to make better decisions.

Failure to Use Outside Research Firms

Some companies have a policy of always performing their own marketing research. For specialized projects in which the firm has little or no experience, outside marketing research firms may be more appropriate. They may also be effective whenever large-scale monitoring of a product's performance is required.

HOW TO MAKE THE MARKETING RESEARCH PROGRAM MORE EFFECTIVE

We strongly suggest that for any project involving a considerable outlay of funds the marketing research department *perform cost-benefit analysis*. As we have said many times in this chapter, the benefit of the information measured in dollars must exceed its dollar cost.

Important data must be emphasized and gotten to the decision maker. He cannot be swamped with an overabundance of information. Only information critical to his function should be given him. Practicing *management by exception* can be helpful here. This means calling to the executive's attention problem areas, such as products not performing acceptably or salesmen who are exceeding their expense budgets.

Primary (or *new*) data should be collected only when necessary. Primary data are costly and time-consuming. Before turning to primary data, marketing research departments should first make extensive use of internal company data, company executives, readily available secondary sources, and informal conversations with the market.

The marketing research department must *function independently*. That is, it must provide executives with recommendations that it believes are correct as a result of its information-gathering operations. It should not tell executives what they want or expect to hear.

This independence is more likely to occur if the marketing research department uses the **scientific method**. This essentially means that scientific methodology is followed when data are collected and analyzed. This includes developing hypotheses, rigorously testing them, and carefully interpreting results. The use of the scientific method helps to increase the possibility of the researcher having more credibility with top management.

Because of the mass of information required for decision making and the need for it to be processed quickly and gotten to decision makers as soon as possible, the marketing research department must *use the company's computer facility*. This is especially true for areas that must be continually monitored, such as the market, competition, and products.

Continuous monitoring is a major task of a specialized kind of marketing research responsibility that is currently emerging in many firms. This is the development of a marketing information system.

MARKETING INFORMATION SYSTEMS

Marketing information systems (MIS) have been developed to fill the need for continuous monitoring of crucial areas of marketing. In particular, periodic reviews of the market, competition, and products are a necessary component for better marketing decisions.

A marketing information system differs from the normal marketing research effort we have discussed earlier in several respects. First, marketing information systems tend to emphasize more an analysis of the *environment*, particularly competition and the market, than does the marketing research function. The latter may stress information for the various functional areas such as advertising and sales.

Second, MIS probably has a greater *time* emphasis because executives need information in time to make crucial decisions about products, markets, and competition. Decisions in the functional areas may not be as pressing.

Third, information gathering under MIS is done on a more *continuous* basis, but in marketing research it is done more as the need arises. A marketing information system would, for example, provide executives with monthly data about a product's performance; marketing research might occasionally be called upon to do this for a product in trouble.

Fourth, MIS stresses more the *what* of information gathering; marketing research tends to emphasize the *why*. Expressed another way, MIS finds out what has happened; marketing research tries to give the reason why it happened. An illustration may be helpful: MIS may indicate that a store's market share has dropped from 20% to 10%. Marketing research may discover that this happened because the store now closes at 6:00 p.m. on Saturday instead of 9:00 p.m.

Fifth, marketing research may *follow* MIS. That is, when MIS determines that something is wrong, such as a decrease in market share, then marketing research would be used to find out why this happened.

Sixth, MIS may make *greater use of computers* than does marketing research because MIS generally has great quantities of information to process and not much time in which to do it.

It is apparent that many companies today realize that MIS is a necessary and important complement to its more traditional marketing research activities. At Bristol-Myers, for example, a sales reporting system can, through the use of a computer, indicate all salesmen who are 10% behind quota.[11] Mead Paper's computer center allows a salesman to tell a customer in his office how long it will take the customer to receive an order. The salesman dials his company's computer center from the customer's office and the computer center provides the answer.

SUMMARY   Although all areas of the environment and each marketing function need the help of marketing research, the *market probably deserves most of the marketing research effort* because an understanding of the market is necessary in developing marketing strategies for *all* of the functions of marketing. For example, it is impossible to plan products and the advertising program without knowing who the market is, what its needs and desires are, and where it is located. In addition, a thorough knowledge of the market is needed in order to monitor the nonmarket areas of the environment effectively. Obviously, it is, for example, practically impossible to assess the strength of the competition unless the market involved is clearly defined.

Time and cost are probably the two most important constraints with which the marketing research department must deal. Time deadlines must be met and information must be gotten to the decision maker in time for him to make effective decisions. Costs, in the form of budgets, must be recognized. Costs are also an important aspect of cost-benefit analysis. In order for information to be obtained, its value (or benefits) in dollars must exceed the dollar cost of acquiring it.

The preliminary investigation step in the marketing research process (outside reading, analysis of internal data, informal talks with executives and discussions with the market) is useful because it provides the researcher with the necessary background information for formulating the rest of the research project. In many instances, this step can also provide researchers with answers to their research questions. Thus, more costly and time-consuming data acquisition methods, such as mail questionnaires, do not have to be used. Other steps in the marketing research process include defining the problems, developing hypotheses, designing the research study, analyzing data, drawing conclusions, and making recommendations.

As we indicated earlier in this chapter, the marketing research effort must obtain much information about the seven functions of marketing. This frequently involves determining the effectiveness of these functions. One measure of effectiveness indicated several times in this chapter is profitability. For example, a firm would like to know which of its salemen are profitable and which salesmen are unprofitable, and so on. The profitability measure is probably the most important measure of effectiveness.

The effectiveness of the firm's marketing research department must be

---

[11] Philip Kotler, *Marketing Management* (Englewood Cliffs, N.J.: Prentice-Hall, Inc., 1972), p. 299.

ascertained. This can be done by seeing if its recommendations are accepted by top management, if the recommendations prove to be correct, if the information it obtains is correct and timely and gotten in time to decision makers, and if their projects are completed within budget and time constraints.

QUESTIONS

1. Which is more important for gathering information, a company's marketing research department or its marketing information system (MIS)? Why?
2. How can the effectiveness of the marketing research department be measured?
3. Why is cost-benefit analysis important in assessing the effectiveness of marketing research?
4. How is brand loyalty measured? Can you think of any other ways to measure brand loyalty?
5. What is the 20/80 principle? Why must marketing research determine if it exists, for example, in a firm's products?
6. Why is the preliminary investigation step of marketing research so important?
7. What are the advantages in using secondary data instead of primary data?

GLOSSARY

Consumer Panel: a sample of a market that records its purchases in diaries so that companies can gather information

Internal Data: data available from the marketing researcher's own company, such as annual reports, purchase orders, and invoices

Marketing Information System (MIS): a system emphasizing computer involvement that continuously monitors the market, competition, and the company's products

Personal Interviews: questions asked of a sample by interviewers

Primary Data: data that must be gathered because they are not already available

Reliability: the accuracy of the data

Response Rate: the number of returned questionnaires divided by the number sent out

Scientific Method: a procedure applied to obtaining information which involves developing hypotheses, rigorous testing of hypotheses, and careful interpretation of results

Sample: that portion of a population contacted in order to obtain information

Secondary Data: data that are already available

Validity: the suitability of data for the research objective involved

Value of Information: the monetary worth of information used in making decisions

CASES

Case 1: David Holmes, Consultant

David Holmes, a college marketing professor, as a result of a study he had conducted of large manufacturing companies, concluded that most companies had insufficient programs for eliminating poorly performing products. He decided to put together a workshop on product elimination and offer his services on a consulting basis. The workshop would be a one-day affair conducted at a company's headquarters and could accommodate up to 20 of the company's executives.

Professor Holmes believed that companies that would be the most interested in the workshop were those that:

1. Had a large number of consumer or industrial products.
2. Had over $50 million in sales per year.
3. Were located in large cities east of the Mississippi River.

Five hundred companies meeting these criteria were selected to receive a brochure indicating the benefits of having a structured product elimination program, as well as the professor's experience in consulting, research, and conducting workshops. The brochure was directed to the firm's vice-president of marketing. If interested, these executives were asked to write the consultant to request additional information. Upon receipt of this request, the professor sent a complete outline of the presentation and an indication that the fee would be $500, plus expenses.

Of the initial mailing of 500 letters, only 5 executives requested additional information. None of these invited the professor to present the workshop.

1. Would additional marketing research have improved the results of the mailer?
2. What other information about the market would have been desirable?
3. In addition to the market, what kinds of marketing research would have helped the professor to obtain better results?

Case 2: The El Sol Manufacturing Co.

A company is manufacturing a new suntan lotion that allows the user to tan rapidly but has properties that reduce the likelihood of sunburn. It took the company's research and development department two years to iron out technical problems.

The product is ready for national distribution in April. Although there was extensive research of the market, some of the marketing executives believe that because of the two-year lag caused by the R&D problem there is a need to re-analyze the market. The executives expressed the concern that market conditions may have changed in two years.

Other marketing executives are pushing for the immediate release of the product. They point out that to delay the introduction would mean that most of the summer season would be over. They also believe that they have a technically superior product that will be accepted enthusiastically by the market.

1. Should the company conduct additional research of the market or introduce the product immediately?
2. If it decides to conduct additional research of the market, what kind of information should it collect?
3. Should the company have continued to monitor the market during the two years the product was being developed?

Achieving Marketing Objectives

After you finish this chapter, you should be able to answer the following questions:

1. What are strategic objectives?
2. What are tactical objectives?
3. What is the relationship of tactical objectives to strategic objectives?
4. What are five major strategic objectives?
5. What are some examples of tactical objectives?
6. How are strategic objectives achieved?
7. How are tactical objectives achieved?
8. Why are external means usually used to implement a different product–different market approach to obtaining strategic objectives?
9. What rules of thumb should be observed in achieving strategic objectives?
10. What rules of thumb should be followed in achieving tactical objectives?

KEY TERMS *Brand Extension   Conglomerates   Forecasting   Growth   Market Share   Product Positioning   Product Protection   Return on Investment   Return on Net Worth   Return on Sales   Secondary Sources   Statistical Method of Forecasting   Strategic Objectives   Survey Method of Forecasting   Tactical Objectives*

INTRODUCTION In Chapter 1 a basic model for making decisions in marketing was developed. The reader will recall that the third step in that model involved establishing objectives and that steps four and five were concerned with how strategic and tactical objectives can be achieved. In this chapter we will discuss steps three, four, and five of this model.

WHAT ARE THE MAJOR STRATEGIC OBJECTIVES OF MARKETING?

There are probably five basic *strategic* objectives that can be established for marketing (these are shown in Figure 6.1). These are major long-run

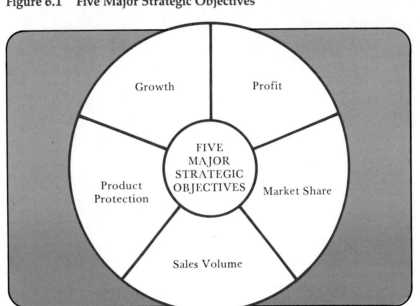

Figure 6.1   Five Major Strategic Objectives

objectives, that is, objectives that usually require longer than one year to achieve. For many companies, strategic objectives exist for the overall firm as well as the marketing department and other departments, such as finance and production.

Profit

Profit is the return that a company receives for taking risks. Some risks are investing in a new company, bringing out a new product, opening a plant in a foreign country, and so on. Profit is probably the most important objective that concerns marketing departments. If companies do not capture reasonable profit, they cannot continue to stay in business, thus providing necessary products and employment.

There are essentially three basic kinds of profit. These include (1) return on investment, (2) return on net worth, and (3) return on sales.

Return on investment (ROI) is the net profit obtained by a firm divided by its total assets (its total investment). For example, if a company had a net

Permission: From the *Wall Street Journal.*

"Gentlemen, the only thing showing a profit this month is the reception room vending machine!"

Preparing to Make Marketing Mix Decisions

profit of $1,000,000 and total assets of $20,000,000, its ROI would be 5% ($1,000,000 net profit divided by $20,000,000 of total assets).

Return on net worth is the net profit attained by a company divided by the assets contributed by the *firm's owners*.

Return on sales is a company's net profit divided by its sales dollars.

What are the normal profit figures obtained by companies in the United States? In 1974 the average manufacturer had a return on sales figure of 5.2%. This is not very high. Interestingly, a survey conducted by the Opinion Research Corporation revealed that the general public believed this figure to be around 30%.[1] In 1970 an analysis of profit figures for 97 of the largest manufacturing firms in the United States showed an average return on investment of about 7%, a return on net worth of about 11%, and a return on sales of about 6%.[2]

Market Share

Market share is the percentage of total units sold of a generic product represented by a single product. For example, if 100,000 recreational vehicles were purchased in the United States and one company sold 10,000 recreational vehicles, its market share would be 10% (10,000 divided by 100,000).

Market share is a frequently pursued objective. Many companies try to get high market shares in their industries. This may be a desirable objective because recent evidence suggests that high return on investment may be associated with high market shares. One study found that companies with less than a 10% market share had an average return on investment of 9%. Those with market shares over 40%, however, had an average return on investment of 30%.[3]

Companies must be careful when pursuing high market shares. It is possible that profitability may decline because the only way one company increases its market share is at the expense of other companies. (If one company's market share increases to 30% from 20%, the market shares for the other companies decrease from 80% to 70%.) Firms frequently increase their market shares by increasing their marketing effort, such as more advertising, more delivery trucks, and more salesmen. These efforts increase costs. If the extra sales dollars obtained are fewer than these additional costs, profits will be less. This can happen if the market to which the additional marketing effort is directed is not very responsive. In other words, the market may be loyal to competitors' products.

Companies must avoid decreases in market share over long periods of

---

[1] *The Wall Street Journal*, May 25, 1976, p. 11.
[2] Richard T. Hise and Robert H. Strawser, "The Validity of Market Share as a Marketing Objective: Some Disconcerting Evidence," *The Southern Journal of Business* (August, 1972), p. 12.
[3] R. D. Buzzell, B. T. Gale, and R. G. M. Sultan, "Market Share—A Key to Profitability," *Harvard Business Review* (January–February, 1975), pp. 97–107.

Achieving Marketing Objectives

time and large decreases in market share from one year to the next because they have been found to be accompanied by declining profits.[4]

Sales Volume

Sales volume, or revenue, is a common strategic objective for the marketing department. Specific dollar targets may be established, such as $10 million, or percentage increases can be stated, such as 20%.

Product Protection

Product protection refers to the extent to which a product can withstand competitors' efforts to weaken its position in the market. This is usually measured by noticing what happens to a product's sales as companies increase their marketing effort. For example, let's assume that the price on Product A is decreased by 30%. As a result, the sales of competitive Product B remain steady or decrease only slightly (say 5%). Product B, thus, enjoys a protected position. Another way to analyze product protection is through *brand loyalty*. This refers to the number of consecutive purchases of a specific brand. The higher the number of consecutive purchases without a purchase of a competitive brand, the greater the brand loyalty. The higher the level of brand loyalty, the greater the degree of product protection that has been obtained. Market share can also be used to represent product protection. A product with a steady or increasing market share illustrates an offering that has probably achieved a protected status.

Product protection is a worthwhile objective because other companies will waste valuable resources trying to compete with such a product. Also, firms with such products may not have to devote as many marketing dollars to them. These dollars can be used on other products.

Perhaps the best way for a company to secure a protected position is to market products that are *different from competitive products on product aspects that are important to buyers.* For example, let's assume that taste is important to beer drinkers and that products now on the market are believed not to taste good. If a firm could develop a beer that tastes good, it would probably soon occupy a protected position.

Growth

Growth is a strategic objective that can take a number of forms, for example, sales, profits, assets, number of employees, market share, net worth, and so on. No matter how the term *growth* is used, it generally refers to *increases* in these performance measures. Thus, a company may talk about achieving a 10% growth (increase) in net worth or a 15% growth (increase) in net profits.

[4] Hise and Strawser, op. cit.

TACTICAL OBJECTIVES

Tactical objectives are objectives that take one year or less to achieve. Tactical objectives are used in the achievement of the long-run (strategic) objectives. For example, a strategic objective may be to increase net profit by $1 million. In order to help achieve this strategic objective, a tactical objective may be to reduce salespeople's expenses by $50,000.

There are numerous tactical objectives that could be developed for the marketing department. Figure 6.2 shows what some of these might be.

DEVELOPING GOOD STRATEGIC AND TACTICAL OBJECTIVES

Many companies do not develop good objectives. Below are some recommendations for establishing objectives.

Objectives Must Be Feasible

Good objectives are feasible, that is, there is a good chance that they can be achieved. An example of an objective that would not be feasible would be to increase a product's market share from 20% to 30% when the company knows that two other companies are bringing out very strong new products.

Figure 6.2   Examples of Tactical Objectives

1. To reduce salespeople's expenses by $80,000.
2. To increase the number of calls by salespeople to an average of 25 per week.
3. To achieve a cost per sales call of $25.
4. To reduce the percentage of salespeople's time spent on paper work to 15%.
5. To obtain an average delivery time of 3.5 days.
6. To achieve a customer out-of-stock percentage of 5%.
7. To reduce inventory costs by 10%.
8. To increase the average number of interviews conducted by marketing research personnel per day to 8.
9. To obtain an average cost per interview of $15.
10. To have 15% of the readers of a magazine remember our advertisement in that magazine.
11. To have 5% of the women between the ages of 20 and 45 remember our product slogan.

Objectives Must Recognize Company Resources

The firm's resources should be studied carefully when the marketing department sets its objectives. These resources act as a brake. For example, if there were no money in the company to hire new salespeople, an objective to increase total salespeople's calls on customers by 20% would be inappropriate if present salespeople were working an average of 60 hours per week.

Objectives Should Be Specific

There should be no misunderstanding about what the desired objective is. Misunderstanding leads to confusion and the likelihood that the desired objective will not be achieved. Figure 6.2 provides examples of specific objectives.

Objectives Should Be Quantitatively Stated

When objectives are quantitatively expressed, those who are charged with achieving the objectives know precisely what their targets are. The reader probably noticed that all the tactical objectives listed in Figure 6.2 are stated quantitatively.

Objectives Should Be Few in Number

The marketing department should not be given a large number of objectives to achieve. It is better if only some of the most important objectives are established. This allows the marketing department to concentrate its time and effort in the most beneficial way instead of dissipating its efforts by pursuing many objectives. Also, the more objectives that are attempted, the more likely it is that the objectives will be in conflict. That is, as one objective is better achieved, another is not achieved as well. An example of this would be the market share and profit objectives discussed earlier. As high percentages of market share are obtained, profit may be reduced.

FORECASTING

Forecasting (predicting) is a very important part of setting objectives, especially strategic objectives that may involve time periods as long as 5, 10, or 20 years. Forecasts provide estimates of conditions that affect the objectives being considered in several ways. First, they help determine whether the objective is feasible. Second, they provide an idea of how high or how low the objective should be set. Let's illustrate these two points with an example.

Assume that a large manufacturer of soap is considering establishing an

"Which do you want, dearie? The near term or the long haul?"

objective of selling 20 million boxes of laundry detergent in 1980. The company does some research and finds that it sells, on the average, one box of this detergent for every four washing machines in the United States. The marketing research department is asked to make a forecast of the number of washing machines there will be in the United States in 1980. Its forecast is 60 million. Since the company expects to sell one box of detergent for every four washing machines, a forecast of 15 million units sold would result (60 million divided by 4 equals 15 million). From this forecast, the company can see that the estimate of 20 million units is probably not feasible and, therefore, it may want to drop the objective to 15 million units.

There are three basic ways that companies forecast: These are by use of (1) statistical methods, (2) survey methods, and (3) secondary sources.

Statistical Methods

We do not have enough space in this text to talk about all of the statistical methods that are available or to show the mechanics of statistical forecasting. We can, however, through a simple example, show the basic **statistical methods of forecasting.**

Many statistical forecasting approaches see what has happened in the

Achieving Marketing Objectives

past and then project the past relationship into the future in order to obtain a forecast. This will be the substance of our example.

Let's assume that a local producer of cookies wants to forecast the number of boxes of cookies it will sell in 1979. In so doing, it assumes that the past sales patterns for cookies sold will continue in the future.

Observing Past Data.   The company goes back ten years and notes for each year the number of boxes of cookies sold. The data are presented in Figure 6.3.

Graphing the Data.   The cookie company then puts the data on a simple two-dimensional graph, as shown in Figure 6.4. The horizontal axis (X axis) represents time (the years 1969 through 1978). The vertical axis (Y axis) indicates the number of boxes of cookies sold. The *dots in the graph* represent the number of boxes of cookies sold for the particular year involved. For example, 10,000 boxes of cookies were sold in 1969.

Representing the General Relationship of Cookies Sold to Time.   The cookie company needs some way to express the general relationship of the number of boxes of cookies sold to time. This is the purpose of the straight line in Figure 6.4. It is used to represent the *average* relationship between the number of boxes of cookies sold and time. (If statistical methods had been used, the line would have been positioned scientifically. In this example, we guessed where this line would be. Even so, it is probably a close approximation of where it would be located if it had been developed through statistical means.)

Forecasting the Number of Boxes of Cookies to Be Sold in 1979.   In order to forecast the number of boxes of cookies likely to be sold in 1979, we simply extend the straight line in Figure 6.4 until it reaches the year

Figure 6.3   Number of Boxes of Cookies Sold, 1969–1978

Year	Number of Boxes of Cookies Sold
1969	10,000
1970	14,000
1971	15,000
1972	18,000
1973	22,000
1974	23,000
1975	30,000
1976	33,000
1977	40,000
1978	43,000

Preparing to Make Marketing Mix Decisions

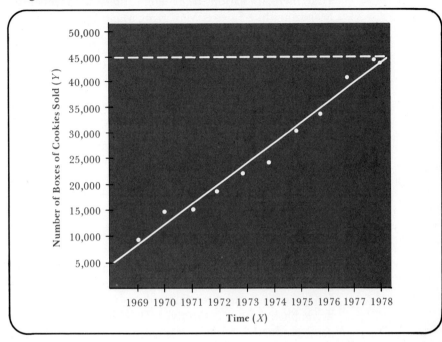

Figure 6.4   Number of Boxes of Cookies Sold, 1969–1978

1979, at which point we see 45,000 boxes of cookies are associated with that year.

Survey Methods

Survey methods of forecasting are often used in making forecasts. They are especially useful if the forecasters do not believe that past relationships are likely to occur in the future. Thus, new trends can be recognized when forecasts are made.

Survey methods are frequently used to obtain estimates of what future purchasing plans are. For example, a manufacturer of machine tools may have its salesmen ask its customers how many machines they expect to purchase over the next year. When the results for each customer are totaled, the manufacturer will have an idea of how many machine tools it is likely to sell. Another example would be a bank's asking its customers if they expect to increase or decrease their savings within the next five years. They might also be asked by how much they expect to increase or decrease their savings. The bank would use these data to forecast its deposits over this five-year-period.

Achieving Marketing Objectives

Secondary Sources

Secondary sources often provide forecasts that can be helpful to individual companies. There are three major secondary sources that firms should use. First, there are various *trade publications* that frequently provide forecasts. Magazines like *Sales & Marketing Management, Industrial Marketing,* and *Chain Store Age* often contain data that are helpful in forecasting. Second, *trade associations* composed of companies in specific industries have as one of their major objectives the development of forecasts. The Iron and Steel Institute, for example, provides projections for its member firms. Third, *government data* (national, state, and local) frequently contain valuable forecasts. At the national level, for example, departments and agencies like the Department of Health, Education and Welfare, Department of Commerce, Bureau of the Census, Department of Transportation, and the Department of Housing and Urban Development are likely to have valuable projections.

DEVELOPING MARKETING PLANS TO ACHIEVE STRATEGIC OBJECTIVES

Marketing plans to achieve strategic (long-run) objectives essentially involve various product–market alternatives. These alternatives are shown in Figure 6.5. Four potential product–market combinations can be used to accomplish strategic objectives. These include same product–same market, same product–different market, different product–same market, and different product–different market.

Figure 6.5 also shows that these four basic combinations can be achieved through internal or external means. An internal approach means that the company implements the basic product–market combination by using current resources (such as salesmen or plant capacity) or adding to them within the already existing company. If a firm acquires or uses another company to carry out the product–market alternative, then it is using an external approach.

The factors that essentially determine if an internal or external approach will be followed are availability of resources and management expertise and experience. If the company has adequate resources, it can follow an internal approach. But if these resources are inadequate (not enough salesmen, not enough production capacity, insufficient warehouse space, for instance), acquiring another company that has these resources may be the only logical alternative to pursue. If management has the necessary expertise and experience for the strategic product–market alternative to be followed, an internal approach may be better. If these are lacking, they may have to be obtained by acquiring a company whose executives have the necessary expertise and experience.

An external alternative tends to be pursued more frequently when a different product–different market strategy is used because current re-

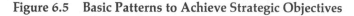

Figure 6.5   Basic Patterns to Achieve Strategic Objectives

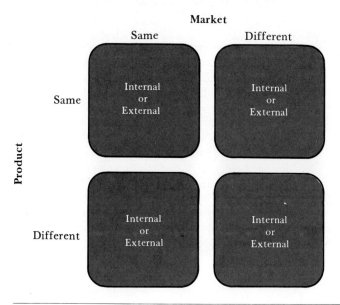

Market

	Same	Different
Same	Internal or External	Internal or External
Different	Internal or External	Internal or External

Product

sources are likely to be lacking and management expertise and experience are generally inadequate.

Same Product–Same Market

There are a number of ways that this product–market combination can be used. One way is to encourage greater use of the product by the current market. For example, a company could persuade consumers to increase the *average size* of its purchase; thus, a restaurant could eliminate a 6-ounce steak and offer only a 10-ounce steak. Or customers could be encouraged to increase their *frequency* of usage. For instance, a distributor of industrial lubricating oils might try to convince its customers to pull maintenance on its machinery twice a year instead of once a year.

Devising *new uses* for current products is an additional approach that could be used. An example is Arm & Hammer baking soda being used as an odor preventive in refrigerators in addition to its normal function in baking.

Attracting competitor customers is an example of the same product–same market strategy. This can be done in a number of ways, such as major product improvement, a lower price, heavier advertising, and so on. The

Avis "We're Number Two" advertising campaign appears to be a major effort to pull customers away from Hertz. Timex increased its market share by offering watches in nontraditional stores, such as drugstores and variety stores.

Same Product–Different Market

Another major approach to achieving strategic objectives is by marketing the same product to different markets. This may substantially increase sales volume and profit. Below are examples of this strategy:

1. Jello being sold to weight-conscious people.
2. Electronic pocket calculators being sold to the mass market, not just to people in scientific and engineering occupations.
3. Bicycles being marketed to adults, not just to children.
4. Gerber selling its baby foods to the adult market.

Another advantage of this strategy is that it does not require the development of a new product. However, the company does have to contend with a new market for the product. If the company is unfamiliar with this market, problems may arise.

Different Product–Same Market

A common strategy is to develop different products for the same market. Here, the company has an advantage of dealing with a market with which it is familiar, but the company has to grapple with a different product.

In some instances, the product will be radically different from already existing products. Sometimes, a slight change or product improvement can be very rewarding. One approach is to make products smaller. For example, smaller refrigerators and washers and dryers have been developed for apartment dwellers. Another is to institute product improvement. Du Pont, for example, added a special coating to a cellophane in order to reduce winter breakage and increase protection.[5] Adding colors can also be effective. The Bissell Company added a line of pastel colored sweepers and reversed a downward sales trend. Until then Bissell's sweepers had been black or gray.[6]

In many cases, distinctly new products are added and directed to the same market. For example, a food processor of canned vegetables may add a new line of canned fruits. A men's retail clothing store may begin to sell shoes. An insurance company may add disability income protection to its normal line of life insurance.

[5] Donald K. Clifford, Jr., "Leverage in the Product Life Cycle," *Dun's Review* (May, 1965), pp. 62–70.

[6] Dik Warren Twedt, "How to Plan New Products, Improve Old Ones, and Create Better Advertising," *Journal of Marketing* (January, 1969), pp. 53–57.

Different Product–Different Market

A company that chooses to use this strategic option must be assured that there is a good opportunity for future sales and profits. Now the company must be concerned with two new different aspects of its marketing operation: the product and the market. In addition, since it will take some time for the company to research and understand the market and product or acquire the new product, the possibility is increased that the market's needs and desires may change.

A classic example of the problems faced by a company confronted with a different product and different market is the manufacturer of industrial tapes that decided to produce and sell a cellophane tape to the consumer market to compete with Scotch tape and Texcel tape. In addition to development and production problems, the company was faced with a bewildering array of marketing difficulties because none of its older products was sold to the consumer market. It knew nothing about using such advertising media as consumer magazines and television. It lacked expertise in selling through drugstores, supermarkets, and variety stores. It was used to developing protective packages, not packages designed to stimulate sales in retail stores.

Because of the company's unfamiliarity with a new product and new market, it may acquire a firm that has experience with such a product and its market. Firms that do this over an extended period of time usually acquire a large number of companies that produce and market a wide variety of different products. Such firms are called **conglomerates.** Textron is a good example of a conglomerate. Its various divisions sell such products as automatic nailing machines for shoe repairing, helicopters, staplers, zippers, home chain saws, watchbands, aerospace electronic systems, and livestock feed.

These firms may be difficult to manage because they are so diverse, but they may prove to be profitable because they recognize opportunities whenever they arise.

RECOMMENDATIONS FOR EFFECTIVE STRATEGIC PLANNING

Now that the reader has some idea of the four basic approaches to achieving strategic objectives, let's look at a number of recommendations that should be recognized. These recommendations are listed in Figure 6.6.

Recognize Trends in the Environment

In Chapter 4, we described a number of developments in the various environments that marketing should recognize. Recognizing these developments is an important phase of the strategic planning process. These developments may either create problems for the marketing department or

Figure 6.6   Recommendations for Effective Strategic Planning

1. Recognize trends in the environment.
2. Recognize opportunities.
3. Take a broad view of the company's reason for existence.
4. Utilize existing resources.
5. Avoid head-on competition with entrenched brands.
6. Practice product positioning.
7. Consider brand extension.
8. Make a definite decision on where the firm is heading.

present opportunities. For example, a firm may lack the technological expertise to develop a new product line; a new law may force a company to remove a certain ingredient from its products and look for an alternative; a government decision may open up new opportunities (for instance, the federal government's decision in 1976 to develop a vaccine for a feared outbreak of 1918-type influenza presented opportunities for four major pharmaceutical firms).

Recognize Opportunities

A company must be constantly on the lookout for new opportunities, for example, developing new products, modifying existing products, discovering new uses for products, attracting competitor customers, and going after new market segments.

Somewhere in the marketing organization the responsibility for recognizing these opportunities must be assigned so that the company may take better advantage of its potential opportunities.

Take a Broad View of the Company's Reason for Existence

A company should not have a narrow view of why it is in existence. A narrow view tends to limit opportunities for achieving strategic objectives. Companies that take a narrow view tend to become product oriented instead of market oriented. This is a mistake. Opportunities exist because market needs are satisfied by current or new products. Companies that focus on products instead of on market needs tend to develop products that fail because the market does not want these products. If a firm focuses on products, it is more likely to explore only a few of the product–market combinations presented above instead of considering all of them. For

Preparing to Make Marketing Mix Decisions

example, the two combinations involving new markets would not be given sufficient consideration.

The classic example of what can happen when a narrow view is taken is provided by the railroad industry. It essentially defined its reason for existence as being that of providing *railroad* service (narrow view) instead of providing *transportation* service (broad view). As a result, the railroad industry failed to provide transportation needs required; this gap was filled by trucks, airplanes, and automobiles. As a result, the railroad industry is not healthy.[7] Contrast this with Continental Can which rejected the notion of narrowly defining the reason for its existence as that of producing steel cans used in packaging. Instead, it took a broader view—based on market needs—and expanded into metal, paper, and plastic lines.[8]

Utilize Existing Resources

Strategic objectives can be better achieved if existing resources can be utilized. Here we are referring to the same quantity and the same type of resources. Being able to use the same quantity of resources to obtain strategic objectives is helpful because additional sales volume may be handled without increasing costs. Thus, a lower price can be charged, making the product more competitive and increasing its chances of success. As an example, new products can often be added without having to increase the size of the sales force or warehousing space.

Using the same type of resource is desirable because the company does not have to contend with unfamiliarity and uncertainty. Companies often lack expertise and experience with new types of resources. They may have to use different advertising media, salesmen, production machinery, and warehouses; the unfamiliarity and uncertainty involved may thwart the company in achieving its strategic objectives. Of course, acquiring other firms that are skilled in using these resources may be a solution.

Avoid Head-on Competition with Entrenched Brands

One very important recommendation is to avoid head-on competition with entrenched brands. These are brands that have secured a high degree of product protection. They are difficult to compete with because they have attracted a loyal core of customers who will probably be reluctant to buy a new brand. This is especially true if the new brand *has nothing new to offer*, that is, if it is a carbon copy of the entrenched product. It has no new and desirable want-satisfying features. In most cases, a "me too" product will not be successful.

A good example of what can happen when a product that has nothing

[7] Theodore Levitt, "Marketing Myopia," *Harvard Business Review* (July–August, 1960), pp. 45–56.
[8] Robert Haas, *Industrial Marketing Management* (New York: Petrocelli/Charter, 1976), p. 126.

new to offer competes with an entrenched product is Lever Brothers' Surf. It lost $24 million in six years competing with Tide and Fab.

Practice Product Positioning

One way that a company can avoid competing directly with an entrenched brand is through **product positioning.** Effective product positioning allows products to compete more effectively. It involves three major steps:

1. Determining from the market the features of a product that are important in satisfying customer needs.
2. Determining the extent to which current products have these important features.
3. If current offerings do not have these features, developing and marketing a product that does.

Let's use an example to illustrate these steps. Assume that a cigar manufacturer finds out that the two most important product features for cigar smokers are mildness and freshness. The firm asks cigar smokers to evaluate the existing five brands of cigars for mildness and freshness. It discovers that these five brands are perceived as being harsh and stale. The company would probably have a successful product if its new cigar would be perceived as being mild and fresh.

Many products are good examples of sound product positioning. The Volkswagen Rabbit appears effectively to combine desirable product characteristics of low cost (under $3,500), economy of operation (41 miles per gallon), and roominess (as much interior as mid-size cars). Aim toothpaste effectively combined taste (a clear gel) and decay prevention (stannous fluoride). Burger King discovered that customers did not like waiting for special orders. Its "Have It Your Way" strategy helped sales increase 38% in one year.

Consider Brand Extension

Brand extension involves putting the same brand name used on currently successful products on new products. The advantage of this strategy is that consumers will have a favorable impression of the new product and will be more likely to buy it. Irish Spring, the brand name for a successful bar soap, was used for a new deodorant. The Mazola brand was extended from corn oil to margarines.

Make a Definite Decision on Where the Firm Is Heading

In obtaining strategic objectives, the firm must know what it wants to achieve and how it wants to achieve it. This means that specific objectives are indicated, plans for obtaining the objectives are developed, and a specific timetable is mapped out.

A company that appears to have violated these suggestions is W. T. Grant, the largest retailer ever to file for bankruptcy. Forced to close its 1,070 stores in 40 states in 1976, it apparently never knew (in recent years) where it was heading and how to get there. Long-run objectives were not developed, the company expanded too rapidly, credit policies were too liberal, unsuitable store locations were chosen, different-sized stores having different layouts were opened, and the company put its own unknown brand name (Bradford) on well-known appliances that it was selling.

DEVELOPING THE MARKETING MIX TO ACHIEVE TACTICAL OBJECTIVES

Earlier we mentioned that the marketing mix is developed in order to achieve tactical (short-run) objectives that are important in obtaining the strategic (long-run) objectives of the firm. We must get a general idea of how this can be achieved. The specifics of various elements of the marketing mix will be covered in Chapters 7 through 15 of this book.

In Chapter 1 we learned that the marketing mix is made up of the following areas: product, advertising, personal selling, channels of distribution, physical distribution, and pricing. A major responsibility is to make specific decisions in these areas so that the firm has the best opportunity to achieve its tactical objectives. We will now offer some ideas that will help in achieving these objectives.

Importance of the Product and Market in Making Marketing Mix Decisions

The product being marketed and the market segments in which it is being sold are major determinants of what elements of the marketing mix should be used and emphasized. The needs of the market are the starting point for developing the product's features (characteristics) and quality level. Both the product and the market should then be analyzed to help develop the most appropriate form of the other marketing mix elements.

The type of product greatly affects the other marketing mix areas. Industrial products, for example, are not usually marketed through channels of distribution. Most consumer products, however, use such middlemen as wholesalers and retailers. Industrial products generally use such advertising media as direct mail and trade magazines, but consumer products tend to be advertised through general magazines, newspapers, and television.

The market dictates the marketing mix. If women prefer to buy perfume in department stores, then perfume had better be available in department stores. If men will not pay more than $39.95 for a certain type of shoes, then the shoe store had better price this item below $39.95. If consumers expect bread and pastries to be fresh everyday, then the bakery must have a large enough fleet of delivery trucks to ensure everyday delivery to the stores.

Need to Make Integrated Marketing Mix Decisions

Decisions in the marketing mix must be made together; they cannot be made separately. The various interactional effects must be considered and the best *combination* of marketing mix selected that will achieve the desired tactical objectives.

Let's use an example to illustrate this point. A company may sell 1,000 units of a product at a price of $10. Its cost per unit is $8. Thus, its total profit is $2,000 since its total revenue is $10,000 (1,000 × $10), its total cost is $8,000 (1,000 × $8), and $10,000 total revenue less $8,000 total cost results in a $2,000 net profit.

Suppose that the company is considering lowering the price to $9.50. At that price, it expects to sell 1,200 units and it predicts its cost-per-unit will be $7.50. If the price were $9.50 per unit, it would have a net profit of $2,400 ($11,400 total revenue less $9,000 total costs).

By looking at only one element of the marketing mix—price—the company, by reducing its price to $9.50 from $10, has increased its profits to $2,400 from $2,000. Suppose that it decided to spend $1,000 for advertising. Since advertising may make the product more desirable in the market, we will assume that the company can sell 1,300 units at a higher price of $11 per unit and that the cost-per-unit will be $8.25. Under these conditions, its net profit would be $2,575 ($14,300 total revenue less $11,725 total cost). (The reader, of course, realizes that total cost is the cost-per-unit of $8.25 times 1,300 units *plus* the $1,000 expenditure for advertising).

The important point of the example is that the firm had the highest level of profit ($2,575) when it considered *two* elements of the marketing mix (price *and* advertising), not just one (price).

Commitment of Additional Effort from the Marketing Mix to a Product Will Increase Sales up to a Point

As we increase the marketing mix effort devoted to a product, we also increase the sales dollars resulting–*up to a point.* For example, as we increase the number of salespeople selling a product or as we increase the number of advertisements, sales dollars will continue to increase, but at some level they will reach a maximum and will decline if additional resource inputs are used. It is foolish to use additional resources beyond this point because sales dollars will decrease and costs will go up. As a result, profits will be lower. *Thus, a major emphasis in assigning marketing mix resources to products is to determine the level of resource input that maximizes sales dollars.*

This concept is illustrated in Figure 6.7, which shows the relationship of number of salespeople to sales dollars. We can see that we increase sales dollars until we have a total of 40 salespeople selling the product. With 40 salespeople, we maximize sales dollars at $40,000. It does not make sense to add salespeople beyond that point because sales dollars will only decline and

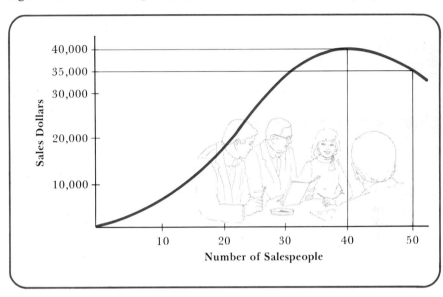

Figure 6.7 Relationship of Sales Dollars to Number of Salespeople

the additional salespeople used will only add to our costs. (The combination of lower sales and higher costs will result in lower net profit.) Figure 6.7 shows that increasing our sales staff from 40 to 50 reduces our sales dollars from $40,000 to $35,000.

Why would sales dollars decrease beyond 40 salespeople? Forty salespeople might be too many to manage effectively. We might not be able to route them effectively so that they call on fewer customers. Or we might require so much additional paper work that the salespeople do not spend enough time with their customers and these customers switch their business to other companies.

Employ Marketing Mix Resources Until Their Additional Cost Exceeds Their Additional Sales Volume

Each element of the marketing mix should be allocated to a product until its additional cost exceeds the additional sales volume it secures. No resource beyond that point should be committed because a lower profit would result.

The reader should examine Figure 6.8. In that figure we are concerned with two elements of the marketing mix: personal selling and advertising. In particular, we want to utilize the number of salespeople and the number of advertisements for a product that will maximize its profits. In both parts

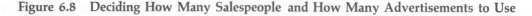

Figure 6.8 Deciding How Many Salespeople and How Many Advertisements to Use

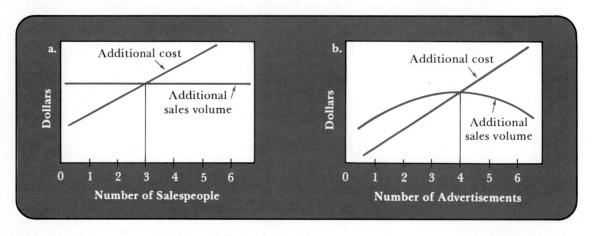

of Figure 6.8 we notice that at first the additional sales volume resulting from adding one more salesperson or one more advertisement is greater than the additional cost, but then the extra cost exceeds the extra sales volume. In Figure 6.8(a), the additional sales volume for one and two salespeople is higher than the additional cost. This means that our net profit is higher. After the third salesperson is assigned to the product, the additional cost is *higher* than the additional sales volume. This means that our net profit is lower, which, of course, is not desirable. Therefore, we would assign three salespeople to the product because this is where our net profit is the highest. To add a fourth salesperson would reduce our net profit; thus, we stop at three.

The same reasoning can also be applied to the problem of how many advertisements to run for the product [Figure 6.8(b)]. There, we see that running four advertisements will maximize net profit.

Effectiveness of the Marketing Mix Is an Important Factor

We must be concerned with the *effectiveness* of our marketing mix decisions as well as their level. For example, we may decide that we ought to spend $50,000 in advertising instead of $30,000, but we need to have some idea of the contribution of that $50,000 to our tactical objectives. The $50,000 might result in 200 new customers if it is spent on new salesmen, but it might result in only 150 new customers if spent on advertising. Thus, the effectiveness of that $50,000 is less if it is allocated to advertising than if it is spent on new salespeople.

Even if the $50,000 is to be spent on advertising, we still must consider its effectiveness. If the $50,000 is spent for magazine advertising, it might result in 2,000 inquiries about our product. If, however, the $50,000 is spent for television advertising, it might result in 2,500 inquiries.

The Level of Effort in the Marketing Mix and Its Effectiveness Must Be Compared to Those of Competition

The greater the level of effort in the marketing mix (number of salespeople, dollars spent for advertising, number of delivery trucks used, etc.) and the more effective this effort (choosing the right advertising medium, hiring the most productive salesperson, buying a fleet of trucks with the lowest breakdown rate), the more likely it is that a company will achieve its tactical objectives. However, the level of effort *for competition* and *its effectiveness* will, in large measure, affect the extent to which these tactical objectives will be achieved. The lower the effort and the less effective it is *in comparison* to the competition's level of effort and effectiveness, the less likely it is that the stated tactical objectives will be obtained. There is a better chance to achieve tactical objectives if the level of marketing mix effort and its effectiveness are greater than those of competitive firms.

In establishing tactical objectives, it is always important to have some idea of the level of competitor marketing mix effort and of its effectiveness. Knowing these will enable a company to establish more realistic tactical objectives that have a better chance of being obtained.

The Marketing Mix Should Be Modified Over Time

A company cannot use the same marketing mix for the same product forever. The marketing mix should be modified over time. These modifications especially need to recognize changes in the markets to which products are directed. For example, if customers now prefer to purchase a product in department stores and not in drugstores, then the channels of distribution must be changed to department stores.

SUMMARY

This chapter has dealt with the objectives that usually concern the marketing department and how these objectives are to be obtained. We learned that the marketing area is generally involved with two types of objectives: strategic and tactical. Strategic (long-run) objectives are those crucial goals of the company to which the marketing department must successfully contribute. These include profit, market share, sales volume, product protection, and growth. These objectives are generally achieved by developing four product–market combinations: same product–same market, same product–different market, different product–same market, different product–different market. These product–market combinations can be implemented through internal or external means. The more management is unfamiliar with the product or market involved, the more likely it is that a company will be acquired (external means) to attain the desired strategic objective.

Tactical (short-run) objectives are goals that assist in achieving the broader strategic goals. These objectives, such as increasing the number of salespeople's calls or decreasing delivery times to customers, are achieved by deciding on the appropriate marketing mix for various products. This involves determining which marketing mix alternatives are most appropriate (such as whether to advertise in magazines or on television). It also involves deciding on the amount of resources to commit, such as the number of salespeople.

Strategic objectives are more likely to be obtained if (1) trends in the environment are observed, (2) opportunities are recognized, (3) a broad view of the reason for the company's existence is taken, (4) existing resources are utilized, (5) head-on competition with entrenched brands is avoided, (6) product positioning is practiced, and (7) brand extension is followed. Tactical objectives must recognize the product and market involved. The specific marketing mix decisions should be made in an integrated fashion by recognizing that the various marketing mix elements are interactional. The point at which additional commitments of resources result in less sales volume or profit should be determined. Marketing departments must attempt to measure the effectiveness of their marketing mix decisions. The level of resource commitments and their effectiveness should be compared with those of competitive companies.

Strategic and tactical objectives must be carefully established. They must be feasible and they must recognize company resources. They should be specific in nature; it is hoped that they will be expressed quantitatively. There should not be a large number of objectives to achieve.

QUESTIONS

1. Which objectives do you believe are easier to achieve, strategic or tactical? Why?
2. Why do you believe that the best way to secure a protected position for a product is to have a product available that is different from competitive products on aspects important to buyers?
3. Why should objectives be expressed in quantitative terms?
4. Under what conditions would the survey method of forecasting be appropriate?
5. Why would a firm use an external approach to achieving strategic objectives?

Preparing to Make Marketing Mix Decisions

6. Would conglomerates in the long run be more likely than more specialized firms to be successful in terms of net profit secured? Why or why not?
7. Why must a company take as broad a view as possible of its reason for existence?
8. Discuss the major steps in effective product positioning.
9. Why is brand extension an effective marketing strategy?

GLOSSARY

Brand Extension: placing brand names from already existing successful products on new products

Conglomerates: a firm comprised of a number of companies that produce and market a wide variety of different products

Forecasting: estimating conditions that will affect the objectives being established

Growth: the extent to which various measures of performance are improved over time

Market Share: percentage of total units sold of a generic product represented by a single product

Product Positioning: developing products that have features highly desired by the market when already existing products do not have these highly desired features

Product Protection: the extent to which a product can withstand competitors' efforts to weaken its market position

Return on Investment (ROI): profit obtained divided by total assets

Return on Net Worth: profit obtained divided by assets contributed by the owners of a company

Return on Sales: profit obtained divided by a company's sales

Secondary Sources: published sources, such as magazines and government publications, that provide forecasts useful to companies

Statistical Method of Forecasting: using past data to make forecasts

Strategic Objectives: major, long-run objectives that require more than one year to achieve

Survey Method of Forecasting: questioning the market about its future intentions to purchase in order to make forecasts

Tactical Objectives: objectives that take less than one year to achieve that are used to obtain strategic objectives

CASES

Case 1: Plasti-Corp Co.

The Plasti-Corp is a small manufacturer of plastic materials purchased by other manufacturing firms. In 1977 its sales were $40 million. Its net profit was $2 million.

John Simpson, the company's vice-president of marketing, is establishing long-range objectives for the company. He has decided that within 10 years the company should attempt to expand its sales volume to $50 million and increase its net profit to $4 million.

In setting these objectives, Mr. Simpson cited a number of the company's strengths: (1) an aggressive sales force, (2) competent, experienced product managers, (3) expanding markets for the kinds of products currently marketed, and (4) a marketing research department that can uncover the needs of the various market segments for plastics. Mr. Simpson knows that the company has many weaknesses that must be recognized when developing plans to achieve these two basic objectives. These include a lack of funds available to finance expansion, a weak R&D department, and a production department that has consistently failed to meet time and cost deadlines.

1. Do you believe that Mr. Simpson's two objectives can be achieved?
2. Given the company's strengths and weaknesses, which product–market combination(s) appear to be the most appropriate for achieving these objectives.
3. Once a decision on the product–market combination has been reached, how should the combination be implemented?
4. What other aspects of the firm's operations should be examined in order to determine how these basic objectives should be achieved?

Case 2: Travelease Corp.

Travelease Corp., a large motel chain, is considering opening a motel in a Florida city of 50,000 inhabitants. A key factor in its decision is an estimate of the occupancy rate for the proposed motel over the next ten years. (The occupancy rate refers to the average percentage of rooms that are occupied.

Preparing to Make Marketing Mix Decisions

The occupancy rate is important because it has a direct influence on revenues.)

Deborah Barnes, an economist with the chain, has been given the responsibility of making the desired forecasts. She believes that her first step is to develop a list of factors that would influence the motel's future occupancy rate. Her preliminary list of factors includes: (1) estimated future population of the city, (2) estimated future traffic flows on existing roads, and (3) approximate location of potential new roads.

1. Do you believe that Ms. Barnes' list of factors is likely to be useful in predicting the motel's occupancy rate?
2. Are there other factors that are likely to be important in predicting the occupancy rate?
3. Once Ms. Barnes has decided on the factors that will predict the motel's occupancy rate, what should her next step be?

PART 3

Marketing Mix Decisions

Introduction to Product Decisions

After you finish this chapter, you should be able to answer the following questions:

1. Why is it important to view products through the customer's eyes? How do customers think of products?

2. How and why are product classifications useful to marketing managers?

3. How can the consumer goods and the industrial goods classifications be applied to marketing strategy planning?

4. Why is the service market booming?

5. What are the unique features of services? Should services be marketed differently from products?

6. What is the product life cycle? What factors influence a product's movement through the life cycle?

7. Who are innovators? Opinion leaders? What are their roles in diffusing new product ideas throughout the marketplace?

Consumer Goods   Convenience Goods   Diffusion Process   Derived Demand   Extended Product   Industrial Goods   Product   Product Life Cycle   Services   Shopping Goods   Specialty Goods   Unsought Goods

The marketing manager works with six components of the marketing mix in developing the organization's marketing program: the product, the price structure, channels of distribution, physical distribution, advertising, and personal selling. The manager must decide on marketing mix factors more or less simultaneously. But for discussion purposes, it is more practical to treat each of the six marketing mix components in separate chapters. We begin with product decisions because the organization's product is the heart of its marketing program.

THE KEY ROLE OF PRODUCT IN THE MARKETING PROGRAM

The product is the medium through which both buyers and sellers attain their exchange objectives. It is through consumption of *products* (goods and services) that consumers realize the benefits they seek. Organizations exist to provide these want-satisfying products to their customers. Through effective customer satisfaction, organizations are able to realize their other objectives—profits, market share, membership enrollment quotas, and so on. Where do the nonproduct elements of the marketing mix fit into the marketing program, then? Essentially, they help *adjust* the product to particular target customer needs. Setting an appropriate price, choosing advertising themes, and creating effective distribution systems and methods may also be absolutely essential to the product's success. In some cases, these factors may override the choice of product in marketing mix importance. On a hot day at the ball park the choice of lemonade, beer, or Coke may not matter to the thirsty fan in the stands, as long as *something* to drink is available and reasonably cold. But while quick and convenient distribution is essential in selling either beverage, the thirsty customer is looking for *product benefits,* in this case, a cold drink to relieve his thirst.

WHAT IS A PRODUCT?

What, then, is a **product?** The answer is not simple and obvious, for what a product is depends on one's perspective. And the choice of perspective can be a most crucial factor in successful marketing.

Perhaps Charles Revson, founder of Revlon, dramatized the differences in product perspective best when he remarked that, "In the factory, we make cosmetics; in the store, we sell hope."

Revson is contrasting the viewpoints of both *producer* and *consumer.* At one extreme, the producer may tend to focus narrowly on a product's physical features and the costs of assembling them into some identifiable form. Thus, a candy bar is viewed as a particular combination of milk chocolate, sugar, nuts, and other ingredients, shaped in a distinctive way,

"But we don't *want* a poignant comment on the hopelessness of the human condition. We want a pretty picture to hang in our living room!"

and paper or foil-wrapped with its brand name prominently displayed. The same ingredients packaged under another brand name may be recognized by the *customer* as a completely different product. Both brands will compete as quick, tasty snacks for everyday consumption.

Shape the candy ingredients into smaller pieces, package one pound of them in a smartly decorated container, and the seller has an entirely different product—a box of chocolates. Viewed now as a gift item, the candy will appeal to very different customer segments. Unlike the candy bars, the gift chocolates may be sold at a prestige price through specialty gift and candy stores. They will sell especially well at Christmas, Valentine's Day, and Mother's Day.

In an **extended product** the basic physical product has been extended through product design, packaging and branding, and services to create unique customer benefits. Also, other marketing elements—their price, advertising, and distribution methods—provide additional customer values and help create separate products for different market segments.

We are now closing in on a definition of **product.** Our perspective will be the market or customer view of product. A product is a combination of physical attributes, services, and symbols designed to supply certain expected benefits, or utilities, to consumers.

By thinking of products in terms of benefits sought by various market segments, marketers are in a position to adjust products to customer requirements and to capitalize on new market opportunities. Furniture leasing firms, for instance, recognize that more and more people don't want to own furniture. They want the *use* of their furniture; they don't want it to "own them." By renting their furniture, young marrieds, the recently divorced, and other people whose tastes, life-styles, and place of residence are changing can save on moving expenses and can update their furniture periodically at much less cost. Furniture leasing has become a $200 million business, at least tripling in sales over the past five years.[1]

Products may be further classified into goods and services. *Goods* are products that have tangible or physical attributes, for example, a washing machine, a factory building, a glass of milk. Strictly speaking, **services** are intangible; they have no physical ingredients. A concert, a dental examination, a Sunday sermon are examples. Clearly, services are consumed for their expected want-satisfying properties.

Classifying Products

Ideally, each separate product that offers unique benefits for different customers should have its own marketing program. But it is often impractical to develop separate marketing programs for each product, just as it often doesn't make sense to market to individual customers. Instead, marketers must classify or group products into product types and market these product types. The thinking here is very similar to our discussion of market segmentation. Products should be classified in ways that are useful in developing marketing strategies.

There are any number of ways to classify products, and each way has its value. For instance, products may be classified by their size, cost, complexity, perishability, and so on. But it is perhaps most useful to classify consumer products in terms of how different consumers view them, shop for them, and use them. For if we know how the consumer sees our products, we have come a long way toward understanding how to market them successfully.

Consumer and Industrial Goods

All products can be divided into **consumer goods** and **industrial goods,** depending on their intended use. Consumer goods are products and services destined for the ultimate consumer. Industrial goods are purchased by

[1] "Rented Furniture: A New Design for Living," *Business Week*, March 14, 1977, p. 107.

organizations for resale or for producing other goods and services. This classification is consistent with the "consumer market" and "industrial market" definitions in Chapter 2. Also, recall from Chapter 2 that consumer and industrial markets usually buy products for very different purposes, and often in different quantities. The industrial buying process may differ greatly from that of the average shopper buying items for personal or family use. So marketing strategies for firms selling products to the two markets will be very different. Even identical products, ballpoint pens, for instance, may be bought very differently depending on whether the purchaser is an ultimate consumer or an organization. Clever advertising and styling will probably be more effective in selling ballpoints to students, but an office buying dozens at a time may be most interested in writing qualities, price, and ease of purchase.

Our ballpoint pen example also points out a limitation of the consumer goods/industrial goods classification scheme: Physically identical goods and services can be classified in either category depending on the purchaser's intended use. So the similarities of how and why identical products are bought by both types of users may outweigh their important differences, as far as marketing strategy is concerned. In such cases, the product classification loses much of its value for marketers.

CONSUMER GOODS

Perhaps the most useful system for classifying consumer products is based on the way that people perceive and buy products. The willingness to shop (effort) and the extent of product preference (loyalty) are two important dimensions for classifying products (Figure 7.1).[2] In terms of the consumer's willingness to shop before purchasing, we can define two basic product types: convenience goods and shopping goods.

Convenience goods are products and services, usually of low unit value, that consumers want to buy quickly and with as little effort as possible. **Shopping goods** are products and services that most people believe should be shopped for and compared before buying.

In terms of product preference or loyalty, products vary between two distinct types: specialty goods and unsought goods.

Specialty goods are products and services that enjoy a preferred status; consumers do not accept substitutes for them and they go to some lengths to find them. **Unsought goods** are just that: people do not seek them out, either because they are unknown or because they are not yet wanted.

Few products fit neatly into one of these four types. Children's sleepwear, for instance, usually is bought rather quickly after very little shopping. Women's dresses, however, are usually examined and compared with others

---

[2] These dimensions are suggested by Ben Enis as refinements of an earlier classification scheme widely reproduced in many textbooks. See Ben M. Enis, *Marketing Principles*, 2nd ed. (Santa Monica, Calif.: Goodyear Publishing Co., Inc., 1977), p. 351.

Figure 7.1 Consumer Goods Classification

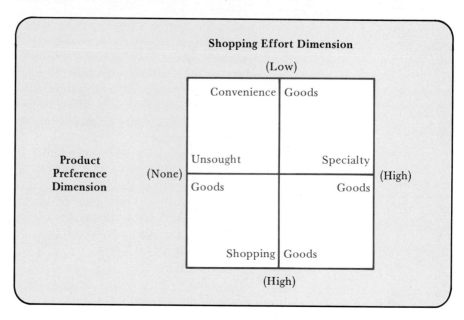

Adapted from Ben M. Enis, *Marketing Principles*, 2nd ed. (Santa Monica, Calif.: Goodyear Publishing Co., Inc., 1977), p. 351.

on style, price, fabric, and fit. But a box of popcorn at the movies involves even less shopping than children's sleepwear. Similarly, for most people, cemetery plots are an unsought good, so much so that attempts to sell them often disturb and anger many people.

At the other extreme, Limmer handmade hiking boots, a specialty good, are so much preferred by enthusiasts that some people are willing to wait for up to three years to buy a pair. Men's formal wear falls somewhere in between. Most men are prejudiced against tuxedos and rental clothing in general. Yet, After Six Company styles and promotes formal wear to successfully overcome men's reluctance to use the product and to develop some brand preference.[3]

Another problem with our classification is that consumers may differ considerably in their desire for certain products and also in their willingness to shop and evaluate before buying. Consider again our chocolate candy example. Boxed chocolates are stocked by convenience stores for last-minute or forgetful shoppers. Other shoppers may compare several brands of boxed

[3] "Stepping Out: Tuxedo Firm Thrives by Promoting Apparel That Most Men Dislike," *The Wall Street Journal*, October 24, 1975, pp. 1, 28.

chocolates on eye appeal and price before selecting one. Still other shoppers may insist on one particular brand and will travel to specialty candy stores or order by mail to get just that brand. Clearly, here are three separate customer segments, each with different buying needs and shopping interests for the same physical product.

Therefore, the marketer is challenged to measure each of the customer segments and perhaps to create alternative strategies for meeting their separate needs. Nonetheless, the product classification scheme is a useful starting point in our thinking about consumer goods marketing.

Convenience Goods

Convenience goods can be viewed as *staple goods, impulse goods,* or *emergency goods,* depending on the consumer's particular buying attitudes and circumstances. *Staple goods* are low-priced items that are used up and rebought frequently, for example, cigarettes, newspapers, gasoline, and most grocery items. Services such as routine dry cleaning, film developing, a one-minute car wash, or telephone number information are staples. We often buy staple goods routinely and without much planning. Buying by brand often becomes important, not only because it simplifies the buying effort, but also because frequent repurchase tends to develop brand preference, and in some cases, intense brand loyalty. Usually, though, the low price of staples makes it easy to try new brands. Widespread distribution is most important. Brands of bread battle for shelf space in grocery stores. Hamburger franchises seek locations on the busiest streets; factors like ease of entry and exit from highway traffic can be critical in attracting a larger share of customers to stores selling staples.

Impulse goods purchases are truly unplanned. Consumers decide to buy them on sight, smell, or some other immediate sensory stimulation. Bakeries use fans to waft the irresistible odor of fresh-baked goods our way. Retailers place impulse items like candy, magazines, and small toys near checkout counters. Some services are bought on impulse, for example, amusement games at fairs (can you think of others?).

Some goods and services are *emergency goods.* They are purchased only when the need is urgent. Alert marketers try to anticipate when and where these needs will occur. Umbrellas during a rainstorm, "fill-in" items that you forget to buy, such as that extra bag of ice for the party, are examples. So is an auto towing *service* when your car won't start.

Convenience food stores exist largely to sell impulse and emergency goods. One convenience store chain reports that half the products they sell are consumed within 30 minutes of purchase, suggesting that location and visibility are even more important for impulse and emergency goods than for staples.[4]

[4] "Convenience Stores: A $7.4 Billion Mushroom," *Business Week*, March 21, 1977, p. 61.

Shopping Goods

Most people see products such as fashion clothing, furniture, and appliances as shopping goods. They compare them on style, fit, durability and price before buying. Services like hair styling or television programs are also shopping goods. People choose a hair stylist by asking their friends for advice and comparing hair styles. We flip the TV dial or thumb through the TV program section and perhaps read the reviews before deciding whether to watch "Johnny Carson" or an old movie.

Homogeneous shopping goods are viewed as being much alike and easy to compare: products like children's tennis shoes, hamburger, or services such as routine car repairs and installment loans. Since low price is the important deciding factor for homogeneous shopping goods, marketers respond by emphasizing price in their advertising, merchandise displays, or packaging.

Heterogeneous shopping goods are seen as being very different in appearance and performance. We buy them only after comparing styles and brands until we are reasonably satisfied and confident in our choices. When value comparisons are difficult, such as durability or trouble-free maintenance in a TV set, shoppers may rely upon brand name as a guideline. Zenith television and Maytag washers are well-known examples.

Marketing heterogeneous shopping goods is complex and challenging. Marketers must determine which of their product's many features are important to shoppers and they must determine how to promote and display these features to best advantage. Since shoppers will want to compare the products before buying, producers and retailers of products such as fashion clothing, small appliances, and used cars prefer to locate near each other in order to make comparison shopping easier and more enjoyable. That's why shopping centers put a dozen shoe stores almost next to each other. As tough as it is to be surrounded by other competing stores, it's tougher still to be left out of a shopping trip altogether.

Specialty Goods

Specialty goods are products and services that provide unusual benefits not found in competitive offerings. Here, convenient location and competitive price are less important than they are for shopping goods. Custom-tailored shirts, very expensive stereo components, a membership in an exclusive club are specialty products and services. So are less expensive items that are in great demand for shorter periods of time, for example, a best-selling novel or tickets to the championship game. In each case, the buyer is convinced about the product or brand he wants and will shop among different sources only if there happen to be several locations or prices for the item.

Specialty goods marketers enjoy significant advantages from having such loyal customers. Therefore, shopping goods marketers work hard to move their products from shopping goods status to specialty goods status and they try to keep them there.

Unsought Goods

At the other end of the spectrum from specialty goods are unsought goods. These are products and services that potential customers don't search for at all, either because the products are unknown or they are unwanted.

Frozen yogurt is an example of a recently introduced product that competes with ice cream and other snack and dessert items. The marketer's task is to move the product out of the "unsought" class. Potential buyers must be informed about the new item, their resistance to the idea of frozen yogurt must be overcome, and they must be convinced that it is equal to or better than ice cream. A difficult task! Eventually, the product may achieve specialty goods status.

Other unsought goods are avoided by most people, either because they don't like to think about the product or because they believe that the product is inferior. Life insurance is a purchase that many people either postpone or avoid completely, even if they recognize a need for it. Life insurance firms rely on aggressive promotion and skillful personal selling to stimulate people to consider buying insurance. If firms are successful, many customers will then wish to compare firms and policies before buying. The insurance agent now faces the task of selling insurance as a shopping good.

Industrial Goods

Glass, rubber, and steel, nuts and bolts, batteries, lamps, vinyl upholstery, cafeteria lunches and insurance programs for workers, these and thousands more products and services are purchased in order to produce and market a single consumer good—an automobile. The fact is that most of us are little aware of the tremendous quantity and diversity of industrial goods that are bought and sold daily. Yet the variety of industrial goods is much greater than that of consumer goods. And they are often much more complex. As a result, industrial goods marketing requires much greater technical knowledge and specialization than is the case for consumer goods.

Industrial *buyers* also vary greatly in size, in the nature of their business, and in the ways they use products. Because their clients' buying needs differ so much, industrial goods sellers usually come to the buyer. Since industrial buyers do little "shopping," a product classification system based primarily on customer shopping behavior is not so useful here. Instead,

Introduction to Product Decisions

industrial firms have developed a rational classification system for industrial goods that is based on how buyers view industrial products and use them in their operations. These classifications of industrial goods include: (1) installations, (2) accessory equipment, (3) raw materials, (4) component parts and materials, and (5) supplies.

Installations are major capital investments for the industrial purchaser. Examples are factory buildings, computer installations, and jet aircraft for an airline. Since they are expensive and long-lived, installations often are bought only after considerable negotiation over several months or even years. Top-level executives of both the buying and selling firms may become involved in the purchase decision. The technical expertise of the sellers, their ability to custom design installations to the buyer's requirements, and the quality of their pre-sale and post-sale service usually are more important than price in winning a sale. Direct sale is typical for large, expensive installations.

Accessory equipment includes products bought to aid in the production operations of an industrial buyer. Portable drills and other hand tools and office equipment (typewriters, filing cabinets, etc.) are examples. Like installations, accessory equipment is bought as a capital investment, but its value is less and its useful life is shorter. Consequently, purchases of accessory equipment are less critical to the direction of the firm and they involve fewer decision makers.

In selling the more expensive equipment bought by relatively few, specialized firms, sellers may market directly through their own sales forces. But more typically, accessory equipment is sold to widely dispersed markets through middlemen.

Component parts and *materials* become parts of other finished products. *Component parts,* such as spark plugs, tires, and oil filters for new cars, do not change further in form, but *materials,* such as steel, rubber, plastic, and glass, undergo further processing in auto manufacturing.

Buyers often contract on a long-term basis to buy large quantities of component parts and materials direct from the seller. The seller's price and service are very important. The product's brand and advertising usually are not important in selling materials, since materials are often standardized, and not distinguishable by the final buyer. But sellers of component parts sometimes try to establish strong brand identity for their products; Timken roller bearings and Firestone tires are examples of component parts of other finished products that have developed their own brand recognition and preference.

Raw materials include farm products, lumber, oil, and other basic commodities. Like component parts and materials, they are used in producing final products. Raw materials usually are standardized in quality so that basic prices are very similar among competing suppliers. In fact, prices often are determined in a central market, rather than set by the seller.

Supplies are short-lived, usually low-priced items that aid in an organization's operations. Stationery, cleaning and other maintenance products, and heating fuel are examples. Since these products are usually standardized, price competition is important and brand insistence is low. Since supplies are bought by many users, and often in small quantities, wholesaling middlemen are used to distribute them. The buying process for supplies is so simple that larger firms may routinely reorder them by computer.

GENERAL CHARACTERISTICS OF INDUSTRIAL GOODS

Industrial goods of all types have several features that are important in their marketing strategies. First, the demand for industrial goods depends on, or is derived from, the demand for final consumer goods. If sales of 10 million cars are forecast, then the tire industry can expect to sell 50 million tires (four each plus a spare) to the auto manufacturers.

Second, the **derived demand** characteristic of industrial goods should be kept in mind when appropriate marketing strategies are being considered. Demand for industrial goods is fairly inelastic. That is, price cutting, advertising, or better service will not sell 60 million tires that year. And a sharp increase in tire manufacturing costs will not decrease sales to 40 million tires (although in the 1977 model year, many new cars were delivered without spare tires because there was a tire supply shortage).

Third, each component part or material used in producing the final product may represent only a small fraction of the total cost of that product. Therefore, the price of any one item will not have much effect on the sales of the final product. The ingredients used to distill a fifth of liquor cost only a few cents, much less than shipping costs and taxes.

Fourth, industrial sellers of component parts and materials still have to worry about their prices. Since products like tires or steel must compete with other very similar items from other suppliers, buyers can choose among suppliers who offer the lowest price. Under these conditions, the seller's reputation for service and product reliability may make the difference in getting the sale.

Fifth, industrial goods sellers are also at the mercy of swings in the market demand for final products. In recessions, consumers put off buying durable goods, which causes manufacturers to stop buying component parts and raw materials, cancel or delay plans for plant expansion, and cut back sharply on purchases of supplies and equipment. In boom markets, everyone scrambles to increase output. Since industrial sellers have little or no control over the final demand, it is critical that they plan for these fluctuations in consumer markets. For these reasons industrial sellers spend much time and effort in forecasting market trends.

The wide swings in output for industrial products can be seen in Figure 7.2 where output for selected years is indicated.

Introduction to Product Decisions

Figure 7.2   Industrial Production Index (1967 = 100) for Primary Metals, 1970–1975

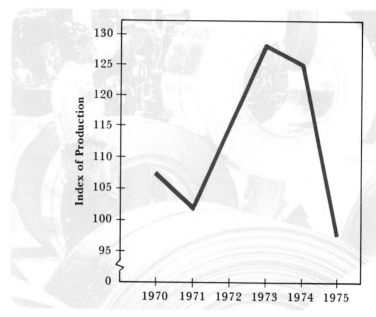

Source: *Statistical Abstract of the United States*, 1976, p. 758.

SERVICES

Consider for a moment just some of the services the average household buys and consumes on any given day. Different members will use the telephone, perhaps catch a bus for work or shopping, play tennis, have their hair styled, visit the family dentist, tune up the car, see a movie, or get a bank loan. In each case, the household is spending money for intangible services instead of for tangible goods. Industrial users buy many services, for example, top-management consulting, marketing research, legal counseling, engineering design, security guards, and window washing services. These are only a few of the services the organization will contract for instead of relying upon company personnel to provide.

Although it may not be obvious, we are in the midst of a service boom. Indeed, our society is often described as evolving from an era dominated by industrial production into a post-industrial service economy. In 1975 services rose to 46% of national personal consumption expenditures.[5]

[5] Current Business Statistics, *Survey of Current Business* (November, 1975), p. 5.

Marketing Mix Decisions

Today, more than half of the labor force in the United States is employed in producing and marketing services. Sixty-eight percent were so employed in 1971, according to one estimate.[6] Services accounted for 44% of all personal consumption expenditures and 64% of the nation's gross national product in that year.[7]

Why Services Are Booming

Why is the demand for services growing so fast? One writer notes three related reasons: (1) increasing prosperity, which leads to (2) a growing complexity in private and business life, and (3) the introduction of many new products requiring added services.[8]

As real income rises, people are willing and able to pay for many services (repairs, education, medical, travel, and so on) that make life more enjoyable and that used to be performed either by the family or not at all. Prosperity enriches but it also complicates private and business lives. Services help deal with this complexity. Most people find that their cars and stereo systems are too difficult to repair themselves. Corporations grow so large and complex that they need service specialists of all types. Thus financial consultants, advertising agencies, transportation systems, electronic communications, and many other services have become essential. New products have many services and create new ones: appliance and auto repair shops, tennis clinics, and mobile home parks all exist to service new products of our affluent, leisure oriented society.

What does this dramatic growth in services mean for marketers of services? First, more and more firms will enter service industries, seeking their bright promise of future growth. New firms will enter fast-growing fields such as electronic communications, legal and tax consulting, renting and leasing, and medical care [the recent growth of commercial (profit-oriented) hospitals is a good example]. Many established firms producing or marketing tangible goods have expanded strongly into services. Sears, Roebuck, a retailer, owns the nation's second-largest consumer insurance firm—Allstate. Gerber, a manufacturer of baby foods, recently introduced a life insurance plan for senior citizens. Without question, the service sector is becoming much more competitive.

Second, because competition is growing, service firms must make their marketing programs as effective as possible in order to capture and maintain a competitive edge. Thus, while the services sector enjoys strong growth, success here requires that services marketing become as creative and efficient as for tangible goods.

[6] Thayer C. Taylor, "Selling the Services Society," *Sales Management* (March 6, 1972), p. 23.
[7] Ibid.
[8] David J. Schwartz, *Marketing Today* (New York: Harcourt Brace Jovanovich, Inc., 1973), p. 534.

There are several reasons why the production efficiency in the services sector is not as high as for tangible goods, for example,[9]

1. The service firm tends to be smaller.
2. The service firm's operating costs are higher. Since automation and other labor-saving devices are more difficult to apply, the service firm must rely on less efficient human labor.
3. The service firm's marketing operations are less sophisticated in sales planning and training, marketing research, and other areas.[10]

Service firms will have to upgrade their marketing operations in the future. To do so, they must recognize the special nature of services and the particular needs and desires of their customers. Many of the same principles for successfully marketing products also apply to services marketing. But not all. Some important differences in services marketing and consumption must be recognized. We will now take a look at some important features of the service markets and then we will note some marketing strategy implications for this important sector.

Special Characteristics of Services

Figure 7.3 lists some of the features of services that are important in their marketing strategies.

Services are essentially *intangible*. Although the consumption of services may also include physical products (auto repair service can include *parts* as well as labor), the service that is bought involves providing certain customer benefits and *not* the transfer of ownership of a good.

Being intangible, services are difficult to mass produce; therefore, their performance tends to be *less standardized* than that of goods. A vacation tour or an educational course are examples. If performance is too variable, the seller's costs and the customer's dissatisfaction may both rise too high. Thus, Holiday Inns claim in their ads that customers will find "no surprises" at their motels. Yet many people want more personal treatment. Here, the marketer can gain by varying his services (hairstyling, for example) to match the customer's desires.

Services are *performed and consumed at the same time* (hairstyling or a bus ride) and are *highly perishable*. A bus ticket offers transportation from one place to another. A bus trip is consumed as it is offered. If the consumer misses the bus, the seat stays empty—the service and the sale are lost.

<hr/>

[9] See, for example, "Why Service Workers Are Less Productive," *Business Week*, November 14, 1964, p. 156; "Services Grow While the Quality Shrinks," *Business Week*, October 31, 1970, pp. 50–57.

[10] William R. George and Hiram C. Barksdale, "Marketing Activities in the Service Industries," *Journal of Marketing* (October, 1974), p. 65.

Figure 7.3   The Services Market: Characteristics and Marketing Strategies

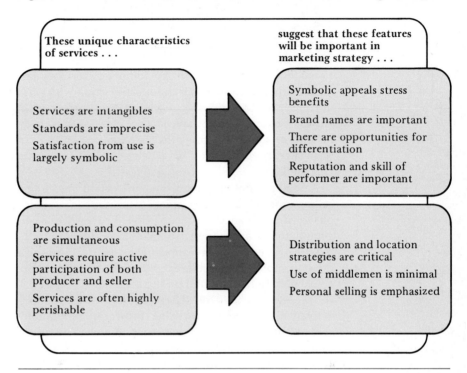

These unique characteristics
of services . . .

suggest that these features
will be important in
marketing strategy . . .

Services are intangibles

Standards are imprecise

Satisfaction from use is
largely symbolic

Symbolic appeals stress
benefits

Brand names are important

There are opportunities for
differentiation

Reputation and skill of
performer are important

Production and consumption
are simultaneous

Services require active
participation of both
producer and seller

Services are often highly
perishable

Distribution and location
strategies are critical

Use of middlemen is minimal

Personal selling is emphasized

Services, then, usually require the *active participation of both the buyer and the seller*. Thus service transactions at the *right time and place* are very important in satisfying both parties.

Marketing Strategies for Services

These above points about some of the unusual characteristics of services suggest that the following factors are important in marketing them:

1. Symbolic appeals to the customer's imagination that stress benefits.
2. Close buyer–seller contact.
3. Reputation and skill of seller.
4. Differentiation of services for unique customers.

Since services are intangible and are consumed as they are being performed, the marketer must appeal to the customer's imagination when he describes his service. The audio equipment dealer can demonstrate the appearance and sound of a stereo system. But the insurance agent must create an image in the prospect's mind of the economic security he will feel by buying a life insurance policy and the worries and hardships his family will face if he should die with inadequate coverage.

Since services are intangible, perishable, and consumed when performed, sellers will want to maintain close contact with customers throughout the buying decision process. Personal selling is often the most effective promotional tool in persuading, in "customizing" services, and in gathering immediate information on customer satisfaction with service benefits. The doctor–patient relationship before, during, and after surgery is an example. Advertising and promotion can also be very effective in symbolizing the benefits of services. Many other services, for example, professional football or theater, spend little on advertising because the media give them extensive free publicity.

A good reputation is even more important in selling services than in selling products because service features are intangible and are not easily observed in advance of consumption. The services of an auto repair shop, a symphony, or an airline are difficult to evaluate until they are consumed. Advice offered by an investment counselor, lawyer, or advertising agency often cannot easily be judged until long after the service is bought and consumed. In fact, reputation in professional services is so important that the professions have relied heavily on word-of-mouth promotion and have actively discouraged advertising. Protecting reputation may be only one reason for discouraging advertising, though. The rules and codes of conduct that regulate professions are now under attack by consumerist groups and anti-trust officials across the nation. Malpractice suits are increasing, and advertising restrictions and pricing practices, in particular, are being declared as anti-competitive.[11]

The service firm's reputation is based largely on the performer's skills. For the auto repair shop, the symphony, or the dental office, the personal abilities of the service performers provide the perceived benefits, establish the reputation, and determine the amount of repeat business.

The intangible, personal nature of many services offers much opportunity for the creative marketer to differentiate his service for various customers. Hairstyling, for example, is often highly "customized." Smaller service organizations may thrive on their flexibility in adjusting to their customer's wants. Taxi service is more flexible than bus service; a concert entertainer can adjust to audience mood, but a movie cannot. Again, marketers who wish to exploit this feature of services must stay in close touch with customers, symbolize service features, and maintain a strong reputation to assure buyers who can compare only while consuming the service.

[11] See, for example, "Closing in on the Professions," *Business Week*, October 27, 1975, pp. 106–8; "Court Voids State Ban on Drug Ads," *Richmond News Leader*, May 24, 1976, p. 1; "The Troubled Professions," *Business Week*, August 16, 1976, pp. 126–38.

PRODUCT LIFE CYCLE

Firms launch their new products hoping that they will grow and prosper for a long time. And many do. But any product's success changes over time. Eventually sales and profit growth will slow, level off, and then decline. Management then will place its bets on other hoped-for winners.

The sales history of a product is called the **product life cycle.** A complete cycle consists of several distinct stages in the product's life. Each stage offers distinct challenges and opportunities; each stage calls for different marketing strategies. Following the life cycle concept, marketers locate the product within a life cycle stage and develop and adjust marketing plans for each stage as the product evolves through its life cycle.

Stages in the Life Cycle

A product's sales history curve, shown in Figure 7.4, is divided into four stages: introduction, growth, maturity, and decline. The product's profit curve is also in Figure 7.4.

Introduction begins when the product is first brought to market. Sales are usually slow while demand is building among channel members. Heavy expenses for introduction often eliminate the possibility of profits at this time.

Figure 7.4   Stages in the Product Life Cycle

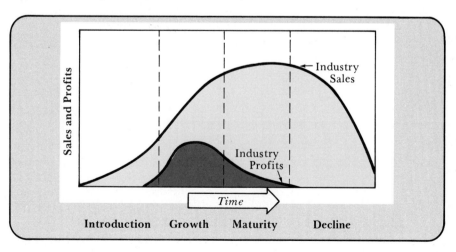

Introduction to Product Decisions

The *growth* stage is a period of rapid market acceptance. Since unit production costs may drop at this time, profits may improve sharply and reach their peak here.

During *maturity* the rate of sales growth slows. Since most buyers have acquired the product by now, much of the sales volume consists of repeat sales. Few new customers are trying the product. Also, competitors have entered the scene during the growth and maturity stages and they are battling for their share of the market. Since this competition may force prices down, promotion expenditures may have to be boosted in order to extend the product's life, which, in turn, will cause profits to fall.

During *decline* sales drift downward as consumers turn toward the newer products entering the markets. Profits continue to fall and may even disappear.

Figure 7.4 is a very general picture of the sales history of products over their life cycles. Not all products pass through this s-shaped sales curve. Within the life cycle of a class of products (such as subcompact autos), the sales curve of a *brand* may be very erratic as a result of specific competitive action or other environmental developments that particularly affect the brand. Sales of the Mazda rotary-engined sedan, for example, declined very suddenly when the energy crunch, dismal reports on the rotary's mileage, and high-mileage claims of competitors all combined to take their toll. The subcompact auto market as a whole was still enjoying strong growth at the time. Some firms are able to reverse declining sales for a time with an extra promotional "burst." Other new products may grow very rapidly to maturity, avoiding the typically slow start during the introductory phase. The "pet rock" fad is an example. This inexpensive novelty item introduced for the 1975 Christmas buying season caught on rapidly. Thanks to lots of publicity in the media, everyone talked about the pet rock; the product instantly became a household word. But like many a typical fad, pet rock sales declined just as suddenly once the gift-giving season passed and the novelty wore off.

Other products seem to go on virtually forever. Ivory soap, introduced in 1879, still shows no sign of dying out.

Why Products Move Through Life Cycles

Product life cycles, then, can be very erratic and difficult to predict. Since a product is not a living organism, we must be cautious in explaining its sales by using a life cycle analogy. A product's life expectancy is not innate, but it is controlled by several factors, for example,

1. Technological advances that bring better products to the market.
2. Political, legal, and other environmental developments.
3. Management decisions on committing its resources to products.
4. Market demand trends and product diffusion rates.

These forces are worth noting further. The product's rate of acceptance in the market (its diffusion rate) is especially important and will be explored in some detail.

Better Technology and Products

Improved technology can make a product obsolete overnight. Thanks to advances in solid-state electronics, the pocket calculator is making the engineer's slide rule a collector's item. Competitors very quickly adopt the new technology when they see that the market takes an interest, for example, as happened in the pocket calculator and digital watch industries. Other electronic products like microwave ovens took years to move into the growth stage. Apparently most consumers who already own modern electric or gas ovens felt that the added conveniences of microwave ovens were not worth their high prices.

Legal, political, and other environmental forces can delay a product's introduction or kill it altogether. As of this writing, the SST still languishes in its very unprofitable introductory stage, plagued by environmental noise problems and high operating costs in an energy conscious market. Ralph Nader's book, *Unsafe at Any Speed,* shoved the Corvair into rapid sales decline. Some artificial sweeteners, red dye No. 2, and many other products declared hazardous to health have been forced off the market despite their popularity.

Management actions, of course, affect product life cycles. Firms may spend heavily to introduce a new product or to boost sales of an ailing product. Or they may stop spending resources altogether on failing products and put the resources saved behind more promising items. We will discuss these and other strategies for managing products over their life cycles in more detail in the following chapter.

MARKET DEMAND AND NEW PRODUCT DIFFUSION

Product life cycles reflect consumer buying decisions. Since consumer influence is so important, we will discuss it in some detail below.

As the product life cycle curve illustrates, sales of most products grow slowly at first and then they are followed by a rapid expansion before they eventually level off. But why does the sales curve take this shape? Apparently because even if a new product is placed on the market in great quantities, not everyone is eager to rush right in and try it. Many people have developed strong purchasing and consumption patterns and they also resist change.

In a product's introductory stage only a few people (consumer innovators) will try the product and experiment with it. Others will wait for more in-

Figure 7.5   The Diffusion Pattern and Characteristics of Adopter Categories

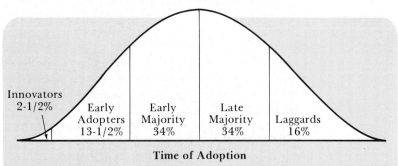

Innovators	Are venturesome; adopt new products without efforts of marketing managers; may not influence later adopters.
Early Adopters	Enjoy respect as opinion leaders in community; adopt early during introduction and growth stages of life cycle, but with some discretion. Important to new-product marketers.
Early Majority	Early majority and late majority make up the mass market. Early majority are deliberative; often seek opinions of early adopters before trying innovation.
Late Majority	Skeptical buyers; adopt only after innovation is well-endorsed; buy when product has moved into maturity stage.
Laggards	Tradition-bound; reluctant to change; they may adopt, if at all, only after innovation is mature or on its way out.

formation before buying. Often these people rely on the experiences of the early buyers. If word of mouth is favorable, sales will take off. Some will buy only after the product is well accepted.

This pattern of new product acceptance is so common that a theory has been developed to explain it. This theory is called the **diffusion process** theory. The diffusion of innovations refers to "the spread of an idea from its source of invention or creation to its ultimate users or adopters."[12] Apparently, the eventual adopters of a new idea or product can be grouped into five categories ranging from innovators to laggards, as shown in Figure 7.5. The proportions of adopters in each category approximate the typical bell-shaped or normal curve (notice the similarity to the product life cycle curve).

[12] Everett M. Rogers, *Diffusion of Innovations* (New York: Free Press, 1962).

Innovators and early adopters are few compared with the early and late majority groups (the mass market for the product). But these early buyers are extremely important to the marketer for several reasons. First, these first buyers serve as a test market. Their reactions to the new product offer valuable clues to adjusting marketing strategy. Second, early buyers frequently serve as opinion leaders. Since they typically are experienced users of specific products, their advice is eagerly sought by less experienced buyers. For instance, tennis and scuba diving instructors frequently give word-of-mouth advice on buying specialized equipment. Realizing the influence these people have, firms selling specialized equipment often seek product endorsements from well-known sports superstars or coaches. Billie Jean King (Bancroft tennis gear) and Jack Nicklaus (McGregor golfing equipment and sportswear) are highly influential, even though their influence is through mass media, not face-to-face, and even though audiences realize that they are paid well for endorsements.

IDENTIFYING INNOVATORS AND INFLUENCERS

Social scientists, studying innovators in everything from birth control procedures to clothing fashions, have established some general characteristics of innovators. In demographic terms, innovators tend to be younger, better-educated, more affluent, and higher in social status. Often, they have higher aspirations, are more mobile and venturesome, and rely more on impersonal information sources than do later adopters. Innovators for one product may not necessarily be innovators for others. Their influence seems to be limited to products for which they have particular knowledge. Innovators may have little direct influence on other buyers. Often their product needs are highly specialized and many of their purchases are experimental. If the innovation does not prove successful, the product expires during the introductory stage. Also, innovators may have little direct word-of-mouth contact with their imitators and little mass media exposure. Therefore, it may be the next group, the early adopters, who pick up the idea from innovators and influence the larger markets. Levi's, for instance, were created in the mid-1800's from denim tent canvas for California gold miners searching for a more rugged material. Over a century later young people made denim a fashion hit. Pants, jogging suits, Vibram-soled climbing boots, and down-filled outerwear originally were highly functional products used for years by athletes and outdoorsmen. All of these products became hot fashion items in the 1970's when certain fashion-conscious young people started wearing them on college campuses.

In modern markets, youth are highly influential in fashions of all types —in casual clothing, automobiles, music, and many other products. More traditionally, fashions often originate among upper socioeconomic classes and then "trickle down" to the mass markets. Designer clothing, jewelry, and home furnishings are examples. But innovations may arise at all social levels and spread across, up, or down social strata.

Using Word-of-Mouth Influence to Introduce New Products

As we have seen, early users may exert a powerful influence on the buying decisions of people. Many firms attempt to design their marketing campaigns in order to take advantage of and encourage word-of-mouth influence. The beauty industry has long believed that a small handful of Americans set the trends for cosmetic buyers. Elizabeth Arden's Chloe fragrance relied on a very few people ("700 rich, thin women") to play Pied Piper to millions of other women.[13] Similarly, R. J. Reynolds Tobacco Company launched its promotional campaign for NOW cigarettes by mailing samples to young women in wealthy urban and suburban New York residential areas. Since the cigarette was positioned as a luxury brand, the firm assumed that this tiny market could be very effective in influencing thousands of other women to try it.[14]

Product Characteristics Influencing the Diffusion Rate

For years the government of India has struggled to gain adoption of modern family planning methods among its population. Using clever promotion, the Wham-O Toy Company saw its hula hoops and Frisbees become national fads within a few months. Although many factors account for these vast differences in adoption rates and levels, the characteristics of the innovations themselves clearly have a lot to do with their acceptance rates. Five general characteristics of innovations are believed to influence the product's adoption rate and the eventual level of acceptance: its relative advantage, compatibility, complexity, trialability, and communicability (see Figure 7.6).

The greater the innovation's *relative advantage*—the degree to which it appears superior to previous ideas—the quicker it will be adopted and the greater its eventual acceptance level (remember our pocket calculator and microwave oven examples). Relative advantages could be lower price, added convenience or ease of use, or many other factors.

The innovation's *compatibility*—its degree of consistency with the adopter's current beliefs and experiences—influences its acceptance rate and acceptance level.

Complexity is also important. The more difficult a product is to understand or use, the longer it takes consumers to accept it, and the lower its acceptance level.

[13] Curt Schlier, "Can High-Fashion Sampling Sell Cigarettes?" *Product Management* (October, 1976), p. 25.
[14] Ibid.

Figure 7.6   New Product Characteristics Affecting Its Rate of Adoption and Level of Acceptance

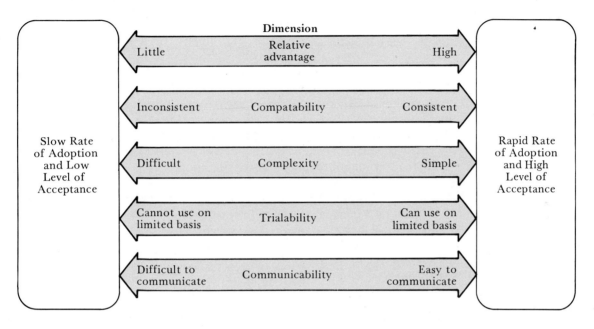

The innovation's *trialability* is the extent to which the product may be used on a limited basis. Consumers find it less risky to try out a new product or service by either sampling it on a trial basis or buying it with return privileges than to take the financial or social risk of buying something that completely fails to satisfy.

Finally, *communicability* of the innovation is important. The more visible its benefits in social situations, or the more readily it can be described or demonstrated, the faster the product's rate of adoption and the greater its ultimate acceptance level.

Frozen concentrated orange juice is a good example of a product whose characteristics allowed rapid adoption and a high level of acceptance. Its convenience advantages were apparent (ease of preparation and storage): It could be stored frozen, then mixed with water and served just like fresh or canned juice; it was compatible with other frozen foods the household was used to buying and serving; it could be bought one can at a time for inexpensive sampling; and its benefits were easily demonstrated to others.

Electronic banking through automatic bank tellers (using plastic credit cards instead of personal checks) was to be a significant achievement in customer convenience as soon as the technology for it was perfected. The

Introduction to Product Decisions

technology was perfected, making electronic banking a reality, but gaining customer acceptance has been unexpectedly difficult. Now it appears that the promised revolution in electronic banking may not come.[15] Our list of product characteristics may suggest why. For one, the relative advantages are not high. Although electronic banking promises greater ease in making deposits, withdrawals, and payments, many bank customers believe that writing checks is already convenient. Also, people fear losing control of their money, security, and privacy with computerized banking. Many customers unfamiliar with computers hesitate to use automatic teller machines. Trialability is also a problem. It is difficult to show consumers its convenience and cost advantages without switching completely to the new system. All of these product characteristics make it very difficult to gain adoptions of electronic banking systems.

The five product characteristics and their examples suggest some marketing approaches for improving the diffusion rate and level of acceptance for new products. Relative advantages must be identified and stressed in promotions. Product complexity and compatibility with existing products and usage patterns should be measured. For instance, soy protein substitutes for meat products, such as artificial bacon, are low in chloresterol and saturated fats, keep better, closely duplicate the real thing in taste, and the price is right. Yet, soy beans are not a well-known consumer food product. Therefore, marketers are careful to tie in the product with familiar and acceptable symbols of real bacon such as brand (Morningstar Farms), appearance (produced in strips and having the texture, color, and taste of bacon), and cooking method. Advertising stresses its close similarity to bacon. Thus, consumers can substitute the artificial product with little disruption of their shopping, cooking, and serving routines.

SUMMARY

Organizations that think of their products in terms of expected customer benefits are in tune with their markets. These firms are in a position to adjust products and product extensions—packaging, branding, servicing, etc. —to customer requirements. In this chapter we developed several product concepts to clarify our thinking about product marketing.

Product classifications offer some help in thinking generally about marketing strategies for matching products to market needs. One useful system classifies goods according to how customers perceive and buy products. Convenience, shopping, specialty, and unsought goods reflect distinct differences in customer shopping effort and product loyalty. Although a particular good or service may not fit neatly into one of these classifications, classifying products this way will stimulate thinking about basic product strategy. The industrial goods classification system, widely used in business, also reflects how customers view industrial products and also helps marketers think about industrial products in an orderly way.

[15] "Electronic Banking: A Retreat From the Cashless Society," *Business Week*, April 18, 1977, pp. 80–90.

Products also include services. Today, nearly half of all personal spending is for services, reflecting the more affluent, complex life-styles of today's organizations and consumers. Services marketing offers considerable challenge as well as promising opportunities for growth. Services are intangible, often nonstandardized, and frequently consumed at the time of purchase. Thus, marketers of services should stress the symbolic benefits of the services, maintain close contact with their customers, and emphasize reputation and performance skills.

A firm's products move through a life cycle of introduction, growth, maturity, and decline. Competition, technological advances, changing market tastes and preferences, and legal and political factors all contribute to management decisions about products. These forces, and the nature of the product itself, interact to make it difficult to predict sales and profits throughout the product's life cycle. But the life cycle concept can help product managers anticipate change and adjust their marketing mix to reflect changes in markets, competition, and costs.

The product diffusion process helps explain how products become accepted in the marketplace. People and organizations differ in their willingness to adopt new ideas and products. Their influence on other potential adopters also varies. Personal influence exerts a powerful force in the rate and extent of product adoptions. Modern marketers attempt to measure personal influence and perhaps incorporate the personal communications between early users and followers as part of their marketing strategies.

The next chapter will examine the marketing tasks of developing and introducing new products, managing existing products, and phasing out declining products in terms of the life cycle concept. Product extension strategies of branding and packaging will also be discussed.

QUESTIONS

1. Why should services be included in the definition of product?
2. A typewriter can be classified as both an industrial good and a consumer good. Why? Does this mean that the classification schemes have no value to the marketer?
3. You view a hamburger sandwich as a convenience good; your friend sees it as a shopping good. Does it matter to the marketer which classification is chosen?
4. Compare the typical marketing mix for an unsought good with the typical mix for a specialty good.
5. Compare the typical marketing mix for installations with the typical mix for component parts.

Introduction to Product Decisions

6. Why might the life cycle for one product be so much shorter than for another product?

7. Why do profits often peak earlier and decline faster than sales during the life cycle of a product?

8. What is the value of the life cycle concept to the product manager?

9. Why is the services market growing strongly? In comparison to the sales growth of products, is this growth likely to continue or fall off over the next several decades?

10. Using the general statements on the characteristics of services and their marketing requirements, compare marketing strategies for a rock concert (service) with strategies for marketing a bicycle (product). How different are your strategies? How similar? Why?

11. Innovators and influencers (opinion leaders) are not necessarily the same people. Explain.

12. What are the general characteristics of opinion leaders? Are opinion leaders in one product class likely to be influencers for very different classes of products?

13. Several years ago, CB radio sales mushroomed almost overnight. Explain why this new product diffused so rapidly. Did word-of-mouth influence and product features determine its rate of acceptance?

GLOSSARY

Consumer Goods: goods and services intended for use by the ultimate consumer

Convenience Goods: goods and services that consumers want to buy quickly and with little effort; staple, impulse, and emergency goods are convenience goods

Diffusion Process: the spread of a new idea or product from its source to its ultimate adopters

Derived Demand: a condition in which the demand for one product is generated (derived) from the demand for some other product

Extended Product: the basic product with its packaging, branding, services, and other features that provide its unique benefits

Industrial Goods: products bought by organizations for resale or for producing other goods or services

Product: a combination of physical attributes, services, and symbols designed to supply certain expected benefits to users

Product Life Cycle: the sales history of a product measured from its point of market introduction to its removal from the market; often classified into introduction, growth, maturity, and decline stages

Services: intangible activities that provide benefits when marketed to users; intangible activities that are *extensions* of products only, such as after-sale delivery, would not be included separately as services

Shopping Goods: goods and services that consumers are willing to examine and compare before buying

Specialty Goods: goods and services that are highly preferred; consumers do not readily accept substitutes for them and they make unusual efforts to acquire them

Unsought Goods: goods and services that are unknown or otherwise not wanted; people do not seek them out

CASES

Case 1: Quik-Stop, Inc.

Quik-Stop, Inc. is a successful franchise organization of 1,200 convenience food stores in over 30 states. The firm has enjoyed remarkable growth in sales and profits over the past 10 years. Its stores are located on high-traffic streets and highways near fast-growing residential areas. While their products can also be found in supermarkets, Quik-Stop stores offer more convenient locations and store hours, quick self-service shopping, and no-wait checkout. The average shopping transaction takes less than 3 minutes. The stores feature prepackaged, nationally branded food and nonfood products that people know and trust, and they stock mostly staples and impulse items that turn over quickly and require little selling effort. Their biggest-selling items are bread and milk, beer, cigarettes, soft drinks, and snack items.

The firm is constantly adding new items to its product lines, especially ready-to-eat snacks like frozen drinks, ice cream, coffee, and hot sandwiches. Several years ago Quik-Stop took advantage of an opportunity to buy out a manufacturer of high-quality chocolates, the Valencia Confections Company. Valencia had been manufacturing boxed chocolates under its label for many years and sold them in prestigious specialty shops and selected department stores throughout the country. Quik-Stop knew that its 1,200 stores reached a wide market for candy and felt the prestige image of Valencia chocolates would provide added benefits to Quik-Stop.

Specially designed lighted display cases of Valencia chocolates were placed on checkout counters in most of the Quik-Stop stores. Quik-Stop's marketing executives hoped that these displays would allow Valencia chocolates rapidly to achieve the high sales volume necessary for success in a convenience food store.

But sales were disappointing. After the first year the chocolates had not achieved the minimum sales turnover rate. Not only were the chocolate displays taking up valuable selling space, but the low turnover of inventory meant that it was difficult to keep chocolates fresh at all times.

Quik-Stop called a meeting to discuss the problem. During the meeting one executive pointed out that the new Valencia chocolate display had not been promoted with banners or window displays and that the chocolates had not been featured in store advertising. The product simply needed more time to attract attention, he argued. The marketing research director proposed that a quick customer and dealer survey be taken before making any decisions. She thought that the survey should measure (1) customer awareness of Valencia chocolates in Quik-Stop stores, (2) how often customers buy fancy chocolates and for what occasions, and (3) how important were brand, price, eye appeal, and other factors in their buying decisions. She also wanted to measure dealer attitudes and opinions. The marketing research director pointed out that more research should have been done before putting Valencia chocolates in their stores, since it was not apparent that people would buy expensive chocolates in convenience food stores.

Top management apparently decided that the acquisition had been a mistake and voted to phase out Valencia chocolates from Quik-Stop stores and to consider selling their chocolate business.

1. Does the consumer goods classification system offer Quik-Stop management any insights into this problem?
2. What specific questions and comments can you offer?

Case 2: The Woodshop

Alfred and Arlo were close friends who shared a common interest in wood-carving and building furniture. Recently they decided to combine their professional experience and training with their love for woodcraft by opening a woodcraft shop for do-it-yourself amateurs. Alfred taught industrial technology courses at the local community college, while Arlo was presently the sales manager for a wholesale hardware and building supply house.

Each was a serious hobbyist who spent his woodworking hours in a well-equipped basement full of expensive benches, power tools, and woods. Alfred knew that woodworking was a booming hobby. In the past three years he had taught several courses in cabinetry, woodcarving, and furniture refinishing at the college and found that the courses attracted people of all ages and occupations. But he agreed with Arlo that the more elaborate power equipment and hand tools were very costly, and that furniture making, especially, consumed a lot of space, making it difficult for many people to really get into woodcrafting. Also, it was difficult to find in local lumberyards a good selection of the more exotic and expensive woods that advanced hobbyists liked to use. Most important, skilled instruction was very helpful to hobbyists who wanted to develop their abilities to the fullest. So The Woodshop seemed a good prospect for filling the needs of the hobbyist.

The Woodshop would offer a complete service for the woodworking enthusiast. A large shop would be well-equipped with the latest benches and tools for rent. Along with woodworking equipment, a complete line of woods, glues, finishes, and other materials would be sold. Finally, classes in all phases of woodcrafting would be offered on a regular basis to encourage people to use the facility and improve their skills. Not only would the shop provide an alternative to buying the expensive equipment and finding the space needed for many woodworking projects, it would offer an environment where woodworking enthusiasts could meet, share experiences, and learn together.

Alfred and Arlo thought that their idea was basically sound. But with only a small budget for advertising, they realized that they would have to build a steady customer base in a short time if their innovative venture was to be successful. They hoped that if they could attract the right people at the start, get them to try out their services, and impress them with the shop, that favorable word-of-mouth would solve their promotion problems. But they were not sure just who to seek out initially or how to encourage favorable word-of-mouth advertising. In fact, they wondered just how difficult or simple it might be to educate the beginning amateur about The Woodshop's concept and to encourage them to try its services.

1. How might favorable word-of-mouth be encouraged by The Woodshop?
2. Do the types of services The Woodshop offers lend themselves well to word-of-mouth promotion, and is rapid growth of The Woodshop likely?

Making Product Decisions

After you finish this chapter, you should be able to answer the following questions:

1. What are the tradeoffs that the organization must consider in choosing among market segmentation and concentrated and undifferentiated marketing strategies?

2. What is the product mix? Can you describe a product mix in terms of its width, depth, and consistency?

3. What factors explain the high failure rate of new products? What can the firm do to reduce the rate of new-product failure?

4. What types of organizational structures have been created to develop new products? What are the distinguishing features of each type?

5. What are some marketing strategies for extending the product's life cycle?

6. What are the major benefits of a formal product elimination program? What series of steps should be followed in a product elimination program?

7. What factors are important in choosing whether or not to establish a brand name for a product? In choosing whether to use a family brand or an individual brand for a product?

8. What are the marketing functions of packaging? Why are packaging decisions becoming more important to the firm?

INTRODUCTION

As noted in Chapter 7, the purpose of marketing strategy is to generate a satisfactory exchange between the organization and its customers. The key element in exchange is the product offer, and the key marketing task in the exchange process is matching product offerings to customer needs in order to achieve mutually satisfying exchanges.

We noted also that what consumers are seeking, and what companies thus must offer, is the totality of benefits achieved through shopping for and consuming the product offer. Not only the physical product, but also the packaging, financing, delivery, customer advice, and before-sale and after-sale services help create the total benefits in the product offer. All of these factors, and others, make up the total product, and all aid in successful matching.

Customers have certain *expectations* about the products they want at any given time. A prospective customer expects that the product will contribute to his desired life-style to some extent. This expectation will lead to product trial, assuming that the consumer is able to locate and can afford the product. But product trial does not automatically mean that the product will be *repurchased*. If the product actually meets the minimum expectations and if the consumer is willing to fit it into his life-style, then repeat purchase is likely. Many first-time customers, of course, do not rebuy if they don't like the product, if they find a better one, or if their wants change.

Usually, only a few buyers find that their expectations are matched totally and repeatedly by the same product. Many other customers have much less brand loyalty and buy a given brand only rarely.

From the marketer's point of view, it is useful to think of the market for any product as being subdivided into three customer groups: core customers, fringe customers, and indifferent customers.

Core customers are those whose product expectations are very closely matched by the perceived characteristics of an available product alternative. The product is just what they want. Core customers are highly brand loyal, and they are not swayed by price adjustments, heavy competitive promotions, or other inducements. They will be among the first to adopt and the last to abandon a product.

Fringe customers perceive the product as somewhat in line with their expectations, but not so much as core customers. Fringe customers will be more cautious about adopting, price-sensitive, and less loyal. Other competing brands might be tried and adopted if the price of this one increases too much or a better product offer comes along.

Indifferent customers are those whose expectations are met only marginally by this product. Other products are just as likely to be chosen. Here is the least loyal customer, the toughest to win and keep. Since the product in question is only marginally satisfactory, this customer will switch loyalties with any perceived advantage in price, brand image, or other features.[1]

MATCHING PRODUCTS WITH MARKETS

One of the important questions the marketer must answer in managing the product/service mix is how carefully or closely must product specifications be matched with the customer's wants? We can tie in the concepts of the core, fringe, and indifferent markets with the concepts of segmentation and undifferentiated marketing strategy options developed in Chapter 2 to help answer this question. There we discussed three possible options in choosing target markets and marketing mixes (including product mix): (1) undifferentiated marketing, (2) concentrated marketing, and (3) market segmentation.

A **market segmentation strategy** assumes that there are a number of customer segments and that the firm essentially aims at the core customers of various segments with distinctive product offerings. Fringe and indifferent customers are welcomed, too, but the firm is less concerned with them.

Concentrated marketing strategy develops a very limited product offering for core customers in one or a very few segments of the total market.

In an **undifferentiated strategy,** the firm offers a single product to all three sectors—core, fringe, and indifferent markets—rather than match precisely the expected benefits of certain core customers.

As we noted in Chapter 2, the marketer must consider trade-offs when he chooses the degree of matching that is best for the firm. Philosophically, the ideal approach is to match core market perceptions very closely. High customer satisfaction provides strong loyalty and thus relative immunity from competition. By contrast, an undifferentiated strategy, in its attempts to satisfy nearly everyone (core, fringe, and indifferent customers), may result in imperfect matching with anyone. The firm will struggle to stay ahead of competitors who may be able to capture the less loyal customers quickly. Heavy promotion expenditures and price cuts will be needed in order to attract customers beyond the core market.

[1] Thomas A. Staudt, Donald A. Taylor, and Donald J. Bowersox, *A Managerial Introduction to Marketing*, 3rd ed. (Englewood Cliffs, N.J.: Prentice-Hall, Inc., 1976), p. 205.

But as noted in Chapter 2, market segmentation can also be costly. Uniquely designed marketing mixes may pile up inefficiencies in production, distribution, and advertising. And if the core market is too small to serve efficiently, the firm may also have to pursue fringe customers.

The Product Mix

Insurance firms handle dozens of different policies. Ringling Brothers Circus shuttles numerous acts in and out of three rings during a single performance. Modern supermarkets may offer well over 10,000 different items, while Sears, Roebuck displays several hundred thousand items in its catalogs. The total composite of all products offered by a particular organization is its product mix. The **product mix** is made up of product lines and product items. A **product line** is a group of products that are closely related in some way: They meet similar customer needs, are marketed together, are distributed through common channels, or are otherwise related for marketing reasons. A **product item** is a specific member of a product line. A Chevrolet K-5 Blazer truck is a product item; Chevrolet's trucks are a product line; Chevrolet's lines of trucks, passenger cars, recreational vehicles, accessories, and replacement parts are its product mix.

The product mix has width, depth, and consistency.[2] The **width** of a product mix refers to the number of different product lines offered by the organization. The **depth** (or *assortment*) of a product mix describes the number of separate product items within each product line. A steak house might offer a dozen different steaks but only one or two seafood items. **Consistency** refers to the relatedness of product lines in production requirements, common distribution channels, customers, or other ways. Cars, trucks, and diesel engines are closely related product lines in General Motors Corporation; City Investing Company's water heaters, magazine printing, insurance, and motel chain show little product mix consistency.

The relationships among these three dimensions of the product mix are shown in Figure 8-1. The organization will consider width, depth, and consistency in matching product items and lines with market opportunities and goals. Ordinarily, decisions involving product mix width and consistency are more crucial than decisions on how many different items should be offered in a product line. A soft-drink bottler could add new flavors of soda (greater depth) to the current line rather easily. But decisions to add product lines (greater width) by packaging candy or pretzels would mean substantial investments in plant and equipment and marketing support. Adding a line of shoes would be inconsistent with the bottler's markets, production facilities and skills, customer image, and trade channels. In fact, alterations in corporate goals and policies would be required as the firm moved in these new directions.

[2] Philip Kotler, *Marketing Management*, 3rd ed. (Englewood Cliffs, N.J.: Prentice-Hall, Inc., 1976), p. 185.

Making Product Decisions

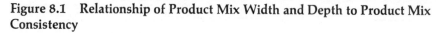

Figure 8.1   Relationship of Product Mix Width and Depth to Product Mix Consistency

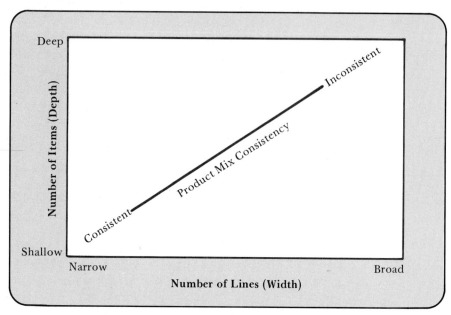

Continual Review and Adjustment Needed

In response to continuous change in the organization's environment, marketers should analyze product lines and items for their current and potential contributions to the total product mix. At any one point in time, the firm that has multiple products will have a product mix that Drucker describes as follows:[3]

1. Tomorrow's breadwinners—new products, or improved present products.
2. Today's breadwinners—current contributors, but yesterday's innovative products.
3. "Repairables"—products capable of contributing if drastic changes are made.
4. Yesterday's breadwinners—once high-volume products, but now sold in small orders as special deals, etc.

[3] Peter Drucker, "Managing for Business Effectiveness," *Harvard Business Review* (May–June, 1963), p. 59.

Marketing Mix Decisions

5. "Also-rans"—yesterday's high hopes; not outright failures, but never quite made it, and probably won't.

A multi-product firm has a balance of products among these types. The task is to keep this balance a healthy one. Too many "today's" and "yesterday's breadwinners" spell trouble ahead. Putting everything into "tomorrow's breadwinners" promises a rosy future, but it is tough on today's sales and profits. Maintaining a productive balance of products requires careful and constant attention to current products and their changing environment. And it also demands that the organization emphasize product innovation.

IMPORTANCE OF NEW PRODUCTS

United Telecom declares in its advertising, "When you're through innovating, you're through." From the Polaroid camera and the Xerox process to corn flakes and bubble gum, product innovation has been the engine that powers companies to success.

There are many ways to innovate in the product mix. The manufacturer may design new or improved products or create new uses for existing products. A retailer may create new merchandise lines—drugstores abandoned soda fountains and added toys, clothing, and small appliances; Sears department stores opened charm schools and bike repair shops, and offered a frozen food home delivery service.

A *new product* will be defined here as any product new to the organization. This would include completely new products, new versions of current products, products that duplicate those offered by competitors, products produced internally, or products bought elsewhere—any product that adds something new to the organization's product mix.

FORCES INFLUENCING NEW PRODUCT DEVELOPMENT

The rewards of new products spur impressive efforts to develop them. Our affluent, growth-oriented economy has encouraged firms in the United States to invest over $20 billion annually in new product development. In 1976 companies listed on the New York Stock Exchange introduced nearly 6,000 significant new products. The rewards of new product development can be tremendous, but the costs are high and so is the risk of failure.

GI Joe and the Six Million Dollar Man made it big in the $175 million market for male toy dolls, but Steve Scout fizzled out. Apparently Steve didn't stir strong enough fantasies of high adventure in the minds of youngsters. Even highly successful, marketing-oriented companies like Procter and Gamble are not immune to new-product failure; of the 16 brands it test marketed in the last decade, 7 failed to win general distribu-

Figure 8.2 A Dozen Examples of New Product Failures

Bricklin sports car
Corfam synthetic leather
Cue toothpaste
Edsel automobile
Frost 8/80 "white" whiskey
Fruit Float canned gelatin dessert
Listerine toothpaste
Quadraphonic sound equipment
Stardust dry bleach
Softswirl instant pudding
Steve Scout toy doll
Tramps cigarettes

tion.[4] The list of well-known product failures is impressively long (see Figure 8.2, for example).

Although it is difficult to measure the rate of new product failure accurately, one authority suggests that about 70% of test-marketed brands of consumer products are not expanded nationally and others either are soon withdrawn or never pay back their original investments.[5] Whatever the exact failure rate, marketers agree that it is much too high and it is apparently not dropping.

The statistics on current failure rates are sobering enough, but a number of factors makes it increasingly difficult to succeed with new products.

Social and Legal Pressures

Spurred by the consumer movement and growing concerns for the environment, government is demanding that new products meet much more stringent criteria. Products must be tested for safety and for ecologically harmful side effects and they must meet stricter requirements in labeling and advertising. Better products may result, but development costs and risks go up.

[4] Peter Vanderwicken, "P&G's Secret Ingredient," *Fortune*, July, 1974, pp. 75–79, 164–66.
[5] J. Hugh Davidson, "Why Most New Consumer Brands Fail," *Harvard Business Review* (March–April, 1976), p. 117.

Marketing Mix Decisions

Longer Developmental Process

Products are staying longer in research and development today. Some product clearances are stretching out to six or eight years or more in order to meet regulations. As a result, fewer products make it to the market, so those that do must pay back their investment much earlier than before.[6]

Shorter Product Life Cycles

Because of faster competitive entry, rapid technological obsolescence, and growing diversity in consumer tastes and life-styles, new products hit their peak and decline more rapidly. A. C. Nielsen believes that 85% of all new consumer brands can expect less than three years of success before their market shares decline rapidly. Product life cycles may be from 40% to 60% shorter than ten years ago.[7] This means a much shorter time in which to recover the growing development costs.

Costly New Product Development Process

Many product ideas must be generated and screened in order to wind up with a few winners. A study of the idea screening and development process for one successful consumer products firm showed that about 600 new ideas must be considered before finally arriving at 30 successful products (see Fig. 8.3).

Shortages, Inflation, and Recession

Recent economic developments have put the squeeze on new products. Products that have potential market appeal have been dropped because the supply of ingredients or packaging materials could not be guaranteed. In other cases, the threat of rapid cost inflation caused management to shy away from introducing new items whose price might not be controllable. These changing costs and risks are forcing some changes in new product development.

Some firms are becoming more conservative and less innovative in developing products. They are putting more effort into redesigning existing products and are seeking new uses for them. One reason is to avoid totally new products that would switch them into costly new materials or questionable sources of supply.[8]

Other firms choose a follow-the-leader strategy, believing that the costs and risks of innovating are too high. Gillette entered the stainless steel razor blade market after it was developed by Wilkinson and captured the

---

[6] "The Breakdown of U.S. Innovation," *Business Week*, February 16, 1976, pp. 56–58.
[7] Ibid., p. 57.
[8] "The Two-Way Squeeze on New Products," *Business Week*, August 10, 1974, pp. 130–32.

Making Product Decisions

Figure 8.3 New Product Mortality in One Major Company

New Product Development Stage	Cost	
Screening and Analysis:		
more than 600 new product ideas	Technical research	$ 30 million
(during a recent, typical 10-year period)	Marketing research	46 million
	Total	$ 76 million
↓ resulting in		
Development:		
118 concepts, of which 31 were eliminated,	Technical research	$ 5 million
at a cost of	Marketing research	5 million
	Capital investment	1 million
↓ allowing	Total	$ 11 million
Test Marketing:		
of the 87 products tested, 47 failed	Total	$156 million*
↓ leaving		

Commercialization:
40 products introduced into the market
Result:
10 commercial failures and 30 successful
products, representing a total investment of $243 million

* This figure was not decomposed.

From Ben M. Enis, *Marketing Principles*, 2nd ed. (Santa Monica, Calif.: Goodyear, 1977), p. 328. Based on data from A. S. Clausi, vice-president for Corporate Research, General Foods Corporation, reported in "The Rebuilding Job at General Foods," *Business Week*, August 25, 1973, p. 50.

lion's share. BIC Pen did the same thing to Gillette's Cricket disposable lighter. Nevertheless, the follow-the-leader approach is dangerous. "Me-too" or "me-three" brands that have no distinct price or performance advantages usually are market failures. They can't attract customers from entrenched products.

Cautious product developers are building in more exacting standards for sales, market share, and profits. Yet other firms are cutting corners wherever they can and are skipping test markets in order to beat the competition to the profitable stage of the shrinking product life cycle.

Today, top management is more involved in new product development. Because risks and costs are escalating, top management is demanding more orderly and effective new product development processes, and it is changing organization structures in order to improve the development process. We will explore both of these trends in more detail in the following sections.

DEVELOPING AND INTRODUCING NEW PRODUCTS

Marketing misfires can be extremely expensive for a firm. Less obvious, but perhaps even more important, good ideas may fail to be developed into successful products, either because the idea is dropped prematurely or the product development is faulty. Either way, the push is on marketing management to devise efficient ways to encourage good product ideas and to eliminate bad ones before they pile up unnecessary costs.

Although the payoff can be high in the new products game, the stakes are being raised. New products represent a considerable investment for the firm. Therefore, it is worthwhile to consider the formal process of new product development.

Although there is no single process that all firms follow, the general procedure for new product development consists of several stages through which innovations will flow from the idea stage to the marketplace. At each stage, key management people are responsible for deciding whether to (1) move on to the next stage, (2) abandon the idea or product, or (3) shelve the idea while seeking more information.

The general stages are included in Figure 8.4 where a general indication of new product development time and money taken by each step is also provided.

Idea Generation

New products start out as ideas. Product ideas can come from anywhere. The firm's new product teams, research laboratories, employees, customers, channel members, ad agencies, government, or competitors may provide ideas that lead to new products. Good ideas can be discovered by chance or from customer analysis. Given the competitiveness of the marketplace and the high cost of product development, the organization's **idea generation** should be purposeful, not just happenstance. Studies during the past ten years have shown that from 70% to 80% of all *successful* innovations were results of market need instead of "pure invention."[9]

[9] "The Decline and Comeback of New Product Introductions," *The Nielsen Researcher*, No. 5 (1975), p. 7, summarizes studies done by MIT's Sloan School of Management.

Figure 8.4 Stages in New Product Development

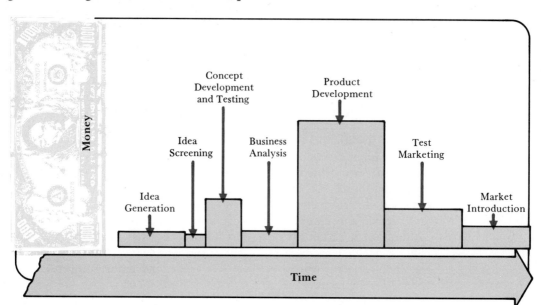

Many firms use checklists, "brainstorming" sessions, and other techniques to generate a pool of ideas.[10] The purpose at this stage is to encourage ideas, not criticize them. That comes in the next stage, idea screening.

Idea Screening

This is the first of several screening stages, the purpose of which is to reduce the pool of ideas. Most ideas will be rejected in early screening because they lack customer appeal (market potential), are too costly, may have negative effects on society, or are inappropriate to the firm's goals and resources. Screening here is not based on extensive product or market analysis. In fact, the product itself usually has not been designed. Checklists or other rating devices may help in deciding whether or not the idea can reach the minimum requirements of any innovation. (Figure 8.5 is a checklist for rating product ideas.)

Concept Development and Testing

The idea now becomes a concrete proposal that is examined for production feasibility and market acceptance. **Concept development** means transform-

[10] Kotler, ibid., pp. 201–05.

Figure 8.5   Checklist for Rating Product Ideas

	Rating			
	Exceptional	Good	Marginal	Poor
Sales volume	X			
Market leadership	X			
Strength of competition		X		
Complements current markets		X		
Complements current production/ technology			X	
Patent protection		X		
Positive social impact	X			
Company image		X		
Resource availability				X

ing the product idea into specific product benefits and images for specific target customers. Perhaps the product idea is a new dog food to meet the high-energy demands of young, frisky puppies as well as the different needs of older, inactive dogs that tend to gain weight easily.

General Foods translates this into a new product concept—a series of four different canned food formulas for the four different stages in a dog's life cycle (later named Cycle I–IV). Preliminary analysis of market potential, production requirements, and profits now begins. The product concept is compared with competing products on product attributes relevant to target customers. (For dog food, these may include price, eye appeal, odor, serving ease, nutritional content, "meatiness," and others.)

Once the product concept is established, **concept testing** begins. Often, small informal consumer groups, called *focus groups*, evaluate word descriptions of the concept and discuss and compare their reactions to the concept's proposed attributes. The opinions and questions of these focus groups can be valuable to the new product team, for they may reveal new insights into how easily people understand the concept, what features they like or find important, and how they describe it to others.

Business Analysis

Business analysis actually goes on throughout the development process. As new information is learned about the product and the market, the company updates the future sales, costs, and profit projections.

Market potential and market share are estimated early in the development process; the estimates are refined as the product concept and target customers are narrowed down.

It is typical for a new product to attract many customers who buy initially out of curiosity but who will not adopt the item. Thus, if the new product is one that should have replacement sales (such as a food or drug item), initial sales levels and the repeat purchase rate must both be estimated.

To determine expected break-even points and return on investment, future marketing and production costs should also be forecast. The product prototype development will offer much more complete information on costs.

Product Development

Until now the product existed only as an idea. If the product looks promising in the initial business analysis stage, the idea is turned into a physical prototype that could be produced in volume. Depending on the technical complexity of the product, this **product development** stage may represent a huge investment in dollars, manpower, and time. The product prototype

Permission: From the *Wall Street Journal*.

". . . What is it dear? . . . I'm busy."

may have to be designed, tested, and redesigned and retested before it meets the production and marketing requirements of the proposed product concept. Also, during this stage the brand name is selected and its packaging is designed.

The prototype is tested both in the laboratory and by potential users. Laboratory testing screens out products that won't go farther. In the research and development laboratory of Heublein, a marketer of alcoholic beverages, 20 researchers dream up hundreds of premixed cocktails, liqueurs, and aperitifs that never make it farther or are shelved for years. (About 1,000 drink ideas come through the lab each year, but 90% of them are discarded as impractical.) The testing process can be time consuming. Heublein's very successful Hereford's Cow, a sweet and creamy drink in several flavors, spent over six years in the lab.[11]

Potential consumers also test the products. At Fisher–Price Toys, three- and four-year-olds are the toy testers. Watching them squeeze, drop, and bang around the new toys helps Fisher–Price decide how to modify their design or whether to introduce them at all.[12]

If the product survives the product development stage, production will begin. Enough quantity will be produced for test marketing or for market introduction if test marketing is skipped.

Test Marketing

In **test marketing,** a product that has been proven effective is put on sale in one or more selected cities that have populations that correspond to the market the firm wants to enter. The product is sold exactly as though it were on sale nationally. Advertising, store displays, and all of the other marketing activities are used just as they would on a full-scale basis to make consumers aware of the product. Many useful insights can be gathered from these test markets, for example:

1. How well does the product sell in actual competition against other brands? Test market sales trends, including repeat sales, can be compared against the goals set for the product. If sales go well in test markets, the firm can be more confident of market success. If sales are disappointing, the product can be withdrawn before making a more costly decision to introduce the product.
2. What kinds of customers buy and how often do they buy? The firm can learn a lot about its target customers here. The firm may be able to find out what kinds of customers buy heavily or very little. This information helps pinpoint target market segments and offers clues to selecting media and designing promotional materials.

[11] "This Work Requires Drinking on the Job: Results Are Mixed," *The Wall Street Journal,* December 17, 1976, p. 18.
[12] "At One Toy Company, the Guys in Research Are 3 and 4 Years Old," *The Wall Street Journal,* December 20, 1972, p. 1.

Making Product Decisions

3. What alternative marketing mixes work best? The firm can experiment with different combinations of marketing mix factors in separate test cities and compare sales results. In its initial test market, Pampers disposable diapers were sold at a price of about $.10 per diaper. This price was based on the costs to produce about 400 million diapers annually. Consumers liked the product but not the price. The company had not been able to discover this problem in earlier consumer testing. At a new $.06 per diaper price, the product sold well in its next test market.[13]

4. Were any serious "bugs" in the design, packaging, etc., overlooked? A baked goods manufacturer discovered that a certain new cookie's taste turned "soapy" after the package sat on the grocery shelf for several weeks. Laboratory testing had not considered this possibility.

Firms run test markets as insurance to protect their large investments in new products. They help reduce the chances of introducing a loser. In some cases, firms may have little choice but to test market. For example, successful test market results may be required if a new food product is to gain access to supermarket shelves.

Test marketing, however, has serious drawbacks. Many firms are discovering that testing does not always pay off. First, test markets are not an infallible predictor of market success. Most packaged goods failures had successful test results. Since the competitive environment, economic conditions, and customer tastes may change quickly, test market data may become obsolete.

There are other problems. Test marketing is extremely expensive—$100,000 and up for a nationally tested brand is typical. Test marketing is time-consuming. Most products stay in test markets from six months to well over a year. Test marketing also tips off competitors who may monitor test results and then rush to market with their own version of the product. Schick's double-edged razor hit the market less than six months after Gillette introduced its Trac II razor to dealers.

To cut development costs and help get the jump on competitors, many firms try to speed up the new product cycle by skipping test marketing altogether. Instead, they concentrate more effort at earlier stages, especially the concept testing and product use testing stages. Computer simulations from concept and product test data are used to forecast sales trends.[14]

Not all firms choose to test market. In industrial markets, sellers may sample their dealers and customers informally, asking them what they like and don't like, what they would want to have, and whether or not they would buy the proposed new product. Large, expensive durable goods, like cars and appliances, cannot be economically produced on a small scale

[13] "P&G Uses Pampers Story to Teach the Consumer About Marketing," *Advertising Age*, April 4, 1977, pp. 41–44.
[14] "New Product Forecasting Techniques May Make Test Markets Obsolete," *Marketing News*, November 19, 1976, pp. 1, 4.

for test marketing. Companies in highly competitive industries, like fashion clothing or toys, feel that secrecy is too important to allow test marketing. It is the mass-marketed packaged consumer goods, where repeat buying and thus brand loyalty are vital, where test marketing enjoys the highest payoff.

Market Introduction

Now the product is ready to be launched in the marketplace. New products in the introductory stage of the life cycle need unusual attention from management. A carefully designed and monitored *rollout* campaign can be critical to later market success.

Products in the introductory stage pose special challenges. Since potential customers are not yet aware of the product, the company should start from scratch to build awareness as well as product interest and preference. The company will advertise very heavily, and for many consumer packaged goods, will use introductory sampling to develop customer awareness and product trial. Promotion expenditures are at their highest during market introduction. Per unit production costs are also unusually high until mass-production volumes are reached. Introductory sales are slow, especially when consumers must learn new shopping and consumption routines. Because of the heavy costs for development and introduction, the new product will not show profits for some time.

Coordinating the introductory program is critical. New products must be on the shelves when the firm's advertising brings buyers into the stores. Managers should track early sales results carefully. The sales trends will be used to establish production and delivery schedules.

If the first products have "bugs" that have to be worked out, they must be found and corrected as quickly as possible. Although the introduction phase is sometimes described as a *shakedown cruise*, today's era of critical consumers and intense competition does not allow much leeway for shoddy product performance.

Strategies for Market Introduction

Some products can be launched slowly and deliberately, priced high, and aimed at the small, innovative market segment that is willing to pay a lot to be the first to buy. Later in the product's life cycle, the price may be lowered and distribution expanded to the mass market. Whenever necessary, the original product is redesigned in order to produce sales at lower prices through mass merchandise outlets or discounters.

The deliberate, market-by-market strategy may rely heavily on favorable word-of-mouth information to boost product trial and adoption. This strategy is appropriate where (1) the product is unique and not easily matched by competitors, (2) target markets are heterogeneous and will pay different prices, and (3) the firm wishes to recover a high gross profit per unit. Best-selling books are often marketed this way: Alex Haley's *Roots*, printed in hardcover, was first sold in bookstores and book clubs at $12.50. When the book finally dropped out of the top ten on *The New York Times* bestseller list, it was offered in a paperback edition at lower prices through drugstore book racks and similar mass outlets.

Marketers may use a different strategy when the potential market is large and repurchases are frequent, consumers are price-sensitive and unaware of the item, and the new product is vulnerable to quick competitive entry. The new product is priced at the current market level or below, perhaps with special introductory offers. Advertising is heavy to all available outlets and customers in order to get quick market penetration. Spending $10 million to promote a new detergent is not unusual. R. J. Reynolds budgeted $40 million over the first six months to introduce its Real low-tar cigarettes.

ORGANIZING FOR PRODUCT DEVELOPMENT

Since new product marketing tasks are very different from managing existing products, many companies have developed organizational structures that centralize responsibility for new products. Several types of new product organizational structures can be noted, for example: (1) product planning committee, (2) new product department, (3) product manager, (4) venture team, and (5) outside new product development specialists.

Product planning committees are the most popular. They often are staffed by top executives from marketing, production, research, engineering, and finance. These executives are managers who have interests and abilities in developing and screening ideas and products. Product planning committees handle product evaluation and approval on a part-time basis, usually turning over approved product ideas to regular product management for further development.

The **new product department,** a small group of specialists working full-time in generating and screening ideas, develops product prototypes up to the introduction stage. As full-time product development specialists, they are often considered superior to the committee arrangement.

The **product manager** essentially acts as a marketing manager for a single product or brand. Supposedly originated by Procter and Gamble in 1927, the product (or brand) manager structure is heavily used today, especially by large, multi-product firms in both consumer and industrial markets.

Product managers usually handle existing products; they may help in developing new products. In many firms they take over new products only at the introductory stage. Typically, they report directly to the chief marketing executive and have complete responsibility for marketing mix planning and programming—advertising, pricing, distribution, and product extensions (packaging, branding, etc.). Although product managers may be responsible for the brand's profits, they have little authority over the line management functions that produce or influence profits, such as field sales or product design. The product management structure is often criticized on the basis of this inconsistency, but its popularity remains strong.

The **venture team** manages the firm's entire new product development task from idea generation to market introduction. Venture teams are made up of specialists from various departments who work together on a full-time basis. In effect, the team operates in an unstructured and innovative manner as a separate small business within the larger company. General Mills, 3M, Dow Chemical, and a growing number of other firms use venture teams.

Obvious advantages of venture teams include their specialization and full-time responsibility for completing a single mission—to develop and launch a specific new product. Less obvious but also important, the venture team approach produces high morale, innovation-mindedness, and independence from traditional bureaucratic management thinking that is geared to more routine tasks.[15]

Outside new product development specialists provide another alternative. These consulting firms perform a variety of services for their clients, from positioning new products and repositioning existing products to taking over the entire new product development and introduction task. William Norton Associates developed General Mills' Crisp 'n Tender batter coating for chicken to compete with the General Foods' Shake 'n Bake. Working closely with General Mills' marketing people, Norton created the product idea and developed it through focus group-oriented concept testing, product and use testing, and test marketing before turning it over to their client for market introduction.[16]

Outside specialists offer up-to-date expertise and independent viewpoints. They are employed on a project-by-project basis, saving the manufacturer the fixed expense of a larger new product development organization.

As we have noted, specialized product development groups, such as new product departments and venture teams, seem to encourage innovation and concentrated effort in product development. And often these organization structures work well. Although they are widely popular today, there are growing pressures on the decentralized, independent management groups, especially product managers and venture teams. The effects of today's new product decisions often reach well beyond the immediate product line. Advertising regulation, pollution, product safety, resource shortages, and other similar factors make the product decision more complex and hazardous. Today, marketing an unsafe product or issuing misleading advertising can seriously harm the entire firm. Seeking better coordination and commu-

[15] Richard H. Hill and James D. Hlavacek, "The Venture Team: A New Concept in Marketing Organization," *Journal of Marketing* (July, 1972), pp. 44–50.
[16] Robert Danielenko, "Those New Product Wizards—How Good Are They?" *Product Management* (September, 1976), pp. 40–44.

Making Product Decisions

nications, some larger firms are shifting the responsibility for new product decisions back to centralized top management.[17]

MANAGING THE PRODUCT/SERVICE MIX OVER THE LIFE CYCLE

Compared with the excitement and challenge of developing and launching a new record album or opening a new restaurant, managing the ongoing product/service mix may seem routine. But all the action isn't in new products. Since the marketing environment is changing constantly, product management is rarely static.

Sources of Change

The sources of environmental change that influence the product mix are endless: economic fluctuations, political actions in domestic and international markets, a new technology, a government ban on a product, a management decision to enter a new market. These events can lead to management changes in everything from long-term corporate goals to the details of selling techniques. Instead of attempting to discuss product mix adjustments for each factor, we will focus on product life cycle changes.

The product life cycle concept is very useful here. It suggests that the product's competitive environment will change in a reasonably predictable fashion. By anticipating this movement, product managers can actively plan and implement new strategies and tactics in order to "stretch out" the product's life cycle. As Figure 8.6 shows, "stretching" efforts may actually rejuvenate sales, hold them longer at current levels, or slow their rate of decline.

Product Adjustments Over the Life Cycle

Marketers can adjust product mix strategy in several basic ways: expand or reduce the product mix; modify the features of current products; and redirect products toward new target markets.

These basic adjustments can be made anywhere in a product's life cycle. Some changes are more appropriate for one stage than for others, as we will discuss.

Growth Stage

Many products do not make it beyond market introduction. For those that do, the growth stage is where the product investment really starts paying off. Sales rise rapidly as early buyers continue to purchase and new buyers are attracted by favorable word-of-mouth and the company's intensive

---

[17] "The Brand Manager: No Longer King," *Business Week*, June 9, 1973, pp. 58–62.

Figure 8.6   Possible Effects of Stretching the Product Life Cycle

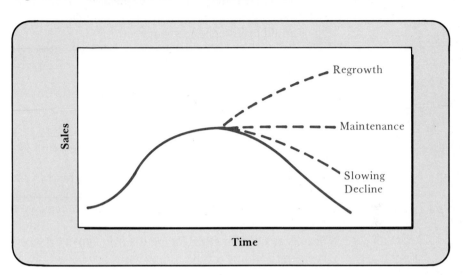

introductory promotional program. The rising sales generate cash flow to recover the large development and introduction costs. Production and advertising costs on a per unit basis drop sharply as the firm realizes economies of scale in buying or manufacturing the new product. The introductory promotion budget is cut back as the new product becomes established in the distribution channels and in consumers' minds. But management can't just sit back and watch sales climb and the money pour in. Competitors are attracted by the growing market. Consumer buying soon slows. Thus, the innovative firm begins to adjust its product strategy to keep ahead of its challengers and to prepare for the eventual slowing rate of growth that signals a maturing market.

During the growth stage the firm tries to keep sales climbing by improving product quality, adding new styles and features, and seeking out new market segments for the product. For example, to keep yogurt sales growing by 30% per year, manufacturers have been experimenting with product variations to expand its narrow market base beyond the 10% of national households who regularly eat yogurt. Adding fruit improved the taste. Then soft frozen yogurt appeared in fast-food outlets in major urban areas. Yogurt makers are hoping that the ice cream–like product, dispensed in cups or cones, will appeal to a much broader spectrum of buyers.[18]

[18] "Yogurt Makers Try a Mass-Market Recipe," *Business Week*, November 8, 1976, pp. 91–95.

Product-mix modifications go hand in hand with other marketing mix adjustments in the growth stage:

1. Opening new distribution channels to reach expanded market segments (frozen yogurt shops appear in shopping centers).
2. Shifting advertising emphasis from building product awareness to brand preference and purchase.
3. Possibly lowering the price to attract more price-sensitive buyers, ward off competition, and reflect lower manufacturing costs.

Maturity Stage

Like it or not, the product's growth rate soon slows and the product enters its maturity stage. The maturity stage demands a lot of management attention. Ordinarily, the product spends more time in this stage than it does in the growth stage, and by now the product has serious competition.

Competitive entry into the slowing market may produce overcapacity in the industry. Firms that have overproduced may boost their promotion budgets and slash prices to the trade and final consumers. Firms may spend heavily to develop more competitive versions of the product. As marketing costs rise and prices fall, profits on the product erode. Weaker competitors drop out while the remaining firms compete for market share.

The maturity stage offers serious challenges to marketers. Management must take the offensive and devise strategies for injecting new vigor into the product.

Firms pursue a number of strategies in the mature stage. Kotler suggests that they usually try first to boost sales of the existing product. Then they modify the product by restyling and adding new features or new versions of the product. Adjustments in product extensions (branding, packaging, warranties, etc.) and in other marketing mix elements (price, advertising, distribution) accompany these product mix strategies.[19]

Market Expansion Strategy. Marketing managers try to increase the consumption by current customers by suggesting *more frequent usage* or *new uses* for the product. This is called *market expansion strategy*. Wineries promote drinking wine with ordinary meals instead of just on festive occasions, and they distribute recipes for cooking with wine. Arm & Hammer baking soda is advertised as a refrigerator deodorant in order to create a new growth phase for the product as the home baking market matures.

Managers may also direct their products toward *new markets*. Johnson's "no tears" baby shampoo was promoted to teens and young adults who need a mild shampoo for every day use. Industries facing mature domestic markets often make a major push in foreign markets. Because the United States soft drink population is aging, Coca-Cola, PepsiCo, and others look to the younger, faster-growing populations of less-developed nations.

[19] Kotler, ibid., p. 237.

Positioning Strategy. A product's *position* is the image that the product projects in the customer's mind relative to (1) other competing products and (2) other products that the company markets.[20]

Seven-Up had a rather broad, indistinct image as a "me-too" soft drink and mixer for alcoholic drinks. With its "Uncola" advertising campaign, 7-Up sought to reposition itself as a clearly different alternative to the well-known cola beverages. Miller Brewing Company repositioned its High Life beer to attract the big-volume drinkers—younger males. Its "champagne of beers" theme attracted women and upper-income consumers, but none of them drank much beer. Miller's bigger success story is its Lite beer. Using ads featuring rugged male sports personalities, Miller repositioned the entire low-calorie beer market away from its previous "diet drink" image to that of a "less filling" beer for big beer drinkers. Again, the earlier segment, diet-conscious women and men, drank little beer anyway.

Repositioning can be achieved entirely through promotion (like 7-Up), but the whole range of marketing mix variables might be involved in the change.

Product Modification and Addition Strategies. Managers may also modify the product in order to attract new customers or improve its performance among current users. As market saturation appears, fast-food chains broaden their menus to include breakfast items (McDonald's Egg McMuffin), ham sandwiches at Burger King, chicken at Arthur Treacher's Fish and Chips. Manufacturers of black-and-white television sets encourage more usage and multiple-set ownership among households through a number of quality improvements and new features: eyecatching new shapes and colors; glare-free screens and more power for outdoor use; miniaturized versions for easy portability; and electronic game features.

In packaged food and household cleaning products, feature improvement has become a routine strategy for stretching out the product life cycle. "New, improved" flavors, citrus and herbal scents, and easy-pour packages flood the market in endless variation.

Style modification, which makes earlier styles obsolete, is popular in products in which aesthetic qualities are an important part of what the consumer is seeking. Clothing and accessories, cosmetics, and furniture are periodically restyled in order to capture buyer interest. The annual restyling of autos has largely disappeared as a result of rising costs and customer disinterest. Critics of style obsolescence have long argued that it unnecessarily wastes consumers' money and society's scarce resources.

Other Marketing Mix Adjustments. To maintain sales and market shares of mature products, managers often turn to other elements of the marketing mix. Detailed discussion is outside the scope of this chapter. The

[20] John H. Holmes, "Profitable Product Positioning," *MSU Business Topics* (Spring, 1973), pp. 27–32.

following examples of strategies may be used alone or in combination with the product modifications already discussed:

1. Price cutting or indirect price cuts through promotional offers, additional customer services, or new lower-priced brands (especially private label or distributor's brands).
2. Adding new market channels, particularly low-margin outlets that attract mass markets through discounting.
3. New advertising appeals, perhaps as part of a product repositioning strategy.

Price-oriented strategies in particular may invite quick retaliation by competitors. Short-term gains by one firm may eventually lead to lowered profits or even severe losses by all. A case in point is the digital watch market. Here, major semiconductor manufacturers like Texas Instruments, Fairchild Camera and Instrument, and Litronix moved in against Timex and the traditional, more expensive Swiss and American watches. Prices on digital watches were slashed from $2,000 to $10 in just over five years as the semiconductor firms took advantage of their technology and production skills to grab huge chunks of the watch market. But profits for all firms slumped in the price war, causing major companies like Gillette and Litronix to throw in the towel and forcing firms like Gruen, a well-known watch manufacturer, to file for reorganization under federal bankruptcy law.[21]

Decline Stage

Product sales may remain stable in the maturity stage for a considerable time. But sales for most products eventually do start to slip. The product enters the decline stage. Sales of fashions or fads, like miniskirts, leisure suits, or pet rocks may disappear very quickly, causing marketers to slash their prices in order to get rid of their inventory. Other products may hang on at low sales levels for years.

While the industry shakeout actually begins earlier, in the market growth and maturity stages, many more firms will withdraw during the market decline stage.

The snowmobile industry is a case in point: There were about 140 snowmobile marketers when industry sales hit their peak in 1969; by the end of 1976 there were only 12.

Marketers make other marketing mix adjustments during sales decline. They reduce the number of product items in the line and they cut out the weaker items. They also withdraw from marginal channels and cut their advertising budgets. The resources they save can then be invested in more

[21] See "The Great Digital Watch Shakeout," *Business Week*, May 2, 1977, pp. 78–80; "Dog Days at National Semi-Conductor," and "Litronix Cuts Out Consumer Products," both in *Business Week*, February 28, 1977, pp. 32, 70–72; "The Electronics Threat to Timex," *Business Week*, August 18, 1975, pp. 42–46.

profitable items. Prices may be lowered, particularly if the firm plans to withdraw instead of attempting to revitalize the product.

Most firms eventually abandon the product. The product may disappear completely, although the remaining products may continue to sell ("laggards" in the diffusion process may have just discovered the product). Some products enjoy a later revival, perhaps selling as a collector's item (almost anything old) or supplying the original needs of a new generation of consumers (Franklin stoves and Raggedy Ann dolls).

Most companies do not have well-developed programs for managing their aging products. There are a number of explanations. New products are more exciting and contribute strongly to the firm's profits, and mature products represent most of the product mix and sales dollars. No one wants to think about the dying products, let alone be responsible for them. In many cases, pride and sentiment get in the way of taking an objective and firm approach to aging products. Abandoning a product may be perceived as admitting management failure. Since their egos and careers are tied to them, the people in management too often find it necessary to rationalize why these products should be revived or kept on even while sales are certain to keep falling.

Developing sound marketing programs and strategies for handling product decline is just as necessary as for other life cycle stages. First, if the slipping product can be rescued through renewed marketing effort, a product revitalization program becomes profitable. If sales decline is inevitable, the firm will find that carrying weak products is costly in several ways. Weak products may have to be propped up with extra advertising or price cuts, and when sales drop, production costs will rise as economies of scale disappear.

The biggest problem is difficult to measure, but it is very real: Weak products tie up assets and management time and energy that could be spent aggressively exploring innovative ideas and developing new products. Management may not realize yet another danger: Inferior products produce unhappy customers and perhaps a negative image for the company and its products.

Strategies for Declining Products

Revitalization Strategy. The firm can attempt to reverse the sales decline by revising its marketing efforts. Actually, the same general approach is used to stretch life cycle stages during growth and maturity. This strategy may be feasible in the decline stage when the product concept is basically sound but has been neglected or mismarketed and has fallen behind more up-to-date, aggressively marketed versions. Ovaltine, a malt-flavored milk supplement popular in the 1930's and 1940's, had been losing badly to changing consumer life-styles and to better-tasting but less nutritious brands. The conservative management had stuck to its original marketing strategy almost to the dismal end. The revitalized marketing strategy included product improvement (chocolate flavor, better texture), new media (television), and extensive advertising and sales promotion campaigns.[22]

Withdrawal of Marketing Support.   Here the firm stresses current profits instead of slowing the sales decline. Resources such as advertising may be cut back or eliminated completely. Marketing support may be concentrated only in the strongest segments and other segments are phased out. The price remains the same or perhaps is raised. Depending on the loyalty of core customers and the remaining competition, sales may stay high enough to cover the lower costs and keep the product in the line.

Product Elimination.   Product elimination refers to the systematic, periodic process in which products are evaluated with the purpose of eliminating marginal offerings. A number of benefits has resulted for firms having product elimination programs, not the least of which is improved profitability. For example, a small candy manufacturer dropped 796 of its 800 items and became one of the most profitable companies in its industry.[23] Another company eliminated 16 products that accounted for 8% of its sales volume; the firm's profit increased twentyfold in 3 years.[24] Other advantages include potential sales increases, reduction in inventory size, and reallocation of scarce resources to more promising products.

In spite of these benefits, there is a good deal of evidence that most firms do not have a sound procedure for deleting marginal offerings. One study of almost 100 large manufacturing firms revealed that:

1. Few firms had a written procedure.
2. Most firms did not use the computer.
3. Few firms assigned the product elimination function to a specific executive.
4. Most firms had dropped only a handful of products over the last five years.
5. Almost half of the companies did not have a replacement parts policy for durable products dropped.[25]

Managing the Product Elimination Program

In order for a company to have an effective product elimination program, the steps shown in Figure 8.7 are recommended.

Periodically Monitor All Products.   All products carried should be monitored periodically. This step involves collecting comprehensive data

[22] Kevin V. Brown, "How to Make a New Product from an Old Product," *Product Management* (December, 1976), pp. 27–31.

[23] Donald K. Clifford, Jr., "Leverage in the Product Life Cycle," *Dun's Review* (May, 1965), pp. 62–70.

[24] Philip Kotler, "Phasing Out Weak Products," *Harvard Business Review* (March, 1965), p. 109.

[25] Richard T. Hise and Michael A. McGinnis, "Production Elimination: Practices, Policies, and Ethics," *Business Horizons*, June, 1975, pp. 25–32.

Figure 8.7   The Product Elimination Program

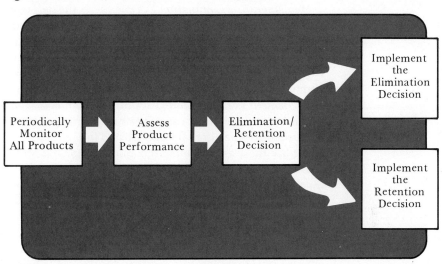

for each product. Some of the most important data to be collected include: (1) product sales in units and dollars, (2) costs associated with each product, (3) market share, (4) inventory levels, and (5) prices charged. From these data it is possible to compute important performance measures for products. For example, dollar sales volume can be matched against costs in order to determine product profitability.

Because the data requirements in this step are enormous, it is advisable that extensive use of a computer be made.

Assess Product Performance.   The data collected from the monitoring step should be used to assess product performance. This means comparing how the product is doing with the objectives stipulated for it. Thus, its actual return on investment would be compared to the desired return on investment. Its current market share should be checked against its desired market share. Its actual net profit as a percentage of sales should be compared with the product's expected profit on sales.

Even though a product's performance may exceed the levels established for it, management should be wary of developments that suggest future problems. Some of these developments are a declining sales volume, decreasing market share, introduction of a superior competitive product, and price declines.

Deletion/Retention Decision.   After assessing the product's performance, management must decide whether to eliminate or retain the product.

The majority of products will undoubtedly be retained. Those that fail to achieve a large number of their most important objectives (especially profit) should probably be dropped. This assumes that management cannot develop approaches that will make the product's performance acceptable.

Implement the Elimination Decision. If the decision has been made to eliminate a product, that decision must be implemented. That is, there are a number of factors that must be considered and accounted for as products are dropped. The most important of these are listed in Figure 8.8. Consideration of these and other factors will result in an orderly product elimination process for the company and its customers.

Implement the Retention Decision. When management has decided to retain a product, it must consider strategies that will *improve* its performance. Some of the alternatives are listed in Figure 8.8. The reader will recognize these as marketing mix modifications. It is obvious that some of these alternatives involve a *decrease* in marketing effort for the product involved. Decreased marketing effort is frequently an effective strategy for a product whose sales will not drop greatly as a result of the reduced

Figure 8.8 Implementing the Elimination and Retention Decisions

Factors to Consider When a Product Is to Be Eliminated

1. When should the product be eliminated?
2. To what other products will the freed-up resources be assigned? When should they be reassigned?
3. Should the current inventory be sold before the product is eliminated?
4. Should customers be notified about the elimination? When should the notice go out? What should the notice say?
5. Should orders be filled after the date for elimination?
6. Are any laws or contractual agreements being violated?
7. Should customers be allowed to return units of the unsold product?

Strategies to Consider When a Product Is to Be Retained

1. Should the price be increased or decreased?
2. Should the promotional budget be increased or decreased?
3. Should the product be modified or should the quality be improved?
4. Should the channels of distribution be changed?
5. Should the advertising media used be changed?
6. Should the product be marketed to new market segments?
7. Should different modes of transportation be used?
8. Should the sales force effort for the product be increased or decreased?

support. In some cases, greater profit will result because the sales decline is less than the decreased costs involved.

OTHER PRODUCT-RELATED STRATEGIES

Buyers of Nikon cameras get more than just a highly capable piece of photographic equipment. They buy the Nikon brand name and its assurance of quality, prestige, and integrity. They buy the assurance of its warranty and its repair service. In addition to the usual camera advice, recent buyers of Nikon cameras are receiving free photography lessons. All of these product extensions, and more, add up to the firm's *total product offer* and the customer's *perceived total benefits*.

The marketer develops strategies for adjusting and communicating his product offer to target customers. We will concentrate here on product related elements that uniquely identify and communicate the product: packaging and branding.

Branding Strategy

Branding Language.   A *brand* is a name, term, sign, symbol, design, or a combination of them used to identify the products of one organization and to differentiate them from competitive offerings. A *brand name* is that part of the brand that can be vocalized—Ford, Blue Cross, Mr. Coffee, Doctor J. A *trademark* is a legally protected brand that allows its owner exclusive rights to its use. A trademark includes the pictorial design as well as the brand name—Charles Schulz's Snoopy cartoon figure on official Peanuts products is an example.

Advantages of Branding.   The consumer relies on branding as an important information source. A brand name on a product identifies the firm and assures the buyer of uniform quality, allowing repeat purchasing with more confidence. Well-promoted brands often suggest higher quality than do unknown brands or unbranded products. Bayer aspirin, Timken roller bearings, and Washington State apples are examples. The buyer may derive recognition and status from displaying prestige brands such as Kuppenheimer or Chivas Regal. Branding offers the firm many important advantages. Brands communicate the product's image quickly and easily (Coke or Levi's.) Brands that project an image of higher quality or status enjoy some protection from the rigors of price competition. Exxon gasoline usually sells for a penny or two more per gallon than other brands. The Gucci name on leather goods, a haircut by Vidal Sassoon, or even a can of beer by Coors may bring a substantial price premium.

Distributors and customers may adopt new products more quickly if they carry an established brand name such as Kraft or IBM.

Choices in Branding Strategy.   Marketers must answer several basic questions when they formulate their branding strategy. Should their products carry brand names? (Most products do, but there are good reasons for not branding.) Should the brand be unique to the product item or should it carry the "family name"? Should the product be branded by its producer or by distributors who market the product?

For branding to be worthwhile, the product's quality must be consistent and reasonably high; the product should be capable of differentiation on physical or intangible characteristics; and the firm must be financially willing and able to support a branding program. Firms not meeting these minimum requirements would do better to invest their marketing dollars elsewhere.

The firm may choose a family brand or an individual brand strategy. A *family brand* is one carried by several items in the firm's product line. H. J. Heinz and General Electric use this approach. Procter and Gamble markets its products under *individual brand* names—Tide, Oxydol, Crest, Gleem, and so on.

Family branding has many advantages. The firm's advertising benefits each product. New product introduction is easier and less expensive because dealers and consumers already know the brand name. This is a big advantage when the firm wants to gain acceptance in mass merchandising outlets like supermarkets, which are very reluctant to drop proven brands from their crowded shelves for unknown newcomers.

But if the firm's products are very *dissimilar* in markets served or in product quality, family branding may do more harm than good. The reputation of a prestige line of watches could suffer if the manufacturer insists on adding a low-priced watch under the same brand name. Similarly, U.S. Time would have difficulty selling very expensive, high-fashion watches under the Timex brand. In both cases, the consumer's previous association of the brand name with a certain price and quality level is transferred to the new product, with unfortunate results. Family branding efforts are also wasted if the firm's products are sold in entirely different markets. Brand advertising will seldom carry over from one market to another.

Products may carry *producers brands* (also known as national brands) or *distributors brands* (private brands). Owning a strong brand gives the firm control over the product's image and, as a result, considerable control over the product's entire marketing strategy. But the brand owner must also develop and pay for most of the brand's marketing program. Usually, the advantages of brand ownership outweigh the disadvantages. Thus, large retail chains like Sears and K-Mart already own most of the brands they handle, and other retailers are following suit, adding to or replacing their suppliers' brands with their own brands.

Developing a Brand Name.   Choosing a good brand name is important and requires careful thought. Below are some rules of thumb that many firms follow in determining a brand name:

1. It should be easy to recognize, pronounce, and remember. Short names like Dash, Tab, and Bic work well; Ignacio Haya cigars may not.

2. It should suggest product benefits. Easy-Off says exactly what the consumer wants to know about the oven cleaner.
3. It should be distinctive. Blue Nun and Exxon are, but doesn't every city have a First National Bank?
4. It should be appropriate for international markets. American Motors' Matador bombed in Puerto Rico where the name translates as "killer."
5. It must be legally protectable. A registered trademark that contains words in general use may not be granted exclusively to a company. The words "Light" and "Lite" created a legal turmoil among competitors in the diet beer market.

This last point deserves further comment. If a brand name becomes the common descriptive term for the product type, the courts may rule that all or part of that brand is generic or legally available for general use. Thus, exclusive rights to the name are lost. Generic names like nylon, cola, and kerosene once were exclusive brands. Most consumers use brand names such as Levi's, Xerox, Jello, Kleenex, Styrofoam, Coke, and Band-Aid as descriptive names. Their brand owners thus face the delicate task of making their brand name widely known and used, but not to the extent that it becomes legally generic. Brand owners that have this problem take deliberate measures to inform the public of their exclusive ownership, such as always using the ® registration symbol with the printed brand name.

Packaging Strategy

Marketing Functions of Packaging.   The product's package essentially performs two major tasks: It contributes to cost efficiencies in storage, handling, and shipping and it aids in customer sales generation. The package must offer good physical protection against spoilage, breakage, and pilferage. It should make handling easier, speed up delivery times, and thereby reduce costs and enable lower prices to be charged.

The sales generating package is often one of the few ways a company can differentiate its product and communicate with its customers.

There are numerous ways that packaging can add value and distinctiveness to products:

1. Improve product display (clear plastic meat trays).
2. Heighten visual interest (record album covers).
3. Encourage multiple purchases (a six-pack).
4. Add convenience (squeeze tubes of cheese for crackers).
5. Provide multiple uses for package (jelly glasses).
6. Enhance prestige (cosmetics containers).
7. Provide an inexpensive advertising medium (cereal boxes).

A single package may offer many of these advantages, and others; consider the pop-tab aluminum beverage can. Packaging may play a vital role in the product's image. Lancer's distinctive wine bottle allows its rather modest contents to be sold in huge quantities at an impressive price. Product repositioning strategy may revolve around packaging changes. One packaging designer suggests that a thermos bottle, a mature staple good, might add a $.10 flotation ring in order to attract boating enthusiasts or color it khaki and add a leather belt loop to attract hikers—both strong growth segments.[26]

Societal Considerations. Packaging's growing influence spreads well beyond the immediate marketplace. Consider the following related issues and trends:

1. *Environmental pollution.* Fluorocarbon propellants in aerosol spray cans, found to deplete the earth's ozone layer, pose a threat to human health. One source estimates that a ban on fluorocarbons would cost the industry $1 billion by 1980.[27] Oregon and other states have banned the throwaway beverage can in order to eliminate the litter eyesore.
2. *Excessive packaging.* Fancy packaging boosts sales, but it also raises costs and wastes natural resources, so charge the critics. The Pringles can is a prime example.
3. *Consumer information and protection.* Modern packaging require-ments encourage product standardization and provide a medium for promotion, which tend to simplify the consumer's information search process. But packaging can also conceal product features and mis-inform consumers. Standards for nutritional labeling, percentage and grade labeling (ingredient quality), unit pricing, shatterproof bottles, and childproof medicine containers are recent trends. They suggest the growing complexity of packaging decisions for the firm, for government, and for consumers.

These trends clearly suggest that packaging decisions are increasing in management importance. Packaging decisions must focus on societal con-siderations and customer needs. And packaging should be included as part of product planning for every product, starting from the product's inception.

SUMMARY

A major product decision is matching products with markets. In doing so, it is worthwhile to consider three kinds of customers. Core customers are those whose product expectations are closely matched with a specific product. Fringe customers' product expectations are somewhat matched with a specific product. Indifferent customers have expectations that are only marginally matched with a product. In pursuing a market segmenta-tion matching strategy, a company provides product expectations that satisfy the core markets of a number of market segments. A concentrated

---

[26] Si Friedman, "The Story of Thermos: How to Improve Your Product's Position," *Advertising Age*, March 21, 1977, p. 41.

[27] Estimates from International Research and Technology Corporation, reported in *Business Week*, May 30, 1977, p. 30.

marketing strategy involves marketing to core customers in one or only a few market segments. When an undifferentiated approach is followed, a company offers only a single product to the core, fringe, and indifferent markets.

The totality of products offered by a company is referred to as its product mix. It is made up of product lines and individual product items. Product mixes can be analyzed in terms of their width, depth, and consistency.

Although new products are critical to the success of most companies, the failure rate for new products is very high. Some of the reasons for the high rate of failure include social and legal pressures, the longer developmental process, shorter product life cycles, the high cost of new product development, and shortages, inflation, and recession. Companies can engage in a number of practices that can help to reduce the level of new product failure. Purposeful idea generation eliminates the obviously unfit prospects, as does a structured screening process. Concept testing secures customer reactions to the new product idea. Business analysis secures estimates of profit, market share, break-even points, and return on investment. Product development involves the creation of the physical product for market introduction or test marketing. Test marketing provides feedback on the product, purchasers, and the product's marketing mix.

Many firms develop specific organizational units to develop new products. These include product planning committees, new product departments, and venture teams. Product managers may assist in the new product development process, and outside new product development specialists may also be used.

The product life cycle is a useful concept for managing ongoing products. A planned series of marketing strategies and tactics over the life cycle can prolong the life of profitable products and marginal products can be eliminated.

Branding and packaging are examples of product extension strategies that can result in better product–market matching.

A structured, formalized product elimination program is a critical aspect of product planning. Such a program can result in improved profits, better use of scarce resources, higher sales dollars, and a reduction in inventory levels. When a product elimination program is being instituted, provisions must be made for monitoring products, assessing product performance, making the elimination/retention decision, and implementing the elimination or retention decision.

1. There is ample evidence that, in spite of the benefits resulting from a formalized, structured product elimination program, most American firms do not have such a program. What factors do you believe explain this situation?

2. What advantages are there in pursuing an undifferentiated marketing strategy instead of a market segmentation strategy?

3. Why do you believe that the failure rate for new products is so high? What can be done to reduce this failure rate?

4. Why would a company use outside new product development specialists instead of internal new product development alternatives to develop new product ideas?

5. Why would a firm want to keep products in the growth phase of the product life cycle as long as possible?

6. What is the major reason why firms engage in product positioning?

7. What are the major reasons why companies use test marketing?

8. Are there any reasons why companies would not want to use test marketing for new products?

GLOSSARY

Business Analysis: the step in the new product process that results in estimates of profit, market share, break-even points, and return on investment

Concentrated Marketing Strategy: a product–market matching strategy in which a single product is offered to core markets

Concept Testing: the process of securing customer reactions to new product ideas

Consistency: the relatedness or compatibility of product lines and product items

Core Customers: customers whose product expectations are closely matched by the perceived characteristics of a product

Depth: the number of separate product items within each product line

Fringe Customers: customers whose product expectations are somewhat matched by the perceived characteristics of a product

Growth Stage: the product life cycle stage in which sales increase rapidly and profits are highest

Idea Generation: the process whereby ideas for potential new products are obtained

Idea Screening: use of checklists or other rating devices to decide if a new product idea has merit

Indifferent Customers: those customers whose product expectations are only marginally matched by the perceived characteristics of a product

Market Expansion Strategy: increasing sales of a current product by directing the product to new markets or obtaining more frequent use or new uses by current customers

Market Segmentation Strategy: A product–market matching strategy in which product expectations are provided that satisfy the core members of a number of market segments

Maturity Stage: the product life cycle stage in which sales increases begin to slow down and profits begin to drop

New Product Department: a small group of new product specialists who work full-time to generate and screen new product ideas

Product Development: the creation of the physical product for market introduction or test marketing

Product Item: a specific member of a product line

Product Line: a group of products that are closely related in some way

Product Manager: the marketing manager for a single brand or product

Product Mix: the total composite of all products offered by a company

Product Planning Committee: a group made up of top executives from various functional areas that works part-time to evaluate and approve or disapprove new product ideas

Test Marketing: marketing a new product in selected cities that correspond to the product's wider market so that information about the product, its purchasers, and its marketing mix can be obtained

Undifferentiated Strategy: a product–market matching strategy in which a single product is offered to core, fringe, and indifferent customers

Venture Team: a less formal, less structured, and more innovative organizational alternative for new product idea generation and evaluation

Width: the number of different product lines offered

Case 1: Granada Food Co.

The Granada Food Company is a large processor of a wide variety of food products. The company is in a very competitive industry in which success (even survival) is largely a function of a firm's ability to develop successful new products. Within the last five years Granada has suffered through a number of new product failures. The only successful new products during this time was a line of cheese snacks packaged in plastic squeeze tubes.

In order to increase the firm's new product success rate, a top-level venture management team was established. Made up of top-level representatives from finance, marketing, research and development, and production, the team was relieved of former responsibilities so that full-time efforts could be given to generating successful new product ideas.

After six months the venture team narrowed an original list of 50 potential new products to 3 products. Given the best chance of success was a proposed line of meat spreads for snacks and sandwiches that would be packaged in plastic tubes. Turkey, ham, beef, and chicken were the flavors being considered.

1. What advantages would Granada gain by introducing this new product line?
2. What are the likely market segments to which this product line should be directed?
3. What else should Granada do before the new product line is introduced?
4. What marketing strategies should be followed if Granada decides to introduce the meat spread line?

Case 2: Midwest Meat Co.

Midwest Meat Co. sells a line of competitively priced packaged meats (luncheon meats, bacon, etc.) under its FlavorFul brand, and beef and pork carcasses for final cutting and packaging by its supermarket chain customers under their own labels. Midwest is a regional packing firm, serving a six-state market area where it also competes with much larger national packers such as Swift, Wilson, and Armour. Its FlavorFul processed meats and unbranded meats are priced competitively with other national and regional brands.

Midwest also sells very high-quality flash-frozen meats to the restaurant trade. This prime-grade aged beef carries a Midwest Meat Co. label and is presently not available in retail stores. But Midwest has noted that several packers are successfully selling flash-frozen steaks to upper-income households and corporate accounts using direct-mail distribution and extensive advertising in prestige magazines and newspapers, gourmet food catalogs, and selective mailing lists.

The average supermarket shopper has been reluctant to buy frozen beef, and the meatpacking industry thus has faced a difficult task in convincing consumers that quality frozen steaks are superior to the fresh meat sold in most supermarkets. Midwest believes that with a carefully conceived marketing effort aimed at the more affluent better-informed shopper, it can successfully introduce its high-quality flash-frozen steaks into selected supermarkets, meat markets, and gourmet food stores.

A critical element in this strategy is branding. Midwest executives have been considering the questions listed below.

1. Should this product be branded by Midwest Meat Co., or sold unbranded to the retail store? If the latter, should the retail store brand it?
2. If Midwest brands the frozen steaks, should the Midwest name (used for the restaurant trade) be used? Should the FlavorFul brand (now on its processed meats) be used? Or is an independent brand superior to a family brand in this instance?
3. What qualities are most important in choosing the brand name for the frozen steaks?

Advertising Management

After you finish this chapter, you should be able to answer the following questions:

1. What advertising decisions is the marketing manager responsible for?
2. How does advertising fit into a firm's total marketing plan?
3. What information is needed to make advertising decisions?
4. How is the company's advertising agency important to the marketing manager and what activity(ies) does the agency perform in getting the company's message to its customers?
5. How much money should a firm spend on advertising? How are advertising budget decisions made?
6. How does the marketing manager measure the effectiveness of the firm's advertising campaign? Is this measure made after or before the advertising appears?
7. Must a firm develop a special organizational structure to accommodate its advertising activities?
8. Can advertising be used for "social good" purposes as well as for product and image promotion?

INTRODUCTION

A basic responsibility of the marketing manager is to ensure that the company's messages reach its potential customers, i.e., the target market. Ultimately, the main objective of any company must be to sell its product or service at a profit. However, the purpose of an individual advertising message may vary from stimulating desired demand to developing an image or overcoming unfavorable publicity.

A principle method by which many companies deliver their messages to groups of customers and, in fact, make their initial contact with most potential customers, is through their advertising. (Advertising is nonpersonal communication through media for which payment is made.) Procter and Gamble spent $445 million in one year (see Figure 9.1) to

Figure 9.1   Top Twenty Advertisers for 1976

1. Procter & Gamble	$445.0*
2. General Motors Corporation	287.0
3. General Foods Corporation	275.0
4. Sears, Roebuck & Company	245.0
5. Warner-Lambert Company	199.0
6. Bristol-Myers Company	189.0
7. Ford Motor Company	162.0
8. American Home Products Corporation	158.0
9. Phillip Morris Inc.	149.0
10. Mobil Corporation	146.5
11. R. J. Reynolds Industries	140.3
12. Unilever	135.0
13. General Mills Inc.	131.6
14. Heublein Inc.	129.1
15. Colgate-Palmolive Company	118.0
16. Richardson-Merrel Inc.	115.5
17. U.S. Government	113.0
18. American Tel. & Tel. Company	112.8
19. Chrysler Corporation	110.0
20. McDonald's Corporation	105.0

*Millions

Source: Reprinted with permission from the August 29, 1977 issue of *Advertising Age*. Copyright 1977 by Crain Communications, Inc.

advertise its products. For expenditures like this, the reader can be certain that Procter and Gamble's management places high reliance on the value of advertising. Since advertising has become a $50 billion industry, it is obvious that many, many other firms share P&G's view.

Advertising is now being used more and more frequently by firms in an attempt to present or explain their attitudes on sociopolitical issues, such as pollution control and environment concerns, collective bargaining positions, proposed legislation, and a host of other issues. Companies realize that in an active newsmaking world they can no longer depend on "free" newspaper space or television time in order to express their views, but that they can be certain that by purchasing advertising space or time they are assured of having the public forum they desire.

Similarly, today we see a much greater use of "image" advertising. Figure 9.2 is representative of the type of advertising a firm—in this case a Cleveland power company—does to tell the public how it is responsive to community needs. Image advertising like this has become commonplace and is used not only to help offset misunderstanding and criticism, but also to help foster a desired reputation or stature for the firm. (Naturally, the latter requires the firm not only to advertise but also to operate in a fashion that matches such image claims if it is to have long-run success.)

Advertising is only one tool that the marketing manager uses. It has definite strengths and weaknesses that depend on the firm, its product(s), and its marketing objectives. If a firm seeks to reach a market segment as a group and can utilize a relatively broad message, advertising can be most successful. However, to reach individual customers with an individualized message, personal selling may be preferable. Limitations of each of the marketing mix tools—advertising, personal selling, physical distribution, channel(s) of distribution, pricing, and product—must be recognized in marketing decisions, and advertising must be used to its best advantage, as must the other tools. Examples of advertising's successful contributions to a firm's marketing efforts are countless; yet one must be aware that advertising alone rarely solves all of a firm's marketing problems.

MARKETING MANAGER'S ADVERTISING DECISIONS

Although the marketing manager in a typical corporation is responsible for a wide range of advertising decisions, most of his activities involve direction instead of actual preparation. Included among his responsibilities are:

1. Determining the role that advertising is to play in achieving the annual (and longer run) marketing objectives for the firm and its products.
2. Establishing specific objectives for the annual advertising campaign(s) and developing a budget that is consistent with these objectives and the funds available for advertising.

Figure 9.2   Image Advertising

One in a series of messages to our customers:

Oil conservation can't do it alone.

Some of the panic has gone out of last year's energy crisis. But the problem is still with us in 1975.

From 1960 to 1970, more oil was pumped out of the earth and burned than in the 70 years before 1960.

And in just the past *three* years, mankind burned that much again! At that rate, by 1980 we'll be burning 70 years' worth *every* year. And after that?

Something has to be done, fast. Oil conservation can't do it alone.

Fortunately, part of the long-term answer is already here. Electricity can be substituted for oil in many applications. Like heating. And rapid transit systems.

And electricity can be produced with *coal* and *uranium*—which are *not in short supply.*

If we are able to build the nuclear power plants we need, we can ease the energy shortage and buy the time to develop alternate energy sources that will make the world less dependent on petroleum forever.

We're rapidly running out of a lot of things.

We'd better make sure that time isn't one of them.

The Illuminating Company

Source: Reprinted by permission of The Cleveland Electric Illuminating Company and *Cleveland Magazine.*

---

3. Identifying the product features and/or consumer motives or concerns that will be featured in all marketing efforts, including advertising.
4. Selecting an advertising agency(ies) to prepare advertising campaigns, including each print advertisement and commercial, that are consistent with the established advertising objectives.

5. Giving final approval to all advertising material prepared by the firm's agency or in-house that carries the firm's sponsorship.
6. Approving media used to deliver the firm's advertising message.
7. Preparing dealer and in-store promotional materials to support the annual advertising campaign(s), including keeping the firm's own sales force and dealers fully aware of these advertising activities.
8. Evaluating the effectiveness of the firm's advertising efforts in achieving the objectives that have been established for it.
9. Maintaining the type of marketing and advertising staff in the firm needed to coordinate and evaluate the corporation's advertising programs and to prepare sales promotion materials.
10. Ensuring that the firm's advertising messages conform to the legal requirements and standards of good taste.

Advertising's Role

At the time the firm's marketing plan is developed, the objectives for advertising, as well as for the other marketing tools, should be established. It should be emphasized that advertising decisions therefore ". . . must take into consideration the rest of the marketing plan with which the advertising effort must be integrated,"[1] and vice versa. All of the firm's advertising activities should be consistent with the objectives that have been established for advertising and should also be *consistent* with and should *complement* the company's total marketing efforts.

Naturally, many will feel that this emphasis and re-emphasis of such a "simple" point seems overdone. However, the importance of tightly integrating advertising into the firm's total marketing efforts can hardly be stressed too much. The greatest difficulty seems to be integrating the advertising and personal selling objectives. Failure to integrate these objectives has caused many firms not only considerable embarrassment, but also unnecessary costs.

For example, if the firm's marketing plan calls for making slight product changes for the year and the use of advertising to attempt to reach a newly identified market segment, then the firm's advertising campaign should be focused on that goal. Planning the advertising campaign without coordinating with this total marketing goal might well lead to using the wrong messages or media. Either mistake would prove costly in terms of lost sales and unnecessary space or time purchases.

Advertising Objectives

Although a firm's marketing objectives ultimately relate to profit, a firm's advertising objectives may be stated in terms of other objectives, such as increased consumer awareness or desired attitude change. In

[1] David A. Aaker and John G. Meyers, *Advertising Management* (Englewood Cliffs, N.J.: Prentice-Hall, Inc., 1975), p. 28.

stating the advertising objectives for the period—normally one year—the marketing manager should be specific so that it is possible to measure the success of the advertising campaign.

Sales. If the objective of the advertising plan is stated in terms of sales, the objective could be a total sales figure, a sales figure for a particular product or territory, or even a percentage change in market share.

If market share is used, the objective may be to increase the firm's market share in total or by product or territory. For example, Pontiac's share of the United States market (excluding imports) was 5.6% for the first of July, 1975, as compared with 7.5% for a comparable period in 1974.[2] If the Pontiac Division of General Motors wanted to increase its share to at least 7.5% for 1977, then part of this responsibility might be assigned to advertising and be included among the stated advertising objectives.

Consumer Awareness. A firm's advertising objective(s) may be to improve consumer awareness of the company, its product(s), or its dealers.[3] For example, market research may indicate that a company's product has a recognition problem. The survey might indicate that only 20% of the market segment to be reached has "heard of" the firm's product or that the firm's product is being confused with that of its competitor. If this is the case, an advertising objective established by the marketing manager may well be to improve this recognition to 50% by the end of the year. Such an objective not only would be appropriate for advertising, but it would also be a measurable objective.

To illustrate, we need only to remember the Goodrich Tire and Rubber Company's campaigns during 1974 and 1975. Goodrich's campaign was designed to overcome the confusion between "Goodyear" and "Goodrich." Patrick Ross, President of Goodrich, reports that as a result of this advertising campaign startling improvements were made in the public's ability to distinguish between Goodrich's name and that of the "manufacturer with the blimp."[4]

Similarly, a company may advertise just to let possible consumers, customers, and the public know that the company does exist. It is not unusual for consumers to be totally unaware of the identity of the manufacturer that produces many of the products they regularly use. This is particularly true when you consider (1) the vast numbers of companies in the marketplace today and (2) the amount of diversification. Company recognition may be important to manufacturers, however, not only because it may assist them in gaining acceptance of their new products, but it may also affect their stock prices and their ability to lobby for and against legislation.

---

[2] "U.S. Auto Sales July 1–10 Fell 5% from 74 Period," *The Wall Street Journal*, July 16, 1975, p. 4.

[3] Frederick E. Webster, Jr., *Marketing Communication* (New York: The Ronald Press Company, 1971), p. 59.

[4] Patrick C. Ross, "Advertising: A Challenge to Management," Unpublished speech at the Tri-States Marketing Conference, Kent State University, May 2, 1975.

A company may also wish to use advertising to identify its dealers. This not only provides information to possible consumers, but it also helps to strengthen the company's ties with its retail structure.

Attitude Change. Just as market research may be used to determine whether or not a firm or its product(s) suffer from lack of recognition, market research might also be used to determine how the public views the company, i.e., its image. Such research may show that 75% of the public sees a particular major corporation as being "cold" or "heartless." In this case, the company might well want to establish as its advertising objective the goal of reducing the percentage of people who see it as "cold" or "heartless" to 25%. In other words, the objective may be to increase the percentage of those who consider it to be "warm" and "concerned."

To achieve this objective, an advertising campaign might be developed that would show how the company's product(s) are used to improve health conditions in less developed countries or how domestically it provides employment or reduces pollution. But these themes must be both accurate and believable if the firm hopes to produce and sustain the desired effect.

Although corporate image improvement may be an important objective of an advertising campaign, an even more significant objective may be an attitudinal change toward the company's product. It has been suggested that improved attitudes toward product characteristics can lead to an increased probability of consumer purchases. Thus, product attitude change may be a most appropriate advertising objective.[5]

ROLE OF CONSUMER RESEARCH IN ADVERTISING DECISIONS

To devise successful marketing strategies, management must have a thorough knowledge of buyer behavior. Previous chapters have provided detailed discussions of buyer behavior and consumer research. The questions that we must answer now are as follows:

1. What role does consumer research play in the advertising decisions of the firm?
2. How may the knowledge of the buyer be translated into an effective campaign?

The following sections will describe the usefulness of consumer research in several advertising decision areas.

Selecting the Advertising Objective

Advertising objectives are the foundation of all promotional efforts. Consumer research can aid management in selecting the appropriate objective. Consumer studies may show that the firm's target audience is not aware of

---

[5] Harper W. Boyd, Jr., Michael L. Ray, and Edward C. Strong, "An Attitudinal Framework for Advertising Strategy," *Journal of Marketing* (April, 1972), pp. 28–29.

its product, does not remember its product, does not like its product (or the company itself), does not want its product, or likes a competitor's product better. Once the specific problem is uncovered, an advertising objective can be selected to focus on the problem(s).

Selecting Product Features and Consumer Benefits

Management must decide which product features and consumer benefits will be featured in its campaign. Advertising should present product features that inform, interest, and gain the attention of the audience. Benefits should be selected that persuade or stimulate the consumer to buy the firm's product. Unless effective product features and benefits are selected, the advertising message will be lost.

Management can use consumer research to uncover the features and benefits that will produce the most effective advertising. For example, an automobile manufacturer may conduct research to select the product benefits that will appeal most to its audience—safety, economy, style, quality, comfort, luxury, or prestige. The appeals used in advertising a Mercedes Benz are very different from those used to advertise a Volkswagen Rabbit.

Several examples of automobile advertisements that feature different product features and benefits are presented in Figures 9.3 through 9.5.

Selecting the Media

The advertiser may use consumer research to decide where the advertising message should be presented. Research can indicate the media habits of the firm's target audience: Do they read newspapers and magazines? Do they read *Business Week* or *Playboy?* At what times during the day do they watch television or listen to the radio?

For example, in a metropolitan area a portion of the firm's target audience may be commuting to work at 7:30 a.m. This would make radio a most appropriate medium for the firm's message.

Evaluating Advertising

Since the target of all advertising effort is the consumer, it is only logical to evaluate the effectiveness of the firm's efforts through consumer research after the campaign is completed. Research may aid management in deciding whether to continue the advertisements, to modify the advertisements, how to modify the advertisements, or to withdraw the advertisements.

Specific methods of consumer research used to evaluate advertising are discussed later in this chapter.

Figure 9.3   A Prestige Benefit

The control center of the Mercedes-Benz 280 — the most copied sedan in the world.

What does it feel like to drive the most copied sedan in the world?

Eight of the world's major automobile makers have either compared their cars to the Mercedes-Benz 280 — or have actually tried to copy it. Your first drive will show you that no one has *copied* the 280 at all.

When you take the wheel of a 280 Sedan, the automobile states its own case. Listen to the engine. It's a sophisticated overhead camshaft six.

Press the 280 into a tight turn. Fully independent suspension gives you uncanny road adhesion. And, because every wheel has its own separate suspension system, bumps or potholes can affect only one wheel.

It's a different story with most of the imitators. Their rear axles are single rigid units. So a jounce on one wheel produces a bounce on its mate.

You get what you pay for

Others have copied the 280's lines and many of its dimensions. But few have attempted to copy the completeness of its standard features. And none has matched all of its engineering features. Features that give you greater safety, comfort and performance. Features that account for the 280 Sedan's price.

Finally, consider this financial fact. Based on the average official used car prices over the past five years, a Mercedes-Benz holds its value better than any make of luxury car sold in America. And even among the Mercedes-Benz models listed, the 280 Sedan's figures are outstanding.

You get what you pay for in the 280: a unique driving experience that is the sum of *all* the reasons why the 280 is the most copied sedan in the world.

Mercedes-Benz
Engineered like no other car in the world.

The 280 Sedan: Rewards you may never have experienced in an automobile.

Source: Reprinted by permission of Mercedes-Benz of North America, Inc.

Using Consumer Research in Advertising Decisions

The usefulness of consumer research depends on the quantity and quality of the data gathered. *Whether or not consumer research is used effectively in making advertising decisions depends on the firm's commitment.*

Many firms and their advertising consultants conduct consumer research. This research is extremely helpful *if the advertiser uses the in-*

Figure 9.4   Price, Performance, Roominess, and Mileage Benefits

Based on Road & Track magazine's consideration
of hundreds of 1975 automobiles:

You're looking at the best car in the world for under $3500.*

There are winners in this world.

And there are losers.

The Volkswagen Rabbit is a winner.

After considering hundreds of '75 cars, the experts at Road & Track named it "the best car for under $3500."

Toyota didn't make it. The Datsun didn't make it. Vega, Pinto, Honda, Fiat—did not make it.

Compare the Rabbit on performance. (From 0 to 50, a Datsun B210 is 60% slower.†)

Compare the Rabbit on roominess. (It has the head and leg room of some mid-size cars.)

Compare the Rabbit on gas mileage.

39 mpg on the highway, 25 in the city. These are EPA estimates of what the Rabbit with stick shift got in 1976 EPA tests.

(The mileage you get can vary, depending on how and where you drive, optional equipment, and the condition of your car.)

No other car will give you the combination of performance, space and economy that you'll find in a Rabbit.

You owe it to yourself to try the best, before you settle for something less.

IT'S THE RABBIT.

*Suggested 1976 retail price $3,499 East Coast P.O.E. Transportation, local taxes, and dealer delivery charges additional. †Source: Agbabian Associates test results.

Source: Reprinted by permission of Volkswagen of America, Inc.

formation gathered. For example, Procter & Gamble discovered that many consumers feel guilty because they do not brush their teeth three times a day. P&G successfully used this information to promote Gleem toothpaste by using the slogan: "For the person who can't brush his teeth after every meal."[6]

[6] Richard H. Buskirk, *Principles of Marketing*, 3rd ed. (New York: Holt, Rinehart, and Winston, Inc., 1970) p. 144.

Figure 9.5   Example of Protection Benefit

BECOME AN OVERPROTECTIVE PARENT.

If there's one time your children should be protected from life's hard knocks, it's when you're traveling along the highway at 55 m.p.h.

Which is why more and more thinking parents choose to travel in the security of a Volvo wagon.

Volvo has crumple zones which collapse at a predetermined rate to help absorb the impact of a collision. The passengers are surrounded by a strong, protective cage formed by box steel pillars.

Even the U.S. government is impressed by Volvo's safety characteristics. They recently bought 24 Volvos for a crash-testing program which will help establish safety standards for cars of the future.

Volvo also has other things to add to your sense of security.

Rack and pinion steering to help you steer clear of trouble. Power disc brakes on all four wheels, instead of just two. A quick, responsive fuel-injected overhead cam engine. 3-point seat belts front *and* rear. And childproof rear door locks to keep the kids in their place.

So when you buy a Volvo wagon, you not only get a big wagon to carry your worldly possessions.

You get a safer wagon to protect your most valuable possessions of all.

VOLVO
The car for people who think.   © 1976 VOLVO OF AMERICA CORPORATION. LEASING AVAILABLE.

Source: © 1976 Volvo of America Corporation.

Nevertheless, many firms that conduct consumer research do not use the information in making advertising decisions or do not communicate it to their advertising agency. To quote one observer:

Too many advertising and marketing strategies are built on the assumption that it is always possible to single out the motives which are the key to any given sales problem. Just talk it over and put your finger on the motive . . . no manufacturer would throw his products together in the haphazard fashion that some manu-facturers fashion their sales and advertising strategies.[7]

Management should conduct consumer research and use it in advertising decisions. It is undoubtedly tempting for the marketing manager to rely on past experience or his own "feel" for the market in making his advertising decisions. However, few marketing managers today would be so unsophisticated as to not fully use all consumer research at their disposal.

ORGANIZING FOR ADVERTISING

To develop an integrated advertising program, management must organize the many activities needed to formulate successful advertising. Basically, the marketing manager must organize so that he will be sure that all necessary advertising activities will be performed and that these activities will be coordinated.

Advertising Management Within the Company

Advertising activities are sometimes handled by the department responsible for sales force operations. It is common to find such an arrangement in a small company or in a company that considers advertising a relatively unimportant part of its marketing mix.

In larger companies or in companies that consider advertising an impor-tant component of their marketing mix, advertising activities are usually handled by a separate advertising department. Here, the head of the advertising department usually reports to the marketing manager or to the vice-president for marketing, but he may report directly to the president of the company.

Although many companies operate their own advertising departments, many companies have outside firms assist them in formulating advertising. These outside firms are usually referred to as **advertising agencies.** Virtually all major corporations and many smaller companies use advertising agencies in addition to their own advertising departments. If a company uses an advertising agency, the marketing manager performs the vital functions of selecting the agency, coordinating its activities, and evaluating its efforts.

The Advertising Agency

The advertising agency is an independent company organized to supply specialized services in advertising and marketing. The traditional advertis-ing agency is an independent business organization. Creative and business

---

[7] Pierre Martineau, *Motivation in Advertising* (New York: McGraw-Hill Book Com-pany, 1957), p. 3.

FRANK AND ERNEST   by Bob Thaves

ACE ADVERTISING AGENCY

HI, THERE! WE'D LIKE ONE SLOGAN AND A JINGLE TO GO, EASY ON THE BUZZWORDS AND NO PUNCHLINE ON EITHER!

Reprinted by permission of Newspaper Enterprise Association.

people develop, prepare, and place advertising in advertising media for sellers seeking to find customers for their goods and services.[8]

Although agencies are most concerned with this traditional function, it should be noted that many agencies are equipped to provide other marketing services. Agencies now offer services in packaging design and many other services designed to aid the firm in its total marketing effort.

Why Use an Advertising Agency?

Even if a firm has a large advertising department of its own, there are several good reasons for seeking the help of an advertising agency:

1. *Number and variety of services.* The company, especially a small company, does not usually have the number and variety of advertising specialists that a medium- or large-sized advertising agency has.
2. *Lower costs for specialized services.* Even though a firm may have the resources to acquire all types of advertising specialists, it may be more economical to use the advertising agency's specialists. An agency can use its staff to provide services to many clients, thus spreading the costs of its staff over many accounts. This may lower the cost of specialized services to any individual client.
3. *Objective viewpoint.* The company may benefit from the objective or outside viewpoint that only an independent firm may be willing to offer.
4. *Experience.* A firm may find an agency's experience with similar firms or products useful in developing its own advertising program.
5. *Pressure to produce effective advertising.* An advertising agency may feel greater pressure to produce effective advertising for the firm than the firm's own advertising department would. Relations between an

[8] Frederic R. Gamble, *What Advertising Agencies Are—What They Do and How They Do It* (New York: American Association of Advertising Agencies, 1960), p. 4.

agency and a firm are very easy to terminate, but it is difficult to get rid of an ineffective advertising department.[9]

All of the above suggest that it is clearly to the firm's advantage to use an advertising agency, and generally most firms do use such an agency. However, there are potential problems that may arise—problems that the marketing manager should be aware of when he uses or selects an agency.

First, there is the possibility that agencies may encourage the firm to *overadvertise*. Since advertising agencies' compensation is usually 15% of the cost to place an advertisement in an advertising medium, its compensation will increase as more ads are placed. Most agencies do not encourage overadvertising because this practice may lead to unhappy clients. The marketing manager, however, should be aware of this potential problem and should maintain strict control over the firm's advertising budget.

The firm should also be aware that agencies typically devote more attention and talent to important clients. The firm that does not do a great deal of advertising may be at a disadvantage if its agency does not consider the firm important. Thus, the marketing manager should select an advertising agency that will consider it important. In such instances, a small advertising agency may be preferable to a major one.

Working with the Advertising Agency

To obtain the best possible service from an agency, management must take steps to ensure a close working relationship between the firm's advertising organization and the advertising agency. Management should first *decide what role the agency should play* in developing the firm's advertising program. How much should the agency participate in developing advertising objectives? Should the agency test the effectiveness of advertising? *Many potential problems between the firm and the agency can be averted by specifying the exact role the agency should play.*

Management should also take steps to establish effective communication channels between the firm's advertising organization and the agency's representative, the account manager. Management must be able to communicate its objectives, suggestions, and criticisms to the agency. Good communication is essential to ensure that the agency representative understands the desires of the firm and can communicate these desires to the creative personnel in the ad agency.

If good communication channels are established, several potential problems can be avoided. The advertising objective formulated by the company and/or agency can be integrated into all phases of advertising activity in the agency, such as preparing research, copy, and illustrations. For example, good communication curbs the tendency of some creative personnel to become involved more with artistic concerns than with producing copy and

[9] William J. Stanton, *Fundamentals of Marketing*, 3rd ed. (New York: McGraw-Hill Book Company, 1971), pp. 548–49.

illustrations in keeping with the advertising objectives and research results. If the advertising objectives are properly communicated to all agency personnel, advertising activities will be coordinated and motivated toward achieving the advertising objective.

Selecting an Advertising Agency

A particularly important decision for the marketing manager is the selection of an advertising agency to handle the firm's account. As of June, 1975 there were 405 member agencies of the American Association of Advertising Agencies. In addition, there are hundreds of other agencies, many of them one-person agencies, located around the country.

Briefly, the selection of an advertising agency requires (1) a careful examination of the firm's own needs regarding advertising service(s) and (2) a systematic evaluation of available agencies that are able to fulfill these needs.

During its self-evaluation phase, the firm determines if it needs only creative or media selection assistance or if it needs a full range of agency services, possibly including marketing research and public relations activities. Next, the marketing manager must determine if he desires an agency that has prior experience in his industry.[10] Finally, he makes decisions on the size of the agency, the specific expertise desired, the location of the agency (proximity to the firm), the age of the agency, and similar issues.

The next step is for each advertising agency to provide its prospective client the information it needs in terms of the above criteria. Finally, competing agencies prepare advertising presentations that provide samples of their creative abilities. After evaluating the alternatives, the marketing manager then chooses the agency best suited for his firm's needs.

ADVERTISING MEDIA DECISIONS

To communicate its message to consumers, the firm must use some form of advertising media. To use media effectively, the marketing manager must answer the following questions:

1. What media are available? What are their strengths and weaknesses?
2. How should advertising media be selected?
3. What criteria can be used to evaluate media?

Advertising Media

In the process of selecting the appropriate vehicle(s) to convey its message, management must consider the characteristics of the available advertising media. A discussion of the major media is provided below.

[10] An accepted advertising agency practice is not to handle the accounts of two or more competing firms.

Newspapers.   Newspapers offer a flexible means of advertising. Newspapers can be chosen to cover a local market or several urban centers. Since almost everyone reads newspapers, newspapers are an effective means of reaching general markets. Closing time (the period of time prior to publication when advertising copy must be submitted) seldom exceeds 3 days for newspapers. Thus, the firm can submit, withdraw, or modify copy up to 3 days before the advertisement is scheduled to be printed. Newspapers are also an excellent means of providing reseller support, such as cooperative advertising agreements in which the firm and its resellers share advertising costs.

However, the life of a newspaper advertisement is very short. There is little opportunity for the reader to get repeated exposure to a single advertisement. Although improvements have been made, newspapers are largely unable to offer the fine reproductions found in magazines, especially for color ads. National advertisers may also find themselves at a disadvantage in terms of cost because local advertisers pay lower rates for newspaper space than do national advertisers.

Magazines.   Magazines provide high-quality color, print, and pictorial reproduction. Magazines allow the advertiser to be highly selective in reaching specific markets. Magazines can be chosen to reach different geographical areas or demographic segments of the market. Magazines have a longer life than newspapers because they present the opportunity for repeated exposure to a single advertisement. Since magazines are often "passed along" to family and friends, a single advertisement may reach a very large readership.

Unfortunately, magazines are less flexible than newspapers in terms of publication deadlines. Magazine copy must frequently be submitted 8 weeks or more prior to publication.

Television.   Television offers a great deal of creative flexibility because advertising messages can be presented through both sight and sound. Excellent opportunities exist for product demonstrations. Television also offers a degree of selectivity because advertising messages can be presented to different geographical areas on different days at different times.

However, television is an *extremely* expensive medium and offers less audience selectivity than other media in terms of age, income, or education. Exceptions are Saturday morning programming that is generally directed toward children, late-night programs for adults, and the so-called soap operas segment of the day for women. In addition, the television message is available to the viewer for only a moment. If a message fails to reach the viewer when it is aired, the promotional opportunity is lost.

Radio.   Of all media, radio has the shortest closing times. Advertising copy can be submitted or changed minutes before it is scheduled for broadcast. Radio provides a high degree of selectivity in terms of geographical coverage and market segment appeal at a low cost primarily because individual stations are able to focus on specific groups through their programming, for example, "all-news" stations or "country/western music" stations. The availability of portable radios allows the advertiser to reach an audience anywhere, especially those traveling by car. Radio also contributes to reseller support efforts.

Outdoor Advertising. Outdoor advertising provides complete flexibility in terms of geographical coverage and the intensity of coverage in a specific market. It can also reinforce advertising presented in other media. A good opportunity exists for the viewer to be repeatedly exposed to the advertising message. It is also an excellent medium to promote widely used consumer products (cigarettes, beer, and gasoline).

Since outdoor advertising is directed toward a mobile audience, copy is necessarily limited to a few words. Outdoor advertising does not permit the firm to be selective in choosing a specific type of audience unless it is concentrated geographically within the community.

Direct Mail. Direct mail is probably the medium that allows for the greatest selectivity in the intended market. Personal letters, booklets, and brochures reach very specific markets with a minimum waste of advertising effort. The most severe limitation in using direct mail is the difficulty in getting and maintaining good mailing lists.[11]

Selection of Advertising Media

Equipped with a thorough knowledge of the advertising media, management must choose the best media for conveying its message. The first consideration involves the type(s) of media to be used: should the advertiser use newspapers, television, or magazines? The second decision involves the selection of specific advertising media. For example, if the firm decides to use magazines, should it advertise in *Reader's Digest* or *Newsweek?*

Selecting Types of Media. In deciding between types of media, the advertiser should consider at least three factors: (1) the *media habits of the target audience;* (2) the *nature of the product and product appeals;* and (3) the *costs* involved in using different media.

Since the firm's goal is to convey its message to a selected target audience, the *media habits* of this audience should be examined. For example, if an advertiser wishes to reach preschool-age children, it is likely to use television. Obviously, any advertising placed in print media (newspapers and magazines) would be ineffective since most children in this age group cannot read.

Another important factor is the *nature of the product and product appeals.* Print media is more useful for conveying complex product appeals; television is most helpful for advertising products that should be demonstrated. For example, kitchen cleaning aids are often advertised on

[11] For a thorough discussion of advertising media, see Frederick E. Webster, Jr., *Marketing Communication,* pp. 463–76.

television because their advantages can be demonstrated. Supermarket chains, such as A&P and Safeway, find newspapers the most appropriate medium for their long lists of food items.

The *costs* of different media should also be considered. Television is an expensive medium; newspaper and radio advertising are much less expensive. The most important factor is not the absolute cost of the media, but the *cost of the media* in relation to the *number of prospects reached.*

Consider Figure 9.6. When total circulation for each magazine is divided into its cost, magazine A has the lowest cost, $.05 compared to $.10 for magazine B. But, if the target market (prospects) is those readers with income over $50,000 per year, magazine B turns out to be the better choice because its cost per prospect is much lower.

Figure 9.7 shows advertising expenditures by major media in the United States and shows the relative importance of the various media. Newspapers, followed by television and direct mail, are the most heavily used media.

BUDGETING FOR ADVERTISING

To plan and control advertising expenditures, management must develop annual advertising budgets. Before advertisements can be developed and presented, the marketing manager must carefully plan the amount of resources to be allocated to advertising efforts.

Figure 9.6   Evaluating Media on a Cost Per Prospect Basis

	Magazine A	Magazine B
Cost for one-page color advertisement	$ 50,000	$ 60,000
Total circulation	1,000,000	600,000
Cost-per-reader (cost divided by total circulation)	$.05	$.10
Circulation with income over $50,000 yer year (prospects)	100,000	200,000
Cost per prospect (cost divided by number of prospects)	$.50	$.30

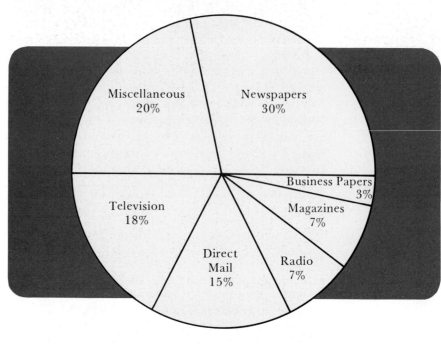

Figure 9.7   Advertising Expenditures for Major Media

Miscellaneous
20%

Newspapers
30%

Business Papers
3%

Television
18%

Magazines
7%

Direct
Mail
15%

Radio
7%

Approaches to Budgeting

Several methods are available to aid the firm in determining the size of the advertising budget. The most common approaches are explained below.

Arbitrary Allocation.   Arbitrary budgeting, that is, budgeting without careful analysis, has often been used. Advertising expenditures may simply be determined according to executive whim or emotion. While less common than several years ago, a few advertisers still do little planning in regard to their advertising allocations.

Percent of Sales.   Many companies set the advertising budget at a specified percentage of sales (either past, current, or anticipated). For example, if a company decides to allocate 2% of next year's anticipated sales of $5 million to advertising, the budget would be set at $100,000.

The percent of sales approach is widely used because it is easy to calculate and understand. It is also a financially safe method because advertising expenditures are directly related to the firm's available revenue.

Even though this approach is simple and financially safe, it *ignores the promotional job to be done.* The focus of budgeting efforts centers on calculating rather arbitrary percentages instead of analyzing the amount of money actually needed to reach the firm's advertising goals. It has the potential of either *overspending or underspending* in terms of achieving such goals. If the firm uses this method, it also makes the mistake of viewing advertising as the result of sales instead as the cause of sales.

Return on Investment. Some observers suggest that advertising expenditures should be viewed as an investment for the firm. Thus, advertising should compete for its share of corporate funds in the same way that other investments, such as plant additions, compete.[12]

Although this approach is logically appealing, it is neither widely accepted nor used. The major problem is in implementing this approach in realistic business situations. Management can usually do little more than estimate the probable returns from advertising dollars spent. Furthermore, the Internal Revenue Service views advertising expenditures as annual operating expenses, not as long-term investments.

Competitive Parity. Firms sometimes establish their budgets by matching the advertising budgets of their competitors. Data on industry advertising expenditures are readily available from advertising periodicals and various trade journals. (Figure 9.8 provides an example of average expenditures as a percentage of sales for various industries.)

The use of competitive parity has been defended for several reasons. This approach considers competitive actions an important part of any firm's operating environment. Widespread use of competitive parity may also prevent advertising wars between firms.

However, the firm using competitive parity may be making several unrealistic assumptions. First, it is assumed that all competitors have similar advertising objectives and resources. It is further assumed that advertising dollars can be spent in an equally effective manner by all competitors. Since no two firms have identical marketing situations, such assumptions reduce the value of this approach.

All-You-Can-Afford. Some companies set their advertising budgets according to what they can afford. This approach may be useful to a firm because it does have the effect of establishing an *upper limit* on advertising.

The all-you-can-afford approach is seldom relied upon exclusively in determining the budget. An advertising budget based on this method alone is seldom related to the firm's advertising objectives. This approach may lead to either underspending or overspending.

Objective and Task. To correctly determine its annual budget, the firm should specify its advertising objective(s), detail the tasks to be performed in order to reach the stated objective(s), and calculate the costs of performing the necessary tasks. This approach is generally considered superior to all others because it clearly relates the budget allocation to the advertising job to be done.

[12] Joel Dean, *Managerial Economics* (Englewood Cliffs, N.J.: Prentice-Hall, Inc., 1951), pp. 368–69.

Figure 9.8 Percentage of Sales Invested In Advertising for Selected Industries, 1976

Industry	Percentage
Agriculture-Crops	2.1
Canned foods	2.9
Chemicals and allied products	1.1
Dairy products	1.9
Distilled alcoholic beverages	5.3
Meat packers	0.5
Motion picture producers	7.0
Publishing	2.0
Railroads	0.6
Real estate	3.1
Restaurant and fast-food chains	2.5
Retail department stores	2.5
Retail furniture stores	4.8
Retail mail order	16.1
Soft drinks	5.9
Textile products	0.5
Trucking	0.3

Source: Schonfeld and Associates, Inc., Chicago, Illinois, by permission.

Unfortunately, several difficulties arise in using the objective and task method. The major one is that firms frequently do not know the effect of advertising dollars on the objective these dollars are supposed to achieve. For example, how many sales dollars will result from one dollar spent on advertising? Also, there may be disagreements as to what objectives should be achieved and how best to achieve them.

MEASURING ADVERTISING EFFECTIVENESS

A very important step in measuring advertising effectiveness is deciding on the specific criteria to be used for judging effectiveness. Should advertising effectiveness be measured in terms of total sales, market share, consumer awareness, or attitude change? The answer should be straightforward if the firm has explicitly stated its advertising objective(s). The measures to be used for evaluation should have been considered at the time the advertising objective was selected.

When Should Advertising Be Evaluated?

Advertisements can be tested *before* they are presented to the public (*pre-testing advertising*) and/or *after* they are presented to the public (*post-testing advertising*).

Pre-testing. Pre-testing provides an estimate of potential effectiveness before an advertisement is actually broadcast or printed. The pre-test may focus on the potential consumer's reaction to the various aspects of the campaign or advertisement—themes, slogans, visuals, or copy—or it may attempt to determine the potential consumer's response to the entire advertisement or campaign. The firm can measure the effectiveness of a proposed advertisement before more funds are invested in the project. If a firm is able to measure the potential performance of an advertisement or campaign, it can decide whether to continue, modify, or withdraw a particular advertisement or campaign before it is presented to the public.

Post-testing. Post-testing provides an estimate of effectiveness after the advertisement has been broadcast or printed. If the firm has good measures of actual performance, it can compare its advertising results with its advertising objectives. Pre-test measures cannot be tied directly to marketplace response, but post-test measures can. The post-test involves an examination of awareness change, sales improvement, or whatever else the objective for the campaign or advertisement may have been. With this information, management can decide whether its advertising should be continued, modified, or withdrawn.

How Should Advertising Be Evaluated?

Numerous methods have been devised to test advertising effectiveness. In choosing which method to use, management should consider the following factors:

1. *When* testing is to be performed.
2. The amount of *time available* for testing.
3. The amount of *management resources and funds available* for testing.
4. The *costs* of testing in relation to the benefits derived.

Frequently the advertiser and/or its agency will hire the services of a marketing research firm to conduct testing. Such expenditures must be judged in terms of improving advertising decisions.

Pre-testing Methods

Direct Ranking and Rating. Consumers are asked to analyze advertisements and other forms of communications by ranking or rating them. Respondents may be asked to rank advertisements in order of their appeal, interest, or persuasiveness. Rankings can also be obtained by asking respondents to *compare pairs of advertisements* one pair at a time.

The main drawback in using ranking methods is the assumption that the advertisement ranked first will be successful. None of the alternatives may be good enough to succeed, even though one or two advertisements may be superior to others.

To avoid this difficulty, various forms of *rating scales* can be used for evaluation purposes. One of the most widely used scales is the semantic differential.[13] Respondents are asked to judge each advertisement in terms of paired polar adjectives such as "interesting—boring" or "hard to read—easy to read."

Readership/Viewership and Recall Measurement. It is possible to screen advertisements by measuring their ability to capture and hold attention. One frequently used method is portfolio testing, which involves exposing respondents to a group of test advertisements. After reading the portfolio, respondents are asked to recall the ads they saw and to recall as much as they can about each ad.

Advertisements may also be tested by using *dummy advertising vehicles*. Magazines that are specially prepared for the test and that include test advertisements are distributed to the respondents to read. Respondents are then asked to recall the ads they have seen in the "phony" magazine.

To test television commercials, television programs containing test commercials are aired in special studios for test groups. Respondents are interviewed shortly after the show to measure how well they recall a specific commercial. In some instances, electronic devices are provided so that the respondents can indicate their reactions to the commercial while it is in progress.

Other Measures. Advertisements are sometimes tested by using *laboratory measures*. Various devices are available to detect changes in the respondent's heart beat, blood pressure, and pupil dilation. These measures are frequently considered to be indicators of the advertisement's ability to gain attention and arouse the consumer.[14]

A less dramatic form of pre-testing involves **test marketing,** described earlier in this text. The entire campaign, individual advertisements, or themes may be tested under real conditions in a limited market. However, advertisements are usually evaluated by using other pre-test techniques before they are incorporated into the test market situation.

Post-testing Measures

Content Analysis and Checklists. Advertisements can be evaluated by using checklists to analyze the specific contents of ads. A firm using this approach decides which criteria should be used to evaluate the ad's theme,

---

[13] For a good description of the semantic differential, see Harper W. Boyd, Jr., and Ralph Westfall, *Marketing Research*, 3rd ed. (Homewood, Ill.: Richard D. Irwin, Inc., 1972), pp. 327–29.

[14] For an excellent discussion of laboratory measures and other pre-test techniques, see James F. Engel, Hugh G. Wales, and Martin R. Warshaw, *Promotional Strategy* (Homewood, Ill.: Richard D. Irwin, Inc., 1967), pp. 302–21.

headline, copy, or illustration. After the message has been presented, the advertisement is evaluated against the selected criteria.

For example, the advertiser may want to answer questions such as:

1. Was the advertisement easy to understand?
2. Did the headline attract attention?
3. Was the advertisement believable?
4. Was the advertising message easy to remember?

Recognition Measures.   In this approach, a sample of readers is questioned to determine whether or not the readers recognize advertisements in a specific magazine or newspaper issue.

The most widely recognized approach to measuring readership is the Starch method. The Starch organization annually surveys approximately 30,000 advertisements in nearly 1,000 consumer and farm magazines, business publications, and newspapers.[15] After questioning selected readers, the Starch organization reports three principal recognition scores:

1. *Noted:* the percent of readers who remember seeing a particular advertisement
2. *Seen-associated:* the percent of readers who recall seeing or reading any part of the advertisement that identifies the advertiser's product or service
3. *Read most:* the percent of readers who report reading at least one-half of the advertisement

The Starch approach permits the marketing manager to evaluate the results of the firm's advertising in terms of readership by men and women. Each element of the advertisement is rated—headline, illustration, and copy. The marketing manager is then able to compare the response to his firm's advertising with the responses to the advertising of his competitors who are advertising in the same magazine.

Recall Measures.   These techniques involve selecting regular users of an advertising medium. Respondents are asked to recall any advertisers or products that have been in a particular issue and to remember everything they can about the advertisements.

Interviewers may or may not aid respondents in recalling advertisements. A good example of the aided recall approach is the *Gallup-Robinson Impact Test.* Magazine readers are allowed to participate only if they can remember at least one editorial feature of the issue under study. Eligible respondents are then handed a group of cards containing the names of advertised brands that appeared in the issue and some brands that did not appear. If the respondent remembers any of the advertised brands, he is asked to recall as much as he can about individual ads. Scores are recorded only if the respondent has recalled the specific advertisement included in the magazine issue and if it is the first time he has seen the particular advertisement.[16]

[15] Ibid., p. 440.
[16] Ibid., p. 445.

Other Measures.   When the firm's advertising objective is increased total sales or market share, *sales response measures* can be used. The marketing manager may attempt to relate advertising effectiveness to the firm's sales or market share. If the sales objective has not been achieved, a careful examination should be conducted to determine why.

However, the firm's advertising personnel and agency may be reluctant to use sales data as a measure of advertising effectiveness. They recognize that a multitude of variables can affect sales results—the product's price, the channels of distribution used, the quality of the product, and competition, for example. Thus, failure to reach a sales objective may not be the fault of the advertising program.

THE RETAIL ADVERTISER

Although the majority of advertising is concentrated at the manufacturer level, retail establishments do use advertising extensively in their marketing mixes. The amount spent on advertising varies according to the type and size of the retail operation. A small neighborhood retailer may spend relatively little on advertising, whereas large retail chains and franchise systems may allocate a large percentage of resources to advertising. The heaviest retail advertiser, Sears, spent about $245 million on advertising in 1976.[17]

The Nature of Retail Advertising

A distinction can be drawn between manufacturer advertising and retail advertising by considering the purpose behind the advertising effort. A manufacturer's advertising *urges the consumer to buy his product* in the store of his choice. The retail advertiser hopes to *get the consumer to buy at his store,* regardless of the products purchased.[18]

Advertising placed by retailers is usually referred to as *local advertising;* advertising placed by manufacturers is usually referred to as *national advertising.* However, retail advertising can be either local or national. The terms "national" and "local" refer not only to the level of the advertiser (retailer or manufacturer) but also to the media used and the way in which the advertising is placed. Newspaper advertisements placed by Sears in local cities are referred to as local advertising since they are *placed by the individual stores.* However, when Sears advertises its men's clothing in a national medium, such as *Sports Illustrated,* it is a national advertiser.

Responsibility for Retail Advertising

The responsibility for retail advertising depends primarily on the type and size of store. In small retail establishments, advertising is normally handled by the *owner or manager* of the store. Larger retail establishments usually

[17] *Advertising Age,* August 29, 1977, p. 1.
[18] Stanton, *Fundamentals of Marketing,* 3rd ed., p. 536.

have a formal advertising department or promotion department that handles the store's advertising.

Retail chains or franchise groups often have a *central advertising department* that establishes strategies, provides assistance to individual stores, and coordinates local programs. The central advertising department may establish the advertising objective, create the advertising theme, and provide sample advertisements for local establishments. In such arrangements, individual local establishments should be given ample authority to adapt centralized advertising decisions to the local marketing environment. Individual stores within the retail chain may serve different consumer markets, operate in different social and economic climates, and face varying degrees of competition.

Some of the conditions that may be imposed by a franchisor on its franchise establishments may be directly related to advertising. These could range from a common outdoor sign, such as the familiar Holiday Inn sign or the McDonald's golden arches, to the use of a common logo. When Dunkin' Donuts announced its new logo in June, 1976, the logo became a part of all its franchise advertising.[19]

Retail establishments may seek help from advertising agencies, advertising service companies, and advertising media. Larger retailers and retail chains are most likely to use advertising agencies. Advertising service companies, which provide only creative skills such as sample newspaper ads and artwork, can be particularly useful to small independent retailers. Many media, especially newspapers, also have advertising specialists to assist retailers.[20]

Retailers frequently receive allowances from manufacturers to advertise their products. In these cooperative advertising programs, manufacturers help in developing their ads.

RESTRAINTS ON ADVERTISING

Advertisers must cope with a growing number of restraints placed on the content and presentation of advertising messages.

Federal, state, and local governments have established laws and other safeguards to oversee advertising activities. In the United States, promotional activities are regulated by several pieces of legislation, such as the Federal Trade Commission Act and the Robinson-Patman Act.[21]

Social attitudes and beliefs can also restrain advertising formulation—especially for certain product classes such as tobacco and alcoholic beverages. Several years ago an agreement was made to eliminate cigarette

[19] *Advertising Age*, July 5, 1976, p. 6.

[20] Don L. James, Bruce J. Walker, and Michael J. Etzel, *Retailing Today* (New York: Harcourt Brace Jovanovich, Inc., 1975), p. 369.

[21] For a good discussion of governmental regulation, see "How Government Regulates Business," *Advertising Age*, November 21, 1973, pp. 144–55.

advertising from television. As a result, the major tobacco companies, such as Philip Morris, British American Tobacco, and R. J. Reynolds, have been forced to depend on other media. In a more drastic move, the Norwegian government recently banned all forms of liquor advertising in its country.[22]

Limits are also placed on advertising by the industry itself. Advertising media, advertising agencies, and trade associations have made attempts at self-regulation through a variety of codes and standards. An excellent example of self-regulation is the Standards of Practice of the American Association of Advertising Agencies. First developed in 1924 and revised in 1962, the code states that members will not knowingly produce advertising that contains:

1. False or misleading statements or exaggerations, visual or verbal.
2. Testimonials that do not reflect the real choice of a competent witness.
3. Price claims that are misleading.
4. Comparisons that unfairly disparage a competitive product or service.
5. Claims insufficiently supported or that distort the true meaning of practicable application of statements made by professional or scientific authority.
6. Statements, suggestions, or pictures offensive to public decency.[23]

ADVERTISING IN NONPROFIT ORGANIZATIONS

The basics of advertising have been presented in terms of the profit-oriented firm that wishes to promote a product, service, or company image. However, advertising can also be used as a tool for advancing social ideas and concepts. Governments, colleges, churches, labor unions, and political parties have used *nonprofit advertising* to promote a multitude of ideas and practices.

Advertising by Governments

Governments have become very active in the advertising business. In 1976, the federal government became America's 17th largest advertiser—spending $113 million for promoting such causes as the Armed Forces, the U.S. Postal Service, and Amtrak.[24] Over 70% of the advertising budget is aimed at military recruiting, which has become a massive problem since the demise of the draft. The U.S. Postal Service uses advertising to urge its customers to use zip codes and change of address forms.[25] Funds have also

---

[22] *Advertising Age*, June 28, 1976, p. 54.
[23] "Standards of Practice," *1975–76 Roster and Organization of the American Association of Advertising Agencies*, p. 18.
[24] *Advertising Age*, August 29, 1977, p. 1.
[25] "USPS Starts Big Ad Drive for Address Forms," *Advertising Age*, June 21, 1976, p. 104.

been allocated to promote U.S. bonds, the Peace Corps, and highway safety.[26]

State and local governments sponsor advertising to promote tourism, publicly owned utilities, port authorities, and corporate investment. The state government of North Carolina has recently appropriated over $1.2 million to promote tourism and industrial development in the state.[27] The local governments of several large urban centers use advertising to create a better image of their cities. Recent campaigns have featured slogans such as "St. Louis has it from A to Z" and "Cleveland is a great place to live."

Foreign governments have also found advertising an effective means of promoting social causes. A notable example is the British government, which became its country's largest advertiser in 1975. The government spent $27 million to persuade its citizens to save energy, wear seat belts, and buy proof-set coins produced by the Royal Mint.[28]

Advertising by Colleges and Universities

Hundreds of colleges and universities regularly use advertising to boost enrollment, promote special seminars and courses, and solicit gifts and endowments. Faced with declining enrollments and rising costs, private and state universities have budgeted unprecedented amounts for advertising efforts. The Wharton Evening School, for example, budgets $7,600 annually for newspaper advertisements.[29]

In promoting higher education, colleges and universities use a variety of appeals. The University of California at Berkeley advertises the "California summer." The University of Maine states that its "recreational opportunities are endless." Many universities tout unusual programs and activities to lure students. The University of Arizona advertises summer tours to Las Vegas and the Grand Canyon. In a similar vein, the University of Colorado offers a noncredit course in mountain climbing.[30]

Advertising by Religious Institutions

Religious associations and churches use advertising to promote church services and programs, present religious programming, and disseminate information about specific religious sects. Thousands of local churches use newspapers to advertise the locations and times of church services and activities. Churches and religious groups regularly present Sunday services

[26] "How U.S. Uses Advertising—A Growing Activity," *Advertising Age*, November 21, 1973, pp. 160–62.

[27] "North Carolina Account Lures 63 Agencies," *Advertising Age*, June 14, 1976, p. 16.

[28] "Government Takes Over as Top British Advertiser," *Advertising Age*, July 12, 1976, p. 87.

[29] "Ads Push Thousands of Public Causes," *Advertising Age*, November 21, 1973, p. 158.

[30] "Beautiful Old Siwash: Schools Wax Eloquent in Vying for Students," *The Wall Street Journal*, July 6, 1972, p. 1.

Figure 9.9   Religion in American Life Campaign

All men grapple with the questions . . .
Why poverty in a land of plenty? Why loneliness
in a world that would join hands? Why war when
the impulse of the heart is to love? The aching
chasm between the real and the ideal, everywhere
provokes the question . . .

WHY?

In a world looking for answers maybe God is the place to start.
God is hope. God is now.

Source: Courtesy of The Advertising Council, Inc.

on television and radio. Much of the media time for religious programs is contributed without charge by television and radio stations. In the United Kingdom all television channels are required to broadcast programs with religious themes for 70 minutes every Sunday.[31]

[31] "The 'God Slot'," *Advertising Age*, June 14, 1976, p. 84.

A great deal of advertising is sponsored by religious associations. A good example is Religion in American Life, Inc. (RIAL), a nonprofit group backed by Protestants, Roman and Eastern Orthodox Catholics, and Jews. With an advertising budget of $200,000 and approximately $27 million worth of donated media time and space, RIAL develops advertising for television, radio, magazines, newspapers, subway stations, and train stations.[32] See Figure 9.9 for an example of advertising by RIAL.

Advertising by Political Parties

In the past decade political parties have become avid users of advertising. In 1972 political parties spent an estimated $400 million for federal, state, and local campaigns.[33]

Although political advertising dates back to the 1930's, political parties have now adopted the more "scientific" approaches used by consumer goods manufacturers. Although candidates still use the traditional campaign techniques such as handshaking, speechmaking, and baby-kissing, campaigns now follow a more sophisticated approach to the political marketing problem—including extensive use of mass communication media such as television.[34]

SUMMARY

Advertising is the principal method many firms use to make initial contacts with potential customers for the purpose of informing them about goods and services and encouraging them to purchase these goods and services. Marketing managers are responsible for a number of advertising decisions, including advertising objectives, selecting the advertising agency, choosing the advertising media to be used, and determining the effectiveness of the company's advertising program. Since a company's advertising strategy is only part of its overall marketing plan, the advertising program must be consistent with and complement the total marketing effort.

To make effective advertising decisions, information about the market must be available to the advertiser. The market's needs and wants are important. Also, the advertiser must get feedback from the market so that he can see how effective his advertising messages are.

Advertising agencies provide a number of advantages. They offer assistance in developing individual advertisements and campaigns. They make available research about media and markets. They provide an objective viewpoint that may often be lacking in a company.

Deciding on how much money to be spent for advertising is an important decision. In general, a company should spend what is required to

---

[32] Edward B. Fiske, "The Selling of the Diety 1973," *Saturday Review*, December 9, 1972, pp. 17–19.

[33] "Ads Push Thousands of Public Causes," p. 158.

[34] For a more detailed discussion of marketing in the political arena, see Philip Kotler, *Marketing for Nonprofit Organizations* (Englewood Cliffs, N.J.: Prentice-Hall, Inc., 1975), pp. 365–88.

achieve the objectives stipulated for advertising. Unfortunately, many companies use less desirable ways of establishing the size of the advertising budget, such as the percentage of sales approach, the arbitrary allocation method, the all-you-can-afford approach, and the competitive parity method.

Measures of advertising effectiveness can be used before or after an advertising campaign is run. Pre-testing, such as direct ranking and rating, recall measurement, and laboratory experiments, provides an indication of the advertisement's potential effectiveness. Content analysis, recognition measures, recall measures, and other types of post-test measures determine a campaign's effectiveness after it has been conducted.

Most large firms have separate departments to handle their advertising function. Since smaller firms tend not to have separate advertising organizations, they rely on advertising agencies for their advertising programs.

In recent years there has been an increase in advertising sponsored by nonprofit organizations. Advertising by federal, state, and local governments is an example. Colleges and universities, religious organizations, and political parties also do a great deal of advertising.

QUESTIONS

1. Define the following terms: advertising, image advertising, and advertising in nonprofit organizations.
2. The marketing manager plays a vital role in the firm's advertising formulation. Describe the specific responsibilities of the marketing manager.
3. Describe how consumer research can aid management in making advertising decisions.
4. Most manufacturers and many retailers use the services of an advertising agency. What are the advantages and drawbacks in using an advertising agency? If a firm wishes to use an advertising agency, how can management select an appropriate agency?
5. Discuss the strengths and weaknesses of the following advertising media: newspapers, magazines, and television.
6. Many firms use the percent of sales method to budget for advertising. What are the advantages and disadvantages of this method? Which of the other five budgeting methods do you consider the best alternative to the percent of sales method? Why?
7. Evaluating advertising effectiveness is a crucial part of the advertising process. Explain pre-testing and post-testing. Why are they important? What methods can be used to pre-test and post-test advertisements?

Advertising: advertising is nonpersonal communication through media for which payment is made

Advertising Agency: an independent company organized to supply specialized services in advertising and marketing; typically receives its income on a commission basis (usually 15%)

Media: print and broadcast organizations used by advertisers to reach their customers; they include magazines, newspapers, radio stations, television stations, outdoor poster companies, and transit companies

Nonprofit Advertising: advertising by organizations such as governments (local, state, or national), colleges, churches, labor unions, and political parties; these organizations were established to achieve clearly defined objectives other than profit, but they still have messages to communicate to the public

Post-testing Advertising: research designed to determine the effectiveness of an advertisement or advertising campaign after its general appearance in the media

Pre-testing Advertising: research designed to determine the effectiveness of an advertisement or advertising campaign prior to its general appearance in the media

CASES

Case 1: Borden, Inc.

Borden, Inc. produces a variety of products: dairy products, consumer packaged goods, and chemical products. One of Borden's most successful products is Cracker Jacks, packaged carmelized popcorn and peanuts.

To promote Cracker Jacks, Borden advertises heavily on TV shows for children. These ads emphasize the good taste of Cracker Jacks.

Borden has now decided to broaden Cracker Jacks advertising to include daytime programs that are usually viewed by housewives and mothers. These ads will urge mothers to buy Cracker Jacks for their children because it includes only natural and wholesome ingredients.

1. Do you think Borden should advertise to both children and mothers?
2. Do you believe TV is the right medium for Cracker Jacks advertising?

Case 2: Advertising by the Professions

Various professions, such as lawyers, dentists, doctors, and certified public accountants long had a history of not advertising. Listings in the white and yellow pages of telephone directories were the closest any of these professions came to advertising. Most of the professions did not attach even the type of work they performed such as lawyers indicating their specialty was taxes or antitrust law. Doctors, however, usually indicated their specialty, for example, orthopedics, pediatrics, or gynecology.

In 1977, lawyers began to advertise. Such advertising was generally limited to an indication of the lawyer's specialty and the fee associated with the attorney's services.

1. Should other professional groups advertise?
2. Besides specialty and fee, what other appeals might the professions use in their advertising?
3. How might the professions benefit from advertising?
4. Are there any disadvantages that might result from advertising by the professions?

The Personal Selling Function

After you finish this chapter, you should be able to answer the following questions:

1. Salespeople need various types of information in order to carry out their responsibilities. What are four major kinds of information requirements?

2. Company goals and goals of the salesperson often clash. Can you identify these different goals?

3. There must be a great deal of cooperation between the sales manager and his salespeople. What are those areas where cooperation is especially needed?

4. The sales manager will secure more cooperation from his salespeople if he can show them how they can benefit from cooperating with him. What are these major benefits?

5. When establishing goals and evaluating salespeople, the sales manager must recognize differences in their territories. What factors should be considered in examining sales territories?

6. The most productive salespeople are those who can effectively manage their time. What can salespeople do to make the best use of their available time?

7. More than anything else, sales managers must deal effectively with people. How can this be done?

INTRODUCTION The company's sales force is one of its most important assets and it is a major component of the firm's promotion mix. Very frequently its effectiveness in large measure determines the extent to which overall marketing objectives will be achieved. This is especially true for firms in which the sales force is a major element of the marketing mix, such as those that market industrial products or various kinds of services (for example, insurance) or those that sell directly to the consumer (Avon). It is also true to some extent for those that sell consumer products to a mass market of consumers in which middlemen are used.

In this chapter we would like to do two major things. First, we want to get an appreciation of the major responsibilities of a salesperson. Second, we want to understand how the sales manager can effectively manage a sales force.

WHAT A SALESPERSON DOES

Although there is a great deal of variation in what salespeople do because there are so many different kinds of selling jobs, there are basic sales activities that most salespeople perform. These include acquiring the necessary information for successful selling, pre-presentation planning, giving the presentation, and performing post-presentation activities. The sequence of these basic activities and their components are shown in Figure 10.1.

Acquiring Information Required for Successful Selling

Before salespeople can begin to plan sales presentations and actually give these presentations to prospects, they must acquire information about their company, the products sold, the competition, and the market.

Salespeople must understand the basic objectives, philosophies, operations, and policies of their company, especially those that pertain to the selling job. For example, salespeople must know how much credit can be extended to customers and how long deliveries will take. It is helpful if they can tell customers how much time will be involved in processing orders. The timing of advertising campaigns should be dovetailed with the sales efforts so that maximum benefit from the sales help provided by advertising can be obtained.

Product knowledge is crucial to success in selling. Complete information

Figure 10.1 The Four Major Responsibilities of Salespeople

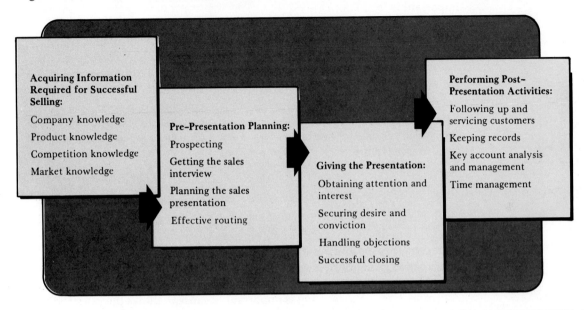

Acquiring Information Required for Successful Selling:

Company knowledge

Product knowledge

Competition knowledge

Market knowledge

Pre-Presentation Planning:

Prospecting

Getting the sales interview

Planning the sales presentation

Effective routing

Giving the Presentation:

Obtaining attention and interest

Securing desire and conviction

Handling objections

Successful closing

Performing Post–Presentation Activities:

Following up and servicing customers

Keeping records

Key account analysis and management

Time management

about the products handled, including sizes, styles, colors, tensile strength, and so on, is necessary. Salespeople must also know why and how their products are different from the competition's products. The sales force must be able to tell customers about the benefits they will obtain from using their company's products and about the after-the-sale service available. They must know the product prices and the discounts from these prices.

Product knowledge is so important that in a survey of 800 sales and marketing executives product knowledge was cited as the most important sales training topic.[1]

Salespeople do a better job when they have knowledge of their competitors. Below are some of the important aspects of competition's operations:

1. Products.
2. Prices.
3. Differences between competitor's products and salesperson's own product line.
4. Tactics and strategies of competing salesmen.
5. Benefits obtained from competing products.
6. Changes in competitor marketing tactics and strategies.

[1] *Sales Management* (March 3, 1975), p. 10.

There are many sources of information that a sales force can use to keep abreast of the competition. Annual reports, and newspaper and magazine articles are excellent sources. Customers are an invaluable source about competitors. Trade fairs and competition advertisements frequently provide important information.

The more knowledge salespersons have about the market for their products, the better job they will be able to do. A sales force must know the needs and desires of the market so that it can show how these needs and desires can be satisfied by the products being sold. Those who make the purchase decisions should be identified. The extent to which customers are satisfied with current offerings should be determined. Salespeople must determine at what stage the prospective buyer is, and they must determine how much resistance they can expect so that adjustments can be made in their presentations.

Pre-Presentation Planning

Once the sales force has the information necessary for successful selling, it is ready to develop plans for making presentations to prospects and customers. Prospecting, getting the sales interview, planning the sales presentation, and effective routing are important aspects of pre-presentation planning.

Prospecting. **Prospecting** is important because it allows the sales force to make effective use of time, it increases the sales volume obtained, and it enables increased compensation. Prospecting refers to a ranking of customers according to their potential sales volume and the likelihood of their purchasing the product. This likelihood (probability) is a result of a number of factors, including how closely the product's features and benefits satisfy needs and desire, how satisfied a prospect is with current products, and so on. A customer who has a potential sales volume of $20,000 and a probability of purchasing of .7 is a better prospect than one who has a potential sales volume of $10,000 and a probability of purchasing of .3 ($20,000 × .7 = $14,000; $10,000 × .3 = $3,000).

In developing prospects, the following sources are available: prospect lists provided by the salesperson's company, referrals from current customers, inquiries from possible customers, and leads furnished from advertising, canvassing, and former customers.

Getting the Sales Interview. The smart salesperson sets up a sales interview in advance. This virtually eliminates the possibility of not having a prospect with whom to talk. Less time will be devoted to non-interested prospects, and the salesperson will have a better idea of what to stress in the interview because he has had time to determine the prospect's needs and desires.

Planning the Sales Presentation. With the sales interview established and prospecting accomplished, the actual sales presentation can now be planned. Products to be presented can be decided upon, as well as product features and benefits that most closely satisfy customer needs and desires. Then the salesperson develops an outline of the presentation (a **planned presentation**) or even goes so far as to determine a word-by-word presentation (**canned presentation**). Canned presentations are more likely to be used in formal presentations to buying committees of large companies.

While the presentation is being planned, the salesperson also considers which audio-visual aids to use and when in the presentation they should appear. Audio-visual aids often increase the effectiveness of a presentation. Popular examples of audio-visual aids include overhead projectors, slides, movies, and filmstrips.

Effective Routing.   Effective routing involves the sequence in which customers and prospects will be contacted. Which streets or highways to be traveled, how long it will take to get from one customer to the next, and how long to stay with each customer are factors to be considered.

In developing the route, a salesperson tries to reduce the travel time because it will result in lower travel costs for the company and more selling time. More selling time should increase sales volume and the salesperson's compensation.

Many sophisticated mathematical models have been developed to aid routing efforts. These minimize travel distance, travel times, and travel costs, although one model dealt with maximizing profits.[2]

Giving the Presentation

In making sales presentations, it is usually assumed that the salesperson wants to obtain the prospect's attention, interest, desire, and conviction in order to make a sale. In addition, handling objections and using successful closing techniques are also important.

Securing Attention and Interest.   The major way that attention and interest can be obtained is by showing the prospect how the product can satisfy his most important need. For example, a salesman might say "Mr. Jones, how would you like to save $200,000 a year in producing cotton towels? Our new machinery can obtain these savings for you."

Obtaining Desire and Conviction.   Desire and conviction lead the prospect closer to making a favorable buying decision. Providing facts and figures is often a good way to secure desire and conviction. Using testimonials of satisfied customers is helpful. Demonstrating the product and getting the prospect to use the product or considering how he would use it are other successful approaches. Visual aids can also help obtain desire and conviction.

Handling Objections.   The good salesperson is rarely disturbed by customer objections because from experience he knows what to expect and can handle the objections. Objections tend to be minimized if the salesper-

---

[2] William A. Lazer, Richard T. Hise, and Jay A. Smith, "Computer Routing—Putting Salesmen in Their Places," *Sales Management* (March 15, 1970), pp. 28–32.

son has done a good job of offering products that satisfy a prospect's needs and desires.

An effective way to handle objections is to agree with the objection—if it is valid—and then try to turn it into an advantage.

An insurance salesman, for example, might say: "I agree, Mr. Jones, that the cost of our life insurance is 10% higher than the industry average, but we are providing much better coverage and 25% higher retirement benefits."

Successful Closing. Successful closing means that the prospect has decided to purchase. There are a number of techniques that are helpful in successful closing. Some of these are listed in Figure 10.2.

The salesperson's job does not end with obtaining a sale. There are a number of post-presentation activities that must be performed.

Performing Post-Presentation Activities

Customers need to be followed up and served. Customers should be contacted periodically so that the sales force can determine if they are satisfied with the product. If they are not satisfied, corrective measures should be taken so that customers will not be lost.

Customer complaints and returned goods should be cheerfully and promptly handled. Any credit problems should be taken care of quickly. The salesperson should ensure that installation, repair, and servicing obligations are being fulfilled.

Keeping Records. Keeping records is considered by most salespeople as an unnecessary evil. In many companies it takes up a large percentage of their total time, often accounting for as much as one-fourth of the working day.

Figure 10.2   Tips for Successful Closing

1. Don't be afraid to ask for the order.
2. Use trial closings during the presentation.
3. Look for closing signals from the prospect, such as questions about price, installation, repairs, and so on.
4. Secure the prospect's agreement of product features and benefits.
5. Review major product benefits prior to asking for the order.
6. Reduce the number of alternative choices for the prospect.
7. Use guarantees and warranties to aid closing.
8. Analyze past-presentations in order to determine which closing techniques work best in various selling situations.

The sales force must keep some records. Management has to know on whom the sales force called; what was purchased; the reasons given if a sale did not occur; and expenses incurred, such as travel, food, and lodging. Many firms are trying to reduce the amount of paper work for their salespeople by giving them more home-office clerical help and by computerizing the processing and analysis of data so that the salespeople will have more time for actual selling and better and more timely information.

Figure 10.3 lists some of the data that should be included in the record-keeping efforts. These data are also helpful when the salesperson is performing the other post-presentation responsibilities.

Key Account Analysis and Management. It is possible to identify key accounts from a salesperson's records. These accounts make up that small nucleus of customers that accounts for large percentages of a company's sales volume and profit, or they are the customers who have above-average sales volumes and profits. A customer may also be considered a key account if in the future it is likely to experience substantial growth in sales volume or profit potential.

Since key accounts are critical to a firm's success, they must receive plenty of attention from the sales force.

Time Management. Effective management of time is a key variable in separating the successful salesperson from the mediocre one. Good time management enables the salesperson to reduce the amount of time devoted

Figure 10.3 Information to Be Included in Salespeople's Records

1. Name of customer called on and his location.
2. Whether the customer made a purchase.
3. The kind of purchase made, including name of item, size, style, and amount purchased.
4. Total dollar sales volume of the purchase.
5. The route taken to make calls and the travel time needed between each customer.
6. The length of time salespeople had to wait to see customer.
7. Reasons why customers bought or did not buy.
8. Objections the customer made during the sales presentation.
9. Customer complaints about the product or the salesperson's company.
10. Expenses the salesperson incurred, such as food, lodging, and gasoline and oil.
11. New products brought out by competition.
12. New marketing strategies of competition.
13. Customer future needs.

to unprofitable activities so that more time can be devoted to direct contact with customers and prospects.

Reducing travel time and waiting time, better routing, making appointments in advance, and making use of unproductive times are important aspects of time management. For example, while waiting to meet with a customer, a salesperson could record the information about the call just made.

Now that the reader has a good idea of what a salesperson's major responsibilities are, we will turn our attention to managing the sales force.

MANAGING THE SALES FORCE

The seven major tasks that sales managers generally perform in managing their sales forces are shown in Figure 10.4.

RECRUITING

There are essentially three major phases of the recruiting responsibility. First, sales managers must decide the *number* of salespeople they need to hire. Second, they must have an idea of the *kind* of person to be recruited. Third, they must be knowledgeable about the various *sources* for salespeople.

Figure 10.4   The Seven Basic Tasks of the Sales Manager

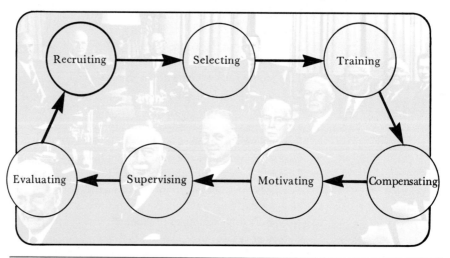

Marketing Mix Decisions

Deciding on the Number of Salespeople

There are a number of ways a sales manager can determine the number of salespeople needed, but we will explain only one of the simpler approaches. The basic data are included in Figure 10.5.

A company has to make a total of 30,000 sales calls during the next year. The current sales force of 100 individuals can account for 25,000 of these sales calls. Therefore, new salespeople need to be responsible for 5,000 sales calls. Since each new salesperson is believed to be able to make 200 calls per year, a total of 25 new salespeople must be recruited (5,000 ÷ 200 = 25).

Kind of Person Needed

The type of person needed is largely determined by the selling tasks that must be accomplished. For example, one kind of salesperson may be required to sell cosmetics in a department store, but another kind may be required to sell pharmaceuticals to doctors.

Sales managers should first develop a **job description** for each of the positions for which they are recruiting. A job description describes precisely what the person in that position is required to do. Below are some examples of the responsibilities of an individual selling machine tools:

1. Making technical sales presentations to prospective purchasers of machine tools.
2. Assisting current customers in installing, maintaining, and servicing machine tools purchased from the firm.

Figure 10.5   Estimating the Number of Salespeople Required

Fact	Number
1. Total number of sales calls needed during the next year	30,000
2. Number of current salespeople	100
3. Average number of calls per year per each current salesperson	250
4. Total number of calls per year for present salespeople (100 × 250)	25,000
5. Number of calls required for new salespeople (30,000 − 25,000)	5,000
6. Average number of calls per year per new salesperson	200
7. Number of new salespeople needed (5,000 ÷ 200)	25

3. Planning and organizing sales calls by establishing travel routes, determining the order to call on current and prospective customers, and deciding how long to stay with customers.
4. Assisting current customers with production problems.

Once the sales manager has decided on the responsibilities to be included in the job description, he then describes the characteristics that job applicants must have in order to perform these responsibilities effectively. This description is called a **man specification** and should list the necessary training, experience, skills, and personal characteristics that are required. The man specification for the salesman of machine tools might include some of the following:

1. Must hold at least a bachelor's degree in mechanical engineering.
2. Must be an effective speaker.
3. Must have at least two years' selling experience of machine tools or similar products.
4. Must have a nice appearance.

After the sales manager has developed the job description and the man specification, he is ready to begin looking for the individuals required. To do this, sales managers must decide which sales personnel *sources* they will want to use.

Sources for Sales Personnel

There are many potential sources for sales personnel. Some of the more frequently used sources include direct inquiries; colleges, universities and high schools; advertisements in newspapers and trade journals; employment agencies; and other firms. The kind of person being sought is an important determinant of which source is to be used. For example, salespeople requiring a technical background are likely to be recruited from colleges and universities that offer engineering programs. Other major factors are the past success in attracting the required people from various sources and the costs associated with each source.

Whatever sources used, the sales manager wants to have a number of qualified people who are interested in the positions available. This means that the sales manager must become involved with *selecting* salespeople, the next responsibility to be discussed.

SELECTING SALESPEOPLE

Selecting salespeople is one of the sales manager's toughest jobs. Two mistakes should be avoided: (1) hiring people who will turn out to be poor performers and (2) rejecting applicants who would have been successful. The sales manager has a number of devices that he can use to help avoid making these errors. These devices will be discussed next, after which we will offer some recommendations that should enable the sales manager to do a more effective job of selecting salespeople.

Selection Devices

Most sales managers use a combination of application blanks, personal interviews, tests, references, and physical examinations during the selection process.

Application Blanks.   Application blanks ask the applicant to provide information. This includes personal information such as name, date of birth, marital status, physical condition, education, address, telephone number, and so on. Perhaps the most important information needed is a complete record of the applicant's past working experience. This information should include companies worked for, titles of positions, responsibilities, salary history, and immediate superiors. The application blank should be carefully analyzed because it may serve as an effective means of preliminary screening. Thus, applicants can be rejected immediately, saving the firm the time and expense of additional contact.

The following are factors that the sales manager should look for on the application blank that indicate he should proceed no further:

1. Excessive job hopping. This may indicate that an individual has had trouble satisfying previous employers.
2. Underqualification. Some individuals will be obviously underqualified and should not be further considered.
3. Overqualification. Some applicants may be overqualified. This could be a possible danger signal. It may indicate that the applicant is desperate for a job. If this is the case, the sales manager should find out why.
4. Higher past salaries than the opening will pay. Although the position itself may not be a step down, a person is unlikely to be satisfied for long if the individual has to take a cut in pay.
5. Employment gaps. The sales manager should be especially concerned if an applicant has been unemployed for any length of time. The reason could be the inability to get another job or a physical or mental health problem.

Personal Interviews.   Personal interviews provide an opportunity for the sales manager to get an idea of how the applicant would be perceived by a prospective customer. The sales manager can determine how sincere the applicant is, how well he or she speaks, how questions are responded to, reactions to pressure, and personal appearance.

Tests.   Some firms put a great deal of emphasis on various tests to help predict applicants' success. These include *aptitude, personality,* and *interest* tests. Aptitude tests, such as mathematical, mechanical, and verbal, may be helpful in predicting success for special types of selling jobs. For example, mechanical aptitude might be an important factor in selling complicated machinery. Some companies believe that various personality factors predict success. Quaker Oats, for example, found that two personality variables, being *active* and *impulsive,* correlated strongly with sales success.[3] Tests that measure interest in people and in sales as a career are also used by some firms.

In deciding which tests to use, the firm must first determine those characteristics and skills most important to the job. Then, a test measuring these skills and characteristics should be given to the *current* sales force. Next, the current sales force should be categorized as to which are good or poor salespeople. Finally, the test results should be examined to see if they can differentiate the good from the poor salesperson. If they do, the test can then probably be used in the selection process.

References. In general, not too much emphasis should be placed on references since almost everyone can give three or four names of people who will say positive things about him. Of course, if references are lukewarm or contain some negative comments, the sales manager should be concerned.

Physical Examinations. Only candidates who look promising should take physical examinations since these examinations are costly. The physical examination is an important step in the selection process, however, because it may save the firm from hiring someone who has a physical or mental health problem.

Tips for Selecting Sales Applicants

Now that the reader has an idea of the basic selection process, he should read the recommendations that should help the sales manager choose the right candidate (see Figure 10.6). Since many of them have been found to be closely correlated with successful selling, they are key factors on which applicants should be evaluated.

TRAINING SALESPEOPLE

New salespeople must be thoroughly trained before they are put into the field. Experienced salespeople must also be trained so that they can do an even better job of selling. Training of the sales force is important because it can help them do a better job, increase their morale, lower selling costs, and improve customer relations. A comprehensive training program should provide help for the salespeople in all of their areas of responsibility.

[3] Clyde Hardin, "Selection Tests: How to Develop Your Own Scoring Key," *Personnel* (January–February, 1960), pp. 64–68.

Figure 10.6 Tips for Selecting the Right Sales Applicant

1. Does the applicant have a past success record?
2. What do previous superiors say about the applicant?
3. Is the applicant articulate?
4. Does the applicant have self-confidence?
5. How does the applicant react to stress?
6. Is the applicant's appearance neat?
7. Is the applicant enthusiastic?
8. Has the applicant demonstrated determination?

Basic Training Techniques

Formal classroom training is the major technique used by many firms. In this setting the sales manager or experienced salespeople share their wisdom with the trainees. Although this approach is inexpensive and does not force the trainee into the field too soon, it lacks reality and does not often obtain the trainee's involvement.

Simulations do obtain the trainee's participation and bring some degree of realism into the training situation. **Role playing** is a simulation training device in which the trainee plays the part of a salesperson making a presentation. An experienced salesperson plays the role of a customer. The Missouri Pacific Railroad, for example, has its sales force describe tough selling situations they have encountered. These become the basis for role-playing exercises.[4] **Cases** are selling situations that trainees are asked to evaluate and to indicate how they would handle. **Games** are popular simulations. One game, for example, stresses effective time management and involves such selling aspects as travel, waiting time, account potential, and the likelihood of making a sale.[5] One of the writers developed a game for use in the sales management course. Participants had to assign their sales force to territories based on their potentials and then the participants had to determine the number of salespeople calling on each account. More experienced salespersons were considered more effective than newer ones. Larger accounts had a lower probability of being sold than the smaller ones. Teams that had assigned the most coverage to any particular account had the best chance of making the sale, but this could be reduced if competition also assigned a great deal of coverage.

[4] "AV Plays a Leading Role," *Sales Management* (August 4, 1975), p. 55.
[5] Stewart A. Washburn, "Salesmanship: The Time Is Money Game," *Sales and Marketing Management* (March 8, 1976), pp. 43–50.

Many firms believe that *on-the-job training* is the best training. After a minimum amount of formal training, salespeople are put into the field. For the first several weeks they are usually accompanied by an experienced salesperson, then they are left on their own, but their progress is closely watched by the sales manager. In this "sink-or-swim" approach, realism is stressed, but the company runs the risk of damaging relations with its customers.

Making Sales Training More Effective

The following recommendations will enable sales training to be more effective:

1. The objectives to be achieved from sales training must be clearly defined. Does the firm want the trainees to memorize a specific sales presentation? What information about the firm's products should the trainees be able to recall?
2. The extent to which the sales training objectives have been achieved must be measured. Participants can be asked if they believe that these objectives have been attained. Or tests can be administered before training starts and after it is finished and the results can be compared. Another approach is to determine how salesmen *perform after* the training compared to their performance *before* the training.
3. The sales manager must realize that all salespeople, even his most experienced people, need training. A recent study surprisingly revealed that only about one-half of the firms contacted had a formal training program for new salespeople and that less than one-half had a training program for experienced salespeople.[6]
4. Training must be continuous. It cannot be done sporadically and it must be planned well in advance.
5. Training appears to be most effective when participants get involved. The training program should be designed to accomplish this.
6. Rules of thumb designed to increase learning should be used. Audiovisual aids should be used. The Charles Beseler Company, for example, developed a series of color filmstrips with a sound narration for a new enlarger. Each salesperson received the sales aid and could learn about the new product on his own time. The total cost was $10,500 (less than one-half of what a sales meeting would have cost) and no selling time was lost.[7] Sessions should be short, repetition should be emphasized, and feedback from trainees should be encouraged.
7. Training should be separated from the day-to-day selling job. Thus, a block of time should be devoted only to training. Training is usually conducted away from the salesperson's home office. For example,

[6] *Sales Management* (March 3, 1975), p. 10.
[7] *Sales and Marketing Management* (September 13, 1976), p. 25.

Inland Steel brought its entire sales force to Chicago for a two-day training session dealing with product knowledge and sales techniques associated with new coil-coated products.[8]

8. If the participants can be shown how the training will increase their performance and income, they will probably respond more favorably to it.

COMPENSATION

In developing a compensation package for a sales force, the sales manager must first decide what he wants the compensation program to accomplish. This decision will determine to a large extent the *type* of compensation and *how much* the total compensation package will cost. In all, eight objectives will be discussed.

In order to understand these objectives, the reader must comprehend the concepts of salary and commission. Salary is a flat payment of money to a salesperson in a time period, such as $12,000 per year. The salesperson receives this payment whether he or she does a good or poor job of selling. (Of course, the salary could be adjusted later.) Pay in the form of a commission is tied directly to the salesperson's performance. For example, if a salesperson were to receive a 10% commission on the sales volume obtained, and if the sales volume were $150,000, the pay would be $15,000 ($150,000 × 10% = $15,000).

Objectives of Compensation Plans

To Attract Sales People.   In order to attract salespeople, the sales manager will probably have to offer a salary above the average for that type of sales position.

To Reduce Sales Force Turnover.   Since the costs of a high rate of turnover (recruiting and training costs) may be very high for the firm, it may wish to pay higher than average salaries in order to reduce the turnover rate.

To Motivate the Sales Force.   A major objective for many compensation programs is to motivate the sales force. Salespeople tend to be more motivated as the percentage of their total compensation in the form of commissions rises. For example, a salesperson whose entire pay results from commissions is likely to be highly motivated since the more sales made, the higher the pay.

To Provide Security for the Sales Force.   If the firm's objective is to provide security for its sales force, then most of the compensation should be in the form of salary. A high percentage of salary also tends to make a sales force stay with the company. However, motivation may be low.

[8] "AV Plays a Leading Role," p. 16.

The Personal Selling Function

To Secure Control Over the Sales Force's Non-Selling Efforts. A compensation program emphasizing salary gives a company more control over its sales force's nonselling efforts. For example, a firm may want its salespeople to spend more time helping customers with their displays. If the salespeople were paid a straight salary, their compensation would not be any less because they are spnding less time in direct selling. A system of compensation that stresses commissions provides less control because any reduction in actual selling time hurts the sales force's pay. Here, the sales force would have some grounds for objecting to an increase in non-selling activities.

To Encourage Various Selling Activities. Compensation can be used to get salespeople to perform various selling activities, such as calling on more new accounts or spending more time with specific customers. One way this can be done is by rewarding the people who do the best job with additional pay.

To Maintain Selling Costs at a Desired Level. The sales manager may decide that his selling costs must not exceed a specific figure, for example, $200,000 per year, or that costs should not exceed, for example, 10% of yearly sales volume. If selling costs exceed these figures, the sales manager could set up a compensation program that takes these figures into consideration.

To Obtain Various Levels of Performance. Various levels of performance can be secured through compensation plans. For instance, if the sales manager wants each salesperson to secure at least $200,000 in sales, he could offer each salesperson who obtains this figure a bonus of $3,000.

Making the Compensation Program Effective

A company should determine what the average compensation is in its industry. This provides a standard below which the firm should not go if it wants to attract and keep good salespeople. Figure 10.7 graphs salespeople's compensation as a percentage of company sales for various industrial products.

The compensation plan should be simple and easy for the sales force to understand. It should be a fair plan, but more important, the sales force should perceive the plan as being fair.

The best compensation plan is the one that provides *some* security and *some* incentive. That is, a portion of the compensation should be straight salary and a portion should be commission. One authority recommends that about 70% of a salesperson's compensation should be salary, and that 30% should be incentive.[9]

The sales force depends on income coming in regularly. Where commission-type compensation exists, income tends to be received irregularly.

[9] Richard C. Smyth, "Financial Incentives for Salesmen," *Harvard Business Review* (January–February, 1968), p. 114.

Figure 10.7   Sales Force Compensation Figures for Various Industries in 1974

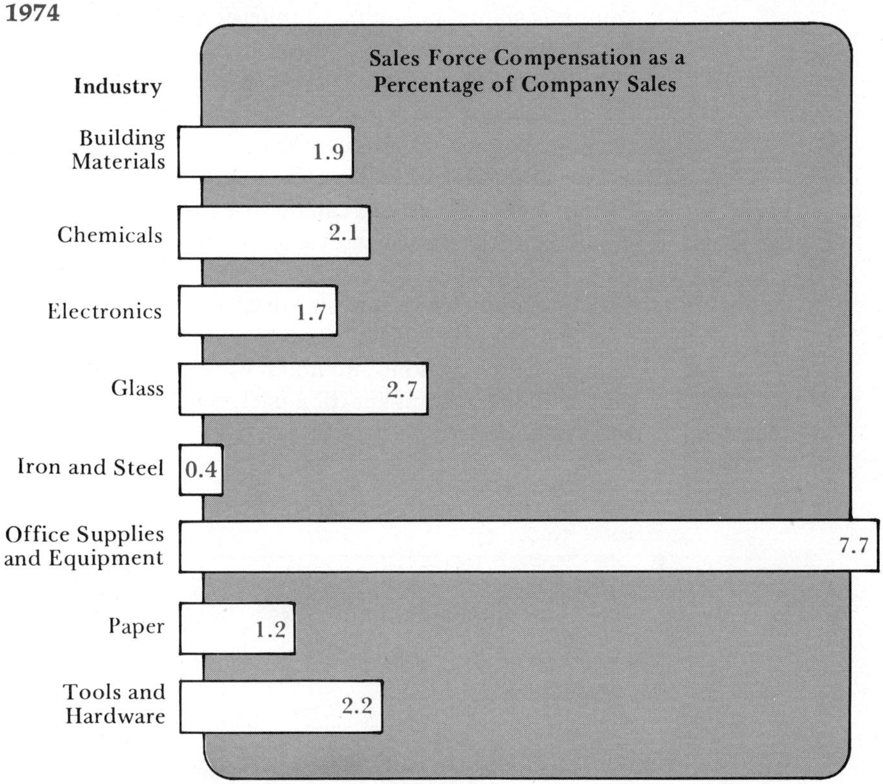

Industry	Sales Force Compensation as a Percentage of Company Sales
Building Materials	1.9
Chemicals	2.1
Electronics	1.7
Glass	2.7
Iron and Steel	0.4
Office Supplies and Equipment	7.7
Paper	1.2
Tools and Hardware	2.2

Source: American Management Association's Executive Compensation Service.

The regularity of income is an important aspect of any compensation program. Many salesmen's wives object to not being able to depend on a set amount of income and have even encouraged their husbands to leave the selling profession.

Salespeople who sell industrial goods should be paid mostly straight salary because there are various aspects of industrial goods selling that can hurt their performance through no fault of their own. For example, there are only a few customers who account for large percentages of the firm's sales volume and there are customers who postpone their purchases.

Salespeople who sell consumer goods can be paid on a commission basis since the sales obtained are more directly a result of their efforts than are the sales of industrial products.

If a company gives its sales force a lot of support in the form of advertising, a lower percentage of the compensation program should be in the form of commissions because the sales obtained may be more a result of the advertising effort than the sales force's efforts.

If the product being sold is clearly superior to competitive products, less emphasis should be put on commissions because the sales obtained may result more from this advantage than from the actual selling effort.[10]

Before concluding this section, we must make a few comments on sales force *expenses*. These include allowances for automobile travel, food, lodging, and entertainment. Generally speaking, a firm should be neither overly generous nor stingy. The company should compare data from various sources so that it can be sure that it is paying the industry average. Figure 10.8 gives some daily expense figures for salespeople employed by consumer products companies.

It appears that salespeople are becoming more interested in *fringe benefits*. These include pension plans, stock options, life and health insurance, and vacations and holidays. Fringe benefits should be considered part of the total compensation package. They are often used to attract and retain competent salespeople.

[10] Ibid.

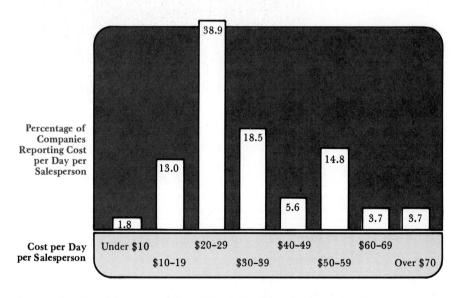

Figure 10.8   Daily Expense Figures for Consumer Products Salespeople in 1974

Source: American Management Association's Executive Compensation Service.

Marketing Mix Decisions

Permission: From the *Wall Street Journal*.

"Skimps a bit on entertaining customers, doesn't he?"

MOTIVATING SALESPEOPLE

Motivating salespeople can be a particularly difficult job for the sales manager. However, it is a responsibility that must be performed successfully if the sales force is to work up to its maximum potential and achieve its own and the company's goals.

The Sales Manager Should Understand Salespeople's Needs

The sales manager must have an understanding of the basic needs that motivate salespeople. These needs include economic, pride, achievement, esteem, and security needs. Although economic needs seem to be the most important for most salespersons, the sales manager should realize that other needs may also be important. This is especially true if his sales force is essentially satisfied with the compensation program. Here, the other factors may be strong motivators.

Goals Must Be Established in Order to Obtain Motivation

Goals motivate salespeople. They provide targets for them to shoot for. Following are examples of goals that could be established:

1. Obtaining certain sales volume figures.
2. Calling on so many customers in one year's time.

3. Calling on so many new customers in one month.
4. Increasing the size of the average order.
5. Reducing travel time by a certain percentage.

Achievement of Goals Must Allow Salespeople to Achieve Their Needs

In order for goals to be effective motivators, the sales manager must demonstrate to the sales force that obtaining the goals will help the salesperson satisfy his own needs more fully. For example, a monetary bonus of $2,000 might be paid to every salesperson who exceeds a sales volume goal.

The Sales Manager and Salesperson Should Jointly Set Goals

The sales manager and each salesperson should jointly decide on the goals to be achieved. If the salesperson is allowed to participate in this decision, he or she will be more likely to be committed to the goals and will be more likely to be motivated to achieve them. Salespeople may even set more stringent goals (in cooperation with the sales manager) than the sales manager himself would have set for the salesperson.

The Sale Force Must Clearly Understand the Goal

There should be no misunderstanding on the part of salespeople as to what their goals are. The goal should be stated as clearly as possible and in quantitative terms. An example of this is to "obtain a $250,000 sales volume for the year 1979." The goals should be put in writing so that there will be no misunderstanding later.

Goals Should Be Neither Too Difficult Nor Too Easy to Achieve

If goals are too difficult to achieve, salespeople will feel that the company is taking advantage of them and will probably become discouraged. If the goal is too easy to achieve, the company's objectives will probably not be obtained because salespeople will not have to exert much effort.

The Sales Manager May Want to Establish Several Goals for the Sales Force

Most sales forces are expected to achieve *multiple* goals because the company itself is pursuing more than one objective. We will have more to say about this in the material on evaluation presented later.

Sales Quotas Are Perhaps the Most Important Goal and Must Be Carefully Established

Most firms emphasize sales quotas when they establish goals. This usually refers to a specific sales volume figure that a salesperson is expected to achieve in one year's time. In many cases, bonuses are not paid if these quotas are not achieved. Quotas are undoubtedly the primary motivator for many firms.

Quotas cannot be the same for each salesperson because of the differences that may exist in each geographical sales territory. Let's keep this factor in mind as we show how a quota should be set. In setting quotas, the territory's *market potential* must first be determined. The market potential is the highest possible sales volume that *all firms* selling in a given territory could expect. In this example, we will assume that a firm selling machine tools believes that market potential should be measured by the number of firms in the territory that are logical purchasers of machine tools. Let's further assume that the average firm could be expected to buy 3 machines each and that there are 400 companies in the territory. Thus, the market potential is 1,200 machine tools (400 × 3).

Next, we would have to determine how many of these 1,200 units we could expect the salesperson to sell. This would be the sales quota. Unfortunately, this is not easy to determine. One way is to see what percentage share was obtained in the past. If this were 25%, then the sales quota would be 300 (1,200 × 25%). Of course, we could move this figure up or down according to, for example, the strength of competition in the territory and how much marketing effort would be provided that territory. If competition were believed to be weak for that year and we were going to spend a lot for advertising, we might specify a sales quota of 400 instead of 300.

Contests as Motivational Tools

Contests are probably the most frequently used motivational tool. In all, it was estimated that $2.9 billion was spent on merchandise and travel awards in 1975, but this figure does not include cash awards.[11] In most cases, the company's objective is to increase sales. During a contest, sales generally are believed to increase 20%, and about one-half the sales force earns some kind of award.[12]

A wide variety of contests have been used, and they are limited only by the imaginations of the sales managers (see the examples in Figure 10.9). These examples show the great range of objectives and incentives (prizes) that can be used. They also demonstrate that *recognition* of the salesperson's achievement should be an important part of any sales contest.

SUPERVISING SALESPEOPLE

Because salespeople are usually on their own and are geographically separated from their sales manager, the sales manager must have a plan for

[11] "A New Role for Incentives," *Sales Management* (April 7, 1975), p. 41.
[12] Sally Scanlon, "Let's Hear It for Recognition," *Sales and Marketing Management* (April 12, 1976), p. 44.

Figure 10.9 Examples of Sales Contests

1. Ford Motor Company sponsored a photo contest for dealer salespeople. Salespeople were to use snapshots of customers and prospects with new and used cars to obtain references and open sales presentations. Those with the best ideas won prizes ranging from shirts to color televisions.
2. Hallmark Cards offered its salespeople a bonus for selling retailers a $150 training program.
3. The Homelite Division of Textron encouraged its district managers to pay more attention to account receivables and encourage their salespeople to obtain new accounts.
4. National Biscuit gives its V.I.P. club members more deluxe accommodations at sales meetings than to its other salespeople.
5. General Electric's Lamp Division mentions top achievers in business publication advertisements.
6. Top performers for Ciba-Geigy's Pharmaceutical Division are sent on three-day vacation trips with their spouses to relax and meet company officers. They are given recognition in the *Journal of the American Medical Association,* which is read by their physician customers.
7. Electrolux has its star salesperson address its sales force at its annual meeting.

Source: Reprinted with permission from *Sales & Marketing Management* magazine, April 12, 1976, p. 44. Copyright 1976.

---

supervision. The plan gives direction and structure. The direction and structure should be related to the *means* that salespeople use to achieve various objectives. For example, if a salesperson is trying to achieve a $200,000 sales volume, some of the following methods might be employed:

1. Calling on 10% more new accounts.
2. Calling on five more established accounts per week.
3. Spending 10% more time with larger accounts.
4. Reducing total travel time by one hour per week.

In supervising the sales force, the sales manager must ensure that these methods are implemented as planned. He must also provide the sales force with the information it needs to carry out its responsibilities and he must establish a mechanism through which he can periodically communicate with the sales force. Below we will discuss some of the more common supervision devices.

Telephone Calls

Telephone calls are an inexpensive approach to supervision. The sales manager can telephone his salespeople frequently in order to find out how they are doing and if they are having any problems with which he can help.

Memos

Memos can be used when the sales manager wants his sales force to have permanent records. Memos can include indications of changes in company policy, information about shifts in the market, changes in the strategies of competitive firms, and new product information. They can also describe the ground rules for a new sales contest, a change in ways to report expenses, new automobile maintenance procedures, and so on.

Reports

Reports probably provide the single most important means of supervising the sales force. Reports provide the sales manager with a wealth of information about the activities of salespeople. After studying these reports, the sales manager can evaluate the performance of each of his salespeople. After the sales manager reads the reports, suggestions can be made on how salespeople can improve their performances. For example, the sales manager might notice that a particular salesperson is doing a poor job of routing. The sales manager could recommend that the salesperson avoid "backtracking" and cluster calls more carefully.

To make the best possible use of reports, a sales manager may want to consider the following:

1. Salespeople usually object to reports if they take too much time to complete. Therefore, reports should require only basic information and should be organized for easy recording.
2. The raw data provided in the report must be used to generate meaningful data. Thus, the sales manager would want to determine the probability of a sale being made (number of sales calls in which a sale occurred divided by the total number of calls made, for example, $30 \div 100 = .30$). He might also want to know the size of the average order (total dollar sales divided by the number of sales made). The percentage of the salesperson's total time required for travel is another figure that is frequently desired.
3. The data in the reports should be put on the computer in order to reduce clerical and computational time.
4. The sales manager should look for positive or negative trends and patterns. For example, the sales manager would be concerned if the average-sized order is decreasing, but would be pleased if a salesperson has been steadily increasing the percentage of time spent in

making presentations to new customers while maintaining good coverage of current accounts.

5. The sales force will be more cooperative if the sales manager can show how they can benefit from filling out reports. If the sales manager can, for example, demonstrate that the salesperson's income will increase by 10% through more effective routing, less resistance will be encountered.

Visits by the Sales Manager

The sales manager should periodically visit his salespeople in the field to see how each is doing, make recommendations for improvement, and be available for answering questions.

EVALUATING THE SALES FORCE

Determining how well salespeople are doing (evaluation) is a critical task for the sales manager because many important decisions depend on evaluation. These include compensation, promotion, and whether an individual will be retained or fired.

Have Objectives Been Achieved?

The best way to judge the effectiveness of salespeople is *how well they have achieved the objectives they are trying to achieve*. For example, sales volume obtained should be compared to the sales volume objective. Assuming that these are fair and that the sales force participated in establishing them, individuals who achieve them should be rewarded more than those who do not.

The sales manager must evaluate salespeople in a number of areas besides those relating to objectives because these other areas have an effect upon sales volumes, costs, and profits. If these are not specified as objectives, then the sales manager should at least be able to compare the performance of his salesmen against some *standard*. One standard is the *company* standard. This might be, for example, average sales volume per salesperson, average cost per sales call, average percentage of quota achieved, and so on. Another standard is the *industry* standard. These standards can also serve as a basis for determining how well salespeople are doing. Figure 10.10 includes a number of standards developed by one of the authors from an analysis of sales activities in the machine tool industry.

Multiple Objectives

Many sales managers want to evaluate their sales forces on a number of different objectives because they feel that it is not fair to look at only one factor. Figure 10.11 presents one way of doing this. It is assumed that we

Figure 10.10   Some Sales Standards for the Machine Tool Industry

1. Average annual salary per salesperson—$10,667.
2. Average annual commission per salesperson—$4,800.
3. Average annual bonus per salesperson—$978.
4. Average annual travel expense per salesperson—$4,167.
5. Total selling cost per mile—$.82.
6. Cost per sales call—$44.
7. Percentage of time devoted to:
   (a) Direct selling—35%.
   (b) Travel—25%.
   (c) Customer relations—20%.
   (d) Paper work—10%.
8. Average number of sales calls made per week per salesperson—16.5.
9. Percentage of calls on current accounts resulting in a sale—27.5%.
10. Percentage of calls on prospective customers resulting in a sale—10%.
11. Forty per cent of salespeople accounted for 80% of total sales volume for each company.

Source: Richard T. Hise, Stanley H. Kratchman, and Thomas A. Ulrich, "Distribution Cost Analysis and Performance Standards for Industrial Selling," in Louis Desfosses (ed.), *Decision Sciences—Education and Applications* (Philadelphia: American Institute for Decision Sciences, 1974), pp. 213–14.

are evaluating salespeople A, B, and C on three factors: sales volume, average size order, and average number of calls per week. Since the sales manager believes that sales volume is the most important factor, he gives it a weight of 5. Average size order and average number of calls per week receive weights of 3 and 2, respectively.

An objective figure is established for each of the three factors. Differences in sales territories must be recognized for all three factors. For example, the sales volume objective ($400,000) for salesperson C may be higher than for the others because the market potential may be higher or competition may be weaker. The average size order may be higher for salesperson A because the territory has larger-sized accounts.

The effectiveness of each salesperson for each factor is found by dividing what each achieves by the objective. This is then multiplied by the weight. The weights obtained for each factor are added for each salesman and divided by the sum of the weights (10) in order to obtain an overall effectiveness. Salesperson C has the best overall performance of 90.0%.

Each salesperson should be evaluated at least twice a year. More

Figure 10.11 Evaluating Salespeople on More Than One Factor

	Salesperson A	Salesperson B	Salesperson C
Factor One: Sales Volume			
1. Weight	5	5	5
2. Objective	$300,000	$200,000	$400,000
3. Achieved	$270,000	$160,000	$360,000
4. Effectiveness	.90	.80	.90
(3 ÷ 2)	($270,000 ÷ $300,000)	($160,000 ÷ $200,000)	($360,000 ÷ $400,000)
5. Performance Level	4.50	4.00	4.50
(Weight × Effectiveness)	(5 × .90)	(5 × .80)	(5 × .90)
Factor Two: Average Size Order			
1. Weight	3	3	3
2. Objective	$500	$400	$300
3. Achieved	$400	$300	$270
4. Effectiveness	.80	.75	.90
(3 ÷ 2)	($400 ÷ $500)	($300 ÷ $400)	($270 ÷ $300)
5. Performance Level	2.40	2.25	2.70
(Weight × Effectiveness)	(3 × .80)	(3 × .75)	(3 × .90)
Factor Three: Average Number of Calls per Week			
1. Weight	2	2	2
2. Objective	30	25	40
3. Achieved	20	22	36
4. Effectiveness	.66	.88	.90
(3 ÷ 2)	(20 ÷ 30)	(22 ÷ 25)	(36 ÷ 40)
5. Performance Level	1.32	1.76	1.80
(Weight × Effectiveness)	(2 × .66)	(2 × .88)	(2 × .90)
Sum of Performance Levels	8.22	8.01	9.00
	(4.50 + 2.40 + 1.32)	(4.00 + 2.25 + 1.76)	(4.50 + 2.70 + 1.80)
Overall Effectiveness (Sum of Performance Levels Divided by Sum of Weights)	82.2%	80.1%	90.0%
	(8.22 ÷ 10)	(8.01 ÷ 10)	(9.00 ÷ 10)

frequent evaluation would, however, allow problems to be recognized earlier.

When problems do arise, the sales manager should stress what can be done to obtain better performance. He should not spend too much time criticizing the poor performance.

The data needed to evaluate performance should be computerized, because it gives the sales manager more time to concentrate on making decisions.

The sales manager should *manage by exception*. The computer can help him to do this. Only those performances clearly out of line should be brought to his attention.

SUMMARY

Salespeople have four major responsibilities: acquiring information, pre-presentation planning, giving the sales presentation, and performing a variety of post-presentation activities. Information about the salesperson's company, products, competitors, and market are especially important because they help in performing the other three functions. The company is usually trying to maximize profits and the salesperson is trying to maximize his income. Unfortunately, this may cause a conflict. The sales manager must resolve this conflict.

There must be a great deal of cooperation between the sales manager and his sales force in establishing goals, determining the objectives of sales training, determining the best way to achieve goals, filling out and evaluating reports, establishing routes, and obtaining and processing information.

In obtaining the cooperation of salespeople in these areas, the sales manager must show them how they will enable him to generate more income. This can be done through such means as freeing up more direct face-to-face selling time, calling on more prospective customers, and making more effective sales presentations.

The sales manager must always recognize the differences in the territories of his salespeople when establishing sales quotas and evaluating them. The major differences are market potentials, strength of competition, and the amount of selling help provided by other elements of the marketing mix, such as advertising.

There appears to be a strong relationship between successful salespeople and their ability to manage their time. Successful time management is generally the result of more efficient routing and better prospecting.

Sales managers should emphasize the human relations aspects of their jobs. They should let their salespeople periodically know how they are doing, allow them to participate in establishing goals, and stress improvement of performance instead of emphasizing poor performance.

1. What must a salesperson do in order to do an effective job of prospecting?
2. Do you believe that successful selling is an art or science? Why?
3. How valuable are references in selecting salespeople?
4. What is the difference between a job description and a man specification?
5. Would you be interested in a career in selling? Why or why not?
6. Do you believe that specific personality types are preferred in selling? Does the type of selling task involved make a difference?
7. Which skills do you believe a sales manager must have in order to be successful?
8. Star salespeople frequently make poor sales managers. Why?

GLOSSARY

Canned Presentation: word-by-word formal presentation usually made to groups of buyers

Cases: simulation technique used in salespeople's training that asks trainees to evaluate and to indicate how they would handle specific selling situations

Commission: payment of money to a salesperson based on the quality of his or her performance

Games: popular simulations used in training that allow participants to compete against each other or against a standard of excellence

Job Description: description of the duties and responsibilities of a sales position

Man Specification: description of the training, experience, skills, and personal characteristics required by salespeople to perform a specific sales job

Planned Presentation: presentation that includes major points to be covered; it does not involve a word-by-word approach

Prospecting: determining which current and prospective customers will help maximize sales volume, profit, and the salesperson's income

Role Playing: simulation training device in which the trainee usually plays the part of a salesperson making a presentation to a customer

Routing: deciding the sequence in which customers will be called on so that travel costs will be minimized and sales volume, profit, and the salesperson's income will be maximized

Salary: payment of money to a salesperson regardless of how productive he or she is

Simulations: training techniques that secure a salesperson's participation and introduce a degree of realism

CASES

Case 1: The Western Inco Co.

Jim Wiley is district sales manager of the Western Inco Co., a large manufacturer of small electric motors. He is responsible for 30 salespeople who are organized into two territories.

At the end of the year he is analyzing the following data on these two territories:

	Territory A	Territory B
Sales volume per salesperson	$100,000	$80,000
Average number of customers contacted per week	30	22
Average number of new customers contacted per month	10	6
Cost per sales call	$50	$60
Cost per mile	$.80	$1.25

1. Should Mr. Wiley be concerned with the different performance levels for the two territories?
2. Indicate and discuss all factors that might explain the differences between Territory A and Territory B.

Case 2: The Tasterite Co.

The Tasterite Company is a medium-sized processor of fruits and vegetables. Seventy-five percent of its sales volume goes through brokers and the rest is sold to institutions (hospitals and schools) by the company's 50 salespeople.

In recent months the sales force has voiced dissatisfaction with the firm's compensation package. Under the current system, salespeople are paid strictly on a commission basis, equal to 10% of the sales volume they obtain. The salespeople believe that most, if not all, of their compensation should be in the form of salary and only a small portion should consist of commissions.

Benton Jones, the company's sales manager, decides to analyze the selling job, the market, and the competition in order to determine if a change in the compensation system would be justified. He believes that the following facts are critical in deciding whether or not to change compensation plans:

1. The company sells to about 200 institutions each year.
2. About 20% of these institutions account for 80% of Tasterite's institutional sales.
3. Extremely tough competition existed for these 200 institutions, especially the largest ones. Thus, a salesperson frequently finds that a number of important accounts during the year might be lost.
4. The company spends $200,000 per year in advertising to its institutional buyers. It believes the advertising is very important in attracting and holding customers.

1. Do you believe that the sales force has a legitimate complaint?
2. Which compensation program is suggested by the factors uncovered by Mr. Jones?
3. What other factors should Mr. Jones consider before he reaches a decision?

Channels of Distribution: Some Basic Concepts

After you finish this chapter, you should be able to answer the following questions:

1. What is a channel of distribution?
2. What are the two major types of middlemen?
3. What is the difference between retailers and wholesalers?
4. What are the three major types of wholesalers?
5. How are merchant wholesalers distinguished from merchandise agents and brokers?
6. What are the major contributions and benefits of middlemen?
7. For what kind of firms are middlemen especially useful?
8. What are the major differences in channels of distribution for consumer goods and for industrial goods?
9. What are some major trends in wholesaling?
10. What are the four major types of retailing establishments?
11. How are chain operations defined? What factors have contributed to their success?
12. What are the major trends in retailing?

Automatic Vending   Broker   Cash-and-Carry Wholesalers   Chain Stores   Channel of Distribution   Concentration   Convenience Stores   Department Stores   Direct Selling   Discount Stores Dispersion   Drop Shippers   Franchisee   Franchisor   Mail-Order Houses   Manufacturers' Agents   Merchandise Agents and Brokers Merchant Wholesalers   National Brand   Place Utility   Private Brand   Rack Jobbers   Retailers   Sales Branches   Sales Offices Scrambled Merchandising   Self-Service   Selling Agent   Shopping Centers   Specialty Stores   Supermarkets   Time Utility   Truck Wholesalers   Variety Stores   Wholesalers

INTRODUCTION   It was brought out in Chapter 1 that one of the major functions of marketing was that of managing channels of distribution. This subject will be discussed in this and the next chapter. In this chapter we must become acquainted with some of the basic concepts of channels of distribution. These include understanding the different kinds of middlemen that make up a channel of distribution, the advantages in using middlemen, the kinds of functions middlemen perform, and trends in wholesaling and retailing. With these fundamental concepts in mind, we will be prepared for Chapter 12 that deals with how channels of distribution can be effectively managed.

WHAT IS A CHANNEL OF DISTRIBUTION?

A **channel of distribution** is the combination of middlemen that a company uses to move its products to the ultimate purchaser. The two major kinds of middlemen that can be employed are **wholesalers** and **retailers.** Wholesalers are middlemen who buy goods and then resell them to retailers, other wholesalers, industrial users (such as manufacturing firms and mining companies), institutions (such as schools), commercial firms (such as hotels), and government agencies. Wholesalers do not sell to ultimate consumers. Retailers sell to ultimate consumers, not to other business firms.

Channels of Distribution for Manufactured Consumer Products

We said above that a channel of distribution is the combination of middlemen (wholesalers and retailers) that a company uses to move its products to the ultimate purchaser. For manufactured consumer products, two major channels of distribution are used (see Figure 11.1). The major pattern consists of a manufacturer using wholesalers who, in turn, sell to retailers who then sell to ultimate consumers. About 50% of all manufactured consumer products are sold through this channel of distribution arrangement.

Figure 11.1   Typical Channels of Distribution for Consumer Products

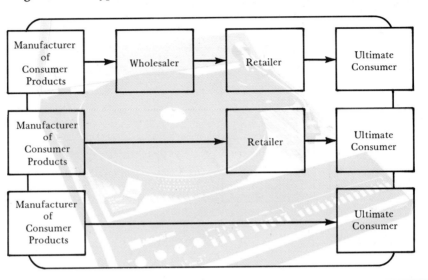

Another important pattern is the manufacturer–retailer–ultimate consumer alternative. In this arrangement, the manufacturer bypasses the wholesaler and sells directly to retailers, who then sell to the ultimate consumer. About 45% of all manufactured consumer products are distributed this way. The third channel of distribution possibility for manufactured consumer products shown in Figure 11.1 is when the manufacturer bypasses both the wholesaler and retailer and sells directly to the ultimate consumer. Although this alternative accounts for only 5% of total manufactured consumer products, it is an important way of marketing such products as cosmetics (Avon), vacuum cleaners (Electrolux), and encyclopedias (World Book).

Channels of Distribution for Manufactured Industrial Products

Two major channels of distribution patterns tend to predominate in the flow of manufactured industrial products (see Figure 11.2). About 80% of this kind of product goes directly from the manufacturer to the industrial buyer. Around 20% first go to a wholesaler and then to the industrial buyer.

In the examples above it can be seen that middlemen are used greatly, especially for manufactured consumer products. They also tend to be important for nonmanufactured products, such as agricultural products. Because middlemen are so important in the marketing of goods, it is neces-

Channels of Distribution: Some Basic Concepts

Figure 11.2   Typical Channels of Distribution for Industrial Products

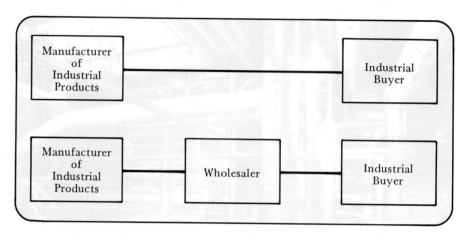

sary for us to understand why. This can be done by examining their contributions to the American economic system.

CONTRIBUTIONS OF MIDDLEMEN

**Middlemen Reduce the Number of Transactions Required,
Thereby Reducing Costs**

Figure 11.3 shows three manufacturers who are each selling to six retailers without the use of wholesalers. There, it can be seen that a total of 18 separate transactions are required, 6 from each of the 3 manufacturers. (We will assume that these transactions consist of deliveries in order to make the example easier to understand. But the reader should realize that we could also consider orders as part of the transactions. These, of course, would flow from the retailers to the manufacturers.)

In Figure 11.4 a wholesaler is placed between the 3 manufacturers and 6 retailers. The wholesaler accepts the shipments from each of the 3 manufacturers and then ships to the 6 retailers. By using a wholesaler, only 9 transactions are now required, instead of the 18 needed when a wholesaler was not used.

This contribution of middlemen is important. Shipments cost money and their costs are reflected in the prices charged for products. If the number of

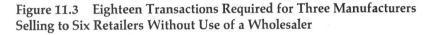

Figure 11.3   Eighteen Transactions Required for Three Manufacturers Selling to Six Retailers Without Use of a Wholesaler

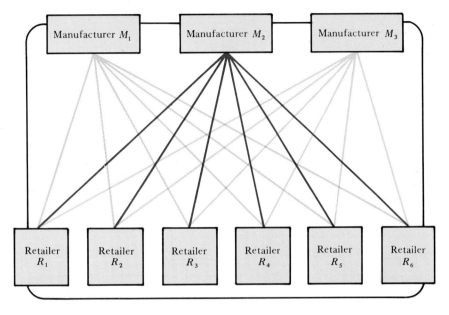

transactions can be reduced, costs will be less and lower prices will result. Our example used only small numbers of manufacturers, wholesalers, and retailers. The cost-saving potentials resulting from the use of middlemen are staggering when one considers that there are 450,000 manufacturing firms in the United States, 2,329,000 retail establishments, and 548,000 wholesaling establishments.

Middlemen Perform Marketing Functions

Middlemen are also valuable because they perform all of the marketing functions that are discussed throughout this text. For example, they conduct marketing research, advertise, employ a sales force, and engage in physical distribution. This means that manufacturers and other users of middlemen can shift the performance of these functions from themselves to middlemen.

Middlemen perform a variety of other functions. They maintain inventories, extend credit and collect debts, and provide a variety of services to their customers.

Channels of Distribution: Some Basic Concepts

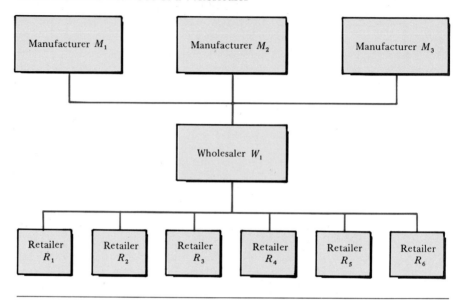

Figure 11.4   Nine Transactions Required for Three Manufacturers Selling to Six Retailers with Use of a Wholesaler

Middlemen Are Specialists

Since middlemen may be specialists in performing specific marketing functions, they are often able to carry them out more efficiently than manufacturing firms can. To the extent that manufacturers shift these functions to more efficient middlemen, the cost of performing them may decrease. Thus, since total marketing costs may be lower, lower prices may result for consumers.

Middlemen Perform the Concentration and Dispersion Functions

Two important functions performed by middlemen are the concentration and dispersion functions. **Concentration** is the consolidating of small lots into larger lots for more economic shipment. Wholesalers perform this function (hence their name *whole salers*). The opposite of concentration is **dispersion,** that is, breaking large lots into smaller lot sizes for convenient purchase by consumers. Dispersion is a function performed by retailers. For example, a retailer will take a case of 24 cans of peaches, break it open, and stack them individually on shelves so that consumers can purchase one or two cans.

Middlemen Enhance the Value of Products

Mainly because they store and transport products, middlemen enhance the value of these products. Through the storage function **time utility** is created. Many products are more valuable to consumers if they can be purchased when consumers want to purchase them. By storing products in warehouses middlemen make products available when customers are desirous of purchasing them. Apples are a good example. They are harvested in the fall, but storage prevents them from spoiling and makes them available throughout the year.

Products are more valuable if consumers can purchase them at convenient locations. This means that these products have **place utility.** This utility is created by middlemen who transport products to stores close to population concentrations.

Middlemen Bring Buyers and Sellers Together

Middlemen play an important role because they bring buyers and sellers together. Middlemen match buyers who are seeking certain products with sellers who are offering these products.

Middlemen Act as Information Sources

Companies that use middlemen like to have the middlemen provide information on the market and competition. Many retailers and wholesalers frequently channel such important information to their suppliers.

Middlemen Save Companies Money

If companies use middlemen, they shift the performance of costly marketing functions to their wholesalers and retailers. Thus, the suppliers do not have to have the financial resources required to perform these functions. This can be a very important benefit for new companies that lack financial backing or established companies that do not have adequate financial resources as they expand their operations.

Middlemen Are Valuable for Companies Going into New Markets

Companies that are trying to sell products in new markets may lack experience with and knowledge of these new markets. Middlemen, however, may be very experienced and knowledgeable about these areas and can, therefore, be used to advantage.

Middlemen Are Valuable for Companies Marketing New Products

New products that are substantially different from existing product lines frequently present problems for the innovating firm. In particular, the firm may not know how to market these additions effectively. Middlemen frequently have the requisite skill and experience and thus are used when new products are ready for introduction.

Middlemen Are Helpful for Small Companies

Small companies generally find that it is to their advantage to use retailers and wholesalers because the companies are not strong financially and they often lack product and market expertise.

Now that the reader understands why middlemen are valuable in our economy and how they can be of assistance to suppliers, such as manufacturers, we must next find out more about wholesaling and retailing institutions. The purpose of this discussion is mainly to familiarize the reader with the various types of wholesalers and retailers and their characteristics. This knowledge is of importance to the marketer when he is deciding whether or not to use middlemen and when he does decide to use middlemen, which types to employ. We will also discuss some basic trends in retailing and wholesaling that affect these decisions. We will first look at wholesaling.

WHOLESALING

Major Types of Wholesalers

There are three major types of wholesaling firms (see Figure 11.5). (We will not discuss petroleum bulk plants and assemblers of farm products because they move highly specialized products and are not nearly as important overall as the other three types of wholesalers.)

Merchant wholesalers, manufacturers' sales branches and sales offices, and merchandise agents and brokers are the most important wholesalers. **Merchant wholesalers** purchase and resell merchandise. The important characteristic of merchant wholesalers is that they actually *take title* to the merchandise they purchase. In general, merchant wholesalers provide a fairly wide range of services. **Merchandise agents** and **brokers,** however, usually perform fewer services than merchant wholesalers do. Merchandise agents and brokers negotiate sales and/or purchases for the companies they represent, but they *do not take title to the merchandise*. Merchandise agents and brokers are paid a commission for the services they render and usually do not represent buyers and sellers in the same transaction.

Manufacturers' sales branches and sales offices are often established by manufacturers separate from their manufacturing operations. These branches and offices enable the manufacturer to perform the wholesaling function himself and are often established when the manufacturer decides not to use wholesalers for all or part of his product lines. **Sales branches** carry inventories of products and customer orders are filled from these inventories. **Sales offices** do not carry inventories. Both sales branches and sales offices serve as offices for salespeople in that territory.

Figure 11.5   Major Types of Wholesalers and Basic Data, 1972

Type of Wholesaler	Number of Establishments and Percentage	Sales Volume and Percentage	Sales Volume per Establishment	Number of Employees and Percentage	Number of Employees per Establishment	Sales Volume per Employee	Operating Expenses as a Percentage of Sales
Merchant wholesalers	289,974 (78.4%)	$354 Billion (50.8%)	$1,221,000	3,023,373 (75.0%)	10.4	$117,088	13.9%
Manufacturers' sales branches and sales offices	47,197 (12.8%)	$256 Billion (36.8%)	$5,424,000	794,691 (19.7%)	16.8	$322,140	7.2%
Merchandise agents and brokers	32,620 (8.8%)	$86 Billion (12.4%)	$2,636,000	208,054 (5.3%)	6.4	$413,354	4.2%

Source: U.S. Department of Commerce, Bureau of the Census.

Figure 11.5 contains some important data: Merchant wholesalers account for 78.4% of total establishments, 50.8% of total sales, and 75.0% of total employees. However, they have the lowest sales volume per establishment and the lowest sales volume per employee. And they have the highest operating expense as a percentage of sales (13.9%). Manufacturers' sales branches and sales offices have the highest sales volume per establishment (over $5,000,000). Merchandise agents and brokers have the greatest sales volume per employee ($413,354), the lowest operating expense as a percentage of sales (4.2%), and the fewest number of employees per establishment (6.4).

Products Carried by Wholesalers

The types of products sold by wholesalers are shown in Figure 11.6. Groceries and related products were the most important merchandise category accounted for by wholesalers; over $106 billion worth were sold in 1972. Other products that had significant sales volume levels were motor

Channels of Distribution: Some Basic Concepts

Figure 11.6   United States Wholesale Trade: 1972 Sales by Type of Operation (in millions of dollars)

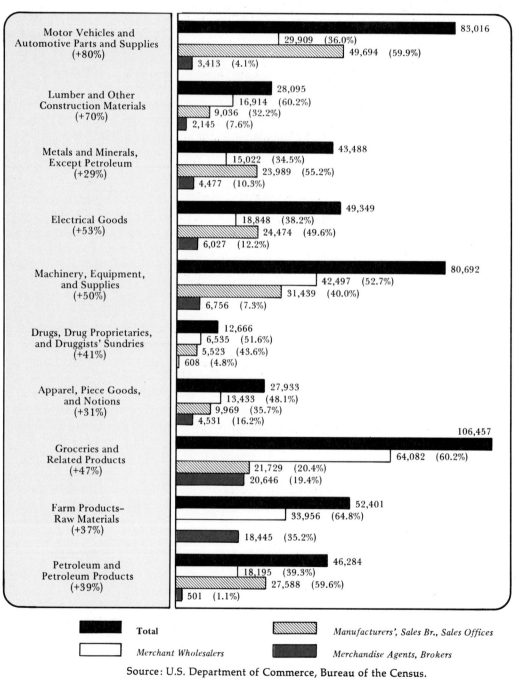

Source: U.S. Department of Commerce, Bureau of the Census.

vehicles and automotive parts and supplies ($83 billion) and machinery, equipment, and supplies ($81 billion).

The left-hand side of Figure 11.6 shows the percentage increase in the sales of the product category between 1967 and 1972. Wholesalers' sales volume in 1972 was 80% greater than 1967 for motor vehicles and automotive parts and supplies. It was 70% greater for lumber and other construction materials. These two product groupings showed the greatest increases between 1967 and 1972.

Figure 11.6 also shows the extent to which sales for these ten product groups are accounted for by the three major types of wholesalers. Merchant wholesalers accounted for over 50% of the sales volume in the following five product categories: (1) lumber and other construction materials; (2) machinery, equipment, and supplies; (3) drugs, drug proprietaries, and druggists' sundries; (4) groceries and related products; and (5) farm products (raw materials). Manufacturers' sales branches and sales offices had over 50% of the sales volume in three product classes: (1) motor vehicles and automotive parts and supplies; (2) metals and minerals, except petroleum; and (3) petroleum and petroleum products. In addition, manufacturers' sales branches and sales offices had almost 50% of the sales volume for electrical goods (49.6%). For most of the product categories, merchandise agents and brokers had relatively small percentages of total sales volume. They did not account for over 50% of any product group; 35% for farm products (raw materials) was the highest figure.

Types of Merchant Wholesalers and Merchandise Agents and Brokers

It is important for companies that use wholesalers or are contemplating using them to know the different types of merchant wholesalers and merchandise agents and brokers that are available. Each type tends to specialize in the sale of specific products, as noted above. Each may offer different services to their suppliers and customers. Each may have extensive knowledge of various markets. Some take full control over the terms of the sale, while others have little to do with the terms of the sale. Some sell competing lines; others do not. Some will specialize in the performance of specific marketing functions. These and other factors are important for a company's channel of distribution decisions and will be discussed in the following sections on merchant wholesalers and merchandise agents and brokers.

Merchant Wholesalers. Figure 11.7 lists the major types of merchant wholesalers and the most important characteristics of each. This figure indicates that there are two major types of merchant wholesalers: those that provide full-range services and those that provide limited services.

Firms that sell through merchant wholesalers providing a full range of service generally are not able to get as high a price for their products than if they sold through merchant wholesalers providing limited services because the full-service merchant wholesaler incurs greater costs than the limited-service merchant wholesaler does. Thus, in order to have sufficient

Channels of Distribution: Some Basic Concepts

Figure 11.7 Major Types of Merchant Wholesalers

Merchant Wholesalers Providing Full-Range Services

1. *Regular wholesalers* provide a full range of services such as carrying inventories, promotion, and extending credit. They generally carry consumer goods and are independently owned firms.
2. *Industrial distributors* are wholesalers who operate in the industrial goods market. They tend to specialize in a limited line of products and may specialize in the kinds of markets they reach.
3. *Rack jobbers* are regular wholesalers who specialize in selling nonfood items, such as toys, records, and houseware items, to retailers. They stock the product for the retailers and mark their prices. Rack jobbers perform the inventory control function for their customers by removing slow-moving items. Generally, they sell on consignment to retailers, which means that the retailers do not have to pay for the merchandise until it is sold.

Merchant Wholesalers Providing Limited Services

1. *Drop shippers* are limited service wholesalers who take title to merchandise but do not take physical possession. The manufacturer performs the transportation and storage functions.
2. *Cash-and-carry wholesalers* do not extend credit to their purchasers and they do not provide purchasers with transportation. Purchasers come to the establishment of the cash-and-carry wholesalers, choose the merchandise they want, pay cash for the orders, and arrange for their delivery.
3. *Truck wholesalers* are limited function wholesalers who generally sell perishables or semiperishable products. Carrying limited stock, they make frequent calls on their customers. Also called *wagon jobbers,* they tend to service food retailers, restaurants, and hotels.

---

margin to cover these higher costs and provide a profit, he negotiates a lower price from suppliers. Companies that have poor financial backing and those that lack marketing expertise are generally more likely to use full-service merchant wholesalers than the limited-service variety because they have neither the money nor the knowledge to perform marketing functions and thus have to pass them on to full-service merchant wholesalers.

The products sold by manufacturers and the markets to which these products are directed are important criteria in determining which type of merchant wholesaler to use. **Rack jobbers,** for example, are important in the sale of nonfood items to retailers; **truck wholesalers** are important in the sale of perishable products to retailers, restaurants, and hotels.

Figure 11.8   Major Types of Merchandise Agents and Brokers

1. *Brokers* bring buyers and sellers together to consummate a transaction. They represent either the buyer or seller but not both. They usually have limited authority over the terms of the sale (such as extending credit) and establishing price. They are paid a commission. Brokers are important in the sale of many kinds of food products.
2. *Selling agents* sell all of a specified line or the entire output for their principals. They usually do not sell competing lines for firms competitive with their principals. They generally perform the entire range of marketing functions and are given control over the terms of the sale and pricing. Selling agents are used instead of a company's own sales force. They are paid a commission.
3. *Manufacturers' agents,* unlike selling agents, do not handle a manufacturer's total output or single product line. They are not given control over the terms of the sale and pricing. Manufacturers' agents are widely used in distributing industrial goods. They are paid a commission.

Companies purchasing through limited function wholesalers often get a lower price because various services are not performed by this wholesaler. However, the purchaser must be able to perform the omitted service economically. For example, a retailer may get a case of peaches for $1 less from a **cash-and-carry wholesaler** than if he ordered from a full-service merchant wholesaler. However, he incurs a transportation cost because the transportation function is not provided by the cash-and-carry wholesaler. If the retailer cannot effectively perform the transportation function, the shipping cost per case may exceed the $1 savings. Thus, the retailer has to be able to hold the shipping cost per case of peaches to less than $1 in order to make purchasing from the cash-and-carry wholesaler worthwhile.

Merchandise Agents and Brokers.   The three major types of merchandise agents and brokers are described in Figure 11.8. As indicated in this figure, brokers, selling agents, and manufacturers' agents are paid on a commission basis. All are independent operations in business for themselves; they are not employees of either the buyers or sellers that they represent. Using brokers, selling agents, and manufacturers' agents offers a number of advantages. These will be indicated in the next chapter.

TRENDS IN WHOLESALING

There are several trends in wholesaling that companies must consider.

Wholesaling continues to be dominated by the larger firm. In 1972 merchant wholesalers with sales of $10 million or more accounted for only

1.7% of all firms, but they represented 45.5% of total sales. In the same year manufacturers' sales branches and sales offices with sales of $10 million or more obtained 97.2% of total sales even though they represented only 24.3% of all firms. Five percent of merchandise agents and brokers generated 46.6% of the sales of this wholesaling category.

Computer usage is being increasingly stressed by wholesaling firms. Computers allow companies to operate more efficiently in a number of ways. Inventory levels that minimize inventory costs can be determined. Unprofitable products can be identified and eliminated. They can order quantities of merchandise from suppliers that minimize total order costs. Management can know almost instantly how many units of any product are on hand. Shipments can be routed so that total transportation costs are minimized.

Additional research of the market is being conducted by wholesalers. Since the results show which new products are likely to be successful, they are in a position to know which products to buy or not buy from suppliers.

Many wholesalers are moving into new quarters or refurbishing existing structures. These, coupled with more efficient materials handling equipment and methods, enable them to move greater tonnages of merchandise at lower costs.

Now that we have a good idea of the wholesaling sector of our economy, we will turn our attention to the second major type of middleman, retailers.

RETAILING

There are four basic types of retailing organizations in the United States. These are stores, mail-order houses, automatic vending, and direct selling.

Undoubtedly, the reader is familiar with the various kinds of stores in which tremendous varieties of merchandise can be purchased. As can be seen in Figure 11.9, stores are the most important form of retailing through which merchandise is distributed to consumers.

Mail-order houses accept orders through the mail for merchandise. This is a convenient means of shopping for people who cannot get out of the house easily or who do not want to contend with having to shop. Of course, there are several disadvantages in purchasing from mail-order houses, including an inability to inspect the merchandise, having to wait at least several days to receive purchases, and running a risk of being dissatisfied.

Automatic vending consists of using vending machines to dispense convenience type merchandise at numerous locations. Candy, cigarettes, sandwiches, soups, chewing gum, and postage stamps are examples of products sold extensively through vending machines. Although their convenient location is beneficial to users, they are often a source of frustration if they malfunction (see Figure 11.10). Automatic vending is frequently a high cost method of selling. Expenses can often be as high as 40% of sales.

Figure 11.9   Major Types of Retailers, 1972

Retailer	Sales Volume and Percentage of Total Sales Volume	Establishments and Percentage of Total Establishments	Number of Employees and Percentage of Total Employees	Sales Volume per Estab- lishment	Sales Volume per Employee
Stores	$459 billion (97.5%)	1,772,345 (91.6%)	11,082,750 (97.6%)	$259,000	$41,420
Mail-order houses	$4.57 billion (1.0%)	7,982 (.4%)	121,976 (1.1%)	$572,600	$37,470
Automatic vending	$3.01 billion (.6%)	12,845 (.6%)	69,897 (.6%)	$234,300	$43,063
Direct selling	$3.98 billion (.8%)	141,294 (7.3%)	84,982 (.7%)	$ 28,170	$46,833
Totals	$471 billion (100%)	1,943,466 (100%)	11,359,605 (100%)	$243,000	$41,462

Source: U.S. Department of Commerce, Bureau of the Census.

Direct selling (sometimes called door-to-door selling) consists of companies having salespeople call on consumers in their homes. Vacuum cleaners, encyclopedias, magazines, cosmetics, and brushes are examples of products that are sold this way. Companies that use direct selling often encounter three major disadvantages. First, salespeople's salaries, commissions, and expenses are often a high percentage of sales, sometimes as high as 50%. Second, salespeople's turnover can be very high. For some direct selling companies, it can be 100%. Third, many consumers are reluctant to purchase from direct salespeople because of some of their deceptive practices.

Figure 11.9 provides basic data for the four major kinds of retailers. Stores are obviously the dominant form of retailing for they account for 97.5% of total retail sales volume, 91.6% of all establishments, and 97.6% of total retailing employees. In general, mail-order houses, automatic vending, and direct selling make up less than 1% of these totals. One exception is that direct selling firms account for slightly more than 7% of total retail establishments. Mail-order houses have the highest sales volume per establishment ($572,600), however, and direct selling has the greatest sales volume per employee ($46,833).

Retailing stores are generally divided into ten major categories and their various subgroups (see Figure 11.11). Figure 11.12 presents additional data on retailing stores. In this figure, the importance of **chain stores** in retailing is demonstrated. Chain stores are firms that own two or more establish-

Figure 11.10   One Way to Get Merchandise from a Balky Vending Machine

ments. Most readers are, of course, already familiar with many chain operations, such as A&P, Giant, Safeway, Acme Markets, Sears, Roebuck, Montgomery Ward, J. C. Penney, and Woolworth. Figure 11.12 shows how chain stores tend to dominate various types of retailing stores since they account for large percentages of sales volume. For example, chain stores account for 97% of department store sales, 84.3% of variety store sales, and 67.8% of grocery store sales. For all retailing, chain stores account for 45.1% of total sales.

The average chain store establishment tends to be larger in size than the independent (one-establishment) enterprise. About one-tenth of all retailing stores are chain operated, but they account for 45% of all retailing sales.

Figure 11.11   Major Types of Retailing Stores

Building Materials and Supply Stores
Hardware Stores
Farm Equipment Dealers
Department Stores
Variety Stores
Miscellaneous General Merchandise
  Stores
Grocery Stores
Meat and Fish (Seafood) Markets
Fruit Stores and Vegetable Markets
Candy, Nut, and Confectionery
  Stores
Retail Bakeries
Other Food Stores
Motor Vehicle Dealers
  Motor Vehicle Dealers—New and
    Used Cars
  Motor Vehicle Dealers—Used
    Cars Only
Tire, Battery, and Accessory Dealers
Miscellaneous Automotive Dealers
Gasoline Service Stations
Women's Ready-to-Wear Stores
Women's Accessory and Specialty
  Stores
Furriers and Fur Shops

Other Apparel and Accessory Stores
  Men's and Boys' Clothing and
    Furnishings Stores
  Family Clothing Stores
  Shoe Stores
  Apparel and Accessory Stores,
    N.E.C.
Furniture Stores
Home Furnishings Stores
Household Appliance Stores
Radio, Television, and Music Stores
Eating Places
Drinking Places (Alcoholic Beverages)
Drug Stores
Proprietary Stores
Liquor Stores
Antique Stores and Secondhand
  Stores
Sporting Goods Stores and Bicycle
  Shops
Jewelry Stores
Fuel and Ice Dealers
Florists
Cigar Stores and Stands
Miscellaneous Retail Stores

Source: U.S. Department of Commerce, Bureau of the Census.

Independent operations account for 90% of all retailing establishments and they generate 55% of total retailing sales volume. Thus, chain operations have a much higher sales volume per establishment ($1,100,000) than do independent operations ($150,000).

Because retailing stores are the means of reaching consumers preferred by most companies, we must look at some of the major kinds of stores. Figure 11.13 lists the 25 largest retailing companies according to sales. Many of the stores in Figure 11.13 are examples of the kinds of stores we will discuss: department stores, variety stores, discount houses, supermarkets, convenience stores, and specialty stores.

Channels of Distribution: Some Basic Concepts

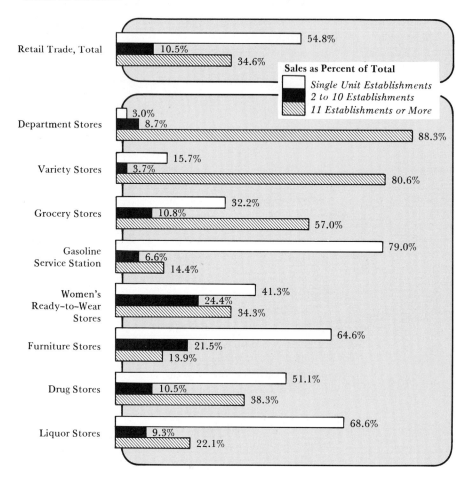

Figure 11.12 Percent Distribution of Sales by Firm Size: 1972 for Selected Kinds of Business

Sales as Percent of Total
Single Unit Establishments
2 to 10 Establishments
11 Establishments or More

Retail Trade, Total: 54.8%, 10.5%, 34.6%

Department Stores: 3.0%, 8.7%, 88.3%

Variety Stores: 15.7%, 3.7%, 80.6%

Grocery Stores: 32.2%, 10.8%, 57.0%

Gasoline Service Station: 79.0%, 6.6%, 14.4%

Women's Ready-to-Wear Stores: 41.3%, 24.4%, 34.3%

Furniture Stores: 64.6%, 21.5%, 13.9%

Drug Stores: 51.1%, 10.5%, 38.3%

Liquor Stores: 68.6%, 9.3%, 22.1%

Source: U.S. Department of Commerce, Bureau of the Census.

Department Stores

Department stores are large stores that sell a wide variety of merchandise organized into separate departments. In each line there is usually a good assortment. The buyer for each department manages that department. Thus, buyers not only purchase merchandise for their departments—their major function—but they also supervise clerks, engage in inventory control, arrange for sales (markdowns), plan promotional campaigns, and so on.

Figure 11.13   The Twenty-Five Largest Retailing Companies (by sales)

Rank (1976)	Company	Sales ($000)
1	Sears, Roebuck (Chicago)	14,950,208
2	Safeway Stores (Oakland)	10,442,531
3	S.S. Kresge (Troy, Mich.)	8,483,603
4	J.C. Penney (New York)	8,353,800
5	Great Atlantic & Pacific Tea (Montvale, N.J.)	6,537,897
6	Kroger (Cincinnati)	6,091,149
7	Marcor (Chicago)	5,280,280
8	F.W. Woolworth (New York)	5,152,200
9	Federated Department Stores (Cincinnati)	4,446,624
10	Lucky Stores (Dublin, Calif.)	3,483,174
11	Winn-Dixie Stores (Jacksonville)	3,265,916
12	American Stores (Wilmington)	3,207,248
13	Jewel Companies (Chicago)	2,981,429
14	City Products (Des Plaines, Ill.)	2,521,400
15	Food Fair Stores (Philadelphia)	2,507,040
16	Rapid-American (New York)	2,346,125
17	May Department Stores (St. Louis)	2,133,235
18	Southland (Dallas)	2,115,768
19	Dayton Hudson (Minneapolis)	1,898,544
20	Allied Stores (New York)	1,813,846
21	Supermarkets General (Woodbridge, N.J.)	1,612,692
22	Grand Union (Elmwood Park, N.J.)	1,611,195
23	Gamble-Skogmo (Minneapolis)	1,590,372
24	Associated Dry Goods (New York)	1,538,849
25	Albertson's (Boise)	1,490,839

Source: Fortune, July, 1977, p. 168, by permission.

Another major characteristic of department stores is that they usually offer a wide variety of services to their customers. Some examples include luncheon rooms, gift wrapping, delivery, nurseries, beauty consultants, and charge accounts.

The traditional department store emphasizes the sale of soft goods, such as men's wear, women's wear, children's clothing, and household items like curtains, blankets, and sheets. Other lines of merchandise commonly carried include books, china, gourmet foods, hardware, cameras, luggage, tobacco products, shoes, jewelry, cosmetics, and furniture. In the past, many department stores carried appliances and sporting goods, but because of increased competition, they have dropped these lines.

Most department store buyers prefer to deal directly with manufacturers and thus bypass wholesalers. Because of their large size, they are often able to get good prices and favorable terms of sale.

Manufacturers should evaluate department stores carefully. One aspect to consider is the image that the department store has with shoppers. This image must be consistent with the manufacturer's products. For example, because of its location, kind of merchandise sold, clientele, store front, fixtures, layout, and clerks, the department store may have a "low-quality" image, which could be damaging to a manufacturer's products if they are "high quality" in nature. Another aspect is to appraise the location of the department store carefully. Many are located in downtown areas of large cities where future growth is likely to be minimal.

Variety Stores

Variety stores are similar to department stores in that they are departmentalized. However, they are not usually as large in size and the assortment in each product line is not likely to be extensive. In addition, they offer few, if any, services. As a result, variety stores tend to have a lower operating margin than department stores. Examples of variety stores include F. W. Woolworth and S. S. Kresge.

Discount Stores

Discount stores appeared in the United States after World War II in response to consumer demand for low prices. In order to achieve these low prices, discount operators located in inexpensive buildings, used inexpensive fixtures, employed few clerks, and offered few services. Their main merchandise line was hard goods, such as washers, dryers, television sets, and radios. They tended to sell major brand names so that promotional costs could be minimized and consumers could easily see the price savings offered.

In recent years discount operations have moved to better locations, improved the quality of their interiors, and have begun to offer some services, such as credit and delivery. These actions have resulted in higher operating expenses and illustrate a phenomenon called the *wheel of retailing*, which means that low-cost retailers gain a competitive advantage when getting started by offering few services so that low prices can be charged. Once they become established, they add services that increase their costs and their prices. Thus, they become vulnerable to new forms of competitors that stress low prices by offering few services. In addition to discount operations, chain store operations in general and supermarkets in particular got a toehold by a low-price appeal, but they had to increase prices as they expanded their services.

Supermarkets

Supermarkets are large food stores that sell dry goods, frozen foods, meats, and fresh fruits and vegetables. They frequently have 20,000 or more square feet of selling area and stock as many as 6,000 different items. In recent years supermarkets have added many nonfood items, including toys and games, housewares, drugs, books and magazines, plants and flowers, and clothing.

Supermarkets emphasize **self-service.** Because self-service allows supermarkets to hire fewer clerks, they reduce their costs and are able to charge lower prices.

We mentioned earlier that chain operations tend to dominate grocery stores, and so it is with supermarkets. Safeway Stores, Great Atlantic & Pacific Tea (A&P), American Stores (Acme and Super Saver), Winn-Dixie, Food Fair, Giant Food, and Grand Union are some of the larger chain stores that dominate the supermarket area.

Convenience Stores

Convenience stores are small-sized food stores that sell a limited line of grocery items, such as milk, bread, pastries, soft drinks, and ice cream. They tend to keep long hours. In fact, many such operations stay open 24 hours a day. Because these long hours provide a convenience to shoppers, convenience stores tend to charge high prices. High's and 7–11 are examples of successful convenience store operations.

Specialty Stores

Specialty stores carry a broad assortment of merchandise in a *single merchandise line*. Examples are candy stores, women's clothing stores, shoe stores, sporting goods stores, flower shops, and toy stores. Generally, their prices are relatively high because they may offer a wide variety of services (such as free alterations). They may also be viewed as specialists in their merchandise line. Because they are specialists, they may charge higher prices.

TRENDS IN RETAILING

There are various trends in retailing that companies contemplating using retailers must consider. Some of the more important trends and their implications for marketing strategies of suppliers will be discussed below.

Channels of Distribution: Some Basic Concepts

Increasing Importance of Chain Operations

We mentioned earlier that chain operations dominate several types of retailing stores and this is likely to continue in the future. For all retailing, chain stores' share of total retail business jumped from 34% in 1965 to over 45% in 1972.

What factors account for this success? Perhaps the most important is *centralized buying*. This means that items are purchased for all stores of the chain at the company's central headquarters. Thus, quantity discounts can be obtained, costs are lower, and lower prices can be charged. Chain stores also have standard store fronts and layouts. Standard store fronts allow customers to identify the chain store easily and standard layouts expedite instore traffic flows and increase sales volume. Standard advertising is also an important strategy used by chain stores. Once the chain has developed effective advertisements, all stores use similar ads and quantity discounts from advertising media can be achieved.

Because of their large size and desire for low operating costs, chain stores usually bargain vigorously with suppliers for low prices and favorable terms of sale. Chain operations, because of their centralized buying, generally require that suppliers make their presentations to buying committees.

Proliferation of Shopping Centers

Large **shopping centers** continue to spring up outside the central cities of large metropolitan areas. Often housing as many as 100 to 200 stores, they offer convenient parking and one-stop shopping for their customers. Frequently, they have enclosed malls so that inclement weather is not a shopping deterrent. As the central cities of America continue to decline, it is likely that shopping centers are going to be increasingly important on the retailing scene.

Most large shopping centers contain one or two large department stores which serve to draw customers to the shopping center. A number of convenience and specialty stores usually complete the shopping center. Real estate developers of shopping centers who lease space to stores generally have a manager who coordinates the marketing activities of the tenant stores.

Increasing Emphasis on Self-Service

Retailers will continue to emphasize self-service for customers. In self-service, customers are given access to merchandise and can inspect the merchandise. If they decide to purchase, they bring the desired merchandise to centrally located checkout stations.

Since in a self-service operation there are fewer clerks, there are lower operating costs for the retailer. For the supplier, however, self-service creates problems. For example, a manufacturer must heavily advertise his products so that they will be easily recognized by customers. Similarly, the products' packages must attract the customer's attention.

Computerization

Because retailers are making greater use of computers, they are maintaining tighter control over their inventories and are thus minimizing stock overages and shortages. Profitability analysis enables retailers to eliminate unprofitable products. Coupled with sophisticated materials handling equipment, computers enable vast quantities of merchandise to be moved with few personnel involved. As a result, costs are lower.

Growth of Private Brands

Private brands are products that are sold in retail stores that carry the retailer's brand instead of the manufacturer's brand (**national brand**). Examples include A&P's Jane Parker brand and Acme and Super Saver's Ideal brand. Private brands appear to be accounting for larger percentages of retail sales. For example, 90% of all Sears, Roebuck merchandise carries its private label. Over 25% of A&P's merchandise is private label. Private brand bread sales for Safeway and A&P soared 288% and 259%, respectively, in 1973. Campbell Soup increased the size of its 1975 advertising budget as a result of the onslaught of private label soups.[1]

Suppliers, especially manufacturers, have a major decision to make when they contemplate whether to market their products under their own brand name or under the private label of their retail outlets. This decision will be discussed in the next chapter.

Scrambled Merchandising

Scrambled merchandising is the term used for the trend for retailers to carry product assortments outside their normal product lines. Thus, drugstores carry cosmetics, toys, games, and gourmet foods. Food stores carry drug items. Variety stores and department stores sell auto supplies.

Scrambled merchandising is so prevalent today that it forces manufacturers to consider new types of retail stores for their products.

Growth in Franchising

In a franchising arrangement, a company (the **franchisor**) lends its company name (or product brand name) to retailers (**franchisees**) who pay for that name and the right to sell the product. In return, the franchisor agrees to give the franchisee the exclusive right to sell the product in a given territory

---

[1] Richard T. Hise, *Product/Service Strategy* (New York: Petrocelli/Charter, 1977), p. 97.

and the franchisor also provides the franchisee with its marketing knowledge. The most important benefit that accrues to the franchisor is that it retains control over the marketing of its products. For example, it can prescribe product quality, store locations, advertising programs, and prices.

An example of a franchise operation is McDonald's, the national hamburger restaurant chain. In 1973 the company had 2,100 outlets, making it the largest restaurant chain in the world. In order to get a McDonald's franchise, $150,000 had to be paid to the corporation, along with 11.5% of gross sales thereafter. The average franchisee made a $60,000 to $70,000 profit annually (before taxes). Exact specifications are developed at central headquarters. For example, each hamburger is 3.875 inches in diameter and weighs 1.6 ounces. Franchisors get help at the company's training facility, called Hamburger U., located in Illinois, on basic and advanced operations. McDonald's research laboratory makes new products and techniques available to franchisees. For example, there is a computer program to make french fries; the method is based on the water content and density of the potato.[2]

Scope of Franchising Operations.   It has been estimated that in 1977 there were about 1,115 franchise companies in the United States with 463,000 individual franchise outlets. Their total sales were about $239 billion annually, accounting for around 31 percent of total retail sales.[3]

Franchising operations are expected to grow rapidly in a number of areas. Figures 11.14 and 11.15 show the areas that experienced the greatest growth in franchising between 1971 and 1977. These figures indicate that most of the growth in franchising was taking place in the services sector.

The entry of many large, well-established companies is spurring much of the growth in franchising. Some examples include:

1. General Foods acquired Burger Chef.
2. Pillsbury took over ownership of Burger King.
3. United Fruit acquired A&W Root Beer and Baskin-Robbins, an ice cream retailer.
4. RCA took over Arnold Palmer Enterprises, which includes driving ranges and dry cleaning shops.
5. Consolidated Foods acquired the Chicken Delight operations.[4]

Legal Problems.   Recently a number of legal problems has arisen in franchising operations. The most important of these will be discussed below.

Most franchising agreements provide that the franchisee be given an

[2] "Marketing the Franchised Hamburger," in Betsy D. Gelb and Ben M. Enis, eds., *Marketing Is Everybody's Business* (Pacific Palisades, Calif.: Goodyear Publishing Company, Inc., 1974), p. 46.

[3] *Franchising in the Economy,* 1975–1977, U.S. Department of Commerce.

[4] Charles G. Burck, "Franchising's Troubled Dream World," *Fortune,* March, 1970, p. 117.

Figure 11.14 Ten Lines of Business in Which the Number of Franchised Establishments Increased the Most Between 1971 and 1977

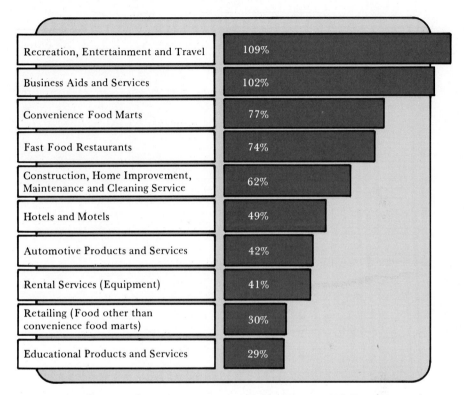

Recreation, Entertainment and Travel	109%
Business Aids and Services	102%
Convenience Food Marts	77%
Fast Food Restaurants	74%
Construction, Home Improvement, Maintenance and Cleaning Service	62%
Hotels and Motels	49%
Automotive Products and Services	42%
Rental Services (Equipment)	41%
Retailing (Food other than convenience food marts)	30%
Educational Products and Services	29%

Source: *Franchising in the Economy, 1971–1973* and *1975–1977*, U.S. Department of Commerce.

exclusive territory in which it is the only firm allowed to sell the franchisor's product. Some people have argued that this is a violation of anti-trust legislation, but in general, the courts have not agreed.

Another common difficulty is that the franchisee is *required* to purchase products only from the franchisor. As a result of the decision in the Chicken Delight case, many franchisors eliminated this requirement from their agreements. Most franchisors now *offer* the availability of products to franchisees. A recent decision in the Dunkin' Donut's case, however, suggests that even this policy may be in jeopardy. The judge ruled that Dunkin' Donuts was so large in comparison to the individual franchisees that merely an offer to provide equipment intimidated them into purchas-

Channels of Distribution: Some Basic Concepts

Figure 11.15. Ten Lines of Business in Which the Sales of Franchised Establishments Increased the Most Between 1971 and 1977

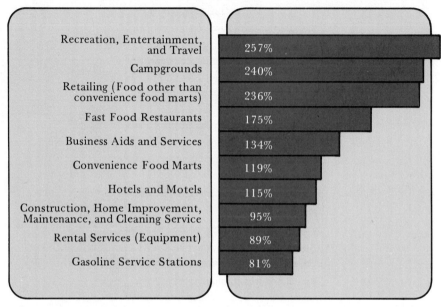

Recreation, Entertainment, and Travel	257%
Campgrounds	240%
Retailing (Food other than convenience food marts)	236%
Fast Food Restaurants	175%
Business Aids and Services	134%
Convenience Food Marts	119%
Hotels and Motels	115%
Construction, Home Improvement, Maintenance, and Cleaning Service	95%
Rental Services (Equipment)	89%
Gasoline Service Stations	81%

Source: *Franchising in the Economy, 1971–1973* and *1975–1977*, U.S. Department of Commerce.

ing, even though franchisees could purchase at lower prices from headquarters than they could elsewhere.[5]

A final legal consideration involves the promises that franchisors make and the information they provide prospective franchisees. Some of these are as follows:

1. Franchisors may show profit figures that are consistently above what the franchisee is likely to make.
2. Expected profits for new franchisees are shown, not the actual profit figures for already existing franchisees.
3. Hidden charges in the franchise agreement may not be mentioned.
4. Prospective franchisees may be led to believe that having a celebrity advertise the franchised product guarantees success. Such, however, has not always been the case. Minnie Pearl Chicken Houses, for example, experienced financial problems in the early 1970's.

[5] *Business Week*, June 16, 1975, p. 82.

5. Franchisors may promise franchisees marketing expertise that they either do not have or do not deliver.[6]

SUMMARY

A channel of distribution is the combination of middlemen that a company uses to move its products to ultimate purchasers. The two major types of middlemen that can be used are wholesalers and retailers.

Wholesalers purchase goods and resell them to retailers, other wholesalers, industrial users, institutions, commercial firms, and government agencies. Wholesalers do not sell directly to ultimate consumers, but retailers do. There are three major types of wholesalers. Merchant wholesalers take title to the products they purchase and generally offer a wide range of services. Merchandise agents and brokers bring buyers and sellers together; they do not take title to merchandise. Manufacturers establish sales branches and sales offices in order to perform the wholesaling function themselves.

Middlemen make a number of contributions to our economy. They reduce distribution costs by minimizing the number of transactions required. They perform all of the marketing functions. Because they are specialists, they efficiently perform these marketing functions. Their operations result in increased value because time and place utility are created. They bring buyers and sellers together and act as information sources. Middlemen can be especially valuable for companies that are going into new markets, small firms, companies that are bringing out new products, and companies that do not have sufficient financial resources.

Firms that market consumer goods tend to use middlemen extensively. In all, approximately 95% of all consumer products flow through wholesalers and retailers. Industrial goods, however, tend to go directly to purchasers and not through middlemen. Around 80% of all industrial goods are marketed directly.

Trends of significance to suppliers are taking place in wholesaling. These trends include an increasing dominance by large firms, more computer usage, additional research of the market, and the purchase of new quarters or renovation of existing facilities.

There are four major types of retailing establishments in the United States. By far, the most dominant of these are stores. Automatic vending, direct selling, and mail order (the other retailing forms) are much less important than stores. Within the stores category, chain operations (operations that have two or more establishments under one ownership) tend to dominate.

The types of stores that are important in retailing include department

[6] Shelby D. Hunt, "Full Disclosure and the Franchise System of Distribution," *Proceedings of the 1972 Fall Conference of the American Marketing Association* (Chicago: American Marketing Association, 1973), pp. 301–4.

Channels of Distribution: Some Basic Concepts

stores, variety stores, discount stores, supermarkets, convenience stores, and specialty stores.

Several significant trends are occurring in retailing. An increased importance of chain operations is likely. Centralized buying, standard fronts and layouts, and standard advertising are major reasons for the success of chain stores. Proliferation of self-service, computerization, increased importance of private brands, scrambled merchandising, and continued growth of franchising operations are other major trends.

QUESTIONS

1. Why are channels of distribution more likely to be used for consumer products than for industrial products?
2. How do middlemen create time utility?
3. What is the major distinction between merchant wholesalers and merchandise agents and brokers?
4. What are the four major types of retailing organizations?
5. Indicate some of the major characteristics of chain operations that have made them successful.
6. What does the wheel of retailing mean?
7. What are the major characteristics of discount stores?
8. What do you believe are the major reasons that explain the success of convenience stores?
9. Why do you think private brands are increasing in importance?
10. What factors do you think explain the growth of franchising in the United States?

GLOSSARY

Automatic Vending: retailing operations that involve machines that dispense convenience type merchandise

Broker: represents the buyer or seller in a transaction and has limited authority over the terms of the sale and price

Cash-and-Carry Wholesalers: limited service wholesalers who do not extend credit or provide transportation

Chain Stores: retailing organizations that have two or more stores under one ownership

Channel of Distribution: combination of middlemen that a company uses to move its products to the ultimate purchaser

Concentration: a function performed by wholesalers that involves consolidating small lots of products into larger lots

Convenience Stores: small-sized food stores that sell limited lines of grocery items

Department Stores: large retailing stores that sell a wide variety of merchandise organized into separate departments

Direct Selling: retailing operations that involve salespeople calling directly on consumers in their homes

Discount Stores: retailing stores that usually emphasize the sale of hard goods at low prices through inexpensive locations and offering few services

Dispersion: a function performed by retailers that involves breaking down large lots of products into smaller lots

Drop Shippers: limited service wholesalers who take title to merchandise but do not take physical possession

Franchisee: a company that pays for the privilege of selling a specific brand or using a particular company name

Franchisor: a company that lends its company name or product brand name to another company that pays for that privilege

Mail-Order Houses: retailing operations that accept orders through the mail for merchandise

Manufacturers' Agents: sell part of a manufacturer's total output; they are not given control over the terms of the sale and pricing

Merchandise Agents and Brokers: wholesalers who represent buyers or sellers in a transaction and do not take title to merchandise

Merchant Wholesalers: wholesalers who take title to merchandise they purchase for resale

National Brand: a product that carries the manufacturer's brand name

Place Utility: having products available where consumers want them

Private Brands: products that carry the middleman's brand (usually the retailer's) instead of the manufacturer's brands

Rack Jobbers: a regular wholesaler specializing in selling nonfood items to food stores

Retailers: middlemen who sell to ultimate consumers, not to other business firms

Sales Branches: manufacturer wholesaling operations that carry inventories

Sales Offices: manufacturer wholesaling operations that do not carry inventories

Scrambled Merchandising: the trend for retailers to carry product assortments outside their normal product lines

Self-Service: limited use of clerks by retail stores in serving customers

Selling Agent: sells all of a specified line or the entire output for a principal; they generally have control over the terms of sale and pricing

Shopping Centers: groups of retail stores that are generally located outside central business districts

Specialty Stores: retailing stores that carry a broad assortment in a single merchandise line

Supermarkets: large food stores selling dry goods, frozen foods, meats, and fresh produce

Time Utility: having products available when consumers want them

Truck Wholesalers: limited service wholesalers carrying limited stock assortments and selling perishable or semiperishable items

Variety Stores: departmentalized stores that sell a fairly wide variety of merchandise but do not carry as extensive an assortment as department stores

Wholesalers: middlemen who purchase goods for resale to retailers, other wholesalers, industrial users, institutions, commercial firms, and governmental agencies

CASES

Case 1: Consolidated Department Stores

A new shopping center is being planned for the south side of a city of 200,000 people located in the southwestern United States. This will be the first large-scale shopping center in this community since River Ridge Shopping Center was constructed on the north side of town 10 years ago.

Consolidated Department Stores is located in the downtown shopping area. The department store's management did not choose to locate a branch in the River Ridge Shopping Center but is considering placing a branch operation in the south side center. Mr. Taylor, the owner, believes that the growth of the city's population on the south side is a major reason for considering to locate there. However, he is concerned by the rumor that a large department store headquartered in the state's largest city plans to put a branch in this shopping center.

1. Should Mr. Taylor be concerned by the possibility of a competitive store being located in the same shopping center?
2. What other information should Mr. Taylor obtain?
3. Should Consolidated locate in the new shopping center?

Case 2: The Ashman Co.

A friend of yours is considering selling common stock in a company that is being formed to manufacture a new line of decorative ashtrays. The Ashman company expects to be capitalized with about $50,000 to start. Management expects to sell these ashtrays in variety stores, department stores, and drugstores throughout the United States.

The company expects to sell the ashtrays directly to these retailers by calling on the buying committees of various chain operations. The director of marketing does not plan to use wholesalers to reach retailers. He feels that wholesalers would not push the product aggressively because they may be selling competitive lines. He also believes that the company will get a better price if it does not use wholesalers.

You believe that the director of marketing has not fully considered the advantages of using wholesalers in distributing the ashtrays. You tell him that in several days you would like to give him a report outlining how his company would benefit from using wholesalers.

1. What would your report say?
2. What kinds of wholesalers would you suggest the director of marketing consider using? Why?

Channels of Distribution Decisions

After you read this chapter, you should be able to answer the following questions:

1. What happens to the functions performed by middlemen when a company decides to market its products direct?

2. What are the two major reasons why companies usually decide not to use middlemen?

3. Under what conditions would a company tend to use middlemen?

4. What factors should be considered when a firm is deciding which middlemen to select?

5. What are the two most important factors to be considered when a company is deciding on the intensity of distribution?

6. What are the major advantages of using specialized middlemen like brokers and selling agents who do not take title to goods?

7. How can companies increase the cooperation they obtain from their channels of distribution?

8. When does a company need an executive to head up its channels of distribution function?

9. What are the major responsibilities of the executive in charge of a company's channels of distribution operations?

Administered System   Channels of Distribution   Conflict
Consignment Sales   Contractual System   Corporate System   Direct
Marketing   Discounts   Exclusive Distribution   Indirect Marketing
Intensity of Distribution   Intensive Distribution   Middlemen
National Brand   Power   Private Brand   Selective Distribution

INTRODUCTION

In the previous chapter the reader was introduced to some of the basic concepts of channels of distribution. There, the reader was exposed to the nature of channel structures and the various wholesaling and retailing institutions. The purpose of this chapter is to extend the coverage of **channels of distribution** by discussing the major decisions that must be made in this area of marketing. These decisions include: (1) deciding whether to use channels of distribution, (2) which channels and which specific companies to use, (3) determining the intensity of distribution, (4) whether to use middlemen who do not take title, (5) whether to place our own brand on products or use the middleman's brand, and (6) how best to secure the enthusiastic cooperation of middlemen. But before we discuss these decisions, we will present the following preliminary topics: (1) channels of distribution and the performance of marketing functions; (2) complexity of channels decisions; and (3) conflict in manufacturer–dealer relationships. All of these have important consequences for making the six major channels of distribution decisions indicated above.

CHANNELS OF DISTRIBUTION AND THE PERFORMANCE OF MARKETING FUNCTIONS

It was indicated in the last chapter that the marketing functions performed by **middlemen** cannot be eliminated. Such functions include, for example, storage, transportation, personal selling, and research of the market. The performance of these and other marketing functions is necessary in order to move products from producers to consumers. These functions can be performed entirely by manufacturers or they can be performed entirely by middlemen. Or the manufacturer and middlemen can share the performance of these functions. The functions cannot, however, be eliminated; they cannot disappear. They must be performed.

If the functions themselves cannot be eliminated, then the *costs* of performing these functions cannot disappear either. These expenditures have to be paid for by either the manufacturer or middlemen, or they can be shared by the manufacturer and middlemen. Or, the cost can be passed on to the consumer. It cannot, however, be eliminated; someone must pay for the marketing functions performed.

COMPLEXITY OF CHANNELS DECISIONS

Channels of distribution decisions are not easy to make. Actually, they are among the most complex of all marketing decisions. This is true for a number of reasons which will be discussed below.

Communications Between the Manufacturer and Middlemen May Be Poor

In many cases, communications between the manufacturer and middlemen may be poor. As a result, either the manufacturer or the middleman is deprived of necessary information required to make effective decisions. In either case, the manufacturer may be hurt. For example, a large publishing house did a poor job of communicating its basic marketing plan to its wholesalers. Therefore, the wholesalers did not aggressively push the publisher's products, and the publisher's sales volume dropped significantly.[1]

Companies Often Do Not Research Their Channels of Distribution

The failure of many firms to research their channels of distribution periodically also means that the firms lack adequate information on which to base decisions. The importance of researching channels of distribution is seen in the experience of a grocery products company marketing a new line of dairy items. A study of how the grocery trade perceived the marketing program of the manufacturer was conducted by a marketing research firm. Such areas as sales personnel servicing, discounts, packaging, and the quality of sales promotional material were analyzed. The president of the firm was surprised to find out how poorly the firm was rated. He commented: "Isn't it amazing that a firm like ours that is successful in sales and profits could score the negatives we did in marketing?"[2]

A large automobile tire manufacturer recently undertook an analysis of the effectiveness of the point-of-purchase material it supplied dealers. The research revealed that the tire dealers did not want the material and usually discarded it. The dealers believed that their biggest marketing problem was getting customers in the door, not selling them once they were inside.[3]

No One in the Company is Responsible for Managing Channels of Distribution

Poor communications and lack of research frequently exist because in most companies an individual is not placed in charge of managing channels of distribution. Thus, there is no one who is ultimately responsible for seeing

---

[1] Reavis Cox, Thomas F. Schutte, and Kendrick S. Few, "Toward the Measurement of Trade Channel Perception," in Fred C. Allvine, ed., *Combined Proceedings 1971 Spring and Fall Conference* (Chicago: American Marketing Association, 1972), pp. 189–93.
[2] Ibid.
[3] Ibid.

that channels decisions are effective. In practice, as a result, these decisions are fragmented. A number of people—such as those in physical distribution, product planning, marketing research, and packaging—make decisions about the channels area, but they lack the necessary overall perspective that would be present if one person were in charge of all decisions affecting channels of distribution.

Channels of Distribution Are in Turbulence

There is a great deal of turbulence within the channels of distribution that adds to the complexity of making channels decisions. One cause of the turbulence is the tendency for all kinds of retailers to carry merchandise outside their "normal" merchandise lines. Thus, some channels become better prospects for a company's products and other channels become poorer prospects. Consider the case of a leading manufacturer of toiletry products that sells exclusively through drug chains. Two-thirds of toiletry products are now purchased through other retailers, but the company will not change its distribution policy.[4]

Another cause of the turbulence is the effort to increase operational efficiency. Computerization of operations is a case in point: Retailers making heavy use of computers have increased inventory turnover, have spotted developing trends sooner, and have identified weak products.[5] Data like these force manufacturers to be on their toes. Retailers, for example, will no longer accept unprofitable or slow-moving products.

Lack of Direct Control

The marketing department is unable to exert direct control over its channels of distribution. Middlemen are independent businessmen who look out for themselves. They may not cooperate with manufacturing firms unless they see benefits for themselves.

CONFLICT IN MANUFACTURER–CHANNEL RELATIONSHIPS

Unfortunately, there may be a good deal of conflict in manufacturer–dealer relationships. Conflict results when the manufacturer or middleman cannot achieve very desirable goals—such as profit—without reducing the possibility of the other firm's achieving its goals. For example, a retailer wants a manufacturer to make emergency shipments of a product if an out-of-stock situation occurs. The retailer benefits from these emergency shipments because he makes his customers happy, they continue to shop his store and his sales and profits remain high. The manufacturer, however,

[4] Ibid.
[5] *Business Week*, July 31, 1971, p. 70.

finds that his profits may drop because he incurs higher transportation costs from having to make emergency shipments in small lots.

If the level of conflict becomes severe enough, it is possible for the performance of the manufacturer–dealer system to suffer. Indeed, its very survival may be in jeopardy.

It is not unusual in conflict situations for either the manufacturer or dealer to gain control over the other. That is, one exerts **power** over the other. Thus, a manufacturer may have power over his dealers, or dealers may have power over the manufacturer. This power is reflected in the ability of one side in the struggle to get the other side to make concessions. Figure 12.1 provides examples of power.

What factors determine who will have power? Some of the more normal factors include:

1. The percentages of sales volume for a particular manufacturer and middleman. For example, let's assume that 30% of a manufacturer's output is sold to a large retailing chain. This output accounts for only

Figure 12.1   Examples of Power in Channels of Distribution Systems

Manufacturer Has Power Over Middleman	Middleman Has Power Over Manufacturer
1. Manufacturer makes no emergency shipments to the middleman regardless of circumstances.	1. Manufacturer makes emergency shipments.
2. No manufacturer salespeople call on the middleman. He is forced to send or telephone his order.	2. Manufacturer sells on consignment basis (middleman does not have to pay the manufacturer for goods until goods are sold).
3. No special discounts are offered the middleman by the manufacturer.	3. Manufacturer provides the middleman with allowances for advertising.
4. No research of the market is provided the middleman by the manufacturer.	4. Middleman consistently does not pay his bill within the allotted time to collect the discount. He takes the discount anyway, and the manufacturer does not bill him for the full price.
5. No unsold merchandise may be returned to the manufacturer by the middleman.	5. Manufacturer is forced to provide free marketing research to the middleman.
6. Middleman must pay transportation charges.	6. Manufacturer provides training for the middleman's salespeople.
7. Manufacturer makes infrequent deliveries to the middleman.	7. Manufacturer must pay transportation charges.

1% of the retailer's sales. In this case, power would tend to be with the retailer. A loss of 1% of his business is not cause for concern, but the manufacturer could ill afford to lose 30% of his volume.

2. Manufacturers, frequently through advertising, have built up such a large demand for their products among consumers that middlemen are pressured to purchase them and grant concessions to the manufacturer.

3. Manufacturers gain power through legal means, such as through *franchising*. In this case, the retailer may be overly dependent on the franchisor. Or, the middleman may sign an agreement to purchase only from the manufacturer.

4. A manufacturer may be the sole source of supply of a product to a middleman because the manufacturer holds a patent or has exclusive rights to the raw materials used in the product.

5. A particular retailer may be the only retailer capable of giving the manufacturer the territorial coverage he needs for a new and important product.

Later in this chapter we will present several ways for reducing the level of conflict in manufacturer–middlemen systems. Next, however, we will deal with the first major channels of distribution decision, whether to even use middlemen to market products and services.

SHOULD WE USE MIDDLEMEN?

The first and perhaps most important problem that a company must deal with is whether it wants to even use middlemen. In some instances, it may be advisable for a firm not to use middlemen. If a company does not use middlemen, we say that it is engaging in **direct marketing.** If middlemen are used, it is engaging in **indirect marketing.**

Perhaps the most important consideration of the firm in deciding whether to use a middleman is *profit*.

Profit

Companies ultimately must look at the effect on profit when they are considering whether to go direct or indirect. Consider Figure 12.2. Here we have a manufacturer that believes he could sell 10,000 units of a product through a retailer. Since the expected price per unit is $1 and the estimated cost per unit is $.80, his net profit would be $2,000.

Suppose that the manufacturer did not use the retailer and sold direct to consumers. Let's assume that he could then sell to them at the $1.20 per unit the retailer would receive. Let's also assume that he could still sell 10,000 units. We *cannot* assume, however, that his cost per unit would remain at $.80 because the manufacturer would have to *perform those*

Figure 12.2   Net Profit for a Manufacturing Firm Selling Through a Retailer

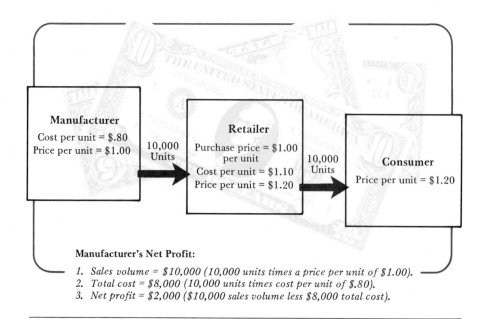

Manufacturer
Cost per unit = $.80
Price per unit = $1.00

10,000 Units

Retailer
Purchase price = $1.00 per unit
Cost per unit = $1.10
Price per unit = $1.20

10,000 Units

Consumer
Price per unit = $1.20

Manufacturer's Net Profit:

1. *Sales volume = $10,000 (10,000 units times a price per unit of $1.00).*
2. *Total cost = $8,000 (10,000 units times cost per unit of $.80).*
3. *Net profit = $2,000 ($10,000 sales volume less $8,000 total cost).*

marketing functions that the retailer would have performed. Thus, the cost per unit for the manufacturer will probably increase. Let's assume that the estimated cost per unit would be $1.05. This means that the retailer's profit would be $1,500, or sales volume of $12,000 (10,000 × $1.20) less total costs of $10,500 (10,000 × $1.05). Given these results, the manufacturer should use the retailer because his net profit of $2,000 would be higher.

It is possible in this example that different figures would exist for the number of units sold and for the price received by the manufacturing firm. The manufacturer, for example, might sell more or less than 10,000 units. The price he receives might be more or less than the $1.20 the retailer could obtain. In making the decision whether middlemen should be used, the company should project the profits likely to result if middlemen are used or are not used. This means that careful estimates of costs per unit, selling prices, and units sold must be made. Net profits for each alternative can be estimated from these data. The alternative having the higher profit figure should be selected.

This kind of analysis is also appropriate for companies already using middlemen but who are considering no longer using them. Profit is the key factor. This approach was used when the Evans Company, a large lumbering firm, decided in 1970 to eliminate its middlemen. Manford A. Orlott, Chairman of the Board of Evans, stated: "The most profitable way to bring forest products to the marketplace is to go directly to the consumer."[6] In 1971 the Evans Company reported a 45% increase in first-half earnings and a sales increase of 19% to $324 million.

Market Considerations

Market considerations are very important in the decision to use or not to use middlemen:

1. The more dispersed the market, the greater the need for middlemen because a market that is spread out is more costly and time-consuming to service. Thus, a company may elect to have middlemen sell to such a market and not incur the costs of performing the marketing functions involved.
2. The larger the size of the market, the more likely the firm can go direct because the potential sales volume is greater with a larger market and the higher cost associated with going direct can be covered more easily.
3. Specific market segments may prefer direct or indirect approaches. Industrial buyers, for example, like to have close contact with manufacturing firms; they do not want to deal with middlemen. Thus, more direct channels of distribution are usually used. Since purchasers of consumer products do not usually need close contact with manufacturers of consumer products, the channels of distribution for consumer products tend to be longer (more indirect).

Product Considerations

The nature of the product determines whether it will be marketed direct or indirect. The more technical the product, the more likely direct marketing will be used because middlemen may lack the expertise and knowledge to market such a product. A new product may have to be marketed direct because channels of distribution may be reluctant to carry it. A product that has a wide spread between its manufacturing cost and its selling price is more likely to be sold direct because there are more funds to cover the higher marketing costs involved. Convenience goods usually use indirect marketing because their market is dispersed, they are not technical in nature, and they usually have a low manufacturing cost–price spread. Shopping goods, however, tend to use more direct channels because their margin to cover marketing costs is relatively high. Perishable and fashionable merchandise, because of the crucial importance of time, tend to use direct channels because the length of time involved in moving the merchandise from producer to the end consumer is reduced.

[6] Ibid.

The Company's Marketing Skill

Sometimes a company does not have the required marketing skill to go direct to the market. It may lack knowledge of the market, it may not be experienced with a new line of products, or it may be deficient in the advertising, personal selling, transportation, and storage areas. When a company lacks marketing skill, it often has no choice but to use indirect means of distribution; middlemen who have the necessary marketing expertise will be asked to market the product.

Companies often find that they need to use middlemen when they are putting a new product on the market because the companies lack the necessary marketing knowledge to do an effective job.

Degree of Control Desired

A major reason why companies use direct marketing is that they want to retain control over the marketing of their products. If middlemen were used, control could be lost since the middlemen would be performing such marketing functions as storage, advertising, analyzing the market, and transportation.

If middlemen were to do an effective job of marketing a firm's products, the company would not object to using them, but many firms believe that they themselves would perform the marketing functions more effectively than the middlemen could. The firms also feel that they would devote more attention to their products than would the middlemen who may have hundreds or even thousands of other products to sell.

Financial Considerations

If a company uses direct means of marketing, it means that the company must be in a sound financial condition because a company that does not use middlemen incurs the costs of performing the marketing functions involved. Thus, it must have sufficient funds to pay for marketing research, advertising, personal selling, transportation, storage, and so on. A firm that is not in a sound financial condition may have to use indirect means of marketing because it lacks the funds to support the performance of marketing functions.

Another financial consideration is that many companies believe that the return on investment is generally higher for research and development and production than it is for marketing. As a result, they prefer not to devote scarce resources in going direct but will instead make use of middlemen and devote more funds to production and R&D.[7]

Figure 12.3 summarizes the conditions under which direct or indirect

[7] Richard S. Lopata, "Faster Pace in Wholesaling," *Harvard Business Review* (July–August, 1969), pp. 130–43.

Marketing Mix Decisions

Figure 12.3   When to Use Direct or Indirect Methods of Distribution

Factor	Indirect	Direct
1. The market	Dispersed Small potential sales volume Consumer market	Concentrated Large potential sales volume Industrial market
2. The product	Nontechnical Low per unit spread between manufacturing cost and selling price Convenience goods Nonperishable and staple goods	Technical High per unit spread between manufacturing cost and selling price Shopping goods Perishable and fashion products
3. Marketing skills of company	Company lacks marketing skills and experience	Company has marketing skills and experience
4. Degree of control desired by company	Company desires little control over marketing of product	Company wants high degree of control over marketing of product
5. Financial consideration	Weak financial condition Company believes that poor return on investment results from marketing operations	Good financial condition Company believes that good return on investment can be achieved from marketing operations

distribution strategies are advised. Companies that have a preponderance of factors suggesting either indirect or direct marketing are probably advised to choose that alternative.

DECIDING WHICH CHANNELS OF DISTRIBUTION TO USE

If a company has decided to reach its market through channels of distribution, it next must choose which middlemen to use. Two major aspects of this decision are important. First, a decision must be made on the *general* type of middlemen through which to market. Several choices are possible: retailers and wholesalers, and various kinds of each (such as drugstores, department stores, supermarkets, merchant wholesalers, selling agents, brokers, and rack jobbers). Second, the specific companies to be employed must be chosen. In making these two choices, several factors must be considered. They are discussed below.

The Market

This market is probably the most critical factor to be considered in deciding which middlemen to select. One aspect is the geographical coverage provided by the prospective middleman. This must coincide with the geographical location of the market in which the product is being sold. If the market is located in Illinois, Indiana, Ohio, and Michigan, the channels of distribution selected must cover these four states.

The type of channel from which the market is accustomed to purchasing the product is another consideration. If, for example, women have generally purchased beauty aids in drugstores, then drugstores probably should be used instead of supermarkets.

The Product

Various characteristics of the product may be important in choosing channels of distribution. Perishable products necessitate middlemen who have refrigeration capabilities. Highly technical products require middlemen who have the necessary experience and expertise. Heavy, bulky products need channels of distribution that have efficient materials handling equipment.

Some middlemen may be reluctant to carry a new product because they are not sure how well the product will be received.

Degree of Channel Cooperation Expected

Some middlemen are more likely than others to cooperate with companies. That is, some will more aggressively push a firm's products. Middlemen will aggressively market a product if they believe that it will be profitable for them. They are also more inclined to carry a product if the manufacturer has, through its promotion program, built up a demand for that product in the market because the middlemen know that they will have an easier time selling the product.

Availability of Channels

Some companies find that their choices of channels are severely limited, for many of the middlemen do not carry certain products. A good example is fashion apparel. In general, only selling agents, brokers, and retailers carry these products. Although manufacturers might like to sell fashion apparel through full-service merchant wholesalers, for example, this middleman alternative does not exist.[8]

[8] Philip McVey, "Are Channels of Distribution What the Textbooks Say?" *Journal of Marketing* (January, 1960), pp. 61–64.

Knowledge of the Market

Middlemen will very often be chosen because they have a knowledge of specialized markets. This is particularly true when a company is selling in a new market in which it has had little experience or knowledge. Here, a firm will seek out middlemen who have sold in this market.

Product Knowledge

Channels of distribution that are experienced in selling the product that a company is marketing will generally be chosen. Some middlemen specialize in selling particular products. For example, brokers often specialize in selling food products. Companies must choose middlemen who are especially knowledgeable and experienced in selling specialized products.

Marketing Expertise

Some marketing skills are more important than others in effectively marketing various products. Advertising may be important for some products; other products may rely on personal selling. Storage expertise may be very important, or rapid transportation may be called for. Potential middlemen should be evaluated on how well they perform the marketing functions deemed necessary for selling these products.

DETERMINING THE INTENSITY OF DISTRIBUTION

A major channels of distribution decision is determining the **intensity of distribution.** Intensity of distribution refers to the extent to which a company wants to saturate existing retail outlets with the product. It is usually measured by the percentage of all potential outlets that a firm wants to carry its products. A high-intensity distribution objective, for example, would be to have 90% of all drugstores in the United States carry our line of cosmetics.

The type of product and the extent to which consumers will exert effort to visit stores are two major determinants of the intensity of distribution. When consumers do not want to exert a lot of effort to visit stores, a high intensity of distribution strategy is appropriate. This is termed **intensive distribution.** For example, convenience goods, like candy and cigarettes, are available in many outlets because shoppers do not want to be bothered with shopping a number of stores to purchase such low-cost items.

Shopping goods, such as women's clothing, generally may be found in a lower percentage of outlets because consumers will exert some effort to compare quality and prices. Thus, **selective distribution** is practiced. Specialty goods may be placed in an even lower percentage of outlets because specialty goods are branded products that are highly desired by cus-

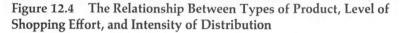

Figure 12.4   The Relationship Between Types of Product, Level of Shopping Effort, and Intensity of Distribution

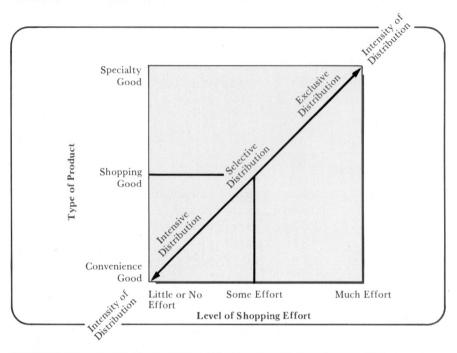

tomers. Therefore, they will go to great lengths to find and visit outlets that carry these specialty goods. In many instances, for specialty goods, **exclusive distribution** may be practiced. That is, one retailer will be selected to sell the brand in a given geographical area. This means that the retailer will have no competitive firms selling that brand in that geographical area.

Figure 12.4 shows the relationship between type of product, level of shopping effort, and intensity of distribution.

USING MIDDLEMEN WHO DO NOT TAKE TITLE

In the last chapter we learned that there are some middlemen who do not take title to products that they sell for manufacturers. Chief among these are brokers, selling agents, and manufacturers' agents. Middlemen who do not take title are a special type of channels of distribution alternative and they are being used more extensively. In the distribution of food, for example, the sales volume of food brokers increased 50% between 1964 and 1969. One-third of the food manufacturers shifted some products to brokers between 1965 and 1970 and over one-half of them indicated that brokers were handling a larger percentage of their sales than they did five years before.[9]

Middlemen who do not take title offer some special advantages to manufacturers, for example:

1. Since they are paid a commission when they sell a manufacturer's products, the manufacturer does not have to pay them until he himself is paid. This is especially beneficial for small or new firms that have limited financial resources.
2. The manufacturer knows his marketing costs with certainty. They will be whatever the percentage commission he is paying. For example, this rate may be 10% of the sales volume sold.
3. Brokers, selling agents, and manufacturers' agents have an intimate knowledge of the markets and they have pre-established contacts with potential buyers. One large food processor, for example, who sold 80% of its sales volume through brokers, indicated that the brokers' knowledge of the market was the chief reason for using them.
4. These middlemen, who do not take title, are important for small companies lacking extensive financial means. These small companies can turn the marketing effort over to agents and brokers and save the expense of having to establish and maintain a separate sales force.
5. They provide the manufacturer with flexibility. They can be used, for example, in market areas where they are strong but not in market where they are weak. They can be used for short periods of time until a manufacturer improves his marketing expertise and then they can be dropped.
6. It is often less costly for new companies to use middlemen who do not take title than to recruit and maintain their own sales forces. For example, a 10% commission on sales of $100,000 ($10,000) is obviously less than it would cost to employ three or four salespeople who might be needed to obtain that level of sales.

There are two major disadvantages in employing these middlemen. First, they may carry competitive products and, thus, not aggressively market some items. Second, at high levels of sales, their cost may be higher than the cost of a company's employing its own sales force. For instance, a commission of 10% on sales of $1,000,000 results in selling costs of $100,000. This figure probably greatly exceeds the cost of employing three or four salespeople. In such a situation, a manufacturer would be advised to drop the middlemen and build his own sales force.

[9] Kathryn Sederberg, "Food Brokers Grow, Offer More Store Calls, Lower Costs," *Advertising Age*, November 1, 1971, pp. 130–31.

PRIVATE VERSUS NATIONAL BRANDS

A major decision that companies must make in their channels of distribution operations is whether they want their products to carry their own brand name (**national brand**) or the brand name of the middleman used (**private brand**). Private brands are frequently carried by large retailing firms, such as A&P and Sears, Roebuck. Companies selling to such firms must decide if their products should retain their own brand name or use the retailer's brand.

Some companies often sell a large percentage of their output to a single large retailing firm which then puts its brand on the merchandise. (Figure 12.5 lists six firms that sell over 50% of their products to Sears, Roebuck). This marketing strategy has both advantages and disadvantages. One advantage is that the manufacturer greatly reduces its risk since it is guaranteed the sale of a large percentage of its output over a specified time. Another advantage is that it may be able to reduce its marketing costs. Since a large percentage of its output is going to one retailer, it may reduce its transportation costs because it can ship in large quantities. The manufacturer may also be able to reduce its expenditures for advertising since it is assured of a purchase for a large percentage of its output. A major disadvantage is that the firm would have to obtain new customers if the large retailer decided not to buy the manufacturers' products.

When a manufacturer decides to allow middlemen to place a private label on its merchandise, it loses control over the marketing of its products. If the manufacturer believes that it can do a better job of marketing its products, it should be reluctant to have its output carry a private brand.

Figure 12.5   Companies with Over 50% of Their Output Going for Sears, Roebuck Private Brands

Company	Principal Products	Percentage of Sales to Sears, Roebuck
1. Warwick	Consumer electronics	89
2. Kellwood	Clothing	80
3. Roper	Appliances, lawnmowers	79
4. Whirlpool	Appliances	62
5. DeSoto	Paint and detergents	56
6. Armstrong Rubber	Tires	53

Source: *Forbes*, April, 1972, p. 49, by permission.

WORKING WITH CHANNEL MEMBERS TO SECURE THEIR COOPERATION

Firms using middlemen must secure the middlemen's cooperation. Unless companies have middlemen that aggressively push their products, they are not likely to be successful. Thus, manufacturing firms and other companies employing channels of distribution must consider how they can secure their cooperation. A number of approaches will be discussed below.

A Salable Product

Providing middlemen with a *salable product* is a major means of getting channels of distribution cooperation. If the middlemen see that there is acceptance of the product in the marketplace, they are more likely to carry it and market it aggressively.

Promotional Assistance

Helping middlemen have an easier time selling a product can be accomplished by providing them with promotional assistance. This help can take two forms. In the first approach, a company promotes its products, such as through advertising. The middlemen benefit because the products are easier to sell. In the second approach, companies provide cash grants to middlemen to be used for advertising purposes. The middlemen place the ads. The amount of assistance usually depends on the amount of advertising dollars spent on the manufacturer's products or the dollar value of the retailer's orders placed with the manufacturer.

Fair Pricing Policies

Offering the product at a reasonable price to middlemen is often an important way to obtain their cooperation. Attractive discount policies also help. **Discounts** refer to a reduction in price available to middlemen because, for example, they purchase in large quantities or they pay their bills promptly.

Market Research Assistance

Middlemen frequently lack market research skills. Middlemen may welcome manufacturer assistance in analyzing their markets and, thus, may push their products harder.

Consignment Sales

In **consignment sales,** middlemen do not have to pay manufacturers for products until they sell them. Merchandise not sold can be returned to the manufacturers. Consignment sales reduce the risk for middlemen. Manufacturers willing to sell on consignment usually expect greater cooperation from middlemen. Consignment selling can be used to get channels of distribution to carry new products. For example, Hanes sold on a consignment basis to get supermarkets to carry "L'eggs" pantyhose. Previously, pantyhose were sold chiefly through department stores.[10] Supermarkets needed the inducement of consignment sales to stock "L'eggs."

Inventory Help

Manufacturers can increase middlemen enthusiasm by providing them with inventory help. Retailers in particular appreciate such assistance. Attractive route girls stock "L'eggs" pantyhose in supermarkets, check inventory levels, and keep display racks dusted.[11] Some manufacturers, like DuPont, Stanley Tool, Colgate, and General Electric hire crews of part-time workers called *detailers* who call on retailers and restock empty shelves and monitor the movement of goods. Retailers appreciate the detailers. As Leon Schwartz, vice-president of Arlans, put it: "We're working on a very lean payroll, and the outside help reduces the tedious and boring aspects of the job in our stores."[12]

Desirable Delivery Policies

Middlemen appreciate manufacturer delivery policies that recognize their needs. Some manufacturers have automatic re-order systems that provide merchandise whenever middlemen inventory levels get low. Manufacturers that make emergency shipments to channels that run out of products can usually expect greater channel enthusiasm for their products.

RECOMMENDATIONS FOR MANAGING CHANNELS OF DISTRIBUTION

In this closing section we offer some recommendations that we believe will help firms to make more effective channels of distribution decisions. These recommendations are presented in a logical sequence in Figure 12.6.

Put Someone in Charge of the Channels of Distribution Responsibility

Large companies that have extensive channels of distribution should have an executive in charge of this responsibility. Effective management of middlemen does not usually occur when this responsibility is fragmented.

---

[10] *Business Week*, March 25, 1972.
[11] Ibid.
[12] *Business Week*, July 22, 1972.

Marketing Mix Decisions

Figure 12.6   Effectively Managing Channels of Distribution

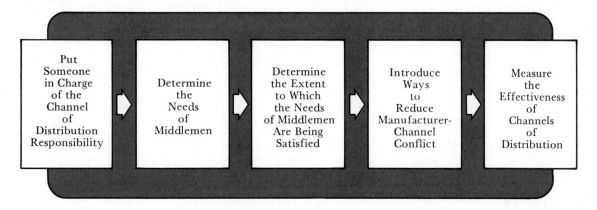

Below are listed some of the major responsibilities of the head of channels of distribution operations:

1. Decides which channels of distribution to use.
2. Examines the effectiveness of individual and various kinds of middlemen.
3. Determines the effectiveness of the company's channels of distribution operations.
4. Determines the extent to which the needs of the middlemen are being satisfied.
5. Develops methods for increasing the cooperation of the channels of distribution.
6. Reduces the level of conflict between his company and the middlemen.
7. Works with physical distribution to make sure that middlemen are receiving orders on time.

Determine the Needs of Middlemen

A company that can satisfy the needs of its middlemen is more likely to get the middlemen's enthusiastic cooperation. Firms should determine what their channels' needs are and which needs they consider to be the most important.

Below are some areas that should be investigated:

1. What do middlemen expect in the way of prices on the products that manufacturers sell them?

2. How frequently do channels of distribution expect delivery?
3. How much time do middlemen expect to elapse between the time they order and the time they receive the order?
4. Do channels of distribution expect manufacturers to make emergency deliveries?
5. How much promotional assistance do middlemen expect?
6. To what extent do middlemen want manufacturers to analyze their markets?
7. Are manufacturers expected to train dealer salespeople?
8. How effectively do manufacturer salespeople service the middlemen?

Determine the Extent to Which the Needs of Middlemen Are Being Satisfied

After a company has determined what the middlemen's needs are and which needs are the most critical, it should find out from its middlemen the extent to which they believe the company has satisfied these needs. Changes can be made if middlemen are dissatisfied.

One example of the value of determining if needs are being satisfied involves a company that discovered that two of its large distributors had dropped its products. It found out that these middlemen were dissatisfied because of the length of time it took to receive shipment once an order was placed. Knowing this would help the company keep its customers. Another company decided to establish a system of expensive, regional warehouses to speed deliveries to middlemen. Analysis of middlemen, however, revealed that they were completely satisfied with the delivery service. Thus, the company avoided a needless, costly investment.[13]

Introduce Ways to Reduce Manufacturer–Channel Conflict

Conflict between companies and their channels of distribution can be harmful. Neither manufacturers nor their channels benefit when conflict is excessive and prolonged.

One way that conflict can be reduced is for manufacturing firms to establish closer contact between themselves and their middlemen. This allows both sides to better understand how they can benefit from each other. Frequently, they find out that they both want the same goals. Ways can be worked out to accomplish these goals through cooperation. Some manufacturing firms establish dealer forum programs through which a panel of middlemen meets periodically with top management, such as manufacturing, engineering, financial, and marketing. These programs appear to be helpful in reducing conflict. Some manufacturers provide comprehensive assistance to their dealers, such as extensive promotion and merchandising programs. When efforts to reduce manufacturer–channel conflict are

[13] Cox, Schutte, and Few, op. cit.

structured and formalized, the channel system is said to be an **administered system.**

When efforts to reduce channel conflict are effected by means of a legal agreement, a **contractual system** exists. The most outstanding example of a contractual system is the franchising agreement that was discussed in the previous chapter.

If administered or contractual systems are unable to reduce the manufacturer–channel conflict, **corporate systems** may be created. Here, the manufacturer itself performs the wholesaling and retailing functions. An example of a corporate system is Hanover Shoes which operates its own retail shoe stores, besides performing the manufacturing function.

Measure the Effectiveness of Channels of Distribution

A company that uses middlemen should measure the effectiveness of the companies making up its channels of distribution. A number of ways that this effectiveness can be determined are listed in Figure 12.7.

Although space does not permit discussion of all these ideas, some of them must be treated. The purpose of examining each middleman according to his sales volume and profit is to identify the middlemen that make the greatest contribution to sales volume and profit. These, then, should become the focus of management's attention because losing some of these companies as middlemen would hurt sales and profits. If a smaller percent-

Figure 12.7   Measuring the Effectiveness of Channels of Distribution

1. Examine each middleman according to sales volume.
2. Examine each middleman according to profit.
3. Determine which companies are aggressively pushing our products and which are not.
4. Determine how many competitive products are carried by each middleman.
5. Determine which middlemen send in orders on time and which do not.
6. Identify the average order size for each middleman.
7. Determine the extent to which middlemen advertise the manufacturer's products.
8. Measure the degree to which channels of distribution practice fair pricing.
9. Determine the ability and willingness of middlemen to work with their customers to ensure their satisfaction.
10. Determine if a smaller percentage of the products being sold are going through current middlemen.

age of products were going through a firm's current middlemen, it would mean that it should consider changing the type of middlemen employed. A company may want to consider reducing the number of times a salesperson calls on middlemen whose orders are small.

SUMMARY

A major decision that companies must make is whether they will use middlemen or go direct to their customers. If the company does not use middlemen, the company will have to perform the marketing functions generally handled by middlemen and will incur the costs involved. The decision whether to use middlemen should be based mainly on profit considerations. The degree to which companies desire to control the marketing programs for their products is another major factor. Companies generally use middlemen when (1) the market is dispersed, (2) the potential sales volume is small, (3) the product is nontechnical, (4) the per unit spread between product price and manufacturing cost is low, (5) the products are nonperishable, (6) the company lacks marketing skills, and (7) the company is in a weak financial condition. Contrary factors would suggest the possibility of marketing direct.

Another major decision that companies must make is which type of middlemen they would like to use. The market, product, degree of channel cooperation expected, availability of channels, the middlemen's knowledge of products and markets, and the middlemen's marketing expertise are factors to be weighed. Middlemen who do not take title to merchandise, such as brokers and manufacturers' agents, offer special advantages, such as a known cost, intimate knowledge of markets, and flexibility.

Companies can secure the increased cooperation of middlemen through several ways, including providing them with a salable product, promotional assistance, marketing research help, and inventory help. Fair pricing policies, consignment sales, and attractive delivery policies are also helpful. Administered or contractual systems are other ways of increasing cooperation and reducing manufacturer–channel conflict. If all efforts fail, companies may perform the channel function themselves (corporate system).

In large firms that have sophisticated channels of distribution systems, an executive should be appointed to manage the channels of distribution function. He should determine the needs of the middlemen and determine the extent to which his company is satisfying these needs. He should develop approaches to reducing the conflict between the middlemen and his company and he also should measure how effective the middlemen are.

1. How can a manufacturing firm gain control over its channels of distribution?
2. Why do large companies that have extensive channels of distribution networks need an executive to be responsible for managing them?
3. If you were the president of a small company that processes tomatoes and you had the opportunity to sell your entire output to a large supermarket chain that would put its brand name on the tomatoes, would you do it? What factors would you consider in making your decision?
4. Which of the middleman's needs discussed in this chapter do you believe are the most important?
5. Many people in the United States believe that the prices of consumer goods would drop greatly if all middlemen were eliminated. Do you agree?
6. What do you believe are the most effective ways a company can obtain the cooperation of its channels of distribution?

GLOSSARY

Administered System: a structured and formalized system by which a firm reduces conflict in its channels of distribution system

Channels of Distribution: the combination of middlemen used by a seller in marketing his products and services

Conflict: pursuit of objectives by companies or middlemen that prohibits or hinders the other firm from achieving its objectives

Consignment Sales: agreements between a seller and his middlemen that the middlemen do not have to pay for the products until they sell the products

Contractual System: system a firm uses to reduce conflict in its channels of distribution system by making legally binding agreements

Corporate System: system in which a manufacturer performs the wholesaling and retailing functions himself

Direct Marketing: a seller marketing his products to customers without using middlemen

Discounts: reductions in prices of goods granted by companies to their middlemen

Channels of Distribution Decisions

Exclusive Distribution: having products available in one retail outlet in a given geographical area

Indirect Marketing: the use of middlemen by a company in marketing its products

Intensity of Distribution: the percentage of appropriate retail outlets that carry a given company's products

Intensive Distribution: having products available in a high percentage of retail outlets

Middlemen: wholesalers and retailers who market products for other firms to consumers and business firms

National Brand: product that carries the manufacturer's brand name

Power: the control that either a manufacturer or middleman is able to exert over the other

Private Brand: product that carries the middleman's brand name.

Selective Distribution: having products available in a low percentage of retail outlets

CASES

Case 1: The RAYNOR Co.

The RAYNOR Co. is a manufacturer of industrial iron and steel products that are sold to other manufacturing firms. In 1976 its sales volume was $85 million. Ninety percent of this volume was sold direct to its customers through the company's 50-man sales force. Ten percent was handled by 6 manufacturer's agents that the company has used for the last 5 years.

In 1976 Warren Jones, the company's director of marketing research, presented the results of a study which indicated a substantial market for cast-iron fireplace sets. The study indicated that the company could expect to obtain from $4 to $5 million a year in sales with this product and recommended that the firm add it to its already existing line of industrial products. Top management indicated that it, too, was enthusiastic about the product, but it wanted to consider carefully the effects of the new addition on the company's marketing operations.

1. What problems do you see in the channels of distribution area for the RAYNOR Co. if this new product is added?
2. Which channels of distribution do you recommend be used in selling the fireplace sets?

3. Do you think that the current sales force should be used to sell the new product? Why or why not?

Case 2: The Eatco Corp.

Daniel Cranston is vice-president of marketing for a large processor of food products, the Eatco Corp. Product lines include cookies, crackers, jams, jellies, cake mixes, peanut butter and pickles. Total sales approach $300 million annually.

About 30% of the company's output is sold to independent food stores and 70% to chain supermarkets. Mr. Cranston had wanted for some time to evaluate outlets because he had been concerned with the low volume of merchandise sold by these independent stores.

The responsibility for evaluating these independent outlets was given to David Thomas, the company's sales manager. After two months of analysis, Mr. Thomas submitted a report to Mr. Cranston. The highlights of his findings were:

1. While independent stores account for 30% of the processor's sales, they make up 50% of the total outlets the company uses.
2. The average-sized order for independent stores is $50, compared to $350 for each store of chain operations that purchases the company's products.
3. Fifty percent of salesman's direct selling time is spent with independents, 50% with chains.
4. Two years previous to the report, 50% of the company's sales volume resulted from sales to independents.

1. Should Mr. Cranston be concerned about these facts?
2. What additional facts should be gathered?
3. Based on the information supplied by Mr. Thomas, what should the food processor do?

Physical Distribution Decisions

After you read this chapter, you should be able to answer the following questions:

1. What are trade-offs? Why are trade-offs important?
2. In what ways can trade-offs be measured?
3. For what kinds of decisions discussed in this chapter can you see trade-off possibilities?
4. What aspects of physical distribution decisions tend to distinguish them from other kinds of marketing decisions?
5. Why are customer service requirements an important aspect of physical distribution decisions?
6. What are probably the two most important measures of customer service?
7. Which are the most important considerations in deciding which transportation modes to use?
8. Why should we look, if possible, at the costs and sales aspects of physical distribution decisions?

INTRODUCTION

Effective management of the physical distribution function helps companies reduce their costs, increase sales, and maximize net profits. These three major objectives will be stressed throughout this chapter.

What do we mean by **physical distribution?** In the first chapter of this book we indicated that physical distribution is that marketing management function that concerns moving finished goods from a company's production area to the purchasers of these products. In general, there are six major functions that are considered to be part of a firm's physical distribution operation: transportation, warehousing, materials handling, inventory control, order processing, and protective packaging.

Transportation

Transportation involves the shipping of finished goods to customers. Several important decisions are involved. For example, the company must decide which *mode* (truck, rail, air, etc.) of transportation to use. For some of these modes, especially trucks, the shipper must decide whether to *own* these facilities, *lease* them, or *use* the services of common carriers. The company must decide the size of the shipment and when the shipment is to go out. It must also decide which routes the transportation modes should take so that costs are minimized and customer requirements are satisfied.

Warehousing

A company must decide whether it wants to use warehouses or ship directly from its factories to its customers. If the company decides to use warehouses, it may want to build or purchase its own warehouses (**private warehouses**) or rent warehousing space in **public warehouses.** If it builds or buys its warehouses, the company must choose between a single-story or multiple-story warehouse. Another major decision is *where* to locate warehouses.

Materials Handling

Finished products must be moved into warehouses, stored, and then moved out of the warehouses when ready for shipment to customers. **Materials handling** operations generally involve the use of such machinery as freight elevators, forklift trucks, conveyor belts and cranes, as well as manpower.

Inventory Control

Inventory control involves determining and recording the location of
finished goods in warehouses. It is vitally important that the number of
units of each kind of product be known. Also important are the customers'
requirements, such as quantities desired and when shipments are wanted.
Since inventories incur costs, such as for warehousing space, taxes, insurance, and materials handling, firms try to minimize these expenses but still
maintain adequate levels of customer service, for example, shipping when
customers need the orders.

Order Processing

As orders are received from customers, they have to be filled. Many
firms request that orders be sent directly to their warehouses. When the
orders are received, it must be seen that the correct orders are sent to the
customers. For example, the right colors, styles, sizes, and quantities of
women's dresses need to be shipped.

Protective Packaging

When finished goods are to be shipped to customers, the goods must be
protected from breakage and spoilage. This is the major purpose of the
protective package.

The above discussion of physical distribution management provides a
brief overview of the decisions that must be made. Some of these topics
will be discussed in greater detail later on. Next, however, we will discuss
the nature of physical distribution decisions.

THE NATURE OF PHYSICAL DISTRIBUTION DECISIONS

Emphasis on Cost Aspects

When physical distribution decisions are being made, companies usually
consider the costs involved. Very frequently the major objective is to
minimize these costs. For example, when companies are deciding which
kind of warehouse will be suitable for their purposes, they make their
decisions on the basis of which alternative will result in the lowest total cost
of handling and storing products.

For most industries, about 55% of their physical distribution costs go
for transportation. About 18% are spent for warehousing, 15% for inventories, and 6% for order processing.[1]

[1] "Physical Distribution: The Right Time, The Right Place," *Sales and Marketing
Management* (June 14, 1976), p. 47.

Sales Emphasis

Although cost is an important aspect of physical distribution decisions, it must be pointed out that these decisions also affect the sales or revenues obtained. Many customers who are purchasing from a company for the first time have chosen the company because it promises good service, for example, frequent deliveries, speed of delivery, and emergency shipments. These customers, and thus, their sales dollars, will be retained because the firm continues to make these frequent deliveries.

Profit Emphasis

Since physical distribution decisions have both cost and profit dimensions, it makes sense to evaluate alternatives on the basis of their profit potential. For example, a company may be trying to decide on the speed of delivery. Speed of delivery will incur costs and affect sales. Sales and costs can be compared for various speed of delivery alternatives (such as two-day vs. three-day delivery times), and the alternative with the higher profit figure could be selected.

Opportunity for Cost Savings

Probably no area of marketing has as good a potential for reducing costs as the physical distribution area. Some estimates place physical distribution costs as high as 50% of total marketing costs. One expert estimates that physical distribution costs increased 40% between 1971 and 1974, accounting for 5.8% of sales in 1971 and 8.2% in 1974.[2] Other experts suggest that the average company could probably reduce its materials handling costs by 20%.[3] What occurred in the early 1970's at Crown Zellerbach Corporation is a good example of what can be accomplished. Through an effort to reduce physical distribution costs, delivery expenses in 1973 were reduced by 5% over 1972. It was able to eliminate 35% of its trucks, and administrative costs were reduced by $20,000.[4]

Trade-offs

Many physical distribution decisions involve **trade-offs.** This means that as one objective in the physical distribution area is better achieved, another one is not achieved as well. Frequently, this means that as one cost is decreased, another cost increases. For example, a company could reduce its inventory costs by storing lower quantities of finished products, but its transportation costs would probably increase because the company would have to ship in smaller quantities and thus would lose the discounts as-

[2] Ibid.
[3] "Distribution Comes of Age," *Dun's Review* (January, 1965), p. 36.
[4] "One Shipper's Approach to Controlling Distribution Costs," *Distribution Worldwide* (December, 1974), pp. 36–40.

sociated with shipping larger quantities. Sometimes the trade-offs involve increasing sales and increasing costs. For instance, a company could provide customers with emergency shipments, which should increase sales because the company is providing a valuable service, but costs would probably increase because the company would be forced to make more shipments.

Figure 13.1 integrates the above concepts by presenting a number of trade-off examples in physical distribution. These will be discussed more fully later in the chapter.

Optimization Needed

Because there are trade-offs involved, there is a need for **optimization.** This means that someone must decide how best to minimize *total costs* if the

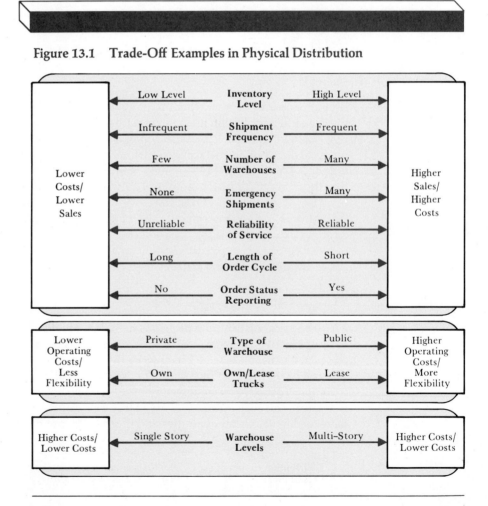

Figure 13.1   Trade-Off Examples in Physical Distribution

Lower Costs/ Lower Sales			Higher Sales/ Higher Costs
	Low Level	**Inventory Level** High Level	
	Infrequent	**Shipment Frequency** Frequent	
	Few	**Number of Warehouses** Many	
	None	**Emergency Shipments** Many	
	Unreliable	**Reliability of Service** Reliable	
	Long	**Length of Order Cycle** Short	
	No	**Order Status Reporting** Yes	

Lower Operating Costs/ Less Flexibility			Higher Operating Costs/ More Flexibility
	Private	**Type of Warehouse** Public	
	Own	**Own/Lease Trucks** Lease	

Higher Costs/ Lower Costs			Higher Costs/ Lower Costs
	Single Story	**Warehouse Levels** Multi-Story	

trade-offs involve costs or how best to maximize total *profit* if the trade-offs involve costs and sales. For example, a decision would have to be made as to the number of purchase orders per year that would minimize the *total* of the order costs *and* inventory costs. The decision maker should not only look at the order costs or the inventory costs separately, but he should also look at them together. Because of this requirement, many companies have placed a well-qualified person at the head of the entire physical distribution operation to examine trade-off situations and make optimum decisions.

Applicability of Quantitative Models

Quantitative models are very helpful in making physical distribution decisions, especially those involving trade-offs. Some examples include *linear programming* to determine the number of units of products to be shipped from various production factories to various warehouses and *queuing theory* to determine how large a firm's receiving area must be.

Utilities Resulting From Physical Distribution Operations

In making physical distribution decisions it is helpful to remember that this function provides time and place utilities (or value). Products lack value unless they are available when people need them. **Time utility** is essentially provided by the warehousing (storage) function. For example, people like to eat peaches throughout the entire year, but as we all know, peaches are harvested only in the fall. Therefore, storage facilities are used to keep peaches available for consumers during the entire year.

Place utility results from the transportation function. Products lack value unless they are available at places conveniently located for customers. Therefore, the products must be moved from manufacturing plants to stores close to where consumers live.

IMPORTANCE OF CUSTOMER SERVICE IN MAKING PHYSICAL DISTRIBUTION DECISIONS

The level of service provided by a physical distribution system to that company's customers is, as mentioned earlier, a key factor in determining if those customers will purchase a company's products and the extent to which they will continue to buy those products. The higher the level of customer service, the more likely customers will initially purchase and will continue to purchase. Thus, the higher the level of customer service, the higher the level of sales expected.

A recent survey of 216 industrial purchasing agents substantiated the above points. Physical distribution was indicated as the second most important reason (product quality was the most important) for an initial

Figure 13.2   Examples of Customer Service

1. Providing reliability of service.
2. Reducing order cycle length.
3. Providing emergency shipments.
4. Reducing out-of-stock situations.
5. Shipping small quantities.
6. Providing frequent shipments.
7. Shipping products fully assembled.
8. Providing packages that benefit customers.
9. Order status reporting.

purchase. Over 50% of the respondents revealed that they had stopped using a supplier because of slow or unreliable service.[5]

Of course, the higher the level of customer service provided (and the higher the sales volume), the higher the cost incurred. Thus, someone in the firm must look at the relationship of sales to costs and decide at which level of customer service profit will be maximized.

A firm should survey its customers and ask them which services they consider the most important. After the company has determined which elements of service are the most important, it should ask their customers how well they believe that the company and its competitors are providing these services. If the results of the survey indicate that a firm is not providing good service but that the competition is, then the firm must take corrective action to improve the level of its service.

The list of customer services in Figure 13.2 indicates the variety of help that companies can provide its customers to obtain and keep a competitive edge. Each of these services will be briefly discussed below.

Providing Reliability of Service

Reliability is probably the most important aspect of customer service. Companies that have high reliability are probably able to gain new customers and retain current ones.

Three examples of service reliability are listed below:

1. The shipment arrives when it is supposed to arrive.
2. The physical condition of the goods is acceptable. There is little spoilage, deterioration, and breakage.
3. When the order arrives, it contains exactly what it is supposed to contain.

[5] "Physical Distribution: The Right Time, The Right Place," p. 48.

One large wholesaling drug firm learned the hard way that reliability of service is very important. The firm, located near a large urban area, decided to close down its older, smaller warehouses in favor of one large, fully automated warehouse located 30 miles from downtown. It was expected that the new warehouse would result in cost savings that would enable the firm to charge its customers lower prices. Unfortunately, the new warehouse resulted in slower deliveries, thereby causing some customers to shift businesses to firms that could provide faster, more reliable deliveries. Customers were more interested in reliability of service than in cost savings.[6]

Reducing Order Cycle Length

The length of time it takes for an order to be received after it has been sent to the supplier is called the **order cycle length.** Order cycle length has been shown to be one of the most important determinants of customer service. Companies that are able to reduce the length of the order cycle will probably increase their sales volume.

The three major determinants of the order cycle are order transmittal time, order processing time, and transportation time.[7] Companies like E. R. Squibb and Lever Brothers have analyzed these components of the order cycle and have experienced positive reactions from customers when the order cycle time was reduced.[8]

Providing Emergency Shipments

Customer good will can often be increased because the shipper is willing to provide emergency shipments. A manufacturing firm that needs a part in a hurry in order to keep its production machinery running will be grateful to the company that provides the emergency shipment. A retail druggist whose supplier ships a drug needed as soon as possible by its customers will be inclined to send future business the supplier's way.

Reducing Out-of-Stock Situations

Retailers often have trouble forecasting demand for the products they sell. If they run out of products, customers may switch to other stores that do have them. Companies that expedite shipments of out-of-stock items to retailers may gain a competitive edge.

Manufacturers also frequently face out-of-stock situations. For example, they may be out of raw materials or semi-finished products needed in the manufacturing process.

[6] Warren Blanding, "Why You Shouldn't Get Involved in Warehousing—Or Should You?" *Sales Management* (August 19, 1974), pp. 36–37.

[7] Richard F. Poist, "The Total Cost vs. Total Profit Approach to Logistics Systems Designs," *Transportation Journal* (Fall, 1974), p. 19.

[8] Edward J. Marien and V. K. Prasad, "Better PD Planning and Control," *Distribution Worldwide* (May, 1972), p. 30.

Shipping Small Quantities

Customers frequently like to receive small shipments instead of large shipments because demand for the items may be more equal to the quantity received. Thus, there is no need to store the items; they can be moved directly to the production area or to the retailer's shelves. As a result, customers save money because they do not have to have costly warehousing space.

Providing Frequent Shipments

Companies that provide frequent shipments are usually appreciated by their customers. Frequent shipments are likely to reduce out-of-stock and emergency situations.

Shipping Products Fully Assembled

Customers appreciate products that are fully assembled when they arrive because customers do not want to spend the time or incur the cost required to assemble the products.

Providing Packages That Benefit Customers

Packages that benefit customers are another example of providing service that customers appreciate. Below are some illustrations:

1. Goodyear Tire and Rubber Company discovered that its container for molded rubber weather stripping was being torn apart in shipment, thereby causing dealers to have difficulty in opening the package. The company redesigned the package, which pleased customers, and saved $12,000 per year in freight bills because the weight of the package was reduced by 21 pounds.
2. Safeway Stores developed Tray-Kwik, a 12-pack corrugated tray for its Craigmont canned sodas, which enabled retailers to remove the top half easily, leaving the bottom half for store display.
3. Vermont Maid syrup was packaged in plastic instead of glass bottles because plastic bottles were thinner than glass bottles and retailers could stock from two to four more bottles in a square foot of shelf space.[9]

Order Status Reporting

Customers want to know the status of their orders. They especially want to know if they will be filled on time. They want to know if the shipper is out of any of the items ordered. The smart shipper will keep his customers informed of the status of their order. This is called **order status reporting.**

[9] "What You Should Know About Physical Distribution Management," *Sales Management* (January 1, 1971), pp. 30–31.

BENEFITS FROM IMPROVING CUSTOMER SERVICE

A number of companies have made improvements in their customer service and, as a result, experienced favorable increases in sales volume and/or profit. For example, the sales of white goods of a large retailer increased 15% when the retailer reduced delivery time. A large chain increased its on-time delivery from 30% to 100% and experienced fewer canceled orders. A chemical manufacturer overhauled its entire customer service program and experienced a 20% increase in sales and a 21% profit increase. A manufacturer made warehousing changes costing $200,000, but it saw its sales increase $5 million and its profits climb $500,000. By reducing and consolidating its distribution centers, a large retail chain increased sales by $100 million and net profit by $10 million.[10]

These examples are concrete evidence that a company's performance can be improved dramatically by providing better physical distribution service to its customers.

We will now focus our attention on a number of specific important physical distribution decisions.

SIGNIFICANT PHYSICAL DISTRIBUTION DECISIONS

In this section we will discuss nine major physical distribution decisions. These are listed in Figure 13.3. The purpose of this discussion is to provide insight into how these decisions should be made.

[10] William D. Perreault, Jr., and Frederick A. Russ, "Physical Distribution Service: A Neglected Aspect of Marketing Management," *MSU Business Topics*, Vol. 22 (Summer, 1974), p. 41.

Figure 13.3   Nine Major Physical Distribution Decisions

1. Locating warehouses.
2. Number of warehouses.
3. Type of warehouse.
4. Materials handling equipment.
5. Mode of transportation.
6. Routing.
7. Size of shipments.
8. Inventory levels.
9. Protective packaging.

Locating Warehouses

Where to locate warehouses is a difficult decision to make because there are so many variables that affect this decision.

The major criterion for locating warehouses is that the location must show a profit. Thus, the company must look at the cost of transporting the products to its customers. It must also consider the customers' service requirements, which, as we know, greatly affect sales volumes.

Costs of Transportation. Costs of transportation are determined chiefly by the total weight moved times the distance that weight is transported. Thus, the greater the weight and distance involved, the higher the total transportation cost.

When considering where to locate a warehouse, a company should determine the location of each of its customers and their total tonnage (weight) requirements. This has been done in Figure 13.4 in which it can be seen that the five customers A, B, C, D, and E are all located close together and that they also account for the five largest tonnage requirements. The two customers that have the smallest tonnage requirements, F and G, are located a distance from the other five customers. Common sense dictates that if the shipper wants to minimize total transportation costs, as represented by weight times distance, he has to locate close to where the greatest concentration of tonnage is. For example, in Figure 13.4 he would be better

Figure 13.4   Location and Tonnage Requirements for Seven Customers

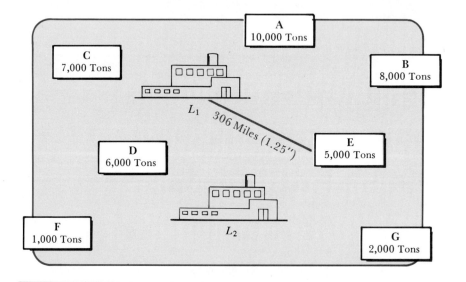

Marketing Mix Decisions

off locating at L_1 and not at L_2 because the total of the weights times the distances and, hence, transportation costs would be minimized at L_1.

In Figure 13.5 the reader can see that the total ton–miles (weight times distance) from location L_1 to the seven customers is 9,544,000 compared to 12,852,000 for location L_2. Thus, location L_1 is better. (In computing these ton–miles, it was assumed that 1 inch represents 245 miles.) For example, in Figure 13.5 it can be seen that there are 306 miles (1.25 inches) between L_1 and customer E.

In practice, the firm would compute the total ton–miles (distance times tons) for a number of different locations in order to determine the location where the total ton–miles is minimized.

Service Requirements by Customers. The service levels required by customers must also be considered because they have such a direct impact

Figure 13.5 Comparing Two Warehouse Locations on the Basis of Total Ton–Miles

From Warehouse Location L_1

Customer	Distance (miles)	Tons	Distance × Tons
A	150	10,000	1,500,000
B	194	8,000	1,552,000
C	250	7,000	1,750,000
D	206	6,000	1,236,000
E	306	5,000	1,530,000
F	600	1,000	600,000
G	688	2,000	1,376,000
			9,544,000

From Warehouse Location L_2

Customer	Distance (miles)	Tons	Distance × Tons
A	438	10,000	4,380,000
B	312	8,000	2,496,000
C	406	7,000	2,842,000
D	175	6,000	1,050,000
E	188	5,000	940,000
F	344	1,000	344,000
G	400	2,000	800,000
			12,852,000

on sales. One key factor is how soon after the shipper receives the order does the customer expect to get the shipment. This time is largely determined by how much distance can be covered by the mode of transportation used. For example, let's assume that customers expect 2-day delivery and trucks can move that merchandise an average of 400 miles per day. The merchandise could be moved 800 miles in 2 days. As a result, the shipper would probably want to establish a warehouse within 800 miles of as many of his customers as possible in order to provide 2-day service.

Number of Warehouses

Deciding on the number of warehouses involves the consideration of trade-off effects. The more warehouses a company has, the better service it can provide customers. For example, having ten warehouses instead of two may allow the company to guarantee two-day delivery times instead of five-day delivery times. This should have a positive effect on its sales volume. Also, the more warehouses available, the lower the total transportation costs since total distance required should be less than if only one warehouse were used. Of course, having multiple warehouses increases the costs of leasing or purchasing the facilities involved.

In recent years there has been a general trend for companies to reduce their number of warehouses. They have found that this did not noticeably decrease the level of customer service, sales were not adversely affected, and they saved thousands of dollars by closing these facilities. A good example is the H. J. Heinz Company that found that it could reduce the number of warehouses from 63 to 34 without jeopardizing customer service and would, at the same time, minimize its physical distribution costs.[11]

Types of Warehouses

Single-Story versus Multiple-Story Warehouses. Single-story warehouses reduce materials handling costs because goods are moved only on the same level, not up or down. Thus, goods can be moved faster and there is no need for expensive equipment, such as elevators and cranes. The major disadvantage of single-story warehouses is the cost of acquiring the land on which they are built. A multiple-story warehouse does not require as much square footage of land space as a single-story building does.

Multiple-story warehouses are more practical when the cost of land is high, such as in Dallas, Tokyo, and New York City. They are also advisable when the emphasis is on storing products for long periods of time and when there is little emphasis on materials handling.

Private versus Public Warehouses. Private warehouses are constructed or bought by a firm for its own usage. Public warehouses are leased.

[11] Harvey N. Shycon and Richard B. Maffei, "Simulation—Tool for Better Distribution," *Harvard Business Review* (November–December, 1960), pp. 65–75.

Figure 13.6   Advantages of Using Public Warehouses

1. No capital outlay is required. For private warehouses, capital outlay can run as high as $2 million.
2. Using public warehouses enables a firm to make use of technological breakthroughs in building and materials handling equipment.
3. Contracts for use of public warehouses can be short term, thereby allowing the user to switch to more favorable locations if desired.
4. Additional space is available in the public warehouse if needed at peak times of the year. Dupont, for example, uses public warehouses for storage of its Zerex antifreeze.
5. Using public warehouses provides various tax benefits.

Private warehouses are built to suit the particular needs of the builder. The layout and materials handling equipment are especially designed for the company and its products. Thus, it is not unlikely that private warehouse operating costs can be as much as 25% lower than the rates charged for the use of public warehouses.[12] Another advantage is that the company exerts direct control over the operations involved.

Public warehouses offer a number of advantages as compared to private warehouses. These advantages are summarized in Figure 13.6.[13] Probably most of them involve the fact that public warehouses enable the user to be flexible in his physical distribution operations; the use of private warehouses restricts his flexibility.

Materials Handling Equipment

Companies have a vast array of materials handling equipment. In recent years this equipment has enabled many firms to drastically reduce the level of manpower required, resulting in lower operating costs.

Forklift trucks are probably the most widely used materials handling equipment (see Figure 13.7). Since they are motorized, they can move goods from one area to another quickly and efficiently. They can also stack pallets. Pallets are wooden platforms on which merchandise rests. The forklift truck is also capable of removing pallets from the tops of stacks.

Containerization is an extension of palletization. Containerization involves special containers that hold a large number of units of a product.

[12] Clifford F. Lynch, "A Case for Public Warehousing," *Distribution Worldwide* (January, 1972), p. 44.
[13] Ibid., pp. 44–46.

Figure 13.7   Forklift Truck

These containers can be easily stored and transported, often from one mode of transportation to the other. Thus, storage and handling costs can be greatly reduced.[14]

Many warehouses make extensive use of conveyor systems to move merchandise laterally. Cranes and elevators are used to move merchandise vertically.

Some companies have developed fully automated warehouses. An example is a 2.25 million-cubic foot warehouse built by Wisconsin Cold Storage Company to house frozen food items. It contains two fully automated conveyor systems, each capable of moving 12,000 pounds per hour. A stacker crane, along with a Rack Entry Module (REM), can stack

[14] "What You Should Know About Physical Distribution Management," p. 31.

standard-sized pallets as high as 50 feet, twice the height usually attained. The stacker crane takes two pallets at a time and elevates them to the desired height for stacking. The REM then moves the pallets off the stacker crane and deposits them on the pile. The stacker crane and the REM can also be used to retrieve pallets. The stacker crane can lift up to 4,000 pounds and has a horizontal speed of 300 feet per minute and a vertical speed of 60 feet per minute. The REM can also lift 4,000 pounds. Its horizontal speed is 120 feet per minute.[15]

Mode of Transportation

The five major modes of transportation that a firm can choose from are pipeline, water, rail, truck, and air. Each alternative has advantages and disadvantages that should be considered. The advantages and disadvantages must be related to the kinds of products a company is shipping and the service requirements of customers. Each mode should be evaluated on the basis of cost and the kinds of services it provides both the shipper and the customer.

Pipelines. Natural gas and petroleum are moved through pipelines. Pipelines are very inexpensive forms of transportation, but they are not as cheap as barges.

Water. Barges transport heavy, nonperishable items such as coal, iron ore, and grain on navigable rivers, the Great Lakes, and the St. Lawrence Seaway. (Freighters are used for shipping similar goods to overseas markets). Although water transportation is the cheapest, it is also the slowest.

Railroads. Railroads are used heavily in the shipment of bulky goods that are low in value in relation to their weight, such as coal, sand, and agricultural products. However, other products like automobiles and chemicals are also frequently transported by railroad.

The **piggyback** is an innovation of great importance to shippers. A piggyback is a loaded truck trailer that is carried on a specially designed railroad flatcar (see Figure 13.8). After the truck trailer reaches its destination, it is hooked up to a truck and moved to customers. The major advantage is that the trailer does not have to be constantly loaded and unloaded; therefore, there are cost savings. Although railroads are a low-cost form of transportation, they are not flexible. They cannot go to as many destinations as can trucks, for example. Also, railroads tend to be relatively slow. For these reasons, many companies prefer to ship by truck.

Trucks. The major advantages of flexibility and speed encourage many manufacturing firms to ship a large percentage of their products by truck. Although the cost may be greater than by rail, the flexibility and speed of trucks are so important in providing good customer service that trucks are

[15] "Wiscold's Fully Automated Warehouse Is Largest of Its Kind Yet Built," *Quick Frozen Foods* (March, 1973), pp. 44–45.

Figure 13.8 Piggyback Train Car

used anyway. It should be pointed out, however, that the railroad cost advantage usually exists on longer hauls and that shipment by truck for short distances (300 miles or less) may cost less than by rail.

A major decision that companies must make is whether to use common carriers or own and operate their own fleets of trucks. Usually, the most significant factor in this decision is not the cost, but the extent to which companies are satisfied with the level of customer service rendered by the available common carriers. If shipments consistently arrive late and in poor condition, firms may be forced to invest in their own fleets.

When the company owns its own fleet, it obtains control over the transportation function. Thus, it should be able to render the type and level of customer service desired. It also has more flexibility in its operations. For example, it can ship when it wants and where it wants.

Sometimes, the cost of shipping by common carriers is prohibitive. Allied Chemical has to ship explosive chemicals from a plant in Utah to customers around the country. Truck common carriers are reluctant to haul these chemicals and, thus, charge high rates. As a result, Allied is considering acquiring a fleet of trucks for that plant.[16]

[16] "What You Should Know About Physical Distribution Management," p. 33.

The major disadvantage in owning a fleet of trucks is the high investment costs. One tractor-trailer, for example, can cost up to $70,000. Because of these high investment costs, many companies are leasing (renting) trucks instead of purchasing them. This eliminates the investment required and it still provides the flexibility and control desired.

Air. Air transportation is the fastest mode available. It is also the most expensive. As a result, high-value items like industrial machinery and automobile parts are frequently shipped by air. When Goodman Equipment Company had to deliver a Conway Mucker excavating machine to Switzerland in the fall of 1975, the buyer specified air freight and was willing to pay the higher costs involved. "The buyer was afraid the snows would come and the machine might not get up the mountain to the site until spring," said Bob Alexander, the company's manager of international sales.[17]

Because of the speed factor, perishable items like cut flowers, strawberries, and asparagus are shipped via air freight.[18]

Many companies use air transportation to make emergency shipments to important customers. The extra cost is justified because of the good will that will result.

Air freight costs have continued to come down to the point where one expert contends that for most manufactured commodities having to go 500 miles or more, air transportation will be used.[19]

Because of the speed of service, companies shipping by air usually obtain a competitive advantage because they can provide better customer service. An example is the Samsonite Corporation that uses air freight to ship luggage from its Denver plant to dealers in Chicago, Los Angeles, and San Francisco. Merchandise is gotten to dealers quicker, dealers do not have to carry as much inventory, and out-of-stock situations can be minimized. Using air freight may also allow Samsonite to eliminate warehouses in these three cities, which would be a considerable cost savings.[20]

Gillette has found that air freight can be an effective marketing tool. In 1970 Gillette shipped its Platinum-Plus razor blades by air to ensure that they would be available in retail outlets when national advertising first appeared.[21]

Routing

Once the transportation mode has been selected, the shipper must determine the routes that the transportation modes should take. For example, truck routing involves decisions on when customers should receive de-

[17] "Physical Distribution: The Right Time, The Right Place," p. 50.
[18] Robert F. Hartley, *Marketing: Management and Social Change* (Scranton, Pa.: International Textbook Company, 1972), p. 533.
[19] "Small Shipments Plague Buyers," *Purchasing* (July 24, 1973), p. 55.
[20] "What You Should Know About Physical Distribution Management," p. 32.
[21] Ibid.

liveries, in what order the customers should receive the deliveries, and which roads should be used in making these deliveries.

Routing may have a number of objectives: First, routes should be developed that minimize the times required to get shipments to customers. This enables deliveries to be made on time, helps reduce the order cycle length, and minimizes out-of-stock situations. Thus, high levels of customer service are achieved. Second, total distance traveled should be reduced. This means that the shipper will incur a lower cost for transporting goods. Third, routes are often established to ensure that larger customers get better service. See Figure 13.9 for examples of different routes according to objectives.

A number of quantitative models have been developed to achieve these objectives. Some require computer analysis because there are so many alternative routes. They are helpful in minimizing the times and distances involved.

Figure 13.9   Routes Differ According to Objectives

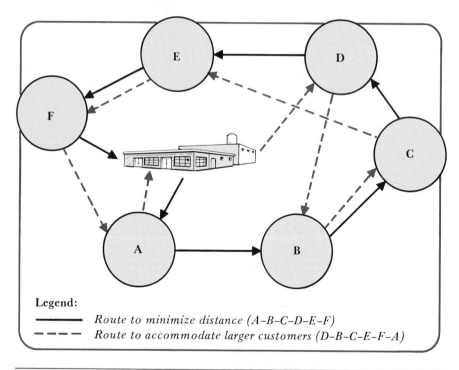

Legend:

——————— *Route to minimize distance (A–B–C–D–E–F)*

— — — — *Route to accommodate larger customers (D–B–C–E–F–A)*

Size of Shipments

This is an important physical distribution decision that has a definite trade-off. On the one hand, customers may prefer smaller shipments because they do not want to invest heavily in storage facilities. Sales may be higher for the shipper. On the other hand, shippers prefer larger shipments because they can take advantage of the quantity discounts offered by common carriers. Railroads charge a lower rate if an entire car is used and truckers charge a lower rate if an entire truck is filled. If a shipper has its own trucks, it prefers to ship them full because it is probably going to incur much the same costs (fuel, drivers' pay) regardless of how full the truck is. Another advantage to the shipper of large shipments is that they may help to reduce the size of the warehousing space required.

Many companies are plagued with what is commonly called the "small-order problem," that is, when a high percentage of orders shipped are made up of only a few pieces or light-weight pieces. One company found, for example, that 40% of its shipments contained four or fewer pieces and 50% weighed less than 400 pounds.[22]

What can shippers do about this problem? One possibility is to delay shipments until customer requirements in a particular geographic area become large enough to fill a truck or railroad car. Another possibility is to eliminate all paper work from small orders by having customers telephone in their orders. Another alternative is to charge more for small orders. All of these alternatives, however, adversely affect customer service, which may hurt sales.

An unusual approach to the small-order problem is the cooperative effort of Noxell (Noxzema products) and McCormick (spices), both located in Baltimore. Four times a week a truck is loaded with Noxell products and then is driven to McCormick where enough merchandise is loaded to complete the truck load. This system allows Noxell and McCormick to get the truck load rate, which saves both companies money.[23]

Inventory Levels

As with many physical distribution decisions, a trade-off exists when the level (size) of the inventory is decided. Large inventory levels allow a high level of service to be provided customers. Shipments can reach customers on time, emergency shipments can be made, and out-of-stock situations can be minimized. Sales, thus, should be higher. However, large inventories necessitate larger warehouse facilities and additional materials handling equipment, which increase the costs involved.

When inventory level decisions are being made, these trade-offs must be recognized. The effect of various inventory levels on sales and inventory

---

[22] C. K. Walter, "Measuring Pick-up and Delivery Costs for Small Shipments," *Transportation Journal* (Fall, 1974), p. 52.
[23] "Physical Distribution: The Right Time, The Right Place," p. 48.

Physical Distribution Decisions

costs must be investigated. Once this is known, the inventory size that maximizes profit can be chosen. Many firms have to use computers to obtain this figure. American Airlines, for example, was able to reduce its inventory level of $3.7 million for the DC-10 while still maintaining a .3% delay factor in deliveries.[24] At Narco Avionics inventory levels were reduced by 60%, but out-of-stock situations still remained low, only .4%.[25]

For companies such as retailers that purchase goods for resale to its customers, the level of inventory is an important factor that must be considered when these companies place their orders.

Whatever the order size, the company must contend with two costs: the cost of placing the order and inventory costs (materials handling, insurance, cost of warehouse space, and so on). These two costs work against each other, that is, there is a trade-off. The smaller the order size, the more orders that must be placed; thus, total order costs increase. Inventory costs decrease because the units purchased do not have to be stored but are moved directly to the production area or to customers. The opposite occurs if the order size is larger. There are fewer orders, which reduces the order

[24] Claudia H. Deutsch, "American Gets MM Off the Ground," *Purchasing* (May 23, 1972), pp. 43–46.
[25] "Computer Helps Purchasing Out of Slump," *Purchasing* (May 23, 1972), p. 6.

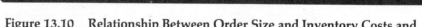

Figure 13.10 Relationship Between Order Size and Inventory Costs and Order Costs

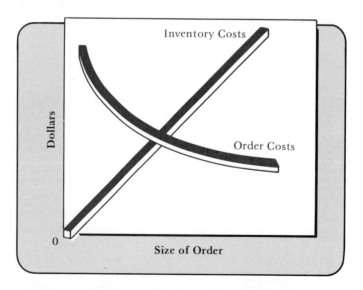

costs, but the inventory costs increase because items have to be stored. The relationships between order size and inventory costs and order costs are shown in Figure 13.10. The following example will also be helpful.

Suppose that a retailer orders a total of 1,000 cases of canned peaches each year. Assume that he usually sells these 1,000 cases fairly evenly throughout the year. At one extreme, he could place one order for the year for all 1,000 cases and thus would incur only one order cost. But, his inventory costs would be high because these 1,000 cases would have to be stored until all were sold throughout the year. At the other extreme, he could place 1,000 separate orders of one case each. In this situation, his order costs would be very high (he now has 1,000 orders instead of one), but his inventory costs would be very low because as each case arrived it could probably be placed on his shelves to be sold and would not have to be stored.

As might be expected, the order size chosen should be the one that *minimizes the total of the order costs and inventory costs.* In this regard, the following equation will provide this optimum order size:

$$EOQ = \sqrt{\frac{2AB}{CD}}$$

where EOQ = "economic order quantity" (the order size that minimizes the total of the order costs and inventory costs);

A = annual demand;

B = cost of placing one order;

C = cost per unit;

D = inventory cost as a percentage.

In the retailer example above the annual demand (A) is 1,000 cases of canned peaches. Let's assume that the cost of placing one order (B) is $5, the cost per unit ($C$) is $10 per case, and the inventory cost as a percentage (D) is 20%. Placing these figures into the equation gives an economic order quantity of about 71

$$71 = \sqrt{\frac{(2)\ (1,000)\ (\$5)}{(\$10)\ (.20)}}$$

This means that in order to minimize the total of order costs and inventory costs, the company should order about 71 cases of peaches each time it places an order. Since it needs 1,000 cases for the year, it would place about 14 orders per year (1,000 cases divided by 71 cases per order).

Protective Packaging

Protective packaging provides several benefits. First, it can reduce the level of breakage and spoilage and thus result in lower costs for the shipper. Second, protective packaging can be tailored to customer needs, thus providing the customer with better service and increasing the sales volume of the shipper. Of course, developing a better protective package costs money which, hopefully, will result in cost savings and increased revenues.

Black and Decker provides a good example of the benefits of protective packaging. Working with Container Corporation of America, it developed a better protective package that also serves as an attractive display case for retailers. Not only did the package increase sales, it also resulted in lower handling costs, less warehouse space, and lower freight rates.[26]

FUTURE DEVELOPMENTS IN PHYSICAL DISTRIBUTION

Probably no area of marketing will undergo as much change in the future as will the physical distribution area. In particular, before the year 2000 there will be a number of potential innovations that may revolutionize the way in which cargo will be transported. Some of these possibilities and other likely future developments will be discussed below.

Compartmentalized Tankers

Compartmentalized tankers would consist of individual units joined together. Such an arrangement would allow different kinds of products to be shipped in each compartment so that a break in one compartment would not affect the merchandise in another. Each cargo could be loaded into its own compartment and then attached to the main body of the tanker. Thus, the tanker would not have to waste time coming into port to be loaded because the cargo would already be loaded. Similarly, the main tanker would not have to dock in order to unload; the detached compartment could be pulled by tug to the port area.

Submarines

Huge submarines could be used to pull submerged or floating barges. These submarines would be unaffected by surface weather. Perishable items could be carried, possibly without the need for extensive and costly refrigeration because at lower depths the water is colder.

Mid-Ocean Floating Warehouses

Floating ports could be located in the oceans where ships could converge to load and unload goods. Ships would not be forced to waste time going into ports and waiting for days to be unloaded.

---

[26] Peter Wulff, *Special Report—Materials Handling*, Vol. 72 (February 22, 1972), p. 40.

Dirigibles

Cargo Airships Ltd. of Manchester, England, has developed a dirigible that travels 100 miles per hour. The cargo would be housed in 20-foot containers. The dirigible could transport up to 500 tons. As the airship hovered over factories and warehouses, helicopters would be used to load or unload cargo. Each ship would have a helipad with a retractable cover where the goods would be loaded or unloaded. The helipad would be serviced by an adjacent freight elevator that would carry goods to and from cargo decks.[27]

Some dirigibles can carry up to 100 million cubic feet of natural gas. Others can handle up to 1,000 tons of freight. The advantage of these airships is that they would be able to reach areas where there are no airfields and no roads. Their major benefits to the shipper would be the ability to carry large loads very inexpensively.[28]

Increasing Use of Quantitative Models

In the future greater use of quantitative models will undoubtedly be made in the physical distribution area. Models will be used to make specific physical distribution decisions, such as which routes a company's trucks should take or what inventory level will minimize inventory costs. Other quantitative models, such as simulations, will be used to develop a complete physical distribution program to maximize profit.

Greater Emphasis on Computer Usage

Computers will be used in conjunction with quantitative tools to make better physical distribution decisions. Computers will also help companies better manage their inventories since the companies will be able to know on a day-by-day basis how many units of each item are on hand. Computers will be used to process customer orders much more rapidly and accurately than they are processed today. Computers, in conjunction with new kinds of machinery, will help perform the materials handling function much more effectively.

Replacing Manpower with Machine Power

Whenever possible, companies will replace costly manpower with machines that will in time enable total physical distribution costs to be lowered. Fully automated warehouses are but one example of what can be done. In these operations, manpower utilization would be minimized and the ma-

---

[27] "What You Should Know About Physical Distribution Management," p. 33.
[28] Much of the foregoing is based on Kurt Schottleutner and Bruce H. Allen, "A Futuristic View of Physical Distribution," unpublished Paper, Virginia Commonwealth University, 1976.

Physical Distribution Decisions

chines would be linked to sophisticated computer systems. Another example is the increased use of machinery and containerization by the maritime industry in the United States in order to replace highly paid longshoremen.

SUMMARY

Physical distribution refers to the movement of finished goods from a company's production area to the purchasers of these products. Trade-offs are an important consideration in this area. Trade-offs mean that as one objective is improved from following a given course of action, another objective is made less attractive. Trade-offs are important because they provide a means for determining the best course of action to pursue. Thus, we choose the alternative that minimizes the total of the costs involved or if costs and sales volumes can be evaluated, we can base our decision on the profit generated. Almost all of the major decisions discussed in this chapter can be analyzed from the standpoint of the trade-offs involved, including order size, warehouse location, number of warehouses, type of warehouse, mode of transportation, size of shipment, and inventory levels.

There are a number of characteristics of physical distribution decisions that tend to distinguish them from other kinds of marketing decisions. For example, most other marketing decisions are not characterized by trade-off possibilities. Also, the possibility of effecting substantial cost savings is probably better in the physical distribution area than in other marketing areas. And we can probably apply a wider range of quantitative models to these decisions than we can to most other marketing areas.

Customer service requirements are an important aspect of physical distribution decisions because they are so closely related to sales volumes. Thus, the higher the level of services provided, the higher the level of sales expected. Although this chapter discusses a number of customer services, probably the two most important are reliability and the length of the order cycle.

Several factors should be considered when choosing a transportation mode. The most important are probably the cost of the mode, its speed, the nature of the products to be shipped, and customer expectations of service levels.

If possible, when we make physical distribution decisions, we should look at the costs involved and the sales to be generated. If we can do this, we have a better chance of basing our decision on the profit expected. Profit is, of course, probably the most important company objective.

QUESTIONS

1. Why must physical distribution decisions recognize sales considerations as well as cost considerations?

Marketing Mix Decisions

2. Why is the level of customer service an important aspect of the physical distribution function?

3. Under what circumstances would a company prefer to use public warehouses instead of private warehouses?

4. What are the advantages of using air transportation?

5. Give examples of trade-offs in the following physical distribution decisions: inventory levels, size of shipments, mode of transportation.

6. In some companies physical distribution decisions are not made by the marketing department. These decisions may be made by the production department or by a separate traffic department. Do you agree that these departments should make the physical distribution decisions?

7. Why must trade-offs be examined when physical distribution decisions are made?

8. Why do you believe that the physical distribution area provides such good opportunities for saving costs?

9. Can a service company, such as a bank or insurance company, benefit from having a physical distribution department? What kinds of marketing decisions would such a department help to make?

GLOSSARY

Containerization: system of using containers that hold a large number of units of a product so that storage and handling costs can be reduced

Inventory Control: involves determining and recording the location and number of units of finished goods in warehouses as well as customer requirements for the goods

Materials Handling: the movement of goods into warehouses, their storage, and movement out of warehouses when ready for shipment to customers

Optimization: the effort to minimize total cost or maximize total profit in a trade-off situation

Order Cycle Length: the time it takes for an order to be received after it is sent to the supplier

Order Status Reporting: a supplier informing its customers when their orders will be filled and delivered

Physical Distribution: the marketing management function that concerns moving finished goods from a company's production area to the purchasers of these products

Piggyback: loaded truck trailers that can be carried on specially designed railroad flatcars

Place Utility: the value that products have because they are available where purchasers want them; place utility is provided by the transportation function

Private Warehouses: warehouses purchased or constructed by a firm

Public Warehouses: warehouses leased to a firm

Time Utility: the value that products have because they are available when purchasers want them; time utility is provided by the storage function

Trade-off: decision in the physical distribution area in which the result is that one objective is achieved more fully while another objective is not achieved as well.

CASES

Case 1: The Highspire Co.

The Highspire Co., a steel manufacturer whose sales are $500 million a year, sells to 20,000 companies located throughout the United States. The company has 10 large regional warehouses to service these 20,000 customers.

Over the last 5 years the company traditionally had 5% of its shipment arrive late. During the last year the company was surprised to find that 15% of its shipments were late.

Concerned with this development, the company's physical distribution executives held an emergency meeting to decide what to do. Ted Jennings, physical distribution manager of the eastern region, believes that the problem is that the company does not have enough regional warehouses to handle its 20,000 customers. He recommended that 6 new warehouses be added as soon as possible.

1. Should the company be concerned with the increase in late deliveries?
2. Do you agree that the late delivery problem is the result of an insufficient number of warehouses.
3. What other aspects of the company's physical distribution system should be examined?

Case 2: The Playco Co.

Playco, a large toy manufacturer, undertakes an extensive analysis of its physical distribution operations. It finds that because of heavy purchasing of toys for Christmas 80% of its total inventory is shipped between July 1 and October 1. It also discovers that 30% of its individual shipments to stores have a value of $50 or less.

1. What do these data mean for the firm's warehousing decisions?
2. What do these data suggest for the company's transportation decisions?
3. What can the company do about their small-order problems?

Introduction to Pricing Decisions

After you read this chapter, you should be able to answer the following questions:

1. Why is price an important variable in the marketing mix?
2. Why is pricing considered to be a "fuzzy" area of marketing?
3. What is a demand schedule?
4. What is meant by marginal revenue?
5. What are marginal costs?
6. Why does a firm maximize net profit for a product when the marginal revenue and the marginal cost are equal?
7. Why is it important to understand the concept of price elasticity?
8. Why must we understand the four basic competitive models?
9. What are the major differences in pricing strategies suggested by the four major competitive models?

KEY TERMS   *Average Total Costs   Coefficient of Elasticity   Demand   Fixed Costs   Marginal Costs   Marginal Revenue   Monopolistic Competition   Monopoly   Oligopoly   Price Elasticity   Pure Competition   Total Costs   Total Revenue   Variable Costs*

INTRODUCTION   This chapter is designed to provide the reader with some basic concepts on the pricing function so that you will be better able to understand Chapter 15 which is concerned with the decision-making aspects of pricing. In that chapter, for example, we will be looking at such pricing decisions as developing pricing objectives, setting prices, pricing new products, and changing prices. This chapter will provide the necessary background material.

A company's pricing policies and pricing strategies are important elements of the marketing mix. Pricing decisions can have significant positive or negative effects on a firm's sales and profitability. No company found this out more to its sorrow than did the Great Atlantic and Pacific Tea Company (A&P), the nation's second largest food retailer. In 1972 it launched its WEO ("Where Economy Originates") campaign that involved reducing prices on thousands of items. In essence, A&P was competing mainly on a price basis. This strategy, however, backfired. Although its sales increased by $800 million in 1972, the company lost over $50 million.[1] In 1975 it essentially abandoned its total emphasis on price by inaugurating its "Price and Pride" campaign, which recognized non-price reasons for purchasing.

It is significant to note that the auto makers turned to the price variable in 1974 and 1975 in an effort to halt skidding car sales. All car manufacturers offered car purchasers cash rebates, which are essentially price reductions. In another example of the importance of price in the marketing mix, Ford and General Motors used deep price cuts in the early 1970's to take a large share of fleet car sales from Chrysler.

Price and Profit

A product's price impacts so strongly on its profit because the price established affects the two basic components of profit: revenues and costs. Along with other elements of the marketing mix, a product's price can either increase or decrease the revenues (sales dollars obtained). Both price increases and decreases may result in higher or lower sales dollars. Since price partially determines the number of units sold, it also determines, to some extent, the costs involved.

Price: The Only Marketing Mix Element in Every Product and in Every Transaction

Another reason why price is an important marketing mix variable is that it is the only element of the marketing mix that comes into play *for every product* and is present in *every buyer–seller transaction*. Some products or services require little in the way of promotion in order to be sold; some products do not have to be stored or transported; but all products and

---

[1] "A&P Counts the Cost of Its Pyrrhic Victory," *Business Week*, April 28, 1973, p. 118.

"Wow! Just look at those prices, George."

services carry a price and price is certainly an important part of every transaction. In fact, it is often the major reason why a transaction either takes place or does not take place. These factors also explain why consumers tend to be price conscious.

Consumers Are Price Conscious

The fact that consumers are conscious of prices for some products is a good indication of the importance of the price variable. This phenomenon has been demonstrated on several occasions. For example, 86% of consumers in one study correctly identified the price of a Coca-Cola six-pack and 91% named a price within 5% of the correct figure. At least one-sixth of the consumers could cite the correct price for half of the products, and one-fourth could give a price within the 5% range.[2]

Pricing Is a "Fuzzy" Area

Despite the importance of pricing, decisions in the pricing area cannot be made with a great deal of certainty. This fact has led one expert on pricing

[2] Benson P. Shapiro, "The Psychology of Pricing," *Harvard Business Review* (July–August, 1968), pp. 14–25.

Marketing Mix Decisions

to conclude that "of all the areas of executive decision, pricing is perhaps the most fuzzy."[3] There are several reasons for this. In addition to the price of a product, there are other factors that affect sales, for example, advertising and personal selling, the level of demand in the market place, and the price of competitive products.

Prices Are Usually in a State of Flux

Another problem for the pricing decision maker is that prices may have to be changed constantly. Price changes may reflect technological improvements, the need to meet the competition's prices, or changing levels of demand in the market. All of these factors appeared responsible for the deep price declines of pocket calculators in the early 1970's. In 1971 they retailed for $240 each; by 1974 the price of pocket calculators plummeted to $19.95.[4]

Increasing Formalization of the Pricing Decision Apparatus

Because of the factors discussed above, many companies, such as Fairchild Camera and Instrument Corporation, are approaching pricing decisions in a more rigorous fashion than they did before. Pricing decisions are being made more and more by high-level employees, often by the chief executive. Some companies are employing more specialists, such as production, finance, marketing, and marketing research personnel. Many companies use computers to improve their pricing decisions.[5]

With these introductory comments in mind, we are ready to discuss some of the basic aspects of pricing.

DEMAND

Essentially, **demand** refers to the number of units of a product that will be purchased at various prices. In general, it is assumed that more units of a product will be purchased at lower prices because a buyer can purchase more units of a product when the price is lower. For example, if a man has $80 to spend for shoes, he can buy four pairs if the price is $20 a pair. He could buy five pairs if a price of $16 a pair were charged. Thus, we can see that at the lower price of $16, more pairs of shoes can be bought (five) than at the higher price of $20 (four).

In order to be able to make intelligent pricing decisions for their products, marketers must have some idea of the number of units that would probably be purchased for a number of likely prices (see Figure 14.1). As the reader

[3] Alfred R. Oxenfeldt, "Multi-Stage Approach to Pricing," *Harvard Business Review* (July–August, 1960), p. 125.
[4] "Pricing Strategy in an Inflation Economy," *Business Week*, April 6, 1974, p. 42.
[5] Ibid., p. 44

Figure 14.1   A Demand Schedule

Price	Quantity Demanded
$20	1
18	2
16	3
14	4
12	5
10	6
8	7
6	8
4	9
2	10

can see, the *demand schedule* indicates the quantity of units that will be purchased for a number of prices. This same information can also be graphed. The graph is called a *demand curve*. A demand curve provides the same information as a demand schedule: It indicates the number of units that will be purchased for each price. It is just a different way of expressing the same relationships.

Figure 14.2 is a demand curve for the demand schedule given in Figure 14.1. The vertical axis (P) is used to represent price. The horizontal axis (Q) is used to represent the quantity demanded at each price. The dots represent each price and its corresponding quantity, as the above demand schedule also does. In Figure 14.2, for example, the dot at point X stands for a quantity of five units being demanded at a price of $12 per unit. The dots in this figure are connected by a solid line to form a demand curve which, in this case, is a straight line. It is designated by the letter D.

REVENUE

In making pricing decisions it is important for the reader to understand the concept of *revenue*. In the following discussion we will be concerned with two revenues: **total revenue** and **marginal revenue.** We will continue to use the demand schedule in Figure 14.1 to illustrate these two revenues.

Total Revenue

Total revenue (or sales dollars) is found by multiplying the price per unit by the quantity demanded. Figure 14.3 lists the total revenue figures for the ten combinations of price and quantity demanded shown in Figure 14.1.

Figure 14.2   A Demand Curve

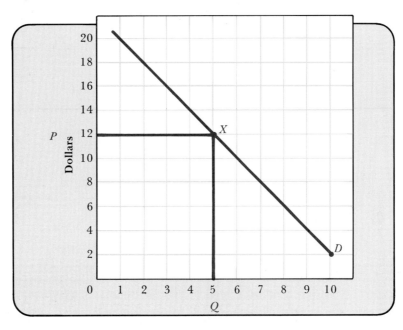

For example, in Figure 14.3 we can see that when two units are demanded (sold) at $18 each the total revenue is $36.

Marginal Revenue

Marginal revenue is an important concept in pricing decisions. Marginal revenue is the *change in total revenue that results when an additional unit of a product is demanded.* The last column in Figure 14.4 gives the marginal revenue for the combinations of price and quantity that we have been using.

The marginal revenue figure is obtained by calculating the difference in total revenue resulting when an additional unit is demanded. For example, when the price is $20 per unit, one unit is demanded; thus, the total revenue is $20. When two units are demanded at $18, the total revenue is $36. Since the total revenue obtained from two units is $36, compared to $20 total revenue for one unit, the marginal revenue obtained is $16. That is, we increase total revenue by $16 in selling two units as opposed to selling one unit.

Let's use another example to make sure that the reader understands the

Figure 14.3   Total Revenue

Price	×	Quantity Demanded	=	Total Revenue
$20	×	1	=	$20
18	×	2	=	36
16	×	3	=	48
14	×	4	=	56
12	×	5	=	60
10	×	6	=	60
8	×	7	=	56
6	×	8	=	48
4	×	9	=	36
2	×	10	=	20

Figure 14.4   Marginal Revenue

Price	Quantity Demanded	Total Revenue	Marginal Revenue
$20	1	$20	$20
18	2	36	16
16	3	48	12
14	4	56	8
12	5	60	4
10	6	60	0
8	7	56	−4
6	8	48	−8
4	9	36	−12
2	10	20	−16

concept. The total revenue obtained for three units is $48. For four units, it is $56. Thus, the marginal revenue (the result of the change in total revenue) is $8 ($56 − $48).

There are two major ideas involved in the pattern of marginal revenues

Marketing Mix Decisions

shown in Figure 14.4. First, the reader will probably notice that as additional units are demanded, the marginal revenue gets smaller. At one unit demanded, the marginal revenue is $20; at two units it is $16; at three units it is $12; at four units it is $8; and so on. This occurs because in order to sell additional units, a lower price is charged and *all* units are sold at the lower price. Second, the reader should realize that eventually marginal revenue becomes a minus figure. This can be seen, for example, in calculating the marginal revenue that results when eight units are demanded. At seven units, the total revenue is $56 ($8 × 7). At eight units, however, the total revenue is $48 ($6 × 8). Thus, the total revenue has *decreased* by $8 when eight units are sold ($56 − $48 = $8). The important concept to be remembered here is that a firm can suffer decreases in its total revenue if it charges lower prices.

In Figure 14.5 we have added the marginal revenue data to the original demand curve shown in Figure 14.2. It is designated by *MR* in this figure.

As we continue our discussion, we will eventually add two more items to this diagram: the marginal cost and the average total cost. With these added to our demand curve and marginal revenue curve, we will be in

Figure 14.5   A Marginal Revenue Curve Added to the Demand Curve

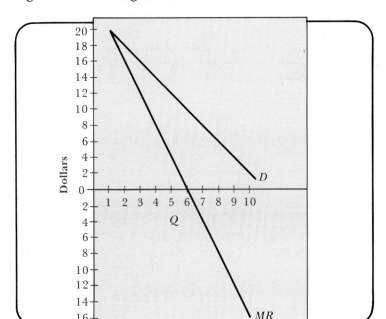

Introduction to Pricing Decisions

a position to determine the price that the firm should charge in order to *maximize net profit.* Before we can do this, however, we must first deal with costs.

COSTS

Whenever a company sells its products, it incurs costs. The following are some examples of costs that exist for most products: research and development, storage, transportation, raw materials, labor, and advertising. The total of these costs must be compared to total revenues so that net profits can be calculated. For example, if a product generates total revenues of $300 and the product costs $250, there is a net profit of $50 ($300 − $250 = $50).

In order to obtain a good understanding of costs, the reader must become familiar with five basic costs: fixed costs, variable costs, total costs, marginal costs, and average total costs.

Fixed Costs

Fixed costs are costs that *remain the same* no matter how many units of a product are produced and sold. Fixed costs do not change whether one unit or a thousand units are demanded.

An example of a fixed cost are the initial research and development expenditures for products. If a company spends $10,000 on researching the market for the product and on developing working models and pilot plants, these costs are constant and do not increase as the number of units sold increases.

Figure 14.6 shows the cost data added to the revenue data already discussed. In this example we will assume that fixed costs are $2. They are listed in column 5.

Variable Costs

Variable costs are expenditures that vary according to the number of units produced and marketed. They are mostly production and marketing costs. The higher the number of units demanded, the more raw materials, labor, and machine time required. Therefore, higher production costs are incurred. Similarly, greater expenditures for marketing are also needed. Thus, in order to sell a greater number of units, more may have to be spent on advertising, transportation, and salespeople.

Column 6 of Figure 14.6 shows the variable costs for our example.

Total Costs

If we add fixed costs and variable costs, we obtain **total costs.** Total costs are shown in Column 7 of Figure 14.6. For example, the total cost incurred when two units are demanded is $30 ($2 in fixed costs and $28 in variable

Figure 14.6   Fixed Costs, Variable Costs, Total Costs, Marginal Costs, and Average Total Costs

Price (1)	Quantity Demanded (2)	Total Revenue (3)	Marginal Revenue (4)	Fixed Costs (5)	Variable Costs (6)	Total Costs (7)	Marginal Costs (8)	Average Total Cost (9)
$20	1	$20	$20	$2	$16	$18	$16	$18
18	2	36	16	2	28	30	12	15
16	3	48	12	2	34	36	6	12
14	4	56	8	2	38	40	4	10
12	5	60	4	2	38	40	0	8
10	6	60	0	2	46	48	8	8
8	7	56	−4	2	61	63	15	9
6	8	48	−8	2	78	80	17	10
4	9	36	−12	2	97	99	19	11
2	10	20	−16	2	118	120	21	12

costs). The total cost is $40 for five units ($2 in fixed costs and $38 in variable costs).

Marginal Costs

Marginal costs are the *changes in total costs that occur when one additional unit of a product* is demanded. The marginal costs are shown in Column 8 of Figure 14.6. To illustrate, the marginal cost incurred in selling the fourth unit is $4. This results from the fact that the total cost for three units is $36. For four units, the total cost is $40 and $40 − $36 = $4.

The reader should notice the pattern of marginal costs in Column 8 of Figure 14.6. At first, the costs become progressively lower, but then after hitting a low point at five units ($0) they begin to increase.

Average Total Costs

Average total costs are found in Column 9 of Figure 14.6. Average total costs are found by dividing the total costs by the number of units. To illustrate, the total cost required for five units is $40. Thus, the average total cost is $8 ($40 ÷ 5 = $8). Another term frequently used for average total cost is *total cost per unit*. This refers to the same calculation— the total costs divided by the number of units.

As the reader looks at the average total cost figures in Column 9 in Figure 14.6, it will be obvious that, at first, average total costs progressively get lower, until they reach a low point of $8 for five and six units. After that, the average total costs begin to increase.

USING TOTAL REVENUE AND TOTAL COST TO DETERMINE THE PROFIT MAXIMIZING PRICE

Total net profit is the difference between total revenue and total cost, or expressed another way, total profit equals total revenue minus total cost. Let's use this approach to find out which price in this example should be charged in order to obtain the most net profit.

Figure 14.7 includes the pertinent data from Figure 14.6 needed to calculate the profit obtained for each price charged. Figure 14.7 shows that the greatest net profit of $20 occurs when a price of $12 is charged. At this price, the total revenue is $60 and the total cost is $40, which results in a net profit of $20.

Another way to arrive at the same conclusion that $12 is the profit maximizing price is to look at the relationship between marginal revenue and marginal cost.

Figure 14.7 Using Total Revenue and Total Cost to Determine the Profit Maximizing Price

Price	Quantity Demanded	Total Revenue	Total Cost	Net Profit
$20	1	$20	$ 18	$ 2
18	2	36	30	6
16	3	48	36	12
14	4	56	40	16
12	5	60	40	20
10	6	60	48	12
8	7	56	63	−7
6	8	48	80	−32
4	9	36	99	−63
2	10	20	120	−100

USING MARGINAL REVENUE AND MARGINAL COST TO DETERMINE THE PROFIT MAXIMIZING PRICE

Figure 14.8 was developed to facilitate the following discussion. The data in this figure were taken from Figures 14.6 and 14.7.

As long as the marginal revenue from charging a lower price exceeds the marginal cost incurred, the firm should go ahead and charge the lower price because the firm will be securing a *higher net profit.* A firm should continue to drop its price until the *marginal cost incurred exceeds the marginal revenue obtained* because then the firm would be *obtaining a lower net profit.*

Let's look at Figure 14.8 in order to understand these principles. At a price of $20, the firm makes a net profit of $2. Let's see what happens if it charges a price of $18. In this case, the marginal revenue is $16 and the marginal cost is $12. That is, the company increases its revenues by $16 and increases its costs by $12. Since the increase in revenue ($16) exceeds the increase in cost ($12) by $4, this means that profit has to be improved by $4. This is exactly what would occur if the firm were to charge a price of $18 instead of $20. In Figure 14.8 the net profit of $6 obtained from a price of $18 is exactly $4 more than the net profit secured when a price of $20 is charged ($2).

Let's look at what happens to the net profit if a price of $16 is charged instead of $18. Since the marginal revenue obtained is $12 and the marginal cost is $6, the company increases its profit by $6 ($12 − $6 = $6).

Figure 14.8   Using Marginal Revenue and Marginal Cost to Determine the Profit Maximizing Price

Price	Quantity Demanded	Marginal Revenue	Marginal Cost	Net Profit
$20	1	$20	$16	$ 2
18	2	16	12	6
16	3	12	6	12
14	4	8	4	16
12	5	4	0	20
10	6	0	8	12
8	7	−4	15	−7
6	8	−8	17	−32
4	9	−12	19	−63
2	10	−16	21	−100

This can be checked by inspecting the net profit column of Figure 14.8 for a price of $18 and a price of $16. At a price of $16, the net profit is $12. This is $6 more than at a price of $18 because there net profit is $6.

The reader will notice that for the next two prices of $14 and $12, the marginal revenue still exceeds the marginal cost. Thus, charging these prices will increase the net profit. Notice, however, what happens if a price of $10 is charged. In this case, the marginal cost is $8 and the marginal revenue is $0, the first price where marginal cost is *greater* than marginal revenue. At a price of $10, then, the net profit will be $8 *less* than it was at a price of $12. Checking Figure 14.8 proves this. At a price of $10, the net profit is $12, which is $8 less than the $20 obtained with a price of $12. Thus, it can be seen that it does not pay to drop the price to $10. The firm should stick with a price of $12 because there net profit is maximized ($20). To charge a lower price would get the firm into a situation in which the marginal cost would exceed the marginal revenue, resulting in lower profits than could be achieved at the *last price where the marginal revenue is greater than the marginal cost.*

It is often desirable to graph the major components that determine the profit maximizing price. These components include demand, marginal revenue, marginal cost, and average total cost. In Figure 14.9 the marginal cost and the average total cost have been added to the demand curve and the marginal revenue already found in Figure 14.5. Figure 14.9 graphically shows what has already been learned about the price that should be charged: At a price below $12 the marginal cost is greater than the marginal revenue. Therefore, profit would be decreased if a price below $12 were charged.

Above the price of $12 the marginal revenue exceeds the marginal cost and, thus, profit would be increased by charging a lower price. It will also be helpful for the reader to realize that at the price that maximizes profit ($12) the price is greater than the average total cost. By consulting Figure 14.9 and Figure 14.6, the reader will see that at a price of $12 the average total cost is $8. Since the price is $12, the net profit per unit is $4 (price of $12 minus average total cost of $8). Since five units are sold at a net profit per unit of $4, the total net profit at a price of $12 is $20 (5 × $4 = $20).

DETERMINING PRICE ELASTICITY

It is very important that the reader understand the concept of **price elasticity.** This concept is significant in helping firms decide whether to *increase* or *decrease* prices. Although we will deal with price increases and decreases in the next chapter, price elasticity must be discussed now because it is such a fundamental concept.

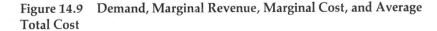

Figure 14.9   Demand, Marginal Revenue, Marginal Cost, and Average Total Cost

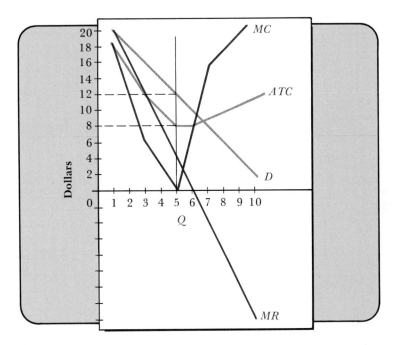

Price elasticity refers to the sensitivity of the quantity demanded to changes in price. *Elastic* demand curves represent situations in which the quantity demanded is very sensitive to price changes; *inelastic* demand curves represent situations in which the quantity demanded is relatively insensitive to price changes.

Elastic Demand Curves

Figure 14.10(a) shows an elastic demand curve. Here, it can be seen that the quantity demanded is very responsive to a change in price. At a price of $10 four units are demanded. A very slight decrease of price to $9, however, results in a very large increase in the quantity demanded (from four to eight units). Similarly, a small price increase from $9 to $10 results in a large decrease in quantity demanded (from eight units to four units).

The more horizontal the demand curve, the more elastic it is. That is, the quantity demanded is more sensitive to price.

Inelastic Demand Curves

Figure 14.10(b) shows an inelastic demand curve. The quantity demanded is not very sensitive to price changes. Here, it can be seen that a very sizable decrease in price from $10 to $5 increases the quantity demanded only slightly (from four to five units). Similarly, a large price increase from $5 to $10 results in only a slight decrease in the quantity demanded (from five to four units).

The closer the demand curve is to being vertical, the more inelastic it is. That is, the quantity demanded is less sensitive to price.

Determining the Coefficient of Price Elasticity

It is helpful to be able to determine the **coefficient of price elasticity,** which tells us *how sensitive* the quantity demanded is to a price change. This involves solving the simple equation below:

$$E_c = \frac{\%\Delta Q}{\%\Delta P}$$

This equation tells us that the coefficient of price elasticity (E_c) is equal to the percentage change in quantity divided by the percentage change in price.

Let's determine the coefficient of price elasticity for the various price changes found in Figure 14.10(a) and (b). Let's first look at what happens

Figure 14.10 (a) Elastic Demand Curve; (b) Inelastic Demand Curve

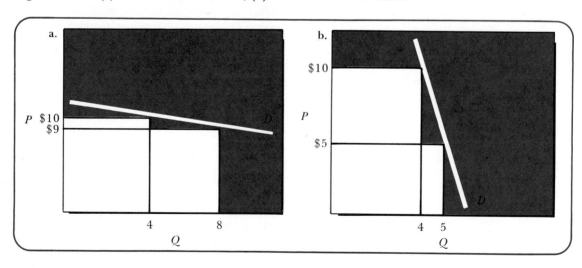

in Figure 14.10(a) when we drop our price from \$10 to \$9. In this case, the coefficient of price elasticity would be 10, which is found as follows:

$$E_c = \frac{\dfrac{8-4}{4}}{\dfrac{10-9}{10}} = \frac{\dfrac{4}{4}}{\dfrac{1}{10}} = \frac{100\%}{10\%} = 10$$

This tells us that a 10% decrease in price would result in a 100% increase in the quantity demanded, or in other words, the percentage change in quantity demanded would be ten times that of the percentage change in price. This demand curve represents a situation in which the quantity demanded is very sensitive to price changes.

Let's see what happens in Figure 14.10(a) when we increase the price from \$9 to \$10:

$$E_c = \frac{\dfrac{8-4}{8}}{\dfrac{10-9}{9}} = \frac{\dfrac{4}{8}}{\dfrac{1}{9}} = \frac{50\%}{11\%} = 4.55$$

In this case, the coefficient of price elasticity of 4.55 tells us that the quantity demanded is again very sensitive to a price decrease. To be specific, a price increase of 11% would result in a 50% decrease in the quantity demanded.

In Figure 14.10(b) the quantity demanded is very insensitive to price changes because the demand cure is inelastic. If we drop the price from \$10 to \$5, the coefficient of price elasticity would be .5:

$$E_c = \frac{\dfrac{5-4}{4}}{\dfrac{10-5}{10}} = \frac{\dfrac{1}{4}}{\dfrac{5}{10}} = \frac{25\%}{50\%} = .5$$

Thus, a 50% decrease in price would generate only a 25% increase in the quantity demanded. Similarly, a price increase would result in a coefficient of price elasticity of only .2:

$$E_c = \frac{\dfrac{5-4}{5}}{\dfrac{10-5}{5}} = \frac{\dfrac{1}{5}}{\dfrac{5}{5}} = \frac{20\%}{100\%} = .2$$

Using the Concept of Elasticity to Decide Whether to Raise or Lower Prices

In the examples above the price changes on the elastic demand curve in Figure 14.10(a) resulted in coefficients of price elasticity greater than 1.0, whereas the price changes on the inelastic demand curve in Figure 14.10(b) resulted in coefficients of price elasticity less than 1.0. This is the test that determines whether a demand curve is elastic or inelastic. If its coefficient of price elasticity is greater than 1.0, it is elastic. If it is less than 1.0, it is inelastic.

Whenever a firm is considering raising or lowering the price of a product, the firm must determine whether the demand curve for that product is inelastic or elastic. *If the demand curve is elastic, the firm should decrease the price. If the demand curve is inelastic, the firm should increase the price.*

To prove these two statements, we must show what happens to the total revenue when price increases and decreases occur. Everything else being equal, a price change should increase the total revenue.

When a demand curve is elastic, a price cut would increase the total revenue. In Figure 14.10(a) a price of $10 would result in four units being demanded. Thus, the total revenue would be $40 ($10 × 4). A price cut to $9 would increase the total revenue to $72 (eight units sold times $9). However, notice what would happen to the total revenue if the price were *increased*. A price of $9 would result in a total revenue of $72, but raising the price to $10 would shrink the total revenue to $40, an undesirable situation.

For the inelastic demand curve in Figure 14.10(b), a price increase would have a positive effect on revenues. At a price of $5, five units would be sold, resulting in total revenue of $25. A price increase to $10, however, would increase the total revenue to $40, because four units are demanded. If the price of $10 is dropped to $5, the total revenue would shrink from $40 to $25.

To summarize: price decreases, not price increases, are advisable when an elastic demand curve exists. Price increases, not price decreases, are advisable when an inelastic demand curve exists.

A good example of a company that had to recognize the elasticity concept in its pricing policy is the publisher of the *New Age Encyclopedia*. In 1976 this encyclopedia was offered for sale at $175, a full 50% reduction from the original price of $350. In its advertising the company announced "an incredible price slash to turn inventory into immediate cash and avoid the high cost of borrowing." Obviously, if there were not an increase of more than 50% in the quantity sold, the company's total revenue would shrink.

FOUR BASIC COMPETITIVE MODELS

The reader must have a knowledge of the four basic competitive models because in large measure they determine a firm's pricing strategy for its various products. Most firms in the United States are multi-product firms; they do not produce and market only one product. For example, it is not uncommon for a manufacturing firm to produce as many as several thousand products or for large supermarkets to sell as many as 6,000 different items. Thus, it is to be expected that these firms may find that the four basic competitive models accurately describe many of their products, thereby necessitating different pricing strategies for different products.

Pure Competition

In **pure competition** a large number of firms produce and market a relatively standardized product. Each firm accounts for only a small percentage of the total units sold in the industry. Because of the relatively standardized nature of the product sold, there is little opportunity to differentiate on the basis of quality, advertising, packaging, brand name, sales promotion, and the product itself. Since each firm has only a small percentage of the total units sold, the firm cannot affect the price by increasing or decreasing the number of units it produces.

Figure 14.11 shows the normal pricing model for products in pure competition.

Horizontal Demand Curve. The first thing that the reader should notice is that the demand curve is perfectly horizontal. This results from

Figure 14.11   Pure Competition

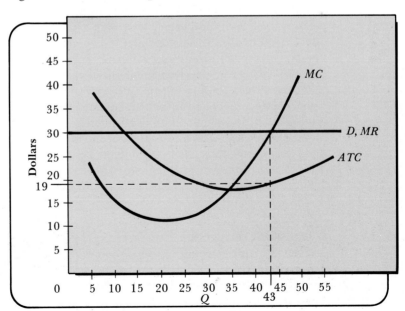

Introduction to Pricing Decisions

the fact that no individual firm can influence the price; it accepts the price as given. No matter how many units the firm produces, it will obtain a price of $30 per unit.

Marginal Revenue and Price Are the Same.   The second thing that the reader should observe is that the marginal revenue (MR) is also $30, the same as the price. That is, the additional revenue obtained from having one more unit demanded will always be $30. To see why this is so, let us observe what the total revenue would be if one unit were sold at a price of $30. Obviously, this would be $30 (1 × $30). The total revenue would be $60 if two units were sold (2 × $30); this would represent a $30 increase over the total revenue of $30 obtained at one unit. Similarly, the total revenue from three units would be $90 (3 × $30), which would be an increase in total revenue of $30 over the $60 existing for two units.

Maximizing Profit.   Where does the firm maximize profit? And how much is this profit? As we explained earlier, the firm maximizes profit when the marginal revenue and the marginal cost are equal. In Figure 14.11 this is where the marginal revenue line and the marginal cost line intersect, that is, at a value of $30. This means that the firm would sell 43 units at an average total cost of $19. Since the price is $30 per unit, the total profit would be $473, that is, the total revenue of $1,290 (43 × $30) minus the total costs of $817 (43 × $19). Another way to see that the total profit would be $473 is to observe that the profit per unit is $11 (a price of $30 per unit minus an average total cost of $19); $11 × 43 units = $473.

Kinds of Products.   Although it is difficult to find examples of products represented by the pure competition model, several products may be close approximations. Some products sold by retail grocery stores, especially staple items, may be as good examples as can be found. These products, such as fresh fruits and vegetables, plain bread, and many canned goods, are difficult to differentiate and are sold by many stores, none of which individually may account for a large percentage of units sold. Industrial supplies, like paper towels and stationery, may be other examples.

An important point to remember is that companies must look at their product lines and determine which ones appear to be represented by the pure competition model. Since the firm probably cannot increase the price, it must emphasize efficient production and marketing practices in order to hold the average total costs *below* the price. If the average total cost exceeds the price, the firm will have a *net loss*.

Monopolistic Competition

Monopolistic competition is characterized by a fairly large number of firms, but not as many as would be found in pure competition. Twenty-five or 50 or so would be an example. Each company accounts for a small percentage of total units sold, but the percentage is high enough for each company to exert some influence over the price. Thus, an important distinction between monopolistic competition and pure competition is that a firm that has products in a monopolistic market *must have a pricing strategy for those products.* Thus, it can vary its price, searching for the price that will maximize net profit.

In a monopolistic market products are not standardized; they are different. In fact, this is a major way that firms that sell monopolistically competitive products compete: They try to develop product differences that will be attractive to the market. This differentiation strategy also allows the firm to exert some control over the price. Customers are receptive to these differences and are willing to pay the higher price.

The Monopolistic Competition Model. The basic model for the monopolistic market is shown in Figure 14.12. By now the reader should realize that the company will maximize profit by pricing where marginal revenue and marginal cost intersect. The reader should analyze the diagram and determine the following where profits are maximized: price, average total cost, net profit per unit, number of units sold, and total profit.

An Elastic Demand Curve. The demand curves for monopolistically competitive products are relatively elastic because they are close to being horizontal. This is shown in Figure 14.12. Thus, the firm can increase total revenues by decreasing the product's price.

Kinds of Products. Firms should analyze their products in an effort to determine which fall into this competitive model. Some products which

Figure 14.12   Monopolistic Competition

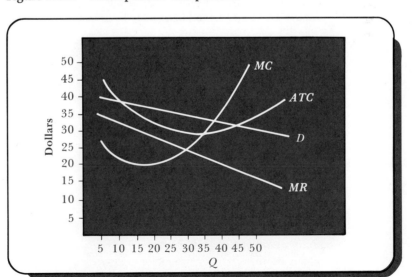

Introduction to Pricing Decisions

are considered to represent this basic competitive model are furniture, men's and boys' suits, millinery, and women's suits, coats and skirts.[6] Each of these products can be differentiated and are produced and sold by firms accounting for relatively low percentages of total units sold.

Oligopoly

Oligopoly is when a few firms account for the bulk of the units sold. Because of the small number of firms involved, no single firm can afford not to be aware of the other firms' pricing policies and since the number of firms is small, it is very easy to keep up with what the other firms are doing. Oligopolistic industries usually have anywhere from four to ten major firms accounting for the bulk of that industry's output.

Since each firm in the oligopolistic market knows what the other firms are doing, each firm is faced with the odd-shaped demand curve found in Figure 14.13. The reader will notice that there are two demand curves, D_1 and D_2. These different shaped demand curves mean that competitive companies will tend to *ignore* any sizable price increase and will quickly *match* any sizable decrease. Rival firms cannot afford to do otherwise.

[6] Cambell R. McConnell, *Economics: Principles, Problems and Policies* (New York: McGraw-Hill Book Company, 1963), p. 495.

Figure 14.13   Demand Curve for Firm in Oligopoly

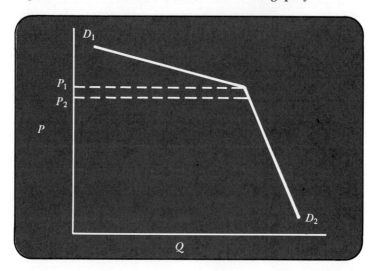

Marketing Mix Decisions

Increasing Price. If one company raises its price, the other companies will not do so because their products are now more attractive because of their lower prices. Thus, the firm increasing its price will find that it will experience a very large decrease in quantity sold, thereby suffering a decrease in total revenue. This situation is explained by the elastic demand curve D_1 in Figure 14.13. (The reader should remember that a price increase when the demand curve is elastic will cause a shrinkage in total revenue.)

A slight increase will probably be all right, but a large one will not. Thus, we have indicated in Figure 14.13 that an increase to P_1 may be ignored.

Decreasing Prices. Firms will quickly match price decreases because they cannot afford to let their competition get a sizable share of their business through lower prices. The reader will notice, as a result, that demand curve D_2 in Figure 14.13 is inelastic. This means that a firm lowering its price will suffer a drop in total revenue because it will obtain only a slight increase in units sold. A small decrease, perhaps to P_2, may be allowed.

Pricing Strategies. Because rival firms in oligopolies tend to ignore price increases and match price decreases, prices in oligopolistic markets for the individual firms tend to be very similar. There may be a little movement, such as that indicated from P_1 to P_2 in Figure 14.13. But, on the whole, prices are very much the same.

Since the price cannot be raised without damaging effects, companies in oligopolies are cost conscious. They have to be sure that their average total cost curve lies below the price where the marginal revenue and the marginal cost are equal.

If all the firms in oligopolistic industries were to raise their prices at the same time or lower them at the same time, their profit would be increased. Because of this, there are strong pressures for these companies to work together to *fix prices.* This is against the law and will be discussed at greater length in the next chapter.

Oligopolistic Industries. Many of the most well-known industries in the United States are oligopolies. Among them are the automobile, tin, steel, aluminum, cigarette, tire, and liquor industries. In addition, companies in other industries may find that individual products also fall into oligopolistic market situations.

Monopoly

In a monopoly market there is only one firm that makes up the industry. The company has been able to keep out competitive firms. This may result for a number of reasons. The government may grant monopoly status as it does, for example, for utilities. Some companies are in a monopoly position because they hold exclusive patents on the products they sell. Or they may own exclusive rights to sources of raw materials. A monopoly can also be created, unfortunately, by predatory means such as cut-throat prices and product disparagement.

Pricing Strategies. Pricing strategies for monopolies are shown in Figure 14.14, which provides the demand, marginal revenue, marginal cost, and average total cost curves for a monopolist.

The demand curve is relatively inelastic for a monopolist because there are no close substitutes for his product. Therefore, if he raises his price, the demand will decrease only slightly and total revenues will be increased. However, counter to the opinion held by many people, the monopolist may not charge the highest price he can. For one reason, this price may not maximize total profit and maximizing total profit is the monopolist's major objective. In Figure 14.14 the monopolist's profit maximizing price is $38, resulting in a maximum total profit of $187. (The reader should verify this by examining the diagram). Another reason why the monopolist does not charge the highest price he can is that a very high price calls attention to the monopolist and this attention may have unfavorable results. For example, the government may not look favorably on such a high price and other firms may be attracted to the industry.

Figure 14.14   Monopoly

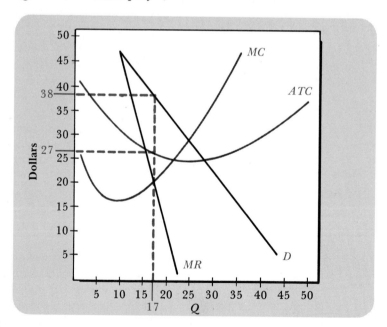

Marketing Mix Decisions

Monopolistic Products. Although monopolistic products are rare, occasionally firms may have a small number that fall into this category. Patents, research and development, and effective marketing programs may help to produce such a product. Despite its monopolistic position, management must carefully plan pricing strategies for such products.

APPLYING THIS CHAPTER MATERIAL TO REAL-LIFE PRICING DECISIONS

The above material is important to the understanding of the basic concepts of pricing. After reading this chapter, the reader will be in a position to better grasp the material provided in the next chapter.

We have stressed the significance of pricing strategies in achieving maximum profitability. In reality, a number of other objectives may be sought. Some of the more important objectives will be discussed in the next chapter.

In practice, it is very difficult for companies to determine the specific price that maximizes profit because they are not able to determine the exact shape of the demand curves for all the products they sell. They may have a general idea of the shape, but seldom can they develop the shape with the precision that we implied in our drawings. Also, it may be difficult to develop precise estimates of costs.

SUMMARY

Many marketing experts consider price to be one of the most important elements of the marketing mix because price directly affects the two major components of net profit—costs and revenues. Also, price, unlike other marketing mix variables is present in every buyer–seller transaction.

Pricing, however, is still a "fuzzy" area of marketing because marketing mix variables other than price affect sales and costs and, hence, profits. Also, it is difficult to obtain the precise demand and the cost data needed to use the standard pricing models.

A demand schedule indicates the number of units that will be demanded at each price. From a demand schedule, it is possible to determine marginal revenue, which is the change in total revenue that results when an additional unit of a product is sold. Similarly, marginal costs are changes in total costs that result when one more unit is sold.

A firm maximizes net profit when the marginal revenue and the marginal cost are equal. At prices higher than the price at which net profit is maximized, marginal revenue is greater than marginal cost. Thus, charging a lower price adds to the firm's net profit. On the other hand, at prices lower than the profit maximizing price, marginal costs exceed marginal revenues. As a result, charging a lower price reduces net profit. Obviously, this is an undesirable situation.

Price elasticity refers to the sensitivity of the quantity of the units demanded to changes in price. We must understand price elasticity in order to determine when it is advisable to raise or lower prices. If the demand curve is elastic, the total revenue will be increased by reducing the price, and the total revenue will be decreased if the price is raised. However, a price increase will result in a higher total revenue if the demand curve is inelastic. But a firm will decrease its total revenue by reducing its price with an inelastic demand curve.

The four basic competitive models are important because they provide pricing guidance for company products that are represented by these models. Although pricing strategies may differ for each market situation, the firm always maximizes net profit by pricing when the marginal revenue and the marginal cost are equal. In pure competition a company does not really need a pricing strategy because the company charges the going price. In monopolistic competition the firm can vary its price. Since its demand curve is relatively elastic, the firm can increase its total revenue by charging a lower price. In oligopolies, a company's price increases will be ignored by the competition and price decreases will be quickly matched. Thus, a firm is confronted with a narrow range within which it can vary its price.

The monopolist has a great deal of freedom in selecting his price. He can increase his total revenue by raising his price because his demand curve is relatively inelastic. He does not, however, charge an excessively high price because the government may not look favorably on such a high price and other firms may be attracted to the industry.

QUESTIONS

1. Why is total net profit maximized when the marginal revenue and the marginal cost are equal?

2. Do you agree or disagree with the following statement? A monopolist, because he is the only firm in an industry, will always price when the marginal revenue and the marginal cost are equal in order to maximize total net profit? Why do you agree or disagree?

3. Why is the average total cost an important aspect of making pricing decisions?

4. Would a product like salt have an elastic or inelastic demand curve? Why?

5. Should a company that is in a purely competitive market charge a low or high price for its product? Defend your answer.

6. How might a company make the demand curve for a given product more inelastic? Why would it want to do this?

7. Can you think of anything a company in an oligopolistic industry could do to give the company more control over its price?

8. What factors besides price affect the quantity demanded for a product at different prices?

GLOSSARY

Average Total Costs: the total costs divided by number of units

Coefficient of Elasticity: an equation that divides the percentage change in quantity by the percentage change in price to determine the extent to which the quantity demanded is sensitive to price changes

Demand: the number of units of a product that will be purchased at various prices

Fixed Costs: costs that remain the same no matter how many units are produced and sold

Marginal Costs: the change in total costs that results when additional units of a product are produced and marketed

Marginal Revenue: the change in total revenue that results when an additional unit of a product is demanded

Monopolistic Competition: the market in which a fairly large number of firms each accounts for a large enough percentage of the industry's output so that each company has some control over price

Monopoly: the market in which one firm *is* the industry and that firm has a good deal of control over the price it establishes

Oligopoly: the market in which a few firms comprise the industry and prices are very similar for all companies because price increases are ignored and price decreases are quickly matched

Price Elasticity: the sensitivity of the quantity demanded to changes in price

Pure Competition: the market situation in which a given price exists for a large number of firms because no firm is able to account for a sizable percentage of the industry's output

Total Costs: the sum of fixed costs and variable costs for any product

Total Revenue: sales dollars found by multiplying the price per unit by the quantity demanded

Variable Costs: costs that vary according to the number of units produced and marketed

Case 1: Throckmorton College

The administration of a small, highly prestigious liberal arts college in the East, Throckmorton College, is contemplating an increase in the cost of tuition. The college draws predominantly students who rank in the upper-tenth of their high school class and score in the upper-tenth on college admissions tests. Their parents' average annual income is generally above $35,000. A large percentage of the college's graduates are accepted into the leading law, medical, and dental schools and into the leading graduate schools.

Tuition fees account for 80% of the college's income. The other 20% comes from gifts, endowments, and federal government grants. So far in the 1970's the college has managed to avoid losses.

In 1977 the tuition was $4,000 per year. The college's board of trustees indicated that it believed an increase to $4,800 per year would be needed to keep the college financially sound.

1. What factors should the board of trustees have considered in making this recommendation?
2. How important are price elasticity, inelastic demand, marginal revenue, and marginal cost in making this recommendation?
3. Do you believe that the tuition cost should be raised to $4,800? Why or why not?

Case 2: The Kelly Car Co.

The Kelly Car Company is a high-volume automobile dealer for one of the nation's "big-three" automobile manufacturers. The company sells high-priced full-sized cars, medium-sized compact cars carrying medium-level prices, and low-priced sub-compact cars. Twenty percent of its sales are full-sized cars, 30% are compact cars, and 50% are sub-compact cars.

The Kelly Car Company's sales manager, Raymond Franks, has followed a rigid pricing policy in the past. The price on full-sized cars is $300 above the cost of the car to the Kelly Car Company, $200 over the cost for compact cars, and $100 over cost for sub-compacts. Last year, the company sold 200 full-sized cars, 250 medium-sized compacts, and 325 sub-compacts. Mr. Kelly, the owner, has supported Mr. Franks' pricing strategies in the past but is wondering if a change might not be necessary.

1. What are the advantages of this pricing strategy?
2. What are its disadvantages?

3. How many dollars did the firm make last year to cover the costs of doing business (costs besides the cost of the cars)?
4. What principles from this chapter does this case illustrate?

Making Pricing Decisions

After you read this chapter, you should be able to answer the following questions:

1. What are the four basic factors that must be considered in developing a pricing program?
2. What are six major pricing objectives?
3. Why do you believe that cost-oriented pricing is a popular pricing approach? What is its major weakness?
4. What is the major advantage of the profit maximization approach to pricing? What is its major disadvantage?
5. What is one advantage of using the break-even method of pricing? What is its major disadvantage?
6. What is one major advantage of marginal pricing?
7. What are the two basic alternatives in pricing new products?
8. What factors should a company consider before it raises the price of a product?
9. How can markup be expressed?
10. How does unit pricing help consumers make better purchase decisions?
11. What is an important advantage of a positive price–quality relationship?
12. What are some of the ways that a company can make more effective pricing decisions?

*Break-Even Pricing   Cash Discount   Cost-Oriented Pricing
Demand-Oriented Pricing   Fair Trade   Marginal Pricing   Markdown
Markup   Penetration Pricing   Price Fixing   Price Lining   Quantity
Discount   Robinson–Patman Act   Skimming Pricing   Trade
Discount   Unit Pricing*

INTRODUCTION

In Chapter 14 we learned that pricing is one of the most important variables in a firm's marketing mix. Now we will devote our attention to the
actual decisions that companies must make in this area. We will be looking
at basic pricing objectives; fundamental pricing approaches; pricing new
products; changing prices on present products; markups, markdowns and
discounts; and special pricing aspects (unit prices, price–quality relationship, odd–even pricing, pricing during inflationary periods, and price
lining). We will also discuss the legal aspects of pricing and will conclude
the chapter with specific recommendations for making more effective
pricing decisions.

BASIC PRICING OBJECTIVES

No matter what pricing objective is desired, there are four basic factors that
must be considered: costs, demand (the quantity purchased at different
prices), competition, and governmental interest and attention. Any or all
of these may be considered when a company decides on its pricing objectives. Let us now look at some of these objectives.

Profit Maximization

Profit maximization increasingly appears to be a major pricing objective.
This was not always true. Many firms used price as a weapon to attract
more customers and increase sales dollars. Profit considerations were not
emphasized. Today, however, rising costs are forcing firms to stress the
profit aspects of pricing decisions. An example of this involves Fairchild
Camera and Instrument Corporation, which in 1974 bowed out of a price
war with Texas Instruments, Inc. Both firms wanted to capture a sizable
market involving control modules for the Polaroid SX-70 camera. Although
Fairchild's price was very close to Texas Instrument's, Wilfred J. Corrigan,
Fairchild's executive vice-president, indicated that the firm's profit per
unit would not be adequate. Mr. Corrigan believes that several years ago
Fairchild would have tried to capture this business.[1]

Profit maximization is an important pricing objective for the Jewelry

[1] *Business Week*, April 6, 1974, p. 44.

Division of Zale Corporation, a large national retail jewelry chain. Its group vice-president, Marvin Rubin, stated, "We are constantly looking for flags that tell us costs have gone up and that we had better re-examine our margins."[2] (Margin is the difference between selling price and cost.) The company uses a daily computer printout that shows the margin for all products handled.

We discussed profit maximization at length in Chapter 14. There we said that a firm maximizes net profit by pricing when the marginal cost and the marginal revenue are equal. We also pointed out some of the difficulties encountered in achieving profit maximization. As a result of these problems, many companies stress the return on investment objective.

Return on Investment

Many companies in the United States have as one of their major pricing objectives the achievement of a particular return on investment figure. In a pioneering study of pricing in American industry it was found that this pricing objective was the major goal of leading firms in oligopolistic industries.[3]

We learned earlier in this text that return on investment is found by dividing net profits by the investment dollars used to obtain the net profit figure. The standard approach to return on investment pricing is for management to stipulate a return on investment figure below which it does not want to go. This might be, for example, 20%. Very frequently this "floor" percentage is what it costs a firm to secure the assets needed to produce a profit. For example, if a firm has to pay a 10% interest charge on $100,000 borrowed from a bank to be used to develop a new product, it would certainly want the profit from this $100,000 investment to exceed 10% because at least this amount would be needed to cover the interest expense.

Securing a High Market Share

Securing a high percentage of market share is frequently a major objective of American firms. (Market share, as we already know, is the percentage of total units sold in an industry accounted for by a specific brand.) As noted previously, a high market share appears to be associated with a high rate of profitability; the average return on investment for companies with less than a 10% market share was around 9%. For those with market shares over 40%, the average return on investment was 30%.[4]

[2] Ibid.

[3] A. D. H. Kaplan, Joel B. Dirlam, and Robert H. Lanzillotti, *Pricing in Big Business* (Washington, D.C.: Brookings Institution, 1955).

[4] Paul N. Bloom and Philip Kotler, "Strategies for High Market Share Companies," *Harvard Business Review* (November–December, 1975), p. 63.

Whenever price is a major factor in generating sales, a low price may attract customers and eventually result in a highly profitable market share. This is apparently the approach followed by Dow Chemical Company, the large chemical manufacturer. "It prices low, builds a dominant market share, and holds on for the long pull."[5]

Precluding Market Entry by Competitive Firms

A low price is frequently a good strategy to deter entry by competitive firms. Most companies thinking about competing with an already existing product will want to price their offering about the same as the product already on the market. If this price is relatively low, the new firm will have to have its average total cost below this desired price in order to make a profit. This cost may not be achieved unless the new company builds a large enough plant to produce a large number of units of the new item. (The reader will remember that the firm's average total cost curve is high when few units are produced, gets lower as more units are produced, and then gets higher.)

As a result of the heavy investment required, many potential competitive firms are scared off. They are not sure that sales will be high enough to justify the heavy investment necessary.

Precluding Unfavorable Governmental Action

A major price objective is that of precluding the possibility of unfavorable governmental action. This is a significant concern for a large number of companies in the United States, so much so, in fact, that one pricing expert said in 1974, "I can't name a major company that hasn't been challenged by the Justice Department on its price."[6]

The inflationary pressures of the early 1970's have resulted in more governmental attention to those practices that result in high prices. Below are some examples:

1. The Federal Trade Commission is carefully watching for any unfair marketing practice that results in higher prices.
2. Agents of the Federal Bureau of Investigation have been instructed to look for price fixing and rigging of contract bids.
3. Several industries are being singled out for intensive investigation by the Federal Trade Commission and the Justice Department, for example, the sugar, bread, coffee, beer, oil, breakfast cereal, title insurance, drug, medical and hospital supplies, and real estate industries.[7]

[5] *Business Week*, op. cit., p. 45.
[6] Ibid., p. 43.
[7] Kenneth Bacon and Mitchele Lynch, "Ford Administration May Really Be Serious About Antitrust Drive," *The Wall Street Journal*, November 18, 1974, pp. 1–6.

Although high prices may disturb the government, low prices are also suspect. This is true when large companies set prices so low that they drive smaller firms out of business. The prices established are usually so low that if the smaller firm matches them, their average total cost will exceed the price. A small firm cannot afford to take such losses for long, but a large firm can because it has the financial backing.

Minimizing the Effects of Competitor Actions

Companies often use lower prices and increased expenditures for promotion to increase their sales at the expense of competitive firms. The companies hurt by this strategy often reduce the effect by lowering their prices. This is more effective when consumers are responsive to the price decreases.

Maintaining Good Relationships with Channels of Distribution

When a large part of a manufacturer's products is sold through channels of distribution (middlemen), the manufacturer must carefully assess the effect of his pricing policies on these individuals. Channels of distribution want adequate margins, that is, the spread between what they must pay for the product and what they can sell it for. If manufacturers can guarantee the middlemen adequate margins, the middlemen will more aggressively sell the manufacturer's product.

Staying in Business

Sometimes a company's pricing objective may be to enable the company to remain in business. After four successful years, in 1974 Mazda car sales plummeted because of higher gasoline prices and low mileage on its models. As a result, its dealer organization was in danger of disintegrating, a serious problem for any auto company. A $500 rebate to dealers and a $500 rebate to consumers were initiated. "The dealer network stayed alive, and so did Mazda, which has brought out more economical cars for 1976."[8]

MAJOR APPROACHES TO PRICING

Although there are a number of approaches to pricing that firms can take, the four major ones used are cost-oriented pricing, demand-oriented pricing, break-even pricing, and marginal pricing. The basic ideas behind each of these approaches is summarized in Figure 15.1, and a discussion of each approach follows.

[8] *Sales and Marketing Management*, Vol. 116 (January 12, 1976), pp. 34–35.

Figure 15.1   Major Approaches to Pricing

1. Cost-oriented pricing: Determine the number of units likely to be sold, calculate the direct cost per unit, and add a percentage to cover overhead costs and profit.
2. Demand-oriented pricing: Price when the marginal revenue and the marginal cost are equal in order to maximize net profit.
3. Break-even pricing: Solve the break-even equation to find the price that results in a desired profit.
4. Marginal pricing: Establish a price so that the revenue obtained exceeds the variable costs incurred so that a contribution to fixed costs results.

Cost-Oriented Pricing

A number of industries use the **cost-oriented pricing** approach. Many service industries and most contractors price on this basis. Wholesalers and retailers tend to consider costs of items purchased when they set their prices. Manufacturers of industrial products made to buyer specifications use the costs of these items to set a price.[9]

How does cost-oriented pricing work? First, the company estimates the number of units of the product it expects to sell. Suppose that this is 20,000 units. Second, the company determines the *direct* costs that are likely to result at 20,000 units. (Direct costs are costs that result from the production and marketing of a product. These might include raw materials, labor, advertising, etc. They are unlike *overhead* costs, such as the president's salary, which are difficult to relate to any specific product.) In our example we will assume that the direct costs are $50,000. Third, we divide the $50,000 direct costs by 20,000 units to get a direct cost per unit. In this case, the direct cost per unit is $2.50. Fourth, we add a percentage to cover overhead costs and profit, thus arriving at a price. If this percentage is 20%, the final price would be $3.00 ($2.50 + 20% = $3.00).

Advantages.   Cost-oriented pricing is relatively easy to use. This is probably its major advantage. One expert believes that this approach often results in a price close to the profit maximizing price, especially when the costs of trying to find the profit maximizing price are considered.[10]

Disadvantages.   The major flaw in this approach is that it does not recognize demand. That is, the decision maker does not know the number

---

[9] William E. Arnstein, "Relating Pricing to Costs," *Financial Executive* (December, 1971), pp. 36–41.

[10] Douglas G. Brooks, "Cost-Oriented Pricing: A Realistic Solution to a Complicated Problem," *Journal of Marketing* (April, 1975), p. 72.

of units demanded at various prices. Thus, the revenue generated at specific prices is ignored. Also, it may be difficult to predict the actual units to be sold in order to determine the direct cost per unit.

Demand-Oriented Pricing

In **demand-oriented pricing** the decision maker estimates the number of units to be sold at each price. Thus, he can also determine total revenue and marginal revenue can be calculated from total revenue estimates. Once total costs are estimated, marginal costs can be developed. Thus, the profit maximizing price is found when the marginal revenue and the marginal cost are equal.

The reader will recognize that we are essentially talking about the basic pricing model discussed in the previous chapter. The advantage of this approach is that it results in a price that maximizes profit. However, as we pointed out in Chapter 14, it is very difficult to know precisely how the demand curve and cost curves will look.

Break-Even Pricing

The reader is probably already familiar with the following basic equation used in **break-even pricing**:

$$BEQ = \frac{FC}{P - AVC}$$

This equation tells us the break-even quantity (number of units sold) that will result in revenues exactly equal to the costs incurred. Thus, the company neither makes a profit nor suffers a loss. In the equation, FC equals fixed cost, P equals price, and AVC equals average variable cost (total variable cost per unit).

Since firms are in business to make a profit, not to merely break even, it is appropriate to use a desired profit figure in the numerator. Thus, we would have

$$Q = \frac{FC + \pi}{P - AVC}$$

In this equation π represents the desired level of profit and Q is the number of units required to generate this profit, given specific values for price and average variable cost.

Our concern, however, is not with finding Q (quantity), but in deciding on P, the price. The same equation can be modified to solve for price. Let's illustrate how this would be done for a specific example. Suppose that it is estimated that the fixed cost of a product is $50,000 and that the company would like a 20% return on this $50,000 investment. (This fixed cost can be considered the same as an investment.) Since 20% of $50,000 is $10,000, we are essentially saying that we would like a $10,000 profit on this $50,000 investment. We will further assume that AVC is $.80 and that we expect to sell 100,000 units. Our problem is to determine the price that will give a net profit of $10,000 if the fixed cost is $50,000, if the profit desired is $10,000, and if AVC is $.80.

In Figure 15.2 we have modified the basic equation to solve for price. The reader can see that the price that the company should charge for this product is $1.40. At a price of $1.40 the company would generate the desired profit of $10,000. The reader can verify that $1.40 is the correct answer by remembering that profit is found by subtracting total costs from the total revenue. In this example the total revenue is $140,000 (a price of $1.40 × 100,000 units) and total costs are $130,000 ($50,000 fixed costs plus $80,000 variable costs, or 100,000 units × $.80). A total revenue of $140,000 less total costs of $130,000 results in a $10,000 profit.

Advantages. Break-even pricing is easy to use and provides some idea of the lowest possible price that must be charged in order to achieve a desired level of profit. In the above example any price below $1.40 would have resulted in less than $10,000 profits being achieved.

Disadvantages. In Chapter 14 we learned that quantity demanded results from the price charged. Yet, when we use break-even pricing, we assume a given quantity first and then we determine the price required to generate a desired level of profit. If quantity demanded is not very responsive to price, however, this may not be a problem. Also, we can experiment with different quantities in order to determine the prices required.

Figure 15.2   Using the Break-Even Equation to Determine Price

$$P = \frac{FC + \pi + (Q)\,(AVC)}{Q}$$

$$P = \frac{\$50,000 + \$10,000 + (100,000)\,(\$.80)}{100,000}$$

$$P = \frac{\$60,000 + \$80,000}{100,000}$$

$$P = \frac{\$140,000}{100,000}$$

$$P = \quad \$1.40$$

Marginal pricing involves setting a price so that the revenue obtained exceeds the variable costs associated with the product. Thus, the fact that the revenues exceed these variable costs means that there is coverage of *some of the fixed costs.*

Suppose that the fixed costs of a given product are $10,000. Let's assume that a price of $1 per unit is charged, that 10,000 units are sold, and that the average variable cost is $.60. Thus, the excess of revenues over variable costs is $4,000, that is, $10,000 revenue less variable costs of $6,000. Obviously, this excess of $4,000 does not cover the $10,000 fixed costs, *but it does reduce it by $4,000.* If this company had not practiced marginal pricing, it would still have to contend with the $10,000 fixed cost, not $6,000.

The major reason for marginal pricing is that the fixed cost exists whether or not the product is sold. To not sell the product at a price of $1 per unit, the firm would have to cover the $10,000 fixed costs instead of the $6,000 fixed costs. Obviously, a firm cannot make a net profit if all of its prices do not produce enough revenue to cover their fixed costs. However, a firm's total profit *from all products* may be increased if it practices marginal pricing. We can illustrate what we mean by assuming that all other products combined in the firm above generated a net profit of $10,000. If the firm did not apply the marginal pricing strategy to the product, the firm would just break even because the $10,000 net profit obtained from the other products would just cover the $10,000 fixed costs for the product. Since marginal pricing would be practiced with this product, only the $6,000 fixed costs must be covered, thus resulting in an excess of revenue over these fixed costs of $4,000. Thus, the company would have a net profit of $4,000 instead of just breaking even.

One company that successfully practices marginal pricing is Continental Air Lines. This airline runs a flight as long as the revenues obtained exceed the direct costs incurred. Thus, there is some contribution to the fixed costs whether the flight is made or not. This strategy has bolstered the company profits such that it suffered only one loss between the end of World War II and 1963.[11]

PRICING NEW PRODUCTS

Two major pricing decisions that must be made involve (1) determining the specific price to be put on a new product and (2) determining how that price should be varied over the product's life cycle. In developing a pricing strategy for new products, firms can use either a *skimming* approach or a *penetration* approach.

[11] "Airline Takes the Marginal Route," *Business Week*, April 20, 1963, pp. 111–14.

Skimming

A **skimming price** is a high price put on a new product so that it can generate high initial profits, especially if the new product has no competition. As competitive products are introduced and as a mass market develops for the item, the product's price can be lowered. The initial high price may create an image of quality and prestige for the new product and consumers will believe that they are getting a bargain when the price is lowered.

There are a number of potential disadvantages in a skimming strategy. First, the high price tends to attract competition because it promises high profits. Second, prices tend to be driven down, thus reducing profits. An example of this is DuPont's Dacron, a polyester fiber. When it was first introduced in 1953, its price was $2.25 per pound. By the 1970's it was $.40 a pound.[12] Third, the initial price may be set too high. This happened to DuPont's Corfam shoes, Cartrevision's home video recording system, a new kind of slag incinerator from Dravo Corporation, and Wella Balsam hair conditioner. When Wella Balsam was introduced, for example, it carried a price of $1.98 ($1.19 was the standard price for cream rinses.) As a result, Alberto-Culver introduced Alberto-Balsam at $1.49, spent ten times as much for advertising, and by 1974 claimed 60% of the hair conditioner market. "We would have liked the profit margins that Wella had with its higher price," indicated Alberto-Balsam's senior brand manager, Randy Trion, "but we just couldn't get enough market penetration at $1.98."[13] Fourth, the skimming approach seems better suited as a short-range strategy than as a long-range strategy. The penetration approach is more concerned with the long-range possibilities.

Penetration

Penetration pricing relies on low prices in order to obtain instant acceptance in the marketplace and, thus, it may result in a stronger long-range position of leadership. Profits may not be very attractive at first because of the low price, but the low price tends to keep out competition, thereby giving the innovating firm a long-run attempt at generating adequate profits.

In some instances, a penetration pricing strategy has resulted in unlocking new markets that companies did not even know existed. For example, when manufacturers began pricing pocket calculators below $100, they moved from the industrial market to the vast consumer market. "Nobody had any inkling that consumers would buy these things," marvels one retailer."[14]

When a low price has been successful in excluding competition, a company may find that it is possible to raise prices and increase profitability.

[12] *Business Week*, op. cit., p. 47.
[13] Ibid.
[14] Ibid., p. 49.

Kodak seemed to be following a penetration pricing strategy when in 1976 it came out with its new instant camera to compete with Polaroid. Kodak's two models were priced at $53.50 and $69.50, compared to $66 and $83 for Polaroid's Pronto cameras. Van Phillips, Kodak's marketing vice-president of consumer products, indicates that this pricing strategy adheres to "our basic marketing strategy of aiming at the mass market only."[15]

When to Use a Penetration or Skimming Price

Figure 15.3 summarizes when to use a penetration or skimming price. A skimming price strategy may be used to advantage when a new product is substantially different from competitive offerings and has features that satisfy important market needs, when price is not important to the market, when the product is not easy to duplicate (for example, when it is protected by a patent), and when management is concerned with a quick return on its new product investment.

A penetration pricing strategy may be used to advantage when a product is not substantially different from other products, when price is very

[15] *Sales and Marketing Management*, Vol. 116 (May 10, 1976), p. 10.

Figure 15.3   When to Use a Penetration or Skimming Strategy for Pricing New Products

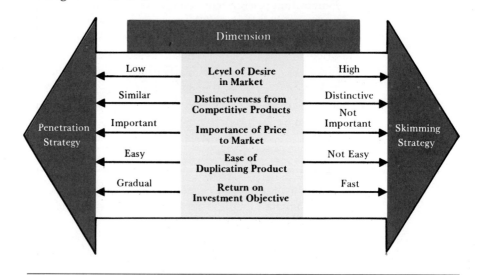

important to the market, when the new offering is easy to duplicate, and when management's objectives stress a more gradual accumulation of profit.

WHEN TO RAISE AND LOWER PRICES

Very seldom does a product's price remain the same forever. Thus, management must be concerned with raising and lowering prices. Although it is not possible to discuss all of the factors that should be considered, some of the most important ones are listed in Figure 15.4 and will be covered below.

Strength of Product

If a product is in a strong competitive position, management can probably raise its price because the market values the product's features and benefits more highly than it does competitive offerings. If a product is in a weak competitive position, management may have to lower its price.

Competition's Pricing Strategies

A firm must always know whether other firms are raising or lowering prices on competitive products. If other firms are lowering their prices, the firm may have no choice but to lower its price, particularly if its product has

Source: Reprinted with permission from the October 18, 1976 issue of *Advertising Age*. Copyright 1976 by Crain Communications Inc.

Making Pricing Decisions

Figure 15.4   Factors to Consider When Lowering or Raising Prices

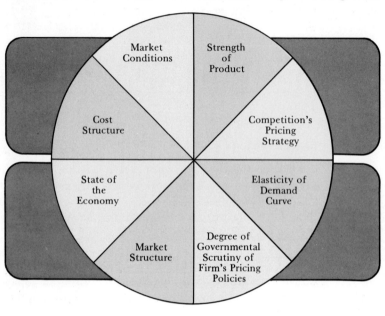

little to offer in comparison with its competitors' products. Price increases by the competition may allow the firm to raise its prices, thus resulting in greater profits.

Elasticity of Demand Curve

The elasticity of the demand curve for a given product should be determined before its price is either raised or lowered. If the demand curve for a specific product is inelastic, a price increase will increase total revenues, but a price decrease will cause total revenues to decline. If the demand curve is elastic a price decrease will increase total revenues, but a price increase will cause total revenues to decline.

Governmental Scrutiny of Firm's Pricing Policies

When a firm is considering either a price decrease or increase, it should also keep in mind the extent to which federal and state governments are interested in the firm's prices. Earlier we indicated that government is becoming more involved in pricing policies, especially the pricing policies of large firms and firms accounting for large shares of their industry's sales.

Market Structure

The product's market structure determines whether its price should be increased or decreased. If a product is essentially in a purely competitive market, the firm is in no position to raise or lower the price. In an oligopolistic market, a significant increase in price will be ignored by the competition and the company's total revenue will decrease. A significant decrease in price will be quickly matched and the company's total revenue will decrease. In a monopolistic market, a significant price increase or decrease may bring about governmental scrutiny. A large price increase may also invite other firms to develop competitive products. In a monopolistically competitive market, a product may benefit from a price decrease if its demand curve is elastic, and it may benefit from a price increase if the demand curve is inelastic.

State of the Economy

Inflation (prices are rising) is probably a strong reason for a firm to increase its prices, particularly if the firm's costs are also increasing and a price increase is needed in order to maintain profit margins. In a deflationary economy (prices are falling) a product's price may have to be decreased because prices for competitive products are also decreasing.

Cost Structure

Companies should investigate the pattern of costs associated with specific products so that they can determine if prices should be increased or decreased. If costs are increasing, for example, because of higher raw material or labor costs, prices will have to be raised if the company wants to protect its profit margin. Falling costs suggest that a company may want to drop its prices and pull sales away from competitive firms.

Market Conditions

Conditions in the market often suggest whether price increases will be possible. If there is an increased demand for the product, price increases are possible. Price decreases are in order if market demand shrinks.

Increases and decreases in the market demand are shown in Figure 15.5. The original demand level is represented by the demand curve D_1. Assume that a price $24 results in 17 units being sold. An increase in demand is indicated by demand curve D_2. The reader will notice that the increase in demand means that the firm can increase its price to $29 and still sell 17 units. A decrease in demand (to D_3) means that there would have to be a decrease in price to $18 in order to still sell 17 units.

Figure 15.5   Increases and Decreases in Market Demand

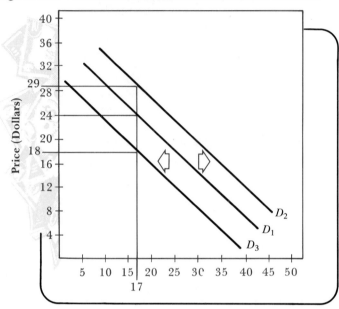

MARKUPS, MARKDOWNS, AND DISCOUNTS

These are three special pricing decisions that deserve attention: Markups and markdowns are especially important to retailers; discounts are considerations for manufacturers and wholesalers.

Markups

Markup is the difference between what a retailer pays for a product and the price at which the product is sold. This difference must cover the expenses the retailer has in selling the product as well as the profit he desires.

Markup can be expressed three different ways: as an absolute figure, as a percentage of cost, and as a percentage of price.

Let's assume that a retailer paid $10 for a dress and put a price of $15 on it. As an *absolute figure*, the markup is $5, that is, the difference in the cost of the item and its price ($15 − $10 = $5). As a *percentage of cost*, the markup is 50% (a $5 markup ÷ $10 cost = 50%). As a *percentage of price*, the markup is 33⅓% (a $5 markup ÷ $15 selling price).

Figure 15.6   Common Markup Percentages on Cost and Price

Markup Percentage on Cost	Equivalent Markup Percentage on Price
10	9
20	16⅔
25	20
30	23
33⅓	25
40	28⁴⁄₇
50	33⅓
60	37½
75	43
100	50

Each and every markup percentage figured on cost will have a unique and corresponding percentage when figured on the price. In the above example the markup figured on cost of 50% is equivalent to a markup on selling price of 33⅓%. Figure 15.6 lists a number of the most commonly used markup percentages. In practice, most retailers figure the markup on the selling price, not on cost.

Markup is an important concept for retailers because it is closely related to profit. The markup has to be sufficiently large to cover the expenses of operating the store and provide an acceptable rate of profit. Most retailers either apply a similar markup percentage for all products received or they use different percentages for related groups of products. Jewelry and furniture, for example, generally carry higher markups than do clothing or food items.

The danger of mechanically applying a markup percentage to merchandise is that the resulting price may not be the best one as far as maximizing profits is concerned. Expressed another way, the resulting price does not recognize demand. Retailers tend to price on the basis of standard markups because it is easy and simplifies record keeping and inventory control.

Markdowns

Very frequently retailers realize that they have put too high a price on some merchandise or they find that seasonal products, like toys, have not sold by the end of the season. In either case, the retailer marks down the items (lowers their prices) and hopes to move them.

A markdown is usually expressed as a percentage of the selling price. All of us at one time or another have been in stores and have seen signs advertising 20% off or 50% off, etc. Most retailers do not have an effective markdown policy. They tend to start off with a low markdown and then increase it even more later if the product does not sell. But this is a mistake because it jeopardizes the selling of the item, and even if the item is sold, it may take a long time to sell it. The best policy is to make the first markdown high enough to move the merchandise quickly.

Discounts

Manufacturers and wholesalers use a variety of discounts to help sell their products. The most important of these are cash, trade, and quantity discounts.

Cash Discounts. A **cash discount** is a reduction in price given to a purchaser for paying his bill within a specified time period. For example, terms of "2/10, net 30" mean that a customer will get a 2% discount if he pays the bill within 10 days and that he has 30 days to pay the full amount if he does not take the cash discount. To show how a cash discount operates, suppose that a retailer buys a case of canned peaches at a price of $7. If his terms are "2/10, net 30," his bill would be $6.86 (a 2% discount from $7) if he paid within 10 days. If he did not take advantage of the 2% cash discount, he would have 30 days to pay the full $7 amount.

Trade Discounts. A **trade discount** is a price reduction offered to various classes of customers. For example, all retailers may be allowed a 20% reduction from the net price. If a set of luggage were priced at $100, a 20% trade discount would result in a price of $80 for any retailer.

Quantity Discounts. In a **quantity discount** the price per unit is determined by the number of units purchased. The more units purchased, the lower the price per unit charged. Below is an example of a quantity discount schedule:

Quantity	Price per Unit
Fewer than 1,000 units	$5.00
1,000 to 1,999 units	$4.75
2,000 to 2,999 units	$4.50
3,000 or more units	$4.25

The granting of discounts is covered in detail by various laws. We will discuss these laws in a later section dealing with the legal aspects of pricing.

SPECIAL ASPECTS OF PRICING

Several aspects of pricing have grown in importance in recent years and, thus, deserve our attention. These include unit pricing, price–quality relationship, odd–even pricing, pricing during inflationary periods, and price lining.

Unit Pricing

Unit pricing has been instituted in a number of supermarkets in order to help confused consumers make price–quantity comparisons. Consumers found it difficult to determine which were the best buys because there were different prices on different-sized packages of a product, or even the same brand. For example, they had to calculate whether a 16-ounce box of soap powder priced at 45¢ was a better buy than a 48-ounce box of the same brand priced at $1.19.

The trick in deciding which of the two sizes is the better buy is to calculate the price per quantity, in this case the price per ounce. The size that has the lowest price per ounce is the better buy. In the above example the 16-ounce box costs 2.81 cents per ounce (45¢ ÷ 16 ounces), compared to 2.48 cents per ounce for the 48-ounce box ($1.19 ÷ 48 ounces). Thus, the 48-ounce size is the better buy.

It might be argued that consumers should be able to make calculations such as these, but many products have odd weights (such as $1\frac{1}{8}$ ounces, 3 pounds 1 ounce, and so on) that make calculations difficult and the average consumer does not want to take the time to make such calculations while in the supermarket.

As a result of pressure from consumer groups, unit pricing is found in many supermarkets today. Under each item on the store shelf is a ticket showing the price per unit. Thus, consumers can tell which can of asparagus costs the least per ounce, which roll of paper towels is the least costly per square inch, and so on.

Although unit pricing does benefit consumers, it does not deal with the quality dimension. For example, one brand of peaches may cost less per ounce than another brand, but this says nothing about how tasty or nutritious the two brands are. Second, the larger sizes are usually the least costly when measured on a per weight basis, but who wants to spend a large percentage of their food budget buying the jumbo size of an item? Or who has the storage space at home for these large sizes, such as a 100-pound bag of sugar? Third, the poor and the ghetto dwellers—for whom unit pricing would be most helpful—are not those making use of unit pricing. It is the middle-class suburbanite who is aware of unit pricing and uses it. (Several studies of unit pricing usage for Kroger, Jewel, and Safeway indicate that only about 30% of all of their customers actually used unit pricing information while shopping.)[16]

Price–Quality Relationship

There has been increasing evidence in recent years of a *positive* price–quality relationship. This suggests that consumers will impute a higher quality to a product if it bears a higher price. More importantly, it means

---

[16] Laurence Lamont, James Rothe, and Charles Slater, "Unit Pricing: A Positive Response to Consumerism," *European Journal of Marketing* (1972), pp. 22–27.

that **more units of a product may be purchased at higher prices,** if quality is important to buyers. This seems to contradict what we said in the previous chapter about more units being sold at lower prices, but what we mean is that there may be exceptions to the general rule. First, let's look at some examples of the price–quality relationship at work.

Examples of Positive Price–Quality Relationship.   Below are a number of instances in which a positive price–quality relationship has either been observed or has been used by astute marketers in their pricing strategies:

1. Patou advertises its Joy perfume as being the most expensive.
2. Chock full O' Nuts promotes its coffee as a costly coffee.[17]
3. A retailer purchased hosiery at 65¢ a pair. He initially priced them at $1.00 a pair. Sales were low. He raised the price to $1.14 and the response was enormous.[18]
4. Many more items of clothing in a large Midwestern department store were sold at a price of $1.77 than at $1.69.[19]
5. The Christmas advertisements in 1967 for Johnnie Walker Black Label scotch indicated that "at $9.40, it's expensive."[20]
6. In the middle 1960's Sears, Roebuck's soft goods were priced low. High-income customers did not purchase soft goods from Sears even though they bought their appliances there. Sears discovered through researching the market that most consumers wanted to spend a higher price for soft goods. Sears raised its prices accordingly.[21]

Products for Which a Positive Price–Quality Relationship Is Likely to Exist.   Whenever it is difficult for consumers to judge a product, they are more likely to judge its quality by its price. Technically complex products (like tape recorders) are difficult to judge.

Products that have high perceived quality differences between themselves and their competing brands are more likely to generate higher sales at higher prices.

Products used as ingredients or parts of other products are likely to have higher sales at higher prices. A chef would not want to purchase a seasoning that would ruin an expensive roast, and a chemical plant manager would not want to quibble over the price of gaskets if he thought that the lower priced gasket could jeopardize his plant's operation.

New products and products that have undergone recent, dramatic modifications are likely to have a positive price–quality relationship because consumers have less experience with them.

[17] Alfred R. Oxenfeldt, "Multi-State Approach to Pricing," *Harvard Business Review* (July–August, 1960), p. 129.

[18] Oswald Knauth, "Considerations in the Setting of Retail Prices," *Journal of Marketing* (July, 1949), p. 8.

[19] Benson P. Shapiro, "The Psychology of Pricing," *Harvard Business Review* (July–August, 1968), p. 16.

[20] Ibid., p. 18.

[21] Wyndham Robertson, "Merchants Fight It Out in a Less Affluent Society," *Fortune*, December, 1974, p. 133.

Products sold by direct mail may have a positive price–quality relationship because consumers cannot examine the products.[22]

In summary, we are essentially saying that products about which consumers feel unsure are likely to have a positive price–quality relationship.

Consumers and the Positive Price–Quality Relationship.   Consumers who are not confident in their ability to choose a product on its merits or who want to avoid risks in purchasing are likely to rely on price as an indicator of quality. People who are prestige conscious are usually not price sensitive.

Odd–Even Pricing

The thinking behind odd–even pricing is that consumers tend to perceive the odd price as not being as high as it really is. For example, odd prices like $1.98, $2.99 and $4.98 are perceived as being closer to $1, $2, and $4, respectively, than they are to $2, $3, and $5. As a result of this downward perception of price, consumers may buy more units of the product, thus increasing total revenues for the firm.

However, if consumers do not view an odd price as being lower and would, therefore, buy as many units at $2 as they would, for example, at $1.97, the company would obtain more revenues by keeping the price at $2.00. Retailers should experiment with their products at various prices in order to see whether odd or even prices should be set.

Pricing During Inflationary Periods

Inflationary periods pose particularly tough pricing problems for marketers. Their costs are rising and their first inclination is to pass them on to their customers in the form of higher prices. This may, however, cause customers to purchase less. Also, the federal government may step in and impose price controls to prevent price increases. This is exactly what happened in the United States in the early 1970's.

What Companies Can Do to Pass on Price Increases to Customers During Inflation.   Some companies during inflationary times require that salespeople secure office approval for any deviation from the list price. If there is no approval, the full price must be paid.

Other firms have *escalator clauses* in their sales contracts involving more than a year. This means that the cost of the products will automatically increase as prices in general go up. The exact price change is usually tied into changes in some specific price *index,* such as the *consumer's price index* or the *wholesale price index.*

Surcharges are also used. This involves increasing base prices by a certain percentage figure. This approach is very popular with companies that use

[22] Shapiro, op. cit., p. 21.

catalogs to sell their merchandise. When the prices quoted in the catalog have to be changed, the company sends its customers a notice that all prices will be raised by a certain percentage. This way the company does not have to issue a new catalog.

Another way of raising prices is to start charging for services that once were free. For example, the customer may have to pay freight charges or he may have to pay for installation and repair service.[23]

In the early 1970's many companies got caught with low prices when the federal government imposed price controls. Unfortunately for them, they could not increase these prices and they also found that controls were not imposed on many of the items they required to do business. As a result, their costs were increasing, but they were not allowed to raise their prices. Thus, their profit margins were shrinking.

After price controls were lifted, companies began taking action to make sure that they would not be caught in the same squeeze should controls be reinstituted. This essentially involved keeping list prices high while giving price cuts. The auto industry's rebate plan is a good example. These were price reductions without reducing the list price. Other firms were more obvious: They simply raised their prices. For example, steel prices rose an average of 45% in 1974 after controls were lifted.

Price Lining

Retailers, especially, practice the pricing strategy of **price lining,** which involves charging different prices for different quality levels of the same product. Thus, the lowest quality carries the lowest price, the next quality level carries the next highest price, and so on. Women's and men's clothing are good examples of products for which price lining is frequently used. Thus, men's trousers might be priced at $8, $13, and $19, reflecting different quality levels measured by type of fabric, how accurate the stated size is, how careful the sewing is, and so on.

Retailers cite a number of reasons for using price lines, for example,

1. The purchasing function is simplified.
2. Price lines facilitate consumer comparisons.
3. Customer uncertainty is reduced.
4. Accounting procedures are simplified.

One of the authors participated in a 1974 study of the price-lining practices and policies involving 179 purchasers of men's ties. The following results were obtained:

1. Eighty percent of the stores had a price-lining policy for men's ties.
2. The most common practice was to have three price lines.

---

[23] Norman H. Fuss, Jr., "How to Raise Prices—Judiciously—To Meet Today's Conditions," *Harvard Business Review* (May–June, 1975), pp. 10–12.

3. The majority of prices were whole dollar prices, such as $3.00, $4.00, or $5.00.
4. The most common percentage price range was 25%.
6. Buyers indicated "market considerations" as the most important factor in determining the number of price lines used and the specific prices used.
7. Very few firms could cite any specific evidence in justifying their price-lining policies.

LEGAL ASPECTS OF PRICING

Some of the most important legislation in marketing deals with the pricing function. In some respects, this legislation is also the most controversial.

The Robinson–Patman Act

The Robinson–Patman Act, which outlaws *price discrimination*, was passed in 1936 as an amendment to the 1914 Clayton Act. Price discrimination means charging some customers a certain price for a product but charging other customers a different price for the same product. In practice, large customers usually pressure their suppliers to grant them lower prices.

Because price concessions take many forms, the Robinson–Patman Act deals with specific types of price discrimination. These include:

1. Granting a lower price to some customers while not offering the same prices to other customers for the same product.
2. Prohibiting quantity discount schedules where the purpose is to grant price concessions to one or a few favored customers. For example, if only one customer purchases more than 10,000 units per year, it would be illegal to have a discount schedule that gives a price reduction for over 10,000 units purchased.
3. Charging illegal brokerage fees. Some suppliers were reducing the price by an amount equivalent to what brokers' commissions would have been had there actually been brokers involved in the transaction. This is no longer allowed; brokerage fees and commissions can only be paid if there is a bona fide broker involved in the transaction.
4. Offering promotional allowances only to a few favored customers. All customers must be offered these allowances on proportional terms. Thus, a manufacturer who normally gives money to support retailer advertising programs would have to offer them proportionally. For example, the manufacturer could stipulate that the size of the advertising allowance would be 5% of the dollar amount of merchandise ordered.

There are several exceptions to the prohibition on price discrimination. Different prices are acceptable if it can be shown that they result from specifically lowered costs of doing business with the firm receiving the lower price. Lower prices may also be justified if they result from an effort to meet the lower prices of competition. Neither of these exceptions has been easy to prove, however.

Fair Trade Laws

In the 1920's and 1930's many small retailers were forced out of business because large retailers sold nationally known branded merchandise below cost in order to attract customers to their stores. The smaller stores could not afford price wars. In addition, many manufacturers did not like seeing their products sold at low prices; they believed that this practice detracted from the quality image they had tried to build.

Because of this pressure, 44 states eventually passed laws forbidding retailers from selling merchandise below the manufacturer's stipulated price. The Miller–Tydings Act of 1937 and the McGuire Act of 1952 are federal laws giving states the legal power to enforce their **fair trade** laws.

In recent years nine states have repealed these laws. And in 1975 legislation was introduced to repeal the Miller–Tydings Act and the McGuire Act. The Consumer Goods Pricing Act outlaws fair trade laws. It is estimated that repeal of existing fair trade laws would allow prices to fall by $2.1 billion annually.[24]

Price Fixing

Price fixing involves competitive firms in an industry getting together and deciding on a price at which they will sell their competitive products. The purpose is to avoid damaging price-cutting wars that hurt sales volume and profits. If prices can be set high enough, sales volume and profits will be protected.

In 1974 the federal government began cracking down on price fixers. (This was to be expected given the inflation experienced in the early 1970's; price fixing keeps prices higher than they would be in a competitive market.) In December of 1974 President Ford signed a new anti-trust bill that made price fixing a felony instead of a misdemeanor. Convicted persons can go to jail for as long as three years and pay a maximum fine of $100,000. Convicted companies may be required to pay a fine as high as $1 million.

A number of large, well-known companies have recently pleaded "no contest" and, thus, decided not to fight federal price-fixing charges. These companies include DuPont, Armco Steel, International Paper, American Cyanamid, Pepsi Cola, Pet, and Sunshine Biscuit. In 1974 the Great Atlantic and Pacific Tea Company (A&P) was confronted with a $32.7 million private suit by six cattlemen alleging that A&P conspired with other retailers to fix prices paid for wholesale beef.

[24] "Farewell to Fair Trade," *Fortune*, March, 1975, p. 94.

In the past, juries were reluctant to convict on price-fixing charges unless specific written documents could be produced verifying the price-fixing schemes. Recently, however, they have proved to be less tolerant of other, more subtle means of price fixing. Because of this, a company should be careful not to:

1. Coordinate discounts, credit terms, or conditions of sale with competitors.
2. Discuss prices, markups, and costs at trade association meetings.
3. Arrange with competitors to issue new price lists on the same date.
4. Arrange with competitors to rotate low bids on contracts.
5. Agree with competitors to uniformly restrict production to keep prices up.[25]

RECOMMENDATIONS FOR EFFECTIVE PRICING DECISIONS

Figure 15.7 offers a number of recommendations that we believe are helpful in making pricing decisions. Each recommendation will be discussed below.

Prices Must Reflect Costs, Competitive Prices, and Demand

Three factors that must be part of any effort to establish prices are costs, competitive prices, and demand. The costs of a product provide a base figure and a firm should never price below this base figure because there would be no net profit. Thus, the pricer must know what the costs are for each product.

Competitive prices for similar products tend to act as an upper limit on prices. Unless a product is definitely superior to competitive products, it is usually not a good strategy to exceed the prices of the competition.

Demand in the marketplace must also be estimated. This essentially means that a firm must have some idea of how many units of a product it can expect to sell at various prices. Using these with cost data, the firm can estimate where the profit maximizing price is likely to be.

Determine the Elasticity of a Product's Demand Curve

A company must determine how elastic the various products' demand curves are. Knowing the elasticity of the demand curve makes it easier to determine if prices should be increased or decreased. As we already know, raising the price when the demand curve is inelastic results in increasing total revenue and decreasing the price when the demand curve is elastic also results in increasing total revenue.

[25] "Price-Fixing: Crackdown Under Way," *Business Week*, June 2, 1975, pp. 42–48.

Figure 15.7 Recommendations for Effective Pricing Decisions

1. Establish prices after determining costs, competitive prices, and demand.
2. Determine the elasticity of a product's demand curve.
3. Decide which pricing objectives are to be achieved.
4. Anticipate potential pricing problems.
5. Constantly monitor the company's pricing program.
6. Realize that product, place, and promotion decisions also affect pricing decisions.
7. Determine the extent to which products have achieved distinctiveness in the marketplace.
8. Attempt to determine which market model is the most appropriate for specific products.
9. Follow a step-by-step procedure for establishing prices.
10. Anticipate possible governmental action.

Decide Which Pricing Objectives Are to Be Achieved

Earlier in this chapter we discussed various pricing objectives. When establishing prices for products (and varying them over time), the pricing decision maker must know which pricing objectives he hopes to achieve. These and other objectives to a large extent determine whether a high or low price will be achieved. For example, if he were trying to preclude competition, he would use a low price. If he wants to establish a quality image, a high price would be more appropriate. Other objectives, such as a desired return on investment, would help to pinpoint the exact price to charge.

Anticipate Potential Pricing Problems

A company's prices and pricing strategies should be analyzed in terms of the problems they cause. A number of important potential problems are listed in Figure 15.8.[26] A company should be aware of these problems and take steps to eliminate them. Failure to do so may result in basic pricing objectives not being achieved.

In order to find out if any of these problems are arising, a company should constantly monitor its pricing program.

[26] Alfred R. Oxenfeldt, "A Decision-Making Structure for Price Decisions," *Journal of Marketing* (January, 1973), p. 51.

Figure 15.8   Potential Pricing Problems

1. Are prices too high in relation to the competition's prices for similar products?
2. Are a company's prices regarded as taking advantage of buyers?
3. Are price changes too frequent?
4. Are too many price choices causing customer confusion?
5. Do the firm's prices seem higher than they really are?
6. Are the firm's prices so low that they attract disloyal customers?

Constantly Monitor the Company's Pricing Program

The following data are required in monitoring a company's pricing program and determining its effectiveness.

1. Record of prices for each product carried.
2. Sales dollars secured by each product.
3. Prices for competitive products.
4. Customers receiving price reductions.
5. Market shares for products in individual markets.
6. Price complaints from customers and salespeople.
7. Customer attitudes toward the company and its pricing program.
8. Number of customers lost and attracted because of the company's pricing program.[27]

Realize that Product, Place, and Promotion Decisions Affect Pricing Decisions

The pricing decision maker should realize that in addition to price, product, place, and promotion decisions also affect demand. Thus, the individual establishing and changing prices should know what the marketing effort is for various products. Without this information, he cannot establish prices that will effectively secure the firm's pricing objectives. As an example, let's assume that it has been decided to spend $50,000 more for advertising a product. With this knowledge, the decision maker knows that because more units of a product will now be sold, he can raise the price and perhaps greatly increase total profits. If the decision maker were not aware of the increased advertising, he might not have even considered a price increase.

[27] This list is based on Alfred R. Oxenfeldt, ibid., p. 51.

Determine the Extent to Which Products Have Achieved Distinctiveness in the Marketplace

Products that have achieved distinctiveness in the marketplace allow the firm some flexibility in pricing. Products that are differentiated from competitive products and that satisfy customer needs and desires may carry higher prices. Products that are only copies of existing products are not distinctive and have little to offer. Therefore, they have to carry lower prices.

Attempt to Determine Which Market Model Is the Most Appropriate for Specific Products

We know from previous material that the kind of market situation—pure competition, monopolistic competition, oligopoly, and monopoly—that exists for a product has a great deal of impact on pricing decisions. These markets help determine whether a high or low price can be charged or if prices should be raised or lowered. Although it is very difficult to determine the market with a great deal of precision, a general idea can be obtained.

Follow a Step-by-Step Procedure for Establishing Initial Prices

Companies should set initial prices by following a specific procedure. We suggest the following (see Figure 15.9):

1. Decide on a basic pricing objective. This usually suggests either a high or a low price. For example, an objective to keep out competition necessitates a low price. An objective of securing a fast return on a product's investment usually means a relatively high price.
2. Estimate the total cost per unit for the product. The product should not be priced below this "floor."
3. Find out what the competition's prices are for similar products. These prices indicate, to some extent, an upper limit on the price that can be established.
4. Determine the extent to which the product is distinctive from competitive products. The more distinctive the product, the higher the price that can be charged, the less distinctive, the lower the price possible.
5. Find out how much marketing support will be provided the product in the form of advertising budgets, speed of delivery, effort to be exerted by the sales force, and so on. The greater this level of effort, the higher the price that can be justified. The lower the level of support, the lower the price.
6. Estimating demand involves a decision as to how many units are likely to be sold at various prices. Competitor prices, distinctiveness of the product, and level of marketing effort affect demand.

Figure 15.9   Step-by-Step Procedure for Establishing Initial Prices

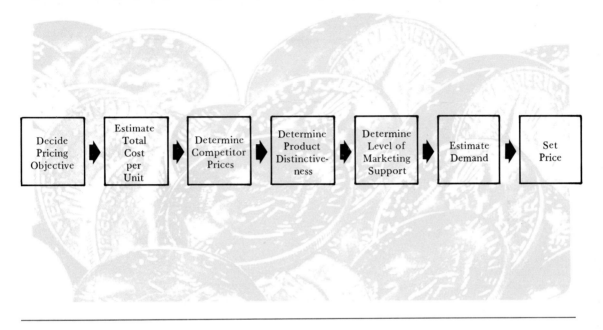

If these six steps are followed, the price setter will arrive at a price for a product that is most likely to achieve the basic pricing objective.

Anticipate Possible Government Action

Potential government reaction to the price must, as far as possible, be determined. In many cases, the potential response may call for either a raising or a lowering of prices.

SUMMARY

The four major aspects that should be considered when a company establishes its pricing objectives are costs, demand, competition, and government interest and attention. These major pricing objectives include profit maximization, return on investment, securing market share, preventing market entry by competitive firms, precluding unfavorable government action, minimizing the effects of government action, maintaining good relationships with channels of distribution, and remaining in business.

Of the major approaches to establishing prices, cost-oriented pricing is popular because it is the easiest to use. Its major weakness is that it does not recognize demand.

Making Pricing Decisions

Profit maximization pricing results in a price that maximizes profit, but the problem here is securing the required revenue and cost data.

Break-even pricing provides some idea of the lowest possible price required to secure a desired profit, but it assumes the same price per unit no matter how many units are sold. We would expect that as more units are sold, a lower price would be charged.

Marginal pricing can be an effective approach to pricing because it may result in higher total profits for all products.

New products can carry a high price (skimming) or a low price (penetration). A skimming approach is designed to generate profits quickly; a penetration approach may help achieve long-run profits and may keep out competition.

When a company is deciding whether or not to raise the price of a product, it must realize that this is more likely to be an effective strategy if the product is competitively strong, competition is not dropping the price on competitive products, the demand curve is inelastic, government will likely not oppose a price increase, the product is a monopoly, and demand is increasing.

Markup is the difference between the cost and the selling price. Markup covers expenses and profit and can be expressed either in absolute terms or as percentages of cost or price.

Unit pricing is a relatively recent phenomenon that helps consumers make better purchase decisions because it indicates the cost per unit of items sold.

For some products, there may be a positive price–quality relationship. This means that more units may be sold at higher prices, thus increasing a firm's total revenue.

In order to make more effective pricing decisions, a number of recommendations should be followed, for example, prices must recognize costs, competitor prices, and demand; basic pricing objectives should be decided; potential pricing problems should be anticipated; a system for monitoring the company's pricing program should be instituted; and a step-by-step procedure for establishing initial prices should be developed.

QUESTIONS

1. Which of the major pricing objectives do you feel are the most important? What conditions should be considered when a company is establishing its pricing objectives?
2. What is the major pricing advantage that results when a product has obtained a distinctiveness from competitive products?

3. Under what conditions might a company be able to expect a positive price–quality relationship for a product?
4. Why are demand, costs, and competitive prices so important when setting an initial price for a product?
5. In establishing initial prices for a product, why do we have to know how much marketing effort is being provided the product?
6. Do you agree with the following statement, Pricing decisions should be made after product, place, and promotion decisions have been made? Why do you agree or disagree?
7. Can you think of any other kinds of companies besides airlines that might benefit from practicing marginal pricing?
8. Would you be in favor of a federal law that would require all grocery stores in the United States to practice unit pricing?

GLOSSARY

Break-Even Pricing: solving the break-even equation to find the price that results in a desired profit

Cash Discount: a reduction in price granted to a firm for making payment within a specified time period

Cost-Oriented Pricing: a pricing approach that adds a percentage to its direct cost per unit to arrive at a price that covers its overhead costs and provides a profit

Demand-Oriented Pricing: setting a price where the marginal revenue and the marginal cost are equal in order to maximize net profits

Fair Trade: legislation that prohibits retailers from selling products below a price stipulated by manufacturers

Marginal Pricing: establishing a price so that the revenue obtained exceeds the variable costs incurred so that a contribution to fixed costs results

Markdown: a reduction in price offered by retailers on a product in an effort to sell it

Markup: the difference between the cost of a product and the price at which it is sold; it can be expressed in absolute terms or as a percentage of its cost or its selling price

Penetration Pricing: placing a low price on a new product so that it will secure quick acceptance and preclude competition

Price Fixing: companies in an industry illegally conspiring to set prices on competitive products

Price Lining: a common practice of retailers that involves charging different prices for different quality levels of a product

Quantity Discount: a reduction in price granted to a purchaser according to the number of units purchased

Robinson–Patman Act: legislation designed to prohibit companies from unfairly charging different prices to firms purchasing their products

Skimming Pricing: placing a high price on a new product so that it can generate high initial profits

Trade Discount: a reduction in price granted to various classes of customers

Unit Pricing: pricing on a per unit basis (such as per ounce or per square inch) in order to help shoppers make better buying decisions; under each item on the store shelf is a ticket showing the price per unit

CASES

Case 1: The Traymore Restaurant

The Traymore Restaurant, located downtown in a city of 500,000 inhabitants, has been approached by a local businessmen's club about providing the club lunch for its once-a-month meeting. The restaurant manager has to decide what price to charge the club members for the lunch. About 30 business executives are expected to attend each meeting. During the last year the club held its meetings at a competitive restaurant.

The restaurant customarily offers two specials of the day on the luncheon menu. These specials change daily and consist of either a meat or a fish dish and two vegetables. A tossed salad may be substituted for one of the vegetables. The price for each special is $2 and does not include an appetizer, beverage, or dessert. The specials are generally regarded by the restaurant's regular customers as being a good bargain.

The regular luncheon menu features a variety of soups, sandwiches, club sandwiches, and platters. Prices are as high as $4.95 for the platters. About 50% of the regular customers select the daily specials and 50% select from the regular menu.

The business executives will be able to select from four entrees for each meeting: roast turkey, hamburger steak, fried chicken, and roast ham. All members will be served the same meal, which will include the meat, a potato, a vegetable, tossed salad or appetizer, roll and butter, beverage (coffee or iced tea) and dessert.

1. What factors should the restaurant manager consider before deciding on a price to charge the business executives?
2. What objective(s) should the restaurant's pricing policy be designed to achieve?
3. What price should be charged? Would you vary this price according to the entree chosen?

Case 2: Juanita's Gift Shop

Juanita Rodriguez recently came to the United States from Mexico, where she had owned and operated a gift shop in Mexico City. From the sale of this shop, she plans to open a similar shop in San Antonio, Texas. Merchandise lines will include pottery, leather belts and handbags, silver jewelry, shirts and hats, and linens. Merchandise will be purchased from Mexico. Sources of supply have been contacted, and a line of credit has been established.

One of her major decisions is the need to establish a pricing policy. In Mexico, her clientele was used to bargaining over prices. Mexican and American tourists, her two major customer classes, appeared to enjoy this shopping give-and-take. From experience, Ms. Rodriguez found that the negotiated price was usually about 75% of her original asking price. This agreed upon price generally provided her with a markup of 30% to 40% over cost of the merchandise, which was sufficient to cover expenses and provide an acceptable profit.

1. Do you believe Ms. Rodriguez should employ a bargaining approach to pricing?
2. What are the risks of this type of pricing policy?
3. Will she be able to assume that the same markup percentage will cover expenses?

PART 4

Implementing and Evaluating Marketing Mix Decisions

Organizing the Marketing Department

OBJECTIVES

After you finish this chapter, you should be able to answer the following questions:

1. What are the most important changes to which the marketing organization must adjust?
2. How can it be determined that the marketing organization expedites communication?
3. What major factors should determine the type of marketing organization to be used?
4. When is the product manager organizational alternative most appropriate?
5. What was the major finding of the study on product managers?
6. What responsibilities does the consumer affairs department usually have?
7. What is centralization? What is the major advantage of centralization?
8. What appears to be the major consideration in motivating personnel?
9. What is intraorganizational conflict? What can be done to reduce it?
10. What is management by objectives (MBO)?

KEY TERMS	*Centralization Customer Organization Decentralization*
	Departmentalization Functional Organization Intraorganizational
	Conflict Management by Objectives Motivation Product
	Organization Span of Control Specialization System 4

INTRODUCTION   In Chapter 1 we learned that the organization of the marketing department is one of the major aspects of the decision-making model. The type of organization that exists and the people in the various positions are critical to carrying out the action plans developed to achieve tactical and strategic objectives. This chapter will present a number of concepts designed to make the marketing organization more effective.

CHARACTERISTICS OF AN EFFECTIVE MARKETING ORGANIZATION

Flexibility

A good marketing organization is flexible. By this we mean that it readily adapts to change. Since change is the constant companion of marketing, the company's objectives will be jeopardized if it cannot respond quickly and correctly to change.

What kinds of changes are there? First, and probably most important, there are changes in the market that the organization must know and to which it must respond. Since consumer needs and desires are constantly changing, the marketing department must be aware of what is happening or suffer the consequences. Companies, for example, that failed to recognize the dramatic consumer acceptance of double knit clothing did not prosper as well as those that did. Second, there are changes in the environment that should be noted and adjusted to. For example, competition brings out new products that threaten the very existence of already established products. Or the government indicates that it will begin investigating various aspects of an industry's marketing operations, such as pricing policies. Or a new technology revolutionizes an industry. An example of this is the recent development of combination glass and plastic bottles in the soft drink industry. These bottles lower the cost of packaging, reduce breakage, and allow bottling of larger quantities (64 ounces).

Achieving Marketing Department Objectives

Whether or not a marketing department's basic objectives are achieved is another test of the marketing organization's effectiveness. At the end of a specific time, usually a year, the department should compare its results with its stated objectives. Thus, it will see if its desired return on investment for various products has been achieved or if the projected market share was reached. Did its salespeople make the number of calls they were supposed to make? Did the company reduce late deliveries to customers to the extent that it wanted?

Factors other than the marketing organization can, of course, cause objectives to be achieved or not be achieved, but this is certainly one of the areas that has a great impact.

Achieving Coordination

The marketing department must coordinate the activities of its various subunits in such areas as new product development. When new products are being developed, marketing research, advertising, and physical distribution may be involved in the process. The marketing organization must be such that each area knows which part of the new product development process it is responsible for and when each aspect is to be completed.

Frequently, the marketing department effort must be coordinated with other departments, such as the production, finance, and personnel departments. A good example is again the new product development process. The marketing organization can facilitate this much needed coordination.

Meeting Time Deadlines

Achieving time deadlines is very crucial to the success of the marketing operation. New products must be gotten to the market as quickly as possible. Test markets must be started on time. Advertising copy must be ready to go to the magazine by a specific date.

An effective marketing organization can facilitate achieving these and other time deadlines.

Expediting Communication

A good marketing organization expedites communication. That is, it gets information quickly to individuals who have to act upon the information. It also means that the communication is accurate.

FACTORS DETERMINING THE NATURE OF THE MARKETING ORGANIZATION

Size of Firm

The larger the company, the more sophisticated its marketing organization, for example:

1. A larger firm has a larger marketing department.
2. A larger firm has more marketing specialists, such as divisional sales managers, marketing research analysts, product managers, advertising

managers, and so on. A smaller firm sometimes has only one person in charge of all its marketing activities.

3. A larger firm has more specialized departments. For example, it may have a sales department, an advertising department, a marketing research department, and a physical distribution department.

4. A larger firm has more layers between the bottom people in the marketing organization and the top layer. For example, between the vice-president of marketing and the individual salespeople are branch sales managers, territorial sales managers, regional sales managers, and the chief sales manager.

5. A larger firm tends to have larger **spans of control.** Span of control refers to the number of subordinates that a superior has under his control. Because larger firms employ more marketing personnel than smaller companies do, there may be a tendency to assign more subordinates to superiors.

The Market

The market is a major factor that must be considered when the marketing organization is established or modified.

The geographical location of the market determines where the salespeople's territories are established. More salespeople tend to be placed where there are heavy concentrations of buyers.

If the market is made up of several large, well-defined market segments, a company may want to have a director of marketing for each of these areas. For example, Campbell Chain has directors of sales for consumer and industrial markets. The American Meter Division of Singer has directors of sales to utilities and industrial firms.

Larger markets (measured by sales volume) generally result in larger marketing organizations. The organizations also become more complex because additional specialists and more departments have to be added.

Type of Firm

The type of firm often determines to a large degree the form of the marketing organization. Raw material industries, such as agriculture and lumbering, tend to emphasize the functions of storage and transportation and minimize such areas as advertising and marketing research. Banks, however, stress advertising and marketing research and are not too involved with transportation and storage.

Products Carried

The type of product has a direct bearing on the form of the marketing organization. Industrial products, for example, tend to be sold primarily through salespeople, and there is not too much emphasis on advertising. The sales department for industrial products tends to be large and elaborate but the advertising department, if any, is small. The advertising department for branded consumer products, however, is usually very large and sophisticated because advertising is a major means of promoting these products.

THREE BASIC ORGANIZATIONAL APPROACHES

The three basic approaches to organizing the marketing department are the product, customer, and functional approaches. Seldom do companies use only one approach. Most companies, especially larger ones, generally use blends of all three approaches.

Product Organization

A number of large, well-known companies extensively use the **product organization** approach. These include Procter & Gamble, General Foods, Lever Brothers, Pillsbury, General Mills, Allied Chemical, Quaker Oats, and Nabisco.

In product organization, individuals are given responsibility for specific products or for groups of products. If they are responsible for individual brands, they are usually called *brand managers*. If they are responsible for a number of products, they are generally called *product managers*.

Product organization is considered to be most appropriate when a company has a number of different products to be sold in one or just a few markets.

Advantages.   The major advantage of the product organization is that attention is given to specific products, especially the important products that account for large percentages of a company's sales. Also, individuals can specialize in marketing one or several products. This cannot be done as easily when numerous products are involved.

Disadvantages.   The product organization tends to be costly because one individual is in charge of one or several products instead of a few people being responsible for a large number of products. Another disadvantage is that there is a tendency for product or brand managers to become too involved with their own products and ignore what is happening in the market.

Basic Kinds of Product Managers.   There are two basic kinds of product or brand managers. First, there are those who are responsible for obtaining profits for their products. Their success or failure is determined by how well their products achieve specified profit targets. Second, there are those who are *not* responsible for obtaining profits. Instead, their job is to effectively coordinate the marketing program for their products, make available important information about these offerings and their markets, and ensure that deadlines are achieved.

Profiling Product Managers and Their Responsibilities. One of the authors participated in a study of 198 product managers from leading companies in the United States. Some of the findings are summarized in Figure 16.1. We believe that the most important finding is the product manager's lack of contact with the market. Less than one-half of the 198 product managers believed that they had much contact with the market. This probably means that their products are not as successful as they would be if the managers knew more about what is occurring in the market.

Figure 16.2 indicates the major decision areas for which these product managers were responsible. They believe they have much involvement with such decisions as establishing goals for their products, the means whereby these goals are achieved, and preparing sales forecasts. The least involvement existed for distribution policies.

Customer Organization

If a firm believes in the marketing concept, then **customer organization** (or market basis) is the logical approach for it to use. Customer needs and wants can be determined and products can be developed to satisfy these needs and wants.

The customer organization appears to be most appropriate when a firm has one or only a few product lines that are sold in a number of different

Figure 16.1   Profiles of 198 Product Managers and Their Responsibilities

1. Product managers tended to be young. Almost three-fourths were under 40 years of age.
2. Their average annual salary was about $26,000.
3. 97% held either a Bachelor's degree (62%) or a Master's degree (35%).
4. 60% of the product managers were responsible for product profits. 40% acted as coordinators and providers of information.
5. 49% were responsible for consumer products, 37% were in charge of industrial products, and 14% were responsible for both kinds.
6. Product managers with profit responsibilities revealed more contact with such areas as production, marketing research, and sales than did those who served as coordinators and information sources.
7. A low level of contact with the market was indicated by these product managers. Only 48% stated that they had much contact with the market.

Source: Richard T. Hise and J. Patrick Kelly, "Product Management in the Mid-1970's," unpublished paper, Virginia Commonwealth University, 1976.

Figure 16.2 Percentage of 198 Product Managers Indicating Much Involvement with Various Product Decisions

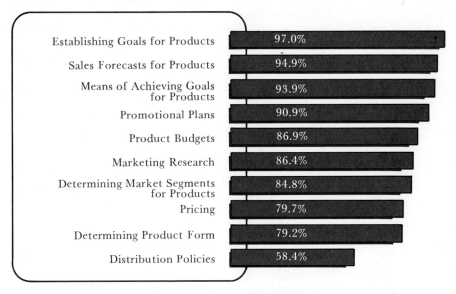

Establishing Goals for Products	97.0%
Sales Forecasts for Products	94.9%
Means of Achieving Goals for Products	93.9%
Promotional Plans	90.9%
Product Budgets	86.9%
Marketing Research	86.4%
Determining Market Segments for Products	84.8%
Pricing	79.7%
Determining Product Form	79.2%
Distribution Policies	58.4%

Source: Richard T. Hise and J. Patrick Kelly, "Product Management in the Mid-1970's," unpublished paper, Virginia Commonwealth University, 1976.

markets. In a customer organization, someone is placed in charge of marketing to these different markets.

What are the markets that might be involved? Some banks, for example, have directors of marketing for commercial customers and retail lines. Railroads are often organized so that specific shipper needs are recognized, including ore, chemical, and fertilizer shippers. IBM has identified hospitals and supermarkets as key customers. Food processors may be organized to cover such crucial market segments as retail stores, schools, hospitals, and restaurants.

Functional Organization

Perhaps the most common form of marketing department organization is the **functional organization.** The department is organized according to the type of functions or jobs that need to be performed.

Whatever the kind of firm, specific marketing decisions must be made in order to achieve basic objectives. These decisions can usually be clustered into specific functions, such as marketing research, advertising, personal

Organizing the Marketing Department

selling, and physical distribution. If these functions are important enough, someone is generally placed in charge of the functional area and reports to the chief marketing executive. If marketing is important enough to the firm, the top marketing individual is usually given the title of vice-president.

Figure 16.3 is an example of a fairly typical functional organization. The four major functional areas of advertising, physical distribution, sales, and marketing research are located in separate departments on the organization chart. Specific individuals head up these departments and report directly to the vice-president of marketing. He and the vice-president of manufacturing and finance report directly to the company's president.

There is not very much detail in this organization chart, but the reader should understand that each of the four departments would have various subunits. For example, the sales department might have a number of regional sales managers. Individuals responsible for advertising testing and copy writing would be found in the advertising department.

We mentioned earlier that most marketing departments are combinations of the three basic organizational approaches. In Figure 16.3 the functional approach is presented, but many firms add to this basic approach product managers who are responsible for various products. It would also

Figure 16.3   Organizing on a Functional Basis

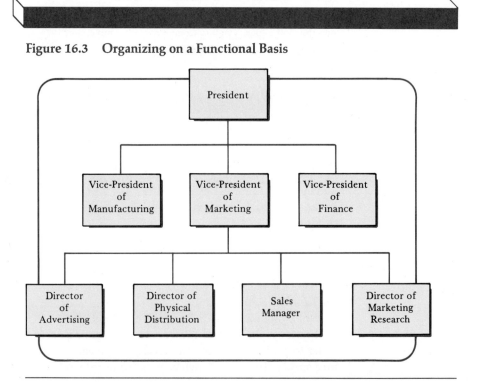

Implementing and Evaluating Marketing Mix Decisions

be possible to include the people who head up the marketing effort directed to particular groups of customers.

IMPLICATIONS OF THE MARKETING CONCEPT FOR MARKETING ORGANIZATION

The specific implications of the marketing concept for the marketing organization are listed in Figure 16.4. The results of a survey of 273 large manufacturing firms indicate the extent to which these organizational recommendations have been adopted.[1]

Having a Need for a Separate Marketing Research Department

If the company adopts the marketing concept, the company must research the market in order to determine what their customer needs and desires are and what products will satisfy these needs and desires. In order to accomplish these objectives, the company should have a marketing research department. In the study of manufacturing firms, about three-fourths of the firms had marketing research departments staffed by one or more full-time employees.

Involving the Marketing Department in New Product Development

The needs and desires of customers should be recognized in new products. Since the marketing department, through its marketing research effort, is aware of customer needs and desires, it should be involved in the new

[1] Richard T. Hise, "Have Manufacturing Firms Adopted the Marketing Concept?" *Journal of Marketing* (July, 1965), pp. 9–12.

Figure 16.4   The Marketing Concept and the Marketing Organization

1. Having a need for a separate marketing research department.
2. Involving the marketing department in new product development.
3. Giving the chief marketing executive equal status with other top-level executives.
4. Giving the chief marketing executive vice-presidential status.
5. Having the chief marketing executive directly responsible to the president of the company.
6. Having the marketing department responsible for marketing functions.

product development process. The survey of 273 manufacturing firms indicated that 77% of the marketing departments had partial responsibility for new product development, 15% had full responsibility, and 8% had no responsibility for developing new products.

Giving the Chief Marketing Executive Equal Status with Other Top-Level Executives

If the firm adopts the marketing concept, the top marketing executive should be given status equal to that provided the company's other top executives. In a manufacturing firm, for example, he should be at the same level as the top man in manufacturing. In 75% of the manufacturing firms surveyed the chief marketing man was placed at the same level in the organization as the head manufacturing executive.

Giving the Chief Marketing Executive Vice-Presidential Status

The top marketing man should be given vice-presidential status if the company truly has adopted the marketing concept. Of the companies participating in the survey, 69% gave vice-presidential status to the chief marketing executive; 43% called him "vice-president–marketing" and 26% called him "vice-president—sales."

Having the Chief Marketing Executive Directly Responsible to the President of the Company

The top marketing executive should report directly to the firm's president because it provides the marketing department with the influence it requires if the marketing concept is to be successful in the company. In the study of 273 manufacturing firms, 71% of the companies indicated that their chief marketing executive reported directly to the president.

Having the Marketing Department Responsible for Marketing Functions

If the marketing concept is to be a success, the marketing department should be responsible for various marketing functions, such as physical distribution, advertising, packaging, and pricing. The study of manufacturing firms found, however, that this was not always the case. For example:

1. Only 18 percent of the companies had marketing responsible for physical distribution.
2. Seventy-two percent of the companies had marketing responsible for advertising.
3. Fifty-three percent of the marketing departments had partial control over packaging, 28% had full control, and 19% had no involvement.
4. Forty-two percent of the marketing departments had full control over pricing, 49% had partial responsibility, and 9% had no involvement.

IMPLICATIONS OF SOCIETAL CHANGES FOR THE MARKETING ORGANIZATION

In Chapter 4 we discussed some of the more important trends in the environment. We pointed out some of the cultural changes that the marketing department must recognize. Among these was consumer insistence that they get a "fair shake." Consumers want products that work, companies that honor their guarantees, products that do not pollute the air and rivers, and companies that are as much interested in society as they are in generating profits.

The increasing clamor by consumers for a fair shake has been encouraged by such consumer advocates as Ralph Nader. These people have been successful in getting a number of laws passed that are designed to protect and benefit consumers. They have also convinced companies to change their practices that are detrimental to customers as well as to initiate such practices as unit pricing that will benefit customers.

These factors have important implications for the organization of the marketing department and will be discussed next.

Consumer Affairs Department

Most companies want to react positively to consumers and many of them have established consumer affairs departments, for example, Giant Foods, General Motors, Motorola, Mobil Oil, Pan American World Airways, and J. C. Penney. Although most of these departments initially were developed with the major purpose of expediting the handling of customer complaints, many now have taken on other responsibilities. J. C. Penney, for example, stresses consumer education. Penney's program explains guarantees to consumers and gives tips on how to shop for clothing. Other examples of educational programs include Gillette's booklets on grooming practice and styling trends, Armstrong Cork's suggestions on home remodeling and redecoration, and Hunt-Wesson's menu-planning service. Stop and Shop has established a consumer board that meets approximately once every six weeks to discuss such subjects as shopping aids and grocery items that should be stocked. The consumer affairs manager at Corning Glass Works reviews the company's product use-and-care instructions to see if they make sense to consumers.[2]

Organizationally, most consumer affairs departments have separate organizational status, that is, they are not part of another department, including marketing. They generally report directly to top management. Handling customer complaints appears to be their major function.[3]

Figure 16.5 contains data on the individuals who head up consumer

---

[2] E. Patrick McGuire, *The Consumer Affairs Department: Organization and Functions* (New York: The Conference Board, Inc., 1973).
[3] Ibid.

Figure 16.5   Characteristics of Heads of 156 Consumer Affairs Departments

1. Three-fourths of the consumer affairs directors have held their current positions fewer than five years.
2. Forty percent of all consumer affairs directors are female.
3. About one-half of the consumer affairs directors have been with their companies for ten years.
4. One-third of the consumer affairs directors came from the marketing area. One-fourth came from customer service. One-sixth came from public relations.
5. One-third of the directors had a business background in college. About one-fifth had liberal arts training. The most prevalent background for women was home economics (one-third).
6. Two-thirds of the companies gave the top consumer affairs individual the title of director or manager. One-sixth accorded the top person vice-presidential status.
7. Female directors tended to be younger than male directors. Thirty-seven percent of female directors were less than 40 years of age, compared to 20% for males.
8. Two-thirds of all consumer affairs directors made less than $30,000 per year. Women were not paid as well as men.

affairs departments. The data are based on a survey of 156 companies.[4] In Figure 16.6, we can get an idea of the kinds of decisions with which such individuals are involved.

More Time Needed in the Legal/Political Area

Because of the passage of more and more laws affecting marketing and the government's greater interest in companies' marketing operations at all levels, firms are finding that their marketing departments must spend more time with legal and political matters. Below are examples of what we mean:

1. Truth-in-lending law: companies must explain credit terms more fully to customers.
2. Truth-in-packaging law: Companies must provide more information about the contents of packages.
3. In the mid-1970's the federal government cracked down on price fixing.

[4] E. Patrick McGuire, *The Consumer Affairs Director* (New York: The Conference Board, Inc., 1973).

Implementing and Evaluating Marketing Mix Decisions

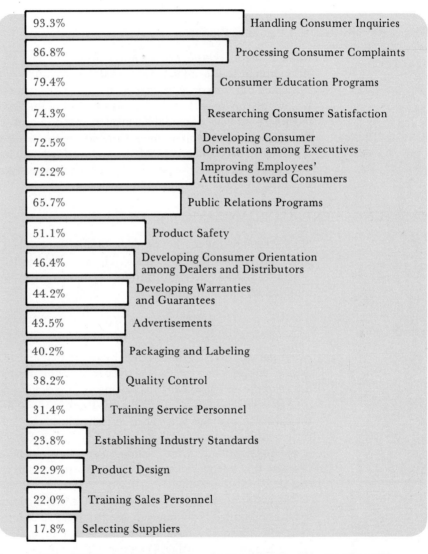

Figure 16.6   Percentage of 153 Chief Consumer Affairs Officers Who Indicated Much Involvement with Various Types of Decisions

93.3%	Handling Consumer Inquiries
86.8%	Processing Consumer Complaints
79.4%	Consumer Education Programs
74.3%	Researching Consumer Satisfaction
72.5%	Developing Consumer Orientation among Executives
72.2%	Improving Employees' Attitudes toward Consumers
65.7%	Public Relations Programs
51.1%	Product Safety
46.4%	Developing Consumer Orientation among Dealers and Distributors
44.2%	Developing Warranties and Guarantees
43.5%	Advertisements
40.2%	Packaging and Labeling
38.2%	Quality Control
31.4%	Training Service Personnel
23.8%	Establishing Industry Standards
22.9%	Product Design
22.0%	Training Sales Personnel
17.8%	Selecting Suppliers

Source: Richard T. Hise, Peter L. Gillett, and J. Patrick Kelly, "The Corporate Consumer Affairs Effort: A Current Status Report," *MSU Business Topics*, Summer 1978.

4. Companies were banned from using such items as DDT, cyclamates, hexachlorophene, and kepone.
5. Advertising of cigarettes on television was banned in the early 1970's.

Because of these and other legal and political developments, marketing departments must spend more time in this area. In the future there will probably be more people who have legal backgrounds in marketing organizations.

More Concern with Social Values of Products

More of the marketing organization effort will have to be devoted to consideration of the social values of products. Products will have to be evaluated in terms of their effects on the environment and users. Society will simply no longer condone products that pollute rivers and the atmosphere, or have potential harmful effects on users. Thus, specialists in the marketing department must work to ensure that if pollution does occur, it does so at safe and acceptable levels. Products will have to be thoroughly tested to ensure that the possibility of hurting users is minimized.

SOME FUNDAMENTAL ORGANIZATIONAL DECISIONS

No matter how the marketing department is organized, there are still many fundamental decisions to be made. These include decisions on specialization, centralization and decentralization, departmentalization, span of control, motivation, and communications.

Specialization

An important decision to be made by top management for the marketing department involves the degree of **specialization** desired. Specialization refers to the extent to which positions in a marketing department are narrow in their responsibilities. In small firms there tends to be little specialization; the owner or manager has broad responsibilities because he has to be concerned with performing all of the marketing functions himself. The owner or manager contends with the marketing research and advertising areas, but in a firm that believes in specialization an expert is in charge of marketing research and advertising.

The major advantage of specialization is that a company obtains the services of skilled individuals in specific areas of marketing. As a result, more effective decisions should be made. An important disadvantage is that specialization is expensive. When specialization is practiced to a large de- ·gree, employees have difficulty communicating with each other because they do not understand the other individuals' responsibilities. Also, the greater the degree of specialization, the harder it is to coordinate the efforts of the specialists involved.

Centralization and Decentralization

If most of the important decisions in a company are made by top executives, the company is practicing **centralization.** If most of the important marketing decisions are made by individuals lower in the marketing organization, the company is practicing **decentralization.**

Advantages of Decentralization.   In decentralization decisions are made by the people who are most familiar with the situation and who should, as a result, make better decisions. For example, a salesperson may know better than the top executives the product needs of customers because he works closely with the customers on a regular basis. Another advantage is that decisions can be made quicker. Time will not be wasted in getting information to a top-level decision maker; the decision maker farther down the line perceives the situation and makes what, hopefully, will be the correct decision. This time factor can be an important consideration when decisions involving the market and competition are concerned. Decentralization also provides a means of evaluating the performance of subordinates. What better way to judge their performance than by how good their decisions are?

Advantages of Centralization.   The most important advantage of centralization is that it allows *optimization.* That is, the decision maker at the top of the marketing organization makes decisions that are *best for the entire marketing department*, not just best for one particular area of marketing. Since individuals at the top are responsible for the entire marketing operation and have access to information from all areas of marketing, they get the "big picture."

Departmentalization

In general, larger companies have more departments on their organization charts than do smaller companies. These departments usually correspond to the important marketing functions that must be performed. Thus, if advertising, marketing research, and physical distribution are important functions, separate departments are generally established to perform these functional areas. This method of organization is called **departmentalization.**

Span of Control

Span of control refers to the number of subordinates that a superior has under his control. If too many subordinates report to one superior, the superior usually has difficulty in coordinating their efforts. He is not able to spend as much time with them as is necessary. The problem is even more severe if the subordinates are performing very different functions or if they are geographically separated from their superior.

When firms try to reduce their marketing executives' span of control, the firms usually end up with a *taller* organization, that is, superiors have fewer subordinates, but the company has more layers of individuals between the chief marketing executive and individuals at the bottom of the marketing department. This situation can cause a number of problems, especially with information flows. The taller the organization, the longer it takes for information to reach its destination and the more likely that the information will be garbled.

In general, a superior cannot usually be effectively responsible for more than five to eight subordinates.

Motivation

Motivation is one of the most troublesome aspects of marketing organization. Motivation here refers to the extent to which an individual will work hard in order to secure the company's objectives.

If individuals are to be effectively motivated, they must see how helping the company achieve its goals allows them to attain their own personal objectives. This can be done in a variety of ways. For example, salespeople can be asked to secure specific sales figures. If these figures are obtained, the salespeople can be given monetary bonuses that satisfy their desire for increased income. At the same time, the company increases the likelihood of obtaining its desired level of sales volume.

Motivating marketing personnel is not easy because different people may be more effectively motivated by different needs. Some may be enticed by monetary inducements. In general, salesmen usually react favorably to the possibility of increasing their incomes. Others, however, may be more effectively motivated by the nature of the job itself. Marketing researchers, for example, may be more interested in having a larger computer and more clerical help than an increase in salary. Other marketing personnel may tend to emphasize the social aspects of their work and, thus, react favorably to motivation schemes that allow them to interact frequently with other individuals. Generally speaking, an effective supervisor discovers what motivates each of his subordinates and uses these motivations to generate enthusiasm. He does not assume that everyone is the same.

INTRAORGANIZATIONAL CONFLICT

Unfortunately, **intraorganizational conflict** appears to be present in almost every company. In most cases, the conflict involves various departments of the company, with marketing often being part of the controversy.

Intraorganizational conflict, or the lack of cooperation between departments, usually occurs because departments are competing for scarce resources, such as budgets and manpower. There are only so much of these resources to go around and departments tend to resent other departments if they do not get what they want.

The marketing department is generally in conflict with production, finance, and research and development. For example, the marketing department would like to have a wide variety of products produced, but the production department would rather have long production runs of a few varieties. Marketing would like to extend credit to nearly every customer in order to get their business, but finance usually wants to tighten up on extending credit for fear of incurring heavy bad debt losses. Research and development tends to stress the technical aspects of products, but marketing is more interested in product features that will satisfy the needs and desires of the market.

Consequences of Intraorganizational Conflict

Intraorganizational conflict is harmful because departments waste valuable time bickering with each other. This time could be better spent in planning how to compete more effectively with other firms. Conflict reduces cooperation among departments and may result in their withholding important information from each other.

Reducing Intraorganizational Conflict

Below are some suggestions for reducing intraorganizational conflict:

1. More emphasis should be placed on achieving company objectives than on achieving individual departmental objectives.
2. Competition for resources should be fair and departments should be given reasons why they are not to receive what they request.
3. Departments should be informed about how the contributions of other departments enable general company objectives to be achieved.
4. Departments should be aware of the problems and frustrations of of the other departments in the company.
5. Departments should interact as frequently as possible with each other. This can be accomplished by having their members serve on various committees or working together on various projects.

EMERGING DEVELOPMENTS IN MARKETING ORGANIZATION

We will close this chapter by discussing some new developments that are likely to become a part of most marketing organizations.

Management by Objectives

Management by objectives (MBO) has been adopted by many companies and there is every reason to expect that MBO will soon become part of the marketing organization. The major MBO steps are shown in Figure 16.7.

Goals. Both the superior and subordinate work together to establish objectives that the subordinate will try to achieve. Few goals should be

"Gentlemen, thanks to an energetic sales force, a whiz-bang ad campaign, and a terrific shipping crew, the cupboard is bare."

established and they should be the most important goals for the firm. The goals should be explicit. They should be written down so that there will be no misunderstanding later. Goals should have a time dimension, that is, a time limit for achieving them.

Action Plan. The action plan is an understanding between the superior and subordinate as to how the goals are to be achieved. The plan should include who, what is to be done (the objective), where, when, how, and how much is required (the resources to be used). The following is a good example of an action plan: Salesperson Tom Smith is to obtain a 20% market share for #10-sized envelopes in the Southeast Pennsylvania territory by December 1, 1978 by increasing his average number of calls per week to 25 within a sales expense budget of $20,000.

Periodic Reviews. Periodically the subordinate should be told specifically how well he is progressing toward achieving his goals. He and his superior should get together several times a year to discuss it. If there are unusual circumstances, the review session should be scheduled as soon as the problem arises.

Appraisal. At the end of the time period the superior and subordinate should appraise the subordinate's performance by comparing the goals with

Figure 16.7   Major Steps in Management by Objectives

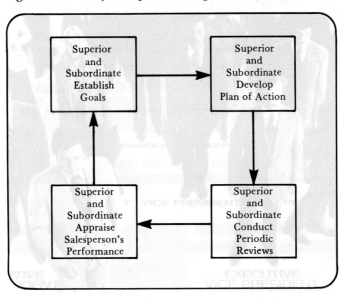

the results obtained. If the goals have been achieved, the subordinate should be praised. If they have not been achieved, the superior and the subordinate must find out why and develop a better action plan.

MBO is beneficial to the marketing organization because it provides the following:

1. Better planning.
2. Increased job satisfaction for subordinates.
3. Greater commitment to goals by subordinates because they have a hand in setting the goals.
4. Improved superior–subordinate relationships.
5. Subordinates with the knowledge of what is expected of them.

Although MBO seems promising for the marketing department, there are some problems, for example:

1. MBO has not had the enthusiastic support of top management, a necessary requirement if MBO is to be effective.
2. MBO in the marketing department has not been integrated with other areas of the firm, such as finance and production.
3. Superiors may not have the necessary interpersonal skills, for example, for coaching and communicating.

Organizing the Marketing Department

4. There is increased time pressure on superiors to implement and install the MBO system.
5. The paper work is excessive.

Futurists

In some firms there may be separate departments of futurists. In other firms futurists may be part of the marketing department.

Futurists attempt to look from 20 to 30 years into the future. They try to determine what our country, indeed the world, will look like then. They try to anticipate long-run changes before they occur so that the firm and its marketing operations are not caught unprepared. Futurists are concerned with human values, population trends, technological developments, raw material shortages, energy potential, the rise and fall of power blocs, and so on. The marketing department should be involved in futuristic thinking because the department can be vitally affected by future developments in the environment.

General Electric has a specific department charged with the responsibility for looking into the future and developing various economic forecasts.

Decreasing Status and Hierarchical Differences

Marketing departments are finding that for some types of jobs it is more effective to play down the status and hierarchical differences that exist among departmental members. Thus, the fact that an individual is superior to another is forgotten and age and experience differences are ignored.

Forgetting these differences enables the group to focus more directly on the task at hand. Subordinates and younger individuals who have less experience feel less threatened and are more inclined to contribute to the group's tasks and objectives. Individuals are appraised for their contributions, not for their rank, position, and experience.

One area where a lessening of status and hierarchical differences has proved helpful is with the *venture team*. This is a group made up of individuals from various departments whose purpose is to develop new product ideas that will be successful. Because creating new product ideas is essentially a creative process, the venture group depends on ideas from all of the members of the group. If rank and status differences are ignored, the contributions from everyone tend to be more effective.

System 4 Orientation

In recent years management specialists have indicated that in the long run a **system 4** organization appears to be the most effective type of organization. Thus, it is proper to suggest that a system 4 approach may also be best for the marketing department.

A system 4 organization is counter to the normal, more traditional organization with which we are familiar (this latter type of organization is called a *system 1* organization). Figure 16.8 lists the major differences between these two systems.[5]

A system 4 organization is difficult to install because it involves new ideas that may be resisted by people who are used to doing things "the old way." This thinking must be overcome, for firms that are embracing the system 4 orientation appear to have greater productivity and higher earnings than firms that are following the system 1 approach. Also, companies that have moved from a system 1 to a system 4 approach (after an initial familiarization period) have found that there is increased job satisfaction among their

[5] Rensis Likert, *The Human Organization* (New York: McGraw-Hill Book Company, 1967), pp. 197–211.

Figure 16.8   System 1 and System 4 Forms of Organization

System 1	System 4
1. Goals are set at the top of the firm.	1. Group goal setting involving subordinates is encouraged.
2. Centralized decision making occurs.	2. Decentralized decision making is encouraged.
3. Communication tends to flow downward.	3. Communication flows downward, upward, and across the firm or department.
4. The control process is located at the top and emphasizes fixing blame for mistakes.	4. The control process is spread throughout the firm and emphasizes why mistakes were made and what can be done to correct them.
5. Motivation emphasizes physical, security, and economic goals.	5. Motivation emphasizes all goals, including social and self-esteem motives.
6. Leadership does not emphasize confidence and trust. Subordinates do not feel free to discuss problems with superiors.	6. Leadership stresses confidence and trust. Subordinates feel free to discuss problems with superiors.
7. Little opportunity for subordinates to have any effect on goals, methods, and activities.	7. Much opportunity for subordinates to have an effect on goals, methods, and activities.
8. Little emphasis on developing through training the human resources of the firm.	8. Much emphasis on developing through training the human resources of the firm.

Organizing the Marketing Department

employees. As a result, a system 4 orientation may be adopted by more marketing departments in the future. However, marketing departments must be aware that shifting from a system 1 climate to a system 4 climate is a long, painstaking process, although the rewards appear worthwhile.

SUMMARY

A major characteristic of effective marketing organizations is their ability to adopt to changes in the market. Because of the market's constantly changing needs and desires, a successful marketing department must be aware of these modifications and develop offerings compatible with them.

Another characteristic of an effective marketing organization is that it expedites communication. This means that information is moved quickly to the intended person and that the information is accurate.

Although there are many factors that determine the type of marketing organization to be established, the four major factors are as follows: (1) the size of the firm, (2) the market for the company's product, (3) the type of firm, and (4) the products carried.

An organizational approach that is becoming increasingly popular is the product manager approach. In this approach the product manager is given responsibility for a specific product or for a small number of products. It is an appropriate organizational approach when a company has a number of different products directed to one or only a few markets. A study of product managers brought out the fact that product managers do not have enough contact with the market.

Consumer affairs departments have been added to many firms as a result of increasing consumer dissatisfaction. These departments were initially established to handle consumer complaints, but recently they have become involved with other areas, such as educating consumers and testing products.

A major aspect of any marketing organization is where the decisions will be made. Some firms prefer centralization (decisions are made at the top by a few individuals). The advantage of centralization is that it increases the possibility of making optimum decisions. Decentralization (decisions are made by individuals lower in the organization) allows for quicker decisions and serves as a basis for evaluating subordinate performance.

Motivating personnel is important if the marketing department wants to achieve its objectives. A good boss finds out which basic needs are important to each of his subordinates and uses them to motivate these individuals. He does not assume that each person can be motivated the same way.

Intraorganizational conflict results when various departments do not cooperate with each other. Unfortunately, there usually is a conflict between the marketing department and other departments, such as finance and production. This conflict may be reduced through such means as emphasizing company objectives instead of departmental objectives and increasing the level of interaction among departments.

Management by objectives (MBO) is a new approach to management that may make the marketing organization more effective. In MBO, superiors and subordinates decide on objectives for the subordinates to achieve. Action plans are developed to achieve these objectives. There are periodic reviews so that subordinates know how they are doing. Finally, the subordinate's performance is formally appraised.

Many firms are using futurists in an effort to predict long-run trends. If these trends can be identified, more appropriate responses to the market and environment are possible.

In attempting to operate more effectively, marketing departments may consider moving to a system 4 orientation, which stresses participation by all marketing employees as well as a relaxing of status and hierarchical differences.

QUESTIONS

1. If a marketing department has a system 1 orientation, how long do you think that it would take to install a system 4 orientation?
2. Under what conditions should a marketing department use decentralized decision making? Under what conditions should it use centralized decision making?
3. Do you believe that the consumer affairs department should be part of or separate from the marketing department?
4. Under what conditions would a customer organization be preferred to a product organization?
5. What are the major advantages and disadvantages of specialization?
6. Do you believe that product managers should spend more time with customers or should they concentrate on such areas as setting goals and developing advertising campaigns?
7. Is there likely to be conflict among such functional areas in the marketing department as marketing research, sales, and physical distribution?

GLOSSARY

Centralization: the approach to marketing organization in which marketing decisions tend to be made by top executives in the marketing department

Customer Organization: the marketing organization in which individuals

Organizing the Marketing Department

are given responsibility for the marketing effort directed to specific groups of customers

Decentralization: the approach to marketing organization in which marketing decisions tend to be made by individuals lower in the marketing department than top executives

Departmentalization: the organization alternative in which various marketing functions are performed by individual departments

Functional Organization: the marketing organization in which individuals are given responsibility for the management of various marketing functions, such as marketing research, sales, and physical distribution

Intraorganizational Conflict: lack of cooperation among the various departments of a company

Management by Objectives: an approach to management that involves having subordinates and superiors working together to establish goals, developing a plan to achieve the goals, and conducting periodic reviews and appraisals

Motivation: the extent to which marketing individuals will work hard to secure the company's objectives

Product Organization: the marketing organization in which individuals are given responsibility for a specific product or for a small number of products

Span of Control: the number of subordinates that a superior has under his control

Specialization: the extent to which positions in the marketing department are narrow in their responsibilities

System 4: an organizational approach that involves high levels of employee participation in such management areas as goal setting, decision making, control, and communication

CASES

Case 1: Southeast Insurance Co.

Bryan Jones is the sales manager for the Southeast Insurance Company. The company employs 200 salespeople.

Last year the company's premiums increased by only 5%, far below the industry average. The company added fewer new customers than other insurance firms did and suffered a loss of 6% of its customers, its highest loss rate in five years.

Implementing and Evaluating Marketing Mix Decisions

Mr. Jones has suggested to the company's vice-president of marketing, James Davidson, that installing a management by objectives system for the company's sales force may be the key to increasing the firm's performance.

Southeast's 200 salespeople are introduced to the idea of management by objectives and appear to be receptive to the idea. As a result, Mr. Jones is requested to develop a plan for installing a formal MBO system.

1. What are the MBO major steps?
2. How long do you believe that it should take the company to install the MBO program?
3. What should the major objectives of the MBO program be?
4. What are the major problems that might be encountered?

Case 2: The Furnco Corp.

The marketing area of the Furnco Corp., a large manufacturer of furniture, is organized on a product basis. The company has six major product lines, each of which is organized as a separate division: office furniture, patio furniture, kitchen furniture, dining room furniture, living room furniture, and bedroom furniture. A product manager heads up the marketing effort for each division, and the managers report directly to the firm's vice-president of marketing.

In each of the six divisions, there are brand managers for various products. For example, brand managers exist for various types of desks, filing cabinets, and bookcases in the office furniture division. In all, the company has 30 such brand managers.

In the past, these 30 brand managers were given little decision-making responsibility. Most decisions for the company's products were made by the six product managers. The 30 brand managers implemented these decisions. For example, they ensured that deadlines were met, and they coordinated the marketing effort with other areas, such as finance and production. They also monitored the market and competition and passed along any important information to their product managers.

In 1978, the company employed a new vice-president of marketing, David Scott. A strong believer in decentralized decision making, Mr. Scott intended to give the 30 brand managers more responsibility for marketing decisions for their products. Chief among these were setting budgets, choosing advertising media, identifying promising market segments, and setting prices.

1. What are the potential advantages of Mr. Scott's plan?
2. What are the potential disadvantages?
3. What information do you believe Mr. Scott should obtain before he decides to install his plan?

Organizing the Marketing Department

17 Marketing Control

After you finish this chapter, you should be able to answer the following questions:

1. What are the major advantages of a marketing control system?
2. What are the major steps in developing a marketing control system?
3. Which of the fundamental control tools is probably the most important?
4. Why is it important for companies to engage in 20/80 analysis?
5. With which objectives are network diagrams most directly involved?
6. What are some ways that marketing control can be made more effective?
7. Why should individuals be shown how they can benefit from the control system?
8. How is management by exception related to marketing control?
9. What is a marketing audit?
10. Who should be responsible for conducting a marketing audit?

KEY TERMS

Budgets   *Critical Path*   *Efficiency Measures*   *Marketing Audit*
Marketing Control   *Monitoring Mechanisms*   *Network Diagrams*
Percentage Analysis   *Performance Improvement Analysis*   *Productivity
Measures*   *Profitability Analysis*   *Standard of Performance*   *20/80
Principle*

INTRODUCTION   The reader will perhaps recall from the first chapter that developing a control system for an organization's marketing operations was the last of the seven major steps in making marketing decisions. It is the purpose of this chapter to discuss marketing control systems in greater detail, with the major emphasis on how control systems can aid the marketing area to better achieve its objectives.

This chapter is not the reader's first exposure to the concept of marketing control. In some of the previous chapters various examples of marketing control were encountered. In Chapter 10 data on salespeople in the machine tool industry were given. For example, we found out how much time the average salesperson spent on paper work. These data are helpful in deciding on a **standard of performance,** one of the major decisions to be made in a marketing control system.

In this chapter we will discuss marketing control in an integrated fashion. The chapter is divided into six major parts: (1) the advantages of marketing control; (2) the six basic steps in marketing control; (3) the seven fundamental control tools; (4) how the fundamental control tools are applied to the seven basic marketing functions of marketing research, product management, advertising, personal selling, managing channels of distribution, physical distribution, and pricing; (5) some recommendations for making marketing control more effective; and (6) the concept of the marketing audit.

ADVANTAGES OF A MARKETING CONTROL SYSTEM

A firm must have a mechanism for determining how effective its marketing area is. It must also formally determine how well it has achieved the objectives stated for the marketing department at the beginning of various time periods. And it must also have some direction and help in obtaining future objectives. Marketing control can help achieve all three of these objectives. In addition, it provides the means whereby performances can be judged and it provides a method of determining how efficiently scarce resources have been used. Perhaps most importantly, a marketing control system can be the basis for improving the performance of marketing personnel.

BASIC STEPS IN A MARKETING CONTROL SYSTEM

The six basic steps required to establish a marketing control system are shown in Figure 17.1 and are described below.

Step One: Decide on Aspect of Marketing Operation to Be Evaluated

The first step in establishing a marketing control system is to decide on the specific marketing aspect to be evaluated. Some examples include:

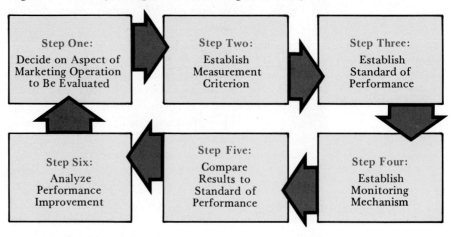

Figure 17.1   Major Steps in a Marketing Control System

Step One:
Decide on Aspect of Marketing Operation to Be Evaluated

Step Two:
Establish Measurement Criterion

Step Three:
Establish Standard of Performance

Step Six:
Analyze Performance Improvement

Step Five:
Compare Results to Standard of Performance

Step Four:
Establish Monitoring Mechanism

1. A salesperson's performance.
2. The effectiveness of marketing research.
3. A new product's performance.
4. The effectiveness of a newspaper advertisement.

In general, a firm usually wants to evaluate *all* aspects of its marketing operations, including people, programs, functions, policies, and so on. Also, the firm may want to evaluate the effectiveness of its *entire* marketing effort.

Step Two: Establishment Measurement Criterion

In the second step some specific criterion must be chosen to represent the marketing aspect designated in the first step. For example, a salesperson's performance may be indicated by the number of new accounts obtained in one year. The effectiveness of marketing research may be measured by the cost per completed interview. Return on investment may be appropriate for measuring a new product's performance. The effectiveness of a newspaper advertisement may be measured by the percentage of newspaper readers who recall the advertisement.

For many organizations, measurement criteria are essentially the major strategic objectives of profit, sales volume, market share, product protection, and growth, as well as the tactical objectives that contribute to the achievement of these strategic objectives.

Step Three: Establish Standard of Performance

The third marketing control step is to establish a standard of performance. This means that the firm should quantify the measurement criteria adopted in Step 2. For example, a salesperson may have to secure 50 new accounts in one year. The cost per completed interview for marketing research should not exceed $20. The return on investment for a new product must be at least 20%. At least 15% of the readers of a newspaper advertisement should recall the firm's advertisement.

In establishing these standards of performance, a company may wish to use its own overall performance. For example, it may find that the average cost per sales call for all of its salespeople is $50. This $50 figure could become the performance standard. Thus, the firm might allow some deviation from this $50 standard (perhaps up to $70), but it would be concerned about any salesperson whose cost per sales call exceeded $70.

Data from outside the firm are often helpful in establishing standards of performance. Figures 17.2, 17.3, and 17.4 list some examples.

Figure 17.2   Performance Standards for Retailing

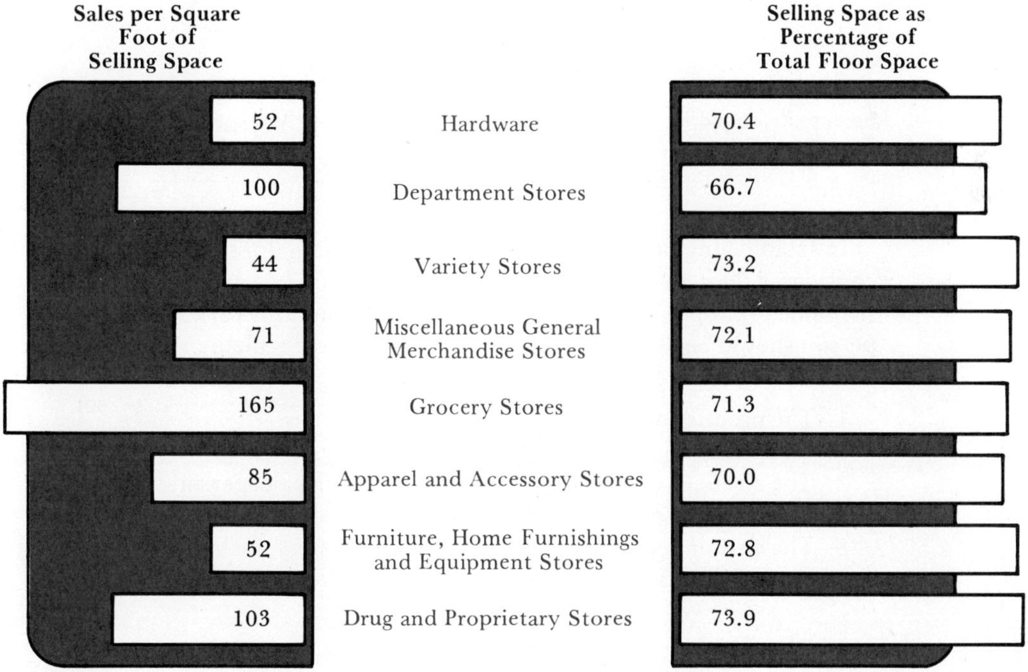

Sales per Square Foot of Selling Space		Selling Space as Percentage of Total Floor Space
52	Hardware	70.4
100	Department Stores	66.7
44	Variety Stores	73.2
71	Miscellaneous General Merchandise Stores	72.1
165	Grocery Stores	71.3
85	Apparel and Accessory Stores	70.0
52	Furniture, Home Furnishings and Equipment Stores	72.8
103	Drug and Proprietary Stores	73.9

Source: U.S. Census of Retailing, 1972.

Figure 17.3   Cities in the United States with Highest Sales Costs (U.S. Average = 100)

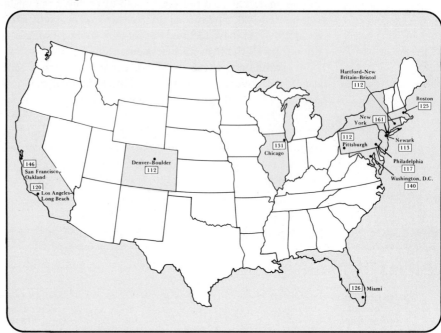

Source: Reprinted by permission from *Sales & Marketing Management* magazine. Copyright 1975.

In establishing performance standards, *individual differences* should be considered. Not all salespeople, for instance, would be expected to obtain the same profit per year. Setting performance standards for each salesperson should be done on an individual basis by recognizing the following factors:

1. The products each salesperson sells.
2. The potential in each salesperson's territory.
3. The strength of competitive products in each salesperson's territory.
4. The strength of the advertising effort for the salesperson's products.
5. The cost of supporting a salesperson in the field, including lodging, meals, and travel costs.

Step Four: Establish Monitoring Mechanism

Step 4 involves developing the means through which performance can be evaluated. This necessitates establishing **monitoring mechanisms.** There are

Figure 17.4   Cities in the United States with Lowest Sales Costs (U.S. Average = 100)

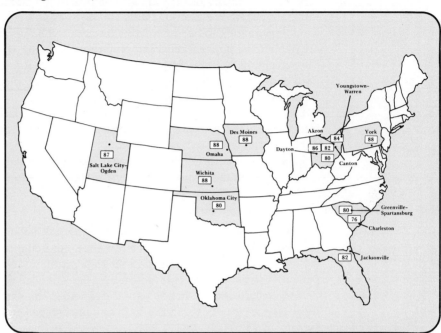

Source: Reprinted by permission from *Sales & Marketing Management* magazine. Copyright 1975.

a number of monitoring tools that can be employed. In Chapter 5 we discussed marketing information systems (MIS). Such systems can be used to record the performance of all marketing areas; for example, they can report monthly sales volumes for all products. Reports are another means of monitoring performance. Some examples of reports are:

1. The sales force at the Mystik Tape Division of Borden's fills out daily sales reports that list the companies called on, the results of the calls, time spent on the calls, miles driven, and expenses incurred. These data could be used to determine the salesperson's cost per mile and the percentage of calls resulting in a sale.
2. The sales force at Helene Curtis fills out forms that cover its entertainment practices and expenses. These forms could indicate whether or not a salesperson's entertainment expenses are out of line.
3. A "Dealer Activity and Inventory Report" allows Eaton's Industrial

Truck Division to determine if dealer inventory levels are too high or to low.

4. Beecham has a form that asks its sales force to indicate if key accounts have added or dropped the company's products.[1]

Various company records are also helpful in the monitoring process. Purchase orders, for example, indicate the sales volume of each customer. Thus, customers can be identified whose sales volumes are so low that they are likely to be unprofitable. Shipping records can be analyzed to determine the percentage of times that orders arrive late. Accounting records can be used to determine the sales volumes of products and their costs, thus providing an indication of their profitability.

Direct observation can also be a monitoring tool. Marketing research interviewers, for example, can be observed so that their effectiveness in conducting interviews can be evaluated.

Whatever monitoring device is used, the results obtained are crucial to the next step in the marketing control system.

Step Five: Compare Results to Standard of Performance

The results obtained through the monitoring process should be compared to the established standard of performance. For instance, the firm can see if Product X has obtained the desired 15% return on investment or if Salesperson Tom Smith has achieved the cost per sales call of $45.

If the results are not in line with the expected standard of performance, it is necessary to engage in the sixth and final step of the marketing control system.

Step Six: Analyze Performance Improvement

Here, an attempt is made to determine why the standard of performance was not achieved. Once the **performance improvement analysis** has been made, corrective action can be put into effect.

Assume that a salesperson has not achieved the desired standard of performance of 25 sales calls per week. In a session with the division sales manager, they both agree that the major reason is that the salesperson spends too much time traveling between customers. The salesperson and the division sales manager then develop a routing scheme to cluster calls in order to reduce the amount of travel time.

FUNDAMENTAL CONTROL TOOLS

In this section we will discuss the seven basic control tools that are frequently used in marketing: (1) profitability analysis, (2) 20/80 principle, (3) productivity measures, (4) efficiency measures, (5) percentage analysis, (6) budgets, and (7) network diagrams.

[1] *Sales Management* (August 18, 1975), p. 14.

Profitability Analysis

A company uses **profitability analysis** to measure the profitability of various aspects of its marketing operations, such as products, salespeople, and customers. The profitability of each can be compared to a desired level. Those falling below the desired level are then subjected to performance improvement analysis.

A profitability analysis for three products is illustrated in Figure 17.5. There it can be seen that Product A is in trouble because it had a loss of $10,000. Products B and C generated profits. If the company specified a return on investment figure of 10% or better, Product B (12%) would be all right, but Product C (5%) would not. If a return on sales percentage of 6% were acceptable, both Product B and Product C would be judged as being adequate.

20/80 Principle

The **20/80 principle** means that a small percentage of a firm's items generally accounts for a large percentage of its sales volume and profit. The reverse of this is also true: A large percentage of items accounts for a small percentage of sales volume and profit.

The 20/80 principle is used very often. Companies find that a small percentage of its products, customers, salespeople, orders, etc. usually generate large percentages of its profit and sales volume. For example, one Sears store got 86% of its volume from only 15% of its open-store hours. A chemical company found that 60% of its sales came from 5% of its jobbers and 75% came from 15% of its sales force. Over 54% of the sales of a

Figure 17.5 Profitability Analysis

	Product A	Product B	Product C
Sales	$100,000	$200,000	$160,000
Less manufacturing costs	70,000	160,000	100,000
Gross margin	$ 30,000	$ 40,000	$ 60,000
Less marketing costs	40,000	28,000	50,000
Net profit	−10,000	12,000	10,000
Investment	150,000	100,000	200,000
Return on investment	−6.7%	12%	5%
Return on sales	−10.0%	6%	6.3%

McKesson and Robbins wholesale house came from only 8% of its products.[2]

Figure 17.6 shows the 20/80 principle for a hypothetical company that has 20 customers. These data clearly indicate the existence of the 20/80 principle. For example, 20% of these customers (the four largest customers in terms of sales volume) account for 73% of total sales. It is also important to notice that this means that 80% (16 customers) obtain only 27% of the company's total sales.

Another significant figure is the *average sales volume* for this firm's

[2] Richard H. Buskirk, *Principles of Marketing* (New York: Holt, Rinehart, & Winston, Inc., 1970), p. 488.

Figure 17.6   The 20/80 Principle

Customer	Cumulative Percentage of Customers	Sales Volume	Percentage of Total Sales Volume	Cumulative Percentage of Sales Volume
A	5	$1,200,000	24.00	24.00
B	10	900,000	18.00	42.00
C	15	800,000	16.00	58.00
D	20	750,000	15.00	73.00
E	25	500,000	10.00	83.00
F	30	400,000	8.00	91.00
G	35	100,000	2.00	93.00
H	40	80,000	1.60	94.60
I	45	60,000	1.20	95.80
J	50	50,000	1.00	96.80
K	55	40,000	.80	97.60
L	60	30,000	.60	98.20
M	65	20,000	.40	98.60
N	70	18,000	.36	98.96
O	75	15,000	.30	99.26
P	80	13,000	.26	99.52
Q	85	12,000	.24	99.76
R	90	5,000	.10	99.86
S	95	4,000	.08	99.94
T	100	3,000	.06	100.00
Totals		$5,000,000	100.00	

largest customers compared to the average sales volume for the company's smallest customers. The average sales volume for the 6 largest companies is $758,333. The average sales volume for the company's 14 smallest customers is only $32,143. Although the largest customers undoubtedly return a profit, it is questionable if the 14 smaller ones do.

It is important for a company to follow the 20/80 principle because it helps the firm to identify *key* products, customers, salespeople, and orders. In the example in Figure 17.5 the company would want to exert a great deal of effort to retain the business of its largest customers. The smaller ones would not be as important.

Productivity Measures

Productivity measures are an important control technique. They enable a company to determine how effectively a given resource is performing. Some examples of productivity measures are:

1. Sales volume per salesperson.
2. Number of completed interviews per interviewer.
3. Cost per sales call.
4. Cost per mile traveled for salespeople.
5. Number of inquiries per advertisement.
6. Number of customer complaints per product.
7. Sales volume per dollar of advertising expenditure.

Efficiency Measures

Efficiency measures determine the effectiveness of the performance of resources. When efficiency measures are used, the output from resources over a given range of these resources are studied. Then decisions are made on how best to use these resources.

Figure 17.7 is a graph of the sales volume obtained by 0 to 20 salespeople. It can be seen that the firm maximizes sales volume by employing 15 salespeople. At that level, sales reach $3,750,000. If it were to have a sales force of 20, its sales volume would be only $2,800,000.

Percentage Analysis

Percentage analysis is an important and frequently used control tool. It can be used to determine the effectiveness of a number of different marketing areas and it is also helpful in analyzing trends over time.

Consider Figure 17.8 in which are shown the percentages of various marketing outlays to total marketing expenditures for 1975, 1976, 1977, and 1978. Analysis of these data reveals several major trends. First, the percentage of total marketing expenditures devoted to advertising increased every year. In 1978 it accounted for 40% of all marketing allocations (com-

Figure 17.7 A Measure of Efficiency

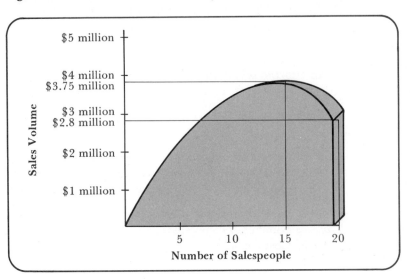

pared to only 20% in 1975). The company should ask itself if it is satisfied with the results it is obtaining from its advertising effort. Second, the percentage expenditure for personal selling decreased every year, from a high of 30% in 1975 to a low of 17.5% in 1978. Is such a decrease in personal selling effort justified or should this policy be reconsidered?

There are other examples of percentage analysis as a marketing control tool. Perhaps the most widely used is market share for individual products. This figure indicates how well products are doing in comparison to competitive offerings. Sales managers often express various aspects of their sales force's job as percentages of their total time to see if they are spending too much time on paper work, traveling, or waiting to see accounts. The percentage of magazine readers who recall information about an advertisement is another example of percentage analysis.

Budgets

Budgets refer to monies allocated to specific marketing activities before the activities are carried out. Frequently used marketing budgets are sales budgets that involve allocations for personal selling and advertising budgets for a company's advertising effort.

Marketing budgets are developed in relation to a company's objectives.

Implementing and Evaluating Marketing Mix Decisions

Figure 17.8   An Example of Percentage Analysis

	Dollar Amount and Percentage			
Item	1975	1976	1977	1978
Total marketing expenditures	$1,000,000 (100%)	$1,500,000 (100%)	$1,800,000 (100%)	$2,000,000 (100%)
Advertising	200,000 (20%)	400,000 (26.7%)	600,000 (33.3%)	800,000 (40%)
Marketing research	100,000 (10%)	150,000 (10%)	180,000 (10%)	200,000 (10%)
Packaging	100,000 (10%)	150,000 (10%)	200,000 (11.1%)	200,000 (10%)
Physical distribution	300,000 (30%)	500,000 (33.3%)	500,000 (27.7%)	450,000 (22.5%)
Personal selling	300,000 (30%)	300,000 (20%)	320,000 (17.8%)	350,000 (17.5%)

The expenditures are a function of the resources believed necessary to achieve these objectives. For example, a company may decide that it will need its sales force to make 8,000 calls during the year in order to achieve a desired sales volume objective of $2,000,000. If the company's cost per sales call is $50, then its sales budget would be $400,000 (8,000 × $50).

Budgets are effective control devices because they force management to determine carefully the level of expenditures required to obtain desired objectives. Thus, budgets guard against the possibility of overexpenditures. They also provide a standard of performance. Unless they result in better achievement of objectives, people who exceed the budget limitations should be held accountable.

Network Diagrams

Time is one of the most valuable resources that the marketing department has. A **network diagram** is an effective control device that helps to ensure that time is used effectively. In particular, it allows the marketing effort to be directed toward achieving deadlines. It also allows specific authority and responsibility to be assigned. And management by exception can also be practiced, that is, management's attention can be directed toward areas in which there are problems.

Let's assume that the Wrenco Company has decided to conduct a one-week sales meeting for its sales force. Management decides that eight specific activities are involved: (1) defining objectives, (2) deciding on the city in which the meeting will be held, (3) choosing the specific facility within the city, (4) deciding on topics to be discussed, (5) choosing speakers for these topics, (6) conducting the meeting, (7) obtaining audio-visual aids, and (8) measuring the results of the meeting. Top management carefully analyzes these eight steps with the objectives of determining which steps should be performed after others are completed and which steps can be performed simultaneously. This analysis results in the network diagram in Figure 17.9. The diagram shows the number of weeks each activity is expected to take. Each activity has been assigned a letter to facilitate the following discussion.

The executives next isolate each path that will link the last activity (measuring results) to the first activity (defining objectives), and then they determine the total number of weeks required for each path. The three paths and their times are:

1. A–B–C–D–G–H = 12 weeks $(3+2+3+1+1+2 = 12)$
2. A–E–F–G–H   = 13 weeks $(3+3+4+1+2 = 13)$
3. A–E–F–D–G–H = 14 weeks $(3+3+4+1+1+2 = 14)$

Path A–E–F–D–G–H is called the **critical path** because it is the *shortest* time in which the *entire* project can be completed. Any activity on this path that takes longer than planned to complete jeopardizes the company's being ready for the sales meeting on time.

Figure 17.9   Network Diagram—Planning for a Sales Meeting

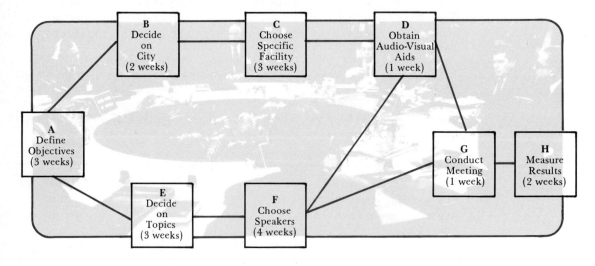

     Implementing and Evaluating Marketing Mix Decisions

It is possible to transfer resources from an activity *not* on the critical path to an activity on the critical path that is experiencing difficulties. In the sales meeting example, activities B and C are not on the critical path. Thus, if choosing speakers is going to take more than the original four weeks, manpower, for example, could be transferred from activity B or C.

Network diagrams are an extremely flexible and valuable tool that can be used to control a wide variety of marketing operations.

USING THE BASIC CONTROL TOOLS IN THE SEVEN MARKETING FUNCTIONS

In the previous discussion of control devices there were examples of how these might be applied to various marketing functions and the organization's overall marketing operation. Figure 17.10 attempts to be more complete. There, we have indicated how these tools might be extensively used to provide the control mechanism needed to manage these functions and the organization's total marketing effort more effectively. The examples provided, however, are merely illustrations. Certainly, many more could be provided. The reader is encouraged to add other examples of control tools for the eight major categories shown in Figure 17.10.

HOW TO MAKE MARKETING CONTROL MORE EFFECTIVE

We believe that instituting and operationalizing a **marketing control** system may be one of the marketing manager's most difficult responsibilities. Marketing control is often resented and viewed with suspicion by those who should benefit from control systems. Because they often resist the installation of control mechanisms, the control system fails to achieve its basic objectives. Following are some recommendations that should help marketing control systems succeed.

Obtain Inputs from Individuals Whose Performance Will Be Evaluated

The people who will be involved in the control system should be consulted frequently while the system is being introduced. Their input about what aspects of their performance should be evaluated and what the standards of performance should be get them involved in the process and may help reduce their resistance.

Show Individuals How They Can Benefit from the Control System

Perhaps the best way to reduce resistance to change is to show how the marketing control system can benefit the individuals involved. For example, salespeople may be shown that a performance standard of having 40% of their time devoted to face-to-face selling will increase their compensation by 15%.

Figure 17.10   Applying the Basic Control Devices to the Fundamental Marketing Functions and the Overall Marketing Operation

			Control Device				
Function	Profitability Analysis	20/80 Analysis	Productivity Measures	Efficiency Measures	Percentage Analysis	Budgets	Network Diagrams
Marketing Research	Determining if the value of the information exceeds its cost.	Determining the small percentage of studies that contributes the most to the company's objectives.	Number of completed interviews per interviewer.	Total value of information according to number of marketing research studies.	Percentage of usable questionnaires received to total sent. Percentage of usable interview responses to total conducted.	Marketing research budget for year.	Diagramming the steps involved in collecting primary data through interviewers. Diagramming a test market.
Product Management	Measuring the profit of individual products.	Determining the small percentage of products that accounts for large percentages of sales volume.	Number of customer complaints per product. Sales volume per unit sold.	Sales volume according to number of products marketed.	Market share for individual products. Percentage of total resources used for each product.	Research and development budget for year.	Diagramming the new product development process. Diagramming the product elimination process.
Advertising	Determining if the sales volume obtained from an advertisement exceeds its cost.	Determining the small percentage of advertisements that accounts for large percentages of sales volume.	Number of inquiries per advertisement. Sales volume per dollar of advertising.	Sales volume over range of advertising insertions.	Percentage of magazine readers who remember an advertisement.	Advertising budget for year.	Diagramming the development of an advertising campaign.
Personal Selling	Measuring the profit of individual salespeople. Measuring the profit contributed by salespeople making calls at various times of the day.	Determining the small percentage of salespeople that accounts for large percentages of sales volume.	Sales volume per salesperson. Sales cost per sale call. Sales cost per mile traveled.	Sales volume over range of salespeople. Sales volume over range of calls on same customer.	Percentage of total time spent by salespeople on paper work, traveling, waiting time, and presentations.	Sales budget for year composed of salaries and commission, travel, food, lodging and entertainment.	Diagramming a salesperson's route. Diagramming the steps in a salesperson's training program.

Managing Channels of Distribution	Measuring the profit of individual outlets and classes of outlets.	Determining the small percentage of outlets that accounts for large percentages of sales volume.	Sales volume per outlet. Sales volume per middleman.	Sales volume as penetration of existing outlets increases.	Percentage of outlets carrying a company's product.		Diagramming the procedure for introducing a new product to middlemen and individual outlets.
Physical Distribution	Measuring the profit of individual shipment sizes and transportation modes.	Determining the small percentage of orders that accounts for large percentages of sales volume.	Ton–miles per truck or railroad car. Ton–feet per forklift truck.	Total storage distribution cost over total square footage of warehousing space.	Percentage of truck capacity used per shipment of orders. Percentage of orders reaching customers within three days.	Transportation and storage budgets.	Diagramming the process whereby customer orders are received, processed, and shipped.
Pricing	Determining which prices maximize net profit or return on investment.	Determining the few prices for a product that account for a large percentage of its sales volume.	Quantity demanded at various prices.	Demand curves. Cost curves.	Percentage of total units sold accounted for by various prices.		Diagramming the process whereby prices are determined for new products.
Overall Marketing Operation	Measuring the profit of individual customers, types of customers, geographical areas.	Determining the small percentage of customers that accounts for a large percentage of sales volume.	Dollars of sales volume per marketing resource used.	Sales volume over range of total man-hours committed to marketing operations.	Percentage of various marketing costs to total marketing outlays.	Total marketing budget for year.	Diagramming the company's overall marketing plan for the year.

Emphasize Performance Improvement, Not the Poor Performance

It does little good for the marketing executive to dwell on a subordinate's poor performance. Instead, the reason why the performance was substandard should be emphasized. Then the superior and the subordinate can develop a plan to improve the performance.

Performance Standards Must Reflect Differences

Performance standards cannot be the same for all salespeople, all products, all customers, etc. For example, for some salespeople higher profit objectives might be established than for other salespeople. These higher standards would result from an analysis of several factors. Perhaps some salespeople are more experienced than others and their customers account for a higher market potential. Or their products are easier to sell because the products receive more advertising effort and competitive products are weaker.

Responsibility Must Be Assigned for Marketing Control Systems

Someone must have the responsibility for marketing control systems. It is probably desirable to involve both top management and operating management in the control process. A combined effort allows operating management to take corrective action when it is required and top management receives the necessary visibility.[3]

Frequency of Review Must Be Realistic

How frequently should performance be evaluated by the marketing control system? This depends on the time period required to provide the most realistic and accurate idea of marketing performance involved. Savings and loan associations monitor their savings positions for branch operations daily. Most manufacturers of consumer and industrial products, however, use monthly or quarterly data.[4]

Computer Involvement Is a Must

In order to effectively process the tremendous amounts of data required, the marketing control system must make extensive use of the firm's computer.

Management by Exception Must Be Practiced

A busy executive does not have enough time to read all the reports that a marketing control system generates. Therefore, management by exception must be practiced, that is, only those critical areas where performance is

[3] *Sales and Marketing Management* (June 14, 1976), p. 41.
[4] Ibid.

substantially below par should be called to his attention. Then plans should be developed to remedy the poor performance.

Cost Versus Benefit of the Marketing Control System Must Be Determined

Marketing control efforts tend to be costly. Thus, there is a need to make sure that their costs do not exceed the dollar value of their benefits. The costs involved may be difficult to pin down. For example, it is not easy to cost the amount of executive time involved. It is also difficult to assign a dollar value to the benefits of marketing control systems, especially since many performance standards are not expressed in terms of sales volume, costs, or profit. Whenever possible, however, performance standards should be converted to sales volume, cost, or profit measures and then compared to the cost of getting the information.

MARKETING AUDIT

The ultimate marketing control system is the **marketing audit,** which is a periodic, complete appraisal of the effectiveness of the firm's entire marketing operations. The following six major areas are usually evaluated: marketing objectives, policies, organization, methods, procedures, and personnel.[5] The appraisal phase in the marketing audit is not limited only to problem areas; all areas are evaluated. This is in contrast to early marketing audits that were usually conducted only by companies in a crisis situation, emphasized solving immediate problems, and were conducted by outside consultants. One such example is the Elgin Watch Company which in 1958 experienced a $2 million loss. A complete audit of products, customers, channels of distribution, and competitors revealed a number of weaknesses that needed attention.[6]

In conducting a marketing audit, attention is first turned to the objectives that have been established. Hopefully, these are obvious, but in many companies they are poorly articulated. Assuming that the company and the auditor agree on the objectives, the auditor should determine the extent to which the objectives recognize the company's opportunities (especially the market) and its available resources.

The auditor's next step is to examine the programs in operation for achieving these objectives. In particular, the auditor wants to find out if the level of resources assigned to the marketing area is adequate in view of the company's objectives. The auditor also wants to determine if various segments of the market are receiving enough attention and whether or not the various marketing activities, such as advertising and physical distribution, are receiving sufficient support.

[5] Edward W. Cundiff and Richard R. Still, *Basic Marketing* (Englewood Cliffs, N.J.: Prentice-Hall, Inc., 1971), p. 580.

[6] Philip Kotler, *Marketing Management* (Englewood Cliffs, N.J.: Prentice-Hall, Inc., 1972), pp. 16–17, 774.

The auditor must next decide whether or not implementation of the marketing programs is adequate. The auditor tends to concentrate on the elements of the marketing mix. For example, the method of scheduling advertisements, the sales force's compensation plan, the method for developing new products, and the routing of shipments to key customers will be examined.

Finally, the auditor examines the company's marketing organization. The auditor is concerned with the effectiveness of vertical and horizontal communication. Another area of interest is the extent to which the various marketing activities are coordinated by the chief marketing executive. The auditor wants to know if the responsibility assigned to marketing managers is matched by the authority provided them.[7]

There are many individuals who can logically conduct the marketing audit. Executives responsible for the activity can be asked to perform a self-audit, or the executive's superior can conduct the audit. Someone from another department can have the responsibility or the company can appoint an audit team made up of executives who have diversified backgrounds.[8] Another possibility is to appoint an individual as the company's *marketing controller* and let him conduct the marketing audit. This is done at the Nestlé Company, where Dr. Sam R. Goodman has served as the marketing controller.[9]

Perhaps the best approach is to have the marketing audit conducted by someone outside the company. An outside auditor may be more objective and someone inside the company does not have to be pulled away from his normal duties.

SUMMARY

Marketing control is the last of the seven major steps needed to make effective marketing decisions. It is valuable because it can help determine how effectively the marketing department and its various subunits have performed and whether or not specific objectives have been achieved. Marketing control allows performance to be judged and can serve as the basis for improving the performance of marketing personnel.

In developing a marketing control system, the following six steps should be taken: (1) decide on the aspect of marketing to be evaluated, (2) establish a measurement criterion, (3) set a standard of performance, (4) establish a monitoring mechanism, (5) compare results to the standard of performance, and (6) engage in performance improvement analysis.

Although all of the marketing control tools are important, profitability analysis is probably the most important because profit is generally considered the company's most significant objective. The 20/80 principle is also important because it enables key customers, products, salespeople, etc., to be identified—those that contribute the most to the firm's profit. Of

[7] See Kotler for an expansion of these ideas.
[8] Kotler, *op. cit.*, p. 779.
[9] James A. Constantin, Rodney E. Evans, and Malcolm L. Morris, *Marketing Strategy and Management* (Dallas, Texas: Business Publications, Inc., 1976), p. 489.

course, other objectives are recognized by marketing control tools. Network diagrams, for example, are concerned chiefly with objectives involving time.

Marketing control can be made more effective through a variety of ways. These include emphasizing performance improvement, not poor performance; setting performance standards that reflect differences; assigning specific responsibility for marketing control systems; and showing individuals how they can benefit from the marketing control system. The latter recommendation is helpful in overcoming resistance to the idea of a marketing control system.

Since marketing control systems tend to generate reams of information, computer usage is a must. Also, management by exception can be practiced if information provided busy executives pinpoints only those areas where serious problems exist.

A marketing audit is a periodic, comprehensive, formalized review of all of a company's marketing operations. Although there are many individuals within a company who can be assigned the responsibility of conducting the audit, it is generally believed that someone outside the firm is more appropriate.

QUESTIONS

1. Can you think of any other important marketing objectives besides time that network diagrams can be used to achieve?
2. Why should a firm use the 20/80 principle to analyze customers, products, and salespeople?
3. Can you think of any aspects of a company's marketing operations besides customers, products, and salespeople for which the 20/80 principle would be appropriate?
4. What are two major aspects of performance improvement analysis?
5. Why is it necessary to determine the critical path in network analysis?
6. Why is it desirable to show individuals how they can benefit from a control system?
7. Why should the marketing control system allow for management by exception?
8. Do you believe that a company is better off by using *internal* standards or by using *external* (industry) standards when it establishes performance standards?
9. What factors should a sales manager consider when he establishes sales quotas for individual salespeople?

Budgets: monies allocated to specific marketing activities before the activities are carried out

Critical Path: the path in a network diagram representing the shortest time in which an entire project can be completed

Efficiency Measures: examine the output of resources over a given range of resources

Marketing Audit: a periodic, complete appraisal of the effectiveness of a firm's entire marketing operation

Marketing Control: evaluating the performance of the firm's marketing operations so that performance can be improved

Monitoring Mechanisms: tools used to evaluate performance

Network Diagrams: sequencing phases of a project in order to achieve time deadlines and assign authority and responsibility

Percentage Analysis: determining the percentage of a total figure accounted for by a specific aspect of a company's marketing operation

Performance Improvement Analysis: determining why performance is subpar and developing corrective action to improve the poor performance

Productivity Measures: determine the effectiveness of the performance of a given resource by expressing a variable on a per unit basis

Profitability Analysis: determining net profit accounted for by various areas of a company's marketing operations, such as individual customers, individual salespeople, and individual products

Standard of Performance: a quantitative expectation of performance

20/80 Principle: a small percentage of a firm's products, customers, salespeople, etc., accounts for large percentages of sales volume and profit

CASES

Case 1: The Donora Co.

The Donora Company is a manufacturer of a large variety of consumer products that is instituting a marketing control system. The manufacturer plans to take two years to implement the system and to do it in a series of planned stages for various aspects of its marketing operations.

The first stage will deal with the company's products. A consensus of marketing executives is that all products should be evaluated according to their profitability. The vice-president of marketing believes that return on investment is the most appropriate measure of profitability. He states that the entire firm obtained a 20% return on investment the previous year and suggests that this standard be applied to all products carried.

The company's product managers believe that the 20% standard should not be uniformly applied to all of the company's products. They believe that each product should be analyzed separately and that various conditions should be considered when different return on investment levels are being assigned.

The vice-president of marketing agrees to consider the recommendations of the product managers. As a first step he requests that each product manager submit a list of the conditions he believes to be the most important in assigning returns on investment.

1. What conditions do you believe should be considered when deciding on return on investment standards?
2. Do you agree with the vice-president's use of the company's overall return on investment figure as a performance standard?
3. Are there other measures of profitability that might be considered as performance standards?

Case 2: Growth, Inc.

Bill Henry, the sales manager of Growth, Inc., a large stockbroker firm, is discouraged by his sales force's performance during the previous year. As a result, he decides to install a marketing control system in the hope that it will raise performance levels.

After a thorough analysis of the sales force's customers, call patterns, costs, and so on, he decides on the following performance standards to be applicable to all salespeople:

1. A cost per sales call of $50 or less.
2. At least 20 calls on new customers per month.
3. A reduction of 10% in the amount of nonselling time accounted for by each salesperson.

The 50 salespeople reporting to Mr. Henry are presented with the new standards at the company's annual sales meeting. At the end of the next year, Mr. Henry does not see a noticeable improvement in the three areas, but he is aware of a higher than average number of salespeople quitting and a decrease in morale of the sales force.

1. Are the standards established likely to be fair standards?
2. What rules for instituting a control system did Mr. Henry ignore?
3. What should Mr. Henry have done differently?

PART 5

International Marketing Management

International Marketing

After you finish this chapter, you should be able to answer the following questions:

1. How large is world trade?
2. Can United States–based firms automatically transfer their domestic marketing strategies to foreign countries?
3. What kind of company is the dominant institution in world trade?
4. What are some significant recent trends in the international environment?
5. What major approaches to entry into foreign markets are available to a company? What factor usually determines which alternative will be pursued?
6. What are the four major alternatives to organizing a firm's international operations?
7. What is meant by the locus of decision making for international operations?
8. What are the two major types of data that must be gathered about foreign markets?
9. What kinds of marketing decisions must a company make in its overseas operations?

INTRODUCTION

American firms are becoming more interested and involved in international business activities. Many see an increased number of attractive markets abroad and they are prepared to respond to these market opportunities either by exporting from the United States or by establishing plants abroad and selling from them. In either case, there is a whole range of new questions and problems with which their marketers must be familiar if these firms are to compete in these markets successfully.

Interest in international marketing has intensified in the late 1970's due to the worsening international trade situation for the United States. For example, in 1977, the United States had a trade deficit of $27 billion. This means that the value of its **imports** (what it purchases from other countries) exceeded the value of its **exports** (what other countries purchase from the United States) by $27 billion. If the United States could do a better job of marketing abroad, it might help reduce or eliminate this deficit.

In Figure 18.1 and 18.2 are indicated some general information about the United States international trade picture: the major types of products exported and imported, and the major countries with which it trades.

Domestic Versus International Marketing

Much controversy has raged through the years over whether or not there is any real difference between domestic and international marketing. Those who say that "marketing is the same everywhere" are very sincere and base their view on the fact that all the same marketing activities, for example, pricing, channels of distribution management, advertising, and product planning, occur whether one is selling in Des Moines or Dakar. Further, they say that in order to understand any market one must be concerned with local customs and laws and that one probably should conduct market research in order to identify market segments correctly. Therefore, they see international marketing as an extension of domestic marketing.

However, such a view is too simplistic for today's world. The same marketing decision activities do occur everywhere, but the complexity of these decisions and the conditions under which such decisions are made tend to increase significantly abroad. Much of the marketing environment that one merely takes for granted domestically becomes "washed out" when operating overseas. In fact, marketers should expect to encounter cultural

Figure 18.1 Exported and Imported Products of the U.S., 1975

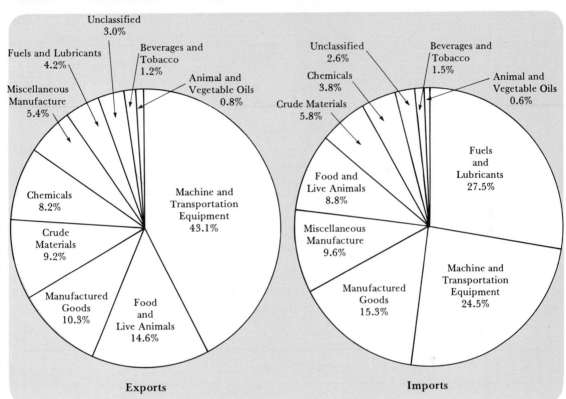

Source: U.S. Department of Commerce.

and legal constraints upon their operations that are very different in both *degree* and *type* from what has previously been experienced. This does *not*, of course, imply that international business should be avoided; the opportunities for most firms are too great to consider such an alternative. Instead, firms must develop the needed expertise in international marketing. Donald M. Hintz, Vice President of Culligan International Company, perhaps stated it best when he noted that 94% of the world's population is located outside the United States and, therefore, there should be considerable sales opportunity overseas for a large share of United States corporations.[1]

[1] Donald M. Hintz, "Internationalizing Your Business," in *Proceedings of Internationalizing Your Business*, ed., J. Irwin Peters (Chicago: DePaul University, 1976), p. 20.

Figure 18.2   Where U.S. Exports Go and Where U.S. Imports Come from (1975)

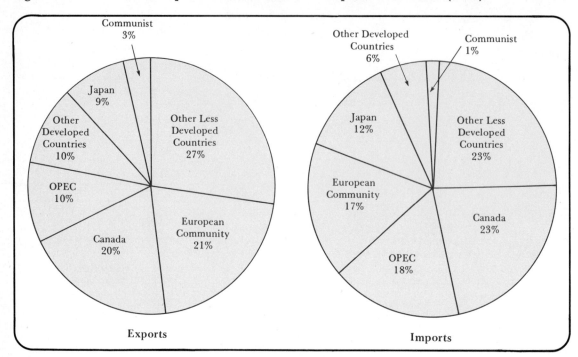

Source: U.S. Department of Commerce.

Growing World Trade

Few people realize the enormity of world trade and the rapidity of its growth. Total world exports alone were an estimated $866 billion in 1975, which is nearly *ten* times the total for 1955. Further, it is often assumed that the United States is the dominant force in such trade activity. Yet, the total exports from the United States ($111 billion in 1976) are roughly only one-third the total amount exported by the European Economic Community (EEC) countries. Still United States business has made great strides in the past few years; in 1955 United States exports were just $14.4 billion.[2]

The MNC

The **multi-national corporation** (MNC) is often thought of first when international business is discussed. Although defined in a number of ways,

[2] *Economic Report of the President* (Washington: United States Government Printing Office, January, 1976), p. 24.

Figure 18.3 The World's Largest Multi-National Corporations

Sales (in billions of dollars)

Gen. Motors	$30.4	Hitachi	$4.4
Exxon	22.1	Du Pont	4.4
AT&T	21.0	General Tel.	4.3
Ford	20.2	ICI	4.2
Royal Dutch Shell	14.1	Toyota	4.2
Sears, Roebuck	11.0	Daimler-Benz	4.2
GE	10.2	Goodyear	4.1
Mobil	10.2	Nestlé	4.1
Chrysler	9.8	Farbwerke-Hoechst	4.1
IBM	9.5	Mitsubishi	4.0
Unilever	8.9	Nisson	4.0
Texaco	8.7	RCA	3.8
ITT	8.6	Kresge	3.8
Gulf	7.6	Atlantic Richfield	3.8
Standard (Calif.)	6.5	Kroger	3.8
A&P	6.4	BASF	3.7
Philips	6.2	Continental Oil	3.6
Safeway	6.1	Fiat	3.6
BP	5.7	Brit. Steel	3.6
J. C. Penney	5.5	Montedison	3.6
US Steel	5.4	Proctor & Gamble	3.5
Standard (Ind.)	5.4	IH	3.5
Nippon Steel	5.4	Eastman Kodak	3.5
Westinghouse	5.1	Renault	3.5
Volkswagen	5.0	Matsushita	3.5
Shell Oil	4.8	LTV	3.4
Siemens	4.7		

Source: E. Christopher Palmer, "Challenges for the Multinational," *World* (Peat, Marwick, Mitchell & Co.), Spring 1974, p. 55.

perhaps the best working definition of an MNC is a firm that has production or service (in the case of banks) facilities in more than six countries and total sales in excess of $100 million per year.[3]

Figure 18.3 lists the world's largest multi-national corporations. The reader will undoubtedly notice that most of these are American.

[3] Gurney Breckenfeld, "Coping with the Nation–State," *Saturday Review*, January 24, 1976, p. 14.

A good example of an MNC is the International Harvester Company, headquartered in Chicago. International Harvester has subsidiaries in 10 countries, manufacturing joint ventures in 4 additional countries, and dealers and distributors in the United States and 155 other countries. With sales of over $2 billion *outside* the United States (roughly 40% of its total sales), this major American-based corporation easily qualifies under our definition of an MNC.[4] Further, International Harvester is no newcomer to international trade for it has been engaged in overseas business since the late 1800's.[5]

The critics of the MNCs were provided considerable ammunition in the latter part of the 1970's by the announcement of bribery incidents involving Lockheed, Gulf, United Brands, and a few other major world corporations. These announcements coupled with earlier criticisms of the MNCs (many of which were totally unfounded) lent impetus to the number of investigations and proposals for regulation. Ignored were the many positive contributions of MNCs to both developed and developing countries and the fact that only a few MNCs were involved in business excesses. Despite this current image problem for the MNCs, these firms will undoubtedly be the forces controlling international trade in the future, unless they are prohibited to do so by regulation.

Trends in the International Environment

There are many dynamic forces at work in the international environment in addition to the growth of the MNCs, for example, (1) the rise of nationalism; (2) the success of the European Economic Community (and efforts by other groups to pattern the EEC); (3) international attempts to regulate trade and stabilize monetary conditions; and (4) a rise in world wide *consumerism* and an increase in marketing regulation.

Nationalism. In the post-World War II era there has been an accelerated pace of decolonization and a rapid emergence of new nations.[6] Many of these new nations have severe economic development problems and they make up the bulk of what has been called the *third-world countries.* At the same time, these countries may be generally characterized as having a high level of **nationalism,** an intense pride in one's country and an antagonism toward its critics or any group that could potentially reduce its independence.

Such a nationalistic attitude can influence virtually every decision made by government officials, businessmen, and consumers. For example, it has

---

[4] *International Harvester 1975 Annual Report* (Chicago: International Harvester Company, 1975), p. 19.

[5] *International Harvester in Russia 1850–1976* (Chicago: International Harvester Company), p. 1.

[6] H. E. Kurt Waldheim, "The U.N. and the Multinational Corporation," *Corporate Citizenship in the Global Community* (Washington, D.C.: International Management and Development Institute, 1976), p. 34.

been suggested that the firms that are willing to establish facilities in Kenya and Tanzania instead of exporting to them will be the ones most likely to benefit from these countries' spirit of nationalism.[7] Such investment would be viewed by the peoples as a confidence in and concern for their country.

Nationalism, of course, is not limited to the third-world countries. During the DeGaulle era France provided a classic example of nationalism in a developed country. In fact, most countries have some nationalistic tendencies, but the problem is one of degree. To the marketer, however, a knowledge of the importance of nationalism is critical.

European Economic Community and Other Economic Groupings. In spite of occasional political and financial concerns, the **European Economic Community** has been a highly successful banding of Western European countries since it was founded in 1957. The original six nations—West Germany, France, The Netherlands, Belgium, Italy, and Luxembourg—were joined by Ireland, Great Britain, and Denmark in 1973. A common market, such as the EEC, is characterized by having no tariffs between members, the same tariffs toward other countries, and a high level of joint economic and political planning. Whether the European Economic Community will develop into a "United States of Europe" is still speculation, but the EEC has certainly been economically successful.

Of special importance has been the EEC's ability to develop special trade ties (preferential treatment) with its members' former colonies and with a host of countries in the Mediterranean[8] and other areas. This has given them special entree for their products in a number of developed and developing markets.

Seeing the success of the EEC, other economic groupings have been established or proposed. These include the Ancon (Andean Common Market), the East African Community, The Asian Common Market, and the Carribbean Common Market. The short-term potential of these groupings is very limited in comparison with the EEC, and to some extent they are merely a linking of countries with common problems. However, regional groupings do increase the size of these markets to the point that they may attract investment from corporations in the United States, Japan, and the European Economic Community.

The presence of common markets is important in the international marketing environment. For example, by locating a production facility in *one* country in a common market grouping, the company has tariff-free access to other countries in the same grouping. Failure to invest in any country in the group would mean that the firm faces the same tariff barrier in all countries. This decision would obviously have an effect on the marketing manager's ability to price competitively.

Trade and Monetary Reform. In recent years steps have been taken to

---

[7] John K. Ryans, Jr., "U.S. Corporate Involvement in Developing Markets: The East African Example," *Pittsburgh Business Review* (July–August, 1972), p. 8.

[8] Marion Bywater, "The EC 'Global' Approach," *European Community* (March, 1976), pp. 20–22.

"Better let me have another gross of the #101 thunderbird ashtrays, two gross of #473 beaded souvenir moccasins, and two dozen #87 turquoise and silver runner pins."

---

regularize world-wide trade and to provide greater international monetary stability. Shortly after World War II some 23 nations (including the United States) negotiated and signed the **General Agreement on Tariffs and Trade** (GATT); this was the first attempt to significantly reduce the tariff and trade barriers around the world. The GATT established formal procedures for continuing tariff negotiations and guidelines for the international trade practices of the participants. Prior to GATT, for example, tariff negotiations were conducted by countries on a one-to-one (bilateral) basis. Some 90 countries now participate in each GATT meeting (GATT rounds) that provides a negotiating forum for reducing specific tariffs for all of these countries simultaneously.

Even though the GATT has had a major impact on world trade barriers, significant tariffs still exist. Other barriers, such as quotas, border taxes, and even outright prohibitions on trade between some countries, still inhibit the free flow of goods and services and produce difficulties for the international marketing manager.

Consumerism and Market Regulation. American businessmen have long been familiar with both consumerism and regulations relating to marketing activities. But too often they think that consumerism is a purely American phenomenon. In actuality, consumerism has been an important factor in many countries, such as Sweden and Australia, for a number of years. Pressures for consumer protection have led to extensive protective legislation and ever active consumer information programs. For example, in Sweden the State Institute for Consumer Information (Konsumentisstitutet, KI), does extensive product testing and publishes the test results in its journal.[9] Such efforts to achieve effective consumer protection legislation will continue to be very strong, especially in the developed countries, and as in the past will lead to many marketing controls.

Some international marketing control legislation prevents using techniques that are acceptable in the United States. International advertisers have been greatly frustrated by the prohibitions on the use of *comparatives* (Product x is better and cheaper than Product y) and their inability in many countries to make meaningful product claims. Under the current interpretation of West German law (Cartel Act, Section I), for example, retailers are not permitted in their advertising to make performance comparisons among themselves and their competitor(s).[10] Thus, international marketing managers must be aware of the prohibitions affecting their advertising and marketing activities in the various countries and they must be sensitive to the growing global importance of consumerism.

ORGANIZING FOR NONDOMESTIC MARKETING

Two dimensions of organizing are important to the international marketing manager. The first concerns the way the firm is organized for *entry* into its nondomestic markets and the second deals with how the firm is *organized internally* to achieve its marketing objectives. In domestic marketing the entry question does not exist and one is immediately concerned with the structuring of the marketing activities within the firm's organizational chart. However, how the firm is organized to enter the market is critical overseas since the method used will have much to say about the degree of decision-making control.

Entry Alternatives

Basically, firms may enter an overseas market with varying degrees of decision-making control over their total operations, including their marketing efforts. The firm that enters an overseas market by establishing a

[9] Hans B. Thorelli, "Consumer Information Policy in Sweden—What Can Be Learned?" *Journal of Marketing* (January, 1971), pp. 50–51.

[10] J. J. Boddewyn and Stanley C. Hollander, *Public Policy Toward Retailing* (Lexington, Mass.; Lexington Books, 1972), p. 418.

wholly owned subsidiary or by having over 50% equity obviously has the greater degree of decision-making control. Perhaps this can best be visualized through the use of a decision-making control continuum (Figure 18.4).

When the firm is *exporting* to a market, it potentially has *no* say on how its product or service is to be marketed, although in practice it can discontinue exporting through an uncooperative middleman. Similarly, by *licensing* the production of its product (and typically by granting the right to use its brand name), the firm has only those decision-making controls that are established in the original agreement. These generally relate to quality control and the territory covered. In either instance (exporting or licensing), the international marketing manager has limited control over the marketing techniques used in the overseas market.

Historically, American firms have tended to prefer entry through the use of **wholly owned subsidiaries.** This entry method provides a maximum of operational control and the greatest protection to a firm's technology and the quality of product sold under its brand name. However, it also entails the greatest risk. Many firms, such as Goodyear International and Sears, have had a long standing preference for entry via wholly owned subsidiaries and this entry arrangement predominates in their overseas investments.

In more recent years, the trend has been toward entry through a **joint venture** arrangement. Among the joint venture's advantages is the fact that it permits sharing the risk while still obtaining a measure of control and participating in the profits in the market. Further, since the joint venture agreement is often made with an existing firm in the overseas market, the

Figure 18.4   Decision-Making Control Continuum

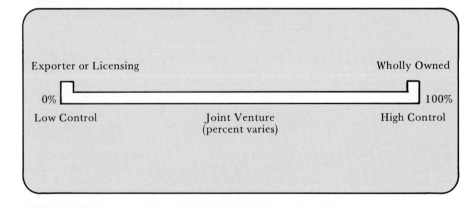

joint venture may have the additional benefits of reducing competition and gaining local market expertise and contacts. An even more recent development is the establishment of *country-company partnerships*. Much of the current overseas activity of General Tire International has occurred through management arrangements with governments in such areas as Tanzania.

An even more compelling factor favoring a joint venture is the foreign investment regulations that now exist in a number of countries. The market in which the firm wishes to enter may simply require the establishment of a joint venture and dictate the percentage of equity that the outside investor may hold. A prime example is Mexico where foreign investors are now permitted to hold only a 49% share of a firm. (This 1973 legislation was not retroactive.) Such laws, as well as restrictions on the percentage of expatriates that can be employed by the firm, are becoming more common, especially in the developing countries. This directly affects the decision-making control of the international marketing manager because his ability to conduct marketing planning becomes restricted.

International Organization

There are several organizational forms that corporations may use to perform their international operations. Many major firms, including MNCs, have separate international divisions or corporations and perform all their marketing and other nondomestic activities separately from their domestic operations. Major MNCs that use this approach include Sears, Roebuck and Company (Figure 18.5) and Goodyear International Corporation.

Factors Influencing Organizational Structure

The five factors that may influence the company organization structure for overseas operations are as follows:

1. The philosophy of top management.
2. The nature of the product line.
3. The relative size of foreign versus domestic operations.
4. The emergence in importance of regional economic groupings.
5. The location of foreign subsidiaries.[11]

Particularly important to the international organization is top management's orientation toward international business. If top management sees the whole world as its market, this affects its entire approach to international business, including its organization structure. If, however, top management sees its international business activities only as an addition to its domestic activities, then it will likely give its international operations only minimal attention and will subordinate these operations in its organization structure.

[11] Arvin V. Phatak, *Managing Multinational Corporations* (New York: Praeger Publishers, 1974), pp. 170–72.

Figure 18.5 Sears, Roebuck and Company International Organizational Chart

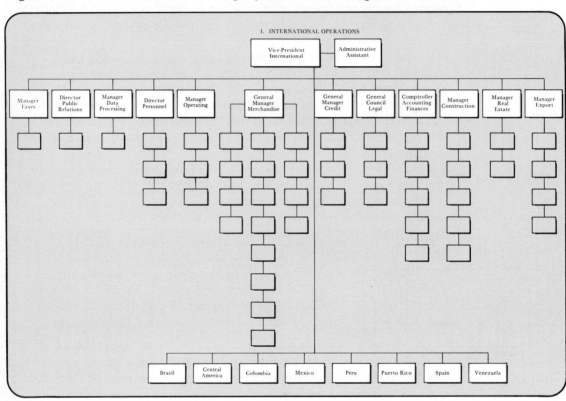

Source: Courtesy Sears, Roebuck and Co.

The breadth and variety of its product line and the homogeneity of its customers certainly influence the firm's organizational structure. For example, a company that primarily manufactures components for original equipment manufacturers, such as AMETEK (1975 annual report), basically appeals to the same industrial market segments everywhere. This is in sharp contrast to a highly diversified company, such as Black and Decker, that sells to many different industrial and ultimate customers.

It was noted earlier that in many firms international business accounts for a very small share of the firm's total business. In such instances, one could expect the international operations to be relatively subordinate in the total organization structure. At the same time, some firms, including such international giants as Philips (Dutch) and Nestlé (Swiss), conduct

International Marketing Management

the major share of their business *outside* their home countries. Such firms, thus, tend to emphasize the international side of their business in their organization structure.

The growth of the European Economic Community and other economic groupings has permitted some firms to move away from country-by-country headquarters to regional headquarters. Currently, Brussels has become very attractive as a regional headquarters location.

Finally, the location of the firm's foreign subsidiaries influences the organization structure. If the firm's subsidiaries are located in areas with marketing structures similar to those of the home country, such as an American firm with subsidiaries in Canada and Great Britain, then geography may be a reduced consideration in the decision making on organization structure.

Alternative Organizational Structures

Clearly, the most popular forms of international organization structure are the **international division,** the **product-line approach,** the **geographic approach,** and the **functional approach.** Rarely, of course, are these forms found in the pure form described here. In fact, each firm has its own particular international considerations and is greatly influenced by the people holding the international marketing positions. However, these four alternatives generally offer the frameworks most often used.

In the *international division* structure, the international operations of the firm are afforded the same level of importance as the various functional divisions of the domestic operations or as the various domestic divisions. In other words, the vice-president for international operations would be at the same organizational level as the vice-president of marketing or the vice-president of finance (whose responsibilities would be strictly domestic) or would be positioned at the same level as vice-president for the Southeast and vice-president for the Midwest (domestic divisions). Historically, firms have tended to use the international division approach when they first become involved in international business activity. This has principally been the case when their international business is conducted primarily through exports and their sales overseas have been small relative to domestic sales.[12]

In the *product-line approach,* the firm has separate divisions for each of its products or category of products and the division product manager is responsible for the products wherever they are sold. Such divisions typically have staff support in all functional areas, *including marketing.* The Celanese Corporation was one of the first United States firms to adopt the product-line approach. It used three broad product categories (fibers and forest products, chemicals and plastics, and consumer products) as its divisions.[13]

[12] Gilbert H. Clee and Wilbur M. Sachtjen, "Organizing a World-Wide Business," *Harvard Business Review* (November–December, 1964), pp. 55–67.
[13] William A. Dymsza, *Multinational Business Strategy* (New York: McGraw-Hill Book Company, 1972), p. 33.

Such an approach is particularly attractive when firms have a highly diversified product offering that reaches widely differing end-users.

With the growth of importance and increased homogeneity in some regions, such as the European Economic Community, several firms have moved to a *geographic* pattern of international organization in which each geographic division reports directly to the firm's chief executive. Corporate headquarters (through the chief executive) retains overall responsibility for world-wide planning and control.[14] Such an approach highlights the differences between regions and the need for special expertise to compete in particular markets. A home office functional staff is usually maintained to provide assistance to all regions. In this approach, North America would be one of the geographic divisions and would have equal line status with the European Economic Community and Middle East divisions. As one would imagine, this approach can result in difficulties if the firm has a wide and highly diversified product line and the approach can also produce staff duplication problems.

Less widely used is the *functional approach*. Here, the various functional areas assume *line* responsibility for world-wide operations.[15] For example, the marketing vice-president would be responsible for every sales office around the world and he would also be responsible for all their marketing efforts. Since each functional division would report directly to the chief executive officer, the burden for all coordination of efforts would rest at the top of the organization. This potentially reduces the critical interaction that is needed between important functional units of the firm such as finance, production, and marketing. In international business, perhaps even more than its domestic counterpart, the decisions relating to finance and production are highly significant to the marketer. Further, the need for information exchange at all levels reduces the viability of this approach in comparison with the product-line or geographic approaches.

Locus of Decision Making

Regardless of the international organizational structure, an important question arises with regard to the location of marketing decision making. In many firms the home office marketing executives retain many (or all) of the major decisions (centralization), but in others most of the marketing decisions are made at the regional or local level (decentralization) (see Figure 18.6). Factors that influence the location of decision making include: (1) the level of local cultural differences, (2) the level of local nationalism, (3) the desire to maintain the morale of its local employees, (4) familiarity of local personnel with products and markets, (5) the firm's method of entry (i.e., the home office may be able to exercise little control where it holds minority equity), (6) regulations on employment of nationals, and

[14] Ibid., p. 31.
[15] Ibid., pp. 34–35.

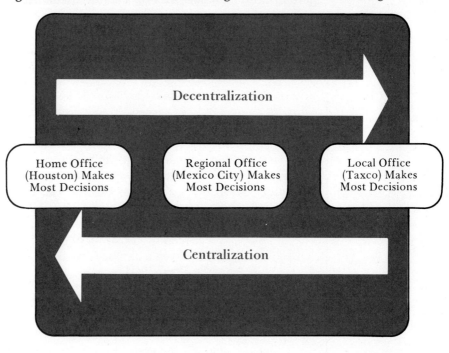

Figure 18.6   Locus of Decision Making in International Marketing

Decentralization

| Home Office (Houston) Makes Most Decisions | Regional Office (Mexico City) Makes Most Decisions | Local Office (Taxco) Makes Most Decisions |

Centralization

(7) whether the area is developed or undeveloped. The impact of these variables on the centralization/decentralization decision can be seen in Figure 18.7 in which the conditions leading to decentralized decision making are indicated.

Manpower Management

Basically, the international firm has need for three types of marketing personnel to staff its nondomestic operations. These include *home office* personnel, *foreign marketing managers,* and other *foreign marketing* personnel, including the foreign sales force.

In the past, home office international personnel in American firms usually had extensive international experience, including rather lengthy overseas assignments. Although this is still somewhat true today, forces are at work that will generally limit this opportunity in the future. In fact, the day of **expatriate personnel** is rapidly coming to a close and most home office personnel will have to gain their experience through a series of short-term overseas trips to solve special problems.

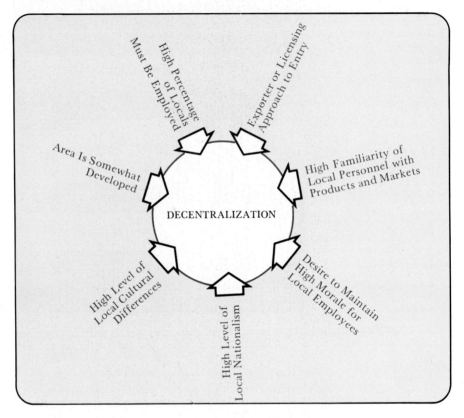

There are many reasons why the use of expatriate personnel is being limited, for example: (1) the rise in nationalism in many countries, (2) the increased number of national laws requiring that all or a high percentage of the firm's employees be local nationals, (3) the cost of sending expatriates abroad, and (4) the shortage of qualified expatriate management personnel.[16] From a cost standpoint alone, the assignment of American personnel abroad has become prohibitive. It is generally estimated that it costs the firm *twice* as much to assign a United States expatriate to a management post abroad than to hire a local manager. In addition, recent changes in the federal income tax laws have made an overseas assignment

[16] John M. Ivancevich, "Selection of American Managers for Overseas Assignments," *Personnel Journal* (March, 1969), p. 189.

much less attractive to the American manager. Thus, it should not be surprising that most overseas marketing posts, and particularly sales positions, will be held by nationals. Americans will be brought in mostly for supervision, advice, or training.

There are circumstances under which a firm may be willing to pay the prohibitive costs of assigning an American to a sales post overseas on a longer-term basis, for example, to sell certain products, the salesperson must have extensive training and perhaps even a special degree; customers may wish to transact business only with an expert; and customers may prefer to deal with an American. Under these conditions, which are more likely found in the industrial field, the firm may wish either to use an expatriate or to send home office personnel abroad for a series of special assignments.

ASSESSING MARKETS AND IMPROVING MARKETING DECISION MAKING

Markets ". . . are *some* people, the people with purchasing power—not *all* people."[17] To correctly assess nondomestic markets and improve marketing decision making, it is necessary to develop those understandings about overseas markets that are relevant to international marketing decisions rather than just information for information's sake. Especially relevant to international marketing are the traditional demographic, socioeconomic, and political factors and an insight into the culture of an area or country.

Traditional Factors

Naturally, one can gain a first impression of a potential market by examining such statistics as its balance of payments, disposable personal income, per capita income, gross national product, demographic data, and literacy rate. These statistics must be coupled with considerations of the language(s) spoken, political system, class system, education levels, and the like, in order to obtain a broad overview of the country and its people. In addition, one would also want geographic and resource information because topography, climate, and availability of ports and a sound resource base also influence the market. For example, Bolivia is not only landlocked, but it is also a mountainous country whose peoples and markets have been separated from normal international trade flows. These factors have influenced the nature and development of this market. An analysis of these concerns alone, however, is inadequate for a viable market assessment and for marketing decision making.

[17] Fred J. Bastl, "Determination of the Export Potential," *Akron Business and Economic Review* (Summer, 1971), p. 5.

Cultural Considerations

A decade or so ago it was said that there ". . . was a time, not so very long ago, when an anthropologist would not be caught dead among marketing men and marketing men would not lend an ear to anthropologists."[18] Although somewhat exaggerated, this statement points to the recognition now given to *cultural considerations* when marketing decisions on foreign markets are being made.

There have been many horror stories about companies that attempt to market products whose colors signified death or illness in some countries or that used product names that were offensive when translated into the country's language. Naturally, a firm trying to market its product in a given country or area wants to avoid such embarrassment, just as it would at home. In fact, recognizing that these potential problems exist and asking qualified nationals about them would likely help to avoid these obvious marketing strategy errors.

The concern here, however, is with trying to better understand all of the factors in an overseas market, including the firm's potential consumers, channel members, company employees, and business associates, that may affect the marketer's success. Since these nationals' attitudes and beliefs are largely attributable to their cultural environment, an understanding of the cultural environment is essential in improving marketing decision making. What cultural factors are important to the marketer?

It is believed that the marketer must be particularly concerned with the *religious, family, educational*, and *social influences* on marketing efforts.[19]

One can easily see how the predominant religion of an area may influence attitudes toward hard work, honesty, and luxury goods and how different family members may influence the purchasing patterns of a household. One need only note the difference between the way the elder is revered in the Chinese family structure in Hong Kong and the way the senior citizen is treated with detachment in the American family structure. Similarly, education (who should be educated and how much) influences the qualifications of salespeople or the size of the middle-income group. The social factor considers not only the importance assigned to reference groups and to status symbols, but also the influence of social pressures in general.

Since each society has its own cultural features, it is difficult to generalize among markets. However, these four cultural considerations just discussed should be analyzed when attempting to better understand individual attitudes in any market. Naturally, other cultural concerns, such as a peoples' sensitivity to the arts, for example, may be a factor for certain firms in individual countries. In such instances, the cultural aspects of a market must be examined in much greater detail than has been implied here.

[18] Maneck S. Wadia, "The Concepts of Culture in the Analysis of Consumers," *Changing Marketing Systems, Proceedings 1967 Winter Conference American Marketing Association* (Chicago: American Marketing Association, 1967), p. 186.

[19] John Fayerweather, *International Marketing*, 2nd ed. (Englewood Cliffs, N.J.: Prentice-Hall, Inc., 1970), p. 24.

By assessing the traditional factors and the cultural dimensions the international marketing manager has a better overall picture of the nature of the market than he would have if he assessed only the traditional factors. This sort of analysis is the first stage in identifying the potential of an area or a country as a marketplace for a firm's product(s).

RESEARCHING NONDOMESTIC MARKETS

International marketing managers must often make overseas marketing decisions without having the type of data that is readily available to domestic marketers. In Chapter 5 marketing research was thoroughly discussed from a domestic point of view. Here we will focus on the information problems the marketer faces when he tries to assess opportunities and plan marketing strategy in nondomestic markets.

Basically, the problems of researching overseas markets can be categorized as follows:

1. The quantity and quality of available secondary data.
2. The cost of conducting primary research and the quality of overseas research firms.
3. The technical difficulties in actually conducting marketing research studies in many developing markets.

The United States is rich in reliable secondary data, a fact that is often unappreciated until one begins to look abroad. For example, the U.S. Bureau of the Census provides extensive information on the economic characteristics of the United States population and breaks this data down by state, city, and so on. In contrast, Kenya was only able (and willing for political purposes) to ask four or five questions of each household when it conducted its major nationwide census in the late 1960's. Kenya, of course, is not unusual in this regard. Many countries do not even conduct a census; they rely on estimates.

Generally, the secondary data available in developed countries, such as Australia, France, and Sweden, is very good both in *quantity* and *quality*. Marketers in developed countries rely heavily on market information for their marketing decisions. It is typically in the **less developed countries** (LDC) where the international marketing manager has difficulties in obtaining adequate, reliable information.

Questioning the Data

There is a tendency to accept published data as being valid and reliable. However, the marketing manager should seek answers to the following questions when he uses secondary data provided by most less developed countries:

1. *Who* collected the data and *why* were the data collected?
2. *When* were the data collected and what research method was used?
3. Are these data consistent with other data on this country?

If, for example, the data were collected by an agency in a less developed country in order to support the country's need for a loan or for a particular project it wished to have funded, then the data might be suspect. The original information may have been collected 25 years ago and data for recent years may be the result of projections from the original data. Thus, it is a good idea to check the data from a country with other sources, such as the Overseas Business Reports (OBRs) that are prepared on a country-by-country basis by the U.S. Department of Commerce or data prepared by the United Nations.

Cost of Collecting Primary Data

Many American companies, particularly the larger consumer goods manufacturers, are accustomed to conducting their own marketing studies in order to obtain specific information on customer preferences, shopping patterns, behavior, and the like. The market potential for these companies is great enough and the need for this information is compelling enough to justify the costs.

If the best estimate of the potential total sales in a particular less developed country is only $150,000 a year, spending $50,000 on researching the market would not be justified. The international marketing manager must weigh the *cost of obtaining* the data carefully in terms of the *estimated potential sales and profit* the country or region might produce. Although cost may be a prohibiting factor in conducting domestic marketing research, the cost overseas is a severely limiting factor in collecting primary data.

Another factor to consider is the availability of competent research firms to conduct the research. Again, there are many excellent research firms in most developed countries. Several major American research firms, such as Burke International, have branches in the leading overseas markets. Many less developed countries, however, have few (if any) marketing research firms and their research personnel may not have the necessary skills to conduct research.

Technical Problems

Some of the more popular methods for conducting marketing research, such as mail or telephone surveys, cannot be used in many areas. Problems of literacy, inadequate postal and telephone systems, and lack of respondent familiarity with the importance of surveys often create severe obstacles for marketing researchers.

In fact, there are even problems with personal interviewing. Often the potential respondent, especially one in a less developed country, is suspicious of the interviewer and may see him as a representative of the government or a tax collector. It must be remembered that in many parts of the world customers are not accustomed to describing why they make a purchase or what color package they prefer. Therefore, customers cannot put their thoughts into words or see little relevance in doing so.

ELEMENTS OF THE MARKETING MIX

Perhaps the greatest distinction between domestic and international marketing lies in the international marketing manager's ability to use the tools of marketing as effectively as he would domestically. Much of the domestic decision-making flexibility in developing pricing, advertising, personal selling, channels of distribution, and product strategy is lost in international marketing decision making, even in the case of wholly owned subsidiaries, partly because of the legal and cultural differences among countries and because of the increased competitive environment, especially in developed markets.

First, let us look at each element of the marketing strategy and discuss the questions that the international marketing manager should answer for *each* country or region where the firm wishes to sell its product(s). By analyzing the market's response to each element of the marketing strategy, the international marketing manager is actually beginning to develop the marketing strategy.

Product Planning

Many product decisions are actually made in the original decision on how to enter the market. If the firm has decided to establish a local plant in a country, either a wholly owned or a joint venture, some thought had to be given to the product(s) to be produced. In Figure 18.8 there are basic product questions that the international marketing manager must be actively involved in answering.

Naturally, a major question deals with determining the product or products to be sold in the market or country. Many manufacturers produce a broad range of product lines and product varieties within lines. A firm may choose to "cherry pick" its line, that is, initially offer only those products that have been most successful in the United States or in a different foreign country. For example, an American household appliance manufacturer may decide to sell electric fans in a West African country, such as Liberia. Although the manufacturer may have many sizes and types of fans that it sells in Europe, in Liberia it may choose to sell only the one that has proven to be most popular among Europeans.

Often, certain product modifications are obviously necessary, such as wiring an electric product for AC instead of for DC for sales in Europe. Other possible changes might be more extensive, for example, drastic

Figure 18.8   Product Policy in International Markets—Key Questions to Answer in Each Market or Country

---

1. What products and product lines should the company sell, e.g., how broad and deep should the product line be for this market?
2. To what extent should the company adapt and modify products to cultural, sociological, and national characteristics for this market?
3. What improvements of existing products should be undertaken and should the firm introduce a new product or products in this market?
4. How should products be packaged and labeled in this market? (Includes a review of existing packaging and labeling laws.)
5. How much emphasis is there on brand names and trademarks? Does the firm wish to use the same brand names and trademarks used in the United States and/or elsewhere in this market?
6. What warranties and guarantees, if any, are desirable or must be offered and what other post-sale service(s), such as repair service, is required in this market?

---

modification in the size of a refrigerator so that it would fit better in the smaller apartment kitchens in Greece. Similarly, decisions on packaging and labeling must be made. These decisions involve putting legally required information on labels.

Many companies, such as Goodyear International, are very concerned about their corporate identifications or trademarks being prominently displayed on their products, in the stores, in advertising, and so on. Other companies, particularly those whose national identifications may actually reduce sales, may choose to use different brand names or trademarks overseas.

Whether or not to offer warranties and guarantees is to some extent related to the product quality. In fact, a company may wish to offer the same quality product it does in the United States, but it may choose not to offer warranties and guarantees in foreign countries because customers do not expect or want them. Similarly, whether or not the firm offers repairs or other post-sale services is not only a product decision, but it also influences the channels of distribution that are chosen.

Channels of Distribution

In most countries the channels of distribution are basically similar. Certainly for consumer products all countries have retailer-type outlets that deal directly with the customer. Typically, all countries also have one or more levels of middlemen performing wholesaler and/or agent functions that connect the manufacturer with the retailer.

At the same time, there are wide extremes in both the complexity of middlemen levels and the size of retail outlets. Japan, for example, is known for having many levels of middlemen for most consumer products and for having a predominance of small specialty stores at the retail level. Kenya and several other African countries have the famous "Mom and Pop" stores that carry a very limited variety of merchandise—often only a few sundry items or one or two shelves of canned foods. These can be contrasted to Stockholm's gigantic store that dominates the landscape and the retail scene.

Figure 18.9 lists six basic questions that must be answered about the channels of distribution to use in any market. Initially, the international marketing manager must analyze the existing channels of distribution for his products and must determine whether or not to use these channels or try to develop an alternative approach. The risk, of course, is greatest when the firm attempts to be innovative. Innovation is usually not advisable unless (1) the current channels are closed to the firm's products or (2) the present channel does not meet consumer preferences. One is reminded of a recent French five-year plan that called for a reduction in the number of small neighborhood shops; these shops were to be replaced by shopping

Figure 18.9 Channels of Distribution in International Markets—Key Questions to Answer in Each Market or Country

1. What is the typical retail and wholesale structure for comparable products in this market?
2. Should the firm use existing channels of distribution or attempt to alter the established distribution patterns in this market?
3. Does the firm wish to sell directly to the retailer or through middlemen in this market?
4. Should the firm attempt to obtain wide distribution at the retail level or rely on exclusive dealerships or outlets in this market?
5. How much channel control does the firm want in this market?
6. What discount structure and credit terms are competitive and appropriate for this market?
7. What is the quality of the available transportation, warehousing, and the firm's other physical distribution needs in this market?
8. How much channel advertising support is necessary and appropriate for this market?

centers. French consumer reactions to this plan were negative and this "innovative" step was not achieved.[20]

Another critical concern for consumer products relates to the desired breadth of the firm's distribution at the retail level. Naturally, to a great extent the decision depends on the product and its consumers, but many firms can choose between selling through relatively exclusive outlets or through a wide number (and variety) of outlets. Tied closely to this decision is the question of how much control of the channel is desired. In order to effectively control the way the product is sold at the retail level, the firm's products must have strong market positions or the firm must provide some special financial incentive to the retailer, such as extended credit or attractive terms of sale. For example, Michelin finds it much easier to control its retail tire outlets in most of Europe than does its American competitors because Michelin has an impressive market share. Other channel concerns include the development of a discount structure, credit terms, and dealer support programs. Financial arrangements must be attractive enough to obtain representation through desired outlets and permit the firm's prices to compete with other firms' prices in the market.

Pricing

In most instances, price has become a *defensive* instead of an *offensive* marketing tool for the firm that chooses to enter a foreign market.[21] Tariff barriers in most countries tend to assure that the exporter cannot do more than match his local competition and often he is forced to price higher than the competition.

For the firm entering a foreign market through the joint venture or the wholly owned subsidiary approach, price strategy can be used much as it is domestically. A recent study, however, has indicated that international marketing managers tend to be more concerned with meeting competitor's prices or with cost-plus pricing than with a more aggressive pricing strategy.[22]

Pricing concerns requiring decisions by the international marketing manager include determining the relative importance of pricing policy in the overall marketing strategy and whether or not to attempt to establish a fairly uniform price in all the firm's markets (Figure 18.10). In addition, the skimming or penetration pricing decision becomes important, especially for new products.

It is probably in this general pricing decision-making area that international firms are most frustrated. Although tariff restrictions inhibit the

[20] James C. Baker and John K. Ryans, Jr., *Multinational Marketing: Dimensions in Strategy* (Columbus, Ohio: Grid, Inc., 1975), p. 168.

[21] Ibid., p. 143.

[22] James C. Baker and John K. Ryans, Jr., "Some Aspects of International Pricing: A Neglected Area of Management Policy," *Management Decision* (Summer, 1973), pp. 181–82.

Figure 18.10   Pricing in International Markets—Key Questions to Answer in Each Market or Country

1. What tariff and dumping laws are applicable in this market?
2. Should the firm establish (or attempt to establish) uniform base prices throughout the world or allow major variations from country to country?
3. What specific pricing approach should be used in the market? (Examples are cost-oriented, competitor-oriented, and customer-oriented.)
4. What are the price regulations (i.e., price fixing and cartel arrangements) in this market?
5. As an overall strategy, is penetration or skimming pricing preferable for new products in this market?
6. What pricing approach do competitors use in this market?

pricing aggressiveness of exporters, lack of information on non-American competitors' pricing policies has tended to have the same effect. Interestingly enough, this problem seems to exist regardless of whether the pricing decision is decentralized to the local level or is retained at the home office.

Advertising

Of all the strategy elements, advertising is perhaps the one most directly affected by the cultural differences among countries. For this reason, a continued controversy in the field of international marketing revolves around the appropriateness of using **standardized advertising,** that is, using the same advertising campaign in multiple markets. Some companies, such as Coca-Cola and Exxon, have been able to use standardized advertising successfully. Perhaps the most famous of such campaigns was the Exxon "Tiger in a Tank" campaign of the late 1960's.

From the standpoint of the international marketing manager, there are several major advantages in using standardized advertising.[23] These include a significant production cost saving and the opportunity to use a successful theme more fully. Despite these advantages, few companies are able to use standardized advertising outside rather compact regions, such as Western Europe. To do so would require the product to have the same appeal everywhere and to have a homogeneous world-wide market segment that it is attempting to reach. Such products could well include expensive luxury

[23] John K. Ryans, Jr., "A Tiger in Every Tank?" *Columbia Journal of World Business* (March–April, 1969), pp. 70–71.

items that appeal to high-income, sophisticated consumers or products, such as Coca-Cola, that have a very basic, universal appeal.

The international marketing manager faces other advertising problems, for example, media availability and government regulation in different areas of the world. Until recently, for example, South Africa had no television and had no plans for television. This was unexpected in such an economically advanced market, but it was another result of apartheid. What this meant in terms of promotion decisions was that TV commercials could not be used in a market where such an advertising medium would be most appropriate for many products. One need only watch the increasing pattern of advertising regulation in such diverse areas as Germany and Australia to see that regulation is a major problem for advertisers.

In Figure 18.11 other advertising questions are asked. A problem in most countries is the lack of reliable media research and circulation/audience data. Circulation, rate, and other media information is now available from *Standard Rate and Data* service for a number of developed markets, including England, Mexico, and West Germany, but it is impossible to obtain circulation figures that are not inflated in many markets, especially in less developed countries. Lack of such basic information, such as the relative circulations of newspapers in a given market, certainly increases the difficulty in making marketing media decisions.

Another major advertising decision is whether to choose an *international*

Figure 18.11   Advertising Policy in International Markets—Key Questions to Answer in Each Market or Country

1. To what extent should advertising themes and campaigns be differentiated from other markets to accommodate cultural, sociological, and national characteristics in this market? (Is standardized advertising a recommended and appropriate alternative in this market?)
2. Should a local advertising agency or a branch/subsidiary of the firm's international advertising agency be used in this market?
3. What media are available and what are their costs and unusual requirements? How reliable are media circulation or audience data?
4. What is the availability and quality of media research organizations?
5. What are the regulations on media advertising that would affect the firm's strategy in this market? What are the regulations on point-of-purchase and in-store materials?
6. What roles do channel members play and what advertising assistance, such as cooperative advertising, in-store promotion, and point-of-purchase materials, do channel members expect?

Figure 18.12 Comparison of U.S. International Agency Executives' and U.S. Advertising Managers' Opinions on Culturally Oriented Advertising Statements

	Respondents	Disagree −5, −4, %	−3 to −1 %	Agree +1 to +3 %	+4, +5 %	N	Total
(1) Basic human nature is the same everywhere; therefore, traditional advertising appeals of economy, comfort, advancement, and social approval are applicable in all markets.	Agency executives	29.3	4.8	43.9	22.0	41	100.0
	Advertising managers	16.0	17.4	43.5	23.1	69	100.0
(2) In practical marketing situations, an individual approach in each country or region is entirely unnecessary.	Agency executives	24.4	56.1	14.6	4.9	41	100.0
	Advertising managers	31.8	29.0	24.7	14.5	69	100.0
(3) Standardized ads can now be readily applied throughout the world because cultural lag between most nations is minimal.	Agency executives	38.5	35.8	25.7	0.0	39	100.0
	Advertising managers	31.8	36.3	27.5	4.4	69	100.0
(4) An international agency preparing the ad in the U.S. can serve its clients as effectively as a local agency in the particular country.	Agency executives	22.5	20.0	45.0	12.5	40	100.0
	Advertising managers	24.7	43.5	24.7	7.1	69	100.0
(5) In most cases, the only major difference between foreign markets will be that of language and idiom.	Agency executives	31.7	36.6	29.3	2.4	41	100.0
	Advertising managers	26.1	42.0	24.7	7.2	69	100.0
(6) Girls in Tokyo and Berlin are "sisters under the skin," on their lips, fingernails, and in their hair styles. Therefore, ads using basic appeals can successfully reach all of them.	Agency executives	23.1	23.0	36.0	17.9	39	100.0
	Advertising managers	13.1	27.5	42.0	17.4	69	100.0

Source: John K. Ryans, Jr. and James H. Donnelly, Jr., "Selected Practices and Problems of United States 'International' Advertising Agencies," *University of Washington Business Review*, Vol. XXX, No. 1, Autumn 1970, p. 53. By permission of the *Journal of Contemporary Business*.

advertising agency with branches in the foreign countries or to choose different local advertising agencies in each market. One study indicates that American-based MNCs are almost equally divided on whether to use international agencies with branches or to use separate agencies in each locale.[24] These MNCs appeared more likely to use local agencies in developed countries than in the less developed countries.

Apparently, the decision whether to use international agencies instead of local agencies is based upon the importance that the firm attributes to country-to-country differences. Figure 18.12 presents the findings of a study of MNCs that sought international advertising managers' attitudes on culture and that compared their responses with those of international agency executives. In addition, it has been found that companies using foreign-based agencies clearly attribute more importance to cultural and environmental issues than do those using the same agency everywhere.[25]

SUMMARY

The total size of world trade is enormous ($866 billion in 1975) and provides excellent opportunities for successful overseas marketing for American-based firms. Despite this potential, firms should not assume that their domestic marketing operations can be successfully transferred to foreign countries. Overseas cultural and legal constraints are two areas that often require different marketing strategies.

Leading the way in international operations are multi-national corporations. These are firms that have production or service facilities in more than six countries and have total annual sales of $100 million per year. Multi-national corporations should recognize significant trends in the international environment that can affect their operations. In recent years, the most important of these have been the rise of nationalism, the growth of the European Economic Community, trade and monetary reform, and consumerism and market regulation.

As companies move into international markets, they must decide how much control over the venture they want to have. If they export or engage in a licensing agreement, little control is obtained. Wholly owned subsidiaries provide 100% control. Joint ventures result in a degree of control between 0% and 100%. In organizing its international operations, a company can use the international division, product-line, functional, or geographical approach. A major organizational decision is whether to centralize decision making in the home office or decentralize it in the overseas office. This refers to the locus of decision making.

Two major types of data should be gathered as a company enters international markets. The first consists of traditional factors, such as disposable

---

[24] James H. Donnelly, Jr., and John K. Ryans, Jr., "How American Companies Advertise Overseas," *European Business* (January, 1970), p. 60.

[25] James H. Donnelly, Jr., and John K. Ryans, Jr., "Agency Selection in International Advertising," *European Journal of Marketing* (Fall, 1972), p. 24.

personal income, balance of payments, and literacy rate. The second involves cultural considerations.

A company that engages in international marketing needs to make the same kinds of major marketing decisions that it makes in the domestic market. Especially important are decisions on products, channels of distribution, pricing, and advertising.

1. Should small companies consider selling in international markets or do you believe that international marketing can only be done by the huge multi-national corporations?
2. Which areas of the world do you think offer the best potential for American multi-national corporations?
3. What is the major advantage of wholly owned subsidiaries as opposed to a firm marketing overseas through the exporting alternative?
4. What four major cultural aspects would you want to consider when you research a foreign country as a possible market for your products?
5. What are the major advantages of having decentralized decision making in overseas operations? What are the disadvantages?
6. Do you approve of foreign countries taking over the property of multi-national corporations, for example, taking over the oil companies?
7. Why are expatriate personnel being used less frequently in overseas operations?
8. What conditions exist today in many foreign countries that would discourage a multi-national corporation from locating there?

GLOSSARY

European Economic Community (EEC): the "Common Market," or nine European countries that have joined together to promote their economic well-being through no tariffs between members, same tariffs toward outside countries, and a high level of joint economic and political planning

Exports: products and services sold to foreign countries

Expatriate Personnel: personnel used in international marketing who are not native to the country where the facility is located

Functional Approach: an international organization structure in which various functional areas assume line responsibility for world-wide operations

General Agreement on Tariffs and Trade (GATT): a formalized attempt by 90 participating countries to reduce tariff and trade barriers around the world

Geographic Approach: an international organization structure in which various divisions are responsible for the marketing effort for a specific region of the world

Imports: products and services purchased from foreign countries

International Division: an international organization structure that provides the chief executive of international operations top-line reporting status in the firm

Joint Venture: the entry alternative to foreign markets that results in degrees of control between 0% and 100%

Less Developed Countries (LDCs): countries that have low levels of income and gross national product per capita

Multi-National Corporation: a company that has production or service in more than six countries and total annual sales of $100 million per year

Nationalism: an intense pride in one's own country and antagonism toward its critics or groups that could potentially reduce its independence

Product-Line Approach: an international organization structure in which a division product manager is responsible for a specific category of products

Standardized Advertising: using the same advertising campaign in different international markets

Wholly Owned Subsidiary: the entry alternative to foreign markets that results in 100% control

CASES

Case 1: The National Preserve Co.

The National Preserve Company is a midwestern manufacturer of preserves, jams, and jellies. The company has been in existence since 1897, and it has been a corporation since 1921.

Sales growth in recent years has been spectacular. Its volume in 1975 was $108 million, compared to $77 million in 1973. Between 1973 and

1975 the net profit was around $3.5 million. Return on investment (ROI) for these three years dropped: 10.1% in 1973, 7.5% in 1974, and 6.8% in 1975.

The company is very conservative. Mr. Thomas Schwartz, its president, is the grandson of the company's founder and the son of its second president. Mr. Schwartz stresses close contact with the firm's 1,300 employees and asks that they maintain neat appearances. Maintaining and improving product quality are the major concerns of Mr. Schwartz. Neither the marketing policy nor the production policy is allowed to detract from this objective; Mr. Schwartz personally visits grocery stores to check on product quality and those responsible for low-quality offerings are politely reprimanded. The company prefers to finance expansions through retained earnings rather than incur debt or issue stock. The company has issued common stock since 1959, but the Schwartz family owns 40% of this stock. The emphasis on retained earnings accounts in part for the relatively low return on investment and the low level on dividends. So that it would not be at the mercy of its suppliers, the firm integrated vertically backward by acquiring acreage in the midwest and California that produces the fruits required for the company's products.

In 1977 the company employed a university professor of marketing as a consultant. The consultant was especially surprised that the company's success was through sole emphasis on domestic sales. The firm did not sell in foreign markets, and it did not have any plans to do so in the future. The consultant believes that future growth may be limited unless the company develops plans to sell overseas.

1. Do you agree with the consultant that the firm should sell its products in foreign markets?
2. Which of its products do you think would be the most appropriate to sell overseas?
3. What kinds of data should the firm gather before it makes a decision to sell in international markets?
4. Are there any aspects of the company's operations that might prove to be a problem if it sells its products abroad?

Case 2: The Divco Corp.

Ranch land in the United States sells for between $100 and $1,000 an acre. Factors that determine the specific price include its yield per acre, whether irrigation is required, how hilly the land is, the size of the parcel (larger parcels may sell for a lower cost-per-acre than a smaller, comparable tract), and so on.

In August of 1977, a ranch was offered for sale in Paraguay. The price was $4,950 for 280 acres. The cost-per-acre was only $17.

The Divco Corp., a conglomerate with $300 million in sales per year, was considering both the acquisition of large-sized ranches and expansion overseas. William Butler, the company's designated individual to head up the overseas expansion, noticed the advertisement offering the ranch for sale in Paraguay. While a ranch of 280 acres was too small for the Divco Corp. to consider purchasing, the availability of ranch land in Paraguay caused Mr. Butler to wonder about the feasibility of acquiring larger tracts, especially since the cost-per-acre appeared to be so reasonable.

1. What facts about Paraguay's general political and economic climate should Mr. Butler investigate?
2. In what facts about the ranching industry in Paraguay should Mr. Butler have an interest?
3. For what questions of a marketing nature should Mr. Butler get answers?

Name Index

Chock full O' Nuts, 458
Chrysler Corporation, 267, 413, 529
Ciba-Geigy's Pharmaceutical Division, 320
Citibank, 59
Citicorp, 149
City Investing Company, 233
City Products, 347
Clausi, A. S., 238
Clee, Gilbert H., 537
Cleveland Power Company, 268
Clifford, Donald K., Jr., 184, 254
Coke, 80, 202, 250, 257, 259, 415, 549, 550
Coleman, Richard P., 93–94
Colgate-Palmolive Company, 267
Commoner, Barry, 62
Consolidated Foods, 352
Constantin, James A., 518
Container Corporation of America, 406
Continental Airlines, 448
Continental Can, 187
Corning Glass Works, 485
Corrigan, Wilfred J., 441
Cott, Ed, 16
Cox, Reavis, 362
Crest, 47, 258
Culligan International Company, 527
Cundiff, Edward W., 517

D

Danielenke, Robert, 247
Darling, John R., 116–17
Dataspeed, 40, 154
Davidson, Hugh J., 236
Davidson, James, 499
Davidson, William R., 113
Davis, Francis, 120
Dayton Hudson, 347
Dean, Joel, 285
DeGaulle, 531
DeSoto, 374
Deutsch, Claudia H., 404
Dirlam, Joel B., 442
Docutel, 120
Donnelly, James H., Jr., 551, 552
Douglas Aircraft, 65

Douglas, John, 83
Dow Chemical, 127, 247, 443
Drano Corporation, 449
Drexel Heritage Furnishings, 54
Drucker, Peter, 61, 234
Dunkin' Donuts, 291, 353
DuPont, 118, 184, 462
DuPont Corfam, 449
DuPont Dacron, 449
Dynsza, William A., 537

E

Eastman Kodak, 118
Eaton Industrial Truck Division, 505–6
Ehrlich, Paul, 62
Electrolux, 320, 331
Elgin Watch Company, 517
Engel, James E., 288
Engel, James F., 96, 103
Enis, Ben M., 205–6, 238, 352
Etzel, Michael J., 291
Evans Company, 366, 367
Evans, Franklin B., 84
Evans, Rodney E., 518
Exxon, Inc., 153, 257, 259, 529, 549

F

Fairchild Camera, 252, 415, 441
Fayerweather, John, 542
Federal Drug Enforcement Agency, 9
Federal Supply Service, 69
Federal Trade Commission Ad, 291
Federated Department Stores, 50, 347
Ferris, Richard, 7
Few, Kendrick S., 362
Field, George A., 83
Firestone Tire and Rubber, 30
First National Bank, 259
Fisher-Price Toys, 243
Fiske, Edward B., 295
Food Fair Stores, 347, 349
Ford, Gerald, 462
Ford, Henry, 43
Ford Motor Company, 257, 267, 320, 413, 529

Friedman, Si, 260
Fuller, R. Buckminister, 61
Fuss, Norman H., Jr., 460

G

Gable, Myron, 126
Gale, B. T., 175
Gallup-Robinson Impact Test, 289
Gamble, Frederic R., 278
Gamble-Skogmo, 347
Gelb, Betsy D., 352
General Dynamics, 131
General Electric, 63, 118, 258, 320, 494, 529
General Foods, 118, 238, 241, 247, 267
General Mills, 6, 247, 267
General Motors, 43, 127, 233, 267, 413, 485, 529
General Tire, 131, 535
George, William R., 214
Georgia Pacific, 30
Gerber, 49, 184
Gillett, Peter L., 94, 487
Gillette, 237, 252, 401, 485
Gleem, 258, 275
Goffman, Erving, 84
Goodman Equipment Company, 401
Goodman, Sam R., 518
Goodrich Tire and Rubber Company, 271
Goodyear International, 534, 546
Goodyear Tire and Rubber, 30, 271, 392
Grand Union, 347, 349
Great Atlantic & Pacific Tea Company, 283, 347, 349, 351, 374, 413, 462, 529
Gruen Company, 252
Grumman Aircraft, 131
Gulf, 529, 530

H

Haas, Robert, 187
Hall, Edwin T., 95
Hallmark Cards, 320
Hancock, Robert S., 120
Hanes, 148, 376
Hanover Shoes, 379
Hardin, Clyde, 310
Hartley, Robert F., 10, 401

Hasbro Industries, 6
Heinz, H. J., 258, 396
Helene Curtis, 505
Hensel, J. S., 62
Hertz, 184
Heublein, 243, 267
Hewlett-Packard, 30, 118
Hill, Richard H., 247
Hintz, Donald M., 527
Hise, Richard T., 14, 126, 149, 175, 176, 254, 303, 323, 351, 480, 483, 487
Hlavacek, James D., 247
Holiday Inn, 291
Hollander, Stanley C., 533
Holloway, Robert J., 120
Holmes, John H., 251
Homelite Division of Textron, 320
Howard, John A., 103
Hunt, Shelby D., 355
Hunt-Wesson, 485

I

IBM, 118, 257, 481, 529
Ideal brand, 351
Illuminating Company, 269
Inland Steel, 313
Instrument Corporation, 415
International Harvester Company, 530
International Paper, 118, 462
Iron and Steel Institute, 182
ITT, 529
Ivancevich, John M., 540

J

James, Don R., 291
J. C. Penney, 347, 485, 529
Jersig, Harry, 7
Jewel Companies, 347, 457
Johnson & Johnson, 49, 250
Joseph Schlitz Brewing, 30
Justice Department, 127

K

K-Mart, 258
Kaplan, A. D. H., 442

Staudt, Thomas A., 232
Stephens, Keith T., 6
Still, Richard R., 517
Stop and Shop, 485
Strawser, Robert H., 175, 176
Sultan, R. G. M., 175
Sunshine Biscuit, 462
Supermarkets General, 347

T

Talarzyk, W. Wayne, 113
Tanner, James C., 152
Tarpey, Lawrence X., 83
Taylor, Donald A., 232
Taylor, Thayer C., 213
Texaco, 529
Texas Instruments, 118, 252, 441
Textron, 131
Tektronix, 118
Thomas, David, 383
Thorelli, Han B., 533
3M, 118, 247
Timex, 118, 184, 252, 258
Toffler, Alvin, 96
Trion, Randy, 449
Turner, Ted, 7

Twedt, Dik Warren, 144, 184

U

Ulrich, Thomas A., 323
Unilever, 267, 529
United Aircraft, 131
United Airlines, 7
United Brands, 530
United States Post Office, 8
United Telecom, 235
Upjohn, 30
U.S. Bureau of the Census, 543
U.S. Department of Commerce, 544
U.S. Steel, 527
U.S. Time, 258

V

Vanderwicken, Peter, 236
Veeck, Bill, 7
Volkswagen, 6, 529
Volkswagen Corporation of America, 275

Volkswagen Rabbit, 6, 188
Volvo of America Corporation, 276
Von Ohain, Hans, 120

W

Wadia, Maneck S., 542
Waldheim, H. E. Kurt, 530
Wales, Hugh G., 288
Walker, Bruce J., 291
Wallen, Theodore O., 96
Walter, C. K., 403
Warner-Lambert Company, 267
Warner, Lloyd W., 90–91
Warshaw, Martin R., 288
Warwick, 374
Washburn, Stewart A., 311
Wasson, Chester R., 78, 94
Webster, Frederick E., Jr., 67, 282
Weiss, E. B., 96
Wella Balsam, 449
Wells, William D., 53, 87, 100, 101

Westfall, Ralph, 288
Westinghouse, 149, 529
Wham-O Toy Company, 222
Whirlpool, 374
Whittle, Frank, 120
William Norton Associates, 247
Wilson, Ian, 96
Winn-Dixie Stores, 347, 349
Wisconsin Cold Storage Company, 398
Woolworth, F. W., 30, 347
Wrenco Company, 511
Wrigley, William, Jr., 30
W. T. Grant Company, 189
Wulff, Peter, 406

X

Xerox, 118, 235, 259

Z

Zale Corporation, 441, 442
Zenith, 30, 208

Subject Index

Italicized numerals indicate pages on which terms are defined.

A

Account executives, 32, 279
Accounting manager, 32
Acquisitions, 149
Action plan, 492, 497
Administered system, *379, 381*
Adopters characteristics, 220
Advertisements, 115, 154, 190, 192
Advertisers, 79, 80, 84
Advertising, *18,* 20–21, 32, 35–*36,* 74, 81, 84, 94–95, 97, 100, 105, 114, 128, 134–35, 153–54, 185, 187, 189, 192–93, 202–3, 205, 249–51, 254, 267ff., *297,* 300, 316, 368, 420, 549–51
  agency, 9, 33, 269, 277–80, 292, 295, 297
    selection of, 280
  appeal, 154
  budget, 153, 268, 283–84, 295
  campaigns, 269–70
  central advertising department, 291
  church and religious, 292–94
  college, 292–93
  consumer research, 272, 274
  cost per prospect, 283
  costs, 270
  decisions, 268, 295
  deceptive, 128
  department, 17
  direct mail, 282
  direct ranking and rating, 287–88
  dummy vehicles, 288
  effectiveness, 154, 286
  evaluating, 273, 287
  expenditures, 283–84
  franchise, 291
  government, 292–93
  headline, 289
  image, 268–69
  labor union, 292
  local, 281, 289
  logo, 291
  management, 32, 159, 277, 286
  media, 33, 189, 270, 273, 279–83, 292, 295
  message, 289
  newspaper, 281–82
  nonprofit, 292–93, 296
  objectives, 268–72, 295
  organization, 277
  outdoor, 282
  political party, 292, 295
  post-testing, 287–89, 296
  pre-testing, 287–88, 296
  professions, 298
  radio, 281–82
  readership-ownership recall, 288
  recall, 289
  recognition, 289
  retail, 290, 291
  restraints on, 291
  role of, 268, 270, 279
  staff, 270
  standardized, 549, *554*
  television, 281–83, 294–95
  theme of, 288
  top twenty advertisers (1976), 267
After-the-sale service, 18
Age distribution, 50
AIO inventories, 100
Air transportation, 155, 399, 401
All-you-can-afford advertising, 285
Aluminized plastic, 121
American business, 127
American industry, 115, 442, 526
American managers, 541
American marketplace, 95
Americans, 9, 17, 97, 127, 133–34
American social-class structure, 90, 92
American standard of living, 9
Annual demand, 405
Annual reports, 159

Queing theory, 389
Questionnaires, 160, 161, 164

R

Racial group, 98
Rack Entry Module (REM), 398
Rack jobbers, 155, *340*, *357*
Radio media, 153, 294
Railroad, 155, 403
   rates, 129
   service, 187
   transportation, 399
Rating product ideas, 241
Rating scales, 288
Raw material, 150, 156, 391, 420
   examples, 210
   shortages, 494
Readership/viewership and recall
      measurement, 288
Real income, 122, *123*, 124, *138*
Recall measures, 80, 289
Recession, 62, 122, 125, 126, 131,
      237
   1974, 126
Recognition measures, 289
Recreation, 134
Recruiting salesforce, 306
Reference groups, 85, *86*, 87, 106,
      107
References, 310
Regional headquarters, 537
Regulatory agencies (federal), 129
Reliability, *151*, *170*
Reliable service, 390, 391
Religious groups, 98
Repurchase, 231
Research and development, 115,
      116, 117, 120, 122, 368, 420
   expenditures, 115–19
Research firms, 33
Resellers, 42, *64*, *67*, *68*
Resources, 11, 29, 190, 194
   allocation of, 136
   existing, 186–87, 194
   scarce, 112, 113, 135
Respectability, 93
Respondents, 160, 161
Response rate, *150*, 160–61, *170*
Retailing, 10, 33, 42, *64*, *67*, 77,
      132, 155, 189, *330*, 332, 342,
      350, 355, *357*, 363–66, 369,
      391, 404–5
   trends in, 349–54
   twenty-five largest companies,
      347
Retiree market, 54
Return on investment (ROI), 151,
      157, *174*, *195*, 285, 442
Return on net worth, 174, *175*, *195*
Return on sales, 174, *175*, *195*

Revenue, 151, 176, 416–17, 428
Revitalization strategy, 253, 254
Risk, 116, 118, 174
Robinson Patman Act, 128, 291,
      461–62, 470
ROI. *See* Return on investment.
Role, *85*, 86, 99, 106, *107*
Role playing, *311*, 312, *326*
Routine response, 78
Routing, 302, *303*, 327, 401–2
   objectives of, 402

S

Safety needs, 82
Salable product, 375
Salary, 31–34, *313*, 327
Sales
   contests, 319
   costs by city, 504–5
   industrial, 315
   information, 325
   interview, 302
   objectives, 322–24
   quotas, 318, 319
   response measures, 290
   standards for machine tool
      industry, 323
Sales branches, 336, *337*, 338, 339,
      355, *358*
Sales dollars, 190, 191
   ratio to salespeople, 191
Sales force, 300–328
   applicants, 310
   compensation for, 315
   evaluation of, 323–25
   expenses, 316
   goals, 317–18
   key account analysis, 305
   management, 306
   memos, 321
   motivation, 313, 317–19
   promotion, 18
   quotas, 318–39
   records, 304–5
   recruiting, 306
   reports, 321–22
   supervision, 319–22
   telephone calls, 321
   time management, 305, 306
   training, 311–12
   turnover, 313
Sales managers, 17, 32, 307, 308,
      309, 317, 318, 319, 321,
      322–25
   basic tasks of, 306
Sales offices, *336*, 337, 338, 339,
      355, *358*
Salesperson, 18, 154–55, 190–94,
      300
   advertising integration, 192

capacity of, 300
characteristics of, 307–8
needs of, 317–18
number needed, 307
personality of, 307–8
ratio to sales dollar, 191
responsibility of, 307–8
selection of, 308–9
sources, 308
training, 310, 312, 313
underqualification of, 309
Sales presentation, 302, 303, 325
   closing, 304
   handling objections, 303–4
   post-presentation, 304
   pre-presentation, 302
   product demonstration, 303
Sales volume, 12, 176, 184, 187,
      191, 192
   forecasts, 16, 146
Same product–different market,
      184, 193
Same product–same market, 183,
      193
Sample, *151*, 152, 160, *170*
   formula, 152
   size, 152, 160
Satellites, 121
Savings data, 132
Schools, 64
Scientific method, 166, *170*
Scrambled merchandising, *351*,
      356, *358*
Secondary data, *164*, *165*, 166, *170*
Secondary sources, *182*, *195*
Seen-associated recognition, 289
Segmentation. *See* Market seg-
      mentation.
Selective distribution, 271, *371*,
      382
Selective exposure, 80
Selective processes of perception,
      80, *107*
Selective retention, 80
Self-concept, *83*, 84, *107*
Self-denial, 96
Self-service, *349*, 350, *358*
Seller, 8, 202, 215, 335
Selling agents, 155, *341*, *358*, 372,
      373
Selling costs, 314
Selling prerequisites, 300, 301
Semi-finished products, 391
Senior citizen, 55
Services, 204, 212–16, 224, 225, 227
   demand for, 213
   examples of, 204
   features of, 214
   growth of, 213
   marketing operations, 214
   marketing strategies, 215